SCIENCE AND CULTURE TEXTS
JOSEPH HUSSLEIN, S.J., Ph.D., GENERAL EDITOR

FUNDAMENTAL SOCIOLOGY

FUNDAMENTAL

C.S.

Sociology

E. J. ROSS
B.Com. (Lond.), A.C.I.S., Ph.D.

THE BRUCE PUBLISHING COMPANY
MILWAUKEE

Nihil obstat: H. B. Ries, Censor librorum
Imprimatur: ✠ Samuel A. Stritch, Archiepiscopus Milwaukiensis
June 24, 1939

To

Reverend A. J. Garvy, S.J.

and

Reverend Edward F. Madaras, S.J.

PREFACE

For many years now, the majority of sociologists have agreed that their science should be of the inductive, positive kind. When Comte first coined the word *sociology*, just one hundred years ago, he fixed its method as the observation, description, and classification of social facts. This stand does not allow for any interpretations of these facts, or permit any judgment of values. Comte did not himself adhere to this method, and neither have many so-called sociologists of the past, but today the positive, inductive method of sociology is, in theory, upheld by most sociologists in the United States, and by the greater number of those abroad. In consequence of this, most sociologists are of the opinion that all social philosophers spin theories by deductive methods without regard to fact, and so they consider all social philosophy to be outside their realm. Very few of them, however, have maintained the methods proposed for them. Some have based their findings on unfounded assumptions, or mere semiproved hypotheses; others have interpreted facts in a wholly unwarranted manner. Indeed, it must be obvious that the inductive method fails insofar as man is not a wholly observable being. The social investigator needs to be aware of the entire nature of man, and to take full cognizance of the findings of other sciences, be they of a scientific or philosophical category; and this awareness is the more necessary according as the sociologist wishes to interpret the facts he discovers, or to effect improvements in social conditions. It is precisely in the interpretation of social facts that the Catholic sociologist considers that he must take into consideration certain principles about man, whose social life he makes the object of his studies. For this reason, therefore, a sociology written especially for the Catholic reader seems to be imperative. Besides this, even were sociology solely of a positive nature, there is a need of considering these positive findings, because classifications are always somewhat arbitrary, and statistics may overemphasize or underestimate certain points of view, and lead the investigator to unintentional but nevertheless incorrect results.

The current book, which is an entirely new presentation, and not a re-edition of the writer's first study, draws conclusions which at times are at variance with the earlier work. Readers will realize that seven years of further study and thought on the subject have inevitably led to a development which it is hoped will make the present book more valuable from the scientific viewpoint as well as from the teaching angle. Of course, certain parts of *A Survey of Sociology* have been utilized, as well as portions of the author's other books: *Rudiments of Sociology, Social Origins,* and *What is Economics?*

So far as the plan is concerned, the book is intended to provide a year's introductory course in sociology, although the subject title may be divided into a half year's course termed Introductory Sociology or Fundamental Sociology, and a later half year's course in Social Problems, Social Pathology, or the like. An examination of the book will readily show where such a division might occur. Part One contains certain basic considerations which seem to be necessary for a study of social life and of the sociological work of others. The major sociological theories and specialized terms which could be logically mentioned in earlier chapters will be found there. By thus introducing some of the technicalities of sociology at an early stage, the writer has hoped to avoid too great a strain on the student's power of assimilation of theories and terms, particularly when studying Chapter 6. Of course the individual instructor may decide to leave a consideration of these more technical topics until after the introductory work has been accomplished. The author hopes that the book will easily lend itself to any desired condensation of this kind, believing it best to err on the side of completeness rather than to have the text too narrow in its scope. Similarly, this Part One could be considerably expanded, either by a more extensive study of social theories, or by a more complete consideration of Catholic social philosophy, and the teachings of the social encyclicals. Part Two examines social life with a view to analyzing the basic social institutions which may be discerned from such a study. Part Three is devoted to a discussion of modern conditions and the major social problems of our times. Parts Two and Three are both planned with the idea that the instructor may be able to expand or curtail the student's study of them, if desired. More attention is paid to economic problems than to others, chiefly because of the many sides of social life which they involve in our modern civilization; partly, too, because sociology instructors usually prefer to discuss the topics of the remaining chapters in greater detail, in courses termed variously: Poverty, Child Welfare, Crime and Punishment, Population Problems, Immigration, Race Problems, the Family, Social Welfare, and similar titles.

In quoting from *Rerum Novarum, Divini Illius Magistri, Casti Connubii,* and *Quadragesimo Anno,* page numbers refer to the volume:

Four Great Encyclicals. Numbers in parentheses are those of the Rev. J. Husslein, S.J., as given the *Rerum Novarum* and *Quadragesimo Anno* in *The Christian Social Manifesto.*

In the preparation of this work, the author is especially grateful for the help given by Dr. Elizabeth G. Salmon of Fordham University; Sister Anne Burns, O.S.B. (who has written the entire chapter on Recreation) and Sister Mary Grell, O.S.B., of St. Benedict's College, Minnesota; members of the Sociology and Anthropology Departments of Yale University and various professors of St. Louis University, under whom she took formal work in sociology and kindred fields; Dom Ernest Kilzer, O.S.B., and the late Dom Virgil Michel, O.S.B., of St. John's University, Minnesota; Reverend A. J. Garvy, S.J.; Reverend Edward F. Madaras, S.J.; Mr. George K. Hunton, editor of the *Interracial Review;* and others, who read the whole or part of the manuscript of this or her other books from which excerpts are taken, and offered many valuable suggestions.

The author also wishes to thank the College of St. Elizabeth, New Jersey, for making available to her the expert secretarial services of Miss Cecile McGurty during two academic years.

April, 1939

CONTENTS

xiii

PART THREE

SOCIAL PROBLEMS

PART ONE

THE BASES OF SOCIOLOGY

CHAPTER 1

SOCIETY AND THE SOCIAL SCIENCES

Social Life Is an Important Subject of Study for Us All

THE familiar we usually take for granted. Generally speaking, a gap must occur in the normal functioning of our daily lives before we become even to the slightest degree aware of the routine mechanism which rules us. If some dear one dies, then we realize how much we depended on his presence. Only when we are deprived of a limb, or our health, or some of our accustomed comforts, do we understand how important they were to us in the past. So it is with social life: because we are social beings we do not realize our dependence upon society, neither do we see the manner in which societies have their rise, maintain themselves, or change.

We are born into the society of the family, helpless, devoid of habits, with merely physical needs for quite a lengthy period of time. As we grow older our connection with society becomes more complex: we belong to a religious organization, various recreation groups, a school group, a work group, a political party; we depend upon various economic groups for the purchase of our supplies and for the wherewithal to earn our daily bread. If we are a citizen of the United States, we learn to eat in a certain manner, to wear the specified types of clothes which are the most acceptable in our local society, to think certain kinds of thoughts (or none at all!) about democracy, racial problems, civic needs. Had we been born a Russian or a Frenchman, or a member of one of the Latin-American Republics, we should have learnt a different set of table manners, and our ideas about clothing, democracy, race, affairs of State, would, in all probability, and in varying degrees, have been different. What makes an American like a feast of fried chicken, pickles, mashed potatoes, corn, and ice cream, when his English cousin might prefer fried steak, fried potatoes, boiled cauliflower, and "trifle"? What is it that makes the girl in the United States need an ever increasing variety of dress, "beauty aids," frequent trips to the movies, while a Chinese maiden is content with the same style of dress that her ancestors wore many centuries ago, and has ideals of close-knit family life very different from those of the average

American of her age? Why do so many Americans hope to acquire a college education, when a much greater percentage of Europeans are usually content to leave school before the age of seventeen? The answer to this problem lies in the fact that we tend to conform to the general ideas and habits of those around us because we are sociable by nature. A study of this social life of ours is surely, therefore, of importance.

Man Is Sociable by Nature and Lives in Society

A number of sociologists claim that man is atomistic and merely "conditioned" to life in society by his association with others from the very moment of his birth. However, it would seem that proof of the statement we have just made — that man is sociable by nature — lies in his aptitude and propensity for society, and also in his need of this group life.

Man's Aptitude for Social Life. The greatest evidence of man's aptitude for society is that in all places and at all times men have been found to live in society. The members of the most primitive tribes of today help each other by many services of mutual aid and often extend this social solidarity beyond their family group. Then there is the gift of speech to be considered. Speech furnishes the means for man to exchange his thoughts and ideas with others. That this communication supplies a universal need is proved by the fact that no people have as yet been discovered without their own language, and the vocabulary of even the most retarded people is quite extensive. It is true that, with the exception of the Andaman Islanders, none of the Pygmy tribes have a language of their own, but converse in the idiom of the neighboring tribes; yet even with these tribes it is highly probable that they once had their own speech, but have in some manner lost it, as is corroborated by the fact that the Andamanese have their native tongue, and further that the Isneg Negritos of Northern Luzon say certain prayers in what may possibly be the remnants of a former language, since this people claim that they have been handed down by their ancestors, even though they themselves do not understand them.[1] Indeed, the language of the most primitive tribes is anything but meager. The most primitive of extant tribes have vocabularies of more than four thousand words, and many are familiar with several times that number. Their language includes expressions which

---

[1] Cf., Vanoverbergh, Rev. E., "Negritos in Northern Luzon," *Anthropos*, Vol. XX, 1925, pp. 417–421.

connote abstract ideas, and they can express themselves in orderly sentences. Although the English and Chinese languages are highly developed and have a very large word content, both are very simple in structure, whereas many primitive tongues are extremely complex, and minute differences are sometimes given expression by means of grammatical forms much more complex than languages of modern civilized nations.

All that man inherits physically, however, is a physical organ and a psychic tendency for speech. Long centuries ago, man had the intelligence to organize sounds into language, indeed, the Bible infers that the first man, Adam, had developed speech. Other than this reference, we have absolutely no evidence of the origin of language as such although, of course, we can trace the development of individual languages, such as the three-thousand-year history of the Indo-European languages. Yet speech existed many hundreds of years before this time, since writing was invented about the year 4000 B.C. Just what idiom the individual speaks is determined by environment, by the long custom of his group.

Further indication of man's aptitude for social life is found in the fact that the full development of his intellectual, moral, and even physical powers is attained only through social intercourse. His finest moral qualities are engendered in family life first, and later in the various other societies to which he may belong. The only child in a family frequently finds it difficult to take his place in later life with other men who have learned under the stimulus of social competition. And the aptitude of all men for love is but the need of expending one's affection on another, and hence but an additional proof of man's aptitude for social intercourse.

Man's Propensity for Social Life. Man has a propensity for social life, the evidence of which lies chiefly in the fact that he normally shrinks from isolation. Man needs to associate with others to be truly happy. A crowd engenders a mysterious but very effective bond of sympathy. It is the lack of this feeling and the deprivation of all communication with others which makes solitary confinement one of the most dreaded forms of punishment. Prisoners left in solitude invent many ingenious ways of communicating with one another. Statistics show that more suicides result from loneliness or lack of sympathy than from any other cause. Those who prefer solitude to society are indeed regarded as abnormal; yet on analysis, they do not live wholly alone, however isolated from man they may appear to be. They have the memory of times formerly spent with men, they commune with nature, or they receive the ideas of others by means of books and newspapers, the victrola, or the radio.

Man's Need of Social Life. Man also needs companionship, not only to satisfy his propensity for social life, but also because his bodily, intellectual, and moral well-being depend on social intercourse. We have shown how the development of man's mental, moral, and bodily powers, depending as they do on complex association with others, is an evidence of the aptitude of mankind for social life. However, we have only to read *Robinson Crusoe,* or give the matter a little thought, to realize that we are all in a state of mutual dependence on others for our material needs. Those of us who lead the simplest lives would have to forgo many things if we lived in a state of isolation and had to depend on ourselves for the necessaries of existence. A certain number of temporal goods are obviously necessary for true progress and temporal happiness. Man depends not only for the comforts of life, but even for his very existence, on the products of co-ordinated effort.

Even in primitive society, we have no record of man being all-sufficing. Work is apportioned among the various members of the family: the men hunt, the women cook and till the soil; or the men till the soil and look after the cattle, while the women perform the domestic duties. As man progresses in civilization, the division of labor becomes more and more apparent, until at the present time few men in modern society "consume" any part of what they themselves produce. An electrical engineer, let us say by way of example, does not produce his food, or his clothing, or his transportation, or his means of recreation. He is utterly dependent for his sustenance on the product of the labor of others, which he procures with the money obtained from his profession as engineer.

Definition of a Society

Man, therefore, is by nature sociable. He lives in society because of his aptitude and propensity for it, and his need of the association of others. Only in society can man realize his rational and social nature. Society or community, however, is group life in general. It is composed of many smaller but autonomous societies or social groups. Strictly speaking, we should also distinguish between groups and societies. The social nature of man may be expressed merely by chance groups assembled for companionship or recreation, for example, a crowd at a theater or at a ball game; or it may be shown by membership in a definite society, such as a family, a parish club, a trade-union.

A society in this latter sense has certain characteristics, chief among which are: there must be a reason for its existence, there must be a certain permanence to be attained through common efforts, and there must be some directive authority. To take these in order:

If a society is to exist for any length of time there must be some reason for it, in other words, it must be established to attain something which the members desire to possess. For example, a trade-union is formed by a group of workers to maintain working conditions and wages at a higher level than would probably be possible if each individual worker had to bargain directly with the employer. A recreational society enables members to buy equipment and to play games in a way which would be impossible for each member individually. A school provides individual students with the means of receiving an education which the majority of them could not obtain if they had to rely wholly on their parents (their natural teachers) or if they were obliged to hire tutors for their private instructions.

Not only must there be a reason for the establishment of a society, however, but the end of society must be attained by a community of efforts; that is, by common means. There must be some sort of social bond between the members; that is, some rights which the members may expect to receive because of their association with the group, or some duties and obligations which individuals, or the group as a whole, must carry out.

There must also be some stability in the association; in other words, a society must have more or less permanence of union. People may gather together for a common purpose — to enjoy the performance of an actor, to listen to a lecturer, or to play a chance game of football — but none of these temporary meetings are societies properly so called. Although they may express the sociable nature of the men who form them, there is no stability of union in these groups.

Similarly, there must usually be some member or members in authority, and some rules to be observed, because our ideas differ so widely that without this directing restraint there would ordinarily be no co-operation between the members, and chaos would be inevitable.

To sum up, we may define a society as a stable union of two or more persons uniting their efforts to obtain a common end by collective action. And, as we have just explained, the elements common to all true societies are: plurality of person, community of aim for the common good, stability of bond, co-operation of effort, and authority. The number of both groups and societies in this world is legion. In general, it is not necessary always to make such a strict differentiation between the terms *group* and *society,* but the technical distinction is, nevertheless, one which should be noted.

Animals Are Gregarious But They Do Not Form Societies

Man shares his gregarious instinct with the animals, but his social nature connotes something more than a mere gregarious instinct. The gregarious instincts of animals are remarkable. They may hunt in packs, or congregate for greater protection against their enemies, and form families for the propagation of their kind. Naturalists, however, have repeatedly demonstrated that animals lack any higher reasoning capabilities, and depend upon instinct for any gregarious organization which may appear to show intelligent planning. Bees swarm, and ants have their colonies, because they are endowed by nature with a hereditary instinct which impels them to act in this manner. They have no free will which would permit them to refuse to obey their instincts and refrain from swarming at the appropriate period. Animals do not appear to distinguish between end and means, or to retain any permanent impression of social influences or tradition, to be handed down to future generations; and they have no highly developed power of adaptation. Animal herdings, therefore, are not true societies. Nature herself has come to their aid in protecting them by imitative devices. We note this particular care of nature in the colors of many birds, insects, and reptiles, and also in the very shape of some animals. And although some animals have an inherited organic manner of communicating certain physical needs, they never organize the sounds of their vocal cords to make intelligible language, with its complicated grammar rules, and to record that language by permanent written signs, as do all humans.

Sociology and Its Branches

Sociology is the science of society. It is a social science which treats of man's relations with his fellow men. It studies human society, its customs and institutions and their development, at all times and places. Its subject matter is social life — the constitution and functioning of the various groups to which, either of choice or of necessity, we and our fellow men belong; and all social dealings, whether they be cooperative or competitive, organized or unorganized. It must by now be evident that we depend upon this phenomenon of social life for companionship, for the development of our mental faculties, for affection, and for the satisfaction of our material needs. Since we are all so very much concerned with it, an intelligent understanding of social life should surely be of interest to everyone, and it is this understanding which sociology aims to provide.

There are two methods which may be employed in the attainment of truth. The first is called the analytic and inductive, or *a posteriori* method. Its aim is to lead the mind by analysis and induction from the immediate appearances, actions, and relations of things, to the necessary intelligible reasons of these appearances, actions, and relations. The inductive method aims at giving an insight into the nature of things. When it succeeds, the result is but very general in character, and not an intuitive vision. But more than that, as all investigations have discovered, these appearances are not very revealing. They are "signs" that hide rather than "signs" that reveal, for their statistical character often gives a false impression regarding the truth of inferences drawn from them. Yet it is very useful for man to analyze these facts, correlate them, and form statistical laws and thus to furnish information about society which is true according to the nature and extent of the investigation. The scientist so occupied may even form theories[2] which will account for the findings, but the more or less probable character of the theories must not, however, be overlooked.

The other method of attaining truth is called the deductive, or *a priori* method, by which the mind is led from knowledge of the intelligible nature of a thing to what necessarily flows from that nature. Without an innate knowledge of things, this method presupposes experience in the general meaning of the term, and a knowledge of specific natures by analysis and induction. Where analysis and induction are revealing we may infer that this or that can be said to be the nature of the thing, and then we may proceed yet further by deduction to say what necessarily flows from such a nature. This is the method of the philosopher.

Now it is difficult to apply these methods with any exactitude to sociology, as "the" method of sociology cannot be said to be determined, as will be amply evident after a study of Chapters 6 and 7 which examine the work of the sociologists of the past. Speaking in a general fashion, we may say that today it is usually understood that pure sociology aims at being a positive science, that is, it seeks its understanding of social phenomena by observing, describing, and classifying actual social facts[3] and conditions; to establish statistical

---

[2] A theory is a verified hypothesis applicable to many related phenomena but not proved to be invariably correct.

[3] A fact in sociology is an observation of social life which can be communicated with precision.

laws,[4] and to propose theories that account for those laws. It uses induction, then, in its most limited sense. It does not intend to be a normative science, and so it is not supposed to be concerned with judgments of values. On the other hand, social philosophy may be said to seek a deeper understanding of man and his social relations, and to deduce certain norms for society in general. Its field may not be large, but it is very essential, and though not of the positive type, yet may be called pure sociology. The reader is asked to refer to the Preface of this book, and to Chapter 7 for a further discussion of the method, to be used in sociology.

Applied sociology is the more practical study, which aims at the active promotion of man's temporal welfare. It studies social problems and their possible solution, and so it formulates principles for social amelioration comformably with the findings of social theory. To do this it needs not only the findings of positive sociology, based upon experience, but also the application of the normative principles of social philosophy. Yet applied sociology cannot depend wholly upon "pure" sociological knowledge, even though the two branches are taken into consideration, but it must also consider the findings of the other sciences which are concerned with man — the findings of medicine and hygiene, of biology, and of the other social sciences, and the teachings of religion. It will be the concern of the next several chapters to summarize the chief facts from other branches of knowledge which the sociologists use when building up their theories and when formulating principles for meliorative programs.

Many sociologists are by no means anxious to provide remedies for present so-called maladjusted social life: they prefer to confine themselves to the classification of available material, and to draw conclusions as to the processes involved, checking these and rechecking them,

---

[4] A law is an observed order of facts, invariable under the given conditions. Man's conduct is never invariable, hence social laws must be clearly distinguished from laws of the exact sciences. The statistical findings of the positive method applied to the social sciences is very marked, and so we must preface any so-called "laws" by such statements as "generally speaking," "other things being equal," and similar qualifications. This is essential because the conclusions of any positive social science may properly be called laws only if each separate set of conditions which influence the result can be measured and controlled; and many of the forces at work in social life can be neither measured nor even predicted. What is generally true about the conduct of men may not be so in any one particular instance. Human beings possess free will; they are influenced by many things, and may act quite contrary to the normal patterns of behavior. Indeed, in all the social sciences the rational, moral nature of man must be taken into account, or only half-truths will be observed, and the formulation of social laws will treat man as an automaton and will therefore be unreal.

and waiting until they know more about the processes themselves before they attempt to remedy conditions by meliorative programs. Even this "pure" theoretical sociology of a positive kind can be, however, most fascinating as well as useful. Yet man with his intelligence most certainly needs to work out laws for society which will lead to social improvement, and applied sociology assuredly has its place among the social sciences.

As with all sciences, various branches of sociology are separately discussed. An introductory course usually considers the basic knowledge needed for a study of the science, discusses some of the broader sociological principles, and outlines the major social problems. Other theory courses are concerned with social philosophy, which as we have said, is a study of what can be deduced by reason concerning fundamental laws of society; or they discuss social psychology, culture, social history, or anthropology, or gather local material for further research or to test existing conclusions. Again, courses may study in detail the sociological principles and processes which seem to be valid according to existing knowledge, or they may consider the history of the various sociological theories or the various methods which may be used in research.

Applied sociology courses may be concerned with a variety of topics, but a knowledge of theoretical sociology is essential to the understanding of social conditions and the problems with which applied sociology is concerned. Urban and rural sociology discuss respectively the problems and processes of city and rural life. Such social problems as those concerning race, poverty, immigration, mental deficiency and insanity, mental or physical health, crime and delinquency, population statistics, are considered separately, or together in a course called variously, social problems, social disorganization, or social pathology. Courses in social ethics consider man's duties toward society, and society's duty to the individual and the various social groups, and, of course, the corresponding rights. In social-work courses are discussed the technical methods of dealing with individuals who are affected by some of the problems dealt with in applied sociology, individuals who have needs due to personal failure or to the failure of the social groups to which they belong.

The Sources of Sociological Data

There are three main sources for sociological observation. First, many sociologists confine themselves to an examination of the modern "civilized" society in which they live, or to the individuals who compose this society. It would seem, however, that to base conclusions solely upon such observations is to risk distortion, because of the difficulty of examining the familiar facts and conditions of our lives with an open and unbiased mind.

An increasing number of sociologists make a study of present-day primitives who have no written history and whose social life is comparatively simple. Our own culture is so complex that it is difficult to arrive at the basic principles which actuate our social life. It is difficult, too, to analyze and regard objectively a culture which we have come to regard as a norm; almost impossible for us dispassionately to distinguish between essential features and those nonessential traits which are perhaps erroneously regarded by us as standards. Since the structure of primitive groups is so much more simple than our own, if, without preconceived notions and in a scientific way we examine the culture of these peoples, it is very probable that we can arrive at a much truer conception of society than if we investigated only the structure of groups to be found in contemporaneous "civilized" communities.

Third, there are the historical peoples of the past, and the manner of living of those peoples about whom we have no history but whose life we can in some measure reconstruct from archaeological remains. Only when the principles of sociology can be tested by the findings of all three of these sociological sources, may they be said to be correct.

The Social Sciences

Sociology is one of the social sciences, so called because they deal with man in his social relations. They are said to be nine in number. As sociology itself, they can each have a positive and a philosophical aspect, but the delineation of each of these aspects and their relations is beyond the scope of this book.

1. *Sociology.* As we have already discussed the subject matter of sociology, we shall proceed with an outline of the other sciences in the social-science field.

2. *Religion,* as a science, is an endeavor to understand by observation and reason the relationship of man to God, and to adjust man's conduct to His supreme Will. It can, therefore, be included in the social sciences. Unaided by revelation, however, man's reason is unable to encompass the full range of truth as it affects his well-being, and is sometimes faulty — for some truths of religion are by nature unknowable to man unless they have been revealed. Hence the study of religion includes not only the systematization of what people believe

about God and the knowledge of right and wrong deduced by reason, but also the truths revealed by God and authoritatively taught by the Church. Religion places the purpose or objectives of life in their true and clear light; it provides the adequate motives and the necessary spiritual means for man to perform his duties and restrain his passions. Comparative religion is a comparative study of the various religions of mankind, and insofar as it deals with primitive religions is concerned with social anthropology, and hence directly affiliated with sociology.

3. *Ethics* deals with the rightness and wrongness of human conduct, and with standards and ideals of morality as evinced by reason. Whereas sociology is chiefly concerned with facts and conditions, ethics is a normative science and deals with motives, purposes, and ends. Insofar as reason can point out the way, ethics shows man how to be perfect morally, and man's perfection is a higher end than his mere temporal happiness. Men live in groups because they have certain ends to attain, and the sociologist must note the moral side of these ends, as furnished by ethics, just as he must take into account the findings of the other sciences. The applied sociologists must of necessity know the norms of right conduct before he can effectually formulate principles of social action and judge existing institutions. As already mentioned, social ethics is often included in sociology courses. This is logical, because although ethics is traditionally a part of philosophy, social ethics considers man's rights and duties in connection with society, and society's rights and duties in connection with the individual and with particular social groups. Social ethics can effectually guide, however, only if it relates the actual conditions of social life, as furnished by sociology, to the norms it lays down.

4. *Psychology*. This science deals mainly with the individual, without any particular reference to social life. It studies the soul and its faculties — will and understanding, and the individual conduct which is the outcome of our mental activity and human habits. Conduct, however, is merely another word for behavior in society, and that branch of psychology called social psychology, which is an examination of the mental side of social life and the individual's relation to it, is often included in sociology courses, and is being used increasingly by sociologists in such applied sociology as the examination of mental deficiency, crime, delinquency, and dependency.

5. *History* describes social events in time and place: it records these events chronologically, and nowadays seeks to interpret them at least insofar as external influences are obvious, and thus to take the place

of sociology in the understanding of social conditions and the explanation of social processes involved. Whereas pure sociology should be analytical as well as descriptive, history is still mainly descriptive. Sociologists can take the facts of history and study their development and perhaps also their possible future trend.

6. *Political Economy or Economics,* is the scientific study of man's activity in providing for such human needs as hunger, shelter, clothing, and education.[5] It deals with man's attempt to earn a living, with man's activities in connection with the consumption, production, and distribution of wealth, and the exchange processes and taxation thereby involved — wealth in economics being a term used to mean all useful material things owned by human beings. It is the science of wealth and of the wealth-getting activities of mankind. Sociology depends on economics for a knowledge of the conditions under which men form economic societies, for example, trade unions and co-operative movements; for the history of economic groups and the economic customs and institutions affecting social life; in particular, it depends on economics when dealing with the problems of pauperism, for these are chiefly due to unequal distribution of wealth. First and foremost man must live, and next in importance is, materially speaking, association with others in a quest for material existence. As we shall explain in a later chapter, economic organization affects social life in all its ramifications. Economists, however, are primarily interested in the theory of the more objective aspect of economic life, such as theories of price, rent, wages, money, and banking. They are interested in social relations only insofar as they enter into the processes concerned with production, consumption, distribution, and exchange. They work, therefore, in a more specific and restricted field than sociologists, who treat of every type of human relations; but they should turn to sociology for possible interpretations of the sociological effect of any economic reforms which they propose. The modern economic system, which treats man as a machine, and transfers employment ruthlessly from one city to another, needs to take into consideration the findings of the sociologist regarding the importance of well-knit family and other social life. Labor economics, or an examination of the problems of human relations in economic life, is sometimes included in sociology courses. And, of course, insofar as man's conception of social justice and charity is the keener or weaker, so will the economic system of a country be better or worse.

---

[5] Economics does not, of course, include a study of the technical processes employed in providing for these needs.

7. *Political Science* deals with politics and law; that is, it describes and analyzes political institutions — their constitution, legislation, and administration. It deals with the nature, forms, and functions of the states and their governments, both in their internal relations and in their associations with each other. As the State is one of the principal societies to which man belongs, and as man's social relations are much influenced by the form of political government and the administration of its laws, sociology necessarily touches upon some parts of political science. The sociologist is concerned with the fundamental aspects of the State, as well as with the evolution of the State group, and the processes involved in this evolution; he is not concerned with the practical details of constitutions, governmental devices, and similar affairs. On the other hand, a government is useful only insofar as it helps man to true temporal happiness; hence political science comes to sociology for its knowledge of how governments have best dealt with citizens in the past, and what may be the probable effect of proposed changes in social institutions.

8. *Demography* describes the actual status of any existing society — giving vital statistics of births, deaths, marriages, crime rates, wealth, unemployment, ill health, and other salient facts concerning social conditions. Sociology may use demographical material as a further check of its conclusions; or it may attempt to make practical use of its already-arrived-at conclusions by studying this material together with similar data of the past, and coming to conclusions as to causes and probable remedies.

9. *Anthropology,* as a natural science, deals with man in his physical relations, with the fact of his physical life and culture. It is chiefly concerned with nonhistorical and preliterate peoples, and it has four main branches. *Linguistics* is an endeavor to discover which languages are related in origin, so that tribes can be classified according to their speech. The social aspect of language as a means of communication is discussed in this branch of anthropology, and the interrelation between language and culture. *Physical anthropology (somatology)* studies the distinguishing bodily characteristics of tribal groups; an attempt is made to establish and classify the biological relations of races, the influence of geographical environment upon man's bodily make-up, and the possible courses of his migrations upon the earth. Somatic anthropology, as this science is sometimes called, may provide some secondary data for sociology, as a physical collaboration of possible findings regarding the diffusion of certain social manifestations or culture traits. *Archaeology* attempts to reconstruct man's material

achievements of the past, and prehistorical archaeology furnishes material clues to the social life of prehistoric man. This science furnishes data as to the relative permanence or the development of culture traits. *Ethnography* or *social anthropology* describes the general culture of social groups, and classifies tribes not only according to their institutions but according to their customs too. As will be evident from later discussions, many sociologists use the recorded observations of the ethnographer almost exclusively, as the basic material for their studies of man's social life.

Before proceeding with a study of sociology proper, it will be necessary to acquire some basic knowledge about man and his place in this universe. The next several chapters will, therefore, be devoted to this purpose.

CHAPTER 2

BIOLOGICAL INHERITANCE

The Importance of the Subject

SINCE sociology deals with man in his social relations, it is obvious that we ought to know something about what makes men as they are. It is true that sociology is not concerned with the individual man's character and temperament, because it deals with social relations and not with individuals as such. Yet it would seem that the basic human characteristics should be known, in order to arrive at a correct understanding of what makes man's conduct what it is. This knowledge seems important, too, because of certain social theories current at the present day. For example, some modern sociologists attribute such social problems as crime and poverty to a bad inheritance, and propose eugenical measures for their elimination; other theorists state that there are superior and inferior races, and advocate the subjugation of the latter; others, again, deny the influence of heredity in conduct and propose environmental measures to modify individual character manifestations, and hence to modify the influence of individual character upon the social character of the groups concerned.

What Heredity Includes

Human heredity means that which goes to make up the individual when he begins life as such. It is the sum total of the potential instincts and the physical, mental, and emotional characteristics which we receive from our forebears at the moment of conception. All the potentialities to be received from heredity are fixed at this time, for in all species that reproduce bisexually, heredity is determined precisely by the union of the two cells — one from each parent. In the nucleus of each of these mature germ cells are twenty-four chromosomes, infinitesimal in size, and each of these chromosomes, in turn, contains a large number of genes which are the real determiners of heredity — the carriers of all our inherited characteristics. These characteristics are very great in number.

The truth of the last statement will be obvious if we consider just a few of the inherited physical traits of any human being, which will differ in at least some small respect from the similar traits of any other person. Each person differs at least slightly from others in the length and proportion of limbs; in the characteristic color and shape of hair and skin; in the shape of the ear and the acuity of its sense of hearing; the precise shape of the nose and its nostrils and its sense of smell. Among the traits of the hand alone, we may cite its specific shape and breadth of palm; the characteristic breadth, length, and position of the fingers; the color and texture of the skin; the size, shape, color of the fingernails; the variations in markings.

It must be obvious that all these characteristics which are peculiar to each individual, and make up his individual physical personality, and all his other inherited potentialities, are not in the fertilized ovum in any formal way; and it must be obvious, too, that the genes are manifold and must be ultramicroscopic in size. Indeed, the genes are merely the carriers of potentialities to develop into certain specific hereditary traits. Each characteristic is determined by one, or by a group, of genes, that is, by the potential factors present in the germ cell. Some of these potentialities are received from the father, some from the mother, in varying degrees, and this accounts for the great differences among members of the same family in physical traits such as height, weight, and in the nervous system, in emotions and other characteristics. How we develop depends, too, upon our environment, our will, and the action of grace in our souls, as will be later discussed.

How Heredity Works

The first question to be considered now is how we inherit those characteristics which are handed down to us biologically by our parents.

a) *Mendel's "laws."* It was an Augustinian monk in Brunn, Austria, the famous Gregor Johann Mendel (1822–1884), who first found actual experimental proof of how we acquire our inherited characteristics. Some of his findings have been modified by later experiment, as we shall show, but in general his discoveries are scientifically accurate. After years of experiment with peas in the monastery garden, he read a paper on the subject before the local scientific society in the year 1865. The findings of this paper, now called Mendel's "laws," were not discovered and given to the world until the year 1900, sixteen years after his death.

Mendel's "laws" may be divided into three principles. First, he said that we inherit one factor for each of our characteristics, both qualitative and quantitative, and these units cannot be divided, but are present as dominant or recessive characteristics. This latter statement is usually referred to as the principle of dominance: that if parents possess contrasting characters or units, they are not blended in the offspring, as Darwin thought, but one will be dominant in the new organism, that is, will be phenotypic, as well as genotypic, and one will disappear temporarily from view, that is, it will be hidden as a "recessive" in the germ plasm and will not visibly appear in the off-spring as a phenotypic characteristic. The phenotypic characteristic will not, therefore, manifest all the genotypic (hereditary) potentialities. Second, the principle of segregation: that either the dominant or the recessive characteristic will be inherited from each parent but not both, so that there are only two factors in the new individual when the two germ cells unite. Hereditary factors therefore remain units and are uninfluenced by any hybrid parent, although differences may come about by a chance combination of genes, as will be explained later. Third, the principle of independent or random assortment of factors in the union of the two germ cells, which is illustrated by the several combinations which can result in the consideration of even two such factors as the color and form of peas with which Mendel experimented, as mentioned in the following page.

Of course, peoples had recognized unit traits before Mendel's time, since the similarity of physical traits between parents and offspring are often very noticeable. After Mendel's discovery, however, it seemed certain that all the very many inherited characteristics of man could be identified and delimited as units, and could be prophesied as to incident according to mathematical performance. And this line of thought, although now somewhat modified, is, in the main, quite true.

Mendel demonstrated his findings by cross-pollinating two pea plants, one of which gave yellow peas and one green peas. Since greenness in peas is dominant, all the peas which resulted from this fertilization would be green, but they would carry a recessive character of yellowness. If these green peas, carrying the recessive of yellowness were cross-pollinated, then 25 per cent of the resultant pea plants would have the dominant green color, 50 per cent would have the dominant green color but would possess the recessive character for yellow, and the remaining 25 per cent would have only the recessive color both phenotypically and genotypically. This conforms to the regular algebraic formula that $(a + b)^2$ equals $a^2 + 2ab + b^2$.

If two characteristics were considered, such as the color and form of round green peas and wrinkled yellow peas, respectively, the ratio would be 9:3:3:1. Nine sixteenths would be round and green; three sixteenths would be round and yellow; three sixteenths would be wrinkled and green; and one sixteenth would be wrinkled and yellow.

For four characteristics, there are sixty-four possible combinations, and it is easily seen that the combinations of human characteristics, being so manifold, are of very great variety.

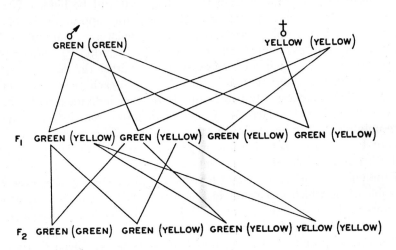

Let us see how Mendel's findings can be applied to the inheritance of sex. First, we must remember that we said that both male and female human body cells contain twenty-four chromosomes. These chromosomes are in the nucleus of the cell, which is formed by a mass of protoplasm (a collection of substances temporarily grouped together in a certain manner). The nucleus itself is composed not only of the chromosomes, but of a fine network of linin which connects the parts making up each individual chromosome, somewhat as if it were thread stringing beads. Actually the female body cell contains twenty-four pairs of chromosomes, and the male cell or sperm twenty-three pairs and one unequal pair. Since it takes two genes to make a characteristic and not four, nature has arranged that in the preparation of these body cells for maturity (so that they are capable of fertilizing each other, and at the same time keeping the species constant) both the ovum and the sperm go through a period of reduction, and half the chromosomes and hence half the genes disappear — otherwise we would have double the characteristics of our parents! The division is longitudinal. For example, in the female the immature ovum containing twenty-four pairs of chromosomes, first divides into two parts, one small and one large. The smaller mass of protoplasm subdivides into two other cells, and both of these degenerate. The larger mass of protoplasm again divides into two unequal cells, and these resulting cells each contain 24 single chromosomes instead of the original twenty-four pairs. The small cell also degenerates and the larger cell is the mature ovum ready for fertilization. If the ovum is fertilized, 24 pairs of chromosomes will result from the union of the sperm with the mature ovum.

If we now consider the inheritance of the chromosomes which determine sex, we shall find that the ovum of a woman contains what is known as a pair of X chromosomes, while in the spermatozoon of a male there is a single unpaired X chromosome and a smaller chromosome called Y which is thought to be rudimentary. If sex, therefore, is represented by the XX chromosomes in the mother and XY in the father, then in the longitudinal division which took place before the time of fertilization, the germ cell would include one of the X chromosomes in the ovum, and in the mature sperm cell there would be either an X or a Y. If a child born as the result of the fusion of the germ cells inherits XX chromosomes, it will be a female. If only one X chromosome is present, it will be a male.

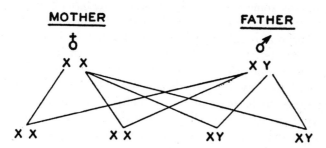

b) *Later experiments.* Since the year 1900 a great deal of experimentation in heredity has taken place. It is impossible to experiment in human heredity in the laboratory, not only for moral reasons but also because human beings mature so slowly that there are only approximately three generations in a century. As will later be mentioned, some work of real scientific value has been possible with "identical twins," but apart from this, all we can know of human heredity is due to whatever information we may have of the last few ancestors of certain people who have accurate family records. Obviously such information is not all-inclusive; it is only possible for a limited number of traits, and even then the danger arises of attributing to heredity what may be due to environment. However, a certain amount of useful information has been obtained from a study of plants, such animals as rats and guinea pigs, which multiply rapidly, and insects, particularly the fruit fly or *Drosophila melanogaster*. The *Drosophila*, for example, with its four pairs of chromosomes and its relatively few characteristics compared to the multiplicity of human characteristics, is particularly useful for study. Obviously, however, one must beware in transferring the findings obtained from plants, animals, or insects, to human beings.

As a result of these recent researches in heredity it has now been discovered not only that each human chromosome contains a large number of genes but, what is of extreme importance, that these genes are not usually unit characters, one for each trait, but that a combination of several genes is nearly always necessary to determine even a simple characteristic. While this fact amplifies rather than nullifies Mendel's "law," it is of immense importance. The genes, therefore, have different functions, and often a character does not depend upon one gene alone, but is a multiple Mendelian factor. For example, eye color is by no means a unit character, but is made up of many different colors, as some eyes clearly show. Characteristics which seem to be determined by one factor may in reality be the result of cumulative factors, because a child may differ from a parent in only one of the smaller characteristics of a larger one such as an infinitesimal difference in the size or color of a ring in the eye. The inheritance of head form seems to obey the Mendelian law, whereas the inheritance of stature seems to be determined by multiple Mendelian factors. This discovery, that we do not inherit many characteristics as units, is seen to be a very important one when we consider the biology of inheritance in further detail.

When the period of maturation takes place in the ovum or in the sperm, there is a meeting of the two hereditary streams of chromosomes contained in these body cells. This meeting is called synapsis. The two chromosomes for each set of genes are very closely juxtaposed at this time, and when they fall apart one or other of the genes, or even whole blocks of genes, may cross over and attach themselves to other genes in the corresponding chromosome. When we remember the large number of genes in each chromosome, it will be seen that a great number of combinations and changes in the genes is possible. The combinations will always result in the new mature ovum and the new mature sperm being unlike the parents. Thus if a pair of chromosomes ABCDE and abcde cross over, the result may be ABcde and abCDE.

In this crossover process, the order of the genes and chromosomes usually remains the same. If, however, the order is changed and, to give an extreme case for example, the genes line up as AcCDE and AbBde, if "c" contains a gene for a characteristic linked with "b," not only will either "c" or "b" be absent phenotypically, but a great change may result genotypically as well. Thus a change in but one gene may result in the disappearance of a characteristic, or in the formation of a characteristic of completely different type. This inheritable change in the size, nature, or distribution of a characteristic in the germ plasm is called a mutation.

Such changes in the material of the genetic system may also occur in other ways. In the synapsis period, the chromosomes are in close relation to each other, and it is thought that they may influence each other by their chemical composition, which may have an effect on the heredity of possible offspring. Similarly, when once an ovum is fertilized, there may be a chemical interactivity of the male and female chromosomes which will also result in some hereditary changes. Experimentation on the fruit fly, guinea pigs, and other animals and insects shows that some genes not only have multiple characteristics, but they also seem to have some factor associated with them which intensifies, weakens, or otherwise modifies other characteristics; or even a so-called lethal factor which seems to make certain other characteristics disappear genotypically and results in speedy death of the offspring. In these experiments X-rays seemed to have some power in changing the genetic constitution, and so it is thought that the radioactivity of the cosmic system may possibly be any agency which produces mutations. Of course, in this one must be careful not to overestimate the importance of work on nonhumans; just because an animal or insect may react in a certain manner, it is not proved that human beings will do likewise.

c) *The inheritance of defects and other delimited characters.* These mutations and changes in the germ plasm lead to many deviations in the offspring from the normal type. It is easy to see that heredity is in a state of flux, and at times may produce what seems almost a new type. It is these factors in heredity which in part explain the great differences in members of the human race. Apart from the definite "oneness" of human beings the world over, and a certain indication as to race whereby we can recognize a member of yellow, black, red, white, and brown races respectively, people differ from one another even physically in a great variety of ways. Not only our physical characteristics, but all our faculties, our memory, power of abstraction, our will, the intensity of our instincts and emotions are peculiar to ourselves. Innumerable strains of inheritance converge in every human being, and chance determines just which combinations of characteristics will appear, so that it is impossible to predict what will be inherited by any certain individual. Genotypically, we all have a tremendous number of genes which do not appear phenotypically and which we cannot possibly determine. Similarly, we may have some phenotypic traits which come from the remote past, and which may appear in us for the first time for many generations.

The latter phenomenon is called atavism, and is explained by the fact that generally speaking inferior or defective genes are recessive characteristics, and not dominant. If, therefore, the parents of a child carry only one defective gene, the offspring may be normal or even superior. But if both parents carry the same defective gene, which is comparatively rare except in the mating of close relatives, then the child may be inferior to both parents. This explains the fact that mentally superior parents may produce children of inferior mentality, and why dull and incompetent parents may have offspring which are of high natural ability. Of course, generally speaking dull parents will have a greater proportion of mentally inferior children than will parents of superior mentality, but many of the world's geniuses, such as Lincoln, Shakespeare, and Napoleon, have come from undistinguished families.

Heredity may result in similarity or in great differences, and it is never possible to predict what an unborn child will inherit except, possibly, in the case of a few characteristics whose inheritance is now more or less accurately delimited, such as albinism, stub fingers, poly-dactylism, hemophilia, color-blindness, piebaldness, twin-bearing capacity, left-handedness, lack of resistance to certain diseases, deaf-muteness, and certain types of feeble-mindedness and epilepsy.

Certain characteristics are positively linked to the X (sex) chromo-somes which not only specify the inheritance of sex, as we have ex-plained, but which determine other characteristics also. The Y chromo-some is rudimentary and seems to have little function, but the X chromosome carries a number of these sex-linked characters, such as hemophilia, color-blindness, and polydactylism. In the following dia-gram showing the inheritance of hemophilia, it is seen that a man who has the potentialities of this disease in the X chromosome will, when marrying a normal woman, have no offspring defective in the first generation in this regard, but some of his daughters may possibly inherit the defect as a recessive (in his male offspring the defect will die out). If a daughter having the defective X chromosome marries a normal man, generally speaking, half the sons will be defective, and half the daughters will probably carry the defect as a recessive.

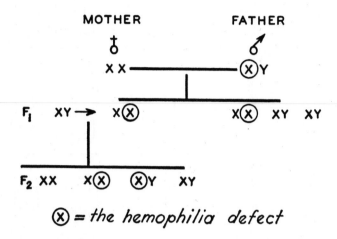

MOTHER   FATHER

$\circledX$ = the hemophilia defect

In hereditary deafness quite a different situation will occur. There are many kinds of deafness, such as deafness of the eardrum and deafness of the middle ear. Deafness is not sex-linked and it is a recessive defect, and only if a person with such a recessive marries a person with exactly a similar recessive defect, will some of the children inherit deafness (in the Mendelian ratio).

Hereditary defects need not show in the offspring. If, for example, ten pairs of genes of the father and the mother respectively are represented by black as defective, and white as normal, it will be seen that if the defects are in different pairs of genes, then genetically the parents may have many defects and the children may receive many genotypic defects, but still the children may be normal phenotypically.

The Characteristics of Man

Having now discussed the mechanism of heredity, we are in a position to examine man's characteristics, and to consider which of these are due to inheritance, and which to environment. The whole question of heredity versus environment (nature versus nurture) is of vital importance to the sociologist, who is chiefly concerned with environmental factors, as we shall later show.

Man shares some of his characteristics with the animals; others are distinctly human.

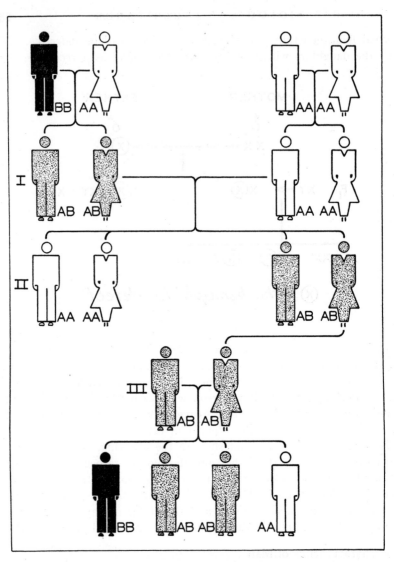

An Example of Inherited Characteristics: Let BB = deafness; AA = good hearing; AB = good hearing with a recessive characteristic for deafness. — I. Two people with good hearing marry, but *one* has inherited a defective gene for deafness, although it is not apparent. II. All their children will have good hearing but half will have recessive characteristic for deafness hidden in their germ plasm. III. If one of the children with this recessive characteristic marries someone with a similar recessive defect, out of four offspring one will have perfect hearing and will never pass on a gene deficiency for deafness; two will have good hearing, with the hidden defect; one will be deaf. This result was shown by the monk Mendel (1822–1884) to be a law of nature.

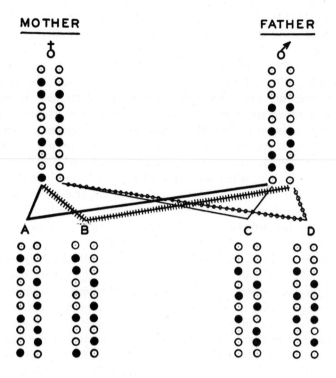

First, we must consider his vegetative and sensitive life. He has a definite bodily form and function which is common to all the members of the human race, so that a man, whether he be tall or short, fat or thin, light or dark complexioned, is always recognizable as a human being, distinct from the other animal creation. With his body he inherits certain physiological and morphological functions. He is equipped with the power of locomotion, with a nervous system, and with certain inborn activities which express themselves in unlearned behavior, that is, reflexes which respond to stimuli with mechanical regularity, such as air-taking, sucking, blinking, digestion, the eliminative processes, sleeping when exhausted, the desire for food and drink when hungry and thirsty.

He has certain lower cognitive faculties, a sex instinct, the exterior senses of sight, hearing, taste, smell, feeling; and also such interior senses as the imagination or the ability to revive sensations, and the memory which depends on associations of ideas about sensory presentations. Man also has a gregarious instinct; and his lower conative faculties, his desires, the ability to feel anger, fear, pleasure, that is, his concupiscent and irascible nature, which seems largely connected with glands.

Although different in form, man shares his vegetative and sensitive life and his power of locomotion with the animal. But his growth and development are very slow compared with the animal. At birth his head and other parts of his anatomy are disproportionate to their relative size in later life (he seems to inherit a proportion-finding potentiality, which functions to a greater or less perfect degree until he is in his teens). Not until he is comparatively old does he reach the age of adolescence, when his power of reproduction is developed, and the secondary sex characteristics such as distinctive voice and growth of hair. At birth the spiritual part of the mind — the intellect and the will — does not function, and it does not reach its highest capacity until adolescence has developed into adult life.

A number of false theories have been fashionable in the past regarding the inheritance of defects. For instance, although we may inherit a weak nervous system which may eventually lead to insanity, we do not inherit insanity as such. Again, the germ plasm is independent of disease — such as tuberculosis, for disease is caused by a germ and it is inconceivable that a germ could be transmitted in the ultramicroscopic genes. We may, however, inherit a certain weakness of bodily constitution which may, under certain conditions, give a favorable environment to the disease or other physical ills.

We do not inherit blood as such, for there is no blood in the germ plasm. We inherit a potentiality of developing one of the four main types of blood, however — the O, A, B, or AB type — and our blood type is thought by some to affect our susceptibility to dental decay and to certain diseases also.

In addition to his vegetative and sensitive life, man has a distinctive rational existence. All living beings have a vital principle, the soul, which directs all their activities, co-ordinates their parts, and perfects them according to their nature. Only in man does this vital principle, the human soul, appear as an active spiritual essence. The vital principle in man, his soul, is a "simple" being, present in every part of his body, and it provides him with his higher cognitive faculty, the mind or intellect, and his higher conative faculty, the will. The mind and will are spiritual by nature, and are, therefore, incapable of being transmitted by physical inheritance. Animals are not endowed with this rational nature, which gives man his distinctive superiority.

Man is dual by nature: he has an animal body with its various powers, but he also has his human soul. This soul, as we said, "informs" every part of his being. Although the soul is distinct from the body, it is not completely dissociated from it as Descartes taught, for it fits the body and may therefore be said to be to *some* extent influenced by the heredity of the body and its development in the environment in which it is placed. There is no doubt but that human beings are all unequal by heredity, mentally, physically, and in emotional control. For instance, man's mind works through his physical brain, and the content of his mind depends upon the senses. Some people are born with sound brain and sound senses, and some are not. Then, too, the action of the brain is much affected by the operation of the ductless glands which we shall soon describe. Man's will is dependent upon both the physical nervous system and the mind.

At birth man's mind is a *tabula rasa,* for nothing comes to the intellect except through the senses, either directly or indirectly by the workings of the imagination. *Nihil est in intellectu quod non erat prius in sensibus.* All the content of man's mind must come from the impressions which he receives by sight, or touch, or smell, or hearing, or taste. But once the impressions have been obtained, man can do what the animal brain does not seem capable of doing. He can excogitate upon them, and from them deduce logical conclusions. He can exercise his judgment and come to swift and accurate appraisals; he can reason and contemplate his own mental states, reflect about himself and about abstract ideas, and he can take and form abstract thoughts and compare concepts. As Dr. Arendzen has admirably put it, man "is something more than matter, being endowed with the spiritual faculty of gazing at himself and observing the sequence of his own modifications. He knows the realities reported by his senses but he also knows that he knows. He is not only conscious of his ever-varying states, but he is conscious of self; he is that changeless something which is the subject of all those variations. Without some fixed and separate point of reference, no movement can be known; something, therefore, in man must remain unmoved, for he has the power of knowing change as change. He is himself indivisible, unextended, a Unit that sees its own unity in the variety of sense perception. Were he divisible and extended, part outside part, he could not reflect, any more than a piece of paper can be folded so as to face itself as a whole. Yet man can be the thinker and, at the same time, the thing thought of. He is, of course, material and subject to all the laws of matter, but he is also something else, which is not that which undergoes the impact of matter. He is what we call a spirit, an entity devoid of the sensible properties of matter including its most radical one, extension in space."[1]

Again, so far as man's will is concerned, it is true that much of his life is dominated by instinct. It is true, too, that he learns simple mechanical actions, such as walking, performing the usual motions of dressing himself, and that he acquires many nonrational actions through habit. But this habit-forming capacity of his, based on his instincts, is, nevertheless, different from any similar power in animals. It is not automatic and certain, but plastic and subject to training. Man is not predetermined, but is responsible for his actions, and every thinking person believes in his own responsibility and holds others responsible for their acts. He can force himself to do what his body does not wish to do. He can control his emotions and his natural impulses. If his will power is sufficiently strong, he can break a habit of long standing.[2]

Heredity, therefore, influences mental traits only indirectly. Mental traits are partly inherited, for they are in part dependent for their development upon the physical side of the brain; but they are partly influenced by environment; they are intensified by feeling, by the frequency of imagination (which can be developed by environment and training). Generally speaking, man will tend to think the thoughts that are easiest, to be lazy, to give in to animal impulses, and not to make an effort to have his mind dominate his acts. But man is not bound to do this. And his intelligence, his rational nature (which ought to dominate all his acts so that he is truly a rational creature), with its powers of consciousness, comparison of experiences and reflections, and his will, with its power of choice and consent, are spiritual capacities and not inherited.

Man's social instinct seems to be an extension of a gregarious instinct which he shares with the animals. We pointed to the use of his mentality in the formation of societies in the last chapter. Obviously, the social and sexual instincts are necessary for our social well-being and to insure the propagation of the race. It is probable, too, that man also inherits a parental instinct, to insure the necessary care of children during the long period of infancy and adolescence. Some theorists think, however, that parental love and care is but the outcome of man's social life within the family, and they show that while some peoples are very solicitous for the welfare of their children, such

---

[1] Rev. J. P. Arendzen, "The Mind of Man and Beast," *The Month*, March, 1935, pp. 225–232.

[2] Conduct is further discussed in Chapter 3.

as the North American Indians, and the majority of the peoples in the world, there are some more or less primitive tribes which put more value upon girls than upon boys, or vice versa. Infanticide was common among the relatively highly civilized Spartans, and exists among many peoples today.

Certain sociologists, influenced by the Behaviorists, whose theories we shall discuss in the next chapter, teach that speech preceded thought, and that it is simply a reflex laryngal movement. Reflection would seem to eliminate this theory. Of course, by being able to give more precise meanings through the use of an enlarged vocabulary, man's speech may enhance his ability to think. Language not only enables third parties to grasp the ideas in a man's mind, but it also fixes the mind of the thinker upon his own ideas and therefore helps to clarify them. Thought does, therefore, depend upon speech in some measure. But to infer that man was at one time without thought, and only later developed speech, is entirely without foundation. And to make thought completely dependent upon speech gives no explanation to the query as to where abstract thought itself originates.

The Ductless Glands

Among the physical characteristics which we inherit, are duct and ductless glands. Accurate knowledge of the ductless glands is of fairly recent origin. As yet we do not know everything about them particularly as, being ductless, the substance they secrete goes directly into the blood stream and cannot, therefore, be easily isolated. Certain of the glands, however, have been fairly accurately delimited as to their function, and it is easily seen that the inheritance of a deviation from the normal in glandular secretion or functioning has a very important effect upon a person's physical, mental, and emotional development. A person equipped with two strong adrenals, pituitary gland and thyroid, would probably be a superaverage person both physically and mentally.

In particular, it would seem that the ductless glands are largely responsible for the universal human emotions and reactions. The emotions play a very prominent role in our life, and it would seem that their reaction may affect not only the visceral system, such as the sweat glands, but our nervous system as well. Overdeveloped emotions such as anger and suspicion may influence our memory, our will, and obscure the intelligence, sometimes even paralyzing the workings of the mind. A crowd is ruled almost exclusively by its emotions and hence does many irrational things. On the other hand, the emotions are valuable as energizers, and sometimes their operation leads a person to a higher level of achievement than he would ordinarily be capable of. Fear, for instance, is a natural emotion, needed for self-preservation, and is only abnormal when out of proportion to the situation. The work of the adrenals is later discussed. The emotions, however, need to be controlled if they are not to have the great disadvantage of interfering with our rational nature and making our conduct unreasonable.

The ductless glands and their known functions may be briefly given as follows:

1. The thyroid glands. These are dark red lobes at the base of the neck which secrete a hormone called thyroxin in very small quantities. The thyroid secretion affects the skin and its appendages: teeth, fingernails, the cornea of the eye. It also affects the stability and intensity of the emotions, as well as intelligence and mental development. Through its influence on the intelligence, the qualities of prudence, tact, and foresight are to some extent connected with the thyroid.

If a child is born with a defective thyroid, so that too little is secreted, it will be a cretin idiot, with no intelligence, small and abnormal in body form, with small legs in comparison with the body, and with very coarse hair. This condition can be overcome by the injection of thyroxin, if the injections are given to the child in the first year or so of its life. If the thyroid stops secreting sufficient thyroxin in later life, the intelligence and the emotions become very slow, and people in an advanced degree of myxedema, as this condition is called, can become the equivalent of idiots.

If the thyroid secretes too much thyroxin, a person becomes too active and nervous, the metabolism rate is too high, and he becomes quickly excitable and exhausted. If the additional secretion is but little, a beautiful fine complexion may result, also bright eyes, beautiful teeth with a bluish shade which, however, may soon decay. It is to be noted, however, that a lack of iodine in the food may result in an imperfect thyroid hormone, so that a thyroid condition is not necessarily inherited.

2. The parathyroids are embedded in the surface of the thyroids. The hormone they secrete is necessary for bodily development, because it controls the calcium in the blood, and if there is a deficiency in the hormone, the calcium balance is increased. It also controls the excitability of muscles and nerves and hence the activity and exhaustion of the individual.

3. The adrenals are two in number: one fits on top of each kidney. Each is composed of two parts, the cortex and the medulla.

The cortex or outer shell seems to have something to do with sex growth or precocity of physiological development. If there is a tumor on the cortex a child may develop full sexual life, with all the secondary sex characteristics, such as a full beard if the unfortunate is a male, as early as the age of five.

The medulla, a spongy substance inside the cortex, secretes adrenalin, which, in very small quantities, increases the number of red corpuscles in the blood, and draws sugar out of the liver, and hence affects the chemistry of acid regulation. The medulla has caused the adrenals to be called the glands of combat. They fit a man for vigorous action. Causing a redistribution of blood in the body, they draw it away from the normal parts, making the ordinary digestive process almost at a standstill, and supply it to the brain, heart, and involuntary muscles. Muscular effort becomes easier, there is less fatigue, the blood clots quickly and so decreases the pain from wounds, the brain processes are clarified. An active adrenal, therefore, makes a person emotionally more active and aggressive, and a more efficient fighter in a battle. If too active, a person becomes very irascible, and physically two types can be noticed. In "red anger," a person's heart beats rapidly, his respiratory rate accelerates, his face becomes purple, his neck swells and the veins stand out, his hair stands on end, his eyes sparkle, his nostrils dilate, and his voice becomes raucous. In "white anger," a person's respiration becomes difficult, his heart contracts, he breaks out in a cold sweat, and violent blows or other external evidence show his interior agitation. Fear, as well as anger stimulates the gland. As the additional blood enlarges the arteries, sometimes people who die from fear or rage do so because of adrenalin trouble. If there is a tubercular medulla (Addison's disease) this affects the pigmentation of the skin, makes it brown, and bleaches areas.

4. The thymus, over the windpipe, a little above and to the right of the heart, is a red-brown spongy mass which controls growth in childhood. It is large during childhood, but usually begins to atrophy at the age of two, and generally disappears about the age of seven, or at least by the time of adolescence. If it secretes too long, although its possessor may be well grown and intelligent, he will remain sensitive and emotional as a child and be of poor physical resistance.

5. The pituitary gland is situated at the base of the brain in a bony depression called the *sella turcica*. It secretes two hormones.

From the anterior lobe pituitrin is secreted, which regulates the growth of the skeleton and supporting tissues, that is, the long bones of the body: the legs, arms, and ribs. If it secretes too much in childhood, before the bones are hardened, gigantism may result. If it secretes too much after growth, it affects the bones of the face, and the size of the hands and feet, and apathy, lack of initiative, and laziness may result. If the long bones close too soon, a person is small and underdeveloped, even a dwarf.

The posterior lobe of the pituitary secretes pituitrin. This affects the nerve cells of the brain, stimulates the muscles, and also affects the sex tone. If it secretes excessive amounts it causes excessive development of the ovary and promotes the production of fat.

It has been thought that the posterior lobe dominates in woman, and the anterior lobe in man, and if the opposite occurs, the woman will have some masculine traits and the male female characteristics.

6. The gonads, which are both duct and ductless sex glands, are called testes in the male and ovaries in the female. They partially regulate the sex appetite, and the endocrine secretions produce secondary sex changes, such as the voice, and, more important, help to differentiate the emotional side of men and women. If overactive, these glands very often lead to hysterical disturbances, and, of course, to overemphasized sex desires. It is for this latter reason that the emotions should not be stimulated by literature, plays, pictures, conversation about sex, for these, in turn, will affect the glands. This is true particularly of adolescents, since it is at this period that the glands become active. The pituitary and the pineal glands also affect sex.

7. The pancreas, like the gonads, is both a duct and a ductless gland. The duct gland secretes pancreatic juice into the intestines. The ductless part of the pancreas secretes insulin which controls the sugar metabolism of the body, and a lack of it causes the disease of diabetes.

8. The pineal body is a gland until the individual reaches adolescence, when it begins to atrophy and becomes a piece of fibrous tissue. Its functions are not yet known, but if it is destroyed the individual develops physically and intellectually too early, and so it is thought that as long as this gland functions some others remain dormant, particularly those which influence the development of sex and adolescence.

It is thought that the spleen and the liver may secrete hormones which regulate the amount of red corpuscles in the blood.

Much of the hereditary differences between men and women seem to be due to the ductless glands. The sexes differ not only in the primary sex differences of ovary and testes, but in such secondary anatomical characteristics as shape of the pelvis, timber of the voice, fat layers, and the like; in physiological characteristics, such for example as greater physical strength and endurance in the male, and his greater number of blood cells, the more rapid respiration and more active nature of the woman, the greater susceptibility of the two sexes to different diseases; the emotional equipment which is the same type yet develops differently. These differences to some extent affect a psychological difference. That woman is the intellectual equal of man has long been proved, although the use of the intelligence, dependent as it is on emotional characteristics, may be different; and a woman often lacks the opportunity and training to develop to her fullest intellectual capacity. Most frequently, too, she has lacked the interest of the male in intellectual development. A man needs to exert himself to succeed in life and thus provide the better for his wife and children. The normal career of a woman is married life and the development of a home, which requires the use of many other faculties besides those of intellect, and does not normally give the same possibility of intellectual expression, so that the woman often lacks the incentive to progress in intellectual pursuits.

Kretschmer's Theory of Character and Body Build

Certain theorists have held that our whole character depends upon inherited body build. Of these the most important is probably Kretschmer (b. 1888).[3] By recording the height, weight, breadth of shoulder, length of leg, circumference of calf, and other measurements of a large number of persons, he came to the conclusion that people could be classified into three types: The *Aesthenic* or *Leptosome* type, tall, slender, slightly built and with relatively narrow chest; the *Pyknic* type, short, thick set, frequently with strong development of the abdomen; the *Athletic* type, middle-sized or tall, broad, and well developed.

In these classifications Kretschmer is not, of course, very original. From the time of Hippocrates, men have been designated according to their "disposition" or their physical appearance. But Kretschmer endeavored to make his classifications on a scientific basis, as a result of careful observation and testing.

Kretschmer also outlines two main types of personalities, the cycloids and the schizoids. The schizoid personality is the deep, nonsurface type, serious, reticent, often unsociable, sensitive and therefore reacting quickly to environmental changes, with an intense appreciation of the finer side of life, but having lots of sorrows and lots of joys. Fre-

---

[3] Cf. Kretschmer, *Körperbau und Charakter* (1931).

quently of commanding will power, the schizoid is nevertheless often nervous and irritable. If these characteristics are well adjusted, then the person is normal; if they are exaggerated, the person may become fanatical, and generally if he becomes insane it will be of the dementia-praecox type of insanity. Aesthenics are said to predominate in the schizoid type.

The cycloid personality, in which the pyknic type is said to predominate, is well adjusted, genial, fond of festivity, goodhearted, friendly, adaptable, placid in disposition, home-loving, and industrious. If such persons become insane, they tend to have the manic-depressive type of insanity.

Athletics may be one or other type. As no two persons are the same, although it is true that certain types do predominate, nevertheless there is nothing really worth while in this analysis. All that can be said is that if a person is of a schizoid disposition, he may develop a certain type of insanity — but, of course, he may never become insane, and if he does, it may be insanity of a different kind. And so, too, for the cycloid. Some races may be relatively more cycloid or more schizoid than others, but again no definite categories can be set up. That our body build depends on glandular development to some extent and that these do affect our emotions and dispositions is true, but our character depends on many varying qualities, as will be seen in another chapter.

False Instinct Theories

At one time it was fashionable to think that mankind was born with many instincts, such as the theory of William McDougall (1871–1938) who lists the following supposed instincts and the emotions he claims they call into being:[4]

1. The instinct of flight and the emotion of fear.
2. The instinct of repulsion and the emotion of disgust.
3. The instinct of curiosity and the emotion of wonder.
4. The instinct of pugnacity and the emotion of anger.

5 and 6. The instinct of self-abasement (or subjection) and of self-assertion (or self-display), and the emotions of subjection and elation (or negative and positive self-feeling).

7. The paternal instinct, and the tender emotion.

Other instincts which he does not ally so closely to the emotions, he lists as follows:

---

[4] Cf. McDougall, W., *An Introduction to Social Psychology,* 21st edition enlarged, 1928, Chapters 3 and 4, pp. 39–103.

1. The instinct of reproduction, associated with sexual jealousy and female coyness.

2. The instinct to seize and swallow food when hungry.

3. The gregarious instinct.

4. The instinct of acquisition.

5. The instinct of construction.

Yet other "general instincts" or "nonspecific innate tendencies" are noted such as sympathy, suggestion and suggestibility, imitation, play; and discussions are made of a great number of sentiments.

Psychologists seem now agreed that such a large number of instincts do not exist, and that it would be impossible for the newly born embryo, for example, to have such incipient instincts as curiosity or acquisition, without being aware of the things in environment about which it was curious, or which it desired to attain. Again, some people, for example, the Hindus, the Kubu of Sumatra, and certain Eskimos, do not seem to be possessed of any combative instinct; and a spirit of aggressiveness seems somewhat lacking among those Greenland Eskimos who win their fights not by a show of anger or revenge, but by satirical songs by both the accuser and the accused, the winner being he who makes most fun of his opponent; it seems absent, too, among the Tlingit and the Kwakiutl Indian tribes of North America, who "fight" with potlatches instead of fists; and among many of the Australian primitives who settle a quarrel by taking one club between them and dispassionately hitting each other on the head in turn until one falls to the ground.

Then there are W. I. Thomas's (b. 1863) *"Four Wishes,"* which are given great prominence in textbooks as the four elemental desires which motivate all human conduct. Our conduct is rooted in four elemental wishes, he says:[5] The desire for new experience, the desire for security, the desire for response, and the desire for recognition. It is true that as a result of our innate ego we might have a desire for recognition, response, and security, but obviously these do not include all the inherited forces in our being. And it must be evident too, that we could not inherit a desire for new experience in the germ plasm, since the child cannot know that new experiences can be enjoyed until he has enjoyed some. True, our mind is of an inquiring nature, if it be well developed, but not all people seem to have any such desire for new experiences, and in any case, if the desire for security is also innate, this latter would surely counterbalance the former. Thomas's "wishes" give us some clues to conduct, but they are not adequate.

---

[5] Thomas W. I., *The Unadjusted Girl,* Chap. 1.

In addition to their ideas of culture, which we shall later describe, W. G. Sumner (1840–1910) and A. G. Keller (b. 1874) of Yale made four social forces in mankind the basis for all social action: hunger, fear, sex, and vanity. They did not specify whether these traits were hereditary or acquired by all men living in human society, but the emphasis on their universal character would seem to imply that Sumner and Keller consider them as hereditary forces. The Yale school, however, is chiefly concerned with the operation of culture, and eschews the psychological aspects of individual behavior.

F. H. Giddings (1855–1931) of Columbia gives undue emphasis to the gregarious instinct, in his ideas about like-mindedness and consciousness of kind as being the most important forces in social causation.[6]

Many other sociology writers have talked of social forces, but as the inherited are grouped with the psychic, it is not the place to discuss them in detail here. We refer to such writers as Lester W. Ward (1841–1913),[7] Charles A. Ellwood (b. 1873), Edward Alsworth Ross (b. 1866), and many of the Chicago school, including R. E. Park (b. 1864) and E. W. Burgess (b. 1886), also give us a variety of psychic forces, some inherited, some not. Ellwood and Ross in particular were greatly influenced by McDougall and Ward: they differ considerably in their ideas in different works, but Ross in his *Principles of Sociology*, 1920 edition, gives a list of primary forces, some instincts, others processes, such as Domination, Competition, Stratification, Accommodation, and the like.

The psychoanalysts also stress heredity, but since they are chiefly concerned with the abnormal, we shall defer a discussion of them until we take up the subject of mental abnormalities later in the book.

Nature versus Nurture

Just what part of man's character and physical endowment is due to environment and what to heredity has been a perennial matter of debate. Although it is very improbable that any complete knowledge will ever be available on the subject, a certain amount of information is now possible by the study of identical twins.

There are two types of twins. Identical twins are those who are produced by a division of the same fertilized ovum. Such twins are always of the same sex and have the same set of genes, so they are

---

[6] Cf. especially, *Principles of Sociology*, p. 17; *Studies in the Theory of Human Society*, p. 29.

[7] Cf. Chapter 6.

really duplications of what might have been but one individual. If such a division took place, but was not completed, then Siamese or other defective individuals are born. The other type is the dizygotic or fraternal. Here two female ova are fertilized at the same time, instead of one, so the twins existed as two individuals from the moment of conception. Since they are from different fertilized ova, their genes are diverse, and they may be of different sex and of marked difference in all other respects as well, just as any two offspring born in different years will differ from each other.

There is no doubt that identical twins can give us many clues as to what is due specifically to environment. If the twins are brought up in the same environment the similarity between them will be very marked, but if it should happen that they are separated and brought up in differing environments, then any differences in them in later life will be due largely to environment. Of course, it is much more in accordance with true social principles that identical twins should be brought up in each other's company, and it is not allowable morally to give possible suffering to human beings for the sake of a mere increase in knowledge. Sometimes, however, identical twins are separated for a variety of reasons, usually because of the death of one or both of the parents when they are young, because of a broken home, or because for some reason or other a relative wishes to take care of one of the two. Psychologists and others who have been able to study identical twins separated under such circumstances have acquired some useful knowledge about heredity, and particularly about the effect of environment upon heredity. One of the most noteworthy discoveries made by the study of such twins is that susceptibility or resistance to disease is almost certainly inherited because identical twins have a remarkable similarity in this matter. It is noteworthy, too, that one identical twin may become insane, and the other not.

While basically it is man's genetic constitution which makes a satisfactorily physical and psychological condition, or the reverse, environment plays such a large part in the development of our inherited predispositions that a chapter will be devoted to its consideration.

CHAPTER 3

CHARACTER, PERSONALITY, AND ENVIRONMENT

WE HAVE now explained the physical basis of man and his character. Yet a moment's reflection will show that neither heredity nor the operation of our own personal mind and will is solely responsible for making us what we are. We have developed habits, ways of thinking, attitudes, ideals, which certainly did not come to us as an inherited endowment. Our personality has remained the same as it was at birth, but the operation of our instincts and emotions, our habits and our character have changed with the years, sometimes for good and sometimes in a regrettable manner. What makes us peculiarly ourselves is due in part to the action of the powers of the soul and of an environment (including grace) upon our heredity. For each one of us our environment is different from the environment for any other human being: this is so, because we ourselves form part of our own environment, and to ourselves we differ from what we are to others; again, the presence of others and of other environment is different to us from what it is to any other person. All environment affects each individual in an individual manner, and it is the continued interaction of environment upon an inherited constitution and of heredity upon environment which gives us our character.

Although the word *personality* is often used today in place of the term *character,* strictly speaking it ought only to be used in one of two senses. Personality is that which designates a human being as differing from the animal: what makes him specifically a man. It also means those individualizing traits of a man which constitute his singularity and differentiate him from all other human beings: in this sense it is a reification of the concept of identity. Personality, therefore, designates a being person, one who is reacting here and now: the essence of man, which remains even if he loses his reason. It is the ego or the "I" of which we are conscious from our earliest years, even though we ourselves are in a vast variety of environments which change, and even though our ideas and types of actions change with the years. The word seems to come from the Latin, meaning an actor's mask through which the voice sounded: *personare,* to sound through, the voice which represented the actual man who spoke his lines. Some modern educationalists talk in terms of personality quotients, which they wish to join to their intelligence measurements, in an endeavor to obtain a picture of a person in all his aspects. Actually, what they mean is an attempt to designate his character, as it shows in the varying situations of everyday life. They are quite correct in distinguishing a man's character from his intelligence, and yet it is to be observed that one cannot estimate character without taking intelligence into consideration.

Character is also something individual and peculiar to its owner. It, too, comes from a stage term, for the word meant in the early Greek theater the fixed mask which was used for each special role. Actually, the word originally meant a notch made in a post, as a recognizable sign differentiating the fields of Kleon from those of Timon. A man's personality, his being, existing person, remains unchanged. His character, under the influence of environment and his mind and will, may change. Character is the expression of the whole man, it is a unity, the sum of his rational faculties, his ideas, his habits, emotional and otherwise. It is the sum total of his heredity, of all the changing roles of environment to which he has been subjected, of the influence of grace, and of the informing presence of the soul in every part of his being. A man's character is judged by his conduct — not by isolated acts, but the sum total of his actions in everyday life.

Before considering environment in some detail, let us discuss what makes a man's conduct what it is.

The Theory of the Behaviorists

Somewhat in protest against the theories of McDougall and other instinctivists, who endowed men's hereditary equipment with too many inborn instincts and emotions, and against the preoccupation of the psychoanalysts with the abnormal, John B. Watson (b. 1878), of Chicago University, gave impetus in 1912 to a new theory regarding the basis of conduct. Stressing the place of habit in man's daily life, Watson has had a large following of sociologists, psychologists, and educationalists in the United States, although he has had little effect upon European thought. The theory of Watson and his followers is called Behaviorism, and is based on the assumption that man is merely a more highly organized animal whose conduct is but habit induced by environment and training. Some of the Behaviorists even go so far as to deny consciousness, and those who admit it do not think it has any effect upon conduct. The soul, and its faculties of mind and will, are entirely ignored, as are also unchanging norms of conduct and the distinction between good and evil.

The Behaviorists admit, of course, the inheritance of certain physiological things: the instinct of sex, the physiological functions of the visceral organs of digestion, as well as of the mouth, arteries, veins, kidneys, and all the glands of the body. They correctly consider that, given the necessary stimulus, some of our responses are hereditary, such for example as the flow of saliva at the sight of food when hungry; the dilation and contracting of the pupil of the eye in a strong light; sneezing; some of the changes in the endocrine system which have much to do with the emotions of fear, anger, and love, and other universal motor, muscular, and glandular activities. The Behaviorists think that all the other activities of man are due to habits formed in environment. For the Behaviorist, man is an automaton: his sense organs receive impressions from the outside world, and his glands, muscles, motor responses, give them back in the form of habitual conduct. He teaches that the nervous system provides man with his capacity to learn and to profit by experience, and that by learning from pleasant and unpleasant sensation our behavior becomes habitual. As a result of habit, given a certain stimulus, a response of a definite nature will inevitably follow. There can be no response without a stimulus, according to this theory, and similarly, if we know the stimulus, that is, the environment, we can predict the response. This theory is often called the S-R bond, the supposed bond which exists between the stimulus (S) and the response (R). Since the same response can be made to a variety of stimuli, or different responses to the same stimulus, learning, they think, consists merely in increasing the number or form of responses to outside stimuli. Our responses can be "conditioned" by environment and training, just as Pavlov conditioned dogs, first by associating colored light with food, and eventually making their saliva flow when the light appeared without the accompaniment of food. If given any healthy child, with full control of his environment they can, they assert, make of him what they choose.

St. Ignatius made a somewhat similar assertion, but he meant that he would train the child not only to virtuous action and in a strong will power, but also to pray to God for grace and aid in the fight against evil.

To the Behaviorist, action which is customary in our group is right conduct, so that unchanging norms of morality have no place, and punishment is merely reformative or deterrent, to teach one whose action does not conform to the group how to make more fashionable responses in the future.

No one would wish to deny that there is much truth in the Behaviorist theory that habit is the basic drive of the majority of our actions. We all act from habit to a greater or less degree, and a great proportion of our conduct is impulsively habitual. Yet the theory is completely materialistic: man becomes merely a more highly organized animal, superior to the beasts merely in that he has learned to use tools and has invented language. Carlyle had the same idea when he said that "man is a tool-using animal with the gift of speech," and more picturesquely and more cynically, Voltaire said that man differs from the animal in "lying and literature." To the Behaviorist, our faculty of speech is simply organic: apart from the ability to weep and to laugh there is, he thinks, little human in speech to differentiate it from animal noises. According to his theory, man learned to speak by organizing his laryngal movements, and after this organization it became possible to hand down his accumulated knowledge, his learned experience, by tradition and in historical records, so that others could adopt them and improve upon them, and experiment with the material things of life where he himself left off. For the Behaviorist, therefore, language sways our thoughts. Even delight is merely a result of conditioned muscular action. Yet man is certainly more than an animal subject to a constant stream of sense impressions, his intelligence gives him the power to stand aside from his impressions and mentally to review them; he has an intellectual capacity to perceive himself and the changes which are occurring in him. Completely materialistic, teaching that man is merely a physical body, entirely conditioned by environment, there is no place for a spirit — for a mind and will — in the rather simplist behavioristic doctrine. For this reason it can only be regarded as an unscientific half-truth, containing valuable clues to the habitual behavior of mankind, but utterly unreliable as an explanation of man as he really is.[1]

What Makes Conduct?

What, then, makes a man's conduct? What makes his actions good or bad? Human conduct is the result of the thinking process of a man under the influence of his will, and aided by grace.[2] Since we

[1] For a summary of Behavioristic psychology, read Allport, F. H., *Social Psychology* (Houghton Mifflin, 1924).

[2] Cf. "And God is faithful, who will not suffer you to be tempted above that which you are able: but will make also of temptation issue, that you may be able to bear it" (1 Cor. 10:13).

cannot measure grace, we must here somewhat ignore it, and say in general that conduct is the result of the ideas in the mind of the individual who, responding to environment, and hampered or helped by hereditary dispositions, performs actions in a certain characteristic way. We are what we think. Strictly human conduct, that is, conduct which distinguishes man from the animal is any activity that is specifically human, that is, performed with rational insight and controlled by the will. There is no unit cause of conduct. Human conduct is a complex thing, due to the constant mutual interaction of the individual and his environment. It is true, of course, that much of our conduct is automatic. There is much value in this, for by making certain of our actions habitual, we can release our mind for the consideration of more important deeds, and for abstract and constructive thinking. A little reflection will show, however, that habit by no means rules our actions. Our mind is continuously working, continuously taking in new impressions from the senses, and in this manner we form habitual attitudes and ideals. As we said, behind our conduct is our mental state.

Our attitudes are certain ways of viewing things — gained from our environment, changed by the working of our mind and our imagination, and somewhat influenced by our physical endowment, particularly by our emotions. These attitudes may be true or false, good or bad, antisocial or constructively of social value. Our ideals may also be good or bad: they are types of excellence which we hope to attain. Every being in its natural state seeks its own perfection, and finds delight in it, so that we all have a strong impulse to strive after pleasure. Now, there are certain norms of right conduct which reason, aided by revelation, tells us we should observe, and there are other norms established by lawful authority, some to insure that the basic moral law just mentioned is carried out, and others less important but nevertheless necessary for the better regulation of orderly social life. These norms we have to obey, the latter to avoid temporal punishment, the former to avoid sin.[3] Now, if our body is not perfectly integrated, so that our mind and our will rule our actions, we shall strive after the pleasure of the senses, or the imagination, or self-satisfaction in the consciousness of ourselves as a person. We shall thus be led to sins of lust or sensuousness, anger, sloth, gluttony; or we shall be proud, or vain, envious, jealous or covetous, in the endeavor to give satisfaction

---

[3] Sin may be defined as self-love of the soul wanting to be independent of God in order to satisfy the cravings of the body and the ego, until finally the soul seeks itself in its intellectual and volitional pursuits as well.

to our ego, to exalt ourselves beyond the position which truth would assign to us. Mental and moral conflicts may arise within us, between our ideals and our acts, between our lower faculties (our impulses and emotions, our concupiscence) and those of a higher order, between the attitudes and ideals of our present surroundings compared with those of the past, or compared with the norms of right conduct which our conscience gives us, or which we have acquired from previous teaching. Our hereditary impulses may be almost overwhelmingly strong, or our inherited nervous system and our will power may be very weak, but always these defects can be overcome at least to some degree. Our mind may be false in its judgment, through ignorance, doubt, or fear, or because it is obscured for a time by our nervous, glandular, or digestive system. We may do actions through habit or through false judgment which we afterwards regret, but surely no correctly thinking person will deny that despite this fact we are conscious of our rational nature, conscious that we are not materialistically automatic like the animals. Before our habits became such, we nearly always began them of our own free will, and always there are actions which are still consciously willed, and consciously thought out with our mind, and carried into action. Our habitual or routine action is not willed, and very much of our conduct, as we have said, is due to habit resulting from our concupiscence, from hereditary impulses or a deranged nervous system; or it is due to environment and training. But all normal persons are capable of willed action, and use their will in making deliberate choices on many an occasion. We are living spiritual beings, not merely physical bodies, and our character is by no means a mechanically induced result. We are not born with unhealthy mental attitudes, and although our emotions and our misplaced pleasure seeking are largely due to the results of hereditary glandular and sense responses, they can be educated to a harmonious integration between thought and action by the control of the will. For this, of course, a favorable environment and grace are needed. That good education and the help of religion are both needed in the molding of character must be very obvious.

What Is Environment?

Since without falling into error of Behaviorism, we admit that environment plays a very large part in the conduct of man let us see what environment is. Environment is any external force that plays upon the individual — the whole surroundings, people, objects, ideas, which affect him. It is of several kinds: Physical environment comprises the objective environment around us, including geographical features, food, drink, drugs, and prenatal influences. Psychosocial environment is the social environment of home and family, neighborhood, school, companions, economic associations: the companionship of man, which is social and at the same time has its psychic aspects. Psychic environment is the environment of such things as ideals, sounds, the influence of books, music, theatrical performances, radios — even the influence of ourselves and our own psychic and emotional reactions, our physical defects and abnormalities.

Physical Environment

Not everything we are born with is the result of heredity. There is an internal environmental influence on the cells of the body: we are not yet sure of the function of the protoplasm which forms an environment for the genes. The organism inherits merely a capacity to develop, for example, to a certain type, if the proper kind and quantity of food is received, and if the endocrine system functions properly. Characteristics are contained in the germ plasm only potentially. Some of these characteristics are relatively fixed early in life, others are very plastic. We cannot determine heredity, but we can very largely determine how that heredity will develop.

At the moment of conception we may receive the potentiality of developing a relatively perfect physical and nervous system. But environment begins to play on us from that time forward. True, we are protected from most types of environment during the prenatal months, and the only connection between mother and child, before birth is the physical resting place she provides for the child, and the food she supplies. If the mother's body provides a certain type of environment which presses wrongly upon the child during its development, it may be deformed. There is no nervous connection between the child and its mother, and no blood connection. The mother cannot influence the child directly by her emotions, or by thinking certain thoughts or looking at certain objects. There is no truth in the tales that if a mother is frightened, the child will be marked with the object which frightened the mother. The mother's function is merely to supply the child with nutrition through a filtered duct. But the nourishment the mother herself takes, her state of health, the condition of her blood and nerves, may affect the type of food she provides for her child, and this will often determine whether an inherited defect will be expressed, and will also fix bounds to the child's development. If the food the mother passes to the child is inadequate, due to ill health, undernourishment, or because she imbibes an excessive amount of alcohol or drugs, then it may possibly be unable to develop properly. It is thought that alcohol in excessive quantities affects both the gonad, in the male, and embryonic life in the female, since the effect of alcohol on experiments with guinea pigs was to increase also the number of stillbirths or of offspring who died of a weakened constitution soon after birth. As we said before, however, an effect upon animals is not necessarily a proof that the same effect will take place with humans, although it has been almost conclusively proved by observation of actual human births that alcohol poisoning as well as lead poisoning does affect the embryonic life of the mother.

The germ of syphilis can affect the child, not only during its journey through the birth passage, but even by penetrating the protoplasm surrounding the developing embryo and thus infecting it before birth. Infection of the latter type has a serious effect upon the child's physique. Gonorrheal infection leads to the danger of blindness in the child, but a compulsory use of a weak 1-per-cent solution of nitrate of silver in every infant's eyes at birth is now practically universal in all civilized countries.

Other diseases, including tuberculosis, can affect the child only after birth. Attempted abortion may permanently injure a child who was originally conceived as "normal." And again, an injury at birth may hurt the child's development — many first-born children are brought into the world with greater difficulty than are later ones, and mental diseases due to injury may result. The combination of heredity plus prenatal environment makes us what we are at birth. But it is very difficult to distinguish the effects of heredity from those of environment. After birth, since food is so important in the growth of the normal body, it has a great influence on a child's development. Rickets and other bodily malformations are well known as being due to faulty diet either through ignorance or conditions of poverty, and a faulty diet may possibly have an influence on the development of the brain and hence the working of the mind. This latter statement is, however, subject to proof. While it is conceivable that mental development should be impaired by lack of correct nourishment, an English investigation of 4,286 boys and 4,474 girls in different schools in that country show that undernourishment, bad teeth, enlarged glands, and diseased tonsils seemed to have little influence on mental development.[4] Yet one cannot know what might be the potential development of

---

[4] Donald G. Paterson, "Personality and Physique," *The Measurement of Man*, by Harris *et al* (University of Minnesota Press, 1930), pp. 163, 164.

individuals in these groups which may have been impaired. Undernourishment and ill health have a marked effect upon the nervous system, and this in turn may very conceivably influence the brain and its development.

Even after complete physical development has been reached, food can have a marked influence on our body as well as on our thought and conduct. The wrong type of food, too much fat, too much iodine, excessive quantities of narcotics and alcohol, coffee or tea, malnutrition, including insufficient minerals, can all influence our digestion and our nervous system. They can possibly make us irritable and also emotionally unstable by affecting our body through the ductless glands in the manner outlined in the foregoing chapter: and frequently at these times the mind does not function at its best. Again, exercise or the lack of it has a considerable influence on our muscles and bodily development.

Care and proper knowledge are also necessary conditions for complete physical development, as is evidenced by the fact that frequently children in the country have a lower type of physique than city children, who, though possibly living in slum conditions, may have high vitality, strong physique, and keen mentality, which may be due in large measure to city maternal and child health programs.

Economic environment has a great influence on man, although not so much as Marx (1818–1883) and the economic determinists would have us suppose. Marx taught that economic conditions are the main forces in the world: that the economic factor, the struggle to earn a livelihood, is the controlling influence in the events of history, a factor which determines the entire "culture" and life of man and out of which all human institutions, including religion, have arisen. This struggle, he held, has led to the various stages of slavery, serfdom, the wage system under capitalism, and must inevitably culminate in socialism. To insist on this last point was the purpose for which the entire theory was invented.

Even earlier than Marx, the social reformer Robert Owen (1771–1858) stressed the influence of economic environment, and he might be said to be an environmentalist.[5] The well-known ethnologist, Father Wilhelm Schmidt, S.V.D. (b. 1868), also thought that economic life was of great importance, saying that the various types of social organization and material civilization which have arisen have been largely determined by the economic life of the people. Various sociologists

---

[5] Cf. Chapter 20.

have also stressed the importance of economic needs: Sumner and Keller base their system on the idea that it is especially hunger or the "food quest" which determines the general social organization of a people;[6] so do Hobhouse (1864–1929), G. C. Wheeler, M. Ginsberg (b. 1899), De Greef (1842–1924), Lippert (1839–1909), Müller-Lyer (1857–1916), Oppenheimer (b. 1864), Veblen (1857–1929), Thurnwald (b. 1869), and others.[7] Unfortunately, these last named almost entirely ignore individual psychology, and the important influence of the soul and its faculties.

That the economic factor plays a large part in human life, we all concede. Many of the world's historical events: wars, scientific inventions, migrations to other lands, and the rise and downfall of nations, can most certainly be connected with economic causes. But neither all culture, nor all events, can be traced to that one source alone.

Looking now at the influence of economic environment upon the individual member of society — again one must attribute to this environment a very important role. Just as good surroundings have a healthy effect upon a child and give him an easy assurance which allows the full growth of his natural endowments, so poverty has a depressing effect upon him and deprives him of that carefree atmosphere so necessary for his development. Poor housing resulting from insufficient economic resources is one of the great evils which has persisted throughout the ages. Yet bad economic environment is not always detrimental. Instead of the bad effects which may possibly arise from poor economic conditions, poverty may result in a strengthening of character, in the acquisition of such virtues as gentleness, patience, sympathy, and understanding, in trust in God and abandonment to His will, and hope of future happiness in heaven, rather than a concentration of interest in mundane pleasures. It may act as the most powerful stimulus to a man to rise from his poverty to greater material comfort. Poverty was the incentive of many an invention which has enriched the world. And on the other hand we must not neglect to note that an excessively rich economic environment may be equally as unfortunate as a poor one. Riches have been the cause of

---

[6] Sumner and Keller, *The Science of Society*, 4 vols.

[7] Hobhouse, L. T., Wheeler, G. C., and Ginsberg, M., *The Material Culture and Social Institutions of the Simpler Peoples*. Müller-Lyer, F., *The History of Social Development*. Oppenheimer, F., *The State*, etc. Veblen, T., *The Theory of the Leisure Class*. Thurnwald, R., *Die Menschliche Gesellschaft in ihren Ethno-Sociologischen Grundlagen. Repräesentative Lebensbilder von Naturvölkern*. De Greef, G., *Introduction à la Sociologie*, etc. Lippert, J., *Kulturgeschichte der Menschheit in ihrem organischen Aufbau* (tr. *The Evolution of Culture*, Macmillan, 1931).

many a wasted life of potential usefulness, and have led many a person to become lazy, cruel, arrogant, selfish, and forgetful of his duties toward God and his fellow social beings.

Geographic Determinism

Just as some socialists have placed too great an importance on biologic factors of heredity, so certain people, called geographic determinists, attribute the whole basis of society very largely to geographic environment. They say that human energy and achievement, religion, sex relationships, occupations, thought, art, crime, character, are all affected by locality, climate, and other geographic features.

An exaggerated idea of the influence of geography belongs to no special time or country. Hippocrates (*circa* 468–370 B.C.), Strabo (*circa* 63 B.C. — *circa* A.D. 21), and a number of other early writers stressed its influence. Ibn Khaldun (1332–1406) a famous Arab philosopher, wrote extensively on the social and cultural effects of climate on temperament and racial characteristics. Strangely reminiscent of the racialist theories of today, he associated light eating with intelligence, and concluded that his own people were superior to all others, not only because of the "temperate" climate of Arabia on account of the waters around the peninsula, but also because of their eating habits. He attributed the historical development of civilization to the effect of physical environment, and stressed the importance of his own people and their contribution to the world.

Next in importance in this ideology is Bodin (1530–1596) who in his *Methodus* and his *Six Books of the Republic* stressed geography and particularly astral influences, as the main factor in the history of mankind. He discussed the differences between peoples who lived in temperate climates and those in hot or cold countries.

Montesquieu (1689–1755) in his *Spirit of the Laws,* also laid great stress on the importance of climate in social development, including religion. Ritter (1779–1859) saw more influence in the topography of the country, and the configuration of its coast line, than in climate. Buckle (1821–1862) contributed little new to the thought of the geographic determinists, but his *History of Civilization* gives us a systematic examination of the influences of geography.

Of the more modern writers, Friedrich Ratzel (1844–1904) wrote the *History of Mankind,* giving one of the best general ethnographical accounts of world peoples. He also made a very thorough classification of the chief elements in physical environment, stressing the influence of geographic environment in molding culture, and how geography affects historical movements which eventually change the culture of a people. He was the first writer to make geography more than a mere account of physical conditions. His work as a pioneer of human geography has been made popular among English-speaking peoples by Ellen Churchhill Semple (1863–1932) who used his cases to illustrate her very comprehensive volumes on the *Influences of Geographical Environment,* and *American History and Its Geographical Conditions,* which show the influence of geography upon society, the state, religion, and other aspects of social life.

Elsworth Huntington (b. 1876) is another popular writer who has written a large number of books to show the influence of climate and other geographical features upon social life. His examples and statistics, however, often seem very inadequate for the conclusions arrived at. Best of all modern historico-geographers is possibly, L. Febvre (b. 1878) whose *Geographic Introduction to History* gives some due place to influences other than the geographic.

The following is representative of the arguments of the geographic determinists:

Those who live in mountainous regions, swamps, islands, deserts, have to struggle to gain a livelihood: their inaccessibility leads to lawlessness, and hence to bravery; their isolation to stagnation. They become independent, individualistic, and "insular" or narrow-minded. Those who live in valleys and great plains, gain their livelihood with ease: they are more easygoing, have many more chances for personal development and achievement, a greater choice in occupational activities, more natural resources to draw upon, and hence a more highly developed culture.

People living near the ocean or at river mouths usually have fertile soil, the products of other lands are brought to them, they develop trade, have the stimulus of contact with those from abroad, become cosmopolitan in their outlook and wealthy, and hence have opportunities of living a life of ease and culture. The sea invites them to discovery and to voyage abroad, and this develops their resourcefulness and their inventiveness. A country with rivers and natural trade routes, such as the passes of the Alps, and the valleys of the Mississippi, the St. Lawrence, Danube, Rhine, are quickly opened up, and early become civilized. A country with many natural harbors, such as England, is similarly favored.

As to soil: the geographic determinists stress that fertile soil and an abundance of forest lands and plant life lead to agricultural pursuits. Infertile soil, they say, leads to a pastoral and a nomadic existence. The presence of mines and quarries quickly results in the growth of townships and the development of industries. Rainfall, as well as latitude, largely determines the fertility of the soil; and cold or hot winds also have their influence. The enormous effect which the Gulf Stream has had on the inhabitability of Europe is frequently stressed.

That a hot climate tends to make people lethargic and noninventive, is another tenet of those who stress geographic influences. The usually abundant vegetation leaves people with less necessity to work, and as a result they are supposedly lazy, and so an easy prey to despots who have greater leadership powers and energy. But they spend much time with others in the open air, which develops social life more than is possible in colder climates, where people stay more within doors, in their own family circle; and this greater social intercourse in warmer climates leads to a greater development of the emotional nature of the people. Very cold climate, on the other hand, gives the inhabitants a hard struggle for a bare existence, with little time for any cultural or social development.

Temperate climates are, of course, considered most favorable for man's development. The soil is usually not so rich as in the tropics, nor yet so poor as in the colder latitudes. Man must work energetically if he is to get a good return from the soil, but the return is ample. His work and the less abundant yield than in the tropics engenders in him habits of industry and thrift, and he has leisure in which to develop both culturally and socially.

There are more crimes committed against persons in summer, it is said, by reason of the more social life led by people at that period, and the effect of heat upon sex impulses; and there are more crimes against property in winter, which is attributed to the greater need of the poor at that period of the year. Generally speaking, also, crime is more prevalent in cities than in the country. Then the climate affects the moods and nerves of people. We grow gay or sad according as the weather affects us. A bright morning will make us hilarious; a dull, wet afternoon may fill us with boredom and discontent. The irritating and enervating heat of summer is said to make suicides more frequent during that period.

Many geographical determinists follow Montesquieu's idea that religion is dependent upon climate, stating that cold climate makes people independent, and resentful of centralized religious control, so that they are preponderantly Protestant; whereas southern people are more submissive to authority and therefore tend to remain Catholic.

It is obvious that some of the above arguments about the influence of geography are very true. Climate and altitude do affect our nerves and temperament, for instance, and have some influence on the incidence of disease, and it suggests the lines of economic development. Geography imposes limits to what is available for use, but it does not necessitate its use. It is but natural that the type of agriculture, herding, building materials which a people develops, and the methods which are used, should be intimately bound up with such physical details as topography, soil, climate, and natural means of communication. Yet peoples by no means develop always in the same manner. The Lapps, for instance, raise reindeer, whereas the Yakuts in a similar climate raise cattle and horses and have no reindeer. Neither peoples could raise the ostrich or the elephant. Some adaptations are needed in many environments, for any material progression; other adaptations may be advisable but man is in no way impelled to use them. Again to give examples from cold lands, we find the Eskimos making intelligent use of their environment and building snowhouses, whereas the Chukchis on the other side of the Bering Strait erect clumsy tents with wooden frames and coverings of hide; and whereas these peoples of the north both attire themselves suitably against the elements, some of the primitives of Tierra del Fuego, in a fairly severe habitat, have not yet invented suitable clothing.

Temperature certainly does not appear to have the influence so often imputed to it, for despite the torrid climate, we have ample proof of a high civilization by the early Sumerians, Egyptians, Indians, and others, while the people living in more temperate climates were still living in barbarism. Nor does climate appear to affect the achievements of those who inhabit cities in the United States, with high summer temperatures and great humidity. And to give yet another example, some very notable men have come from the cold, bleak climates of Scotland and of Scandinavia.

Frenay, who made an exhaustive study of the subject says: "There is no correlation or only an insignificant one between suicide and climate."[8] There are, in fact, fewer suicides in hotter southern countries than in colder ones. And as for religion, there are fewer members of the highly organized Catholic faith in the south of the United States and in the south of England, than in the northern parts of these countries. The Catholic population of the cold countries of Poland and Lithuania is over 75 per cent of the total, and the number of Catholics in Holland and Germany, both northern countries, amounts to over one third of the population. Practically the whole of Belgium

---

[8] Frenay, Rev. A. D., O.P., *The Suicide Problem in the United States*, p. 126.

professes the Catholic faith. Neither can the differences in character
and culture between the French and the Germans, or the English and
the Irish be explained by any geographical peculiarities.

Favorable geographic factors naturally enrich human life, but they
can in no way be said to dominate. Seemingly insurmountable limitations of former times have been largely overcome at the present day
in all advanced civilizations by the many phases of modern inventions.
Man's ingenuity has made uninhabitable deserts fertile, and fertile
plains gloomy oil districts; it has led to the cutting of a continent in
two to make a seagoing passage possible between the Atlantic and
the Pacific; it has made inaccessible places but a few hours distant,
by train or airplane, from civilized parts; and it has made the use of
synthetic products quite commonplace. The spread of literature, the
newspaper, the radio, have made even the most remote spots isolated
no longer. Indeed, examples of man's domination over nature are too
numerous to attempt to pick out a few representative illustrations.
The limitations of physical environment are but relative.

Psychosocial Environment

It will be evident to the reader that man's environment is not merely
objective. There is a social environment provided by the people we
live with, the social groups to which we belong. Our social environment has a very great influence on what we are, and do, and think.
Man is greatly influenced by the various groups with which he is
associated. Brought up in a group of ruffians, it is extremely unlikely
that he will be refined. He will hardly become an ardent nationalist
if brought up in a group of revolutionaries. In this almost inevitable
influence lies the importance of the study of group life. "Tell me your
companions, and I'll tell what manner of man you are," or as the
proverb puts it: "Birds of a feather flock together."

Most important of all social groups and societies to which a
person belongs is the family. We are born into this group and in it
we normally spend the greater part of the most important years of
our life. Because we are men, we inherit a capacity to learn; what
we learn is determined very largely by our environment, and it is
particularly in early childhood that the developing mind receives its
most vivid impressions and its most effective training. If a child is
formed to good habits in the home, in an atmosphere of love and kindness, with a normal healthy development of all social qualities with
his parents, brothers, sisters, and companions, then very probably the
defects and propensities to evil which he may have inherited will be

largely eliminated, and his good qualities will develop. Brought up in an environment of indifference, where the parents exercise little self-restraint, where there is quarreling, anger, and other vices, a child's bad qualities are likely to be brought out and his good ones stunted. His social environment here will tend to have a bad effect upon him rather than a good one.

Then there is the neighborhood, in which the child usually seeks his companions at play. Wholesome recreation with good companions develops not only the body but also the mind. It engenders self-reliance, self-control, fidelity to ideals, a respect for law; and it is a great leveler of caste and race. This is true, of course, for adults as well as for the young.

Nor must one forget the school group, which has an influential socializing effect since in it the majority of children spend many hours daily for at least eight to twelve years of their life. Not only does the school teach youth, as does the play group, to be self-reliant, self-controlled, and to formulate high ideals, and to have a respect for law, but it also imparts specialized knowledge which enables the student to be a good citizen, and to train for an occupation in life. Religious training and a sound education, coupled with the social influence of teachers of high ideals and moral integrity, further the development afforded a child by his home and play group to a very considerable degree.

Again, there is the work group, to which the majority of persons must belong in later life. Dull, monotonous toil, with poor wages, unpleasant working conditions, and a lack of friendly co-operation between worker and employer, must of necessity affect the employee adversely, engender an antisocial spirit within him and make him less fit physically and mentally to be of value in the world. On the other hand, a good socializing effect on the employee is bound to follow varied, interesting work, in pleasant surroundings, with congenial fellow workmen, where the worker is encouraged to take a pride in his attainments, where he has the opportunity to advance in his profession, is paid an adequate wage for himself and his family, and is encouraged in a spirit of friendly co-operation with his fellow workers and employers.

In addition to the influence of the important social groups and societies of family, neighborhood, church, work group, school, and play group, one must not overlook the environment provided by each of the other minor groups or societies to which a person usually belongs. Infinite in variety, the social contacts provided by these groups all wield an influence, more or less profound, on the continuously developing character of their members.

Mental or Psychic Environment

So far we have talked of such external environment as the physical and the social, both of which, and particularly the social, has some effect upon the mind, and hence upon conduct. There is, however, a much more important environment which plays upon men, and that is the psychic environment. From his earliest childhood a person learns to conform to the thoughts, to the attitudes, ideals, habits, sympathies, and traditions of his group. Gradually he learns to feel, to think, to judge as his neighbors do. His social instinct, coupled with his desire to express himself (to satisfy his ego) ever leads him to desire to conform to the standards of those around him — to win their approval and their admiration, either by strict conformance to the traditions of the past, or in conformity with the desire of the group to follow a leader to changed customs and pastures new.[9] In other words, he wishes to belong to what Sumner (1840–1910) called the "in" or "we" group; he experiences what Giddings (1855–1931) terms "consciousness of kind,"[10] the "we-feeling" of Cooley (1864–1929), and fears the feeling of isolation, ostracism, and inferiority if he belongs to the "out" group, those not socially acceptable. Gumplowicz (1838–1894) gives the term *syngenism* to the sentiment of attachment or union resulting from being born and reared together, and it was he, too, who invented the term *ethnocentrism,* to express the feeling of unity which exists among people bound together by ties of nationality, race, or culture, and who emphasized the struggle between races.

It is such psychic influences as these which lead a crowd to act

---

[9] In some Bohemian circles it is fashionable to go against accepted opinion, but to run counter to the opinion of others is precisely to conform to the ideas of that particular group. It is noteworthy that those who are powerful because of a position of authority, riches, or personal qualities, are less constrained to conform to accepted standards than other people, although vanity may lead them to do so, and duty may require their conformity.

[10] E. Giddings defines consciousness of kind as "a state of consciousness in which any being, whether low or high in the scale of life recognizes another conscious being as of like kind with himself" (*Principles of Sociology,* p. 17). In amplification of this definition we read: "When the individuals who participate in pluralistic behavior have become differentiated into behavioristic kinds or types, a consciousness of kind, liking or disliking, approving or disapproving, one kind after another, converts gregariousness into a consciously discriminating association, herd habit into society; and society, by social pressure which sometimes is conscious but more often perhaps unconscious, makes life relatively hard for kinds of character and conduct that are disapproved" (*Studies in the Theory of Human Society,* p. 291).

irrationally at times. All groups aim at like-mindedness within their sphere, for a group functions in perfect unison only when all its members are in accord; and homogeneity simplifies the task of government. This social or group mind has been very much emphasized by some of the sociologists. Giddings notes it: "The social mind is the phenomenon of many individual minds in interaction, so playing upon one another, that they simultaneously feel the same sensation or emotion, arrive at one judgement and perhaps act in concert. It is, in short, the mental unity of many individuals or of a crowd."[11] Durkheim (1858–1917), Le Bon (1841–1931), and others have so exaggerated the influence of the common ideas of a group upon the individual that they talk of a group to which the members must and will conform without thought of motives or consequences. In other words, they consider society, as well as morals, a sentiment of sociality, as being something apart from and above the individual, transmitted psychically as part of the social heritage. While it is, of course, true that a man very frequently acts in an irrational manner, particularly when with a group,[12] nevertheless he is always capable of using his reason and his free will, and he is by no means constrained to act against his principles and his ideals, when these differ from those of the group.

Not only is man influenced by group ideas, he is, too, molded by the environment of the attitudes and ideals engendered by the books and newspapers he reads, by the current fashions in art, music, dances, dress, theater, and concerts of all kinds. At the present time the German Nazis are making full use of all psychic and other environment to impose an entirely erroneous race theory, as well as a feeling of national unity upon the German subjects. Unless a man has very strong personal ideals, or unless he be highly educated, of strong individual views, or of commanding will power, he is certain to be influenced by the spirit of his times. The influence of many a good home, school, companions, is diluted, sometimes almost nullified, by the contrary attitudes and ideals engendered by the current literature, motion-picture theaters, radio, and other factors. Again, the pernicious influence of many of our commercial amusements and materialistic literature is, of course, happily mitigated by the influence of good taste in music, literature, and other arts, and high ideals and noble sentiments engendered in the home and school.

Added to this *zeitgeist* around us, there is the psychic environment

---

[11] Giddings, F., *Principles of Sociology*, p. 134.
[12] Examples of unintelligent group behavior are to be found in La Piere, R. T., *Collective Behavior* (McGraw-Hill, 1938).

which we provide for ourselves. We are influenced by our conduct, by our views on our physical and mental defects and abnormalities — our beauty or our ugliness or our "ordinary" looks, our height and weight and general appearance, our intelligence and our achievements or our failures, all, insofar as they do not conform to average norms, create a spirit which will influence our conduct in society. If we are well-integrated persons, our characters will be admirable types; insofar as there is a disequilibrium between the higher and the lower abilities of our nature, and between our ideals and our acts, or our ideals and attitudes and those of the persons around us, we may or may not develop a good social character.

The provision of good education is an important factor in man's psychic environment, which can counteract many other harmful influences. Everything possible should be done to promote public libraries stocked with the best of books, good schools for young and old, good public concerts, educational lectures, and other educational facilities which will enable a child or an adult to have a greater fund of knowledge, develop his intelligence, his will power, his ideals, and preferences of the right kind, which will give him a deeper understanding of his fellow men and of society, and fit him better to take his place as an influence for good in the world.

It is precisely in the psychic realm, too, that religion exercises its most powerful influence, providing the motives for right conduct, and furnishing the means to help human frailty somewhat to attain to the lofty ideals thus established. The Catholic Church realizes the uses of emotion as a help to the formation of good habits and as deepening intellectual conviction. Emotional appeal alone is bad, insofar as it belongs to the lower faculty of man's nature, and the Church stresses the intellectual aspects of religion, and its true end. Mindful, however, of the value of symbolism and of attuning all the senses to higher aims, the Church gives her members the aid of beautiful, as well as meaningful services, good church music, light and color, even the smell of incense and of flowers. In recent decades many Catholics lost the former ideals of good taste in these matters, but the growth of the Liturgical Movement has already seen its fruits in the growing awareness of congregations in those parishes where the Church's services have been restored to their rightful place, and where the people are instructed how to participate in them intelligently and with all the powers of their being.

A different aspect of environment will be discussed in the next chapter.

CHAPTER 4

MAN AND CULTURE

What Culture Is

IN THE two preceding chapters we have concentrated mainly on man as an individual. Yet in sociology the interest is not so much in the individual as in society as a whole. Man is a social being, and society is made up of individuals each with their varying character, living in physical, social, and psychic environment. Here we shall discuss man and his environment as a social unity.

Man differs from the animals not only in the possession of human intelligence and purposive will, and in the power of speech, but also in the fact that from the time he first appeared upon the earth he supplemented his hereditary, physical, and psychic potentialities by material culture, habits, and techniques, which increased his comfort, power, and safety. During the course of the many centuries he has lived upon the earth, he has left behind him many monuments: buildings, furniture, implements, above all, accumulated inventions. More than this, he has acquired habits, and has left their manner of development behind him, too, handing them down, not by biological inheritance, but socially, through teaching them to the oncoming generation by word or in writing. He has thought deeply about many things, abstract as well as the concrete, and has perpetuated these also in the written or the spoken word.

This accumulation of material, social, and spiritual things, habits, and ideas, which are an expression of man and yet outside himself, is what the sociologist calls by the term *culture*. Culture to the social scientists means all the social institutions, customs, and ways of living which are peculiar to any group; and all the manifestations of the social habits of a community. It is not used by the sociologists and anthropologists in the sense of a cultured man; it does not mean cultivated or civilized; instead, it denotes the way of life of a people — their particular civilization. There is a primitive Pygmy culture, a modern culture of the English. Yet more strictly, perhaps, in the latter connotation we should say a culture of the Londoners, a culture of the men of Devon, a culture of every other localized place in England—

or to continue with examples, the culture of the people of Boston, the culture of the South, of movieland, of the farmers of the Middle West. These separate cultures, in turn, participate in the general culture of the English or the inhabitants of the United States, whereby the English or the American way of life is distinguished from the culture of the French, or the Basques or the Japanese, or even from the culture of the Americans or English of any epoch than our own.

Culture differs, but a difference from the culture of our modern western world, for example, does not necessarily mean that it is of a lower order.[1] A low material culture may be accompanied by a high moral order; a high material culture, such as ours, seems at present to be rather decadent in moral worth.[2]

E. B. Tylor (1832–1917) first used the word *culture* in this sociological sense in the year 1871, and his definition is the most frequently quoted and the best known: "Culture or Civilization," he says, "taken in its wide ethnographical sense, is that complex whole which includes belief, art, morals, law, custom, and any other capabilities or habits acquired by man as member of society."[3] Built upon man's habit-forming capacity and his intelligence, culture is, therefore, a uniquely human phenomenon, which is socially inherited by each generation.

The culture of an ethnographical group includes all the social institutions, customs, and ways of living which are peculiar to it; and all the manifestations of the social habits of the community. And since these ways of living are so extremely diverse and complicated, culture, too, is a highly complex thing, including thoughts and feelings and activities of every kind.

Culture differs in all social groups. All people have their own peculiar habits, customs, and reactions — their culture; all families and all other social groups, have their peculiar culture, too. The human

---

[1] For a discussion of culture differences in general, see Boas, F., ed., *General Anthropology*, pp. 464, 465; Lowie, R. H., *Are We Civilized?*

[2] To the Catholic, a culture is of a high order only when individual and social life is *fully* developed. Thus, for the individual it should mean the development of the whole man: bodily, to adequate health and functioning; mentally, to an appreciation of the beautiful, that is, the true and the good, both physically and morally, to the adequate fulfillment of duties to God, to self, and to society. Socially, true culture promotes the well-being and happiness (taken in the completest sense of recognition of the real end and dignity of man) both of the group, and of individuals.

[3] Tylor, E. B., *Primitive Culture*, Vol. I, p. 1. Spencer (1820–1903) was the first sociologist, however, to use cultural data as the main source for his writings. He initiated the cultural approach to sociology and was the first to see culture as a whole. So far as Tylor's definition is concerned, the reader should note that if man acquires culture "as a member of society," culture cannot be the cause of societies, as so many of the cultural sociologists infer.

race has the same basic heredity and the same human needs, but each human being is subjected to the influence of the culture around him from the moment of his birth, and outward expressions of needs and other habits develop differently with each social group. Kissing may seem to us a natural expression of affection, yet it is unknown to some peoples, as for example, the Eskimos. We weep for sorrow, and the Maori and Andaman Islanders have ceremonial weeping for joy. When an American sneezes, his tongue remains in its normal place, and if he follows accepted standards of politeness, he will put up his hand to shield his mouth; if a member of the Hopi tribe sneezes, he puts his tongue out. Most people who use tea, drink it, but the Tibetans roll it into balls with butter and salt and use it as food.

We all form habits which become almost second nature to us, so that we do not even realize that they were imposed on us from outside, and that others do not think or feel as we do. And as a result of the habits we form, we feel prejudiced toward what is unusual to any of our senses. The great variety of food which most peoples have is largely a psychologically induced need, due to acquired habits of taste and desire. Milk is considered essential to good health in the United States, and in many European countries, but it is rejected by many of the peoples of Asia. Consider any two American colleges: both may belong to the same standardizing agency, say the North Central, yet each will have its distinctive spirit, due to the beauty of or utility of the buildings and their architecture; to the size of the groups and the extent to which they are socially knit together; to the personality of the teachers, the types of students who preceded each of the incoming classes, and to the traditions, customs, and habits which have been developed. Notice the difference between the members of any two religious communities, how the walk, and mannerisms and even facial expression of a Jesuit differs from that of a Dominican; how a Benedictine nun differs from a member of the Franciscan order; yet all these people have the same basic motivation for their manner of living.

The Culture Trait

An examination of the culture of various social groups shows clearly that it is really composed of a large number of traits or units of culture, such as single habits or artifacts, and that such traits are closely bound together, and interpenetrate each other. Note, for instance, the large number of individual culture traits which go to make up the customary scene of an American family at breakfast, an English group at afternoon tea, a college group at a ball game, or a group of Catholics at Holy Mass or at a Benediction service. Notice how the Chinese or the American manipulate table implements, their way of holding the cup and of drinking, the habitual expressions employed to greet each other at a meal, or to show satisfaction, or to ask to have things passed to them, or to refuse food offered; consider, too, all the numerous differing objects present on the table. Note all the multitudinous details of the form and structure of an automobile, as well as the numerous actions connected with driving it; see how the very facial expression of a man changes when he drives a car from what it is when he is merely a passenger in it. All these tangible and intangible things are culture traits.

If even one of these traits is removed, the others are affected, and the environment becomes different. Man must adapt himself not only to physical environment and to other men and ideas, but also to the sum total of the social heritage (including the physical, of course) which we call culture. The removal of a trait may lead only to a temporary annoyance, or it may result in complete social disintegration. Witness, for instance, how people are often dissatisfied in new surroundings, however intrinsically pleasant they may be, and even if the culture differences be but slight, such as a customary greeting of "Hi, there!" in place of: "Good day!" or even "Hello!" Notice the frequent ennui and awkwardness of a man accustomed to working in an office all day, when he retires while still in good active health; yet one who has spent most of his life in the country, or who has provided himself with reading and other hobby habits, in earlier years, will find plenty to do with his leisure time. Occasionally a poorly balanced individual will be so unable to adjust to a change of environment and habits that he or she becomes a "mental problem," or even quite insane. And these isolated, individual disturbances are as nothing compared with the disastrous effects of some of the acts of certain colonial administrators or missionaries in backward countries, who have sometimes abolished primitive customs which seemed to them foolish, perhaps even repulsive, without realizing the place these customs occupied in the preservation of order or morality. Once the customs were gone, effective restraint on bad conduct, or incentive to good endeavor was sometimes completely absent, and occasionally the result has been almost complete social disintegration.

Folkways, Mores, and Institutions

When customs become habitual to a number of members of a group, for example, etiquette of various kinds, sociologists usually call these *folkways* — a term first used in a peculiar sociological significance by William Graham Sumner (1840–1910) in 1906.[4] When these folkways are considered essential to human welfare, generally by the development of ritual, then mores are said to arise — another term first used sociologically by Sumner, in his book on *Folkways*. According to Sumner, however, and a number of other sociologists, all our institutions are merely important mores whose culture traits have been long considered permanent, and they include as such, monogamous marriage, any form of religious worship, a special type of government, and the like.

Now, it is very true that many of our mores and institutions are but the result of long-established custom. Yet it is equally true that certain of our mores and institutions are by no means sanctioned merely by tradition and long use. In all primitive cultures, as also in the culture of all other men, certain cultural institutions in addition to speech are remarkable for their universality. These are: marriage and the family, religious worship, some attempt at the organized division of labor, at least an incipient state form, and private-property ownership. There is, too, a remarkable similarity in basic moral codes. Although even the very universality of these institutions and norms of conduct would seem to point to the fact that they must be "natural" to man, arising out of the needs of his human nature, and a divinely implanted moral law, other reasons must be given to make any valid proof of their universal need — reasons which will be explained in later chapters. Yet, of course, it is only the essence of these institutions and norms, their general character, which is essentially the same in all cultures. Their form or content varies somewhat among nearly all peoples, so that the folkways or even the mores attaching to them — but not their essential attributes — may justly be said to have arisen merely out of custom. It remains true, however, that those sociologists who teach that even the essentials of these institutions are "evolved," must be in error, as will be clearer after the reader has studied Part Two of the book.

Basing their ideas on certain results of inductive research, on the Bible, on the teachings of the Church, and on the findings of philosophy, Catholic sociologists consider the following truths as certain: that the family and the State are "natural" primary societies; that the institution of private property is a "natural one"; and that the Catholic Church is a supernatural primary society. The Church and the duly

---

[4] Sumner, W. G., *Folkways, A Study of the Sociological Importance of Usages, Manners, Customs, Mores and Morals* (Ginn & Co., 1906).

constituted State are considered "perfect" societies, that is, sovereign in their own power, and not in any way dependent upon a power other than God alone. In the natural sphere, of course, the family is considered more important than either Church or State since it is prior to both and the latter are composed of none other than families and their individual members. Certain Catholics are of the opinion that Occupational Society (the regulation of labor, and its organization into groups which function within civil society) and International Society (organized harmonious co-operation between nations) are also natural societies. The usefulness of both these societies would indeed seem to show that they are primary. Certainly this would be so for economic organization. As for international society — just as the individual cannot exist without the family, and just as the family needs group life and the State for its protection and its fuller development, so States need each other. International society should logically be the natural development of civil society, and it may thus be considered as at least remotely primary. But whether these two societies are "natural" as well as primary may well be debated. Two other primary groups are educational society and recreational society. All of these important social groups are discussed more fully in later chapters.

The Culture Complex and the Culture Area

The culture of every people is, as we have shown, composed of a large number of traits, which most frequently group themselves into what is called technically a culture complex — a cluster of culture traits which seem to move together. Such might be said to be all the manner of etiquette connected with the satisfaction of hunger, which vary with practically every nation in at least some small particular. Herskovits[5] (b. 1895) has described the "cattle complex" of East Africa, showing how cattle enter in all the important events of life, in birth ceremonies, religious ceremonies, marriage and the like, and how they consequently play a much larger part with East African natives than, for example, with ourselves. Clark Wissler (b. 1870) has given us details[6] of the "horse complex" of the Plains Indians, and the "maize complex" of other North American Indian tribes.

Each culture trait has its own history of development, but as each combines with other traits, it continues its history as a unit with these

---

[5] Herskovits, Melville J., "The Cattle Complex in East Africa," *American Anthropologist*, Vol. XXVIII, n.s., pp. 370 *et seq.*
[6] Wissler, C., *The American Indian.*

other traits, and forms a culture complex, which has its own history in time and space.

When a particular type of culture complex is typical of a well-defined geographical area — when a culture conforms to one general homogeneous type within this area, then a culture area is formed. The term *culture area* was first used by Wissler,[7] who found ten such areas among North American Indian tribes, and five among the original inhabitants of South America.

How Culture Developed: The Importance of Today's Primitives

An important question to consider is the manner in which any people adopts culture traits, or a complex of traits, in any area previously without these culture items. In the very early days before the Fall, the culture of Adam and Eve embraced a high degree of moral order, but it is very unlikely that it was characterized by any high scientific, mechanical, and aesthetic development — in fact all archaeological evidence would seem to point to the exact contrary, although, of course, we have no means of arriving at any knowledge of the manner of life of the first human society, other than from the scanty Biblical account. Yet although we can get little from history, and from archaeology only a few material clues to the life of some of the earliest inhabitants on the earth, as we mentioned in the first chapter, ethnologists think that certain primitive tribes of today can give us a clearer conception of man's early social life than any other social groups of which we have record. The culture of a few primitive peoples seems to indicate a survival from archaic times, although very few can be put into this category.[8] The few there are may be found only in the remote corners of the earth, in inaccessible forest and mountain fastnesses. They live the simplest kind of social life, untouched by what we call our modern civilization. They are merely food gatherers, living on fruit, nuts, roots, and such fish, reptiles, insects or other animals as may be available to them. They are not food producers. Their clothing, tools, and weapons are of the simplest. Simple as their material, political, and social life may be, it is nevertheless noteworthy that each has its distinctive culture: ceremonialism and elaborate magical formulas and taboos are particularly evident. Indeed, they have certainly developed somewhat through the ages, and the very fact that the simplicity of their culture would point to stagnation

---

[7] *Ibid.* (1917 edition), p. 51.
[8] Cf. The theories of Rev. Wilhelm Schmidt briefly mentioned in the previous chapter, and again later.

for a very long period of time is evidence that we cannot draw any exact inferences from the lives of these primitive peoples as to the life of our first parents. They do, nevertheless, provide us with some clues, and there is a remarkable similarity of the basic social institutions in the lives of all of them, as we shall later show.

Turning now to the development of culture, it seems probable that when Adam and Eve began life upon the earth, their intelligence was directly inspired by God toward the utilization of at least some of the many natural products which surrounded them. God walked with Adam in the Garden of Eden.[9] And at that time man was probably instructed in certain norms of conduct, the basic primary institutions. As for culture in general, man's natural intelligence would eventually lead him to discoveries of more possibilities in nature's products, and gradually he invented many a habit and manner of self-expression. Eventually, when the people dispersed to different parts of the world, they took with them the original culture as it had developed in the first place of man's habitation on the earth. This process is called by the sociologists a fission of culture.[10] In the culture area which would be formed by each of the migrant tribes, the archaic culture would, of course, survive. Undoubtedly, however, a series of improving inventions and discoveries would arise. Despite the lack of originality in the majority of men, and despite man's tendency to take things as he gets them and to conserve them by the inertia of habit, tradition, and taboos, many changes would inevitably take place with the years. Culture existing at any one specified period of time, from which further inventions and discoveries spring, is called a culture base. From this base man nearly always elaborates or changes in at least some small degree the traditional habits and ways of life. A small difference in environment, additional products of nature or the absence or rarity of products formerly used, would lead persons in different tribes to discoveries of some products or forces previously unobserved — and to inventions, or the purposeful creation of some new process or combination of former culture traits. In this manner, different cultures would develop. Those who led a nomadic existence, who kept herds, would develop inventions and a manner of life, and different thought from those who lived a sedentary agricultural existence. To some extent at least, culture depends on the resources of physical geographical environment, and this was more true of primitive peoples and in ancient

---

[9] Gen. 3:8.

[10] Another example of fission would be the development of the English language and of Sanskrit from the same Indo-European base.

times than in the modern civilizations of today. Development was probably, therefore, very slow in early times. Indeed, development is hampered in any culture by the stabilizing effect of custom and tradition, which may nullify many an innovation. It is particularly noteworthy that many of the relatively undeveloped "primitives" of today have surrounded their institutions and their folkways and mores with a number of taboos and religious or magical sanctions which have their values, but their disadvantages to development are very great.

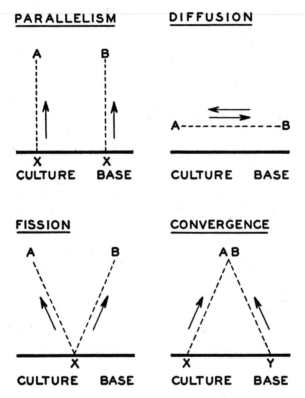

Four Ways Culture May Develop

Parallelism and Convergence

The name *parallelism* is given by sociologists to a case where two groups in different regions independently develop closely similar culture traits, that is, similar inventions or manners of living. If this growth arises from an original element of culture which they had in common, the parallelism is said to be secondary. Primary parallelism implies a strictly independent origin, where the original culture received could not possibly have been instrumental in bringing about the similarity of two particular culture forms.

For some years near the end of the past century it was fashionable to trace many of our social institutions as having gone through a series of parallel developments, rather than as having their origin in a single early source, or having at some time or other developed through contact with other peoples. These theorists were the unilineal evolutionists, who thought that as human nature is always the same, all men would inevitably develop certain culture traits along certain lines, have the same culture history, and independently arrive by well-defined and similar stages to the same results. The same theorists also considered that everything about man, not only his body, but his whole culture has evolved from lower animal forms, through a primitive brutish-human state, to the higher civilization of the western world today. Herbert Spencer (1820–1903), worked out detailed (yet, of course, quite imaginary) stages of development for religious, social, and political organizations. His *First Principles* was published in 1862 and preceded Darwin's ideas of natural selection and the survival of the fittest. A whole host of writings of sociologists and anthropologists followed Spencer's lead. All these writers dogmatically asserted the results of their entirely hypothetical thinking. They taught that the family progressed from primitive promiscuity, through matriarchy or mother rule, where the mother is most important, then through polygamy and the patriarchal family, down to monogamous forms. For religion there is a whole series of progressions, from primitive atheism to monotheism. For property, they confidently assert that originally men held all things in common. These assumptions were built upon the so-called methodical observations of the culture of primitive tribes, and the inferences which might be drawn from these observations. But often the most superficial, secondhand travelers' tales were used, or facts were stretched to fit predetermined theories. Most modern anthropologists contend that the social evolutionists are mainly in the wrong, and that they are unscientific, and a glance at any modern ethnographical work will show that the record of modern anthropological fieldworkers is worthy of scholarly attention. Their theories will be mentioned again later in Part Two.

Yet, of course, some culture traits have been invented or discovered independently by people in different culture areas, particularly where the same or similar materials were at hand, or where people developed a manner of life which required that the same tasks should be performed. On the other hand, similar environments may be utilized for quite a different cycle of inventions. As Lowie says: "Environment cannot explain culture because the identical environment is consistent with distinct cultures; because cultural traits persist from inertia in an unfavorable environment; because they do not develop where they would be of distinct advantage to a people; and because they may even disappear where one would least expect it on geographical principles."[11] Invention depends upon so many factors, not only upon opportunity and need, but also on observation and imagination and an appreciation of the particular situation. Generally speaking, inventions are more frequent where material culture is rich, for the very variety of forms suggests small changes and additions. It is dependent upon existing culture, but the same invention in different culture areas or culture complexes may have quite a different cultural history and spring from quite a different original culture base. Such a situation, the independent development of similar culture traits from dissimilar origins, is called by the sociologists convergence.

Diffusion

No civilization, however, is the product of a single people. The greatest factor in the development of cultural life seems to be the normal tendency of culture traits to spread themselves by means of social contact with other peoples, through borrowing, or migration and interaction, called by the sociologists acculturation[12] or diffusion. Not only does culture change because of internal changes in the course of time, but culture moves in space as well, because of diffusion, that is, because of influence from the outside. The independent origin of inventions is very rare. Often seeming parallelisms are, instead, the same idea spread originally by diffusion, but the connection is lost to history. Oftentimes migrations of the past are completely lost to us. For instance, the world over there are similar accounts of a big flood at some early period of the world's history. While some single origin of the stories of the North American Indians is rather obvious from special details of their myth — on the other hand, the universality of the account in the Bible, in Babylon, Sumer, among the Greeks, and with so many primitive peoples of today would seem to infer a previous his-

---

[11] Lowie, R. H., *Culture and Ethnology*, p. 62.

[12] The term *acculturation* is now usually confined to the results of cultural contact, whereby modern Western culture is brought to primitive tribes; for example, the imposition of certain Western ways by the Belgians upon the peoples of the Congo, or by the British government throughout its colonial empire.

torical contact by diffusion, or at least survivals from earlier times as a result of fission.[13]

The borrowing and diffusion of culture is constantly taking place. At the beginnings of the race, various tribes branched off from the parent stock, took with them a culture base, and developed cultures of their own, as we have already mentioned; later they would come in contact with each other again, through trading, intermarriage, war, or migratory wanderings. Ideas would be borrowed from each other, and the combinations would give rise to new inventions and to other ways of living and of thought. No one particular trait can be considered a peculiarity of any culture area, for culture traits travel widely on account of human intercourse. Geographic environment does not necessarily handicap the development of a culture trait which, easy in the region from which it came, might nevertheless be adopted in a new environment despite difficulty in maintaining it. One could perhaps cite the comparatively recent introduction of very thin silk stockings by women living in the colder parts of the United States and in Canada. Yet, of course, geographical conditions do sometimes limit the distribution of a trait — the habit of skiing in the winter, for example, could never become a widespread sport in Louisiana or in the British Isles. Such is the nature of man, that whenever he travels he takes his cultural habits with him, but he also generally assimilates some of the culture traits of the people among whom he visits — he brings culture by migration, and adopts culture by the borrowing process. For example, the American abroad may take with him an insistence on the provision of drinking water with his meals, and some of the people among whom he lives may likewise adopt his habit; but he may bring back with him to his own land a habit of needing afternoon tea, or a particular foreign gesture of the hands, or a lifting of the eyebrow, which may become a habit in his group. The early American colonizers brought many features of European civilization to the American Indian tribes, but they borrowed tobacco, the canoe, snowshoes, toboggans, the use of rubber, potatoes, tomatoes, maize, squashes, peanuts, chocolate, the turkey, and many other foods from the peoples whom they conquered.

Frazer (b. 1854) and others have pointed to the origin of many of the Christian rites in Jewish and even pagan ceremonies, thus stigmatizing Christianity as a mere accretion to former religious types. In

---

[13] An excellent discussion of this latter connection is to be found in Caiger, S. L., *Bible and Spade: An Introduction to Biblical Archaeology* (London: Oxford University Press, 1936).

this, of course, they show an ignorance of the fact that Christ "did not come to destroy"; that the early Christians, realizing perhaps unconsciously the importance of existing Jewish and pagan culture traits and their influence on the lives of the people, took these traits and merely gave them a different and higher significance.

We have many instances of a quick spreading of a culture trait when once it is invented. The wheel was invented in Babylon about 3300 B.C., the true arch existed in that country in 3000 B.C., and the horse was brought there by an Asiatic tribe about 2000 B.C. The use of the wheel and the horse spread much more rapidly than did the true arch. Tobacco, used for many centuries in America before European conquests there, was introduced by the Spanish and the English into Europe, was taken by the Portuguese to India and other parts of Asia, and very rapidly spread round the world, being reintroduced into America by way of Alaska within two hundred years. Yet note that writing was invented about 4000 B.C., the Egyptians developed the pure alphabet about one thousand years later, but it was long after that period before this form of writing became very widespread. Paper was invented in China at a fairly early period, probably about the time of Christ, it was not introduced into Europe, through Arabia, until the twelfth century, but then its use spread very rapidly.

The Culture Threshold and Social Control

Although there are slow changes in culture, the theory of gradual change in the development of all culture traits is now considered entirely erroneous. As Goldenweiser (b. 1880) says: "Not that slow changes have been proved to be non-existent, but experience with historic and prehistoric communities has shown that sudden mutations, cataclysmic and revolutionary, are wont to cut into the more orderly chain of historic events. Such imitations are inventions, religious revivals, happy thoughts, features borrowed from outside and the like."[14] The fact is that people do not borrow traits until they are ready for them. "Culture, it seems, is a matter of exceedingly slow growth until a certain 'threshold' is passed, when it darts forward, gathering momentum at an unexpected rate."[15] The term *cultural threshold* is now used technically to mean the point at which a trait can be borrowed after a certain level of culture is reached, or the place in a certain series of inventions where a final innovation can be made either because the

[14] Lowie, R. H., *op. cit.*, p. 78.
[15] Goldenweiser, A., "Diffusion and the American School of Historical Ethnology," *American Journal of Sociology*, Vol. XXXI, July, 1925, p. 19.

prior inventions themselves or some other factor has made the time ripe for it. Chapin (b. 1888) has used the term *cultural horizon* somewhat in the sense of the cultural threshold but with a wider meaning, to denote a general stage of development necessary before any new cultural pattern is possible[16] — as, for example, a period when a great number of similar inventions are made for the same things within a very short period of time. An example of the cultural threshold is seen in the invention of a stocking knitting machine in the time of Queen Elizabeth, which could not then be used because the Queen prohibited it, to avoid the unemployment of hand knitters, and was not introduced again until over a hundred years later. Other instances could be cited of machinery existing in France, England, and elsewhere from the thirteenth century onwards, and yet the widespread use of machinery and the manifold inventions connected with its employment began only one hundred and fifty years ago. Napoleon saw no utility in Fulton's steamboat, even though he was offered its exclusive use. Were they to meditate on the matter, the peoples of Europe must surely recognize the superiority of the many "services" provided in the United States by department stores, certain libraries, and other public places; yet hygienic and easily available drinking fountains and other facilities have not yet been adopted there. If the cultural horizon or threshold is not reached, a trait will never spread among a particular people.

Culture does not change uniformly, and even when it is transmitted, modifications will frequently occur. The external form may remain, but the meaning may be changed, as for example, when the Indian ceremonial use and setting for tobacco was completely discarded by the Europeans and those who received the culture trait by diffusion through Europe. No trait is completely static, because people are dynamic. Society selects the culture traits which it adopts. The people of the Near East discovered the possibilities of the domestication and milking of cattle, yet whereas the Zulu use the meat only, we use both milk and meat, but neither the Zulu nor the Americans and Europeans consume almost the entire content of the animal, including its stomach, as do certain of the Eskimo with their reindeer. With the widespread use of literature, the radio, quick means of travel, culture traits are disseminated much more rapidly throughout the "civilized" world than was possible in former times. Yet the culture of each region continues to differ in a few or many respects from the culture of any other district on the earth. Differences are particularly pronounced between

---

[16] Chapin, F. S., *Cultural Change*, p. 349.

the different ethnic groups, with their long specialized culture history behind them.

Herbert Spencer (1820–1903), as mentioned before, wrote of the survival of the fittest in culture traits, and about their selection by the people, just before the publication of Darwin's doctrine. This idea has been developed by many other sociologists, and especially by A. G. Keller[17] (b. 1874) who based his work on that of W. G. Sumner whom we have also already mentioned, and is of the opinion that whenever a variation occurs in the culture of a people, unconscious social selection takes place before the trait is rejected or else transmitted socially as a folkway or mos. Sumner gave the name *Syncretism*[18] to the selection which determines which of the mores will survive and which perish, saying that it is usually the strong component group which sets the standards which others imitate. Keller taught that it is a strain toward consistency which keeps advances in certain traits from getting out of line with the rest, and which helps the weight of tradition to exercise its full influence without unduly hindering progress when the time is ripe for it. He thought the selection of a social variation was almost always automatic, and that unless a graceful adjustment is made to changing times, social disorganization ensues. Many other sociologists, distinguishing between the social and the cultural, make culture something superorganic, and a completely extrahuman determinant of human behavior.[19] In this they go farther than do the psychological theories of Durkheim and Le Bon, mentioned in the last chapter, for these latter writers include all culture as a determinant of mankind and do not confine themselves merely to the consideration of a supposed "superindividual" social mind.

It seems true that the distinction between the social and the cultural is a valid one. It is frequently correct, also, that in large part changes in culture may be unthinking, and are, indeed the logical outcome of the culture of the past. Sumner and Keller have shown, with truth, that changes in culture are not haphazard events, but are inevitably linked up with the social habits and culture of the past. It is true, too, that we make use of folkways, mores, and institutions to exercise over people what is known as social control.[20] Fear of being ostracized by the group

---

[17] Keller, A. G., *Societal Evolution*.   [18] Sumner, W. G., *Folkways*, Chap. 2.

[19] Cf. Keller, A. G., *op. cit.*, also Kroeber, A. L., "The Superorganic," *American Anthropologist*, n.s., Vol. XIX, 1917, pp. 163–213; Stern, B. J., "Concerning the Distinction Between the Social and the Cultural," *Social Forces*, Vol. VIII, 1929, pp. 264–271; Durkheim, *et al.*

[20] Edward Alsworth Ross first popularized the more specific sociological sense of the term "social control" in his book *Social Control* (1901).

is a very powerful form of this control. Laws, punishments, rewards, taboos, all exercise control to keep the individual in line with cultural tradition; so, too, as mentioned in the last chapter, do the group ideas expressed in literature, art, music, the theater, and all other group activities. All peoples seem to have worked out elaborate ceremonial rites to take place at all the crises of life — birth, marriage, death, the admission to membership in social groups — and these have a very strong and important influence in molding a person's thought and action.

But culture is by no means wholly a mechanical thing. It can be spread only through persons, and it is the outcome of human thought, and of the interaction of all the individual human beings who compose society, with their varying heredity, and their varying environment, even though there are certain universal human traits, and certain aspects of environment which are common to large numbers within a social group, or even large numbers of social groups. Culture has no meaning unless it is allied to the behavior of living human beings. Boas (b. 1858) shows this very clearly when he says: "It has been claimed that human culture is something superorganic, that it follows laws that are not willed by any individual participating in culture, but that they are inherent in the culture itself. It seems hardly necessary to consider a culture a mystic entity that exists outside the society of its individual carriers, and that moves by its own force. The life of a society is carried on by individuals who act singly and jointly under the stress of the tradition in which they have grown up and surrounded by the products of their own activities and those of their forebears. . . . The forces that bring about the changes are active in the individuals composing the social group, not in the abstract culture. . . . Laws of development, except in most generalized form, cannot be established and a detailed course of growth cannot be predicted."[21] Readers will not forget that although we may be very much influenced by environment, heredity, and habit, nevertheless man not only has an intelligence which makes the culture, but he has an intelligence and a will by which he can avoid domination by the culture which surrounds him. In ignoring the psychology of the individual, Sumner and Keller have too much overemphasized the automatic influence of culture.

Culture Lag

The course of growth of a trait cannot be predicted not only because of the human element in culture, but also because of what has been

---

[21] Boas, F., *Anthropology and Modern Life*, p. 235.

called a *culture lag*. This term, invented by W. F. Ogburn (b. 1886)[22] means the interval between a change in material culture, or a change in one type of immaterial culture and not in another. Culture lags are particularly prone to occur when a culture trait is adopted or developed rapidly, as is so often the case today. Higher education, or scenes in motion-picture theaters may give many a person a desire for material goods which he cannot procure, and dissatisfactions will then occur. Sometimes certain traits remain long after the reason for their existence has ceased to be a custom. Such would seem to be the case with many of our irrational superstitions, such as considering a black cat or a horseshoe as "lucky," throwing spilled salt over the left shoulder, refusing to walk under a ladder even when it is not being used by a painter with a dangerous paint pot. Yet it must be noted, too, that certain culture traits may seem meaningless to the uninitiated and therefore considered as "lags" whereas they may have a deep and true significance, as, for example, the ceremonies of the Catholic Church with all their beautiful symbolism. And again, it is sometimes said today that theological concepts and ethical ideas are lagging behind scientific and technical progress,[23] whereas this may by no means be the case, but rather that certain individual scientists and technicians have been unable to integrate their findings with the truths of other branches of knowledge, and lack an integrated philosophy of life.

Culture lags and moral conflicts between norms of conduct (true or false) and group customs (false or true) are, however, the most important causes of our social problems. Spencer, however, went too far when he said that all evil results from nonadaptation to conditions,[24] as must be evident from the above remarks.

Walter Bagehot (1826–1872) better known as one of the first editors of *The Economist* in England, and author of *Lombard Street* (1870) may also be said to have had some ideas of the culture lag, in that in his sociological work, *Physics and Politics* (1872), he talked of the inheritance of culture and its restraint by what he termed the "Cake of custom."

The Age of Culture Traits: Age Areas; The "Kulturkreistheorie"

It has been thought that the relative age of the culture of existing peoples can be discovered by close scholarly attention to certain criteria as regards their culture traits, that is, that we can tell not only

---

[22] Ogburn, W. F., *Social Change.*
[23] Cf. Stamp, Sir Josiah, *The Science of Social Adjustment,* p. 57.
[24] Spencer, H., *Social Statics,* p. 2.

diffusion in space, but also give the age of certain culture traits in specific culture areas.

In the absence of history, the wide distribution of a trait is supposed to be an index to the fact that it has existed over a very long period of time, and that intensive development of a trait is an indication of its place of origin. The great similarity between the material culture of sometimes very diversely situated peoples, led certain German museum directors, at the end of the past century, to realize the folly of the unilineal evolutionists, and to postulate the diffusion of cultures. These pioneers were Ratzel, who first arranged museum materials in their cultural setting, and Frobenius (b. 1873) who in 1898 and the following years, while comparing West African cultures with those in Melanesia, developed Ratzel's investigation by showing that not only single culture traits, but whole organized systems had seemingly migrated. Then in 1904 the two anthropologists Ankermann (b. 1859) and Graebner (b. 1877), while equipping a Berlin museum in similar fashion, discovered that Ankermann's materials from Oceania bore a great similarity to Graebner's from Africa. The results of their findings were published in the *Zeitschrift für Ethnologie* (Vol. XXXVII) in 1905, and from then onwards, what has been known as the *Kulturkreistheorie*, the culture-cycle theory — the German historical method — was established, in an attempt to determine the whole culture history of mankind. Father Wilhelm Schmidt, mentioned in the last chapter, is the greatest exponent of this new school at the present time, and he has greatly developed it.[25] The main idea of those holding the *Kulturkreistheorie* is that man in general is uninventive, and when groups of men wandered off from the early home of man upon earth, they took with them not isolated cultural elements, but whole clusters of culture traits, both of the material and the spiritual kind — in other words, a culture complex.[26] In order to trace the historical connection of the

---

[25] Father Schmidt's theories may be found in the following: Schmidt, Rev. W., *Der Ursprung der Gottesidee*, 6 vols., 1912–1936; *Handbuch der Kulturhistorischen Ethnologie*, 1937. *The Origin and Growth of Religion* (London, New York, 1931); *High Gods in North America* (Oxford, 1933); Schmidt, Rev. W. and Koppers, Rev. W., *Völker und Kulturen*, Vol. III of *Der Mensch aller Zeiten* (Regensburg, 1924). Biographical data, a more complete bibliography, and a synopsis of Schmidt's method and work is to be found in Ross, Eva, J., "Do Primitives Fill a Gap in History?" *Central-Blatt and Social Justice*, Vol. XXXI, Nos. 10, 11, January-February, 1939, pp. 301–304, 339–342. A critical study of Graebner's and Schmidt's theories is also to be found in Kluckhohn, C., "Some Reflections on the Method and Theory of the Kulturkreislehre," *American Anthropologist*, n.s., XXXVIII, 1936, pp. 157–196.

[26] It must be remarked, however, that Father Schmidt takes into account the effect

many more or less distinct primitive culture areas, and to determine their age, the *Kulturkreis* theorists take each fairly well pronounced area in turn. They carefully examine the physical characteristics of the people, and all material, social, ethical, and religious criteria, as also oral traditions (legends), travelers' tales, the monographs of professional ethnographers — checking, testing, and controlling all direct and indirect sources of every kind. As a result of this work, two or more culture areas in different parts of the world may show such striking similarities that their origin from a single source is considered by them to be almost certain. After an examination of many thousands of criteria, an elaborate history of the development of culture has been worked out by Father Schmidt and his followers, but although much valuable information can be obtained from an examination of this work, not only on diffusion in space, but also on the relative age of various cultures, it would definitely seem that their conclusions are too schematic to give us any correct picture of the early development of culture.

In England, G. Elliot Smith (1871–1922) and Perry, joined later by Rivers (1864–1922), adapted the diffusion ideas of the *Kulturkreistheorie* to meet their own theories, and have developed somewhat on different lines. They adopted the idea that man in general is uninventive and that hence few culture traits arise independently more than once; but they developed a theory that favorable climatic circumstances led to the early development of culture in Egypt, and later spread throughout the world, usually losing some of its traits in the diffusion process.

The theories of these two historical schools must be distinguished from the American Historical School of Anthropology, for the latter stay chiefly with the factors of diffusion within the Americas; theorizing as to the general development of culture they consider to be outside their scope as historians of backward peoples, at least until such time as the individual culture history is independently worked out for each area.

Of all the age-area theories it may be said that widespread culture is not necessarily the oldest (as witness the spread of tobacco within recent historical times); it may, indeed, have remained stagnant in a very small geographical area, as did the Basque and the Celt languages,

---

of environment of all kinds upon the original culture. He is careful to note that this original culture has been changed not only by present surroundings, but by other environment which might have affected the tribe in its wanderings to its present habitat, and by the workings of different human intelligences.

the oldest in Europe, and with the least distribution. And the origi-
nators of a culture trait do not necessarily possess it now: Christianity
is not widespread in Palestine, and it flourishes most in other parts of
the earth. Culture does not even move always in cycles, as Wissler and
the *Kulturkreis* theorists and others think, for as Wallis has pointed
out, the Eskimo language is linear over the north of North America,
and has not moved in a cycle at all.[27] And there is always the danger of
inferring a historical connection from similarities which may be due to
other reasons.[28]

Conclusion

To sum up: man is influenced by culture to a very great degree, but
he is not completely dominated by it. There is need, therefore, of more
thoughtful individuals: a need, too, of more thoughtful leaders with a
strong belief in religion and the true norms of morality; and a need of
good literature, music, dramatic productions, so that man, who is a
creature of habit and imitative impulses may not adopt culture traits
which are regrettable.

Cultures vary, and we shall rid ourselves of many foolish prejudices
and unfounded notions of the superiority of our own culture if we will
examine a few accounts of primitive ways of living.[29] Yet certain institutions seem to be universal, and therefore merit the more careful
study which we shall give them in Part Two of the book. How culture
developed is one of the major problems of the cultural sociologist and
of the anthropologist. Material culture most certainly progressed from
lower levels, but the primary social institutions of mankind seem to
have had a higher level at the earliest stages of civilization, if we take
present-day primitives as our criteria, as well as the records of history.
There is no doubt but that much valuable information can be obtained
from a study of primitive tribes, but whether we can trace the exact
course of prehistoric times, as Father Schmidt claims to have done, is
very much open to doubt.

---

[27] Wallis, W. G., "Magnitude of Distribution of Centrifugal Spread and Centripetal
Elaboration of Culture Traits," *American Anthropologist,* n.s., Vol. XXX, pp. 755–771.
[28] Cf. Sapir, E., *Time Perspective in Aboriginal America* (Canada: Geological Survey,
Memoir No. 90, 1916), p. 38.
[29] Such accounts may be found in issues of the *American Anthropologist,* the
Annual Reports of the Bureau of American Ethnology, Anthropos (which includes
articles in English as well as German and French), the *Journal of American Folklore,*
the *Journal of the Royal Anthropological Institute, Primitive Man,* and similar sources.

CHAPTER 5

THE ORIGIN OF MAN

Evidence of Prehistoric Times

HAVING discussed the nature of man and the ways in which he acquired his culture, and having shown the use of studying present-day primitive tribes, it remains for us to ascertain what we can know of man and his culture in the days of prehistory.

Evidence as to prehistoric times is derived from archaeology, geology, and paleontology. Archaeology we have already defined. Paleontology is the science which examines fossilized remains of the past, and geology fixes the approximate period of the formation of the rocks which contain the fossilized remains. These sciences show that man lived upon the earth for a long period before the times of recorded history, and we shall now outline what they can tell us of early man and how he lived. Obviously our knowledge of these matters is limited, for we are dependent upon geological strata and fossil remains for an indication of the earliest times. So far as fossils are concerned, a large number of plants, animals, men, and cultural objects never became fossilized or petrified. Fossilization requires favorable circumstances — the remains must be protected from predatory animals; and they must be in a river bed, cave, or other sheltered spot. Obviously, too, very little about social organization can be discovered by this means, because all we can find is some of the material artifacts which man left behind him, and some of the different types of flora and fauna which existed upon the earth.

Times Prior to the Advent of Man

Geologists have found that the oldest rock strata, which were formed during the period they call the pre-Cambrian era shows practically no fossil remains although there is indirect evidence of primitive forms of plant and animal life. If the earth evolved — and this is a question which we shall discuss later in the chapter — then life was only in the beginning stages at this time, many millions of years ago.

The next oldest strata of rock are also many millions of years old. The era of its first existence is called by geologists the Paleozoic or primary old age, and sometimes the age of primitive plants and animals. Traces of this era are found in rock strata in various parts of the world. According to age, it has been divided into several periods, called respectively the Cambrian, or oldest Paleozoic period (farthest removed from our time), the Ordovician, the Silurian, the Devonian, the Carboniferous, and the Permian. In the earliest rock strata of these times fossil remains have been found of corals, sea lilies, and such primitive animals as mollusks and trilobites; later in the era there are traces of fish of various kinds and in the Carboniferous period there are the first traces of amphibians. The Carboniferous period was also the time when coal accumulated in great quantities. At the end of this era, in Permian times, fossils show that spiders, insects, and reptiles resembling mammals were in existence, and there were great coniferous forests.

Then followed, still some millions of years ago, what has been named by the geologists the Mesozoic or middle recent era, the age of reptiles. This epoch may have been five million or more years ago and it has been divided into three periods in order of time, the Triassic, Jurassic, and Cretaceous. In the rock strata of the Triassic period have been found now extinct reptiles of immense proportions, such as the Dinosaur; later, in the Jurassic period, fossils of wingless birds and small mammals are found; toward the end of the Mesozoic age, flowering plants, and higher insects existed, and reptiles had become specialized.

The next era revealed to us by geology dates back some two million years ago, and it is usually spoken of as extending to about 500,000 B.C. (readers should note that all dates prior to about 20,000 B.C. are only approximations, and there is still much scholarly dispute about them). Geologists have called this the Lower Cenozoic or Tertiary period, the age of mammals, divided in order of time into Eocene, Oligocene, Miocene, and Pliocene periods. In the Eocene period fossils show the rapid development of birds and mammals into specialized classes, the four-toed horse existed and there were cereals and flints. In the Oligocene strata there are traces of ape life. Fossils of the Miocene period show that at this time there were anthropoid apes and the rhinoceros, in addition to the previous forms of plant and animal life. In the Pliocene strata the horse had only three toes, and there were also the camel and the giraffe. This brings us to the close of the Tertiary period during which no trace of man has been discovered. A number of flint stones dating, it is said, toward the end of the Tertiary era, are thought by some to have been purposely shaped. The stones are therefore called eoliths or dawn stones. On the presumption that they indicate the presence of man upon the earth, from this time onwards not only geologists and paleontologists, but also anthropologists are interested in the rock strata. The Tertiary geological period is therefore also known as the Eolithic culture period, although these stones are accounted for by some scientists as formed by the action of the elements, and not by man.

Early Evidence of Man's Habitation of the Earth

The Tertiary era was followed by the Quaternary or Upper Cenozoic geological era, called sometimes the Pleistocene period. This era is thought by most geologists to cover a long period of time. Its duration differed in different parts of the world and so, as we said above, dates are very much disputed and can be regarded only as approximations which may or may not be correct, this is particularly true of the earliest date assigned to the era, for estimates vary from 300,000 to one million years, not to mention the position of those who refuse to accept these figures, on the basis that we cannot know the rapidity with which physical changes may have taken place at earlier periods. This observation should be borne in mind in connection with all the geological figures given in this chapter.

This Pleistocene period is full of interest for the anthropologist because of the positive remains of artifacts as well as human skeletons giving incontestable evidence of man's habitation on the earth during these times. The period is divided by the anthropologists into three culture stages, called respectively the Lower Paleolithic or lower old stone age; the Paleolithic; and the Upper Paleolithic. Each of these stages has various subdivisions, named after the places where rock strata with fossil remains of the period were first found. Geology, as well as changes in plant life and in human and animal skeletons, show that in most parts of the world relatively rapid changes in climate took place in this period. Huge glaciers covered a great part of America, Europe, and Asia at four separate times. Geologists divide up the Pleistocene period according to the climate. There were four Ice Ages or Glacial epochs, which alternated with three interglacial warm periods; and were followed by one postglacial or Holocene period which is the period in which we now are. The great changes which took place are indicated by the fact that fossils of semitropical and arctic fauna and flora are sometimes found in different strata at the same place. They were probably caused by astronomic changes, which brought about climatic differences as well as the redistribution of land and water masses. Yet during these times Northern Africa and what is now known as Mesopotamia (Iraq and the surrounding country) seem to have had abundant rainfall and tropical climate until the Middle Pleistocene or Paleolithic period, and even after the climate became dry, the rivers Nile, Tigris, Euphrates, and Indus enabled the peoples of the Egyptian and Babylonian areas to maintain a continuous culture, so that they had a high civilization 4000 years B.C., at a time when people in Europe were still illiterate.

Lower Paleolithic Culture

Taking the periods of this Quaternary or Pleistocene epoch in order, we shall first consider the Lower Paleolithic or first glacial period. This is called the Pre-Chellean culture period, though only some very rough flint *coup de poings* or fist hatchets have been found in Europe, to witness man's tool-making capacity — and some have doubted their man-made character. Evidence of the bison, saber-toothed tiger, one-toed horse, and other animals are found in Europe also.

Near Trinil, on the Island of Java, a Dutch army surgeon, Dr. Dubois, found a skull in 1891 which, to judge by the fossilized mammals associated with it, and other evidence, seems to belong to the middle Pleistocene period, although some have dated it earlier. Due to the conflicting opinions about the date of this epoch, no date can be assigned to it. The skull is low, and dolichocephalous (long rather than broad) and anthropologists say that its possessor had an erect carriage. Some people consider it to be the skull of a human, and call its possessor *Pithecanthropus erectus*. Other skulls were discovered in 1936, 1937, and 1938. Their cranial capacity is not much smaller than that of a small woman of today. There is much controversy in scientific circles as to whether the skulls may correctly be attributed to an animal-like human, in a supposedly halfway state of evolution from an animal origin to humankind (a missing link), or whether they are the skulls of animals. The evidence seems too slight for any definite conclusion to be drawn from it at the present time.

In 1921, however, a number of fossilized bones near Peking were discovered, which also seem to belong to the early middle Pleistocene period, although the exact date is unknown. Among these remains two teeth were recognized in 1926, and another tooth in 1927. In 1928 part of two lower jaws and numerous fragments of skulls were found, parts of which were reconstructed. Fossils of giant stags and boars were also unearthed. In 1931 well-shaped stone and bone tools, as well as charcoal were found, and thousands of hackberry seeds, showing that men used fire and tools in these early times, and probably hunted, scraped skins, and collected berries. Finally in 1936, a complete brain case was discovered, called the Peking "man" or *Sinanthropus pekinesis*. In all, fragments of twenty-four skulls have been recovered, and their lowness somewhat resembles the Java remains. It would seem that they are remains of true humans, and not "missing links," and that these individuals were possibly cannibals who preserved only the skulls, for no other bodily parts have been found.

Following this first glacial epoch of Quaternary (Pleistocene) times, the earth became warmer and the ice sheet retreated to the North. The waters of the lowlands then evaporated, and the fauna and flora indicate a warm tropical climate in this first interglacial period. In this later Pre-Chellean culture stage, we find traces of forests in England, with such trees as the beech, elm, maple, pine, and spruce, and evidence of the rhinoceros, the elephant, and the tiger. In France there is evidence of the rhinoceros, the hippopotamus, and the saber-toothed tiger.

At Piltdown, on the River Ouse, in England, a Mr. Charles Dawson discovered between 1911–1913 certain fossils of this or a later period (the geologic age is uncertain), which have been thought to indicate a possible "missing link," though they may be the remains of a real human. First, part of a brain case was found in a gravel pit, and then later two nasal bones, a tooth, and half a lower jawbone were found near the skull, although they may not have belonged to it. A stone hand ax was near by, indicating the presence of man at the time. The remains have now been assembled into a female skull. This reconstruction indicates a brain which approximates that of the modern human, and a jaw which seems more like that of an ape. Although scientists disagree on whether this is a human relic or a "missing link," or merely animal remains, and whether the jaw belongs to the skull, the title of *Eoanthropus dawsoni*, the Piltdown dawnman, has been given to it.

Then followed what is known as the second glacial period. Immediately preceding this time may be placed the Chellean culture period, so called because of the discovery of fossils of the time at quarries at Chelles-sur-Marne in France. Stone hand axes or cleavers, awls, scrapers, and other implements were found here, more advanced than any previous tools. In 1907 a fossilized lower jaw was discovered at Mauer, near Heidelberg, which may belong to this period. The jaw was heavier than most modern human jaws and the teeth were large and retreating, yet seem to be human, though the evidence is inconclusive. The skull and limb bones were never found, but some people are of the opinion that the jaw, being suggestive of an ape type, belongs to an early development of man from a supposed ape ancestor, and provides a missing link. Obviously there is nothing conclusive to prove this hypothesis about the so-called *Homo heidelbergensis,* or "Heidelberg man." No tools were found on the site, although rough spear-shaped hand axes of this period have been found in England, France, and Belgium.

After the second Ice Age followed the second interglacial epoch, known also as the Acheulian culture period, from the quarries at St. Acheul, near Amiens in France. In this place were found improved flints, borers, and scrapers or crude knives, probably used for scraping fur.

Paleolithic Culture

Then followed what may be called the Paleolithic period proper, which includes a third glacial period, thought by geologists to have begun possibly some 150,000 years ago, followed by a third interglacial period which is dated back some 75,000 years by them. The culture of these later times has been called Levalloisian and Mousterian, from Levallois and Moustier, near Les Eyzies, in the Dordogne, France. The cold, wet climate of the later period is obvious from the animal and plant remains. Reindeer, the woolly rhinoceros and woolly mammoth were plentiful as far south as Italy. In France we find remains of such animals as reindeer, sheep, and cattle; and a variety of trees, including the maple, sycamore, birch, and pine. Charcoal remains indicate the first traces of fire which have so far been found in Europe, and there were many finer and thinner edged tools of flint. It is interesting here to note that hand axes found in Africa, dating back to lower Paleolithic times, are much finer than these improved Mousterian implements. A good many human skeletal remains were found at Le Moustier, either belonging to this period, or to the following Aurignacian period. These skeletons were covered with red ocher, and were buried facing in a certain direction with what appears to be offerings placed near them, probably intended to be of use to them in the future life. We may, therefore, consider that human beings lived upon the earth at this time, caring for their dead, which is interpreted as an indication of belief in life after death, and hence of the existence of religion. These skeletal findings at Le Moustier, which probably belong to the end of the third interglacial epoch, commonly dated by geologists to have taken place some 25,000 or more years ago, have their counterpart in many places in the world. Remains of a race of men which seem later to have died out, called the Neanderthal race, have been found not only at Le Moustier, but also at Neanderthal in Germany (where the first recognized specimen was discovered in 1856), at Weimar in Germany, at Gibraltar, where actually the first skeleton had been excavated in 1848, at La Chappelle-aux-saints (Corrèze), La Ferrassie, and La Quina in France, in Spain, the Channel Islands, Belgium, Jugoslavia, the East Indies, and in caves at the foot of Mount Carmel in Palestine. Scientific reconstruction of the remains show that in general the Neanderthal man was short (the male was about 5 feet 4 inches in height, and the women shorter). His knees were bent, possibly due to his prolonged squatting over the fire during this inclement period. His chest was large, his chin receded or he lacked a chin, his forehead sloped back, he had protruding brows, and he was dolichocephalic. It must be noted, however, that the skeletons of women and children show much less heavy brows, as also do skeletons found at Gibraltar and Weimar. The Neanderthal man cared for his dead, and at La Ferrassie evidence of religion may be conjectured by the existence of stones which may possibly have been regarded as sacred. The reindeer, lion, hyena, bear, horse, and lemming existed at this time. Man used bone and reindeer horn. Awls, blades, javelin points, and wedges have been discovered. Simple painting and carving give the first indications of man as an artist.

In 1921 a skull and various limbs were found in Rhodesia in South Africa which some consider to belong to the Pleistocene period, though not to the Neanderthal race. As the remains were not fossilized, however, they may be Neolithic, or later.

Upper Paleolithic Culture

Following the Paleolithic epoch, came the Upper Paleolithic. The fourth glacial period was the earliest, and the culture of the time is called Aurignacian, thought by most scientists to date back some 13,500 years, and merging into a cool postglacial period. The Upper Paleolithic epoch also includes the Solutrean and Magdalenian culture periods: times of rising temperature.

In the Aurignacian period, known because of the discovery of seventeen skeletons (which were later lost) at Aurignac, France, in 1852, we find crude frescoes and sculpture, the use of bone, reindeer horn, and ivory, and gravers for art work on these materials; finer and sharper flints and scrapers; bone needles, javelin points, and dart throwers.

The Solutrean culture period probably flourished some 13,000 years ago, and is named from Solutre, near Macon in France, where a number of remains were found. Five skeletons of this period were discovered in a small rock shelter at the foot of some cliffs in the village of Cro-Magnon, France, in 1868. Other skeletons similar to the Cro-Magnon have been found at Obercassel in Germany, in the Bas-Pyrénées, and on the northern coast of Spain. The Cro-Magnon were definitely men like ourselves, perhaps coming from Asia or North Africa where the climate had been more favorable than in Europe, for the latter had just passed through the fourth Ice Age. The men were very tall, being over six feet in height, and the women had an average height of about five and a half feet. Both the skull and the brain seem very similar to that of modern man, but the face was broader than present European types. The Cro-Magnon buried their dead in long barrows. They had bone needles and harpoons, and beautiful leaflike arrowheads; they made flints sharp by pressure instead of the percussion method evidenced by all previous remains; they had whistles and flutes, and bracelets and necklaces of shells and animal teeth. Presumably they ate much horse meat because heaps of bones of small horses have been found. They were hunters and fishers, and the animals of the period include the reindeer, the woolly rhinoceros, arctic fox, cave bear, cave hyena, wolf, bison, stag, and elk. There is no evidence that they practised agriculture or domesticated animals.

In this same Solutrean period, there possibly existed another type of people, called the Grimaldi. Definitely human skeletons, differing from the Cro-Magnon, yet possibly of the same race, have been found at the Grotte des Enfants near Mentône, France, and in other parts. These Grimaldi were tall, broad-faced people whose physical proportions and facial characteristics were typically Negroid; this accounts for the view of a number of anthropologists that Europeans came to Europe by way of Africa.

Following the Solutrean period, and still in the Upper Paleolithic epoch, was the Magdalenian period, so called from findings at La Madeleine, near Les Eyzies, France. This period — usually dated back some 10,000 years — has been divided into six cultural stages. At this time the herds of bison, reindeer, and horse disappeared from southern Europe, probably because the rising temperature made hunting grounds into forests. The Cro-Magnon of the Magdalenian period have left behind them in France and Spain evidence of culture more advanced than any heretofore found in Europe. Like their predecessors, the Magdalenians were hunters and fishers, because fishhooks, arrows, and harpoons have been found, but in this period we also find the first traces of harpoon points made of reindeer horn, and bone spear throwers and javelins. They lived in caves, used fires, sewed skins, made artificial light in crude stone lamps, and buried their dead. That they possessed imagination and high artistic skill is evidenced by the engraved decorations on tools, weapons, and ornaments, and their beautiful cave frescoes. There is evidence of belief in a god of fertility.

Neolithic Culture

Following this period we come into recent times, with the advent of the Neolithic or New Stone Age, preceded by a transitional stage, both geologically and culturally. The geologic Mesolithic period, when the climate was warm and humid, is calculated to have occurred between the years 12,000 or 10,000 B.C. The Mesolithic culture itself, whatever date is assigned to it, is usually placed in two categories. First, the Azilian, so called from findings at the Mas d'Azil, in the Ariège, France. Rubbish heaps give some indication of crude pottery being made. There were bone, horn, and stone implements, painted pebbles, and the bones of many animals. A painting of something that looks like barley gives the first definite, but still not conclusive, evidence of agriculture. The second culture period is called the Tardenoisian, from findings at Fère en Tardenois, in the Aisne district, France.

While the typical culture of the New Stone Age is not found in Europe until about 6000 B.C., the peoples of Egypt, the Tigris-Euphrates Valley, and other places in the near East had already merged into historical times by at least the year 5000 B.C., and there is no doubt, of course, that the culture known to us definitely by historical records spread from these parts. By this time the people of this area were shepherds and agriculturists; they had the potter's wheel, and made fine pottery; they used copper, polished axes and other stone implements, and made delicately carved vessels far in advance of any European artifacts of the time. The beginnings of writing are also evident in Egypt.

The Neolithic period in Europe is characterized by the domestication of animals and by agriculture (which had existed in Egypt long before their advent in Europe). The people of these times used polished stone implements, the wheel, and pottery; there was spinning and weaving of flax and wool; they buried their dead in rectangular stone tombs or dolmens; they manufactured crude boats, traveled and engaged in commerce (relics of Mediterranean goods have been found in the north of Europe). They placed stone monuments in circles (cromlechs) as at Stonehenge and other places, or in parallel rows (alignments) as in Brittany and elsewhere, but the reason for these monuments is not clear. Crude sculpture of the female form gives some indication that a goddess of fertility was worshiped.

Remains of this Neolithic culture in Europe are found in England, France, Greece, Northern Italy, Scandinavia, and Switzerland. First, there might be said to be the early Neolithic or Campignian culture of about 8000 B.C. The people of this time used the bow and arrow; they made crude pottery and bone, horn, and stone tools; and they had domesticated the cow, sheep, and pig.

Dating back to about 7500 B.C., although some archaeologists place this date much later, is the Neolithic culture of Denmark, on the shores of the Baltic. These people left rubbish heaps or kitchen middens behind them, and from the various strata of this debris, their life can be fairly well reconstructed. Their diet consisted largely of shellfish, but bones of other kinds of fish and of animals show that there was some variety. They had domesticated the dog, made crude pottery, and chipped and polished flints into axes and other tools.

At a time of drought in Switzerland, in 1853–1854, the waters of many of the lakes receded, and revealed some remarkable remains. Petrified wooden houses built on wood piles driven into the lake were found. The inhabitants of these houses had domesticated the dog, goat, pig, sheep, cow, and horse. For the first time in the history of man in Europe we find evidence of a varied diet, for in addition to the animals, charred remains of wheat and barley loaves are found, and the stones or seeds of cherries, plums, apples, pears, and grapes as well as acorns, beechnuts, and other plant foods. The Swiss Lake dwellers used flax and spun linen on looms; they made crude pottery; chipped and polished flints and had bone awls and polishers. The piles of their houses were made of oak, birch, and beechwood, which must have been cut with flint axes. They had wheels made of sections of tree trunks. Skeletal remains show that they were very skillful at head operations, and the inference is that they practised other types of medical science.

Late Neolithic Culture

Late Neolithic times are divided into three culture periods, characterized by the use of metals. First, the Copper and Bronze Age, which dates from before 3000 to 2000 B.C., in Egypt and Asia, and from 2000 to 1000 B.C., in Europe. In Europe bronze (an alloy of copper and tin) was first used on the Isle of Cyprus and from there its use spread to other peoples. How metals came to be used is a matter of conjecture; either outcroppings of the pure metal were beaten into tools, or some metal ore may have accidentally been reduced at a campfire. As tin and copper are frequently associated with each other in mines, the invention of bronze was merely a matter of time.

What is known as the early Iron Age began in Egypt and Asia about the year 1300 B.C., and in Italy about 1000 B.C. In Europe this age remained from about 1000 to about 500 B.C. The height of its development seems to be at Hallstadt in Germany, where pocketknives, very similar to those of today, had blades fitting into bone handles.

About 500 B.C. the later Iron Age began in Europe, characterized by the artifacts found at La Tène, where scissors, the potter's wheel, glazed pottery, and glass were unearthed.

Racial Origins

We have now briefly traced the history of the earth so far as it is revealed to us by geology, paleontology, and archaeology. The history of later periods is for the most part now available from the reconstruction of more complete archaeological findings than for earlier times, and from recorded history. Actually, however, the earliest accurate records (the Egyptian) are only available from about 4000 B.C. From about 3500 B.C., onwards we have records for Babylonia and Assyria though these were for some time only pictographic; for India, from about 1500 B.C., and for China, from about 1300 B.C. Grecian history dates from about 1000 B.C., that for Rome, from about 750 B.C., while that for Persia and the Celts is available from about 500 B.C. The history of other peoples is lacking until about the time of Christ.

There still remains to be discussed in this chapter the question of how and where the various races upon the earth originated: a subject about which there is little exact data.

A race, in the strict sense of the word, is a group of people who have certain inherited physical characteristics (with but a limited range of variability) which differentiate them from other groups.[1] Of course, no race is uniform in its genes, but the people of a race have a number of genes in common, and the similarity within the different groups enables us to distinguish them by the usual classifications of Caucasian, including Europeans, Persians, Arabs, and the peoples of India; Mongoloid, including the Chinese, the Japanese, and the Central Asiatic peoples; African or Ethiopian, including Negroes; American Indian peoples; the Malayans and the Polynesians; the Australoids. The races are distinguished not only by color of skin, but by general physique, and such characteristics as the straight hair of the Mongoloids and

---

[1] The word *race* is used in the popular sense to describe a social group identified with certain inherited characteristics.

North Americans, the wavy or curly hair of the Caucasians, and the woolly hair of the Negroes. Other distinguishing features are the position and shape of the nostril, the nasal profile, the shape of the lips, the difference in sweat glands which give the distinctive racial odors, the epicanthic fold over the inner corner of the eye in the Mongoloid races, and the shape of the skull.

Within the very general race classifications given above, peoples differ widely, resembling one another only in a general way. Each race has many subdivisions, or smaller groups, with certain additional genes in common. The Negroids of Africa, for example, have many distinctive physical types, such as the tall, slender Nilotic Negroes, the short Pygmies, and the Hottentot. There are marked differences between the Chinese and the Japanese peoples, although both belong to the Mongoloid race. In Europe, the "typical" Alpine peoples are stocky, brachycephalic, and brown haired; the "typical" Nordic is blonde, tall, and dolichocephalic; the "typical" Mediterranean type is dark, short, and dolichocephalic; many European Russians have certain Mongolian affinities.

Actually, races are a composite of other races and of subdivisions within the race itself, which in part explains the marked variations within each race, and among the different peoples of each race. There are Negroes of so-called "pure" stock, for example, who have a fairer skin than some so-called "pure" members of the white race; and there are white people whose facial contour is very similar to the Mongoloid. Innumerable further examples might be cited. Nations are still more intermixed: for example, France and Germany both have two distinct types, the Nordic and the Alpine, in addition to other intermixtures.

The intermixture between peoples of differing physical characteristics began long before the time of history, for ever since historical times the races have remained more or less stable as regards these body types. The Bible tells us that we are all descended from Adam and Eve. Apart from the certainty of this revelation, however, there is an increasing agreement among scientists in support of the fact that mankind had a monogenetic origin, and not a polygenetic one. By this, of course, is meant that man is descended from an original pair, and that there were not at the beginnings of the race divers pairs from which the different races came. This "oneness" of the human race is evidenced by the fact that all peoples have the same characteristics which distinguish them as men from the rest of animal life, all can intermarry,[2] all have the same bodily temperature, approximately the

---

[2] It is worthy of note, however, that although marriage between two people of a different race (miscegenation) is biologically possible, nevertheless difficulties are

same span of life, the same emotional powers, the same power of abstract thought, and the same basic social organizations, and many other cultural resemblances.[3]

When the races became differentiated not only into the primary racial stocks, but into the various subdivisions, is mostly based on conjecture, although there is a certain amount of supporting evidence, and the history of some of the comparatively early migrations has been definitely ascertained. The Bible fixes the original birthplace of the human race as between four rivers. Two of these are known: the Euphrates and the Tigris; the other two, the Pison and the Gehon, cannot be traced by these names, but are considered by some to be the Nile and the Ganges or the Indus — a wide territory which would include Egypt and Asia Minor. Most archaeologists and physical anthropologists are now agreed that the cradle of mankind was probably in Asia or Africa.

Comparatively early in the sequence of man's presence upon the earth, various groups must have left the original home of man and wandered to other parts. Some migrated to Europe, and some to Asia. Others went to Africa and, presumably by means of a land bridge over the Bering Straits, men eventually entered the Continent of the Americas and journeyed as far south as Tierra del Fuego. Innumerable subsidiary migrations took place, with the resultant fusions or inhabitation of one territory by two or more different groups of peoples. The Celts were in possession of parts of Europe before the Greeks or the Romans. The Dravidians, who had been preceded by a now unknown people, inhabited India before the Caucasians settled there. History records for us how Abraham left the Kingdom of Ur, became a wandering shepherd, and lost much of the high civilization of his former home; and how the Jews lived in the same territory with other peoples, but rarely intermarried with others, and even preserved a pure monotheism despite the prevailing paganism of surrounding tribes.

---

sometimes present. Marriage between people of slightly diverse races often leads to the genes supplementing each other in such a manner that the offspring is physically superior to the parents, though the opposite result may also hold true. Great divergency between the physical characteristics of the parents, however, may lead to a serious lack of bodily harmony, such as big hands with small arms and other disproportions.

[3] If man had a polygenetic origin, the similarity of the basic social organization, the "natural" societies which we have mentioned, would be difficult to explain on the basis of diffusion alone. Some theorists even suppose that man evolved in different parts of the earth from different species of apes! The uniformity of the basic social institutions would then be even more difficult to account for; and propagation by racial intermarriage would seem to be impossible.

As to *how* racial differences occurred, various theories exist. Some theorists, postulating the evolution of man's body from lower animals, have considered that the different races have been present from the very time when man supposedly evolved from the anthropoid apes. They are of the opinion that the Caucasian race and chimpanzees descended from common stock, as also the Negroes and gorillas, and the Mongoloids and the orang-outangs. There is no supporting evidence for this polygenetic theory, and against it we may cite the "oneness" of the human race, whereas the morphological differences between the three species of ape are much greater than between any of the races of man.

Other theorists attribute the differences in racial colors to climate, saying that in tropical countries those with heavily pigmented skins would tend to survive, because they could withstand the rays of the sun more easily than light-skinned peoples. Similarly, eventually those with dark skins would probably die out in the North, unless they in some way supplied the deficiency of the sun's actinic rays, and vitamin D for example, by eating certain types of raw fish, as do the Eskimos; light-skinned people would get more of the actual rays of the sun and might be able to survive without the aid of special diet.

Sir Arthur Keith, C. R. Stockard,[4] and others have thought that racial characteristics are largely due to the stabilization of glandular defects through heredity. They postulate, for example, that the brown pigmentation of the Negroes is due to an inherited disease of the medulla of the adrenals; that the steatopygia of the Hottentot women may be traced to a defective pituitary inheritance; and that the African Pygmies and the Mongolian peoples have a thyroid deficiency. This solution does not appear to be supported by actual facts. The average peoples of the different races are normal in bodily and mental health, and to explain race differences from observation of the result of a pathological condition in white peoples can have little scientific validity. For example, Mongolian peoples as a group could in no way be said to compare with "Mongolian idiots" among the white race, a condition due to a lack of thyroxin secretion. The theory leaves one with the problem as to how the supposed differentiation in function of the glands developed.

Yet other theorists attribute race differences to the action of the hormones on different sets of genes which have become stabilized by long intermarriage, but they do not postulate a necessary glandular

---

[4] Cf. Keith, A., "The Evolution of Human Races in the Light of the Hormone Theory," *Bulletin of Johns Hopkins Hospital,* Baltimore, Vol. XXXIII, 1922, pp. 155–159; Stockard, C. R., *The Physical Basis of Personality, et al.*

defect; or they point to the possibility of the occurrence of large mutations eventually becoming fixed by tribal intermarriage.

Darwin (1809–1882) in his *Origin of Species,* 1859, explained the evolution of animal types by natural selection and the survival of the fittest. He was of the opinion that on account of use or disuse of certain parts of the body, and for other reasons, minimal differences would occur, which would be inheritable. In the animal kingdom, he thought, those who inherited these differences would tend to have more chances of being preserved, and thus of perpetuating themselves by heredity, whereas eventually the less specialized members of the same species would be killed or die out. The "fittest" would therefore survive. So far as man is concerned, certain sexual preferences would lead to the mating of peoples of a preferred type, and the type would then tend to become stabilized in any particular area. This theory explains how types may be preserved, but it in no way explains the origin of the type, for acquired characteristics cannot be inherited; sunburn, tattoo marks, circumcision, and mutilations are not passed on to the offspring of those who have acquired these modifications. It postulates that variation by change would always be in the direction of progress, whereas in fact gene mutations are by no means always progressive.

There is some evidence from genetics that mutations in the gene are responsible for inherited differences in physical type. Experimentation with the fruit fly, the *Drosophila melanogaster,* has shown that mutations have occurred which could be passed on to the offspring in settled type by inbreeding, and some of the new present types have capabilities which were lacking before. Not all the mutations were progressive, however — some were lethal and resulted in extinction of the type. And it must be noted that although over four hundred new types were produced, the percentage was not very great when one considers the thousands of specimens which have been bred. Moreover, all the variant types are always recognizable as fruit flies, and have not evolved into any other class.

While it is very possible that some of the differences in racial type are due to mutation, others were probably caused by specialized food habits and other cultural aspects of the different local groups. This latter theory has been upheld by Boas, one of his most famous studies being the observation of the children of certain European Jews and Sicilians, some of whom were born in Europe, and some in the United States. Whereas the usual head form of the Jews born in Europe was brachycephalic, and that of the Sicilians dolichocephalic, the children of these people born in the United States tended to be mesocephalic.

They also tended to be taller than their parents and the other European-born siblings. The explanation of this phenomenon seemed to be the fact that the American-born babies were allowed greater freedom of movement than were the ones brought up in Europe, there was more physical exercise in the later educational program, and the food eaten differed considerably in most of the families studied. If changes in type occurred in this manner, the fixing of these differences was probably due to close tribal intermarriage. During their migrations certain people would probably remain isolated for long periods of time, and would intermarry among themselves. Physical peculiarities would thus become stabilized. As Boas says: "An isolated community that remains subject to the same environmental conditions, and without selective mating, becomes after a number of generations, stable in bodily form."[5] This enforced intermarriage might later be adopted into the culture of the group as the accepted form, since it is notable that primitive peoples of today tend to interbreed within a small locality, even when bands of the same peoples live in an adjoining territory.

Modern Race Theories

From quite early times we have records of the peoples of one race considering themselves to be superior to all others. Thus Aristotle thought that the people of the North lacked intelligence because the Greeks had a superior political organization, and Ibn Khaldun assigned superiority to the Arabians because their cultural achievement at the time was in many respects superior to the European. Modern racial theories assign superiority to the white race in general, and to the "Nordics" in particular, although Italian Fascism has initiated a racial campaign in favor of the Italians. These modern theories began with the superiority assumed by the white race in the days of the slave trade and of colonial expansion. They were fostered not only by Darwin's doctrine of the survival of the fittest (since the whites arrogantly took it for granted that they were the "fittest" upon the earth) but also by the vogue set up by the writings of Count Arthur de Gobineau (1816–1882) whose *Essay on the Inequality of Human Races* (1853–1855) was designed to show the superiority of the white race. Houston Stewart Chamberlain (1855–1926), an Englishman who adopted German nationality, enlarged upon these ideas in *Foundations of the Nineteenth Century* (1899) which was designed to show the superiority of the "nordic Teutons" among the so-called "Aryan"

---

[5] Boas, *Anthropology and Modern Life*, p. 131.

peoples. Among other racialists might be cited G. Vacher de Lapouge of France, and Otto Ammon of Germany, who both enlarged upon "Aryan" theories and said that scientific measurements showed that dolichocephalics had a greater aptitude for success than brachycephalics. In the United States, Madison Grant in *The Passing of a Great Race* (1916) and Lothrop Stoddard in *The Rising Tide of Color Against White World Supremacy* (1920) emphasized ideas of the racial superiority of the white race, and particularly of the Nordic, and had much influence on later immigration laws which discriminated against certain peoples.

To begin with, the idea of Aryan superiority in early times is based on the work of Max Müller, who applied the word in a purely linguistic sense to mean the Indo-Iranic languages, of which Sanskrit is the oldest known. The word itself has no racial or anatomical signification, and therefore is of no ethnic consequence. But so far as ancient times are concerned, if any peoples can claim "superiority" it ought to be the Egyptians and the peoples of Asia Minor, who had a highly developed material civilization while the original forerunners of the present white race of Europe were but savages. As regards European peoples, first the Greeks and then the Romans enjoyed a high civilization; the civilization of modern times is, indeed, built upon the remnants which survived after the Roman Empire had been destroyed by the barbarian tribes of the North, including the overrated Nordics. Nor are there any really "pure" types of any stock, for there have been numerous intermixtures in the course of history, and, more important, before historic times.

Even granting that one can separate the various races and, to some extent, the various peoples, there is little upon which the much vaunted superiority can be based. We have mentioned how European civilization was of late growth, and that it centered around the eastern Mediterranean long before the more northern peoples became civilized. In view of the ideas of Nordic superiority it must be said that the Celts were civilized some time before the Teutons, and the civilizations of India, China, and of the now extinct Aztecs and Incas of Central America, date back a very long period of time.

Those who hold that man is descended from the anthropoid ape, point to the fact that the Negro resembles the higher anthropoids more closely than the Caucasians in cranial capacity, length of arm, receding forehead, and prognathous jaw. Yet of all the races the Negroes are farthest removed from the ape type, with their thick, red lips in contrast to the ape's thin bloodless ones, with their woolly hair, and their lack of body hair. Actually, the white race more closely resembles the ape than any other racial type in hairiness of body. And so far as size of skull is concerned, by no means does a large brain always indicate intelligence. Some brilliant white men have had very small heads. Women's brain cases are smaller than men's, yet their intelligence is certainly not inferior to that of the male. For that matter, too, many of the Eskimos, the North American Indians, and the Kafirs, less advanced in civilization, have larger skulls than the Europeans, as have also many of the Chinese.

As for present achievements, it is true that in material advancement the white race has exceeded all others, and that there is therefore an actual criterion by which to pass judgment. Yet the fact of material achievement is not necessarily an indication of intrinsic superiority. For example, Lévy-Bruhl[6] and others have popularized the idea in certain circles that the primitives, with their extremely backward culture, are less intelligent than more highly civilized peoples. Yet even the most primitive peoples of today make efficient tools, showing that they can reason from cause to effect, and also by analogy from effect to cause. All primitives give evidence of abstract thought in their vocabulary, and many in their proverbs and other philosophy. They show clearly that they are possessed of such characteristic operations of the human mind, in addition to abstraction, as perception, memory, and control of impulses by the will.[7] Although it is true that we have made such vastly improved material progress, it certainly does not appear that present-day primitives are in a prelogical state; rather it is certain that their intellectual gifts differ from ours, if at all, in degree only and not in essence. Our superior cultural achievement seems much more probably due to the greater experience we have had, the large populations, the wider area in which we live, the close contact with those of other cultures, personally and by means of the radio, the press, and other modern ways, all of which has helped to develop our intelligence in higher spheres and has led to an enormous output of material invention within the past hundred and fifty years. We are not necessarily more intelligent because we use electric elevators, oil-driven motor ships — indeed, few of those who use them are in the least acquainted with the principles which make them work. A wider life increases quickness of wit and resourcefulness, but does not presuppose that the people are intrinsically more intelligent.

---

[6] Cf. Lévy-Bruhl, *La Mentalité primitive*, 1922; *L'Âme primitive, Myth primitive*, 1935.

[7] Cf. Ross, E. J., *Social Origins*, pp. 29–38.

In the United States the question of race superiority largely involves the supposed lesser intelligence of the Negroes. In mental tests given in the various school systems, Negroes have nearly always been shown as scoring lower than white children. The findings, however, do not present a true picture of the situation, as will be discussed in Chapter 27.

Was There Evolution?

We must now discuss the important question as to how man himself originated, and whether or not the earth evolved and all things on it. Various theories about this problem have been held, roughly divisible into two categories, the theory of the non-evolutionists and that of the evolutionists.

The non-evolutionists hold that inorganic matter and the different classes and species of plants and animals, including man, were all specifically created by God at different times, and that evolution has taken place only in minor details. The literal interpretation of the words of the Bible support this theory. The Bible describes the different creation scenes, including the definite and separate creation of man. A learned Protestant, Bishop Ussher, interpreting the word *days* as literally twenty-four hours, and taking the genealogies provided in the Bible in strict sequence,[8] estimated that the world was created only 4,004 years before the time of Christ, a view held by many Churchmen for some time. He made this erroneous conjecture before the modern research in geology and paleontology, and in view of the findings of these sciences, as discussed earlier in the chapter, his opinion is, of course, preposterous. It is now generally accepted that when the inspired writer of Genesis refers to "days," he did not mean that these consisted of but twenty-four hours, but that he referred to periods of time, each extending over many thousands of years. It is of particular interest to Catholics to note that St. Gregory of Nyssa, St. Augustine, and other Fathers of the early Church held a theory of "emergent evolution" — that life evolved progressively from created inorganic matter to the present state in accordance with a well-designed plan of the Creator — and this idea was held by many Christian scholars until about the thirteenth century.

In opposition to the non-evolutionists, are the evolutionists. We shall first give an outline of the general evolutionary theory, and then distinguish between "mechanical" or atheistic evolution, and an "emergent evolution" which postulates the existence of God as a Creator.

---

[8] Actually, it is most probable that note is made only of the important members of a family, and that several generations are often omitted in the phrase that "X begat Y."

In general, evolutionists are of the opinion that there is sufficient evidence in support of their theory that inorganic matter and organic matter were not separately created, but emerged by a long-continued process of change which was generally progressive but not necessarily so. Even as early as 1755, long before the time of any explicit evolutionary thought, Kant was of the opinion that the mechanical laws which explained the present working of the world could also explain its origin and development. He held that the earth began as a primal nebula, a mass of inorganic material which began to converge under the influence of gravitation and its chemical reactions, and that in converging it acquired a rotating movement. We also find a like notion in Laplace, who thought that the primal nebula was hot — a huge gaseous mass which broke off from the sun and in the course of time cooled down. As it lost its heat, it contracted, the gases turned into liquid which covered the plains that resulted from the subsidence, so that seas resulted. The evolutionists think that gradually, as the earth cooled in the course of time, the waters settled down, organic life appeared, and evolved into the present classes and species. The Catholic priest Abbé Lemaître, of the University of Louvain, Belgium (who does not, however, subscribe to any mechanical evolutionary theory), has a theory of an expanding universe, with the idea that the universe began as an exploded atom.

Evolutionists account for the presence of organic life upon the earth by the gradual development of undifferentiated matter into differentiated, from the inorganic to the many-formed organic life. In general, they think that lower animal life must somehow or other have developed by spontaneous generation, and that later man evolved. The experiments of such scientists as Pasteur and Tyndall would seem to have shown that the present evidence for this theory is invalid. The findings of geology and paleontology indeed show in a general way that simple forms of life upon the earth came first. We can further trace a progressive development within certain species, such as the horse. Comparative anatomy also shows that the nervous system becomes progressively more developed as we go up in the biological scale. But the fact that simple forms of life and not complex types, appear in the oldest rock strata, does not prove that animals and plants actually *evolved* from lower forms. And although animals and plants can be arranged in groups, there is discontinuous variation, and paleontology shows that classes of organisms formed groups in very early times even as today.

Granted that there is much evidence in favor of evolution of the plant and lower animal kingdom, there still remains the problem of the possible evolution of man.

Some of the earliest skeletal remains which have been found would seem to point to structural resemblances to the ape, particularly the skull of *Pithecanthropus erectus,* and *Eoanthropus dawsoni,* the jaw of the so-called *Homo heidelbergensis,* the *Sinanthropus pekinensis,* and the forehead and jaw of the Neanderthal men. On the other hand, with the exception of the Neanderthalers, there is no certainty that these remains are those of human beings. However, even should these findings be human remains, it still remains to be proved that such characteristics as a small cranial capacity and projecting teeth in a prognathous jaw (giving a small facial angle) are evidences either of an animal origin, or of a lack of intelligence. Neither should one forget that the Cro-Magnon and Grimaldi men were of fine physique, and had a large cranial capacity. The Neanderthalers were certainly characterized by a prognathous jaw but this fact is not necessarily evidence of animal descent. Neither does decrease in size and position of jaw and teeth of modern man necessarily show a higher evolution from a more apelike type, for the change might be due to difference in diet. The toughness of food in the days before refined cooking and varied diet might have caused the jaws and teeth to be large and specialized to perform the required functions.

Those who believe in evolution from an apelike type sometimes account for the change in facial angle by man's more highly developed intelligence: this supposition is, however, purely imaginative. We have evidence of early man's intelligence in the tools, paintings, and other artifacts which he left behind. Even if man developed physically from low beginnings, the inference is positively in favor of the fact that from the time he was man, he was an intelligent creature endowed with intellect and will and so capable of only accidental development. We find that parrots can be taught to say certain words by habit, but they do not compose sentences to show thought, or any evolutionary development of intellect. Yet even humans who are deaf and dumb can learn to communicate their ideas, and, as we said in the first chapter, the most primitive of peoples today have a fully developed language. Paleontology shows us the evolution of the dog, and proves that he was man's companion before the time of historical records, but dogs have never given any outward signs of communicating their mind by speech, whereas man can learn a language and progress in quality of speech. This speech and its progress arises from the intellectual power, which in turn can be more highly developed through the precisions of a refined language. Intellectual power may develop marvelously in contact with other intellects. But there is a vast difference between maintaining that the intellect as a principle can develop, and saying that the intellect can develop as a power.

All through the times of recorded history, humans have been born with the potentiality of thought — the intellect itself has not developed, but the mind has certainly developed in contact with concrete wisdom which could be learned. Language is a help in this development, and is necessary for the handing down of culture. There is no evidence in animals of this human intelligence and the power of language; nor is there evidence of any connection between the human and the animal mind, and there is no trace of any lower stage of human intellectual development — a time when man did not make tools and by their use improve his comfort.

As regards a comparison between actually existing anthropoids and man, it is true that there are striking resemblances between man and the gorilla, the chimpanzee, the orang-outang, and the gibbon. Anatomically, all parts of the ape's body are found in the same relative position as in man; but in addition to this, the pattern and intricacy of the brain are similar; both have the same chemical composition of blood; both have a prolonged period of embryonic development and postnatal growth and have a very similar prenatal development; and both lack an external tail.

Several differences, however, are certainly of importance. The anthropoid ape's skull shows a relatively small brain case, whereas the human brain case is relatively large; and so far as man's facial angle is concerned, he has a positive chin, and the ape has not (although it must be noted that most of the Neanderthalers and the Peking "men" lacked a chin); and man's forehead is usually high, whereas that of the ape is low and slopes backward (again it must be noted that the Rhodesian man and the chimpanzee have about the same forehead profile, the Java, Peking, and some Neanderthal skulls are almost as low, as also are some skulls of people today). Yet as we have shown, the size and shape of the head is not necessarily of importance in ascertaining intellectual capacity. So far as intellect is concerned, apes studied by Kohler and Yerkes have shown that they can perform actions suited to an end, but they have never given any signs of human intelligence with its power of abstract thought and its expression by means of language. There are, however, other differences between the ape and man. Man's body is relatively hairless,[9] while the ape

---

[9] Note that many Pygmy Negritos retain the embryonic lanugo throughout life.

has a thick covering. Man walks erect, and his pelvis is basin shaped outward to permit this erect carriage. The gorilla, gibbon, and chimpanzee can stand, but they walk with knees bent, and the ape's pelvis in general is more like an inverted basin. Man's spine has a distinctive double curve. Man has short upper limbs compared with the longer ones of the anthropoid. The position of man's large toe and thumbs is different, though not at the early stages of the individual's embryonic development; man's hands are not as specialized as the ape's, and his feet are primarily adjusted for support, whereas the feet of the ape are mainly prehensile organs. Moreover, a "missing link," a creature in the halfway developmental stage between man and the ape has never been found. As we have shown, none of the remains thus far discovered have been clearly ascertainable as such, and there is no such evidence in recorded history.

Other supposed evidence of evolution is furnished by embryology. For example, there is a very remarkable similarity of embryonic development in the pig, the rabbit, the ape, and man. Evolutionary development is supposed to have left its traces on man's heredity, and it is argued that these higher animals and others repeat in their embryonic growth the adult stages of lower animal life. In support of this theory, it is a fact that so-called gill slits are present in the embryos of both mammals and birds at one period of their development — a supposed indication of a common origin and an evolution from early fish life. During prenatal growth, also, the human embryo possesses a tail which recedes into the vertebral column before birth.[10] Sometimes a development from the caudal filament remains as a soft external tail after birth, a phenomenon which also persists in the orangoutang and chimpanzee. Again, the human infant is covered with hair (called the lanugo) from six months until shortly before birth, and sometimes even after birth. At one period during embryonic development the ear of the human is pointed and resembles that of certain of the anthropoids, and there are other significant resemblances which are too technical to detail here.[11] So-called vestigial organs are also

---

[10] Note by the General Editor: The phenomenon of the embryonic tail, as biologists are aware, is merely the result of a more rapid growth at first of the spinal column in the embryo, as compared with the lower members of the body. No evolutionary significance attaches to it. We may add that the entire Recapitulation theory, interesting though it is, has long ago been scientifically repudiated, but lives on as vigorously as ever in certain sociological and other textbooks.

[11] For further embryological data see Schulz, A. H., "Embryological Evidence of the Evolution of Man," *Journal of the Washington Academy of Sciences*, 1925, Vol. XV, pp. 247–263.

cited in support of this theory, but whereas most of these were formerly considered useless, the greater percentage has now been found to have a high value in human development as, for example, the ductless glands discussed in Chapter 2.

Further evidence in support of evolution is provided by genetics or experimental breeding. We mentioned previously that positive changes in hereditary characteristics have been observed in the *Drosophila melanogaster,* sometimes caused by selective breeding, but mostly due to mutations followed by selective breeding. The obvious changes in man from the original type to the racial types of today are, as we said, probably due to mutations, as well as to changes in diet and culture habits. If man has descended physically from the animal, therefore, it is very probable that large mutations occurred in the past, due to geological disturbances or some other cause, and that these mutations then became fixed by inbreeding. Certain difficulties in the way of acceptance of this theory can, however, readily be cited. For example, if a change in species was due to mutation, either two or more of the species were so changed, of differing sex, or else cross-fertilization between the two was possible. Yet the fact remains that at the present time crosses between two species not of the same genus are either nonproductive of offspring, or else the offspring is infertile — as the mule, the hybrid resulting from a cross between the horse and the ass.

Catholic Views on Evolution

Although it is seen that paleontology, geology, archaeology, comparative anatomy, embryology, and genetics all furnish a certain amount of evidence which may seem to point to evolution, it must be evident to the reader that none of this accumulation of data furnishes any incontrovertible proof for it.

The Church herself has made no pronouncement on the subject of evolution in general (although from time to time individuals within the Church have condemned the evolutionary hypothesis) for she is not concerned with the settlement of scientific subjects as such. Her business is to save souls and to safeguard revelation. Pope Leo XIII has, however, stated: "We declare that every wise thought, and every useful discovery, no matter from whom it may come, should be gladly and gratefully welcomed,"[12] and in the same spirit, Pope Pius XI set up an Academy of Scientists. Since truth could not possibly con-

---

[12] *Aeterni Patris,* August 4, 1879.

tradict truth, the Church has nothing to fear in the advancement of science.

As we mentioned earlier in the chapter, St. Augustine and others of the early Church Fathers upheld a doctrine of what is called "emergent evolution." Some scholars even see in the Bible supporting evidence for the evolutionary hypothesis: for they point out that in the story of the "days" of Creation it is recorded that light appeared on the earth, the seas were divided and vegetable life existed before the sun, the moon, and stars were evident (even as they would first show through the gradually disappearing vapors during the time of the cooling of the gaseous mass, if it be true that the world began in this manner); they also show that the creation of fish came first, then birds, and then beasts (the same order of appearance which seems clearly evidenced by geology and paleontology). That some scholars like Bishop Ussher have seriously erred in the interpretation of the Biblical account of the Creation and of the Flood,[13] does not take away from the account its concurrence with modern scientific discoveries.

So far as the "creation" of man is concerned, certain limitations must be noted. The word *Adam* itself resembles the Hebrew word *Adamah*, meaning soil. The Biblical words are these: "The Lord God formed man out of the dust of the earth, and breathed into his nostrils the breath of life."[14] Many other references in Scripture also point to man's origin from dust or slime.[15] These words are, of course, capable of two interpretations. There may have been a direct creation of the first man out of dust or mud, after the rest of the world was created. On the contrary, there may have been an intermediate creation of man's body, for it may have evolved from the primary dust of the world until the time when a higher animal developed into the being which became the human, Adam. This latter evolutionary hypothesis in no way detracts from God's glory. A miracle is never inferred if natural causes are sufficient to account for any condition. If man's body evolved by gradual stages from a primal nebula it would seem that God would thus manifest His power even more than by the

---

[13] The flood story in the Bible indicates that "All things wherein there is the breath of life on the earth, died" (Gen. 7:22); because of the distribution of fossil remains, either the flood referred to was before Paleolithic days, or the word *earth* must be taken to mean nothing more than the immediate neighborhood in which Adam lived. Archaeological remains at Ur indicate an extensive flood in Babylon before the year 3000 B.C. (cf. Caiger, S. L., *Bible and Spade,* pp. 14, 26). Ussher's date for the flood as 2348 B.C., cannot be accepted.

[14] Gen. 2:7.

[15] Cf. Gen. 3:19; Job 10:9; Jer. 18:6; Isa. 45:9; Isa. 29:16; Ps. 102:14; Wisd. 15:7; Rom. 9:20.

direct creation of man by a sudden miracle. If this were so, God would have given the nebula at the time of its creation the power to evolve, through all the intricate stages, until such time as it evolved a man. That God created the first nebula, if the world evolved in this manner, must be obvious. The beauty and harmony of the structure of the organic world in an almost endless multiplicity of forms clearly shows the plan of an intelligent Creator.

It is in this latter viewpoint that "emergent evolutionists" differ from those who hold the atheistic notion of mechanical evolution. Mechanical evolution implies that the earth and everything upon it evolved without any creative design, by inevitable physicochemical laws. If the world came into being in this manner, without creative design, the present structure would be merely the result of a chance organization. In these circumstances there would surely have been at least as many nonuseful as useful changes, and the present harmony would not exist. Mechanical evolution presupposes, too, the evolution of man's intellect, a fact which, as we have shown, can in no way be proved and is, moreover, impossible, since the intellect is spiritual by nature and could not evolve. Finally, herd evolution, which is the form in which human evolution is often proposed, must be definitely rejected by the fact of the transmission of original sin from *one* man only, to the entire human race. This implies that in human evolution the body alone could have been directly of animal origin, before the soul was breathed into it.

While evolution, therefore, has not been conclusively proved, it is certainly not opposed to the Sacred Scriptures, except within given limits, and Catholics may hold the evolutionary doctrine provided they do not question the literal historical sense of those statements in the first part of Genesis which concern the "peculiar creation of man, the formation of the first woman from the first man, and the unity of the human race."[16]

1. Catholics cannot believe in mechanical evolution, but must follow the lead of reason, as confirmed by revelation, that God at least created the original nebula with the power eventually to evolve a body fit for the reception of a human soul.

2. Catholics must believe in the separate creation of each man's soul, since the soul, with its faculties of intellect and will, is spiritual by nature and must be directly created by God Himself, even if the body was only indirectly created, through the evolutionary process.

---

[16] Biblical Commission, *Enchiridion*, Denziger-Bannwart, June 30, 1909.

3. On the authority of Scripture, Catholics must believe in some special intervention for the formation of Eve's body.

4. On the authority of Scripture, too, they must believe that all men (of all races) are descended from Adam and Eve, and that the whole human race inherits the consequences of their loss of the original state of grace. This fact is presupposed in the doctrine of our redemption by Christ. Through one man we lost our supernatural rights to sanctifying grace, to the sonship of God, and to heaven; therefore one Man was to redeem us: Christ.

CHAPTER 6

BRIEF HISTORY OF SOCIAL THEORY

Introduction

SOCIOLOGY is a comparatively new science, for it is said to have had its rise only in the year 1839, with the invention of the term *sociology* by Auguste Comte. Throughout the ages, however, men have been interested in social life, and many persons of ancient times have given mankind systematic theories about the societies in which they lived, or have proposed utopias for the better organization of the social life of their times. Although the reader who is but beginning a study of sociology will not be able to evaluate these theories until he has made a fairly wide reading in sociological literature, it seems worth while to mention a few of the most important names, and the works for which they are most famous. Any such enumeration, however, is necessarily limited in scope and incomplete. How limited is the discussion here will be obvious to anyone who examines some of the histories of social thought which have been written. Since this book is primarily intended for the American reader, when mention is made of modern trends in sociology we shall emphasize American sociologists rather than those of other countries.

Early Times

As far back as people have left written records, we find that philosophers wrote and taught about social life and its necessary principles and precepts. Thus we find records of the social thought of the early people of Egypt, of Babylonia, and Sumer (cf., especially the Code of Hammurabi, *circa* 2050 B.C.), of East India, China, and other ancient civilizations. The social thought of ancient Greece and Rome is so rich that to select individual names would mean to neglect some of equal importance. Of course all educated people must be conversant with the works of Plato (427–347 B.C.) and of Aristotle (384–322 B.C.). Aristotle's influence on the philosophic thought of the Middle Ages and on the Neo-Scholastic philosophy of the present day is too well known to comment upon here. As we mentioned in Chapter 3, some of the early Greeks were geographic determinists, stressing the influence of geography on the social life of the people. The chief contribution of the ancient Romans to social thought is probably that of the Roman Codes of law and of the writings of Cicero (106–43 B.C.).

Jewish and Christian Social Thought

The Old and New Testaments, and the many works which have been written to expound and amplify their teachings will give the reader ample material on the social thought of the Hebrews[1] and of the Christians. Indeed, most histories of social thought present the work of Christ merely as that of a teacher of a "social" gospel, ignoring His chief mission of individual salvation.

Since the beginning of the Christian era, St. Paul's writings are a prime source for Christian thought, and among the many other Church Fathers of early times, who occupied themselves with social problems, in the second century we find Pope Clement I writing to the Church in Corinth on the necessity of order and discipline, and St. Justin writing on marriage, Christian charity, and the need of submission to establish authority. Tertullian (A.D. 160–230) wrote numerous works on matters related to social life and marriage. St. Augustine (A.D. 354–450) is especially known to sociologists for his *De Civitate Dei,* the City of God, which defends Christian social ideas and is regarded even by non-Catholics as an influential piece of writing on the true social outlook of man.

Christian writers on social questions are too numerous for us to list them here. Yet we cannot overlook St. Thomas Aquinas (1226–1274) who by means of pure reasoning and experience, together with the teachings of revelation, epitomized Catholic social teaching in his *Summa Theologica* and his *De Regimine Principum.* Neither ought we to forget the *De Monarchia* of Dante (1265–1321); and the influence of Bellarmine (1542–1621), Suarez (1548–1617), and others on the political thought of their times. We shall refer to later Christian thought in the next chapter, and, of course, the present book aims at presenting the Catholic view of social life, as well as the findings of the best secular sociology.

The Utopias

Progressing rapidly in our scanty survey of the social thought of the centuries, the *Utopia* of St. Thomas More (1477–1535) must be

---

[1] Cf. Husslein, Rev. J., *The Bible and Labor.*

mentioned as an important fanciful work. It would assuredly disturb the author, however, if he knew that his work has been studied for practical purposes by the Russian Communists of today. The views on marriage and religion, as expressed in *Utopia*, are almost certainly intended merely as a logical development of a "natural" state, and did not reflect the supernatural viewpoints which led the author to abandon his influential position as Chancellor and to lay down his life for his religion of Catholicism in 1535. Indeed, at the end of the book, More reports concerning the mythical narrator of his tale: "I cannot agree and consent to all the things he said."

Of the other Utopias, the best-known works are *New Atlantis*, by Sir Francis Bacon (1561–1628); *City of the Sun* by the Dominican monk Thomas Campanella (1568–1639) and *The Commonwealth of Oceana*, by Harrington (1611–1677). In much more recent times William Morris (1834–1896) wrote *News from Nowhere* (1890), and Edward Bellamy (1850–1898) wrote *Looking Backward* (1888). Both have had an extensive influence on modern idealistic social thought.

Machiavelli

One of the most important works in the history of social theory is the well-known book by Machiavelli (1469–1527) entitled *The Prince*. This book, giving principles of government for a successful ruler, is a realistic analysis of the facts of governments of the past, together with some shrewd psychological analyses of mankind. Machiavelli is important as an early example of many modern pieces of so-called social research, where the "whole" man and his true purpose of existence is neglected, to the detriment of any truly human norms of action. He is considered by some as the founder of modern political science (as opposed to the politics of Aristotle) in that he introduced inductive methods into the study of government and statecraft. He only used his historical examples, however, to bolster up his theory of politics: that ethics has no place therein, that expediency knows no moral law, and reasons of State provide sufficient justification for injustices to citizens — axioms which had been the guiding spirit of many a ruler before his time (as his copious examples bear witness) and which assuredly, but no less wrongly, are the moving principles of many a modern nation today. *The Prince*, now read merely for its historic interest, has been considered a dominant factor in the political policies and philosophic outlook of such important people as Cromwell, Bacon, Catherine de Medici, Rousseau, Hobbes, Hume, Montesquieu, and Napoleon.

Early Protestant Thought

Of great importance, too, because of their influence on practical social thought, are the teachings of Protestantism as originally expounded by Luther (1483–1546) and Calvin (1509–1564), particularly the latter's *Institutes of the Christian Religion*. With their trend toward individualism and away from a consideration of man as a social being, it is quite probable that Max Weber (1864–1929) and R. H. Tawney (b. 1880) are correct in attributing to them and especially to Calvin, the ideational foundations for modern capitalism.[2] Certainly, Protestantism led to the idea of national independence in place of the international viewpoint of the universal Church.

Philosophical Influences on Social Thought

For the moment it seems necessary to overlook the chronical development of social thought, to give a brief indication of important philosophies.

Following Machiavelli's lead, the Englishman Francis Bacon, whose *New Atlantis* we mentioned previously, advocated that philosophy should be of an experimental kind, rather than of the speculative order, and can be said to be the founder of modern English empiricism.

A little later, we have René Descartes (1596–1650) in France, whose subjective rationalistic stand of clear and distinct ideas and mechanistic universe has so profoundly influenced all modern thinking and ultimately though not intentionally caused the downfall of metaphysics and the rejection of revelation.

In his *Essay Concerning Human Understanding*, John Locke (1632–1704), to whom we shall refer again in the next paragraph, thought that all knowledge comes from human experience, and he disavowed Descartes' idea of innate thought, although he followed the introspective method advocated by him.

As a logical consequence of Locke and also of Berkeley (1685–1752), followed the utterly empirical and skeptical conclusions of David Hume (1711–1776), to whom we shall later refer. Emmanuel Kant (1724–1804), attempting to reconcile the dogmatic rationalism of the Cartesian stand as found in Leibnitz (1646–1716) with the skeptical conclusions of the empirical school, overstressed the subjective condition of science.

Although these philosophers lived at varied periods, each must be

---

[2] Weber, Max, *Protestant Ethic and the Spirit of Capitalism;* Tawney, R. H., *Religion and the Rise of Capitalism.*

correlated with theories of society because of their profound influence, in their respective times, on the outlook and method of such early sociologists as Montesquieu, Condorcet, and Comte.

Social-Contract Theorists

Although differing in their premises and conclusions, Hobbes (1588–1678) in the *Leviathan* (1651), Locke (1632–1704) in *Civil Government* (1689), and Rousseau (1712–1778) in his *Social Contract* and *Emile* (1762), extended the doctrine of individualism (the untrammeled liberty of the individual) which had such a great influence on political and economic thought and ended in the nineteenth-century extension of democratic governments and the liberalism of *laissez faire* (the idea of "letting well enough alone," of preserving individual liberty at all costs, even at the expense of the socially weak and powerless; it being presumed that eventually the survival of the fittest would be the best for society). All three of these social-contract theorists were chiefly interested in politics. Hobbes thought that a state formation became necessary to suppress antisocial (atomistic) instincts of man. His idea was that man in a State of Nature lived in such intolerable conflict that he made an irrevocable contract to form an artificial man, a commonwealth, so that he might live in harmony with his fellow men. From this state, said Hobbes, all rights and duties emanate, so that his theory involves state absolutism in the ethical as well as in the political sphere.

Locke was the more moderate of the three. His idea of the "State of Nature" was a time of ideal liberty for man, but he thought that man formed a contract with his fellows to live in civil society, because he needed protection in the exercise of his liberty. The State was to interfere with his liberty as little as possible, and was merely to prevent license and to safeguard his rights to life, liberty, and property. Each of us, he thought, has the right to punish those who violate the natural law, and he was of the opinion that the government should be changed if it exceeded its authority. His theory led directly to political *laissez faire* and was taken over by Voltaire.

Rousseau inconsistently united these two theories: he thought that the absolute surrender of the individual to the group was necessary for a peaceful government, so although he was adverse to all subordinate groups within the State, he advocated a political absolution in order to secure liberty. He was of the opinion that originally man lived in an ideal condition, absolutely free, but nonsocial. He made a contract to live with others in society, and so lost his freedom by the artificial restraints imposed by social life and organization. But since the contract he made was an agreement among equals, he did not contract with a sovereign, and hence the people in the State are collectively the sovereign.

Early Sociologists

Montesquieu (1689–1755) already noted for the importance which he attributed to climate in social development, tried by inductive methods and the description of concrete facts to show in *The Spirit of the Laws* that certain social laws are deep rooted in the nature of man, that man has a natural tendency toward association, and that the ordered development of civil society is derived from fixed laws. He stressed that society is an organic whole of interrelated parts, an idea made use of by many sociologists later, and because of this and his relatively inductive and comparative method, he is thought by some to be logically the "father of sociology" rather than Comte.

Condorcet (1743–1794) in his *Sketch of an Historical Picture of the Progress of the Human Mind* also wished to be inductive, and to transfer the method of physical science to the social sciences. He is of interest, too, in that he prophesied a continuing intellectual, moral, and physical improvement in man, an idea of which the unilinear evolutionists made much in later days.

David Hume (1711–1776), as we have shown above, is classed with the philosophers rather than with the sociologists. He is noted especially for his *Treatise of Human Nature,* 3 volumes, published between 1739–1740, on which his fame chiefly rests. In this work, with telling logic, he reduced our knowledge of human nature to a pure empirical level, and, perhaps more than anyone else, influenced the trend of empirical thought in France, thus leading to the positivistic stand of Comte.

Adam Ferguson (1723–1816) to some extent used the comparative ethnographic approach to social problems, in that he gave examples from history and particularly from ethnographic reports of simpler peoples in an attempt to show that progress is natural to man, and also that borrowing inventions from others is of importance in social progress.

The economic theories of Saint-Simon (1760–1825), Charles Fourier (1772–1837), Robert Owen (1771–1858), Louis Blanc (1813–1882), and Proudhon (1809–1865) and others we shall refer to in some detail in Chapter 20 on proposed economic reforms. Saint-Simon is of more interest to sociologists than the others because he stressed the positive method of observation, experiment, and generalization, and perhaps did something to set the very prevalent antireligious viewpoint of sociology. Comte was Saint-Simon's secretary for many years, although he abandoned this position when Saint-Simon wished to put some of his ideas into practical effect, as Comte was only interested in the theory of society.

Reverend Thomas Robert Malthus (1766–1834) should also be mentioned here. In 1798 he anonymously published an *Essay on the Principles of Population,* and after further years of research he republished the essay under his own name in 1803. Having studied population statistics for various countries of the world, both ancient and modern, he came to the conclusion that population tends to increase in geometric progression, while the means of production only increase arithmetically, thus:

Population increase: 1, 2, 4, 8, 16, 32, 64, 128, etc.
Production increase: 1, 2, 3, 4, 5, 6, 7, 8, etc.

As a result of this tendency, he foresaw a terrible time of starvation and famine, and he recommended that checks to population should be established — the poor laws should be abolished; people should marry later, and should use restraint so as to limit their families. The entirely unlooked for results of his restraint theory, as it is now applied to birth-control ideas, should by no means be attributed to Malthus. And although his theory of ratios was scientific enough according to the knowledge available in his day, it is by no means correct. He was unfortunate in that he lived just prior to many important events and discoveries. For example, it was after his time that the world witnessed the development of such vast areas as the United States, Canada, and Australia, not even now fully cultivated; the use of large-scale mechanical methods for the extensive cultivation of large tracts of land; the adoption of scientific farming which increased yields and made more intensive farming productively possible; the discovery of improved methods of preserving perishable foods by canning them, by refrigeration, and the extensive use of substitutes, such as wood pulp for the making of clothing and oil and electricity in place of coal.

Auguste Comte

Auguste Comte (1798–1857), who was the son of Catholic parents but became a freethinker at an early age, is generally considered as the founder of sociology and of positive thought. Obviously a follower in the footsteps of Condorcet and Saint-Simon, he emphasized the need of a system of sociology by means of a scientific methodology of observation and classification, and he advocated the complete abandonment of philosophic methods. His chief work is the six-volume *The Positive Philosophy* (1830–1842) translated in two volumes by Harriet Martineau, and a *System of Positive Polity,* 4 volumes, 1851–1854. He did not follow his own prescription of inductive and comparative methods, and the utilization of the findings of other sciences, and although he made use of some historical facts, and outlined what he thought was the actual state of the sciences at his time, his sociological work is largely the figment of his own brain and merely of historical value at the present day. Postulating that man has progressed from low beginnings to a higher order, he gave the following stages to society, emphasizing an interpenetration of geographic, spiritual, economic, and political factors: First, a theological stage, where he thought man was first a fetich worshiper; that he then developed polytheism as a religion and with this the institution of slavery; and that finally monotheism arose, which he thought developed into Catholicism, side by side with a militaristic political order. The next stage, in his opinion, was a metaphysical stage, where abstract supernatural forces were the motivating ones, leading to Jesuitism, Protestantism, Deism, and to the study of politics and economics. Finally, he thought a stage of reason was coming into being, where positive philosophy or the science of sociology would arise from a universal hierarchy of knowledge. In this hierarchy, Comte gave first place to mathematics as the pre-eminent science which would furnish positive philosophy (sociology) with both its origin and its method. Then followed in order, astronomy, physics, chemistry, biology, and finally the new science, sociology. Comte was the first to isolate sociology from the other sciences, to show that it could be a science, and to give it a name, that is, to coin the word *sociology* (a knowledge of society). He divided this new science into two branches: social statics, or the investigation of the laws of society; and social dynamics, the theory of social progress. He was anxious to reform the society of his day, and he emphasized that the family was the original social unit and was normally monogamous (ideas which he most probably retained from the Catholic doctrine of the schools where he had received all his formal training). He thought, however, that the individual was absorbed in society. Ever since the days of Comte the study of society has retained the name *sociology,* although many sociologists have regretted the wide application which can be given to the word, and wish that it could be confined entirely to the "scientific" inductive (positive) methods advocated by Comte. While many sins have been committed in the name of philosophy, and particularly in the name of social philosophy, the stand taken by many so-called scientific sociologists, that all philosophy is useless, is, of course, ridiculous. They ignore the fact that philosophy, if conducted by true scientifically deductive methods, has its use and positive need in a well-rounded-out whole.

The Trend of Sociology After Comte

From the time of Comte onward, sociology, therefore, came into its own as a social science. As we said, however, the scientific method proposed was not carried out by Comte, and neither was it followed by many of those who came after him. Actually, many so-called scientific sociologists are more wedded to a philosophy (and generally speaking a wholly imaginative and erroneous philosophy) than most of their readers are aware. Apart from a very few modern sociologists who stress individual psychology to the extreme, sociology has been a complete breaking away from individualistic schools of Protestantism, and of the political thought of the eighteenth and nineteenth centuries; and for most sociologists it has also led to a divorce from *laissez faire* economic notions. Some of the sociologists, it is true, think with Hobbes that man is atomistic by nature; but all agree that only in society did man find his true expression and happiness. Many sociologists, however, have gone to the extreme of merging the individual in society, as did Comte and some of the many later sociologists whom we shall note in the following pages. Some of these wish to improve present conditions; others, more or less deterministic, do not see any possibilities of improvement. This so-called mechanistic determinism of man by his social environment even led such writers as Spencer and Sumner, to advocate extreme *laissez faire* as the only means by which society could work out its own problems. Marx had a somewhat similar notion, though he wished to aid the natural and "eventual" outcome by a revolution. With these ideas, of course, the Catholic sociologist has no part. In his view of the whole man, as well as the whole of society, he is much more truly scientific than some of these so-called scientific sociologists.

Herbert Spencer

Herbert Spencer (1820–1903) is undoubtedly the most influential of the earlier sociologists. As we said in Chapter 4, he worked out detailed, and, of course, quite imaginary, stages of development for religious, social, and political organizations. Although he denied taking any ideas from Comte's work, most critics are agreed that he made use of Comte not only in adopting the terms *social statics* and *social dynamics,* but also in his likening society to a physical organism (called biological analogy). As did Comte, he paid no attention to the individual, but studied society as a whole. He tried to absorb the individual organically into society, and talked of every society having a sustaining, regulating, and circulating system. Society, he said, is "an organism which undergoes continuous growth."[3] He also made use of the evolutionary ideas to be gained from Malthus's so-called law of population, and stressed that the evolution of human institutions has been uniform, gradual, and progressive. In this he was the founder of the school of unilinear evolutionists, to which we have already referred in Chapter 4, and whose theories on marriage and the family, religion, and property, we shall refer to in more detail in the appropriate chapters of the next section.

Spencer was perhaps influenced by Ferguson in his use of ethnographical material as the main sources for his ideas, but he did this much more consistently than did Ferguson, and with a great show of scientific induction. (See his *Descriptive Sociology* for the ambitious framework under which his secretaries and followers have classified ethnographical and historical data.) He may, therefore, rightfully be called the first of the modern cultural sociologists, although these latter are generally much more discriminatory than was Spencer in the choice of their sources, and they do not usually try, as he did, to fit their sources into any prearranged framework. Spencer also seems to be responsible for the idea developed by later sociologists of the supposed superorganic nature of culture, for the idea is inherent throughout his *Principles of Sociology,* although he did not define it. He thought that the workings of culture and unilinear evolution were so mechanical, by means of a supposed natural selection and survival of the fittest, that he did not think progress could be forced, and he was therefore an advocate of extreme *laissez faire.* As mentioned in Chapter 4, his ideas predated Darwin's work, although he was probably much influenced later by Darwin (1809–1882), whose *Origin of Species* and *Descent of Man* had such profound influence on sociological literature, as is evident from the writings of the unilinear sociologists and those of some of the cultural schools. Particularly in Volume Two of his

---

[3] Spencer, H., *Principles of Sociology,* Vol. I, p. 462.

Principles, Spencer stressed the importance of ceremony as a means of social control, an idea which also probably gave fruit to much of the work of the later cultural sociologists. His theory of the origin of the family from low beginnings is in line with his other theories of evolution, and his ideas that religion evolved from a primitive fear of ghosts will be noted in the Chapter on Religion. As we said, since the theories of the other unilinear evolutionists were discussed in Chapter 4, and will be mentioned again in later chapters, we shall not consider them here.

Extreme Biological Analogy Theories[4]

Out of Spencer's idea of likening society to a biological organism, and influenced doubtless by the theories of Darwin, many sociologists have stressed this analogy, talking of the necessity of all societies growing, maturing, and decaying in a mechanistic manner, which inherently, though not specifically, denies the intellect and free will. The main theorists in this category are the Russian, Lilienfeld (1829–1903), the German, Schaeffle (1831–1903), Fouillée (1838–1912) and Worms (b. 1869) in France, Ward (1841–1913) in the United States, and also Oswald Spengler (1885–1935) a German.

Lilienfeld taught that the only difference between society and an organism was in degree. He invented the term *social pathology,* and talked of diseases of society being similar to insanity; diseases of justice to be like delirium; and political diseases to resemble paralysis. Schaeffle likened the various social groups to bodily parts, called houses, epidermal tissues; economic groups, the nutritive process of society, and making similar farfetched analogies.

Ward was much more moderate in his terms than these men, and his sociology had many more ideas than just the biological. He was a scientist in the Federal Government service until 1906, and before he resigned from his scientific work and began teaching sociology at Brown University, he had already written a number of sociological works as well as many highly regarded scientific researches, and was, too, the first President of the American Sociological Society in 1905. For Ward, sociology was mainly a study of the forces of society and their control, and he was the principal originator of the idea of "social forces" which many other sociologists later developed.[5] These ideas

---

[4] Cf. Barnes, H. E., "Representative Biological Theories of Society," *The Sociological Review* (London), Vol. XVII, 1925.

[5] Cf. House, F. N., "The Concept of Social Forces," *The American Journal of Sociology,* Vol. XXI, 1925, 1926.

ally him to the psychological school as well as the biological. He classified the chief forces which made society under two main headings. Essential forces were ontogenetic or preservative (seeking pleasure and avoiding pain), and philogenetic or reproductive (sex desires and parental and conjugal love). Other important, though nonessential forces were enumerated by him as the sociogenetic, aesthetic, emotional, and intellectual. Ward talked of the sympodial evolution of society, meaning that society branched out like a strawberry plant rather than a treelike branching or like the upward progress postulated by the unilineal evolutionists. With Ward's name is also connected the term *synergy* by which he meant the constructive energy of nature, or the systematic and organic working together of the antithetical forces of nature; and *telesis* meaning a conscious striving to improve man's temporal lot. Ward particularly stressed the value of education in scientifically working for the welfare of society, showing how education could give what he called telesis or purposeful direction to social trends.

Spengler, who has had a great influence in the development of Nazi ideology, claimed in his *Decline of the West*, that societies grow, have a period of constructive maturity, and then, after a period of decline, finally decay. He traced the rise and decline of such civilizations as the Sumerian, the Egyptian, the Chinese, the Grecian and Roman, and the Mayan. Postulating that each of these civilizations went through similar stages, which he designated by the four seasons of the year, he prophesied the complete decay of Western civilization, which he said began its upward swing about the year A.D. 900, and is at present rapidly declining. In his ideas of the organic unity of each culture, Spengler was much influenced by Hegel.

Conflict Theorists

Also interested in social forces, but maintaining that social life progresses by means of conflict so that conflict is the main force to be considered, are the two well-known Austrian sociologists, Gumplowicz (1838–1909) and Ratzenhofer (1842–1904). Both were chiefly concerned in the formation of the larger social group of the State and have little interest in smaller groups. As mentioned in Chapter 3, Gumplowicz stressed racial conflict, and the value of ethnocentrism which arises from what he terms syngenism or the sentiment of attachment which results when people are born and reared together. Ratzenhofer stressed such interests as the racial, physiological, individual, social, transcendental interests, and others, and it is from him that the

American sociologist Small drew many of his own ideas. The philosopher Nietzsche (1844–1900) and the Russian Nowikow (1848–1912) are also to be classed among these conflict theorists. They may, too, be said to belong to the psychological school of sociology, since they are interested in sentiments and mental interests.

With these conflict theorists may also be placed Karl Marx (1818–1893) whose theory of class struggle is discussed in some detail in Chapter 20 on Proposed Economic Reforms, and such other economic determinists as Oppenheimer (b. 1864), Veblen (1857–1929), Thurnwald (b. 1869), De Greef (1842–1924), and Lippert (1839–1909). Lippert and Thurnwald, both German sociologists, stressed the cultural approach; the former was very much imbued with the doctrines of the unilinear evolutionists, but Thurnwald is one of the better modern ethnographical writers. Oppenheimer's main ideas center around State formation: first, he thinks, there was a societal evolution through conflict, but later co-operation arose through ethnic amalgamations, and so the State came into being. Veblen's *Theory of the Leisure Class* (1904) is chiefly concerned with showing the economic factors which determine modern social life.

Le Play

Quite different in his approach to social life and its problems is the French Catholic, Le Play (1805–1882), whose idea of the correct method of sociology was a quantitative analysis of actual social facts. A metallurgist by profession, he journeyed six months in each year from 1830–1853, in all European countries as far as the Ural mountains, and made a series of detailed monographs on the family in its varying organizations in different European countries. For the statistical value of his first book, *Les Ouvriers Européens* (1855) the Academy of Sciences in France awarded him a prize which he used to establish the *Société internationale des études pratiques d'économie sociale,* for world-wide study of family life and the publication of such researches as monographs. Stressing the importance of geographic environment and the manner of earning a living, on family and other social life, he drew up a classification of information to be obtained, and established a methodology for the collection of these family monographs. In this his contribution to practical inductive sociology has been great, and he may be said to have inaugurated the social-service method of investigating social facts, and hence to be the inspirer of numerous social surveys which have been made since his time.

Le Play had the Catholic idea of the family as the most important unit in society, and of group solidarity. He stressed the importance of the family and the home as a social institution to be preserved for the good of stable society, and he was particularly interested in what he called the *famille souche* or "stem society," by which he means a patriarchal family with a due amount of individual liberty and individual-property ownership. He thought that social life was at its best when there was mutual co-operation between such families and the individuals composing them, in a spirit of altruistic religion.[6]

The best-known disciples of Le Play are Victor Branford (b. 1864) and Patrick Geddes (1854–1932). Geddes, said to be Darwin's favorite student, was one of the founders of the English Sociological Society (which calls its headquarters: Le Play House) and directed the work of this society into its present channels of regional surveys integrating geography, history, and city planning.

W. I. Thomas

One of the most important sociologists in the United States is W. I. Thomas (b. 1863). Thomas elaborated the modernistic approach at the University of Chicago, and advocated a complete examination of the modern culture of various small groups which could be isolated within the larger groups of our present-day civilized communities. From a study of individual people in their whole cultural setting he wished to draw up social laws. He stresses individual motives, and may therefore be said to have a psychological approach. We have already spoken of his theory of four wishes as innate social forces at the end of Chapter 2. As a result of his work in this direction we not only have the valuable *Polish Peasant*, which he published with the collaboration of the Polish sociologist Znaniecki, but a whole series of monographs about modern American city life has been published by Chicago University, which could prove useful material to the cultural sociologists when the time comes for them to test their theories and laws from modern history and modern life. We refer to such monographs as *The Hobo* by Anderson, 1923; *The Ghetto*, by Wirth, 1928; *The Gold Coast* and the *Slum*, by Zorbaugh, 1929; *The Saleslady*, by Donovan, 1929. Although his emphasis is the more specialized one of delinquency, Clifford R. Shaw (b. 1896) and his work, such as *The Jack Roller*, might also be classed with these works. Thomas's interest in individual psychology takes him out of the class of cultural sociologists, yet it must be said that he is somewhat in line with these in that he examines by inductive

---

[6] See Zimmerman, C. C., and Frampton, M. E., *Family and Society* (New York: D. Van Nostrand Co., 1935), for an exposition of Le Play's theories on family life.

methods the whole culture of the groups to which the individuals he is studying belong.

Other Psychological Sociologists

Sociologists who are interested in the psychological approach differ widely from each other. Under this heading may be included all those who stress individual instincts, drives, forces in a virtually exclusive manner. Of these, we have already taken the conflict theorists.

At Chicago, in addition to W. I. Thomas other sociologists adopted the idea of social forces. We may chiefly name R. F. Park (b. 1864) and E. W. Burgess (b. 1886) who take over Thomas's four wishes and add to them many such other forces such as sentiments, ideas, and public opinion.

Of all social psychologists, William McDougall (1871–1938) may perhaps be said to be the most extreme, for he bases all his social psychology on a long series of instincts which he lays before the reader without any scientific proof. These we already mentioned at the end of Chapter 2.

Among other sociologists who are interested in psychology may be listed Albion Small, Edward Alsworth Ross, Giddings, Pareto, Bogardus, Ward, and others. Bogardus (b. 1882) takes attitudes as the determining forces in social life. Small (1854–1926), the founder of the Chicago School of Sociology, was also one of the founders of the American Sociological Society, and the editor of the *American Journal of Sociology* from its inception until his death. As before mentioned, he drew much of his inspiration from Ratzenhofer, and in his most important work, *General Sociology* (1905), he stresses man's major interests as food, sex, and work, and his minor interests as wealth, sociability, knowledge, beauty, and rightness.

Edward Alsworth Ross (b. 1868) was also much influenced by Ratzenhofer in his earlier days, as well as by Ward. In his earlier books, *Social Control* (1901), *Foundations of Sociology* (1905), and *Social Psychology* (1908), he stresses such series of social forces as egotic, affective, recreative, cultural, religious, ethical, aesthetic, intellectual, sympathy, sociability, wealth, and even worries. His term *social control* has been widely used in a sociological sense. In his later work, *Principles of Sociology* (1920), he makes instincts the prime factor in social life, and is there chiefly interested in the processes which he considers as all important in the shaping of social life, such as socialization, stratification, co-operation, and the like. These "forces" have been widely used by writers of sociological textbooks.

F. Giddings (1855–1931) considers sociology as a psychological science. He followed Gumplowicz, through Ward, and we have already discussed in Chapter 2 his idea of consciousness of kind. He is the author of a number of books on sociology, and a large number of his students from the University of Columbia have become important as sociological theorists. Among these we may name Gehlke, Gillin, Lichtenberger, Odum, and Ogburn. In addition to his ideas on the importance of instincts, and to the importance which he ascribed to psychological forces in society, Giddings may be said to be somewhat a geographical determinist, and in his *Principles of Sociology* (1896) he also outlined what he thought was a sequence in social life: first zoogenic association; then anthropogenic society, or the development of the social mind, that is, the so-called transformation of man from the use of animal instincts to the human mind; third, ethnogenic association, or the development of the family, clan, and tribe; and finally demogenic association, or the development of the national state.

Vilfredo Pareto (1848–1923) also belongs to the psychological sociologists. His chief sociological work, *Trattato di sociologia generale,* published in 1916, was published in English as *Mind and Society,* 4 volumes, in 1935. Differing entirely from the evolutionists, Pareto's main idea is that society has only appeared to change, but that actually it has remained the same and it is only a change in the ruling classes and the ruled which has taken place. He is of the opinion that sentiments are the mainsprings of conduct, so that all society is conditioned by them. However, he calls the outward manifestations of these sentiments, residues — common instincts developed in society — and he says that it is these which actually determine human behavior. From these residues, derivations are supposedly made, although these, he claims, are usually illogical verbalisms. Pareto prophesied the Great War and in his stressing of the value of the middle classes as rulers, and predicting their rise, he is considered the "father" of Italian Fascism.

The Freudians, with their idea of sex as the main determining force in the world, and the theories of the other psychoanalysts about the psychological conflicts which supposedly determine human conduct, are discussed briefly in Chapter 23.

Other psychological theorists may be said to be Gabriel Tarde (1843–1904) who stressed the importance of imitation in social life, and Gustav Le Bon (1841–1931) who was chiefly interested in the psychological effect of crowds. Durkheim (1858–1917) also belongs to this category. In Le Bon and Durkheim, however, we get back again to cultural determinism as will be evident to those readers who have read Chapters 3 and 4. Lévy-Bruhl (b. 1857) is chiefly noted for his theories that primitive peoples are lower in intelligence than ourselves, and that their thought is illogical.

Denying the importance of inheritance, including an inherited mentality, the Behaviorists and such sociologists as Bernard (b. 1881), Ogburn (b. 1886), and Ellwood (b. 1873) stress the influence of environment in the determination of social life. The reader is referred to Chapter 2 for a discussion of Behaviorism.

Robert Morison McIver (b. 1882) must be placed in a class by himself, although in his early work, *Community* (1917), he builds society upon a scheme of interests, with their corresponding associations — classifying them (but with many ramifications) as general, specific, and derivative, as well as discrete and common. McIver's general work, and especially his: *Society: Its Structure and Changes* perhaps represents the best of the non-Catholic social philosophies.

Similarly, Charles Horton Cooley (1864–1929) is out of line with the psychological school, although he talks of interests, and of the social importance and public opinion and of not belonging to an "out" group. One of the pioneer sociologists in the United States, he is chiefly notable for his classification of primary face-to-face groups of family, play group, and school, and his emphasis on the role of the primary group in conditioning the child to social life. Chiefly an armchair theorist, however, his philosophic thought is of a rather shallow order. His chief works are: *Human Nature and the Social Order* (1902), *Social Organization* (1909), and *Social Process* (1918).

The Cultural Sociologists

The cultural school of sociologists mainly use the recorded observations of the ethnographer and of the archaeologist as the basic material for their studies. Proceeding by inductive methods, cultural sociologists aim at analyzing the complete social life (the whole culture) of a large number of primitive and semiprimitive tribes (the simpler-culture peoples) and from the facts thus obtained to arrive at certain scientific conclusions about social interaction. As explained in Chapter 1, primitive tribes are considered because primitive social life is less complex than our own; because the observer can examine it without the emotion and blindness which is sometimes present when one tries to analyze the culture of one's own community. The relative simplicity of primitive culture also enables results to be obtained much more easily than is possible with a consideration of the many ramifications of our own social life. Our ways of life have grown complex because we have received ideas of variations in our culture from so many different sources, not only in time but also in space. In the course of time, our people have received a heritage of intercourse much wider than any the primitives might have had; and our present methods of communication are so extensive, that if we consider our complete social relations they may indeed be said to be world wide. Primitives live in small groups in isolated places, so that their way of living is largely the result of natural growth and is little influenced by ideas from without. The data of the cultural sociologists is therefore chiefly furnished from ethnography and archaeology, although they do sometimes make use of historical and demographical material to check their conclusions and to find supporting evidence therefor. Later, when researches in primitive life are completed, the cultural sociologist should logically examine the culture of more complex groups — a work which the Chicago school has already undertaken as regards modern life, but not regarding historical civilizations of the past.

The founder of this school may perhaps correctly be said to be Herbert Spencer, although it is to Tyler that we are indebted for the first satisfactory definition of the term. Sumner and Keller, to whose theories we have already referred in Chapter 4, also belong to this group. William Graham Sumner (1840–1910) taught the first university course in sociology in the United States at Yale in 1875, using Spencer as a textbook, and influenced in his ideas later by the German, Lippert (1839–1909). His best-known sociological work is *Folkways,* wherein he used the words *folkways* and *mores* now current in sociological literature. His successor at Yale, A. G. Keller, developed Sumner's ideas in the 4-volume work *The Science of Society,* which forms the basis of Yale's sociological studies. Keller further developed the Darwinian idea of automatic adaptation in social life. To this cultural method of sociology, Sumner and Keller added the theory that the four main interests and basic hereditary drives which motivate social life are hunger, fear, sex, and vanity.

The important contribution of Spencer, Sumner, and Keller lies in the method which they proposed: the collection of a large number of facts concerning the social life of primitives, and the scientific interpretation thereof. The criticism to be made of their work lies, however, in a number of their interpretations. At times these interpretations undoubtedly go beyond the conclusions warranted by the facts, as in their theories regarding the disappearance of cannibalism, the evolution of religion, and the like; sometimes, too, the interpretations are based on implied postulates which can be seriously questioned, for example, the assumption which they seem to make that social life is in no way determined by the psychological make-up of man and by his faculty of free will. The department of sociology at Yale continues to employ the method proposed by Sumner and Keller in the line of pure theory, with many more useful results at the present time. Maurice Rea Davie (b. 1893) and others also carry on at Yale an examination of modern conditions in the realm of applied sociology which are not necessarily always allied to the cultural studies made there.

Durkheim and others, who, following Spencer's ideas of the super-organic, have stressed the so-called superindividual element in culture are, of course, entirely too mechanistic; and their divorce of culture from individual psychology cannot be upheld by anyone who realizes the value of the individual, albeit the individual is most certainly a member of society and greatly influenced by all the environment which surrounds him.

F. S. Chapin, to some extent allied to the cultural school of sociology, is chiefly noted for his theory, based on examples from history and archaeology, of synchronous culture cycles. He believes that each cultural form has its own law of change, which is wavelike and rhythmical. Material culture forms change with relative rapidity, he thinks; whereas non-material culture traits move more slowly, so that more lags are apparent. While some traits are passing through a period of integration, others are declining, others disintegrating, and others attaining a phase of equilibrium; but as both material and non-material culture traits move within the cycles of national civilizations, of necessity these latter are relatively slow and ponderous in their movements. Chapin also invented the term *cultural horizon,* to which we referred in Chapter 4, and somewhat in line with Ogburn, he had a theory of "societal reaction patterns" — that laws are merely a reaction to bad adjustments. His conclusions, however, seem to be based on far too few examples to warrant any acceptance of them.

Pitirim Sorokin (b. 1889), the Russian head of the Department of Sociology at Harvard University, is also interested in culture cycles, although in many ways his work is to be classed with the psychological type of sociology. Sorokin is working for a pure inductive science of sociology, and in his recent massive work in three volumes: *Social and Cultural Dynamics* (1937) he draws on the history of every type of culture in an attempt to show the rise and decline of cultures according to whether "sensate" or "ideational" ideologies are in the ascendant. He has drawn up elaborate tables to summarize his theories of cultural adaption[7] and he conceives of our present age as an overripe "sensate" one, soon to decay in favor of an ascending and superior ideational civilization. Again the conclusions arrived at do not seem to be entirely warranted by the facts.

To the writer it seems as if the *modern* cultural school of sociology has most chances of doing really worth-while work toward an understanding of society, though this work may be of little avail unless a deeper understanding of man and his social relations be arrived at by taking into consideration the findings of the social philosophers. We shall now turn to the writings of Catholic social thinkers, whose work has largely been of a philosophical nature rather than of the inductive kind.

---

[7] Sorokin, P., *Social and Cultural Dynamics,* Vol. I, p. 97.

CHAPTER 7

BRIEF HISTORY OF SOCIAL THEORY:
THE CATHOLIC POSITION

Catholic Sociologists — Theoretical and Practical

CATHOLIC writers on sociology and social philosophy are so numerous that we can give brief mention to only a few. We have previously made a brief survey of Catholic writers of the early and Middle Ages. Here we shall confine ourselves to the nineteenth and twentieth centuries, from which we have already outlined the work of Le Play and Father Schmidt. First, we must mention the Vicomte de Villeneuve-Bargemont (1784–1850) whose three-volume work *Economie politique chrétienne* showed up the dangers of capitalism as early as 1834.

Another outstanding name at the beginning of the last century is Frédéric Ozanam (1813–1853) who initiated the Society of St. Vincent de Paul in 1833, with the idea of the sanctification of its members by mutual encouragement in a Christian life and the visitation of the poor in their own homes. In this latter connection Ozanam began a new philosophy in social work. The guiding spirit of these visits to the poor was to be sympathy and service — an attempt to understand the needs of the poor, so that they could adequately be provided for, and a realization that the friendship which the poor could offer them was a rich return for their aid. The work of the St. Vincent de Paul Society is extremely flourishing in the United States, in Canada, and in most other Christian countries today.

Chronologically, next in importance is Adolph Kolping (1813–1864), a shoemaker who became a priest in 1845, and who established in 1849 the famous Catholic Journeymen's Guild, a social organization to provide young craftsmen with the means of developing social self-help. Just previous to the present regime, nearly two thousand Kolping societies in Germany provided the young apprentice worker with a home, technical instruction, and a priest guide. What the situation is at the present time is difficult to say.

Next we may mention the famous Bishop of Mainz, Wilhelm Emmanuel von Ketteler (1811–1877), who was an ardent supporter of producers' co-operative programs and private profit-sharing schemes at the beginning of his career, somewhat similar to Lasalle's ideas, though he wished to help establish them without State aid. Later, he took up the cause of the workingman from a different angle, and advocated State aid to enable the workingman to better his economic condition. But although he demonstrated the evils of individualistic ideas of property ownership, he did not fall into the error of socialism, and he maintained the natural rights of the owner of property legitimately acquired. In 1873 he drew up a program of basic principles for German Catholics in politics, which included protection of the workers against capitalistic greed, legislation for shorter working hours, better health conditions, and inspectors to see that protective laws were carried out.

Baron Karl von Vogelsang (1818–1890), who became a convert to the Church in 1850, was prominent in Catholic circles of Austria from 1860 until his death. He founded the *Monthly Periodical of Christian Social Reform,* and was one of the original members of the *Union de Fribourg,* which we shall shortly describe. He stressed the social functions of property, and urged the co-operation of worker and employer in true functional groups. He stressed, too, the need in his country of co-operation between Church and State for the proper functioning of these vocational organizations.

Franz Hitze (1851–1921) a priest, was very important in German politics and the social legislation of his time. His main ideas are contained in his book *Capitalism and Socialism* (1880) wherein he chiefly advocates a return to the corporate guilds of the Middle Ages as a necessary combative of State socialism. In collaboration with Franz Brandts, a textile manufacturer, he established the *Society for Social Culture and Communal Betterment* in 1881, to foster a better coordination between industrial employers and their workmen; and in 1890 he and Brandts (1834–1914) also established the *Volkerverein* or *People's Union,* a central organization for Catholics to insure their instruction in Catholic social principles.

Windthorst (1812–1891) was a German lawyer who became interested in politics in 1848. He was elected president of the politically important Centre Party in 1874, and as a layman who was the sole opponent to Bismarck in the Reichstag, was largely instrumental in bringing about the end of the Kulturkampf. He urged protective legislation for workers, and stressed the duty of the State to establish boards of arbitration for the settlement of industrial disputes.

Reverend Henry Pesch, S.J. (1854–1926), was the originator of the theory of Solidarism in his *Lehrbuch der Nationalökonomie.* The details of this theory are difficult to outline, as they are somewhat involved.

In general, he worked out somewhat more theoretically the teachings of von Ketteler, Hitze, and others. He wanted to overcome the present dichotomy between the classes by the establishment of a vocational order, where human labor would be considered as of more worth than capital, and where labor and capital would work together. Pesch stressed the need of all social organizations, including the economic, to be bound together by their common national interests, under the authority of the State. His nationalistic ideas were mitigated by his urging the abandonment of imperialistic policies, and by his desire to see due regard paid to the principles of religion, including the claims of charity and justice. Pesch has had a large following, called Solidarists, who claim that it was precisely from the doctrine of Solidarism that the *Quadragesimo Anno's* central theme is taken. In general the chief defect of Solidarism is its idealism coupled with its lack of a clear-cut practical program.

Charles Périn (1815–1905) a Belgian professor at the University of Louvain, and Frédéric Le Play (1806–1882), whose theories we have already discussed, are considered the most outstanding writers in the French language on nineteenth-century Catholic thought. In contrast with Le Play's conservative and practical approach to social problems, Périn stressed in his *Des lois de la société chrétienne,* 1875, and *De la richesse dans les sociétés chrétiennes,* 1861, the need of a moral reform rather than any practical economic or other sociological program.

Impressed by the work of the German Catholics, Count Albert de Mun (1841–1924) and Colonel de La Tour du Pin (1834–1924) started workers' circles or clubs in centers of communism in the outskirts of Paris and elsewhere. These circles were linked up into a national organization which, under the editorship of de La Tour du Pin, founded the review *Association Catholique,* an important journal which existed from 1876 to 1915. De Mun's method of organizing these circles was much too paternalistic at first, but he became more democratic in later years. De La Tour du Pin confined himself largely to editorial work and writing about the Church's doctrine regarding democracy. Like the Germans, he was interested in the growth of the organization of trades into corporate vertical unions.

Another influential Catholic figure in France was Léon Harmel (1829–1915), whose model Christian factory at Val des Bois near Rheims, with its profit-sharing, and democratic government by employer and workers joined in works' councils, was imitated by other employers in the north of France, and was somewhat responsible for the development of French social legislation, including family allowances. French employers had made a pilgrimage to Pope Leo XIII in 1844, and a large labor pilgrimage of employers, workers, and priests had been made in 1887. From 1889 onward, Harmel organized a succession of workers' pilgrimages to Rome, and these had the effect of putting Pope Leo XIII in intimate touch with the needs of the workingman and the current development of industrial democracy.

In Switzerland Bishop Mermillod (1824–1892) of Geneva and Lausanne is an outstanding figure in the development of Catholic social doctrine. In 1882, Bishop Mermillod, Bishop von Ketteler, Father Kolping, de Mun, de La Tour du Pin, Harmel, and other theorists and practical reformers formed a private group to examine social questions of interest to the worker. Out of this committee there developed in 1885 the *Union de Fribourg,* under the leadership of Bishop Mermillod whose seat was in the Swiss city of Fribourg. The object of this union was to examine questions relating to labor, property, and the organization of society, with a view to the amelioration of industrial conditions, to repress the abuses of industrialism, and to urge the corporate organization of industry within each state.

In the United States, Cardinal Gibbons of Baltimore actively took up the workers' cause. The Knights of Labor trade union had been condemned in Canada, but through the influence of the Cardinal, who journeyed to Rome for the purpose, it was approved by the Holy See.

In England, Cardinal Manning became known for his sympathy to the workingman not only by his writings, but particularly when dock strikers in London invited him to intervene on their behalf — a task he satisfactorily accomplished. Bishop Bagshawe of Nattingham was also noted for his economic interests: he was in favor of land reform, and greater State intervention. A layman, Charles Stanton Devas (1848–1906), made some outstanding contributions to English Catholic literature in the general economic and sociological field.

Bishop Mermillod was made a Cardinal in the year 1890, and during the following months which he spent in close touch with Pope Leo XIII (1810–1903) in Rome, the famous "Workers' Charter," the encyclical[1] letter *Rerum Novarum* was written, and published in 1890. The rights and duties of man as a member of society, as a citizen, as a worker, and as an employer, are so clearly set forth in this encyclical, and with such foresight that its principles are as applicable today as at the time when it was first issued.

---

[1] An encyclical is a circular letter sent by the Pope to the Bishops, to be read to the faithful, on any matter about which the Pope may wish to instruct us. The opening words of the letter give it its title.

Indeed it is to Pope Leo XIII that we are chiefly indebted for the exposition and development of Catholic social theory in modern times, in whose footsteps Pope Pius XI has closely followed. Prior to *Rerum Novarum*, Pope Leo XIII had already shown himself most keenly interested in social problems, and had issued such encyclicals as *Inscrutabili Dei*, 1878, on the present ills of human society; *Quod apostolici muneris*, against socialism and communism, 1878; *Arcanum Divinae Sapientiae*, on Christian marriage, 1880; *Diuturnum illud*, on the authority of the State, 1881; *Immortale Dei*, on the Christian constitution of states, 1885; *Libertas Praestantissimum*, on Liberty, 1888; and *Sapientiae christianae*, on duties of Christian citizens, 1890.

Since the publication of *Rerum Novarum* very much literature has been forthcoming from Catholics, to explain the Catholic position on social thought and social problems. Among the encyclicals of social importance issued afterwards, we may note the *Graves de communi* of Pope Leo XIII on Christian democracy; that part of the *Motu proprio*, of Pope Pius X (1835–1914) dealing with Catholic Action for priests and laity, 1903; the *Divini illius magistri* and *Mens nostra*, 1929, on the Christian education of youth by Pope Pius XI (1857–1939); and, by the same Holy Father, the *Casti Connubii*, on Christian marriage, 1930; and the *Quadragesimo Anno*, 1931, written in commemoration of the fortieth anniversary of *Rerum Novarum*. *Quadragesimo Anno* is the most important social encyclical since the time of *Rerum Novarum*. It shows wherein Pope Leo's ideas were in some measure adopted; wherein, to his own detriment, man has failed to embrace them. Pius XI affirms the doctrine enunciated by his predecessor, and lays down yet further rules for the guidance of mankind, including important statements about the advisability of establishing vocational groups for the right ordering of industry. Following *Quadragesimo Anno*, Pope Pius XI issued such encyclicals as Atheistic Communism, *Divini Redemptoris,* in 1937, and Germany and the Church, *Mit brennender Sorge* also in 1937.

In addition to the literature which has been written on these matters, to explain and elaborate the encyclicals and other Catholic social teaching, Catholics have a vast record of more recent achievement in social matters. At the beginning of this century, French Catholics began the famous democratic movement called the *Sillon,* later put under discipline; the *Action Populaire,* an important organization conducted by Jesuit fathers for research and for popular exposition and leadership in social thought and work; and an annual "Social-Study Week." After the War, both the *Action Populaire* and the Social-

Study Weeks, or *Semaines Sociales* were revived with notable success. In 1931 a French Catholic, Mounier, founded a new periodical, *l'Esprit*, as a vehicle for his social thought called *Personalism*. The movement is by no means so important as those just mentioned but it is gaining ground in certain circles. Built largely on traditional Catholic doctrine, this theory stresses the value of the individual person, but shows that only by communitarianism or true notions of social duties as well as rights, can the individual person gain true liberty. The idea of man's vocation in life is particularly stressed, as the true explanation of the fundamental equality of man, despite his differences.

Belgium has furnished not only a number of outstanding Catholic writers, but in 1920 the *Union de Fribourg* was revived by Cardinal Mercier (1851–1926) under the title of International Union for Social Studies. A synthesis of Catholic social teaching has been issued by this International Union, called *A Code of Social Principles*. This code was translated into English by the Catholic Social Guild, Oxford, in 1929, and a revised issue was published by the same institution in 1937. The International Union has also issued a Code of International Ethics likewise translated and published by the Catholic Social Guild in 1937. In the practical field, Belgian Catholics are particularly noteworthy first, for the outstandingly successful agricultural co-operative, the *Boerenbond Belge*, or League of Belgian Peasant Farmers, whose membership includes a very large proportion of the farmers of the country; second, for the social-work organization for Catholic women which is very well organized and highly successful; and third, for the famous *Jociste* youth movement for agricultural as well as industrial workers, which has spread throughout Belgium, France, French Canada, England, and elsewhere, and has affiliated sections for students.

Two other outstanding continental Catholic social movements should be mentioned. One, the International Federation of Christian Trade Unions, founded in 1920, with its headquarters in Holland, and which grew from under a million members in 1934 to nearly one and a half million in 1937, despite the withdrawal of the large German contingent since the Nazi regime. The other is the Grail youth movement, which stresses the social importance of women and hence strives to develop the potentialities of its members for social usefulness and to form their characters along the lines of the best Catholic thought. This movement, which originated in Holland, has spread throughout Holland, England, Scotland, Australia, and other countries.

In England, the chief organization for the dissemination of Catholic social teaching is the Catholic Social Guild, founded in 1909 by a group including Archbishop Keating of Liverpool, Monsignor Parkinson, Rector of Oscott Seminary, Reverend Charles Plater, S.J., Miss Margaret Fletcher, Mrs. Virginia Crawford, Mr. Leslie Toke (an ex-Fabian socialist), and others. It was Father Plater (1875–1921) who set the tone of the Guild by stressing the need of the publication of literature and the establishment of workingmen's study clubs in every parish — a work which the Catholic Social Guild has carried out from the first. In 1920 a regular annual summer school was established, similar to that of the *Semaines Sociales* in France. In 1921 the Guild established a Catholic Workers' College under the direction of Father Leo O'Hea, S.J. (b. 1881), where workers who gain scholarships are given a two years' training in Catholic social principles, and also study for a diploma in economics and political science from the University of Oxford. The Principal, together with Father Lewis Watt, S.J. (b. 1885), and others have continually extended the work and influence of the Guild in England and among English-speaking readers.

In the United States, the large number of degree-granting Catholic universities and colleges, and their extension courses are the chief vehicle of Catholic social thought. For some time the teachings and writings of the professors in the universities was the usual Catholic approach of the nineteenth and twentieth centuries. The main emphasis was, therefore, that of *Rerum Novarum:* the modern application of Christian philosophical principles particularly in regard to labor and its related problems. This socio-philosophical emphasis gave rise to such books as *A Living Wage* (1906) and *Distributive Justice* (1927) by Monsignor John A. Ryan (b. 1869) of the Catholic University in Washington; the *Social Mission of Charity* (1921) by Father William J. Kerby (1870–1936); *The Christian Social Manifesto* (1931) by Father Joseph Husslein, S.J. (b. 1873); and *Man and Society* (1930) by Monsignor Francis J. Haas (b. 1889). The National Catholic Welfare Conference, established during the War as the National War Council, has a Social Action Department headed by Monsignor Ryan and Father McGowan (b. 1892). In addition to the publication of numerous pamphlets on social matters, and also the monthly review *Catholic Action* this Social Action Department holds annually various two-day industrial conferences in different parts of the country; and an affiliated Peace Association holds an annual conference in Washington. In 1937 an annual week's summer school for Catholic workers was inaugurated in Washington by the same organization. These conferences and the summer school are somewhat analogous to the *Semaines Sociales* and the Catholic Social Guild Summer School. The

Paulist Press, the International Catholic Truth Society, the St. John's University Press at Collegeville, Minnesota, and the American-German Catholic organization in St. Louis — the Centralverein — likewise issue a number of publications to spread Catholic social doctrine. A noteworthy step in the propagation of Catholic social principles has been the establishment of diocesan summer schools for priests in various parts of the country in recent years; the National Catholic Action meeting in Milwaukee in 1938, with another held in Cleveland in the summer of 1939; and the National Catholic Rural Life Conference. The work of the Englishman, Henry Somerville (b. 1889), now living in Toronto, author of *Studies in the Catholic Social Movement* (1933) and other books, ought also to be mentioned, and also the now famous co-operative movement and study-club plans of the St. Francis Xavier University, Antigonish, Nova Scotia.

Contemporaneously with this emphasis on the moral responsibility of labor and capital, a religious movement which emphasized the social meaning of the liturgy began to receive a hearing. This liturgical movement, as emphasized by Dom Virgil Michel, O.S.B. (1890–1938), and his Benedictine associates through the monthly periodical *Orate Fratres,* gave a dogmatic theological turn to the relation of labor and capital. This ideology is the motive power behind the recent teachings of those Catholics, interested in social problems, who limit their current writings almost wholly to applying the religious doctrine of the Mystical Body of Christ to the social scene. Such are Father Paul Hanly Furfey (b. 1896), of the Catholic University in Washington, in his *Fire on the Earth* (1936) and *Three Theories of Society* (1938); Dorothy Day, Peter Maurin, and their associates of *The Catholic Worker;* the editors of *The Christian Front,* and others.

The Method of Sociology

We have just given a brief survey of the major writers on Catholic social thought during the past hundred years. The question now arises: How do the Catholic ideas differ from those of others? Is the Catholic sociologist truly scientific in the positivistic sense; is he a social philosopher of more or less acumen and intellectual achievement; or again, is he a social philosopher with his tenets already laid down for him by the Church?

The answer to these queries lies chiefly in the delimitation of the field of sociology, as discussed in Chapter 1. If sociology is a pure positive science, then its work is merely to collect facts and to draw probable conclusions from them, and it is in no way concerned with judgments. Now, it must be obvious to the reader of the past chapter that sociology is still in the formative stage, and "the" method of sociology is not yet determined. Many sociologists, with some show of inductive science, have gathered vast arrays of social facts and from them have drawn conclusions. Other "sociologists" have done no more than arm-chair thinking, usually of a very inferior order. Even the majority of the so-called "scientific" sociologists, the positive schools, have seem-ingly been unconscious of the fact that they, too, have built their theories around a philosophy, or they have taken unproved facts as postulates,[2] and have drawn conclusions on mere hypotheses,[3] or on evidence of the slimmest kind.

It is unfortunate that many sociologists, influenced by the anti-religious evolutionism of the ex-Catholic Comte, by the liberalism of last century, and the hypotheses of Darwin, have formulated opinions upon the assumption that it has been definitely proved that the world and everything in it, all animals, including man, have evolved; and that not only has man evolved physically, but that even his intellect is merely conditioned by external enviroment. They have erected their theories upon the idea that man is his own master; that there is no God; that there are no norms of conduct (no rules of justice and charity) and no eternal verities which man must take into account; that, therefore, there are no duties to God or to man — many of them hold that society can decide at any epoch what is right and desirable, so that we are merely subject to chance laws; that there is no funda-mental meaning in life, but the fittest must survive; that man has within himself all the means necessary to perfect himself; that the exaltation of State or race are important, rather than God and the attainment of happiness in the future life: Lévy-Bruhl has even pro-nounced that sociology will supplant religion.[4] Some sociologists have felt that they can decide upon useful present norms and present their programs for improvements in society based on their own ideas, and have stressed the need of co-operation and humanitarian ideals. Others,

---

[2] A postulate is a truth or fact which is either evident in itself or for which ample proofs are available if one wishes to study them in detail. Were proofs already satis-factorily established by experts in other fields, in need of being proved all over again, superfluous duplication of work would be unlimited.

[3] A hypothesis is a mere supposition made as a basis for reasoning or as a starting point for investigation; for example, that atoms are composed of ions and electrons, or that evolution is probable. The scholar always takes care not to mistake a hy-pothesis for an actuality. Conclusions based on hypotheses of another branch of knowledge would give information only in accordance with the nature of the hy-pothesis, and might easily result in error.

[4] Lévy-Bruhl, L., La Morale et la Science des Moeurs, pp. 198, 199.

as we have seen, have assumed the existence of social forces, and have been of the opinion that all adjustment is so automatic that any attempt at meliorative programs is foredoomed to failure. It must be very obvious to the reader of sociological literature that none of the sociologists have been purely descriptive and entirely without some ideas of values. Even those who have most professed to follow inductive methods and to make sociology an exclusively positive science, have not maintained this aim in actual practice.

To the writer it seems that if sociology is to be more than a mere reporting science, and to be interpretative in its scope, then it must include also social philosophy. Many of the exponents of Catholic social thought discussed earlier in this chapter have been social philosophers and nothing more. Many, however, have done much good inductive work, and have interpreted their findings in the light of the norms laid down by social philosophy. In turn their social philosophy has taken as postulates truths established in other fields of knowledge. The Catholic sociologist, therefore, differs from the majority of the sociologists whose work we outlined in the last chapter, chiefly in that his theory is not based on working hypotheses alone; but he integrates his inductive work with a social philosophy based on certain postulates, and thus he can interpret social facts in the light of reason, and produce a well-rounded theory of use in guiding societal organization.

The Postulates of Sociology

The Catholic sociologist, therefore, does not regard sociology in the narrow positivistic sense, and in his work he presupposes the following, which he considers to be satisfactorily proved by philosophy, by historical events and documents, by revelation and in other ways:

1. That God exists, who is the Creator of all things, man included.[5]

2. That Christ, the Son of God, established the Church to which He gave divine authority to guide men in matters related to their supernatural destiny.

3. That man has a spiritual soul which is immortal; hence he has an eternal destiny.

4. That man is endowed with a free will.

5. That man is not only subject to physical (necessary) laws, but also to the moral law.

---

[5] The existence of God as Creator is proved by philosophy, hence the sociologist must recognize a general moral dictator; and if revelation is said to have been given, the sociologist as an intelligent being, must study it. The Catholic position takes it for granted that we are under a true revelation.

6. That man is a social being, and has certain rights and duties which are common to all mankind.

Proof of these postulates are beyond the scope of sociology and will not be given here.[6] On account of their intimate relation with social life, however, it seems necessary to discuss the last two postulates at greater length.

Postulate 5. *Man is by nature subject not only to physical (necessary) laws, but also to the moral law.*

It will be best first to describe briefly the different kinds of law. *Law* according to St. Thomas is "an ordinance of reason, promulgated by him who has charge of the community, for the common good."[7] Every created thing has its own finality; that is, it must have been created for a particular purpose. The function of law is to direct all creation to the end for which it was created. Divine law comes from God directly, and according to its particular form it is called eternal law, natural law (physical and moral), and divine positive law.

Eternal law, to quote St. Thomas again, is "the divine reason itself, directing the actions and movements of all existing things."[8] It is the act of will whereby God wishes that all beings should direct their actions according to reason and to their proper end. This eternal law does not govern all creation in the same way. Man was created to enjoy God forever; all creation other than man was created to furnish man's needs. Yet all creation, living and nonliving, rational and irrational, is subject to the eternal law. If the eternal law did not exist for any one particular being or thing, then that being or thing would itself not exist, since its existence would not be willed by the Creator; that is, it would not have any end to justify its existence.

The eternal law is in God: the natural law is a participation of the eternal law and is expressed in creation. It may be known by reason, as being in the nature of things.

In regard to irrational creatures, the things of nature, and also the physical side of man, these laws of nature are known as the *physical law*. Physical law is the creature's natural inclination to its proper end and act. Reason discovers these laws by observation, experiment, and induction; for example, the laws of astronomy, physics, chemistry, biology, gravitation or attraction, weight, and many others, including some which perhaps are as yet undiscovered.

---

[6] The reader is referred to a good elementary exposition of philosophy, if proofs of the above are desired. Certain proofs are found in the author's earlier book, *A Survey of Sociology,* Appendix I; or Ward, M., and Sheed, F. J., *Catholic Evidence Outlines.*
[7] St. Thomas, *Summa Theologica,* 1–2, q. 90, a. 1.
[8] *Ibid.,* 1–2, q. 93, a. 1.

Only on his physical side is man subject to the physical law. There is no doubt that he has to conform his use of the things at his disposal (his own faculties included) to the purpose for which they were intended, according as his rational study of their nature discloses to him. But even when he has discovered this order of things, he is not forced by a physical law into the observance of that order: he is, owing to his free will, capable of accepting it or rejecting it. Thus, what in irrational beings is physical order and law, becomes for man in all except automatic physical functions, moral order and law.

Moral law, therefore, is the eternal law in its application to rational beings, that is, to man, and it is imprinted in man's conscience.[9] Conscience interprets the natural law for us; we are under its authority, and our mental integrity is impaired if we refuse to do what, after due reflection, is presented to our mind as right and therefore necessary. The natural moral law is summarily expressed in nine of the ten commandments (that on keeping the Sabbath is a positive divine law). God has deigned to reveal to us, in this way, even the natural law, in order that man's reason, so prone to error, may find a confirmation for its natural conclusions in God's own words.

Positive law applies solely to man, as does the moral law, and may emanate either from God or from an authorized human legislator. It is a dictate of reason in harmony with the natural law, and determining what is left indeterminate in it, promulgated by him who has care of the community for the common good. The precepts of the natural law written in our conscience are only general principles. Man needs more particular determinations of some of these principles. Human positive law, therefore, is a man-made law applied to particular needs. Its determinations may be changed according to the needs of the times, but they are binding only insofar as they are not opposed to the natural law. If in conformity with the natural law, the positive law may prescribe punishments to those who publicly refuse to abide by the dictates of conscience (and its interpretation by positive law) and thus promote good order in society. It also provides other necessary guidance for the promotion of good order, as, for example, traffic laws, and laws in regard to voting or the payment of taxes. There is also a divine positive law: the old Mosaic law, and the law of Christ, which purified religion, perfected and superseded the Mosaic law, and emphasized once more the social nature of man and man's important place as the center of the moral universe.

---

[9] Conscience is the practical judgment of the mind upon the morality of certain acts in the particular circumstances in which one may be placed.

As to the necessity for postulating that man is thus subject to law, it is obvious that all but the exclusively positivistic sociologists must base their principles and interpretations of human conduct on the natural law. If laws are promulgated which prevent man from developing according to his nature — which prevent the correct worship of God, and prevent true freedom of association where the social order is not thereby impaired, then grave injustice is done to the individual and chaos will eventually ensue.

Postulate 6. *There are certain rights and duties which are common to all mankind.*

Where there is a law, there is a duty for man to observe it; and where there is a duty, man has a right to expect full liberty in conforming to his duty and to discountenance anything that might hamper him in the exercise of this right. Rights and duties are the necessary consequence of a moral law, and it is impossible to study human relations without a thorough understanding of their nature and extent.

A *right* is an inviolable moral or legal authority to have, to do, to demand, to omit, or to acquire something. A *duty* is a moral obligation to do whatever the law commands, and to omit what it forbids. Rights and duties are always correlated: one is impossible without the other, for if someone has a duty to perform, it is because someone else has a right to the thing to be performed. And it should be noted that unless a man be conscious of his own rights he will never thoroughly realize the extent of his duties toward his fellow men.

All rights and duties arise from the moral law, although they are sometimes proximately dependent upon human law. That is to say, a legal right or duty is immoral and not binding if it is not in accordance with the natural law. For example, a man has a right to the integrity of his limbs, and any legal enactment which would deprive him of them under certain unnecessary circumstances, as for example, the sterilization of the "unfit," is not in accordance with the natural law and hence is immoral. Similarly, a legal duty to drive an automobile on the right side of the road is valid, because it in no wise interferes with the natural law; a legal right to divorce one's wife or husband at will is immoral, because by the moral law each partner has a right and a duty to the maintenance of the indissolubility of the marriage bond: "What God hath joined together let no man put asunder."[10] Man has a right to earn his living in an honorable fashion, and any law is unjust which would deprive him of that right merely

---

[10] Matt. 19:6.

on account of difference of opinion as regards politics or creed, or because of race hatred or false notions of race.

Of all visible creation, man alone is capable of having rights and duties. A right is a moral power, and a duty is a moral obligation, hence it is clear that only one who is capable of performing moral acts can have moral rights and duties; and since duties and rights are correlative, neither animals nor anything else in the visible creation other than man, can have rights. They cannot know rights, so therefore they cannot wish to exercise any rights nor protest against the violation of any rights. Thus, to bring up the well-known controversial question, *vivisection* is not morally wrong in itself. Since animals have no rights, and since the lower order of creation exists for the service of the higher, it follows that man, being the king of the material universe, is authorized to use the universe for his benefit. Yet vivisection is wrong when suffering is caused which would in no wise advance science or be useful to man in some other way, for although man has no duties toward animals and plants, nevertheless he has duties in regard to them. First, toward God, for he must use all God's creation in such a way as befits his rational nature. Second, toward himself, as a rational being. Third, toward his fellow beings, who may need those things created for man's use. And although it may be contended that children or the insane do not possess rights because they are incapable of reasoning, this argument is false. Their nature is inherently or radically capable of performing duties and is essentially rational, even though that rational nature is not yet developed, or may have become defective.

Just as man has rights and obligations, so also have lawful associations of men, since man is by nature and necessity a social being, as we have explained. A lawful society is capable of contracting obligations and of being held responsible for them: it is therefore capable of possessing rights. But which are the various classifications of rights?

Innate rights are those which are ours by birth; as for example, the right to live, to be free, to acquire property, to integrity of limb. All other rights are acquired. These again may be subdivided: (1) Those which are acquired under certain conditions independently of any positive law, e.g., the mutual rights of husband and wife under the marriage contract; or the right to an article bought under ordinary market conditions. (2) Those which may be given by positive law, either divine, e.g., the positive right of the parish priest to be supported by his parishioners; or human, e.g., the right to vote under certain conditions. Some rights are public, e.g., the rights of the State or of the Church, and all social rights; others are private, e.g., the rights of individuals. Some are positive, in that they confer something; others are negative, in that they enjoin that certain things should not be done. Some are inalienable, and cannot be renounced by the owner, e.g., the right to life; others alienable, and can be renounced, e.g., the right to marry, or to continue to own one's legal property. Some are absolute, which all persons must regard, e.g., the right to live, the right of possession of a good legally owned; some relative, where only a few persons are involved, e.g., the right of parents to the obedience of a child, the right of an employee to a living wage from his employer, and the right of an employer to a full day's work for a full day's pay.

We said in the foregoing that a right is inviolable, but we should also note that it is limited. Since rights are correlative they are dependent, sometimes for their existence, sometimes for their extent, upon the term or terms of the relation. Thus right is limited by duty: a right of an urgent character is superior to that of a less urgent; a right conferred by positive law is controlled by the natural law; a lower right is subject to a higher one.

All men, as such, have equal rights and duties, for all are equal in that they have the same nature, the same Creator, and an immortal rational soul intended for the same destiny.[11] In the use of the universe, therefore, man is limited by the coequal dignity and rights of his fellow men, be they of his race or nationality or creed, or widely differing from them. The most important rights inherent in men might be given as follows:

1. *The Right to Life.* (*a*) A man has the right to be born; hence abortion is murder. (*b*) A man has also the right to individual and private self-defense; hence intentional slaying can only be lawful in self-defense; infants have a right to their life being preserved by their parents; war is justified only for social and public self-defense. The question of the deprivation of life by capital punishment is treated in the Chapter on Crime. (*c*) No man has the right to end his own life; hence suicide is never justified: God is the only author and master of life, and He alone may end it directly or by legitimate authority. In some cases where death may result from self-defense, in war, or in an effort to save others, the purpose of the action is not, as in suicide,

---

[11] This equality is emphasized by membership in the Church, the Mystical Body of Christ: cf., "For you are all through your faith sons of God in Christ Jesus. For all of you who were baptized unto Christ have put on Christ. In him is neither Jew nor Greek, neither slave nor free, neither male nor female; for you are all one in Christ Jesus" (Gal. 3:28). "Where there is neither Gentile nor Jew, circumcision nor uncircumcision, Barbarian nor Scythian, bond nor free. But Christ is all and in all" (Col. 3:11).

one's own death, but the attainment of a legitimate end. (*d*) Since it is man's duty to maintain life, he has a duty to work, if he is not otherwise provided for, and a right to live by the fruit of his work. He has, therefore, a right to a living wage, so as to maintain life at a reasonable standard of comfort, "For the laborer is worthy of hire."[12] He has also a right to adequate time for rest and recreation to enable him to recuperate the forces spent in labor, that he may be the better able to work again. And furthermore, he has a right to an education which will fit him for work.

2. *The Right to Liberty.* A man has a right to liberty, and a duty to maintain the liberty of others. Toward God man is free, but not independent. If he disobeys the dictates of his conscience, i.e., the natural moral law or if he disobeys the precepts of the positive divine law or that human law which is in accordance with the natural law, he destroys the harmony of his being and abuses his freedom. And if in so doing, a man injures his fellow men, then he loses his right to personal freedom, and he may in justice be imprisoned, or may forfeit even his right to live. But his fellow men must not violate his conscience, or make his freedom a mere name. Hence a man has a right to the liberty of his own opinion, if it is not opposed to truth or to the moral order; to liberty of propaganda (not only manifesting his opinion externally, but seeking to influence others to accept the opinion which he honestly holds); to the exercise of his natural rights, to marry or to remain single, as he pleases; and to the performance of his duties toward God, which includes the right to follow his conscience, and freedom of religious worship. As social life becomes more complex, progress may require a more perfect organization of mutual help rather than an increase of individual liberty.

3. *The Right to Truth.* A man has the right to maintain his bodily life by nourishment, so also has he a right to have his mind and will nourished with truth. Hence he has a right not only to the particular training which constitutes for him indispensable equipment to earn a living, but also a right to provide his mind with a knowledge of the truth. He has, too, a right to that tolerance which will permit him to receive an education according to his religious belief: for whatever be his religion, for him it represents the truth, though one should note that the right to tolerance which a person has for his erroneous belief derives from the person, since error, of itself, has no right. As a corollary to these rights, those in charge of education and religious instruction have the duty of eschewing falsehood and imparting only the truth.

---

[12] Luke 10:7; cf., also Matt. 10:10; 1 Tim. 5:18.

They have the duty of ascertaining in advance that their teachings are based on principles of right thinking. Negligence in this is a serious breach of duty; for a student cannot discriminate between the false and the true if he is instructed in falsehood by those whose duty it is to impart the truth. Every Catholic child, therefore, has a right to a Catholic education, and Catholic parents are grievously negligent if they send their children, without just cause, to non-Catholic schools where, all too often, instruction is given with much disregard of truth.

4. *The Right to Live Socially.* Man is a social being, and as such has a natural right to join with other men to form groups, so long as these groups do not violate the natural law. We discussed man's aptitude and propensity for social life, and his need of it, in the first chapter.

5. *The Right of Authority.* This is a social and not an individual right. Authority is a social necessity, since groups of men cannot come together in harmony and sustained unity of purpose without a leader and a guide. True individual liberty can only be accomplished within society by its partial sacrifice for the common good; for although men are theoretically equal, in the concrete they all differ in health, strength, mental ability, will power, and other moral qualities. Indeed, the intellectual or moral superiority of some men would imply a natural fitness to govern, particularly as progress is impossible without the exercise of initiative. Insofar as authority is socially necessary it is, therefore, a social right: for human authority is based upon the order of nature, so that ultimately "there is no authority that is not from God."[13]

6. *The Right to Property.* Man, too, has a right to ownership, since the earth was created for him, and the ownership of private possessions would seem to be necessary for right order and for protection against the tyranny of others. And the ninth commandment definitely confirms this right, by forbidding us to take what is another's.[14] Yet though all men have an abstract right to ownership, they have not all the same concrete right, and it is the concrete right which it is the duty of the State to determine. That the capitalistic order, as at present constituted, is socially and morally wrong cannot be denied, for it has as its basis the concentration of wealth in the hands of a few, while leaving a great proportion of mankind without proper participation in the fruits of production. On the other hand, compulsory collectivism is equally wrong, both morally and socially, since it seeks to deny man his

---

[13] Rom. 13:1.
[14] Deut. 5:21.

lawful ownership of productive goods, and strives to give the sole right of possession to the State. This right of property is discussed at much greater length in the special chapter on the subject and in the chapter on proposed economic reforms.

7. *The Right to Justice.* A man has a right to justice: distributive, legal, and commutative. St. Thomas has defined justice as: "a habit whereby a man renders to each one his due by a constant and perpetual will."[15] Commutative justice is that which governs the relationships existing between individuals. Distributive justice governs the relationships of the community to the individuals which compose it. It is connected with giving the individual what is his due, and hence is concerned with the equitable distribution of all the benefits and the burdens of the State among the citizens, according to their merits and their needs. It involves the equitable distribution of wealth, including just taxation. It involves, too, the meting out of retributive punishment. Par excellence, distributive justice should be the virtue of those who govern.

Legal or social justice in its subjective aspects governs the relationships between the individual and the group. Objectively it concerns the co-ordination of human efforts to accomplish the common good. The common or social good implies more than each individual attaining his individual good. Pope Pius XI gives an excellent short summary of the basic Christian teaching about social justice in his encyclical *Divini Redemptoris,* showing that each individual must seek not only his own good, but must likewise contribute his share to the common good. If this is accomplished, then, of course, distributive justice is also effective, and each individual will be able to procure all that is necessary for the exercise of all his functions. Social justice requires that all those better endowed than their fellows with ability or wealth, should share their greater apportionment of material or immaterial goods with their fellow men. It involves, therefore, man's duty to use his time and gifts to good advantage,[16] and also the handing down to future generations all the accumulated scientific and other knowledge which has been received from the past.

Closely allied to social justice is the virtue of charity. This is an essentially Christian virtue, which involves the individual giving to society more than is strictly required from him in justice. Christ taught that man should not only render to his neighbor what is his due, but

---

[15] St. Thomas, *Summa Theologica,* 2, 2ae, Q, 58, a. 1.

[16] Cf. 2 Thess. 3:10: "If any man will not work, neither let him eat." Note, however, Pope Pius XI's interpretation of this passage pp. 20, 21 (*QA,* 23).

that he should love his neighbor as himself.[17] Here we cannot do better than quote the words of Pope Pius XI:[18] "Charity cannot take the place of justice unfairly withheld, but, even though a state of things be pictured in which every man receives at last all that is his due, a wide field will nevertheless remain open for charity. For, justice alone, even though most faithfully observed, can remove indeed the cause of social strife, but can never bring about a union of hearts and minds. Yet this union, binding men together, is the main principle of stability in all institutions, no matter how perfect they may seem, which aim at establishing social peace and promoting mutual aid."[19]

As we stated that the rights of man imply corresponding duties and responsibilities on the parts of others, perhaps it will be well to quote briefly the more important headings under which may be classed man's natural duties:

1. *Toward God,* man owes the duty of worship; acceptance of His will and submission to it as manifested in divine revelation; and the fulfillment of his moral duties. These duties are the only human duties which involve no correlated right on the part of man. But true worship of God implies an understanding and carrying out of man's duties toward himself and his fellow men.

2. *Toward himself* man owes the preservation of life, and health, both physical and moral. He also owes to himself the proper utilization of his powers and possessions whether spiritual or material. He must be jealous also of his honor and reputation. But before all else man owes himself the duty of self-respect. Self-reverence implies an absence of all slovenliness: it means not only a neat personal appearance, a clean and tidy house, the performance of useful work, and the practice of thrift so as not to become dependent on others; it means, too, the cultivation of abilities and the performance of actions at least moderately well.

3. *Toward his fellow men* man owes first, justice, and second, charity, as we have just explained.

Catholic Social Theory

The last two postulates of the Catholic sociologist have been out-

---

[17] Mark 12:31; cf., also Matt. 25:31–46.

[18] *Quadragesimo Anno,* p. 44 (*QA,* 46). In quoting from *Rerum Novarum, Divini Illius Magistri, Casti Connubii,* and *Quadragesimo Anno,* page numbers refer to the volume: *Four Great Encyclicals* (New York: Paulist Press). References in parenthesis are to the paragraph numbering of the *Rerum Novarum* and the *Quadragesimo Anno* of Rev. J. Husslein, S.J., in *The Christian Social Manifesto.*

[19] Cf. *Parable of the Talents,* Matt. 25.

lined at such length because of their importance for a correct viewpoint on social life and because those readers who were not acquainted with the findings of philosophy might not fully understand their social implications.

Believing in the above six postulates, as truths clearly established by other branches of knowledge, the Catholic sociologist's view of society obviously differs from that of most of the sociologists whose views we have discussed. It is true that up to the present very few Catholic writers have taken sufficient note of the inductive side of the science, and were either social philosophers, or applied sociologists interested in the theory of social work rather than in the science of sociology. On the other hand, the Catholic writer who makes use of truths arrived at by deduction to interpret his inductive findings, is not necessarily less scientific than the non-Catholic. As we said, all sociologists have been more or less remiss in their so-called scientific approach to social problems. The Catholic sociologist may with advantage employ the positive method, examine social facts scientifically and from them draw scientific conclusions. He does not, however, fall into the error of taking as a hypothesis the supposed fact that man is merely an automaton, nor does he regard man as an accident in the world; life has a meaning for him, and he regards man's most important duty as that of gaining his eternal destiny. For the Catholic, all else is subordinate to this end, so that no laws which sacrifice the eternal (and this includes laws which go against the natural law) are to be preferred, even though material gains by them may seemingly be very great. No Catholic sociologist considers that a custom is to be considered "right" simply because it is prevalent or expedient. The general conclusions and social laws which he will draw from his observations of social phenomena will mean for him nothing more than the fact that in certain matters men have more or less universally followed their natural inclinations and the dictates of reason. He will always remember, however, that mankind is a fallen race, and may therefore have arrived at some social practices at variance with the conclusions not only of social philosophy, but also of moral theology which, moreover, takes the fall of man into account. The Catholic sociologist does not fall into the error of merging the individual in society. He takes full account of the dignity of the human person, and considers the good of the individual as prior to the good of society, when a good of any higher order is in question. On the other hand, the Catholic sociologist is not an individualist; he does not forget that man is a social being, and that the individual is not so important as the social good when a good of any lower order is concerned. Ever since the time of St. Paul, the social doctrine of the Church has been that of the Mystical Body of Christ: all mankind, linked in the brotherhood of man through the Church, of which Christ is the head, working together for the common good.[20]

For the attainment of this common good, as explained in Chapter 4, Catholics consider that the family is the primary group to which man belongs, and a "natural" (necessary) society. They also consider that the State is so essential to man's development that it, too, is "natural"; and they have no part in theories which consider the State as merely the result of a man-made contract, whose power is merely the aggregate of individual rights ceded to it; neither do they think it the chance product of evolutionary growth, nor merely the outcome of a conscious effort on the part of man for mutual amelioration. They consider, too, that the Church, a supernatural society, is divinely appointed to teach man the way of salvation; and that in their separate spheres both State and Church are "perfect" societies entirely independent of any power but God alone. Although the Church needs the protection of the State to function within society, yet because the end of the Church is of such paramount importance, Catholic theorists never consider it as subordinated to the State. Most Catholics consider "occupational" society and "international" society as necessary for well-ordered social life, but whether or not they are "natural" is, as we said, in Chapter 4, still a matter of opinion and debate. On account of the interrelation of the various interests in economic life, most Catholics are in favor of a greater mutual co-operation between these interests, either by corporative organization, by the extension of co-operative society, by a "distributive" State, or by some other means, to which we shall refer again when dealing more specifically with economic problems.

We are now in a position to begin our sociological study of the principal social institutions, and the rest of this book is an attempt to present a sociology, a science of society, which is not only scientific from the inductive viewpoint, but which also takes into consideration what the Catholic considers as basic postulates, and the findings of social philosophy, necessary for the rational consideration of any of man's activities.

---

[20] This idea of society as the Mystical Body of Christ is not comparable to the theories of the biological analogists and others who consider society as a social organism and neglect to note man's necessary personal dignity and freedom functioning within the social organism.

PART TWO

SOCIAL INSTITUTIONS

CHAPTER 8

MARRIAGE AND THE FAMILY

Introductory

HAVING now discussed the basis of individual and group conduct, the knowledge of man which is furnished to us by prehistory, and some idea of the varying theories of society which have been held in the past or are still being considered as valid, we are now in a position to make an actual study of human society. We shall draw our conclusions from an examination of the social life of prehistoric peoples (where this is possible), the nations of history, the primitives of today, and the higher civilizations of modern times, as well as from the truths which are evident from common-sense reasoning. If we pay more attention in the next few chapters to the ways of life of the primitives or those of relatively primitive culture it is because the author is convinced that the methods of the cultural sociologists are more productive of results at the present time than the methods of any other sociological school or system.

As we already explained, at the beginning of Chapter 4, out of all the complexity of social customs we may discern several basic institutions which have arisen — certain standardized forms within which man works out his basic human needs. It is these basic institutions which we shall discuss in this Second Section — leaving a consideration of modern social problems to Part Three.

The individual institution of marriage has led to a continuous relationship which is to be found among all people. This relationship is called the family. It is the institution of the family which we must first consider, for the family is the most important of all social groups — the social cell around which have been built all other social institutions, primary as well as secondary.

The Importance of Marriage and the Family as a Social Institution

To insure self-preservation and self-propagation, Divine Providence placed in man two tremendously powerful instincts: the appetite of hunger and sex desire. Sexual appetite is as necessary to insure the sexual functions, as the hunger appetite is necessary to insure eating

for bodily strength. This sexual desire was implanted in man, therefore, to give him an incentive for sexual intercourse, in order to insure
the propagation of the race. This intensely strong impulse also enables
two persons to support each other's foibles and idiosyncracies, and to
overlook the rough places in life. It supplies, too, the necessary incentive for any man or woman to undertake the arduous task of bringing
up their children for an eternal destiny, of working to supply food for
them, and of undertaking all the anxieties and worries commonly endured by parents for their children — sickness, education, and responsibility toward God for their eternal salvation. So arduous is this
latter task that to assist parents to carry on the work which they thus
undertake, parental love also develops, although whether this is a
latent instinct, or a natural outcome of close social union within the
family is a matter of debate, as discussed in Chapter 2.

Marriage is the divinely appointed control for this important sexual
instinct — to insure the propagation of the human race, and the rearing
of children so that God may be glorified through them; to foster the
mutual comfort of husband and wife; and to allay concupiscence,
which is inborn in every human being for the reasons above stated.
Marriage is both a contract and a continuing state, and the latter
results in the establishment of a family, the social institution which
provides a stable foundation for a married pair. A family may be described as a society which, originating in marriage, includes those
who are closely related by ties of relationship and who usually live
together. Generally this domestic society consists of parents and their
children; sometimes other dependent relatives are included, and in a
few countries permanent servants are also considered to be members
of the family for which they work.

The family is the most important of all social groups, and marriage
and the family, as socially recognized institutions, are to be found
among all peoples. Man formed domestic unions before any state or
other group came into being, and at all times it is to the family and to
no other society that we look not only for the perpetuation of the
human race, but for the insurance of its very existence. For most of
mankind, the family is an essential factor for their virtue and happiness. Not only does the family provide this important need, insure the
continuity of the human race and the proper education of children,
but it is in the family that there are also preserved the important traditions and accumulated culture of society. Family love is also one of
the most powerful incentives for a man to continue energetically in
his task of earning a living for himself and his dependents.

The Family Is a Natural Society

The family possesses all the essentials of a true society. It certainly seems intended to be a permanent union of a man and a woman for the definite primary end of the propagation and education of children, and for the secondary end of satisfying the mutual need of the two sexes, and of fostering conjugal love and rendering mutual assistance in their married life. Where servants are included in this category, it is in virtue of the assistance they give to the family in carrying out its functions.

The family or domestic society is also a natural society. It is natural to man to have a propensity to sexual life, to affection for his mate, and love for his offspring. In the wise dispensation of Providence, all of this has been implanted in man's nature as a necessary condition for the continuance of the human race. Man, unlike the brute creation, has been given an aptitude and a need for the more permanent union of domestic society. His very qualities of affection, tenderness, parental love impel him to want a more lasting union than that afforded by any state of sexual promiscuity, or even polygamy, and his nature craves for a more intimate companionship and love than that afforded by the uncertainties of ordinary social life. Moreover, infancy and childhood need many years of care and help, and naturally postulate for the parents permanency of union, at least until their primary and secondary ends of marriage shall have been adequately attained.

The family assures that women and children will have the necessary assistance of the male, and that the aged and the infirm will be taken care of.

The Principal Forms of Marriage

As has just been said, the functioning of socially controlled marriage and family is found among all peoples — the only difference being that the control is largely traditional among the primitives, and rigidly fixed by law of Church and State in more highly civilized countries. Everywhere the family is the primary social unit, although among small primitive tribes it is almost merged into a group of families.

There are two principal systems of marriage, which it will perhaps be best to define before continuing our discussion.

1. The only form of marriage which is to be found in all social groups is monogamy. Monogamy is the marriage of but one man and one woman during the lifetime of either, marriage with a second person being allowed only on the death of the first partner. Where any

other form of union is prohibited, strict monogamy prevails; where the majority in a group are monogamous, but where, nevertheless, some members have more than one mate, without being considered as offending against good morals, dominant monogamy may be said to exist.

2. Polygamy is a term used to describe both polygyny, which is the marriage of one husband to several wives, as is, for example, sanctioned under the Mohammedan law; and polyandry, which is the union of one woman to several men. As a recognized form of marriage, polyandry is comparatively rare, although it is to be found in Polynesia, among the Todas of southeastern India, among the Hima of Uganda, in Tibet, and among certain Eskimo and Chukchi. Where all a woman's husbands must be brothers, as in Tibet, the custom is termed fraternal polyandry; where the husbands are unrelated to each other, the term nonfraternal or Nair polyandry is used to describe this lower form. In Ceylon the practice of polyandry among the Todas was prohibited by the British Government in 1860.

Some writers include a third system which they call "group marriage" — a system of relative promiscuity under which an entire group of women is allowed to have promiscuous sex relations with an entire group of men, although not with men or women of another group. Such a condition is found in very few instances in the world. It is nothing else than a phase of sexual promiscuity and is not marriage at all, although it may possibly be a degeneration from a former practice of polyandry. From the start it should be clear that plural sex relations are *not* plural marriage in the sense of setting up more than one social unit of the institution we call the family; and we should also realize that the institution of the monogamous family does not necessarily mean monogamous sex relations. As we have explained, marriage implies a socially recognized alliance between two individuals for the procreation of children. It is a fixed bond with mutual duties, and although some people may have promiscuous sex relations, nevertheless they may be monogamous as regards marriage and the family.

Marriage Customs

Within the two systems of marriage which are to be found in the world — monogamy and polygamy — society has regulated marriage in various ways, and many varying though relatively unessential customs can be observed.

Many of the primitives have very strict social rules for exogamous or endogamous marriage. Exogamy is the system which has been the general practice of mankind; that is, nearly all peoples demand that in the choice of a partner in marriage a person go outside his immediate social group of close relations. Endogamy is the term descriptive of the practice of enforced marriage within one's group. The two terms were invented by John Fergusan McLennan (1827–1881) author of *An Inquiry into the Origin of the Form of Capture in Marriage Ceremonies* (1865) and of *The Patriarchal Family* (1885). McLennan thought, however, that originally there was promiscuity, then polyandry. In the latter stage he thought that early in the history of the race there was a scarcity of women, due to female infanticide, and eventually men were forced to seek a wife outside the group, which finally developed into a rigidly enforced exogamy and monogamous marriage.

How exogamy arose is uncertain. Possibly it was invented by man in early times to introduce women from other tribes, to increase property ownership or strength, or to promote friendly alliance between two tribes; it may have arisen from the capture of women slaves and an observation of the stronger children who may have resulted from the union, who would be of great advantage in time of war. Or perhaps it came about in an effort to avoid sexual relations between blood kin before marriage, and to make family life more peacefully satisfying. However it arose, for the later protection of the race, a horror of incest seems to exist among all mankind.

It must be said, however, that tribal exogamy is necessarily rare among primitive tribes, and almost of necessity tribal endogamy exists. Usually, however, marriage outside of one's immediate family is insisted upon by primitives. Where there is endogamy, marriage is generally regulated not only as to which kin one may or may not marry, but also as to within which tribal subdivision it is allowed or forbidden to look for a mate. These regulations are a safeguard which prevent the physical defects which might be intensified by a too close intermarriage within the family or clan, and seem to be an attempt at least at exogamy. Inbreeding is not necessarily harmful; and it is obvious that at the early beginnings of the human race intermarriage was necessary and had a dispensation from God Himself when He bade Adam and Eve to "increase and multiply." At this time, when man was more perfect than he is today, no great amount of harm could have resulted.

Where tribal endogamy exists the tribe is usually, though not necessarily, divided into a number of sibs or clans. Most members of the American Anthropological School use the word *clan* in the restricted sense of a unilateral matrilineal sib, where descent, property, and inheritance is traced through the mother, while they use the word *gens* for a unilateral paternal organization. The word *sib* is therefore used as an expression descriptive of both the clan and the gens, although many anthropologists do not make this distinction and use the word *clan* as a broad term indicative of any unilateral family grouping. In the more highly civilized countries of the present day, although we are patrilineal as regards name, we consider descent as bilateral.

Where the sib system exists, a person of one clan or gens must usually marry someone of another group. The different clans are often divided into sections, and marriage under this form of sib endogamy is sometimes so complicated that it almost amounts to complete exogamy. The Dieri of Australia have two exogamous moieties or groups, the Materi and the Kararu, and marriage must always be with a person of the opposite moiety, and is strictly forbidden to any of the following relations, either through marriage or through Pirauru marital privileges to be later described; mother, child, brother, sister, father, father's brother, father's sister, mother's brother, mother's sister, brother's child, sister's child, father's brother's child, father's sister's child, mother's brother's child, mother's sister's child. The Seneca Indians in North America have two moieties or phratries, each divided into four classes, and marriage is forbidden within one's moiety as well as within certain subdivisions of the opposite class. Among the Arunta in Australia each clan is divided into two moieties, each of which is divided into four parts. A person must only marry a member of a defined subdivision of the opposite moiety. A child is never considered as belonging to the moiety of his parents, but again, he cannot marry anyone in the subdivision to which his parents belong.

Not all primitives, however, are arranged on the unilateral-sib plan. The unilateral sib does not exist among such primitive peoples as the Yahgan of Tierra del Fuego, the Andamanese, the Chukchi, and many others. The Andamanese, for instance, are not obliged to go outside their group for a mate, but they are forbidden to marry blood kin.

Sometimes marriage is much more strictly endogamous. It may take the form of cross-cousin marriage, such as among the Toda of India, where a man may only marry the daughter of his father's sister, or his mother's brother. Among the Masai the smiths form an important endogamous caste, and the ruling classes are strictly endogamous in Polynesia. These two latter systems in particular are based on aristocratic pride, or as an effective means of keeping wealth and power within a certain group, much as we, too, with our wider society to choose from, have our genealogies, and are frequently constrained to marry within our social "set."

Some tribes are stratified by age distinctions, and a person is restricted in the choice of a mate to his (or her) own age grade, in which his membership depends on the year of his birth, or the time his initiation took place at adolescence. Sometimes everyone belonging to the same age grade is called "mother" or "father" of younger members of the tribe, even though there be no actual relationship. And often extramarital rights are allowed to those of the same grade, which may seem to be group marriage, though it actually is not.

In some tribes child marriage exists, as among the Kurnai and the Dieri tribes of Australia, and among the Toda, where a child is often married at two to three years of age, though she remains with her parents until the age of fifteen or thereabouts. A Dieri girl is allotted to her future husband by the father or headman during her infancy and is bound to marry him later. Sometimes a bride must bring a dowry to her husband, but much more frequently a bride price is paid by the would-be husband to the girl's father. Among the Fan, where women are considered as mere chattels, hardly as belonging to the human race, the bride price is very considerable. Sometimes a childless wife can be divorced or sent back to her people in disgrace, or the husband can marry a second wife if there are no children by the first. In some tribes a father has strict duties to provide for his wife and children, in others he has no such obligation. Because primitives do not always store up wealth for future consumption, there is always some social arrangement for the care of widows and their young children. Among the Yoruba, where the levirate was once in force — a term we shall shortly explain — at a man's death the wife and concubines are divided among the sons as their wife or concubines, but no son may take his own mother to wife. A Bantu widow becomes the property of the brother of her dead husband. Among the Dieri a widow is inherited by her late husband's eldest brother or, if there be no brother, then by his nearest male relative, although inheritance of name and totem are through the female line. Yet in some tribes, the inheritance of a widow may be a privilege and not a matter of economic duty of provision for widow and child. In tribes where women do a large part of the work, the addition of a woman to the household is an economic acquisition, hence she is inherited like other property. Among the multitudinous other varieties of marriage and family customs, mention may be made of the Ona, where the man can never speak to his father-in-law; among the Fan and the Shilluk the much more common mother-in-law taboo is in vogue. While marriages among primitives are very frequently "arranged," even in childhood, a Hopi girl, for example, can arrange her own marriage with perfect freedom.

The mention of freedom in love and marriage brings us here to differing customs within our own modern peoples. Whereas marriages are still "arranged" for their children by parents in many of the Catholic countries, marriages for love are much more usual at the present day. While free choice of a life partner, arising out of deep and true affection, is the ideal for responsible human beings, it is of interest to note that "arranged marriages" are frequently more successful than marriages undertaken by children without parental advice, and, of course, much more satisfactory to the families of the young couple. In modern popular usage the word *love* has been degraded by an undue emphasis on the physical element — the sex desire which man shares with the animal. But in its true and adequate sense, human love is a passion which under the guidance of right reason and the control of the will (aided by grace), seeks its good in the union of one person with another. It includes the love of God, our supreme good, and the love of parents, children, friends, and fellow men, thus embracing the love of local or national groups. In one of its purposes, the propagation of the human race, it also includes that special love of a man and woman that requires an intimate conjugal union for the establishment of a family. In its exercise under the dictates of reason as to its object and manner, love thus becomes a virtue; and in its radical permeation of our whole nature, beyond that of any other passion, this union of the affections is productive of the greatest and most lasting happiness. It is, indeed, this essentially human desire of exclusive intimacy and lasting companionship, which most insures stable monogamous marriage. There may be "love at first sight" in that mysterious spontaneity which impels to union, but it becomes true love only when sanctioned by unhampered reason. Many modern "romantic" marriages, where a pair marry for sentimental love alone, on short notice, and without conscious intelligent choice and thought of the practicalities of life, end in marital unhappiness and frequently in the breakup of family and home. Where parents choose, or help to choose, the life partner for their children, they will be much more likely to avert possibly unsuccessful marriages by exercising prudence and foresight in choosing a suitable person, accustomed to the same social and cultural traditions, and trained in worthy ideals.

Two well-known family organizations are the patriarchal and matriarchal regimes. In the patriarchal family, which is often polygynous as among the Bambara of the Sudan, the father is head not only of his immediate family, but also of the families of his grown-up sons and daughters. Abraham and other early Biblical characters provide us with an illustration of the power of the patriarchal family head — the oldest living male in this type of family. The patriarch of this extended family was responsible for everything, and members received from him directly, or from other members at the father's command, everything necessary for their mental, moral, and physical growth. He was the early ancestral priest. The older members of the family co-operated for the education and all the other needs of the younger members.

In the matriarchal family, the authority is not quite so centralized. Matriarchy is a system in which property, name, and inheritance are traced through the female line, and in which the husband usually lives with the wife, or in a special man's house, as among certain American Indian tribes and the Khasi of Assam. It is fairly common among primitive tribes, though by no means universal. Strangely enough, matrilineal organization was unknown among modern scholars until its existence was brought to light by the Swiss Jurist, Johann Jacob Bachofen (1815–1887), who wrote *Das Mutterrecht* to describe it in 1861, but who, like McLennan, had erroneous ideas about the origin of family life. Where matriarchy exists, its form varies in the different tribes, and the reasons for it seem to vary, too. Sometimes it seems to be present because the women form the more stable element in the family, or because the men and youths live in special men's houses, and for this reason name and property are traced through the mother because there is a more intimate bond between her and her younger children. Sometimes it may be due to the fact that the father expects his daughter to bring her husband to live with her parents to add to the economic well-being of the household. Another reason is possibly to insure the unity and purity of the family. As Bishop LeRoy (1854–1938) says: "If the chief has his sister's son for successor, he is certain to have one of his own blood, whereas with the son of his wife, who can tell?"[1] Among the Melanesians, however, where matriarchy is found, succession to the chieftainship is patrilineal. Matriarchy does not mean mother rule strictly so called. In almost all known cases of matriarchy, there is matrilineal organization only. Property, name, and inheritance may be traced through the female line, but the mother's brother usually wields the authority in the household, a fact

---

[1] Rt. Rev. Bishop A. LeRoy, *The Religion of the Primitives*, p. 69.

which explains the statement just quoted from Bishop LeRoy. The avunculate is the term given to this type of family organization, although it is not restricted to tribes organized matrilineally. Under the avunculate there are quite special relations between a nephew and his maternal uncle. Often he inherits the latter's property; and where cross-cousin marriage exists, the nephew must often marry the maternal uncle's daughter and go to live in his household. In certain Melanesian tribes a magician is bound to pass on his knowledge to his sister's son, and among the Hopi Indians the sister's son inherits the office of a priestly uncle.

Another strange custom connected with marriage is the levirate, described in the Bible,[2] and existing among the Chinese, the Arabs, the Hindus, and also the Arunta of Australia, the Ainu of Japan, and other tribes. This institution is one whereby a widow left without children has a claim to be married to her deceased husband's brother. Usually, the child of such a union bears the name and takes the property not of his father, but of his mother's former husband. The levirate clearly recognizes group obligation in connection with matrimony, and it is usually an adjustment to other conditions as well. Where it exists among primitive tribes, it is nearly always an economic adaptation, providing means of caring in a satisfactory manner for the widow's material needs. In the Bible it is seen to be the result of a desire of the Hebrews to be connected genealogically with the future Messiah. Similar practices existing among the Hindus and the Chinese are equally as obvious to be associated with a fear that the family might die out, and domestic worship of ancestors be discontinued.

The couvade is another peculiar marriage custom among certain primitives whereby the father observes a number of taboos about the time of his child's birth and sometimes for a long period afterwards. During this time, he must refrain from certain occupations or from eating certain types of food, to avoid harm to the child. Usually he has to retire to bed at the time of birth. Sometimes he must even simulate the pains of childbirth; and often he is waited upon by his wife as if he were the mother.

Theories of the Origin of Marriage

The unilineal evolutionists based their ideas on the theory that the moral life of man has developed in the same manner as his industrial life — from the simplicity and paucity of primitive times, to the complex material civilization of today. They say that at the beginning of

---

[2] Deut. 25:5.

the human race man was more like the animals from which he was supposed to have sprung, and so he indulged in promiscuity or group marriage. In the course of time they consider that polygamy developed as a social institution. Sir Henry Maine (1822–1888) thought that then the patriarchal family arose, but most evolutionists hold contrary views and assert that first there was that form of polygamy which is called polyandry, and concurrent with this there is supposed to have been a universal matriarchy. Then after polyandry, in point of time, polygyny and the patriarchal family is supposed to have developed. Finally monogamy became the customary marriage form. As this latter type need not be the final stage in the evolutionary process, it is interesting to speculate on what would be considered the next type. This sequence of family types is supposedly based on scientific observation of the primitives and of the higher animals, as well as on marriage customs described in early historical records.

The theory which, though modified, has had a long vogue, was originated by Bachofen in *Das Mutterrecht* (1861). Morgan (1818–1881), author of *Systems of Consanguinity and Affinity of the Human Society* (1869) and *Ancient Society* (1877), and discoverer of kinship systems among the Iroquois, which he originally studied merely as a basis for a secret society, presents an extreme case of unilinear evolutionism. He thought that all peoples went through the same phases in the so-called development of marriage, and wrongly supposed that unilateral kinship systems existed among all peoples, and hoped that he could thereby prove the oneness of the human race from a racial viewpoint. Although Morgan proceeded in seemingly inductive manner, he made many errors due to such fundamental misinterpretations as that punuluan marriage in Hawaii was a group marriage, and that when a man called his wife's sister by the same term as his wife, then he had sexual relations with her, even though this might be merely a lack of verbal expressions for a particular type of relationship. Morgan's so-called steps in the evolution of marriage are: first, promiscuity; second, the consanguine family, the intermarriage of brothers and sisters, thus forming an endogamous family within a small group; third, punuluan marriage, several sisters with each other's husbands, and several brothers with each other's wives having marital relations with each other; fourth, syndyasmian marriage, or temporary pair marriage (monandry); fifth, patriarchal marriage, one man having several wives; sixth, monogamic marriage, one man with one wife.

Modern anthropologists have completely abandoned this conception of the evolution of family life, and the revival of the idea by Briffault

(b. 1876) in *The Mothers* (1931), has affected certain sociological thought rather than the notions of the anthropologists.

Refutation of the Evolutionist Theories

To take the evolutionary theories in order, we may first consider the possibility of promiscuity at the beginning of the race. History gives us no clue of such a state among early peoples, and if we go to modern-day primitives for our data we certainly do not find any supporting evidence for this theory. Promiscuity as a social institution does not exist: there is always a certain degree of social regulation over sex relations, and a family bond is at least to some extent observed. In other words there is always to be found a recognizable individual marriage which lasts beyond the mere act of reproduction. As we said before, plural sex relations is not plural marriage. Yet we must take special care not to minimize the fact that while marriage among the primitives is always arranged in accordance with a specially regulated system, promiscuity does exist in many primitive tribes before marriage. On the other hand, in some cases strict premarital chastity is supposed to be observed, as among the Kachari, where the bride price is also paid. And sometimes the daughters of the more wealthy parents are kept strictly chaste, for example, the girls of the better class in the Yoruba tribes are betrothed in childhood, and must be virgins on marriage. Most primitive tribes permit a great deal of postnuptial as well as antenuptial freedom, but this sexual promiscuity outside the marriage bond does not necessarily take from marriage its monogamous character, any more than such occurrences in our own society justify our being called a non-monogamous people. The married men of some tribes may divorce a childless wife, lend their wife to a visitor, or even exchange wives; in Polynesia the wife of the eldest brother is shared among the rest, but these extramarital privileges do not make the persons to whom they are granted partners in the marriage, and even a monogamous union may be upheld. In some primitive tribes adultery is severely punished; among the Ona of Tierra del Fuego it is even said to be entirely unknown.

Similar statements may be made in regard to group marriage. Where it exists, it is not a primitive condition, but a degeneration from a previous state of individual marriage[3] and, as we have said, nothing else but a phase of sexual promiscuity. Where the levirate is found, or where extramarital rights are granted, a marriage may be of special

---

[3] Cf. Goldenweiser, A., *Early Civilization*, p. 24; Lowie, R. H., *Primitive Society*, p. 62; Tozzer, *Social Origins and Social Continuities*, p. 139 *et al.*

interest to a group but the marriage itself is between the two individuals concerned and is not group marriage. For instance, monogamous marriage exists among the Australian Dieri, the wife being called
a "Noa." Side by side with this form of marriage is a definite permission for the husband and wife to exercise marital rights in connection
with certain women or men (as the case may be), of the opposite
moiety. This has sometimes been called Pirauru marriage. A woman
"married" to a man in this way is not called his "Noa," but her children are regarded as the children of their father, and the Noa treats
them kindly. This is not true marriage, because a woman needs her
Noa husband's consent before she can allow a Pirauru man to have
relations with her. If a Noa dies, a female Pirauru cares for the
children.

Although among certain primitives divorce is sometimes easily procured, this is not usually so where there are children. The Andaman
Islanders forbid divorce and must observe strict lifetime fidelity. Only
in exceptional circumstances is divorce allowed to certain Australian
primitives, to the Vedda, or to the Semang. Considering the rigid legal
codes which we have built up in our own civilization, based upon the
authority of Scripture, it is remarkable how many primitives have instituted customs of monogamy which have long prevailed.

Ideas of the existence of original polyandry seem to be based on
very flimsy evidence. In almost all the cases of which we have record
of polyandry, a reason for it can be found. Sometimes economic conditions are too scanty to enable most men to afford a wife and her
children and so they share a wife with others. Sometimes there is a
scarcity of women due to female infanticide (boys being considered of
greater utility in later life, in tribal warfare or to collect food), or to a
disaster of some kind, such as war or the taking of slaves, or some
other disturbances in the balance of the sexes. The institution of
matriarchy is supposed to be a vestige of earlier polyandry, or even of
a supposed primitive promiscuity. Those who hold this view have
varying speculations as to how matriarchy arose. Some say it came
about because of the uncertain parentage of children under promiscuity, others think that it took its rise from the fact that early man
did not know the facts of procreation, and did not recognize paternity.
This lack of knowledge of paternity is true of the Arunta, yet these
people hardly fit in with the hypothesis of primitive matriarchy, for
they are patrilineal. And although matriarchy is more widespread than
polyandry it can by no means be called a vestigial remains of it, for
there is no maternal organization among such primitives as the

Arunta, the Philippine Negritos, the Pygmies of Central Africa, the Kubu of Sumatra, the Yahgan, the Andamanese, and the now extinct Tasmanians. And where matriarchy *does exist,* a reason can usually be found for it.

The couvade is also supposed by some evolutionists to be a vestigial remain of an earlier polyandry — a transitional stage by which the father openly recognizes his paternity. Although the couvade exists in many North American tribes, in Brazil, in the West Indies, and among the Yahgan of Tierra del Fuego, it is by no means universal. Rather than being a remnant of a former matriarchal or polyandrous regime, it is probably to be associated with imitative and sympathetic magic.

In Tibet, which is famous for its polyandry, monogamy brings a man prestige, and the wealthier men who can afford it are strictly monogamous, and only the poorer ones share the expenses of a family with other men. To some extent polyandry resembles matriarchy in that it conserves continuity of property and name. And it must be noted that where a woman has several husbands, one of them is usually the chief one, or else she spends a certain length of time, a month for example, as the sole wife of one of the husbands before going to the next husband again to spend a period of time exclusively with him.

A biological argument against both polyandry and also polygyny is that since the sexes are born in more or less equal numbers, there would not be enough women to go round in universal polygyny, nor men in polyandry. Polyandry is often against the unity of the family, for paternity is uncertain, and so none of the men may give the children the affection of a father, or bring them up and educate them in the best manner; and a sympathetic understanding and mutual assistance of husband and wife is also less sure. Against the theory of primeval promiscuity and polyandry it has also been argued that if each woman at the early beginnings of the race had many husbands she would tend to become sterile and the race would probably have died out long before the next stage of the so-called evolutionary process would be possible. This argument, however, has not been proved.

We may sum up the situation, by quoting Lowie, who says: "There is no fixed succession of maternal and paternal descent; sibless tribes may pass directly into the matrilineal or the patrilineal condition."[4] Rivers pointed out that in parts of Oceania a change from matrilineal to patrilineal descent has taken place within historical times, but as Lowie maintains this "does not prove the priority of matrilineal

---

[4] Lowie, R. H., *Primitive Society,* p. 185.

descent anywhere else, say, in Australia, or Siberia, or America; and even in Oceania the matrilineal condition may in turn have been superimposed on an earlier paternal one."[5] And again, as the same author correctly states, "In Australia, there is not the slightest indication that matrilineal people like the Dieri enjoy a poorer culture than the patrilineal Arunta."[6]

We come now to the question as to whether the original form of marriage and the family could have been polygyny, or at least whether polygyny is a stage in the "evolution" of marriage to monogamous forms.

While polyandry is rare among the primitives, at least what might be called a moderate polygyny is rather prevalent, and much more prevalent still among tribes who cannot be classed as true primitives and yet who are not very high up in civilization. Polygyny does not *per se* interfere with the true end of marriage, and hence not all polygynous unions offend against the natural law. Under the Old Law it was, indeed, sanctioned, seemingly becoming customary among the Jews at the time of Abraham. There is no sign in the Bible, however, that Jewish polygyny had divine approval. The Levirate, a form of monogamous sororate, became polygyny only if the deceased man's brother was already married. There are indications, indeed, that with the Jews polygyny served somewhat as a protection for some women, although it was by no means a desirable state for a woman at any time.[7] A special form of polygyny sometimes found in connection with matriarchy is called the sororate. Under the sororate, which is very widespread among primitives in North and South America, the husband of the one sister of a family has the right to consider the others

---

[5] *Ibid.*, p. 180.

[6] *Ibid.*, p. 181.

[7] Cf. Exod. 21:7–11: "If any man sell his daughter to be a servant, she shall not go out as bondwomen are wont to go out. If she displeases the eyes of her master to whom she was delivered, he shall let her go: but he shall have no power to sell her to a foreign nation, if he despise her. But if he have betrothed her to his son, he shall deal with her after the manner of daughters. And if he take another wife for him, he shall provide her a marriage, and raiment: neither shall he refuse the price of her chastity. If he do not these three things, she shall go out free without money." Cf. also Deut. 21:10–14: "If thou go out to fight against thy enemies, and the Lord thy God deliver them into thy hand, and thou lead them away captives: And seest in the number of captives a beautiful woman, and lovest her, and wilt have her to wife: Thou shalt bring her into thy house. And she shall shave her hair, and pare her nails. And shall put off the raiment wherein she was taken: and shall remain in thy house, and mourn for her father and mother one month. And after that thou shalt go in unto her, and shall sleep with her; and she shall be thy wife. But if afterwards she please thee not, thou shalt let her go free; but thou mayest not sell her for money nor oppress her by might; because thou hast humbled her."

as inferior wives. This sororal polygyny, however, is a privilege connected with marriage, and not a polygynous marriage.

A certain amount of wealth is usually necessary for the existence of polygyny for it is expensive to keep several wives with their families. Only wealthy Mohammedans practise it. Among the Bambara it is general because it is limited only by the man's ability to provide a house, clothing, and food for all, and these are easily come by in the Sudan. Yet only one of the women is considered as the true wife, and the rest are her slaves. If the customary marriage is by purchase or exchange of gifts polygyny in a primitive community is almost impossible, for wealth is not usually accumulated. Generally speaking, polygyny can be accounted for by special economic and social conditions, or by excessive ideas of the importance of property and male authority. Wealth to support a larger family, and an excess of marriageable women, as also a tendency to lust which some men, with loftier ideals, will always be found to condemn, are necessarily prerequisites to polygyny. Among some more or less monogamous tribes a second wife is permitted when the first is childless, and a few rich people have two wives, but generally strict monogamy prevails. Among the Mekeo Papuans, not only is polygyny limited to the rich, but the first wife of a rich man may object to his having plural wives and win her right to his undivided home. Often where polygyny is to be found in primitive society it is because the first wife has herself insisted on having other wives to help her with the housework, or because if only a few men can afford more than one wife, a number of them will give her and her husband prestige. The wife then remains the principal wife — the wife of status; though legally wives are entitled to equality of treatment, the others are subordinated to the first or "great" wife and even tyrannized over by her as among the Ainus, or treated as mere servants, as among the Kai, the Chukchi, and the Koryak. Because of the marriage custom, the children of these inferior wives are legal, and have a claim to inherit property, although they are socially inferior. The secondary wives may really be said to be concubines, so that plural marriage strictly so called is not in question, as it would be if we were considering Mohammedan polygyny. A system which considers only one wife of status, and the rest as *de facto* or even acknowledged concubines, is often given the name of monogyny.

Monogamous peoples will, in general, surpass polygynous ones in material and moral progress, chiefly because there is little real solidarity in a polygynous household. When the women are old, they will often be discarded for other wives, and perhaps left without resources;

there is sometimes but a slight bond between father and children, and he, in turn, may suffer from poverty in his old age. Even where true polygyny exists, one wife is usually favored more than the others, and although plural wives may live together harmoniously, there is often an atmosphere of jealousy and strife within the polygynous household, and the children will have to submit to the varying authority of each of the several wives. Even if the propagation of the race and the rearing of children are satisfactorily accomplished in polygamy, the other ends of marriage and the family are not. The family is more than a physical union. The moral union of husband and wife and the reciprocal love which makes marriage the most beautiful of all human relations, cannot be present, for the husband's affections are divided, and the husband lives a life apart from each of his wives. At least the greater part of the beauty of family life, love, devotion, and true affection cannot be present. The wife must necessarily be, not the equal, but inferior to the husband. Under polygyny she is often merely the tool for the lust of the man, and hence she cannot be the object of the reverential love of her children which is her position in the ideal monogamous home. While the practice of polygynous marriage will not necessarily lead to a complete lack of cohesion within the State or impede a certain level of civilization, sooner or later any State must suffer from widespread polygyny. For the State is but a composition of families, and if family life is disharmonious, the unity of society as a whole must inevitably suffer. As Bishop LeRoy wrote: "The family among the primitives of Africa, as among all others, is the central pillar on which, along with religion, all social life depends. If the family is strongly constituted, the tribe prospers; if its bonds are lax, the tribe grows weak; and if, as happens on the coasts, and in the European centers, it is disorganized, the tribe disappears."[8]

If we examine the life of the real primitives, we find that the family is at least preponderantly monogamous among them. The Andaman Islanders, the Semang Pygmies, the Negrito tribes, and some of the primitives of Tierra del Fuego observe strict lifetime fidelity. Most of these peoples and, in addition, the Ainu, the North Central Californians and several others even have legends of the origin of the human race from a single pair. Among the primitives other than those enumerated above, occasional polygyny is allowed, but they do not practise it as a universal custom, and so it may be said that they observe a more or less strictly monogamous family life, quite comparable to our own.

---

[8] Rt. Rev. Bishop A. LeRoy, *op. cit.*, p. 62.

Customs differ, there may be no rice or confetti or old boots attached to motor cars after the marriage ceremony; the bride-to-be may even show a strange reluctance to marry even the man of her choice, and pretend that it is necessary to be carried away by force. In general, however, there is little difference between the primitive family and the family of modern civilized countries. Apart from superficial differences, marriage and the family as social institutions are much the same the world over: among all peoples we find monogamy if not exclusively dominant, at least the *de facto* prevalent form of the domestic union. Monogamy coexists with all other forms and is the only form of marriage recognized and permitted among all peoples. Yet although from the life of the primitives we can form some idea of the common tendency of mankind even in archaic times of forming such a basic society as the monogamous family, we cannot draw moral principles from such a tendency. In addition to these anthropological arguments, we have already given some of the psychological and biological proofs which may be adduced in support of a statement that the family was originally intended to be based upon monogamous marriage. Let us now take the Christian teaching regarding it.

God's Purpose and Plan in Marriage

We have definite Scriptural authority for the assumption that God intended marriage to be monogamous and not of any other form. The Church did not create marriage and the family, for it existed long before the Church's existence. However, the Church has developed a definite teaching in regard to this most important institution, based on the teaching of Christ and His Apostles in this regard. First, in the Old Testament it is clearly stated: "Wherefore a man shall leave father and mother and shall cleave to his wife; and they shall be two in one flesh."[9] Second, we have the direct words of Christ on the subject, and we must remember that His words are also good historical testimony, for Christ told the Jews and they did not contradict Him, although they had expert historical knowledge of the subject at issue, that Moses allowed them divorce because of the hardness of their hearts, but that "it was not so from the beginning."[10] And again He said: "Therefore shall a man leave his father and mother, and the two shall become one flesh: so that they are no longer two but one flesh."[11] And He uttered the definite command: "What God, then, hath joined together let no

---

[9] Gen. 2:24.

[10] Matt. 19:8. Scripture quotations in the chapter are from the Westminster Edition.

[11] Mark 10:7, 8; cf. also Matt. 19:5, 6.

man put asunder."[12] And again: "Every man that putteth away his wife and marrieth another committeth adultery; and he that marrieth her that is put away from her husband committeth adultery."[13] And St. Paul writes: "To the married I give this charge — nay, not I, but the Lord — that a wife depart not from her husband (but if having departed, let her remain unmarried, or be reconciled to her husband), and that a husband put not away his wife."[14] St. Matthew, it is true, is sometimes interpreted as giving the impression that Christ allowed divorce in the case of adultery, according to His statement at the time of the Sermon on the Mount,[15] yet a brief examination will show that the meaning is really quite clear: If a man puts away his wife, and she has already committed adultery, then he is not the cause of her adultery. But if he divorces an innocent wife, then he is placing her in temptation, and is clearly responsible if afterwards she commits adultery. Indeed, to make His meaning quite clear, Christ added: "and he that shall marry her that is put away committeth adultery" — a phrase which leaves no ambiguity. The conversations, as recorded by Mark 10:2–12, and Luke 16:18 omit the so-called qualitative "except it be for fornication." It seems evident, therefore, that the Apostles definitely understood Christ to mean that marriage was to be indissoluble: "And He saith to them: Whosoever putteth away his wife and marrieth another, committeth adultery against her: and she, if she put away her husband, and marry another, committeth adultery."[16]

It is to Christ Himself that society owes the restoration of the ideal of monogamy. He wished to restore marriage to what it was "in the beginning" before the "hardness of heart" had led to divorce, polygyny, and concubinage, which existed everywhere among the wealthy classes at His time. His teachings were continued by the Apostles, and we find Christianity propagating a new doctrine — stressing the fact that marriage is of a religious character, that it must be definitely monogamous, and cannot be dissolved by divorce or any other custom: "What God hath joined together, let no man put asunder."

The Catholic Church has never set aside the teaching of Christ and His Apostles. It has always stressed the virtue of monogamy, and has never sanctioned polygamy, concubinage, or divorce. Christ raised mar-

---

[12] Mark 10:9; cf. also Matt. 19:6.
[13] Luke 16:18.
[14] 1 Cor. 7:10, 11.
[15] Cf. Matt. 19:9: "And I say to you whoever putteth away his wife, except for impurity, and marrieth another woman, he committeth adultery: and he that marrieth her that is put away committeth adultery." Cf. also Matt. 5:32.
[16] Mark 10:11, 12.

riage to the dignity of a sacrament, and the Church has always maintained this. It has held that all men are equal, slave and freeman, and hence that a slave's marriage is as valid in the eyes of God, and his or her person as sacred, as that of the free. More than this, the Church has pointed out the ideal relations between husband and wife which, if maintained, would give the family a foundation of mutual love and harmony.[17]

Showing that husband and wife have the same duties and the same rights toward each other, that they no longer belong to themselves, but to one another, the Church raised woman from her degrading pagan position to a place of equality with man — making her man's associate, not his subject.[18] Indeed, the essential and distinguishing features of Christian marriage are the indissolubility of the matrimonial bond, the inviolability of conjugal faith, and the mutual love and respect which husband and wife owe to each other. True, the man is given the authority in the household. But every society needs authority, as we have already shown in another chapter. A man is not handicapped physically and emotionally by childbearing; his greater physical vigor imposes on him the duty of protecting his wife and children; the average man seems more guided by reason than the average woman who is, however, usually endowed with finer susceptibilities and powers of affection, so that the two usually complement each other. Too, the man usually has a greater opportunity of weighing all sides to an issue, for, generally speaking, the woman is more confined to the home than the man, who must go outside the home to earn the living for the group and represent the family in society. Authority, however, is not given to a man so that he can selfishly exert his egotistical nature, but for the common good of the family: "Wives, be subject to your husbands as to the Lord," said St. Paul,[19] but he adds: "Husbands, love your wives as Christ also loved the Church and delivered Himself up for her . . . even thus ought husbands to love their wives as their own bodies. He that loveth his own wife loveth himself."[20]

"The man is the ruler of the family, and the head of the woman; but because she is flesh of his flesh and bone of his bone, let her be subject and obedient to the man, not as a servant but as a companion, so that nothing be lacking of honor or of dignity in the obedience which she pays. Let divine charity be the constant guide of their mutual relations,

---

[17] Cf. Eph. 6:32.

[18] It is noteworthy that among nearly all true primitives woman has a position of dignity and often of equality in the home.

[19] Eph. 5:22.

[20] Eph. 5:25, 28.

both in him who rules and in her who obeys, since each bears the image, the one of Christ, the other of the Church."[21]

The Church has also taught children to love and reverence their parents, and to obey them, since authority is necessary for the right conduct of society. It has enjoined parents not to exceed their authority and usurp the natural rights of the child; yet similarly it has warned them not to allow their children to grow up without parental "discipline and correction": "Children obey in the Lord your parents for this is just. . . . And ye fathers, provoke not your children to anger, but rear them in the discipline and admonitions of the Lord."[22] Only when grave injustice is done to them, may children be released from their duty of obedience when under age, as for example, when parents attempt to force them into a state of life against their will. The duty of love and reverence does not cease with adult life.

As for the Christian ideal in choosing a partner in marriage, we cannot improve upon the words of Pope Pius XI, who has written as follows: "To the proximate preparation of a good married life belongs very specially the care in choosing a partner; on that depends a great deal whether the forthcoming marriage will be happy or not, since one may be to the other a great help in leading a Christian life, or a great danger and hindrance. And so that they may not deplore for the rest of their lives the sorrows arising from an indiscreet marriage, those about to enter into wedlock should carefully deliberate in choosing the person with whom henceforward they must live continually: they should, in so deliberating, keep before their minds the thought first of God and of the true religion of Christ, then of themselves, of their partner, of the children to come, as also of human and civil society, for which wedlock is a fountainhead. Let them diligently pray for divine help, so that they may make their choice in accordance with Christian prudence, not indeed led by the blind and unrestrained impulse of lust, nor by any desire of riches or other base influence, but by a true and noble love and by a sincere affection for the future partner; and then let them strive in their married life for those ends for which the state was constituted by God. Lastly, let them not omit to ask the prudent advice of their parents with regard to the partner, and let them regard this advice in no light manner, in order that by their mature knowledge and experience of human affairs they may guard against a disastrous choice, and, on the threshold of matrimony, may receive more abundantly the divine blessing of the fourth com-

---

[21] Leo XIII, encyclical *Arcanum Divinae Sapientiae.*
[22] Eph. 6:1, 4.

mandment: 'Honor thy father and thy mother (which is the first commandment with a promise) that it may be well with thee and thou mayest be long-lived upon the earth.' "[23]

Marriage is truly holy only when the members are themselves holy. Just as preparation is needed for such states of life as those of teacher, doctor, nurse, stenographer, engineer, so preparation for the vocation of marriage is essential, and in particular it would seem that practice in self-denial and in the virtue of charity is of especial worth. Marriage requires mutual surrender between husband and wife, and calls for much restraint and self-denial both in personal relations and in the arduous duties of earning a living, of making a home worthy of the name, and of bringing up children in an adequate manner.

Far different from this ideal Christian reparation for marriage is that modern institution called "companionate marriage" — which is, of course, no marriage at all — where a couple live together some time before deciding whether or not they wish to make the union legally permanent.

Thus we find Christianity restoring the family to unity and indissolubility, giving precepts to lasting and harmonious relations between all the members, and creating forever an ideal of monogamy; parents and children living in mutual harmony and charity in the stable family home, which is the inner sanctuary of all social life; parents caring for their children not only because they continue themselves in the child, since the child, by heredity, is something of themselves, but also because the child is a precious gift, for whose spiritual, physical, mental, and moral development the parents are strictly accountable to God.

Before closing this chapter perhaps it will be well to add a word concerning the Church's attitude toward celibacy. Some have interpreted the words of St. Paul: "It is better to marry than to be on fire with passion"[24] and the dignity which the Church has accorded to consecrated virginity, as meaning that marriage is but tolerated. Nothing could be further from the Church's ideas.

It is true that consecrated virginity has been pronounced "the better part." We have the words of Christ: "For there are eunuchs who were born so from their mother's womb, and eunuchs who were made such by men, and there are eunuchs who have made themselves such for the sake of the kingdom of the heavens. He that can take this in, let him take it in."[25] And St. Paul, himself unmarried, has much to say on

---

[23] Pope Pius XI, *Casti Connubii*, pp. 115, 116.
[24] 1 Cor. 7:9.
[25] Matt. 19:12.

the subject; and it seems best to quote him extensively: "Now concerning virgins, I have no commandment of the Lord, but I speak my mind, as one by the mercy of the Lord, rendered trustworthy. I think therefore that this state is good on account of the present distress — that it is good for a man so to be. Art thou bound to a wife? Seek not to be loosed. Art thou not so bound? Seek not a wife. But if thou marry, thou hast not sinned; and if a virgin marry, she hath not sinned. Yet such as marry shall have affliction in the flesh. But I spare you. . . . My desire is to have you free from care. He that is unmarried hath a care for the things of the Lord, how he may please the Lord; but he that is married hath a care for the things of the world, how he may please his wife, and he is drawn different ways. So also the unmarried woman and the virgin hath a care for the things of the Lord: that she may be holy both in body and soul, whilst the married woman hath a care for the things of the world, how she may please her husband."[26]

Consecrated virginity is, however, a counsel of perfection, for "him that can take it." Most people will fulfill God's designs for them in the married state: such is the ordinary vocation for mankind. And marriage is sacred from the very nature of wedlock, since as Pope Pius XI says: "It is the means of transmitting life, thus making the parents the ministers, as it were, of the Divine Omnipotence," and he continues: "To this must be added that new dignity which comes from the sacrament, by which the Christian marriage is so ennobled and raised to such a level, that it appeared to the Apostle as a great sacrament, honorable in every way (Eph. 5:32; Heb. 13:4)."[27]

Marriage, therefore, is a divine institution, raised by Christ Himself to the dignity of a sacrament. To maintain *virginity* is essential for the unmarried; *chastity* is essential for all, married and single. Just as it is sinful to overeat, so it is sinful to abuse the sexual impulse even within the married state. And the Church enjoins chastity, as distinct from virginity, upon both her married and her unmarried members. The reason for this ideal of bodily purity is beautifully expressed by St. Paul in the First Epistle to the Corinthians, Chapter Six: First, our bodies have been made partakers in the life of grace in the name of Christ: "But ye have washed yourselves clean: but ye have been hallowed, but ye have been justified in the name of the Lord Jesus Christ and in the Spirit of our God. . . . For God through His

---

[26] 1 Cor. 7:25–28; 32–34.
[27] *Casti Connubii*, pp. 100, 101.

power hath raised the Lord and us too shall He raise up."[28] Second, our bodies are members of the Mystical Body of Christ: "Know ye not that your bodies are members of Christ? Am I, then, to take the members of Christ and make them members of a harlot? God forbid! . . . But he that cleaveth to the Lord is one spirit with Him."[29] Third, our bodies are temples of the Holy Ghost by reason of the redemption of Christ: "Know ye not that your body is the temple of the Holy Spirit who is within you, whom ye have from God? and ye are not your own, for ye have been bought at a price. Glorify God, then, in your body."[30]

Education within the family, and modern-day problems of family life will be discussed in later chapters.

---

[28] 1 Cor. 6:11, 14.
[29] 1 Cor. 6:15, 17.
[30] 1 Cor. 6:19, 20.

CHAPTER 9

THE STATE

The Family Needs the Co-operation of Others for Its Economic and Social Welfare

AT THE beginnings of the race the family was adequate to care for human needs. As needs and inclinations grew, however, something more than the family became necessary. Families require the assistance of other families to satisfy their social instinct and their want of protection, mutual co-operation, and fellowship. The single family would normally be powerless to protect itself from attack and the violation of its rights, and needs the assistance of others for protection and self-defense, and for the maintenance of peace. Similarly, if each family had to be self-supporting and provide for its own requirements, there would be little time for those with abilities in craftsmanship or the arts or sciences to follow their true avocation. Nor could the single family provide the means of communication, roads, mail service, education, trade facilities, and many other worth-while things of life, without the assistance of others in like need. Hence, although the family is the basic social unit of society, it is not a perfect society in itself, for it is impossible for it to exist independently of the co-operation and help provided by other families associated with it. For mutual protection and the promotion of their well-being, therefore, families and individuals group themselves into a larger society which is known as a State.

Definition of a State

A State is a civil society, usually characterized by a certain degree of homogeneity in race, language, social and cultural ideals, which distinguishes it from other states. Its function is to protect the rights of the individuals who compose it and to promote their well-being. It is made up of four elements: a given population or community, that is, an association of individuals and families and all the municipalities, counties, and other civic groups to which they belong; a defined territory in which they live; freedom from foreign control; and a government — an agency through which the common good of the people is realized. Other ties, such as a common economic life, local exogamy law, common danger from enemies, also keep a civic group united in the community of interest which is the prime reason for the State's existence.

Although the words *State* and *nation* are frequently used synonymously, actually, they have not the same meaning. The word *nation* is derived from the Latin *nascor, natus,* meaning birth and referring primarily to the common origin of a people. We keep this original sense of the word *nation* when speaking of one's nationality, as fixing the place of one's birth. Where a State is formed by peoples of one race, as for example, Japan, then it is called an ethnic State or nation. Yet a nation (people who live in a unified fashion within the State) is not necessarily made up of the same race, for various races can make up one nation, as in the United States. Every State is, indeed, a nation, although sometimes people of the same nationality belong politically to different States, such as the Polish peoples of pre-War days, who did not have their own State, but belonged to Germany or to Russia. In such examples as the latter, nationalities sometimes clash with true nationalism. Peoples forming a State by mutual consent or by domination, without regard for origins of blood relationship, are said to be a demotic society. Just as unity of race is not a necessary criterion of a nation, neither is unity of language a necessary mark of one; for example, the Flemings and the Walloons have very dissimilar languages, yet they both form part of the Belgian nation.

The word *State* comes from the Latin *status,* meaning something fixed and established, hence primarily the organization and government of a people. It includes the nation, but it is something more than a mere collection of individuals. It is a harmonious and more or less permanent political organization of the families of the nation and the individuals who compose them. As we stated earlier, these peoples must live in a defined territory, be free from foreign control, and have a government. A State may be a city State such as Athens, or Ancient Rome; or Florence, Genoa, and Venice in the Middle Ages; or it may be a nation, or an empire. A State may be formed on the basis of a religious creed, as in Geneva under Calvin; or of a common political creed, as in Russia today (although this statement might be contested if one has regard for the ignorance of the majority of the people); or it may be bound neither by a common race, nor by common religion, nor by common ideas on politics, as in the United States, and still be a peaceful State.

Patriotism and Nationalism

To carry out its functions in the highest degree, the State needs the support of nationalism: the strong and genuine feeling of unity between the citizens of a State. True nationalism is allied to patriotism, which is the love of a man for the country of his birth, his *terra patria*, and is a highly desirable and admirable trait. Yet despite the beauty and the utility of patriotism and true nationalism, the word *nationalism* today is usually used in another sense, in opposition to the term *patriotism*. Nationalism is generally used now to connote a false and excessive nationalism, called by the opprobrious terms *jingoism* and *chauvinism*, which takes its root in national pride and egotism, and breeds international injustice, hatred, and war. This false nationalism reverses the idea that the State exists for the good of the citizens, and makes an exalted nationalism more important than the common good. It resulted from the individualistic ideas engendered by the Reformation, which replaced the international viewpoint of the Catholic Church. It was fostered by the Mercantilist economic philosophy which sought to make the State independent, self-sufficient, and powerful, and measured the wealth of the country solely in terms of accumulations of material wealth. It was further promoted by the liberalistic ideas of the Contract theorists mentioned in Chapter 6, and by the ensuing economic ideas of *laissez faire*. As Pope Leo XIII has shown, patriotism may degenerate into a vice: "That very love of one's country and of one's race, which is a powerful source of many virtues and acts of heroism when it is regulated by the Christian law, becomes no less a germ of injustices and numerous iniquities if, transgressing the rules of justice and right, it degenerates into immoderate nationalism."[1]

Types of Government

There are many types of government, but they may be broadly classed under three main divisions:

1. A monarchy, where the supreme political control is in the hands of one person, whose office may be elective or hereditary. Monarchies are of two types: (*a*) the *absolute,* where the ruler holds absolute and despotic sway, as in the time of the Roman Emperors; (*b*) limited. A limited monarchy may be constitutional,[2] such as existed in Medieval Europe, where the fundamental laws of the State limit the ruler's

---

[1] Pope Leo XIII, *Urbi Arcano Dei.*

[2] Of course, the term *constitutional* does not always imply that a formal written document calls the State into being, as in the United States.

power, and where the ruler also consults the nobility, the clergy, and the representatives of the people in matters of government. It may likewise be of the parliamentary type of government, where the rule is in the hands of the parliament or governing body, and where the king, while nominally appointing executive ministers to rule the country, actually can select only those approved by the majority in parliament. This type of government approaches an oligarchy or a democracy, despite the fact that the head of the country is a king. Where one person is given exclusive power by election or usurpation of office, a dictatorship rather than a monarchy results. A dictator, and even an absolute monarch is, however, usually dependent upon the party which either put him in power or which helps him to maintain his power.

2. An oligarchy. In an oligarchy or aristocracy, the government of the State is in the hands of a few people, membership in the ruling class being determined by birth, wealth, or intelligence.

3. A democracy is a State where the government is in the hands of the people, either directly or indirectly. Direct democracy would mean that all citizens would have to pass a vote on each governmental issue. However, indirect democracy is the only existing form at present, that is, the people have indirect control rather than direct, for they elect a body of representatives to form a government, and delegate all or nearly all of their power to deputies. Democracies are of many types, some approaching an oligarchy or even a monarchy in form. In Russia, under the Bolshevist government, only the working class is given voting rights, and unskilled artisans in the towns have the most privileges, and, moreover, the General Secretary of the Communist Party has almost complete power. In Fascist Italy, control of both government and business is organized through the fourteen "corporations" of employers and workers, under the direction of Mussolini, who has, in many respects, a dictator's powers. Many Catholics are upholding a democratic "Corporate Order," as proposed by Pope Pius XI in the *Quadragesimo Anno*. Such an order is above all, an economic organization, and if sanctioned politically it would seem that a democratic State might come into being, adequately organized for the economic welfare of the people, as well as for the other ends of the State's existence, with room for individual freedom too. Details of such an organization are to be found in Chapter 20. It is to be noted, however, that the organization described by the Pope is economic and not political in form.

4. As a fourth type of government one should note the theocracy of early Jewish times, of Calvin's Geneva, and of the New England

Puritans in the United States. When the Church absorbs the State, a theocracy ensues, but the Church is not usually anxious to exert civil authority.

Although a strongly centralized government seems neither necessary nor, perhaps, advisable, for the proper carrying out of the State's needs of the provision of protection and aid for its citizens, nevertheless even a dictatorship may at times be the chosen or best form of government for a particular State. In actual practice, whether a government is a monarchy or a democracy, it is usually in the hands of a small influential group. If this group strives to carry out the functions of the State, is competent to do so, and is subject to some form of control by the community, then it is usually satisfactory. Uncontrolled absolute power, or even governmental power of any kind, is almost necessarily abused, because it is only human that the ones who exercise the power should tend to be convinced that the public good coincides with their own individual good. A State is therefore best governed when the politicians who form the governing body are efficaciously controlled by other groups by means of a system of checks and balances. Most modern States have their governing officials controlled by law; for example, the power of the government of the United States is limited by the authority committed to it by the Constitution, and the Constitution and the Supreme Court check the laws passed in Congress. It is further thought by a growing number of citizens that a State is better governed when minorities are proportionately represented in governmental assemblies. An election system of Proportional Representation has already been tried in certain cities in the United States.

The Christian Theory of the State: A Natural and Perfect Society

The Christian theory of the State is that it is a natural or fundamental human society, because in it are fully expressed man's aptitude and propensity for authority and submission to authority; and in it is also found the full expression of the universal and therefore human need to gather into groups for protection and for the promotion of social welfare. In civil life alone can man attain his full material, intellectual, and moral development, further his interests and protect his rights and liberty from the encroachment of others. Just as the monogamous family is a natural society, because it is needed for the very propagation of the race and for the proper upbringing of children, so to live in civil society or the State is also necessary for man and therefore must be part of the design of the Creator. The State is, indeed, a perfect society, as is also the Church, because, once constituted, it does not depend upon any higher power other than God alone, although, of course, it must observe the natural rights of man, individually and in other societies.

Authority in the State

We have already stated that authority is one of the four essential elements of the State. This is so because authority within the State, expressed through a government, is absolutely essential for the maintenance of order, since no group of men can for any length of time harmoniously and with advantage pursue a common end, however necessary this end may be, without any center of direction. Since authority is, of its very nature, essential to the State, it must be according to the law of nature, hence it comes from God. As Pope Leo XIII expressed it:

"As no society can hold together unless someone be over all, directing all to strive earnestly for the common good; every civilized community must have a ruling authority, and this authority, no less than society itself, has its source in nature, and has, consequently, God for its author. Hence it follows that all public power must proceed from God. For God alone is the true and supreme Lord of the world. Everything, without exception, must be subject to Him, and must serve Him, so that whosoever holds the right to govern, holds it from one sole and single source; namely, God, the Sovereign Ruler of all. 'There is no power but from God.' "[3]

Although it is natural for man to belong to a State, because he has a propensity, aptitude, and need for more extensive social co-operation than that provided by the family, and although authority within the State is necessary and, if duly constituted, from God, yet God did not determine in whom or in what form of government man should vest this civil authority. The opinion most widely accepted by political scientists and philosophers is that the authority necessary for the right conduct of the State (civil authority) is first vested by God immediately in the people. The people, however, cannot all exercise it, for chaos would result. They are therefore bound by nature to organize into a State, and in forming civil society (the State) they transfer their authority to the ruler or rulers to whom they entrust the reins of government, according to the form decided upon. The government of a State thus derives its power from God, through the people.[4] This au-

---

[3] *Immortale Dei*, pp. 2, 3.

[4] Some philosophers, however, are of the opinion that authority comes directly from God to those who are designated to exercise it, and not through the people and their

thority or power is conferred on the ruler or rulers in the measure and after the manner in which the people desire to confer it when they establish their particular form of government. But once they have designed the authority of the State, they are bound to obey it in all matters which are in accordance with the laws of the State and the natural law.

What determines State membership. Everyone has a duty to promote the well-being of the State to which he belongs. On its side, the State has the duty to accept the people within its territory, and most men, on reaching the age when they might decide to adopt a nationality other than that of their birth or the choice of their parents, usually, without hesitation, continue their allegiance to the State of which they are already members. Yet it must be noted that a man can choose the State to which he may wish to belong, provided the State of his choice would be willing to accept him, and therefore some people transfer their allegiance to states other than that of their birth, as do immigrants who become naturalized as citizens of the United States, Canada, Australia, and elsewhere.

Type of governments. The State is, therefore, the whole people organized for government, with the authority necessary for the orderly conduct of this organization. When a State exists, this authority is no longer in the multitude but in the ruler or executives who succeeded to power. The government may procure this power through inheritance, through election by the people of their representatives, or in any other fashion decided upon by the people in establishing a definite State, or acquiesced in by the people if a new form is imposed upon them by force. Any one of the types of government previously mentioned is legitimate, provided the general welfare of the members of the State is insured, and provided no laws are enforced which are against the natural law and interfere with man's natural right and duties.

Limitations to the power of the State. The last statement is of great importance. Although the State is sovereign in its own sphere, and has the power to enact laws and to enforce their observance, even, where necessary, by force, the authority of the State is not unlimited.

First, the State is limited by the measure of power conferred on it by the people. Then, too, the State itself is merely a unified body of persons who compose it, and since all men are moral beings, the State is a moral being as well, and hence it is subject to the moral law, and

---

natural organization into civil society. Thus in the matter of life and death (exercised by a judge, etc.) they claim that the authority *must* come directly from God, for He alone has power over life, saying that no man or group of men possess such power.

cannot do what it would be immoral for individuals to do. It cannot, therefore, make laws which are contrary to the natural law and the common good.

"The right to rule is not necessarily bound up with any special mode of government. It may take this or that form, provided only that it be of a nature to insure the general welfare."[5]

Again, the State exists solely for the use of man because man has need of it to live a full and complete human life. It is, therefore, limited in its power by the natural rights of individuals and of groups of individuals. The individual and the family both existed before any State came into being, and it is the State's duty not to injure or usurp their rights, but to safeguard and promote them. These individual rights of man were outlined in the postulates discussed in Chapter 7. Similarly, since man has a natural right to social life, he has a right to form any social group or society he chooses, provided it be not dangerous or subversive of the natural law. The State must therefore preserve and protect the right of any lawfully constituted society, however small.

In certain cases the rights of individuals and smaller groups must be subordinated for the good of the community or nation, but in working for the common good, individual liberty and other rights should not be sacrificed unless it is clearly for the benefit of all. It should be noted that the common good is not necessarily the good of the majority.

Finally, the State must not interfere with the Church's authority in matters pertaining to faith and morals, but must protect its rights because the Church has a right to exist as a lawful, natural, and perfect society. This is true also because man's supernatural interests have been entrusted exclusively to the Church, and the State, existing for the good of men, must in nowise hinder his eternal welfare, for this is of more importance than anything else in the world. Both Church and State are independent societies, but must necessarily collaborate for their mutual welfare. Religious societies other than the Catholic Church, insofar as they are sincere in their quest for eternal verities and the social organization of worship of God, are entitled to the same consideration.

Revolt against existing authority. As for the important question as to whether or not the citizens of a State can overthrow an established government, the Christian theory is that they can do this only, if they are justifiably dissatisfied with the existing form of government, and

---

[5] *Immortale Dei,* p. 3.

cannot by legal processes substitute another. If a change of government cannot be effected by law, revolution is justified only if the revolt against the existing government is necessary for the common good (because, for example, the government has become substantially and habitually tyrannical), if all legal processes to effect a change have been tried unsuccessfully, if there is a reasonable hope of success, if the means taken are not disproportionate to the gravity of the governmental disorder and if the international common good is adequately safeguarded. Since the State is a natural society, it is perpetual by nature, so that although a change of government may occur, the new form must carry out the just obligations which its predecessor undertook with other States, for example, the payment of debts previously contracted.

Functions of the State. The chief general functions of the State are:

First, the State must protect the rights of individuals and groups which compose it, and in doing this must protect the rights of everyone, not merely those of a majority, or of the rich and influential.[6]

Second, the State must promote the well-being of its members. Whenever a work that is not primarily an affair of the government can be satisfactorily accomplished by private initiative and smaller societies the State should not interfere with that work. If the State undertakes unnecessary tasks, it is in no way promoting social well-being. Man should be free to undertake that which he thinks best, provided it be lawful;[7] and if the State leaves smaller groups to do what they can, it will then have greater freedom to carry out its other duties.[8]

Duties of the State. It is the duty of the State to do whatever is necessary to carry out the above functions. The chief duties of the State are therefore as follows:

1. Religion: the State should foster and protect religion by its laws, and it should not enact any measure to compromise its safety, for man's eternal welfare is of prime importance.[9] Yet faith is a free act and the unbeliever who is in good faith must be protected.

---

[6] Cf. *Rerum Novarum*, pp. 18–21 (*RN*, 26–29).

[7] Cf. "There are times, no doubt, when it is right that the law should interfere to prevent association; as when men join together for purposes which are evidently bad, unjust, or dangerous to the State. In such cases the public authority may justly forbid the formation of associations, and may dissolve them when they already exist. But every precaution should be taken not to violate the rights of individuals, and not to make unreasonable regulations under the pretense of public benefit. For laws bind only when they are in accordance with right reason, and therefore with the eternal law of God" (*Rerum Novarum*, pp. 28, 29; *RN*, 38).

[8] Cf. *Rerum Novarum*, p. 31 (*RN*, 41); *Quadragesimo Anno*, pp. 26, 27 (*QA*, 28).

[9] Cf. *Immortale Dei*, pp. 4, 5.

2. Protective services: The State should exercise its "police" powers for the maintenance of internal peace, order, and safety, and for the preservation of the community from external encroachments that would overthrow its security. It should provide an army, a navy, a police force, and judicial service. It should have adequate legislation for the protection of rights and the enforcement of duties, and should provide preventive and reformative measures for prisoners and juvenile delinquents. It should preserve health by the provision of sanitation and general health laws, such as for street cleaning, quarantine of infectious diseases, and against adulteration of foods. Where satisfactory provisions are not privately made, it should also preserve health by the provision of parks and recreation centers, sanitary inspectors, health measures for workers and school children; by the maintenance, where public aid is necessary, of hospitals for the care of the insane, feeble-minded, defectives, and all dependent incurables; and by health and accident insurance.

3. Preservation of a high standard of morality: The State should suppress vice, and for this reason it is its duty to pass laws against immoral conduct and incitements to immorality, such as pornographic literature and plays.[10]

4. The operation of public works and the conservation of natural resources: Provision must be made for roads, bridges, canals, post offices, and public utilities; also for the upkeep of national parks, the preservation of beauty spots, afforestation schemes, and the like, where these cannot be satisfactorily maintained by private efforts. "It is understood that the right of supervision by the State is to be exercisable when private organizations are entrusted with the maintenance of public services, and whenever the public interest calls for it."[11]

5. Education: the State must foster education and supply the defects of private educational systems. It may thus establish universities, museums, libraries, art galleries, zoological gardens, and other educational facilities. It must not put itself in the place of the family, however, but merely supply its deficiencies and perform part of the disciplinary powers formerly exerted by the parents alone.[12]

6. The enactment of social legislation to regulate economic life: All men should have an opportunity to participate in the public prosperity. As Pope Pius XI expressed it: "The exigencies of the common good finally must be regulated with a view to the economic welfare of the

---

[10] Cf. *Casti Connubii*, p. 118.
[11] *A Code of Social Principles*, 2nd edition, 1937, p. 49.
[12] *Divini illius magistri*, pp. 49, 50.

whole people."[13] The State should take such positive action as the regulation of imports and exports, coinage, banks, corporations, privately owned public utilities such as electric light and power companies, street-car corporations, etc. It should safeguard the worker by providing legislation to insure Sunday rest, hygienic working conditions, security of employment, the payment of a living wage, the protection of trade-unions and other private but legitimate social groups. The State should also combat unjust speculation, protect consumers against fraud, conduct research, and provide commercial information which cannot be readily obtained from private sources. It should encourage industry (a) negatively, by putting no obstacle in the way of legitimate, wholesome employment and its profit; (b) positively, by the protection of patents, the encouragement of private associations, and by giving rewards to real benefactors of mankind. The "Corporate Order," upheld by many Catholics as an ideal economic organization is, as we said, discussed in Chapter 20. It is economic rather than political in scope.

7. The relief of destitution and care for all dependents and defectives: The State must provide hospitals for the sick, homes for the dependent poor who cannot be cared for in other ways, financial assistance to the needy, old-age pensions, and the like. These services should, however, be provided by the State only insofar as they may be necessary. "It is the duty of the public authority to supply for the insufficient forces of individual effort, particularly in a matter which is of such importance to the commonweal, touching as it does the maintenance of the family and married people. . . . Wherefore, those who have care of the State and of the public good cannot neglect the needs of married people and their families, without bringing great harm upon the State and on the common welfare. Hence, in making the laws and in disposing of public funds they must do their utmost to relieve the needs of the poor, considering such a task as one of the most important of their administrative duties."[14]

8. Administrative and representative services: The State must provide municipal and governmental administrative departments, and also a diplomatic corps for its dealings with other States.

Rights of the State. Within the limitations of the natural law and its Constitution, the State as a whole has the following rights:

1. The right to do anything necessary for the common good, understanding that it is not morally wrong.

---

[13] *Quadragesimo Anno,* p. 24 (*QA,* 27).
[14] *Casti Connubii,* p. 117.

2. The right to expect citizens to co-operate with it fully in the exercise of its duties toward the common good, for this is an end which is the very *raison d'être* of civil society.

3. The right to expect citizens to obey its laws; and to punish transgressions for the common good.

4. The right to conscript men for military service, when necessary for the defense of the country.

5. The right to exact taxes, to secure the requisite finances to carry on its work. Although, as Pope Pius XI wrote, it is "unlawful for the State to exhaust the means of individuals by crushing taxes and tributes."[15] The *Code of Social Principles* expresses a very sound viewpoint on taxation: "Taxation laws which are just and justly applied, are binding in conscience. So far as the common good allows, distributive justice requires that taxes should not be directly proportionate to incomes, nor levied on a scale increasing at a constant rate, but on a scale whose rate of increase gradually diminishes until at the upper limit it approximates to a proportional tax. Such a tax may be called 'progressive.'

"In theory the ideal would be a single progressive tax on income. But in practice a part of the public revenue must be obtained through indirect taxes, which are more willingly accepted and do not so easily become oppressive.

"Direct taxation has, however, the advantage of asking from the citizens a conscious sacrifice which gives them an interest in public affairs.

"In regard to the choice of taxation, the legislator should have regard to these three rules:

"*a*) To avoid taxes which bring manifestly harmful results and those which admit of fraud, since the latter encourage habits of evasion.

"*b*) When imposing new taxes, to tap sources of revenue rather than funds which are economically sterile and otherwise unreasonable. In any case, established forms of taxation are generally adjusted by their methods of application, or by reactions that bring about by degrees an equitable distribution of these public charges.

"*c*) Sumptuary taxes, on luxuries or undue extravagance, such as taxes on liquor, tobacco, and amusements, deserve to be encouraged. Even if their result is not great, the moral lesson they teach enlightens and strengthens the public conscience, and serves the common good at least to that extent.

---

[15] *Quadragesimo Anno*, p. 17 (*QA*, 17).

"Very high taxes on legacies, though justifiable in exceptional circumstances, undermine the principle of property. They scarcely differ from confiscation, and hinder the building up of national reserves."[16]

The duties of citizens. Since citizens need the co-operation of the State to protect their rights and to promote their well-being, they in turn must co-operate with the State in its efforts to fulfill its duties to other citizens. In general, the citizen has the following duties to perform in regard to the State:

1. He must comply with all civil laws which are in conformity with reason. It must be noted, however, that "For reasons of prudence and for fear of a greater evil to society persons may obey a law that is not binding in conscience; but if such a law formally prescribes acts or omissions contrary either to the natural law or the positive divine law, then each one ought to obey God rather than men."[17]

2. He must respect public authority, both public officials and the laws they enact, for "There is no power but from God."[18]

3. He must be patriotic and loyal to his country, lending the State sincere co-operation in its work for the common good and doing all he can to contribute to its security and advancement. By promoting the common good he is, of course, also promoting his own good, since as a part of the State, he is himself affected by the welfare of all the citizens within the State.

a) He should have a natural love for his country, springing from the same eternal source as his supernatural love for the Church, since God ordained both civil and religious society.

b) He must pay the taxes justly demanded of him, thus taking his share in the financial burden of the country. The State needs money to carry out its functions for the benefit of the citizens. Each citizen, therefore, should pay his fair share of the costs of this burden, in accordance with his ability to pay. A tax is each man's social obligation in this matter, expressed in terms of money.

c) He must not live in indifference to the government of the country, but must use the greater or less share in government that has been accorded to him, in order to avoid a majority vote in the hands of those who have possible less correct notions of justice than he has himself. Every citizen should try to form intelligent opinions on all public matters, and if he has a vote, there can be a very positive obligation, binding under conscience, to use it. If he does not do so, he helps to weaken the control of the people over the executives.

---

[16] *A Code of Social Principles,* 2nd edition, 1937, pp. 59, 60.
[17] *Ibid.,* p. 29.
[18] Rom. 13:1.

Political Suffrage

Having now discussed the Christian theory of the State it will be well to turn to the question as to whom should be given a voice in the government of a country.

As stated in Chapter 7, a man's rights may be divided into those which are his by nature, and those which are acquired. By nature man has the right to life, to liberty, to justice and truth, to the acquisition of property, and to social equality. As a member of the State man retains these natural rights, but, as we have said, the State has the higher right to restrict them under certain conditions, for the common good. Man as a member of the State has also two acquired rights: political and civil. Over these rights the State has such control as is given it by its constitution. It has a right to regulate their exercise both positively and negatively, as it has also the right to determine their very existence in given instances.

The right to vote is classed generally among political rights. A man has a right to social equality, but he has not the natural right to vote, and he would be deprived of no inherent right if the State could rule justly, and for the common good, without allowing him a participation in the government. In our present age, it is universally considered advisable (except in totalitarian States) that members of a community should have some control over those who govern them, and this check on governmental power is usually provided for in the State's constitution. Yet granted that in most modern States the determination of laws and their execution — that is, the election of representative officials — is by vote, it is a matter of debate as to whom the vote should be given.

Some are of the opinion that the vote should be allotted to man, as an individual. On the other hand, others argue that the State is composed primarily of families, and not of individuals and that the vote should therefore be given to the married man, as representing the family. Adherents to this latter argument concede that unmarried men may be given a vote, on the presumption that they will eventually marry. But they deny full citizenship to women: (1) Because unless the husband dies she will never be the head of her family, for authority cannot be divided between the two and, as Scripture puts it, women should "be subject to their husbands."[19] Woman is not equal to man, they say, but rather the sacred ministry of a woman, to give birth to children for the continuation of the race, in its own manner puts her on

---

[19] Eph. 5:22.

a higher plane and involves a reverence which would be lowered were she given social status and equality with man. (2) Because marriage and motherhood is the natural course for a woman, and if she follows this course she will rarely be self-supporting; yet self-support should be one of the conditions of citizenship. (3) Because woman's physical strength is not sufficiently great for her actively to undertake the defense of her country, or the enforcement of its laws. Therefore she cannot fulfill completely the duties of citizenship. Most modern States, however, now give the right of suffrage to man as an individual; that is, both men and women get an equal vote.

But whichever theory is held in a State, the following provisos are lawful: (1) The right of suffrage may be conferred, limited, and withheld at the pleasure of the people acting in their sovereign capacity. That is, an individual's capacity to vote, in age or educational requirements, may be determined by the general body. (2) An individual forfeits his right to vote by acting against the common good, thus proving himself incapable of exercising his vote justly. (3) An individual may, by consent or implicit delegation, entrust his right of suffrage to another.

Theories on the Origin of the State

Historically we have the story of the rise and formation of many an actual civil society. States have come into existence in the past by mutual consent, by force, or as the result of habit or other circumstances. Geographical environment, natural resources, unusual opportunities, or lack of opportunities, have all played an important part in the later growth of States into large or smaller territories, and also in their social composition. But although city states of Ancient Greece, the United States of America, Canada, the South American Republics, and many others came into being largely by the process of aggregation which we have just described, this is by no means true of all States. Some of them have been greatly influenced and absorbed by domination from outside nations, as witness the history of Great Britain, and of most of the European countries.

Yet although we have so many examples of the rise of States within historical times, we have, of course, no record of the origin of the primeval state.

Early anthropological theorists postulated the growth of all civil society through the same stages toward a strongly centralized State, basing their ideas as usual upon a so-called scientific examination of present-day primitive tribes. History nullifies these theories of unilineal State development, as does also an examination of primitive society, whose organization we shall discuss in a later paragraph.

A number of theories trace the rise of the State to a social contract made at some early time, but the authors of these theories have merely tried to carry out a philosophical idea by imaginative happenings; they sometimes made use of legends in their attempts to rationalize their theories, but in no way did they pursue historical investigations. The most important of these theorists are Hobbes, Locke, and Rousseau, to whom we have already referred in Chapter 6. Whereas the Catholic doctrine stresses the positive work of the State in watching over the good of the citizens, these contract theorists thought the State merely a necessary evil, whose restraint was to be exercised as little as possible. They stressed the need of personal liberty, without realizing that true liberty is only possible in well-ordered society, because various states of anarchy ensue, according as necessary authority is more or less absent. Since the State, with its authority, is so essential for man to preserve and perfect himself, its origin must be looked for in the very nature of man. The State, in one form or another was certainly intended by God from the beginnings of society, and cannot have been a mere voluntary concession of man, for if this latter were so, man could take away what he freely conferred on the State, thus bringing an end to all authority and introducing universal anarchy.

Out of the individualistic philosophy of the voluntarists or contract theorists, came the doctrine of liberalistic *laissez faire*.

Adam Smith (1723–1790) and the Classical School of economists were the initiators of this theory. All men are equal, they said; hence, all have equal rights and should be allowed the widest liberty, only restrained by civil authority insofar as such restraint is necessary for safeguarding the liberty of others. Believing, in general, that the State is evil, and its function merely one of restraint, they taught that the State should function merely as judge and preserver of external juridical order, exerting its authority solely in order to insure: (1) that justice is carried out in the execution of contracts legally entered into by private individuals; (2) that individual liberty is respected and competition allowed to function naturally; (3) that life, liberty, property, and health are safeguarded and protected insofar as such protection does not interfere with others' rights. The State should not interfere, they maintained, in the relations between capital and labor, in industry or private initiative of any kind, since such relations are freely entered into by the parties concerned, and the interference of public authority would be calculated to deprive private initiative of its force.

Now, it is obvious that while all men are equal politically, as well as from certain spiritual points of view, there is no equality in other respects, for each has been endowed with varying degrees of health, wealth, opportunity, talent, and temperament. Under the policy of *laissez faire,* which characterized the early history of capitalism, and exists to some extent even today, the weak are left unprotected while stronger, wealthier, more intelligent men can so exert their influence over the State as to exploit the weak for their own betterment.

A *laissez-faire* system, indeed, leads to the very opposite of what the adherents of the theory would have intended, for it denies protection to the poor and the weak, so that these latter are deprived of their freedom by the domination of the rich and the strong. Under such a system the best interests of all (the common good), which is the end of the State, can in no wise be pursued. While freedom is essential to the highest development of the individual, and while overgovernment tends to weaken the character of the individual, all restraints are not evil, for character is not developed by liberty alone, but by discipline and proper restrictions. Moreover, it is the duty of the State not only to redress injury done to an individual, but to safeguard him by wise protective measures. Unrestricted competition is, of course, a great menace to the welfare of society.

Hegel (1770–1831), who is to a large extent responsible for the present-day conception of the totalitarian State, enunciated his well-known dialectics, the theory of changes and movements. According to him the whole course of human history is simply the evolution of a Universal Spirit (according to necessary and inevitable laws). History, therefore, is merely a manifestation or phase in the dialectical evolution of the "idea" or World Spirit. Every idea embodied a partial truth, he thought, which formed a thesis; but because this phase of society would only be partly true, an antithesis or conflict would rise, to be followed by a synthesis between the two which would, in turn, provide a thesis for a renewed antithesis or conflict. In Hegel's view, the highest manifestation and evolution of this "idea" was the State, wherefore the State is the highest human institution, and is the fount and origin of all rights including the family, religious worship, private-property ownership, and all others. In the Hegelian concept, then, all individuals and all social institutions derive their importance and the justification for their existence from the State; hence they must serve and exalt the State. The State becomes for them the supreme end of human action, the personalization, as it were, of the nation. The result is a kind of pantheistic worship.

As we shall show in Chapter 20, Marx (1818–1883) took Hegel's idea, divested it of its pantheism, and substituted for the spiritual ideas of Hegel, the idea that class domination for economic reasons represents the thesis of each new dialectical process. His idea was that the exploiting class of any period keeps the exploited in subjection by means of the State. Instead of considering the State as all the citizens organized under authority, he thought of it as a separate entity, an instrument in the hands of the particular exploiters of any given period. In the final stage of Marx's dialectical process, therefore, there would be no State, for there would be no ruling class and no need of domination. In the meantime, however, the Bolshevists are seeking to aid and speed up this supposed necessary historical evolution by extreme domination of a party for the avowed purpose of a present working-class rule. The result is an extreme instance of what is now called Totalitarianism, where the purpose of State is considered all important, and citizens are considered to exist solely for the good of the State. The philosophy of the totalitarian State, therefore, is the extreme opposite to the Christian theory that the State exists for the sake of the people.

Hegel's doctrine is evident in the theories of Gentile, Croce, de Sanctis, and Spaventa, who, together with Pareto are largely responsible for Mussolini's Fascist State. Hitler undoubtedly took his Nazi program from Mussolini. Fascism largely partakes of the qualities of the Russian totalitarian State theory, even though its specifically avowed purpose is to uphold a moderate capitalism, and to combat not only *laissez-faire* capitalism, but particularly communism. In Germany, Italy, Japan, and other totalitarian countries, the citizen has been declared the creature of the State. The State has been glorified as a mystic entity, and its head is considered the incarnation of it, and is clothed with totalitarian authority in the name of the State party. Yet instead of aiming at class war and working-class predominance, as in Russia, the fascist countries strive, rather, to bring about class co-operation. In place of invoking class interest, therefore, the Fascists exalt an ideal of nationality, as a so-called "Aryan" racial unity in Germany and a political group in Italy.

The Christian idea of the origin of the State, and one which appears to be the most logical, is that there have been no set stages for the State's emergence and one should speak not so much of the origin of the State as of the emergence of governmental bodies to enable the State to carry out its functions which, with the greater complexity of social life, become more complex and involved. Christians see in the

State a natural and gradual evolution from a single family organization, through clan grouping, to a larger civil group. Indeed, the Old
Testament quite definitely suggests the State's rise in the patriarchal
system — the banding together of families related by blood under the
authority of an elder for the reasons stated in the first paragraph of
this chapter. Then, for the same reasons, several groups or clans probably joined into larger communities, occupying a definite territory and
speaking a common language, thus becoming a tribe. In this way
ethical or genetic societies were formed by aggregation, their chief
social bond being a real or fictitious blood relationship. Later some of
these tribes developed into still larger societies, to form a folk or
ethnic nation. On the other hand, some tribes divided and developed
variations in language and custom, and probably these did not become
closely associated with other tribes until much later in their history.

The State Among the Primitives

Following our plan of seeing what an examination of primitive and
semiprimitive social life has to add to the knowledge which we can
get from reason, we find that even among the most primitive peoples
men are organized into co-ordinated groups with some kind of authority, and with definite territorial and linguistic ties. The primitive
"State" is indeed primitive. There is, of course, no question of specified
forms of government divided into legislative, executive, and judicial
branches; there are no ministries or organized party systems. Yet
among all peoples at least a rudimentary State form is to be found: a
small community within a definite territory and with a certain amount
of effective authority. The political unity of such a group is particularly
manifest in time of war.

The simplest form of "State" organization is found among the Eskimos, the Veddas, the Yahgans of Tierra del Fuego, the Semang Pygmies, and the Andaman Islanders, where the isolated family with
clearly defined property rights in land is the only real unit of political
organization. But the family must here be regarded in a wider sense
than is customary among ourselves, for it includes all relations. For
example, the Andaman Islanders are divided into groups of about
twenty to fifty persons each, and each has strict territorial rights over
approximately sixteen miles, and rigidly excludes uninvited trespassers.
Respect is paid to older members in all these simpler communities; or
a man may win the respect of the group because of his personal qualities of leadership, or special ability of some kind, and so he may be a
de facto chief without legal authority. Among the Yahgan a temporary

chief is elected at festival times, when he is given full power; sometimes the shaman or medicine man has a very great influence, as
among the Eskimo and the Semang. Some tribes have two chiefs, one
of whom has power in peace time, the other in time of war. It may
therefore be truly said that a political organization, based on solidarity
of kinship, exists among these simpler peoples. Rarely, however, does
a chieftain of a group have the power to impose his will upon the
members of the tribe when these act collectively.

Other primitive groups are "governed" by a local council, with or
without a chief. Among the Ainus, a hereditary chief of each local
group has a moderate amount of power, although his proposals or commands can be vetoed by the council, which is attended by all the members of the group. Among the Dieri, there is a general council of
initiated men, but an inner council of warriors, heads of bands, heads
of totem groups, and orators, has the most real authority; and although
the authority of this council is absolute, the headman exercises more or
less authority according to his eloquence, bravery, number of relatives,
and similar considerations. Where sib organizations exist, they usually
provide a simple state form. These organizations are more than mere
family groups, for they organize primitive court machinery for the
judgment of criminals, and act together in such emergencies as war and
care for the needy. Members of the sib or union of sibs are usually
controlled by a council of heads of families, possibly presided over by
a chief who may have the leadership of the group, without any necessarily expressed or inherited authority. Each local Arunta grouping has
a totem chief who is an acknowledged leader, although he consults a
council of elders on all important matters, and the sib organization as
such does not perform any governmental functions. The Iroquois (who
are not, however, to be classed with those of mere primitive culture)
have their sibs, but for governmental purposes they have a federated
democratic community in which the women have an important part.

Age grades, with their initiation ceremonies at the important periods
of life, are sometimes more important than any village council in the
exercise of civil power. Where they exist, the function of the family in
training the child is often taken over at an early age by these social
groups. Often, as among the Bambara, there is a leader for each age
grade, and those in the highest age grade govern the whole group.
Where age grades are organized into secret societies, the power is
usually in the hands of those who have gained prestige by means of
their personality, or, in more developed communities, because of their
wealth. As an example of the latter situation, the Banks Islanders may

be cited, where position in the age grades is by purchase, and government is therefore by a plutocracy.

Among the simpler peoples of more developed culture, a wide variety of governmental forms may be found. Hereditary wealth sometimes forms the basis of a ruling patrician class, as among the Haida Indians, the Maidu Indians of California, the Yurak, and certain peoples of Polynesia and Micronesia. Wealthy men in the Yurak tribes pay large sums for their brides, and in this way they gain prestige and governing power. The smiths among the Masai warriors exercise power as a hereditary class. In Polynesia, accumulation of property by his own efforts may give a man authority, but hereditary chieftains wield most of the power, for if a patrician destroys his wealth, the plebian must be able and willing to destroy a like amount, if he is not to return to his original status. Ultimately, therefore, birth is more important than wealth among these people.

Sometimes chieftains of almost despotic authority are to be found among more developed communities, although, as we said, the chieftain of a primitive group rarely has absolute power. It is considered a sacrilege to defy a chief in Polynesia, for he is supposed to be possessed of *mana,* or sacred power. The Shilluk, tribes in Uganda and Baganda, and certain other African groups, have kings whose power may be very great. Among the Shilluk, however, as soon as a king becomes ill he is killed off and his place is taken by another.

Among the real primitives, however, it must be emphasized that the State is usually such a simple organization that its government is hardly in evidence at all, even though among certain peoples it may take more complicated forms. Yet at least a rudimentary State exists, for everywhere we find families congregated together for the common good, bound together by intermarriage, a common kinship organization, and a common territory and language, and under some form of authority.

Punishment for disobeying authority or tribal rules, does not seem to be given by any fixed institution among the primitives. Usually, the sanction of tradition, the power of public opinion or possible ridicule, and taboos, are effective means of social control. Reverence for, or fear of, breaking taboos is, as it were, the chief juridical instrument of the State. Where punishments are inflicted, however, strangers usually receive harsher treatment, and the consciousness of group solidarity among members of primitive tribes is clearly evidenced in the distinction which they usually draw between themselves and outsiders. This latter distinction may sometimes go so far as to regard lightly the property rights of other communities, whereas such rights may be respected where those of the local group are concerned.

It is of interest to note that in many primitive tribes the tribal organization carries out some of the functions of working for the common good which the modern and much more complicated State also performs for its members. Many of the nomad tribes carry their sick and helpless people with them in their wanderings; and when they find it impossible to continue caring for them, they are abandoned only after as much food as can be spared is left to enable them to live as long as possible. Even at the cost of great inconvenience and self-sacrifice, food is nearly always set apart from the general produce of the chase for the old, the sick, and the disabled.

While, therefore, all theorizing on the historical origin of the State is pure guesswork, we can say that among modern primitives at least, there is always a well-defined group of people in a more or less fixed territorial domain, with linguistic ties; and how better could the common good be developed than by organizing life so that the sick, the aged, and the needy are taken care of, and by all living together in harmony? As for the need of protection, or rather almost the lack of this need among the primitives, Schmidt seems to present the correct viewpoint when he says: "the relations of the various families with each other are as a rule neither hostile nor even unfriendly. It is especially to be noted that the very idea of wars of conquest, wars to gain possession of the hunting grounds of another tribe is generally so remote from their mentality that these people cannot even imagine it."[20]

There Are Many Problems Connected with the State at the Present Time

Since human nature is fallible, it is obvious that neither the State nor the citizens fulfill their duties perfectly. Charity and justice are not clearly recognized in the world, by either citizens or all the governing body of officials. There is much political corruption, graft, favoritism in tariffs, secret agreements and treaties with individuals and other States. This condition of affairs naturally militates against fair and equitable service being rendered by the State to all its citizens and to all those who have dealings with it. It likewise makes it difficult for the citizen to maintain a fitting respect toward officials whose dishonesty is known to him, and to obey laws which he knows are unjust.

The inhabitants of the State themselves are frequently indifferent

[20] Eyre-Schmidt, "Primitive Man," *European Civilization* (Oxford University Press, 1934), p. 50.

to their duties as citizens: they do not keep themselves informed on public affairs, and they either vote haphazardly, or even neglect to use their vote at all. Individuals and groups likewise often carry out their functions imperfectly, so that the State must step in to fill the gap. From this arises the danger that officials will assume too much power, and a further danger that they will abuse that power, as we stated in the paragraph describing the function of the State. The direction of group life in all its multiform phases should, wherever possible, be left to the initiative of individuals or private groups. If all citizens did but carry out the dictates of social justice and charity, the State could then confine its activities to those tasks which private initiative is unable to accomplish satisfactorily. Relieved of a multiplicity of un- necessary duties States could be more efficient and come nearer the ideal than any which exist at the present time.

CHAPTER 10

RELIGIOUS SOCIETY*

The Church Is a Supernatural Society

WE HAVE now studied the two most important societies necessary for man to lead a natural life as a creature: the family and the State. Another primary society, which is supernatural rather than natural, is religious society.

The word *religion* is commonly supposed to be derived from the Latin *religare*, implying the bond between God and His creatures. As used by sociologists, it means a social bond by which men, conscious of their helplessness and desirous of a continued existence after death, feel united in the worship of a transcendent power. Religion should be a high monotheistic form. Most of the present-day Christian and Judaic religions, and Mohammedanism, with its borrowed tenets of revelation, are monotheistic. There is a natural religion attainable by all, and actually attained by many to whom a knowledge of revealed religion has not come. Most peoples who are unaware of a revealed faith have a natural religion of some kind — perhaps grossly distorted by magic and paganism and so-called revelations, or perhaps distorted hardly at all. Pure monotheism, belief in an uncreated exclusively Supreme Being, by no means characterizes all religions, so religion may only be said to be universal if we take it in the wider sense of theism, by which men believe in transcendent power, which they therefore consider as superior to themselves; a power which they worship; a power to which they consider they owe duties, and whose help they petition, not only individually but socially as well. And it should be noted that the obligation of paying honor and praise to a higher power, inherent in all religions, carries with it the implication that the non-observance of nature's laws dishonors the higher power [God] who is the creator of these laws. Included, therefore, in religion, is an observance of nature's laws which may be called morality or ethics.

Even the most primitive peoples usually show a need of expressing their dependence on the Creator by some form of outward worship in

---

* The author is indebted to Sheed & Ward for kind permission to use in this chapter material taken verbatim from her book *Social Origins*.

196

common with their fellows [religious society], and have a more or less clear notion of the natural moral law, with sanctions for its disobedience. There are many religious societies in the world, and Catholics believe that God Himself ordained that man should belong to a religious society, for as we stated in Chapter 7, they take as a postulate that He founded the religious system of the Israelites, which Christ His Son later replaced by the Catholic Church, saying: "Thou art Peter; and upon this rock I will build *My church,* and the gates of hell shall not prevail against it."[1]

It is the Catholic belief that membership in this Church is necessary, not only that man may realize his social nature by worshiping God in common with other men, but also because God has made the Catholic Church the depository of truth and the official means of salvation. Catholics maintain that whereas the ideas of individual men often err, and man frequently misinterprets the dictates of his conscience, strict adherence to the teachings of the divinely founded Church cannot but lead him to his last end.

The Church is, therefore, a primary, and supernatural society. More than this, it is a perfect society, because, like the State, it is sovereign in its own sphere, and does not depend on any power other than God. Yet the State, whose aim is the material and temporal welfare of its members, belongs to a sphere inferior and subordinate to the Church or religious society, whose aim is the spiritual and eternal welfare of her members. Hence, the State must not interfere with the Church authority in matters pertaining to faith and morals, but should protect its right to exist as a lawful, natural, and perfect society. This duty devolves upon the State also because man's supernatural interests have been, as we said, entrusted exclusively to the Church; and the State, existing for the good of man, must in nowise hinder his eternal welfare which is more important than anything in the world.

The Religion of the Primitives

What is the religion of the primitives? It may be said that *in general* the primitives are more or less monotheistic in their belief. While they do not worship a Supreme uncreated God, possessing all the heights of virtue and power to the complete exclusion of other gods, yet almost without exception they do believe in a Supreme Being, and usually attribute to Him almost theological concepts.

With few exceptions, the real primitives have the idea of God as the

---

[1] Matt. 16:18.

creator. They make Him eternal, omniscient, all good, even the principle of good. To give just a few examples to illustrate the primitive idea of these attributes of God: The Fuegians say that God is like the wind and cannot be grasped; the Yahgans term Him "the good old one," also "the slayer in the sky" because He sends death; the Ona God is a most powerful being, who punishes the people with death, but who is also invoked for good weather, to heal the sick, and to perform other works of mercy. To every Pygmy the Supreme Being is omnipotent, lord over all other beings, with no one who can approach Him in power. The Batwa tribe of Ruanda in Africa call God "Imana" and say of His omniscience that there is nothing Imana does not know about, He knows everything, even the secret sins of thought. The Ainu call their God "the upholder," "protector," "inspirer of the world." The Koryaks call Him "the overseer," "the power," "He who is outside." Puluga, the God of the Andaman Islanders, is especially characterized by sympathy and readiness to help; He is considered never to have been born, to be immortal, invisible, omniscient, and the creator of all things except evil, which He punishes. The Euahlayi of Southeast Australia say that Baiame, their Supreme Being, could not be seen, but only heard and felt, and for both the Aranda and the Kurnai tribes in Australia, God is the supreme deity. The Isneg Negritos of Northern Luzon say that God is distinct from all others, invisible, omniscient, unmarried, who never dies, and who punishes evil and rewards good.

Although we thus have striking testimony that very many of the primitives do believe in a Supreme Being, it must be admitted, as we said above, that exclusive monotheism among the primitives is very rare. In nearly every case we find mixed up with evidences of monotheism, magic, or nature worship, or totemism, or manism, or fetishism, sometimes a combination of these, or even a hierarchy of gods. Sometimes a monotheistic god will be confused with a mythological hero, and will be considered to interfere with the world in a very human way. Sometimes the Supreme Being is an "otiose" deity, as among the culturally more developed Yoruba and the Bambara: one who rarely intervenes directly in the affairs of men, so that prayers are rarely addressed to him although they may be addressed to lesser gods. These are facts which, of course, need some explanation.

First, however, we may definitely confirm what we said above, that the vast majority of primitive peoples do believe in a Supreme Being, and in an afterlife; and consider the Supreme Being as all powerful, omniscient, and invisible, who punishes good and rewards evil. Often other features are merely additions to the religion, and they are rarely essential to it. Second, many of these features are not religions at all, although the rise of religion is attributed to them by the evolutionists. Third, it can be shown fairly conclusively, it is thought, that religion could not have taken its rise from any one of them. Much less could religion have originated from atheism. Atheism in the evolutionary sense cannot mean a denial of God, for denial presupposes an affirmation. If one takes the atheism to mean ignorance of God, then one has to resort to pure imagination to explain why man changed his idea from *dis*-belief to the universal existence of religion today, in the wider sense given to religion in the definition above. Man *might* have come to a knowledge of God by reason, as we shall later discuss, yet it is usually safe to take the Hindu saying as a principle that *ex nihilo nihil fit* (out of nothing comes nothing), and one may well ask what made man change his ideas if, at the beginning, he did not believe in a God. Neither is there any evidence in primitive religions that their religion was invented by themselves. The reader must note, however, that whether or not primitives believe in God and have a relatively monotheistic religion has no fundamental bearing on the truth or otherwise of the existence of God and the claims of the Church to be the divinely appointed "religious society." It was brought out at the Annual Conference of the American Catholic Anthropological Society in 1934, that anthropological research shows that there are several peoples, primitive and semiprimitive, who have not so far been found to have a religion, or even any traces of a former religion. It was emphasized at this meeting that the universal existence of religious belief is not a necessary or even a very valid proof of the existence of God and man's need of religion. (Magical practices are equally as universal!) For these facts, the arguments of philosophy, the historic continuity of the Judaic and Christian Churches, and many other proofs are available. Yet, even as regards tribes for whom no religion is claimed, such as the Navaho, one is inclined to question the findings of the anthropologists who make these claims, for some of these tribes do believe in a future life, or in punishment for ill doing, and their beliefs may very likely be a degenerate vestige of former more articulate belief.

Primitive Morality

We said that most primitives have a more or less clear notion of the natural moral law. Before proceeding with our discussion about religion, it seems best here to discuss briefly the question of natural ethics, as with nearly all peoples moral conduct is most intimately bound up with a religious system or with religious ideas.

Spencer, Durkheim, and others of the evolutionist school have said that morals have evolved. At first there was a period of no restriction, they say, then obedience to a leader became necessary to insure order; courage came to be esteemed, kindness to others, regard for the property of others (and in connection with this they think that the notion of chastity in women arose, for she was considered the property of the man she married, and only if she had been previously chaste might she be said to belong wholly to him); and gradually customs of morality grew up, and were accepted by all. This idea of "what is customary, what is acceptable, is right" is also inherent in the *mores* concept of Sumner and others.

Of course, if these theories were correct, then there would be no norm for morality, and the science of ethics would not only differ in every locality but would frequently change in the same community. Just as we do not need any quasiconfirmation from social anthropology for the existence of God, so also we do not need to have any of our standards of morality approved as it were by the conduct of the primitives. Nevertheless, it seems interesting to note that on the whole the standards of morality of present-day primitive races do compare favorably with our own. Notions of the evil of theft, murder, lying, unkindness to parents, anger, infanticide, even adultery and other vices are to be found among practically all of them. Most peoples have severe punishments for murder and theft, and often enough for adultery. These punishments are most frequently imposed by the local family or tribal council, though sometimes they are privately administered, as among the Fan, with no "governmental" intervention. Not seldom, trial by magic, including severe and often ludicrous ordeals, is resorted to. Often, however, norms of morality are clearly linked to individual responsibility toward the Creator, or to the religious society. We find that God is considered as the author of the moral code among all the Pygmy races, the Ainus, the people of Tierra del Fuego, and many others. Most of the primitives believe not only in the survival of the soul after death but also in the punishment of bad conduct and the reward of good, although with some of them this future happiness is said not to be linked up with religion or any God. And although certain types of conduct which are considered as good or bad might not conform to our standards, as we said, the moral code of the primitives is surprisingly similar to our own in all basic particulars. This moral code is usually regarded as being jealously guarded by God, or by the chief god of a hierarchy of gods, and sacrifices are even made in propitiation for wrongdoing. It is indeed a theory of Andrew Lang (1844–1912) and this is more plausible than the theories of the evolutionists, that early monotheistic religion became vitiated when man felt the need of some-one whom he could "square," since the "equal father of all men can-not be 'squared,' to make himself useful to one man rather than another." For, as he says, "A moral creator in need of no gifts, and opposed to lust and mischief, will not help a man with love spells or with malevolent 'sendings' of disease by witchcraft; will not favor one man above his neighbors. . . . Ghosts and ghost-gods, on the other hand, in need of food and blood, afraid of spells and binding charms, are a corrupt, but, to man, a useful constituency."[2]

The Theories of the Evolutionists

A sociological study of religious society can take two forms. Either it can be the practical one of showing its place in the social life of any peoples, and its influence on particular groups; or it can be the theoretical one of speculating how religious societies other than the historical arose. It is with this latter aspect that we shall be concerned here. Ever since the time of Comte, who was of the opinion that religious society took its rise in fetish worship, sociologists have been concerned with the origin of religion and of religious society.[3] Most sociologists have been evolutionists in this respect, although their ideas as to the supposed growth are very varied. They nearly all say that man was at first atheistic, with or without the accompaniment of magical practices. They argue that man cannot have had any high form of religion when he first emerged from the animal state from which they think he evolved, and they postulate for him a prelogical existence, when he could have had no conception of a deity at all. Sir John G. Frazer (b. 1854) believes in the origin of religion in magic. Sir John Lubbock (Lord Avebury, 1834–1913) thought with Comte that religion originated in fetishism. E. B. Tylor (1832–1917) who was the first evolutionist to work out a well-rounded, if erroneous, theory on the subject, was of the opinion that man first came to a notion of souls through dreams, ecstasies, and hallucinations, and then he endowed all nature with a soul and by this means came to a notion of religion. This "animism," he says, "characterizes tribes very low in the scale of humanity, and there ascends, deeply modified in its trans-

---

[2] Lang, Andrew, *The Making of Religion*, p. 257.

[3] For lack of space, reference to the theories of innate ideas as expounded by Plato, Descartes, Leibnitz, and others is omitted.

mission, but from first to last preserving an unbroken continuity, into the midst of very high modern culture."[4] Others, such as Spencer, thought that manism, that is, ghost worship, or the propitiation of ghosts of departed ancestors, gave rise to religion. W. Robertson Smith (1846–1894), Durkheim, F. B. Jevons (b. 1858), McLennan (1827–1881), Reinach (1858–1932), and others thought that religion developed from totemic practices. From these various initial stages, the evolutionists trace the growth of religion to polytheism, and finally to monotheism.

All these writers use anthropological research as the basis of their so-called inductive studies. Much erudition is to be found in their works, and many facts of great value as source material for the cultural sociologist who makes use of anthropological data. Yet the "facts" are often taken from inaccurate sources, and frequently they are distorted to fit into preconceived theories, or meanings are misinterpreted or given undue emphasis. For this reason we shall proceed to show what anthropological data really furnishes as regards the religion of present-day primitives, after which we shall examine each of the major evolutionary theories, with a view to showing wherein lies the error of the thought involved.

Magic and Religion

Let us first take the question of the possible rise of religion from magic. Magic is the art of manipulating the forces of nature by certain techniques and formulas that are outside of nature but which sometimes have a religious appearance. It includes incantations, charms, sorceries of all kinds. Always a technique is employed in connection with magic — a mystic form of words or a ritual mode of conduct; and if the art is correctly applied, the results are supposed to be infallible. Sir James G. Frazer devoted his whole treatise *The Golden Bough* to a discussion of the supposed outgrowth of religion from magic. He distinguishes between Homeopathic or Imitative Magic and Contagious Magic. In Homeopathic Magic, the person exerts the magic on the principle that like produces like — that if he whistles, he may produce a wind, or if, as among the Dyaks, a woman wishes to procure the easy delivery of a child, the magician must simulate a woman in travail. In Contagious Magic, association of ideas is the principle, that is, by the supposed "law of contiguity" things which have once been in contact with each other continue to act on each other even when they are far distant: for example, the idea that one can harm a man

---

[4] Tylor, E. B., *Primitive Culture*, Vol. I, p. 385.

by doing harm to something he once possessed, as a tooth, or nail paring. Frazer thinks that it is not the end that is to be condemned in magic, but the means. If the means employed is the scientifically correct one, then science and not magic would be the consideration. If the means employed is wrong and foolish, then magic is concerned. In this latter case, Frazer conceives that when early man discovered that the magical ceremonies did not effect the results they were designed to produce, then he realized his inability to manipulate natural forces at pleasure. At this point Frazer supposes that primitive man imagined that the forces of nature themselves were possessed of spirits which were more powerful than he; and out of abject fear of these forces came propitiatory worship, that is, religion. Frazer thus makes religion the antithesis of science. He says that he arrived at this conclusion "deductively from a consideration of the fundamental ideas of magic and religion," and "inductively by the observation that among the aborigines of Australia, the rudest savages as to whom we possess accurate information, magic is universally practised, whereas religion in the sense of propitiation or conciliation of the higher powers seems to be entirely unknown."[5] He says, too, that religion is diverse, whereas magical practices are essentially the same wherever they are found; so that magic, the invariable, must be older than religion (an argument which Father Schmidt and some of the diffusionists might also logically give!).

Now, Frazer's hypothesis is false for a number of reasons. It is true that magic has a certain affinity to religion in that on the emotional side both religion and magic have "a certain awe or reverence or fear or affection toward the beings or force with which they deal, an emotional stirring," as it were, and "on the volitional side, both religion and magic include a practical or conative attitude toward supernatural beings or forces, or both."[6] Both magic and religion have ritual and mystery in common, and the supernatural character of magic is expressed in the abnormal character of the magician. But most frequently magic tries to force and use the invisible world for man's own nefarious ends, in spite of religion and against religion. Magic involves no social relationship, whereas religion implies a twofold communion, first a striving to get into communication with higher powers by means of worship and intercession, which should be, and is, a phase of worship; and secondly, a communion of man with man. Magic is by nature impersonal, and it is compulsive, unethical, and essentially utilitarian. It

---

[5] Frazer, Sir J. G., *The Golden Bough,* one-volume edition, p. 55.
[6] Cooper, Rev. J. M., *Primitive Man,* Vol. 2, Nos. 3, 4, July–Oct., 1929, p. 34.

is generally used to control the forces of nature and make them useful for one's own end, to the disadvantage of others. Religion is persuasive and propitiatory; it is beneficent, constructive, and lifts up the mind to higher and nobler ends, petitions and does not demand. There is no control implied in religion, as there is in magic. Nor could religion have evolved out of fear of nature and natural forces. Fear is a feeling, and man's intellect, not his feeling, is necessary to give him an idea of a personality superior to himself. Schmidt gives an admirable refutation of the possibility of fear alone giving rise to religion, when he shows how courage and curiosity are human feelings just as much as fear, and says "in the presence of any strange or 'fearful' phenomenon, a man will be stimulated by his courage and curiosity to endeavor to find out the nature of the phenomenon in question, and its cause. If, then, primitive man was in point of fact terrified by certain natural phenomenon he would naturally endeavor to find out their nature and their cause, and this he could only do by the exercise of his *reason* as distinct from his emotions. . . . Even allowing that fear may have played a part in the origin of religion, we can see that this part must have consisted mainly in the stimulation of man's reasoning powers, and the use of the principle of causality."[7] Primitive man uses his reasoning powers and applies science when he makes fire, handles his bow and arrow, uses the wedge: he does not resort to magic for these things. Magic is something apart from science, just as it is apart from religion.

By its very properties, magic is not religion. It may be bound up with religion, but always religion is found superior to it, even when existing side by side with it. There is, indeed, very little magic to be found among the extremely primitive Halakwulup of Tierra del Fuego, or among the Pygmy races who are ethnologically older than the Australians whom Frazer uses as the principal ethnological source for his theory. Although magic exists among many of the primitive North American Indians, the Australians, the African Bushmen, the Samoyeds, the Eskimos, the Koryaks, and the Ainus, it is not nearly so prevalent among these peoples as among their neighbors who have a higher grade of civilization in other things. And even among the Australian tribes cited by Frazer, it is now recognized that the Euahlayi have a high god called Baime, to whom we have previously referred; the Deiri have a good spirit, the Creator, and petition sky

---

[7] Messenger, *Studies in Comparative Religion*, article by Schmidt, Rev. W., Vol. I, p. 26. Of course fear very frequently has a paralyzing effect on the individual, but it is contrary to nature to postulate a universal and continuing effect of this kind.

dwellers for their needs, and the Kurnai make use of magic but very infrequently. Magic and sorcery are notably less common among real primitives than among those of higher culture, and often where magic does exist, no special meaning is attached to the absurd things which are characteristic of it, but those who make use of it ascribe the so-called effective force in magic practices "as being imparted and attached to them by the *personal* Supreme Being, and His omnipotence is the explanation of their mysterious power."[8] Often, too, magic rites are to coerce some spirit or minor deity, and not the Supreme Being. The Bantus employ magic in this fashion, but they do not believe that the Supreme God can be affected by it.

How did magic originate, it may well be asked. Magic is not science, any more than it is religion. Rather magic is a perversion of religion as well as of science. Both magic and religion are a recognition that science has its limits, and that man's intellect and skill are at times impotent against the forces of nature. Perhaps man made use of magic as well as a plurality of gods, in an effort to escape from the inconveniences of the stern moral law, in order to obtain benefits which the Father-God apparently refused to give, as Andrew Lang thought probable.[9] Possibly various writers are correct in calling it a pseudoscience, by which, working on a false conception of causality, primitives adopted the ceremonies which constitute magic, with the thought that they could thus threaten the spirits which govern natural phenomena. Whatever it was, however, primitives do not exercise magic to the exclusion of religion, nor does it seem possible that religion in any way arose from magic.

Fetishism

Another widespread theory as to the origin of religion is that of universal early fetishism. The word *fetish* comes from the Portuguese *feitiço*, a charm, from the Latin *factitius* something made, something magically artful. De Brosses, in a book published as early as the year 1760, thought religion had sprung from fetishism, and fetishism from fear, and his theory was revived by Comte and later by Sir John Lubbock (Lord Avebury).

A fetish is a natural (material) object, without any value in itself — a stone, a tooth, a shell, a serpent, a piece of wood carved in a particular way — which object is believed to be possessed of personality,

---

[8] Eyre, *European Civilization; its origin and development,* article by Schmidt, Rev. W., Vol. I, p. 46.

[9] Cf. Lang, A., *op. cit.,* p. 247.

that is, of spirit and power, and thus is supposed to be able to aid its possessor to attain desired ends. It is not considered to be animated by spirits, but to be possessed of mysterious power either in its own right, or because it is supposed to be the temporary dwelling place of a spirit or god. Prayers and sacrifices are addressed to the fetish, not as the object itself, but as to a symbol of the power which it possesses. The fetish is placated, petted, or ill treated, according as it does the possessor's will or not. Sometimes its power is said to diminish, or even to disappear. Fetishism, therefore, cannot be religion, which demands an attitude of inferiority toward a superior being.

There are three known kinds of fetishism: (1) Fetishes, that is images, which enclose relics of the dead, and which get their power from these relics — a form of ghost worship; (2) fetishes which exercise a protective influence toward their owners, and have power to give the possessor an advantage over others — many primitives attach a piece of the umbilical cord around the neck of the newborn child for this purpose; (3) fetishes made especially to satisfy revenge and to work black magic.

Despite ritualistic functions in connection with fetishism, it is essentially individualistic, and *very* antisocial. The fetish is supposed to promote the interests and desires of its possessor, and not those of the community; it is used for the private end of the owner, and is destructive of the good of others. Religion, on the other hand, is essentially social. It must be said, too, that since the personality of which the fetish is possessed is by no means necessarily permanent — since fetishes are often found to lose their power to lead the owner to success, and are then discarded in favor of some new ones — it is hardly possible that out of fetishism could have developed a notion of the gods. And Lowie calls our attention to the connection between fetishism and magic: "There is now considerable evidence," he says, "that precisely in some of the regions where fetishism flourishes most, *viz.,* in West Africa, the power of the fetish is derived not from an embodied spirit but from, say, some magical substance that is smeared over it and is inherently endowed with supernatural potency."[10]

The classic home of fetishism is West Africa, but we can, indeed, find it in many parts of the world. Yet there is little of fetishism to be found among those of real primitive culture. The Fan have their fetishes, as well as their minor gods and totems, but they believe also

---

[10] Lowie, R. H., *Primitive Religion,* p. 117.

in a creator who ranks above all others. Fetishism is much more to be found among peoples whose culture is a little higher in the order of age, such as the West African of Upper Guinea, the Dravidians of Southern India, the Pueblo, Sioux, and Crow Indians of North America. And nowhere does religion consist of fetishism alone. Fetishism is merely a debased form, an excrescence of religion, a barnacle on it, as it were. It seems impossible that religion could have taken its rise from the practice. As Max Müller (1823–1902)[11] says, "it has never been proved that fetishism in Africa or elsewhere has ever in any sense of the word a primary form of religion, neither has it been shown that fetishism constituted whether in Africa or elsewhere, the whole of a people's religion."[12]

The Theories of Animism and Animatism

Animism is the term given by Tylor to his idea of the origin of religion which, together with the animatism or mana concept of R. R. Marett of Oxford (b. 1866), is a theory still very highly favored by many anthropologists. Tylor thought that man first came to a notion of souls from dreams, ecstasies, or hallucinations. Once he had arrived at a notion of his own soul, he transferred the idea to other humans, then to animals, and to the inanimate world. Because of shadows, reflections in the water, because of the action of the wind and other natural phenomena, primitive man is supposed to have endowed all nature with a soul or spirit, and, through fear of these natural forces, he came to worship them. More than this, Tylor thought of primeval man as linking up his idea of nature and spirits, of the future life, and the order of heavenly bodies into a single, coherent, and systematic view of the world, or what he repeatedly refers to as a "philosophy of nature."[13] After this period of endowing all natural objects with souls, and the deification of nature, the author of this concept thought that there developed, in turn, ghost worship, fetishism, polytheism, and finally monotheism.

Animism, therefore, is the universal, systematic philosophy which √ Tylor supposed was held by primeval man, that all nature (not only plants and animals, but also inanimate nature, sticks, and stones, the sun and moon and stars) is temporarily or permanently inhabited by living personalities or spirits which should be feared and worshiped.

---

[11] Max Müller of Oxford University, was particularly famous for his Sanskrit studies and his work on the Vedic songs.

[12] *The Origin and Growth of Religion*, p. 101.

[13] Cf. Schleiter, F., *Religion and Culture*, p. 86.

Why the primitive should come to link up the idea of an indwelling soul in this way is unanswered by those who hold the animistic theory. Of course, there is chemical activity in nonliving matter, but to consider that early man exaggerated this activity in such a manner as to liken qualitative difference to quantitative degree, so as not to distinguish between animate and "inanimate" things is very farfetched indeed. Then, too, if every living and nonliving nature object had a spirit which was worshiped, the primitive could not possibly have any idea of the law and order in the universe (which must indeed be evident to him) for if he gives a power of determinism to all manifestations without exception, nature could not possibly act harmoniously. Yet, on the other hand, animism is too intellectualistic in its concept. Is it possible that in primitive times all men, without exception, possessed this religious *weltanschauung?* As Schleiter points out: "All ethnological evidence tends to show that no such systematization of experience has ever taken place; on the contrary, we have abundant evidence to prove that very heterogeneous beliefs, arising from diverse sources, may exist side by side without ever coming into conflict."[14] As we said earlier in this chapter, side by side with religious and semi-religious ideas of many diverse kinds, there does exist among primitives of today, an almost universal conception of a Supreme Being. False intellectualism plus fear could hardly have resulted in this widespread theism which we now find.

Of course, there is no doubt but that nature worship is indeed found among the primitives, and is especially prominent among the West Coast Africans and in parts of Melanesia. These people, however, by no means endow everything around them with a soul; they may think that the sun and the moon and the wind have souls for, indeed, they often have a keen poetic imagination; but they do not give a soul to every nature object with which they come into contact. Max Müller has shown that much of animism is merely a poetic conception of nature and so is not religion at all. He, together with Father Wilhelm Schmidt, W. Robertson Smith, Lowie, and others all show too that animistic fear is neither universal nor especially primitive. All that investigation seems to show is that there is a little more animistic fear among certain primitive peoples than is usual in later cultures. In general, however, it may be said that animism may form a phase or aspect of religion, but it is not necessarily religion, and nowhere is it the whole religion. The Crow Indians, for example, or the Ainu and the

---

[14] *Op. cit.,* p. 86.

Andaman Islanders all show a certain animism in connection with their religion, but still they have a Supreme Being who is higher than all other spirits, including all nature spirits, and who is wholly unaffected by the lower worship accorded to these lesser deities. We may, it seems, definitely conclude that religion did not take its rise from animism.

Marett, who contested the animistic theory, extended the idea. He wishes us to distinguish between animism, which attributes a spirit to all plants and natural objects, and his own idea of a prior animatism, whereby he thought that primeval man attributed intrinsic psychic power or personality to certain men, or natural objects, but that this power, though a potency of high order, was in no way connected with a ghost, or soul, or spirit. His idea is really closely allied to a conception of magic and also to fetishism. Deriving his theory from some notions of the Polynesians and some of the North American tribes, he said that primitive man came to associate luck or success with certain persons and objects. Successful men, or men who differed markedly from the rest, such as epileptics and those possessed of psychic powers, were found to possess *mana* (a Polynesian word meaning something superhuman or mysterious, beyond human ken), expressed as *Manito* by the Algonquin tribes, *Wakanda* by the Sioux Indians, and *Orenda* by the Iroquois. He who has *Orenda,* for example, is always happy, always prosperous, has mysterious power, because he partakes of the spirit of the gods. Things which seem to be particularly associated with success come also to be considered as possessed of this special magic power and potency (here a certain alliance with fetishism seems evident). In Marett's theory, such persons and objects became taboo (from the Polynesian word *ta,* meaning marked and *bu,* an adverb of intensity). Out of this primitive conception of mysterious force came animism, magic with shamanism, and ghost worship — worship of ancestors who were especially possessed of the lucky *mana* power.

This *mana* concept has had a wide vogue. It seems faulty, however, for the various reasons set forth in opposition to the theories of the magic origin of religion, of fetishism, animism, and ghost worship which is next to be discussed. It is by no means to be found among all the primitives, and neither does it explain the almost universal belief in a Supreme Deity.

Manism or Ghost Worship

Another theory as to the origin of religion is Herbert Spencer's Ghost Theory, to which Tylor's animistic ideas gave origin. This seems to be a resurrection of the theory of the Greek Euhemeras of about 300 B.C., who saw in the gods merely deified human beings, to which anthropomorphism the name *euhemerism* is given.

Spencer's idea was that by reason of his dreams about departed relatives, early man came to the notion that these relatives were still alive, and in a spirit world; that if food were given to them they would be able to continue to live in the world of shades, and would be well contented and willing to aid those left on earth; if not propitiated, being spirits they might be powerful, and do their living relatives much harm. From fear and propitiation of the dead, ancestor worship is said to have arisen. Then later a worship of spirits in general came about. Later still, the people would think of certain ancestors or tribal chiefs as more important and more influential in this world, and hence probably more potent in the next. Thus polytheism is supposed to have originated. Finally, from this host of deities one mythical or actual ancestor would outrank the rest, ultimately leaving religion as a monotheistic concept.

The sacrifices which are found among some of the primitive tribes are supposed to have arisen from magic rites in connection with ghost worship, because, it is said, sacrifices are always of food, and with ancestor worship food is so often placed in or on graves, to propitiate the dead. Yet it must be noted that primitive sacrifices are by no means always concerned with food. The Pygmies of Africa do not sacrifice food at all, but they offer the first blades of grass to God. The Semang Pygmies make an incision in their leg, take the blood and throw it up to the heavens as a sacrifice of propitiation, to appease the Almighty who sends the thunder, they think, as a sign of His displeasure. And with most primitives the idea behind the sacrifice is homage, and sacrifice is concerned with the spiritual connotation rather than with the physical content of the food. There is, indeed, too great a transition needed to link up positively with each other sacrifice and the appeasing of the dead.

Then, too, ancestor worship is by no means universal, and is, indeed, entirely absent in many parts of the world. There are peoples who do not believe in ghosts, and have no religious care of the dead, who know nothing of ancestor worship, and yet have a notion of God. Such are the southeast Australian tribes,[15] the Andaman Islanders, the

---

[15] The primitive Dieri of Australia bury their dead, and say that cremation would debar the spirit from re-entering the terrestrial domain. Instead of ghost worship, the body is deprived of the fat adhering to muscles of the face, thighs, arms, etc., and partaken of by all near relatives to make them forget the one who died.

peoples of Tierra del Fuego, and the Bushmen. "It is safe to say," we read in Lowie, "that the lack of ancestor worship is a significant negative trait of North American religion."[16] The Ewe have a seeming ancestor worship, yet they believe in a future life when they will live again with their dead ones in mutual equality, so no true ancestor worship is present here. We do find the Pygmies, the peoples of Tierra del Fuego and others deserting their camp when a death takes place, but this is not so much for fear of the dead, as for fear of the Supreme Being who has visited them with death; and probably also to escape pestilential contagion. With most of the primitive peoples, the Supreme Being has no wife, and no family; and as Andrew Lang so aptly pointed out to us, ghost worship and dead ancestor worship is impossible before the ancestor is dead and is a ghost, yet the "Supreme Being of savage faith, as a rule, never died at all. He belonged to a world that knew not death."[17]

China is the classic home of universal ancestor worship, where sons are valued so much more highly than daughters because of their duty to pray for their departed parents — yet up to the fall of the Manchurian Dynasty in 1915, the Emperor made sacrifice and prayer to the Supreme Being, and the head of the empire has recommenced this practice. Worship of the one Supreme God was confined to the Emperor; as the ruler and father of the people he was considered the link between them and God, and there is no trace of an ancestor ever being considered as having become the god.[18] The Chinese cult of ancestors seems, too, to be reverential regard rather than religious worship. Among the primitives, there are really few traits of ancestor worship, although the Ainu do have a definite ancestor cult. Father Schmidt tells us that "ancestor worship is very feebly developed in the oldest cultures, while a monotheistic religion is already clearly and unmistakably to be found there . . . the highest development of ancestor worship does not come till the most recent times, and even then the ancestors almost always remain clearly differentiated from the gods and inferior to them. Even in later times, ancestor worship has by no means a universal distribution."[19] Where ancestor worship is found, it seems rather obvious that it is a degradation of man's traditional knowledge of the immortality of the soul.

---

[16] Lowie, R. H., *op. cit.*, p. 175.
[17] Lang, A., *op. cit.*, p. 186.
[18] Cf. Windle, Sir Bertram, *Religions Past and Present*, p. 64.
[19] Schmidt, Rev. W., *The Origin and Growth of Religion*, p. 71.

Totemism and Religion

Another famous theory of the origin of religion is the idea that totemism is the key to its development. The word *totem* was first made known in English literature by McLennan, the discoverer of exogamy, in his book *Primitive Marriage* in 1866. The word comes from the language of the Algonquin Indians, *Nindotem* meaning one's close of kin or relation, and it is related to the Chippewa Indian word *Ototeman,* which also means relationship by consanguinity.

In its most general form, totemism is an emotional attitude of members of a group toward some animal, plant, or natural object, the idea being either that all members of the group are descended from the totem animal or plant or that their first ancestors were in close contact with it. There is thus a feeling of relationship between the members of the same totem group, and this group totem is passed by heredity from one generation to another, just as we inherit our father's surname. Sometimes there are multiple totems in the same tribe, such as among the Fan, which has individual totems and group totems connected with organized religious groups, and in addition to these, totems connected with each family, phratry, and tribe, as well as a "national" totem. Sex totemism is an example of multiple totemism, where a totem belongs either to all the females of a tribe, or to all the males, to the exclusion of the other sex. Another type of multiple totemism is that in which some members of the tribe belong to one clan, moiety, or phratry, and claim descendancy from one totem, and others belong to another division and have another animal ancestor. A common totem is not always a sign of kinship, because, for example, a member of the Arunta may acquire a totem by reason of the spirit which is supposed to be reincarnated in him; and although among the Mashona of South Africa totems are inherited patrilineally, there is no absolute evidence of relationship, for names and totems seem, in the past to have become somewhat confused with names of areas, mountains, and real ancestors. Where the inheritance of a family totem exists, however, as among many North American Indian and primitive Australian tribes, it is usual to find a prohibition against a member of one totem group marrying anyone with the same totem. Most of the Dieri tribes, for instance, have two exogamous groups each with twelve totemic subdivisions. In some tribes, where these totemic subdivisions exist, there is a taboo against marrying a person belonging to the same totem group, even though no blood relationship exists; but in other tribes this prohibition is absent. Two of the subdivisions are held in greater esteem than the rest, and parents strive to have their children marry into them. It is easily seen that clan or phratry totemism of this kind is a social institution to insure a form of exogamy in marriage.

In addition to the more usual clan, family, and sex totemism, where the totem is inherited at birth, some tribes also have individual or personal totems, which are acquired. Such a totem is not inherited, but is usually adopted in connection with puberty rites. A boy, for instance, is sent out into the forest or into the desert to fast and pray, and then he either chooses, or sees in a dream, the animal or plant which is to act as his personal guardian spirit, and give him supernatural aid and comfort throughout life. Among the Arunta and Dieri of Australia, the totem is acquired at birth.

Usually a totem animal or plant is treated with reverence and respect, yet it is regarded as an equal, not as a superior or god. Usually, though not always, it is feared, and must not be used or touched or injured in any way, but must be carefully preserved; and if a noxious animal such as a snake is a totem, it must not be killed. At other times, however, the totem animal is eaten, and the particular qualities attaching to it, bravery and strength, for example, are supposed to enter into the eater. Among the Kariera of Australia, each tribe is divided into several groups, and each group has an animal totem and is responsible for supplying the tribe with that animal for food.

Most readers have seen reproductions of the totem poles of the North American Indians, which are about ten, fifteen, or even twenty feet high, usually of red cedar, and with heads and animals, birds, or plants carved on them, beginning at the top and going down almost to the base. These carvings express the myth origin or totem animal of each family in a clan group, and are usually placed outside the village or in front of the chief's house.

McLennan, Robertson Smith, Jevons, Reinach, Durkheim, Freud, and others believed that religion took its rise in totemism. Robertson Smith saw evidence of totemism in the names of the tribes of Israel, and in the animal sacrifices of the Jews, asserting that the animals were totem animals which were considered identical with God, sacrificed and eaten. Biblical scholars have successfully refuted this theory, and it may also be noted that sacrifice cannot be derived from totemism, for the Pygmies and the Arctic peoples, for example, have no trace of totemism, yet they have their sacrifices, as before referred to. Freud thought that the God of today was merely a sublimated physical father: that in early times men transferred a supposed phobia for their parents to an animal species, and then they came to think of themselves as related to these animals, and that from eating their flesh in connection with religious rites, sacramental communion developed. Of course, this is merely a Freudian cerebration, for Freud did not use any inductive material upon which to base conclusions. Durkheim was of the opinion that when people gathered together in crowds they developed a crowd consciousness, which came to be recognized as a social force which could sway one as it willed; in other words, he thought that the concerted action of a crowd was a separated entity, which forced one to do actions wholly foreign to one's intellectual consciousness. This superwill of the crowd became crystallized in a symbol, he thought, taken from the realm most comprehensible to man, the natural world of plants, animals, or other natural objects. This symbol is the totem, and it supposedly represents the superwill of the crowd, and is therefore above man, and comes to be worshiped, and finally regarded as God. Ceremonialism, built around a totem, is therefore the supposed origin of religion. Again this theory, which is purely the result of Durkheim's own fertile imagination, needs little refutation.

It is indeed, comparatively easy to disprove the beliefs of those who contend that religion took its rise in totemism. First, although totemism is of very wide occurrence, not only in North and South America, but in Australia, Melanesia, Africa, New Guinea, and seemingly among the prehistoric peoples of southwestern Europe, nevertheless it is far from universal. The most usual form of totemism is associated with clan organization, yet although we find the clan and family everywhere among the Pygmies, for example, there is no totemism among them (their guardian spirit is individual, not connected with a group). Neither do we find totemism among the peoples of Tierra del Fuego, the Pygmoids, the Kurnai of southeast Australia, the Ainu, the primitive Eskimos, the Samoyeds, the Chukchi, and the Koryaks. There is not a trace of totemism in the majority of world religions (despite the imaginative interpretation of Robertson Smith and Durkheim that sacramental communion is a relic of previous totem rites), and none of the great deities bear the name of an animal or plant to show that they had in any way a totem origin. Therefore, since all peoples have not passed through a totemic stage, and since so many primitives show no evidence of it, it is hardly possible that totemism was at one time universal, and much more certain that it is of later growth than the primeval. We may well ask where nontotemic peoples acquired their notions of religion if religion necessarily evolved from totemic rites.

Then, too, although totemism may result in animal worship, yet totemism itself is not a part of religion. Totemism is social rather than religious. Religion, as before explained, is social in that it creates a social bond in the union of worship; but the worship and the intercession which are a part of worship, are religion's most important aspects. Totemism is important in anthropology because it underlies the family organization or a minor State group, and has some relationship to the exercise of marriage. But just like fetishism, magic, animism, and other possible origins of religion which we have discussed, totemism is certainly posterior to religious belief and not anterior to it. Among those primitives and other races of early culture where totemism is found it is, indeed, essentially connected with their social organization, and is not concerned with their religion. It seems to have grown out of practical needs of exogamy, of distinguishing by name between group and group. Perhaps through lack of multiple-language forms, primitive speech was unable to distinguish between an animal and a person named after that animal, and in the course of centuries, ancestors named after animals became confused with the animals themselves. Perhaps totemism has some connection with early magic rites; it is, for instance, very possible that totemism arose with the use of magic to produce fertility of animals.[20]

Frazer strongly opposed the idea of the totemic origin of religion although as previously explained, he developed an erroneous magic theory of his own. He shows how the eating of the totem animal by the Aruntas was a magic rite in connection with the food supply, and the totem was not reverenced as such.[21] The animals on the Haida Indian totem poles are neither worshiped, nor are they regarded as ancestors; they are merely supposed to have heraldic signification.

Totemism could not have developed inevitably out of ancestor worship, as some other theorists would have us believe, for as Lang pointed out, among the Australians, where totemism flourishes, "the names of the dead are usually tabooed, there is hardly a trace of prayers, hardly a trace of offerings to the dead, and none of offerings to animals."[22] And he emphasizes the fact that among the Australians, there are "no totems."[23] We may quote Frazer again: "On the growth of religion the influence exercised by totemism appears in some societies to have been considerable, but in others, perhaps in most, to have

---

[20] Cf. Messenger-Schmidt, *op. cit.*, Vol. I, p. 15.
[21] Frazer, Sir J. G., *Totemism and Exogamy*, Vol. IV, p. 231.
[22] Lang, A., *The Secret of the Totem*, p. 23.
[23] *Ibid.*, p. 136.

been insignificant. In the first place, as I have already observed, true totemism is not a religion at all; for the totems as such are not worshipped; they are in no sense deities, they are not propitiated with prayer and sacrifice. To speak, therefore, of a worship of totems pure and simple, as some writers do, is to betray a serious misapprehension of facts. . . . Religion always implies an inequality between the worshippers and the worshipped, it involves an acknowledgment, whether tacit or expressed, of inferiority on the part of the worshippers . . . pure totemism is essentially democratic; it is, so to say, a treaty of alliance and friendship concluded in equal terms between a clan and a species of animals or things; the allies respect, but do not adore each other."[24]

In confirmation of the above, here is what Goldenweiser, the authority on this subject, concludes: "Totems are not worshipped. Animal and plant worship and the deification of nature are not totemism. Almost everywhere, in fact, these forms of religion exist side by side with totemism."[25] And further, "Totemism (is a) peculiar combination of a certain type of religious attitude with a form of social organization."[26]

Polytheism and Mythology Among the Primitives

Now finally we come to races of polytheism among the primitives and to a consideration of the possibility of the rise of monotheism through polytheism. Polytheism unlike magic, is really religion, because worship and propitiation of higher powers are its essential elements. However, it cannot be proved from a study of social origins that religion began with polytheism, nor that all religions have passed through a polytheistic stage. Many primitives do not have any polytheism at all, as has already been shown. There is, indeed, hardly a trace of any gods other than the Supreme God among the Kurnai of southeast Australia, the Negritos of the Philippines, the peoples of Tierra del Fuego, the Samoyeds, and the African Negrillos. And where a seeming polytheism is to be found, among the Ainus and one of the tribes of southeast Australia and most of the Algonquin Indians, for example, it is generally recognized that there is really an essential monotheism, because these other gods are subsidiary gods only, subordinated to the Supreme God.

---

[24] Frazer, Sir J. G., *op. cit.*, Vol. I, pp. 27, 28.
[25] Goldenweiser, A., *Early Civilization*, p. 287.
[26] Goldenweiser, A., article on Cultural Anthropology, in Barnes, *History and Prospects of the Social Sciences*, p. 224.

The growth of this seeming polytheism may be due to the dividing up of the separate powers of God, attributing them to subsidiary gods; or to the transformation of the evil being into an independent though lesser god; or to the creation of wives and children or other relatives for the Supreme Being, as an outcome of astral mythology. Yet in this latter connection it may be said that many of the primitives, the African Negrillos, the Samoyeds, the primitive Eskimos, the peoples of Tierra del Fuego, and nearly all primitive races of North America, have absolutely no conception of relatives for the Supreme Being or, as we said before, of polytheism.

As for mythology: Max Müller traced the origin of religion in nature myths. Deriving his theory from the Vedic nature poems, he saw in mythology a disease of language, resulting from the attributing of sex to such words as light, life, the soul, the good, as being male; and darkness, death, the body, and evil as being female. From the endings of words came a confusion of names, he thought, resulting in a combination of gods, in polytheism. But though the subject of these early Vedic songs was a host of nature gods, yet one of these was always temporarily supreme, and the embodiment of all the virtues of the other gods of nature who, in their turns became supreme. To this ever present supremacy of one god all the time, Müller gave the name *henotheism* or *kathenotheism,* and in it he saw the beginnings of the development of monotheism.

Andrew Lang was one of the leading exponents of Max Müller's nature-myth theory of religious origins, just as earlier, although one of Tylor's leading pupils, he exposed the fallacies of the animistic concept. Lang saw in mythology a primitive explanation of the world about us.[27] He thought that most probably primeval men turned the familiar facts of everyday life into imaginary histories; that, realizing the importance of the family, and religion and other societies in their social life, men perhaps argued that at one time they must have been without these institutions, and so they made myths about the gods or the ancestors who introduced these social forms into their way of life. With fragments of real history, Lang thought they thus wove imaginative happenings into fantastic tales.

Judging by the life of the present-day primitive, it would seem that early men first thought of God as a loving Father. Then, using their imagination too greatly, and feeling more powerful as their inventions of the mechanical arts increased, their feelings of reverence and

---

[27] Cf. Lang, A., *op. cit.,* p. 41.

dependence on the Supreme Being became weakened. Afterwards they would imagine God on a level with themselves, and so they created stories to account for the origin of man, the origin of death, the beginnings of the tribe, and other facts unknown to them. Yet although men may have become vainglorious about their powers, it would seem that they would progressively come to realize their helplessness and dependence on the higher power who sent the drought and the rain, frosts and excessive heats, and the other vagaries of life. Speaking of the herders, who have the most highly developed mythology, Father Schmidt has imagined that their dependence on God was not obscured but "it rather grew into something immense, corresponding with the immensity of their herds, and into something terrible and fatalistic with the rapidity with which misfortune could rush upon them."[28]

However mythology arose, it seems indeed that mythology itself is primitive philosophy, theology, pseudohistory, science, poetry, legend, but of its nature it certainly is not religion; and in no possible way, it seems, can the Vedic songs give us any real insight into the origin of monotheistic religion from a possible earlier polytheism.

Theory of the Origin of Religion

From the above examination it appears that we can definitely reject the theories of the unilinear evolutionists, who all postulate that religions have inevitably passed through several of the stages we have outlined. First, there can be no inevitable psychological law to necessitate the correlation of the various stages of religious worship, as is postulated by them. Secondly, we have shown that magic, animism, ghost worship, fetishism, all differ so profoundly that each must have had a separate origin. We have also shown that although they are associated with religion, they are by no means the whole of religion, but exist side by side with it. Sometimes, as with magic and totemism they are not religion at all, although certain religious attributes have sometimes been added to them. As Father Cooper says: "In general it would seem that the farther we go back into the prehistoric times, the less do we find of magic, manism, and animism. They do not disappear, but they are simpler, less exuberant, less complex, as we pass from more recent to more remote prehistoric days. We do not, on the other hand, find any such definite thinning out and attenuation of theism as we go farther back."[29]

---

[28] Messenger-Schmidt, *op. cit.*, Vol. I, pp. 22, 23, Essay on the "Religion of the Later Primitive Peoples."

[29] Cooper, Rev. J. M., *Primitive Man*, Vol. 2, Nos. 3, 4, p. 48; cf. also Rt. Rev. Archbishop A. LeRoy, *The Religion of the Primitives*, p. 304.

"An exclusive and intolerant 'ethical' monotheism is rarely if ever found among uncivilized peoples," says the same author, "but a form of theism, or Supreme Being worship approaching in a greater or lesser measure to such monotheism, is found very commonly among uncivilized peoples."[30] Theism, of course, is a religion of one Supreme God without, however, excluding the existence of lesser gods.

As mentioned at the beginning of this chapter, the primitives have almost theological attributes for their Supreme Being. They do not have fully developed prayer, but they do have a wealth of ceremonies, which they follow strictly in every detail, according to their traditions; and while not all of them have sacrifice, yet sacrifice is to be found in many of the primitive races, among the Asiatic and African Pygmies, the Bushmen, the Ona, the Vedda, and many of the Arctic peoples.

If we have disposed of the evolutionary theories of how religion evolved, the question, however, still remains to be answered: How could man have come to know God easily and clearly without revelation? And if he once knew Him, how did he turn to other beliefs? Why is it, as Archbishop LeRoy asks, that China today has a less precise knowledge of God than ancient China had, and with all their highly developed mythology, why was the religion of the ancient civilizations of Greece and Rome less pure than that of the primitive Negroes of Africa today?[31]

If, as we have said, modern-day primitives are as intelligent as are we when it is a question of brain process, then it would seem most probable that primeval man, too, could most certainly reason from effect to cause, else he would not have been a *man*, a responsible creature, for responsibility depends precisely on the possibility to reason, to connect cause and effect. He could early come to the conclusion that there must be an all-powerful maker of the things which he himself could not make, and over which he had no control. By the law of causality, from a perception of the wonders of the external world, he could come to recognize that there was an all-powerful prime mover, therefore; in other words God. It seems unreasonable to discount revelation to man at the beginning. As Briault says:[32] it is hardly conceivable that after God created man he left him without any instruction, to discover Him as best he might. God must have spoken to him most intimately in many ways, *multifariam multisque*

---

[30] *Ibid.*, p. 38.
[31] Rt. Rev. Archbishop A. LeRoy, *op. cit.*, p. 301.
[32] Cf. Briault, M., *Polytheism and Fetishism,* pp. 183, 184.

modis, "in divers manners," as St. Paul writes in the first verse of his Epistle to the Hebrews, following this with a brief account of the history of the Jews; and man's thoughts must have turned to Him in love, gratitude, worship, petition. But man's knowledge of God must have become varied as races went away from each other and developed materially. Probably, then, man identified God with his manifestations in nature, or man became proud and independent and resorted to magic practices, or developed protective spirits of his own, or myths developed as in the section on this subject we imagined they must have come. There seems much logic in Archbishop LeRoy's words: "The human species migrated from the original spot where it first appeared, at a period which science is powerless to determine in a precise manner. There had been put into its possession a fund of religious and moral truths, with the elements of a worship, the whole rooted in the very nature of man, and there conserved along with the family, developing with society. Each race according to its particular mentalities, its intellectual tendency, and the special conditions of its life, gradually established those superficially varied but fundamentally identical forms that we call religions. Everywhere and from the beginning there were attached to these religions, myths, superstitions, and magics which vitiated and disfigured them and turned them from their object."[33] St. Paul describes the degeneration of religious belief in his own way in the first chapter of his Epistle to the Romans, where he says: "For the invisible things of Him, from the creation of the world, are clearly seen, being understood by the things that are made; His eternal power also and divinity, so that they are inexcusable. Because that, when they knew God, they had not glorified Him as God, or given thanks: but became vain in their thoughts, and their foolish heart was darkened."[34]

Whatever the origin of religion, so far as its later development is concerned, we have the unbroken record of monotheistic worship among the Jews and the history of the Catholic Church which the Catholic sociologist holds as a postulate to be the proved supernatural and perfect society wherein alone by following its precepts, man can be sure of giving to God the rational worship which is His due, and of attaining his final end.

---

[33] Rt. Rev. Archbishop A. LeRoy, *op. cit.,* p. 319.
[34] Rom. 1:20–22.

CHAPTER 11

PROPERTY

Definition and Classification of Property

NEXT to the family, the State, and the religious society, the most important social institution in this world is that of private property ownership.

Property is an object or "good" which one has the stable right to use, retain, or dispose of, subject only to certain prior rights to be discussed later. Ownership is the right to use, hold, or dispose of such a good.

In philosophy a "good" is the right object of any faculty, and particularly the object of the will. In sociology the word *good* is restricted to the economic sense of a commodity or service (e.g., the service of a doctor or teacher) capable of satisfying human economic wants. Some goods are tangible, like land, buildings, tools; others are intangible, like services and skill, and titles or claims to copyrights in names, songs, formulas of various kinds. A good in this economic sense has value in use or utility, and it may also have value in exchange. Value in use is the importance which a person ascribes to a good as a condition to the gratification of his wants. Although this value in use often depends upon the basic physical characteristics of a good supplied by nature, it is largely subjective, and pertains to the relation between goods and individual men. Some goods have value in use but no value in exchange. A ragged schoolbook, a lock of hair, a picture painted by a world-renowned artist, a photograph, may be highly valued by one person, and yet may be unappreciated and considered as not of use and therefore of no value by the rest of the world. When goods have value in exchange, a more objective value is placed on them. The objective value pertains to the relation between goods and goods, that is, the power of a good to command other goods in exchange for itself. This power is, again, somewhat dependent on the subjective value which people put on it. The value in exchange of a good may be high because it is procurable only in small quantities and is considered desirable by many. Or its value may be low even if large numbers of people want it, because it may be very easily obtained, like a piece of paper or a loaf of bread in normal times and under ordinary conditions. The value in exchange of goods, both commodities and services, fundamentally depends upon their scarcity, coupled with the satisfaction to be derived from them. Sometimes, of course, the actual price of goods (price is value in exchange expressed in terms of money) is unduly high because of the large profits secured by semi-monopolies.

There are various ways by which goods can be classified which are of importance only to the economist. The sociologist, however, who wishes to understand the various theories of socialism must keep in mind one of these classifications; that is, the division of goods into consumption and production goods — according as they are consumed to satisfy some direct want of the user, or are "enjoyed" only indirectly, being employed to produce other goods. Food and clothing are examples of the first. Factories and their machinery, or even a simple spade, are examples of the second. Since every producer is a consumer as well, there are very many more consumers than producers in the world: very young children, the infirm aged, and the disabled do not produce, and neither do many others who continue their education beyond the normal period, or who have an income from past production on which they live without directly producing anything themselves. But everyone, to remain alive must be a consumer — the smallest child is one, with his need of clothing, food, toilet articles, medicines, doctor's or midwife's services.

Refutation of Evolutionist Ideas on Property

According to some of the evolutionists there was originally communal ownership of all things, and our so-called property rights came into being only as a result of the expression of vanity and greed, by means of conquest or unfair advantage taken by some people over others. Yet nowhere can we find proof that when the earth ceased to be a common good, property in land and other goods took a collective form. History tells us that from the beginning of their recorded history the Israelites owned property; and likewise the Chinese, the Greeks, the Romans, and the Egyptians (Joseph bought all the land of Egypt, and after the inundations of the Nile all land was surveyed to fix property boundaries).

King Hammurabi left us records of a highly organized system of property ownership in the laws which he had engraved on a stone pillar about 2050 B.C.,[1] when Abraham went out from Ur and began a

---

[1] Cf. Chilperic, Edward, *The Oldest Laws in the World* (London: Watts & Co., 1906).

nomadic tent life. We read of the penalties of stealing the property of another:[2] "If a man steal the goods of a god, or a palace, that man shall be slain. And whoever receives the booty at his hand shall be slain also. If a man has bought silver, or gold, or a man slave, or woman slave, or ox, or sheep, or ass, or anything else, from the hands of a child, or slave of another man, without elder or contract, or receives them on deposit, that man shall be considered a thief: he shall be slain. If a man has stolen an ox, or an ass, or a sheep, or a pig, or a goat, either from a god or palace, he shall pay thirtyfold. If he is a plebian, he shall render tenfold. If the thief has nothing to pay he shall be slain." The penalties for theft of all kinds and from different classes of society take up many continuing statutes of this law code which, discovered only in the year 1901, gives us an accurate picture of social life, including commerce, industry, and finance four thousand years ago. There are, too, records of individual land ownership from the earliest times in Gaul and Germany.

Turning now to property ownership among the primitives, and semi-primitives, nowhere do we find that they own all things in common, as would seem to be expected if the conclusions of the evolutionists were correct. Rather, we discover the opposite to be the case.

Let us first consider the question of land ownership. Undoubtedly it is true that no primitive individual has any exclusive property in land, yet frequently tracts of land are very clearly marked out for exclusive family use. For example, among the Dieri, definite limits are placed on the hunting grounds of single families, groups of families, and tribes, and the sons inherit the use of the hunting grounds of their fathers. Sometimes land is held in common by a tribe, for the use of the component families and their members. Yet, of course, these clans of tribal groups are only larger families, and joint ownership in a family cannot be called communism. The joint ownership is, too, readily understood when we realize that although the range of their wandering is limited the primitives are, nevertheless, nomads, and settle in one place only for short periods of time. Some nomadic tribes do not seem to have any idea of exclusive rights in land, but that ownership in land is recognized by many of these groups as is evidenced by the fact that tribal or clan collective ownership is very rigidly enforced as against all outsiders. The Ona of Tierra del Fuego are divided into about thirty patrilineal groups comprising from forty to one hundred persons, and the land is divided among these groups in a very precise fashion so that each has strictly delimited hunting grounds. The An-

---

[2] *The Code of Hammurabi,* statutes 6–7.

daman Islanders, divided into bands of about twenty to fifty persons each, have strict territorial rights over approximately sixteen miles for each band, with a rigid exclusion of uninvited trespassers.

Among tribes a little more advanced in material culture, we find that the Okanagan of British Columbia own tribal property in common, but the bands kept their property distinct and had to ask the chief's permission to hunt, fish, pick berries, or dig roots on the land of another band, and then only at the proper season. The Coeur d'Alène Indians of what is now the State of Idaho, on the other hand, more nearly approached tribal communism in land, although, again, the various bands had certain private rights. The following ethnographical report about these latter peoples is of some interest: "Land was communal or tribal, and the same applied to rivers and lakes. The whole country was considered the property and food preserve of the tribe. However, parts of the country in proximity to villages of bands were seldom used by outsiders, for they depended on this territory for the gathering of roots and berries, and for everyday fishing and hunting. Besides, these grounds were under the control of the band chief. Nevertheless the more distant parts of each band territory were considered tribal and not band territory; and even the 'home ground' of each band was free for any member of the tribe to use, as long as the chief of the band was notified and his regulations were followed. Every part of the tribal territory was free to all members of the tribe for travel and later on for pasture, and also for gathering of food, hunting and fishing, when traveling from point to point.

"Each band chief was in charge of the 'home territory' of the band, and regulated the gathering of roots and berries therein. As each important kind of fruit ripened, he sent persons from time to time to inspect the crop at different places. When on any ground a sufficient quantity of berries was ripe, he declared the ground open for berrying, and the women went in companies and gathered the crop. This gave all the women an equal chance, and prevented jealousies, quarrels, and the picking of immature berries. The same regulations governed the digging of camas and all important roots. Some of the large cama and berry grounds distant from the settlements of any band were in charge of chiefs of divisions and were opened by them at the proper time for digging or picking. These places were free to all the members of the tribe, and people from all bands resorted thither. All, however, had to obey the orders of the divisional chief, or, if he were not present, of the camp chief. It seems that there were no restrictions regarding times for fishing and hunting, for these matters regulated themselves by the seasons, the weather, and the habits of the different kinds of game and fish. It seems that there was no private or family property in fishing places, eagle cliffs, etc., and it is very doubtful if deer fences were privately owned. In some cases these appear to have been band property."[3]

Sometimes we find coupled with tribal ownership of land a clear recognition of the individual use of it. Among certain Malay Negritos of Zambales, and with the Banks Islanders, planting land which is cleared away by an individual belongs to him, although other land is held in common. And among the Malay Negritos the produce of what a man plants is his private property even if it be a tree and he be absent from the district for many years. Among the Kai the sons inherit the fruit trees which were personally planted by their father, and among the Fan trees always go to the eldest son. The Thompson River Indians and the Maidus of California hold land in common, but a deer fence or fishing station belongs to the man who did the work, and he can pass on the product of his efforts to his heirs. Land among the Yoruba of Southern Nigeria belongs to the community collectively, and is vested in the chief. The chief distributes it among the families, and once a man has land allotted to him, he cannot be dispossessed and the usufruct is inherited by his children. Although the land itself cannot be sold, houses, trees, and crops upon the land can be disposed of for gain, with the consent of the chief. If, however, a man allows his allotted land to become overgrown with bush or forest, it reverts to the tribe. Among the Bambara of the French Sudan, land is said to belong to the local protective spirit of the property. Some of this property is used in common, but some is used by individual families or groups of families. The usufruct of land, though seemingly precarious, is, in fact, perpetual, and the eldest living male head of the family who has descended from the founder in direct male line, has the usufruct of all the family lands for the benefit of the family. When a woman marries she acquires the right to the usufruct of her husband's family goods, and retains this right after he dies until, at her death, it reverts to the eldest living male descendant. If no males survive, the land and other property is divided among all the surviving daughters. If there are no children, division is made among the collateral males and, failing these, collateral females, or their descendants.

Obviously, in view of the above citations, we cannot say that even as regards land tenure, true communism exists among primitive tribes,

[3] Teit, J. A., "The Salishan Tribes of the Western Plateaus," *Annual Reports of the Bureau of American Ethnology*, XLV, 1927–28, pp. 162, 163.

although it must be said that many primitives and semiprimitives have very strict rules against the sale of land, so that there is only a limited ownership right. Among the Ewe and the Haida tribes, for example, the land is considered to belong not only to the living members of the tribe, but also to the dead.

As for movable tangible goods, individual property rights are seemingly always respected. The Dieri bury all trinkets, weapons, or decorations owned by the deceased with his corpse. The Ainu indicate ownership of weapons and household goods by individual property marks. Among the Yoruba, property is inherited at death, although a little, and especially dowries and drink, is put in the grave. The wife's and the husband's property are considered separately. The wife's property is exclusively hers, and the daughter's usually divide equally her ornaments, clothes, flocks, and other possessions. The sons inherit the husband's property equally, and the widow herself is inherited with this although a man never marries his mother. Purely personal property can be given away during the lifetime of the owner, but family property in the usufruct of land is strictly inalienable.

Although food is often shared in common among the primitives, and large game may be divided among the whole tribe, certain parts of food are often individually owned. For example, we read of the Coeur d'Alêne Indians: "Hunting parties generally divided the game in the following manner: The skin, brisket, and one side piece of the animal belonged to the man who had killed it. The other side piece went to the hunting chief. The rest of the carcass was the common property of the hunting party, and was divided equally among all the hunters by the chief. In small hunting parties of friends the division was about equal. A man hunting alone owned the whole animal, but he often gave part of it to his neighbors or friends. In buffalo hunting parties, as a rule, each hunter owned all he killed, and he took as many of the skins and as much of the meat as he wanted or could handle. Whatever was left was the property of whoever wanted it, and all could help themselves without restriction. When only a few buffalo were killed, and the people were short of food, the meat was divided by the chief like other game."[4] And again we read: "Skins and meat of trapped animals, when the traps or snares were private belongings and the trapper was unassisted belonged to the man who trapped them."[5] A similar division of parts of an animal, recognizing the killer's prior rights, takes place among the Kurnai and many other primitive peoples.

[4] Teit, J. A., *op. cit.*, p. 162.
[5] *Ibid.*, p. 163.

"We do not know of a single tribe," writes Boas, an authority in the anthropological field, "that does not recognize individual property. The tools and utensils which a person makes and uses are practically always his individual property which he may use, give away or destroy provided he does not damage the life of his family by so doing"[6] (that is, make his family dependent on others). Of course, no storing up of vast accumulations of property is possible among the primitives — their life is too simple, and they do not usually prepare for distant contingencies. "Sufficient for the day," or at most, "for the winter," is their economic philosophy so that they see no point in the accumulation of clothes or utensils.

Here, however, a word might be said about the "potlatch" of certain of the North American Indian tribes, of a more highly developed culture, such as the Haida and the Kwakiutl, and of some of the Eskimos who borrowed it from the Northwest Coast tribes. According to this custom, a person will amass property, chiefly blankets, for many years, often lending them out at interest. When a sufficient amount of property has been acquired, the goods lent out are called in. (Among the Kwakiutl interest on a blanket loaned for a year is 100 per cent, for example, ten blankets must be returned for every five borrowed. The percentage of interest is less for shorter periods, but is rarely less than 20 or 25 per cent. Public accountants check the loans.) Then, after a festival of many days' duration, the accumulated property is distributed among the guests, and all, even slaves, receive their quota of blankets, the donor being left with hardly any property at all. Yet, it is to be noted that, on the *do ut des* principle, he who gives at a potlatch expects to acquire at the potlatch of another. Blankets are sometimes forced upon those who attend the feast, and always they must be repaid at interest at a future potlatch. The Kwakiutls have copper plates of little intrinsic value, but each with its own distinctive characteristics which represent so many thousand blankets each. The greater the number of blankets given at a potlatch, the greater is the ceremonial value of the copper. A man who throws a copper of value into the sea has more prestige than he who gives it to others, to be returned with interest value later.

Some of the evolutionary writers have seen in this potlatch custom a transitional stage in the evolution of property ownership. Yet as was pointed out in *Social Origins*[7] the reason for the potlatch is very evidently the gaining of social esteem by what might be called an

---

[6] Boas, F., *Anthropology and Modern Life*, p. 227.
[7] Ross, E. J., *Social Origins*, pp. 67, 68.

orgy of generosity; and rather than indicating a disregard of property rights, it seems to recognize a right to dispose of one's own possessions. Potlatches confirm our assertion that the private ownership of goods is clearly recognized in primitive society.

Some of the primitive tribes even extend property ownership to intangible possessions. We even find the idea of copyrights and patents in primitive society, in evidence of which Lowie gives the following example. "Among the Kai . . . as in the Andamans, a poet is the absolute owner of his composition. No one else may sing it without his consent, and usually he exacts a fee for granting it. Similarly, there is ownership of magical formulas, the instructor being entitled to compensation. Certain carvings, too, must not be copied without special leave. Even personal names are in a sense a form of patented property, so that a young man adopting a name already held, presents his elder namesake with a gift by way of conciliation."[8]

Strict laws governing the passing on of *property* after death are also proof of the primitive's clear idea of man's rights of private ownership, even though the right may be limited by certain restrictions. Among the Fan, more primitive than the more highly developed Bambara and Yoruba tribes already mentioned, property is inherited only in the male line, and goes to a man's sons and brothers and, failing these, to the father's brothers and their sons. With the Ainu of Japan all property except female apparel and household goods goes to a man's sons, and if there are no sons, then to the husband of his eldest daughter. Primitive inheritance laws differ, of course, from our own. Sometimes, because they are considered members of different sibs, a husband and wife do not inherit from each other, but a brother inherits from his brother, and a sister from her sister. Some tribes hand down property through the last born of a family, and others have primogeniture laws. Yet these differing situations are to some extent duplicated among modern civilized peoples, for some estates are entailed, and in some countries property is divided among all the heirs, whereas in others the law of primogeniture prevails.

There is, therefore, abundant evidence that the private ownership of property is clearly recognized by all primitive races. Yet it must be noted that the primitives can teach us many a lesson on the right uses of property, and we certainly cannot get any confirmation from primitive customs for our present-day unsatisfactory division of property, with its vast accumulations in the lands of the few, and the poverty of the masses.

---

[8] Cf. Lowie, *Primitive Society,* p. 236.

Many arguments can be adduced to prove the right of the private ownership of property, other than these just outlined from social anthropology. The anthropological argument is, indeed, by no means the principal one, and is chiefly useful insofar as it destroys false evolutionary theories.

Proofs of the Natural Right of Private Property Ownership

Much more conclusive reasons can be given to prove that man is intended by nature to acquire, possess, and enjoy, as an individual, both consumptive and productive goods or property, and that the institution of private property ownership is a practical necessity arising out of man's human character:

First, since life is man's dearest possession, he must procure the goods necessary for his sustenance.

Second, acquisitiveness is a human trait which seems almost universal, and to put forth his best efforts in labor, a man needs more than a bare daily sustenance. By nature, man needs an incentive to work, a motive power to give him courage to continue his labor, and for the majority of men this incentive is best provided by the possibility of amassing property which he can dispose of as he pleases, either as consumption goods or, as production goods to yield future consumption goods or purchasing power therefor.

Third, man is by nature a social being, and in exercising his sociability he must live in harmony with his fellow men. To avoid quarrels, to maintain peace among men, and to assure a wise administration of goods and production, stable rights of private ownership seem very necessary. "Innocence could live from a common purse, not ordinary man. Communism was a lost ideal left behind in the garden."[9] Man is more careful with his own goods than with goods belonging to the community, and is more content with individual ownership than when possessions are matters of joint concern and must be shared with others. Then, too, the larger the society, the larger would be the aggregates of collective property to be administered for the good of all, and the greater the difficulty of checking the private greed and injustice which might characterize the administrators. Generally speaking, the private ownership of property is a necessary condition of human freedom, to protect the individual against the possible tyranny of his fellow men, of his employers, of the State. Collective ownership may be satisfactorily practised by some few religious or other groups, with supernatural ideals and motives, but universal collective owner-

---

[9] Cf. Jarrett, B., *Social Theories of the Middle Ages*, p. 122.

ship would necessarily lead to disorder — surely contrary to nature's intent.

Fourth, the foremost relationship into which man enters as a social being is the family. He has, therefore, the right to marry and raise a family, and a duty to provide for his family which, on account of the vicissitudes of life, may often be done only by amassing some property for them. As Pope Leo XIII says: "It is a most sacred law of nature that a father must provide food and all necessaries for those whom he has begotten; and, similarly, nature dictates that a man's children, who carry on, as it were, and continue his own personality, should be provided by him with all that is needful to enable them honorably to keep themselves from want and misery in the uncertainties of this mortal life. Now, in no other way can a father effect this except by the ownership of *profitable* property, which he can transmit to his children by inheritance."[10]

Fifth, man has many contingencies to meet, such as accidents, ill health, old age, death, and the leaving of dependents. The latter cannot be provided for unless man saves up goods for the future; and to economize for "a rainy day" he must have the right to amass not only consumptive property, but productive capital also. If he had not this right, and suffered misfortune, he would become wholly dependent on the will and charity of others, and he could not leave his dependents any property. While many primitive tribes of today seem willing to undertake collectively the economic needs of their less fortunate members, to expect others to forego the consumption of wealth for the sake of the unfortunate is to look for a high degree of unselfishness and charity not always to be found in the human character. Besides, under modern conditions of city residence, many people are not acquainted with their neighbors and their needs.

Sixth, man is endowed with intelligence, and he has the right to use his intelligence to foresee the contingencies just mentioned and to provide for them. Unlike the animal, he does not live merely for the present. He has the right, therefore, not merely to consumptive, but also to productive, property which is not consumed in the using. And since intelligence and other moral qualities are perfectible, he has also the right to his own property to enable himself or his dependents to spend what time is necessary to perfect these gifts by study, travel, and in other ways. This is impossible without a store of goods with which to maintain life while devoting one's attention to pursuits other than the gaining of a living. Man's nature demands this improvement

---

[10] *Rerum Novarum*, p. 7 (*RN*, 10).

of his moral qualities. For the obviously gifted this need might be taken care of by collective funds given in the form of scholarships. Yet many a man's genius is not evident until his mind has been long trained, or he has long sought after the expression of intangible ideas. These moral qualities are now frequently lost in the poor who have only scholarships available to them, and on the other hand, they often materialize among the well-to-do who have the property ownership which affords them leisure for experiment with potential gifts and aptitudes.

Finally, there is God's sanction for private property in the two commandments which presuppose its existence: "Thou shalt not steal"; "Thou shalt not covet thy neighbor's goods . . . nor anything which is his." Christ had friends among the rich, such as Lazarus and his family, Zacheus the tax collector, and "certain women who had been healed of evil spirits and infirmities . . . and many others who ministered unto Him of their substance."[11] And when asked about the payment of taxes on wealth, He took "a coin of the realm" and said: "Render unto Caesar the things that are Caesar's."

Christ and Socialism

Certain Socialists claim that Christ Himself was in favor of the communal ownership of goods, and that it was practised by the early Church.

Actually, Christ Himself never preached it. True, He was ever on the side of the weak and the oppressed, and He pronounced it exceedingly difficult for a rich man to enter into the Kingdom of Heaven. However, He did not condemn riches, but only the abuse of them, that is, an inordinate attachment to material goods. A man may be rich and still be detached from earthly possessions; another man may be poor, yet set all his store in the acquisition of earthly gain. Christ had many friends among the rich, as we have just shown.

Yet He did praise those who gave of their possessions to others: "For I was hungry, and you gave Me to eat: I was thirsty and you gave Me to drink: I was a stranger and you took Me in: naked and you covered Me."[12] And although the rich young man of the Gospel was not told to renounce his riches as a necessary corollary to his entrance into life everlasting, he was later invited to sell his possessions — not as a precept but as a counsel of perfection.[13]

---

[11] Luke 8:2, 3.
[12] Matt. 25:35, 36.
[13] Matt. 19:16–21.

Voluntary collectivism has always been an ideal of the Church, to be carried out by those who wish to live in freedom from the cares which the ownership of material wealth involves. Human nature being what it is, voluntary collectivism will never be universal. The collectivism of the early Church was not even concerned with the common ownership of the means of production, distribution, and exchange. Rather, it was a common charity fund, administered for the good of all. Those who practised it did so for greater devotion. It was voluntary, and in no wise obligatory; and strictly speaking it was confined strictly to Palestine. Many Christians must at least have retained some of their goods, for they are mentioned as giving alms.[14] We read of Mary, the mother of John surnamed Mark, as owning a house, whither Peter went after his miraculous deliverance from prison.[15] And again, Ananias and Saphira were rebuked for telling a lie, not for retaining their property. "Whilst it remained, did it not remain to thee? And after it was sold, was it not in thy power?"[16] The collectivism of the members of religious orders at the present day is this type of voluntary collectivism — a community of possessions voluntarily undertaken.

The Christian Conception of Property Ownership

Private property ownership has been shown to be an institution which is universal and permanent, and which seems to respond to a natural need of man. This is so because from the practical viewpoint, human character and intelligence, and the varying moral qualities, natural endowments, education, and opportunities of each man would seem to make the use of private property a necessary tool for the stable and orderly use of natural resources. It seems, therefore, to be better for human welfare than the collective ownership of goods. As Pope Pius XI has said: "The right to own private property has been given to man by nature or rather by the Creator Himself, not only in order that individuals may be able to provide for their own needs and those of their families, but also that by means of it, the goods which the Creator has destined for the human race may truly serve this purpose. Now, these ends cannot be secured unless some definite and stable order is maintained."[17] Yet the precise form of private property may vary from time to time according to the needs of individuals and families, and the development of the common good, and the State may

---

[14] Acts 9:36.
[15] Acts 12:12–14.
[16] Acts 5:41.
[17] *Quadragesimo Anno*, pp. 15, 16 (*QA*, 15).

legitimately own types of private property which might, perhaps, in private hands, be abused to the social detriment. Pope Pius XI very clearly expressed this in the *Quadragesimo Anno*:

"History proves that the right of ownership, like other elements of social life, is not absolutely rigid. . . . It is plain, however, that the State may not discharge this duty in an arbitrary manner. Man's natural right of possessing and transmitting property by inheritance must be kept intact and cannot be taken away by the State from man. . . . The prudent Pontiff had already declared it unlawful for the State to exhaust the means of individuals by crushing taxes and tributes. . . . However, when civil authority adjusts ownership to meet the needs of the public good it acts not as an enemy but as a friend of private owners; for thus it effectively prevents the possession of private property, intended by Nature's Author in His Wisdom for the sustaining of human life, from creating intolerable burdens and so rushing to its own destruction."[18]

The Christian conception of wealth is that it is a sacred trust, and not an evil; that it involves the duty of aiding the poor out of what is superfluous fortune, but that it is only the abuse and not the right use of it which is to be avoided. As Pope Pius XI himself wrote: "The investment of superfluous income in searching for favorable opportunities of employment, provided the labor employed produces results which are really useful, is to be considered, according to the teaching of the Angelic Doctor, an act of real liberality particularly appropriate to the needs of our time."[19] And again: "those who are engaged in production are not forbidden to increase their fortune in a lawful and just manner: indeed it is just that he who renders service to society and develops its wealth should himself have his proportionate share of the increased public riches, provided always that he respects the laws of God and the rights of his neighbor, and uses his property in accord with faith and right reason."[20]

It is Christian teaching that property must be both justly acquired and put to proper use. The latter obligation imposes two duties on the rich: the duty of justice, and the duty of charity. A man has a right to goods which he legitimately possesses, but justice requires that he should give a starving man the means of sustenance. So far as charity is concerned, we cannot do better than quote the words of Leo XIII: "No one is commanded to distribute to others that which is required

---

[18] *Ibid.*, p. 17 (*QA*, 17).
[19] *Ibid.*, p. 18 (*QA*, 18).
[20] *Ibid.*, p. 43 (*QA*, 46).

for his own necessities and those of his household; nor even to give away what is reasonably required to keep up becomingly his condition in life; 'for no one ought to live unbecomingly.' But when necessity has been supplied, and one's position fairly considered, it is a duty to give to the indigent some of the surplus. 'That which remaineth give alms.' It is a duty, not of justice (except in extreme cases) but of Christian charity — a duty which is not enforced by the human law. But the laws and judgment of men must give place to the laws and judgment of Christ, the true God; who in many ways urges on His followers the practice of almsgiving — 'It is more blessed to give than to receive'; and who will count a kindness done or refused to the poor as done or refused to Himself — 'As long as you did it to one of My least brethren you did it to Me.' Thus to sum up what has been said: Whoever has received from the Divine bounty a large share of blessings, whether they be external or corporal, or gifts of the mind, has received them for the purpose of using them for perfecting his own nature, and, at the same time, that he may employ them as the ministers of God's Providence, for the benefit of others."[21]

There is no doubt, however, that the words of Pope Pius XI are very true, that "the vast differences between the few who hold excessive wealth and the many who live in destitution constitute a grave evil in modern society."[22] To remedy this situation, both Pope Leo XIII and Pope Pius XI have urged in their encyclicals that men should carry out their duties in charity and justice, which would involve a "mutual agreement" between capital and labor such as would result in "pleasantness and good order," and would lead to the payment of a living wage. If this ideal condition could be brought about, there would still be inequalities, for, in fact, nature does not seem to have intended that strict equality should prevail: men differ in their capacity for work, in their capacity for acquiring wealth and keeping it when once it is acquired; then again, some men have more spending propensities than others, and some have more demands upon their resources. But though there would still be the rich, and "the poor will be always with us," both classes would be united in a bond of fellowship, in a way almost impossible to envisage at the present time, and a more equitable division of private property would be brought about without any of the injustices of compulsory collectivism.

On the other hand, the Church teaches that man's right to own property is only a general right. If a man does not possess anything,

---

[21] *Rerum Novarum*, p. 13 (*RN*, 19).
[22] *Quadragesimo Anno*, p. 21 (*QA*, 23).

no one has deprived him of any concrete right and he can only demand possession of any goods in the one grave instance if he is starving, lacks all means of subsistence, and is refused alms; then he can take the goods he needs without injustice, provided they are not necessary for their owner. In such circumstances, since every man has a right to life, he has a right to preserve his life by taking necessary food or its equivalent from another. In all other cases "it belongs to what is called commutative justice faithfully to respect the possession of others, not encroaching on the rights of another and thus exceeding the rights of ownership."[23] The right to property, therefore, must be made definite by first occupancy, with the necessary application of industry (in the case of unappropriated land or goods),[24] or by purchase, inheritance, donation, or other lawful means. "For God has granted the earth to mankind in general; not in the sense that all without distinction can deal with it as they please, but rather that no part of it has been assigned to anyone in particular, and that the limits of private possessions have been left to be fixed by man's own industry and the laws of individual peoples."[25] Man's right to own property does not, therefore, mean that his possession of particular types of property is inalienable, unlimited, and without control. It is one thing to have a right to possession, and another to enjoy that right as one pleases — when one lives in society where other people have rights too.

So far as the State is concerned, as Leo XIII has written: "The right to possess private property is from nature, not from man; and the State has only the right to regulate its use in the interests of the public good, but by no means to abolish it altogether."[26] The State, then, has no right of ownership over the property of its citizens, but by virtue of its authority it may at times subordinate the rights of the few to the rights of the many, where the welfare of the community so requires. In promoting the general development of the community, therefore, it has the right of "eminent domain," that is, it has a right of jurisdiction or control of property, and within limits it can extend or restrict ownership for the sake of the common good, and so also it can tax property and limit the profits on its use. In the name of the commonweal, the State may dispossess a man of his property, and convert it to

---

[23] *Ibid.*, p. 16 (*QA*, 16).

[24] It seems but just that first occupancy should give exclusive right of ownership only to that part of the land which a man and his family can cultivate. It is noteworthy that Pope Clement IV gave permission to strangers to cultivate one third of the estate of any man who preferred not to cultivate it all himself.

[25] *Rerum Novarum*, p. 5 (*RN*, 7).

[26] *Ibid.*, p. 27 (*RN*, 35).

the use of the public, if such action seems reasonable and necessary. To protect the citizen in his right to private property, however, the constitutions of the various States require that the right of eminent domain be exercised only when compensation is made to the owner, for if property is forcibly taken from the owner without compensation there would be a violation of rights. However, the State could not purchase all or a majority of the enterprises within its jurisdiction without the use of force, and any wholesale dispossession of property and conversion for the use of the public would be not only unconstitutional, but bureaucratic and paternalistic, since the State would not be promoting the common good, but would be usurping functions that could almost certainly be satisfactorily carried out by others. The right of "eminent domain" must in no way be confused with the theory which makes the State all-powerful.

Regarding the inheritance of property and taxes thereon, the *Code of Social Principles* mentioned in Chapter 7 gives the following viewpoint:

"The right of inheritance, like the right of ownership, to which it is closely allied, has a two-fold character, individual and social. This is particularly so when it is a question of property changing hands within the family circle, in view of the close ties that unite members of the same family and the particular purpose of family property.

"The State, therefore, cannot directly or indirectly suppress inheritance without gravely injuring social interest and attacking the inviolable rights of the family. Nevertheless, it has the right to adapt the degrees of relationship that may inherit to the actual organization of the family.

"It is desirable that the State should reduce the duty as much as possible, and even abolish it, in the case of succession in the direct line. It is, moreover, desirable that testamentary rights should be allowed to the head of a family sufficient to ensure the passing on of small undertakings intact within that family."[27]

Single-Tax Socialism

All socialist and communist theories attack in some measure man's natural right to private ownership. These we shall discuss in more detail in Chapter 20. It seems, however, that we should mention one type of socialism here, the single-tax system, for it is particularly concerned with private ownership in land, and yet claims to be one of the most moderate of socialistic tenets.

---

[27] *Code of Social Principles,* 2nd edition, 1937, p. 48.

PROPERTY   237

The originator of this theory was the American journalist Henry George (1839–1897), who published the famous book *Progress and Poverty* in 1879 and who spent more than twenty years as a traveling lecturer and propagandist of the idea. Henry George and his followers attack the receiving of rent on land by private owners. They are of the opinion that material progress is always accompanied by increasing poverty of the worker, and that rent absorbs the whole benefit of progress. They say that economic rent is a social product, the owners do nothing to produce rent as such, and the earth was given to all mankind to move around on and derive sustenance. The only title to ownership, they assert, is from productive labor, so the present system of landownership in the hands of a few is unjust, and this free natural gift should be divided among the community. This can be done, they think, by the application of a single tax on land, to represent the rent value of the land, and to take this away from the owners. The yield from this tax would be so great, they are sure, that all other taxes for governmental needs would be unnecessary, and so there would be a single tax, that on the rent of land. Landowners could stay on their land as before, and enjoy interest on the capital expenditures on buildings and so forth, and wages of management, but the rent would go to the State, to compensate the masses for being excluded from the land, and to enable them to obtain the value of the products of the land. Because of the impossibility of procuring rent, George thinks that many landlords would be willing to sell their land at a low cost; workers would then be able to afford to purchase land, which would diminish the number of industrial workers, whose wages would then be increased. Thus poverty would be greatly diminished.

Although there is an element of truth in the foundations of the Henry George theory, it has many flaws.

First, not all land is rent-bearing from a commercial viewpoint, for some people own land as a consumption good and do not expect to make a gain from it in industry or commerce.

Second, it takes away a man's property without due compensation.[28] If a man has a natural right to own property, as we have just shown, then he has also the right to the product to be derived therefrom. When a person works upon property which is not his own, a title is given to the product upon which the work has been performed only by con-

---

[28] George specifically states (*Progress and Poverty*, Book VII, p. 1): "If private property in land be just, then is the remedy I propose a false one: If, on the contrary, private property in land be unjust, then is this remedy a true one." No Catholic can subscribe to George's theories, therefore, without modification.

tractual agreement. Again, there can be little question now of original occupation of land, for land at the present time is rarely owned by persons who originally acquired it. Land is bought as an investment by some people instead of building factories or other buildings on leased lands, or instead of purchasing partnerships or securities. When land is acquired by purchase, the purchase price is usually the capitalized value of the normal rent. If rent were taken from present landowners, they or those who left them the land, would have paid high prices for nothing, which would be, in effect, a very unjust capital levy. They could not sell the land at its capitalized rent value, for no such value would exist. They could only sell it at all, if there were competitive bidding for it for consumptive or business use. Effective ownership in land would therefore be abolished for all who did not need it for actual use. Landowners, including the small farmer possessing but a few acres and the worker who had secured his little property in the city, would be the exclusive payers of taxes, whereas those who leased or who lived in hotels and earned their income in other ways would go tax free, except insofar as the tax would be incorporated in the lease price.

Yet to possess a piece of land for his own certainly gives a man confidence and an incentive to thrift and self-respect. Although it is true that in the large cities land is often in the hands of financial magnates, most of the other land in the United States belongs to the middle class and not to an idle landowning class. From the social viewpoint, landed property owners are powerful factors in the stability and progress of the nation. Without some hope of rent, it is doubtful whether the settlement of America would have been so rapid as it was. The social value of private ownership of land has always been recognized and encouraged by the United States Government, and to abolish it would undoubtedly do social as well as individual harm. Indeed, one of Pope Leo XIII's strongest recommendations for the cure of modern economic ills is the extension of small property holdings. "If working people can be encouraged to look forward to obtaining a share in the land," he says, "the result will be that the gulf between vast wealth and deep poverty will be bridged over, and the two orders will be brought nearer together. Another consequence will be the great abundance of the fruits of the earth. Men always work harder and more readily when they work on that which is their own; nay, they learn to love the very soil which yields in response to the labor of their hands, not only food to eat, but an abundance of the good things for themselves and those that are dear to them. It is evident how such a spirit of willing labor would add to the produce of the earth and to the wealth of the community. And a third advantage would arise from this: men would cling to the country in which they were born; for no one would exchange his country for a foreign land if his own afforded him the means of living a tolerable and happy life."[29]

If people had originally placed the land in the hands of the governing authority, for the benefit of all, such a system might possibly be better than our own, yet Pope Leo XIII was against such a plan, and as he mentions in the quotation above, it is notorious that people take better care of their own individual property than that of a group. From the economic viewpoint, too, it is doubtful whether land would be put to its best and most productive use, and would be conserved for future generations by judicious crop rotation, if long leases and profit in the form of rent were not forthcoming.

Henry George also argued that as we have progressed materially, so landownership has become more concentrated in the hands of the few, rents have increased, and therefore the less money is available for capital and labor. This argument is not wholly true. High rents may be paid for store premises in fashionable shopping centers, for instance, where the turnover of goods and profits thereon may allow high interest rates and wage payments. It is not true that rent has absorbed the whole benefit of progress, neither is it true that the receipt of rent by the landlords is the sole cause of poverty. Many people are poor because of the bad organization of industry, commerce, politics, or because of physical and moral handicaps. Material progress has not benefited landlords only, for many workers and certainly many capitalists have improved their position by the progress of our times. Even if it were true that paying rent to the landlord impoverishes the people, it is difficult to see how an improvement would be effected by paying it to the State, except insofar as other taxation would be diminished. It is evident, too, that material progress in any district does not necessarily mean increased rent on land there, for the progress may be due to the use of materials coming from other countries. And whenever the rent value of land is increased by population pressure, or by such government improvements as roads, sanitary conveniences, and the like, the taxable value of the land is always increased, so that a large portion of the additional rent is, in fact, appropriated even now by the State authorities. Here it must be admitted, however, that where increase in the value of property is clearly due to the recent growth of the com-

---

[29] *Rerum Novarum*, pp. 26, 27 (*RN*, 35).

munity, or to recent improvements undertaken by the State, and particularly where it is due to the landlord's taking advantage of people's need of shelter, then an attempt to tax all the ascertainable increased rent due to these facts would be very desirable, and one would here contest the arguments of Henry George's followers.

In this latter connection, however, a very practical difficulty to Henry George's plan exists. It would be extremely difficult for the collector of the rent tax to calculate the exact yield on farm land, owing to the chance effects of unfavorable weather; it would also be difficult to differentiate the rent yield from the yield due to other factors: interest on capital, expenditures on sanitation, transportation, desirable locality, superior managerial ability in planning the use of land, finding suitable tenants, and the like.

Another practical difficulty is that the tax yield under the proposed Henry George system would be more or less fixed, whereas government financial needs fluctuate.

The more moderate Georgists, not denying the right to landownership, merely wish the State to take the surplus whenever land is sold at a higher figure than that which we originally paid for it. If this higher figure were due to urban amenities, such as good roads, or the provision of transportation, sanitary conveniences, electricity, and the like, a tax of this nature might be very desirable, although it would be extremely difficult to ascertain in how far the increased sales value was due to other causes. Yet if the State were to receive the increased sales value, obviously no one would be willing to pay a higher price than the original value, unless there were several competitors eager to have the site for business purposes, or for security of possession as a consumption good with possible hereditable transmission. Furthermore, if landowners had to pay the capital appreciation on their property to the State, it would be just that the State should compensate the landowner who sold his land for less than the price previously paid for it. For nowadays as many acres of land decrease in value as have an enhanced valuation placed upon them. Any sizable city has its derelict houses in districts which were once fashionable or bore high rent yields.

Although many followers of George still exist, which is the reason for devoting so much space to this theory, on the whole serious economists do not in any way subscribe to the practical application of his theories, even if they admit that there is much truth in the fact that many landowners receive high rents for no service rendered to mankind. Yet it is equally true that the same criticism can be leveled at many stockholders and many entrepreneurs of business enterprises. Only too frequently men have interpreted their right to own private property, in the grossly exaggerated sense of a right to excessively large profits, rent, interest, or industrial power, at the expense of the propertyless laborer and the unprotected small owner. The Catholic doctrine of man's natural right to own property is, of course, quite otherwise.

CHAPTER 12

OCCUPATIONAL SOCIETY

Work Necessary for Man

MAN must work in order to live. There is no gainsaying this statement. God gave the earth to man to provide him with sustenance, but despite the abundance of the fruits of the earth, man would soon die if he did not seek his food and provide himself with shelter. "And the Lord God took man, and put him into a paradise of pleasure, to dress it, and to keep it."[1]

To lead even the simplest life man must hunt, fish, gather in fruits, and labor in many other ways to avail himself of nature's supplies. Many of nature's goods need complicated services to make them of use; for example, it is not enough that cotton be grown, but it must be picked, and ginned, and spun, and woven, and bleached, and dyed before it can be used for making a dress. Most of man's requirements can be provided for only by work. Before Adam's fall, seeking the wherewithal to sustain life was a pleasurable occupation: since that time the earth has yielded man life only "in the sweat of his face."[2] Yet work is none the less honorable for being arduous. Although in pre-Christian times work was regarded as dishonorable by all except the Jews, Christ Himself rendered it noble and dignified it in His own person and His Gospels.[3]

Man is bound to work for four main reasons: (1) He has a duty to himself to maintain his own life.[4] (2) He has a duty to provide for those dependent upon him. (3) He has a duty to contribute to the general welfare of society. (4) He has a duty to God, not only to preserve his own life, but also to use the gifts of nature and to develop his faculties conformable to the divine will.

Despite man's obligation to work, however, not all men are bound to provide for their own sustenance, or that of their dependents. The rich, for example, have a right to live on the proceeds of their riches. Neither

---

[1] Gen. 2:15.
[2] Gen. 3:19.
[3] Cf. *Rerum Novarum*, p. 14 (*RN*, 20).
[4] Cf. 2 Thess. 3:10: "If any man will not work, neither let him eat." Note, however, the qualification in the next paragraph. Cf. pp. 20, 21 (*Q4*, 23).

is there an obligation to work hard during all one's waking hours. A certain amount of recreation and rest is essential; social intercourse or the pursuit of the arts may afford us great pleasure and yet be our duty; and it is at least advisable to have leisure time for personal development.

But no one may be idle, for, as we have just stated, man has a duty to lead an honest and useful life in society, and a duty to use the gifts of nature and to develop his personal gifts and faculties. Work, indeed, develops not only physical and mental powers, but moral qualities also, and all labor, if done for a good purpose, has a high moral quality. And if we are fortunate to work at the type of labor for which our gifts and aptitudes best fit us, then work becomes a pleasurable occupation, for men are always happy when they are doing what they are able to accomplish with relative ease and notable skill.

The Division of Labor

From the earliest times man had discovered that he does not live "by bread alone." Evidence of the existence of deer, ox, bison, the horse, and other animals in some way connected with man goes back to pre-Chellean times. In the late Paleolithic period we find evidence of barley, harpoons, arrowheads, and fishhooks. By the neolithic times man had domesticated the cow, the sheep, the pig, the goat, and the dog, and there are clear traces that agriculture was carried on. Spinning whorls were discovered in the ashes of the Aurignacian caves.

The most primitive peoples of today are food gatherers, but usually the men provide the flesh food by snaring and hunting, fishing or gathering shellfish, and the women collect the vegetable products. Next in order of material development come the peoples to whom Schmidt assigns the title of "primary grade" who, he says, represent the late paleolithic *coup de poing* and bone civilization. If this analogy is correct as regards economic organization, then early man quickly developed different types of economic organization. For among the present-day peoples of the "primary grade" we find that some are nomadic cattle raisers, and others have developed agriculture. The cattle raisers often breed such animals as reindeer and horse, and among this group women do not have the position of equality which they enjoy in the most primitive tribes, because they are no longer needed economically to collect vegetable foods and other provisions.[5]

---

[5] Schmidt, Rev. W., "The Position of Women with Regard to Property in Primitive Society," *American Anthropologist,* n.s. XXXVII, 1935, p. 246.

The agricultural peoples, represented by the primitives of East and West Australia, Central Melanesia, parts of Indonesia, East and West Africa, North and South America, have a high development of agriculture, and women usually predominate in the economic and social organization.

It is highly probable that Father Schmidt[6] and others are correct, that after man had first differentiated himself in tribes, some developing agriculture, and others herding, then peoples from the different types of economic life intermarried as time and circumstance arranged. This intermarriage of peoples with differing economic life brought about all the combinations of early economic organization.

So far as actual historical records show, far back in history we find that some tilled the soil, and others hunted, and discovering that he had needs other than the material, man soon gave part of the fruits of his labor to such specialists as the priest, the medicine man, and those who administered justice in the tribe. First there was probably a simple family division of labor, as there is today among the most primitive tribes. Later a friendly co-operation grew within the tribes and eventually, in the course of time, specialized trades grew up. While the majority of families would still care for their own needs, others with special aptitudes for certain tasks, would devote their labor to the different arts and crafts, to government and other necessary work, receiving goods or money in return.

Definition of Occupational Society: A Primary But Not a Natural Society

The division of labor soon led to an elaborate organization of economic life. In an earlier chapter we defined occupational society as the regulation of man's labor and its organization into groups which function within civil society, that is, within the State. Occupational society is, as we said, a primary society because man has not only an aptitude and propensity for it, but also a fundamental need of it. It is not a natural society, because whereas natural societies have, of necessity, an exigency in nature, and this exigency is proximate in domestic, religious, and civil societies; in occupational society it is comparatively remote. In earlier times it might even have been denied that occupational society was primary, since it would have been possible

---

[6] Father Schmidt claims to have scientific proof of such a development from his careful examination of primitive tribes of today although it would seem that his picture of early development is too schematic to be taken as a reliable picture of prehistoric times.

for all except the very young, the aged, and the infirm to grow crops or to gather fruits and kill wild animals for sustenance. Yet although man might be able to exist without the organized division of labor, this co-operation enables each of us to specialize in certain tasks and thus to be more useful in this world, to produce more wealth, to enjoy more goods, and frequently to develop our gifts and aptitudes in a manner which gives us greater joy in satisfactory achievement.

Occupational society is a constituent element of civil society, and functions within that group as remotely natural. This Pope Pius himself indicates when he says:

"Just as the citizens of the same municipality are wont to form associations with diverse aims, which various individuals are free to join or not, similarly, those who are engaged in the same trade or profession will form free associations among themselves, for purposes connected with their occupations."[7] And again he says "For as nature induces those who dwell in close proximity to unite into municipalities, so those who practice the same trade or profession, economic or otherwise, combine into gilds or organizations. These groups, in a true sense autonomous, are considered by many to be, if not essential to civil society, at least its natural and spontaneous development."[8]

Economic Systems of the Past

The systems which man has devised for the better organization of the division of labor, as shown by ethnographical reports and historical records, have been of diverse kinds.

We find in the Book of Genesis that Abel was a shepherd, while Cain, his brother, tilled the soil. And later, toward the close of the antediluvian period we find the first mention of industrial organization, when we read that Tubalcain was a hammerer and artificer of every work of brass and iron, while his half brother Jubal "was the father of them that play upon the harp and organs."[9] When Solomon built his temple, the Jews, being then agricultural people, exchanged with Hiram of Tyre their wheat, barley, oil, and wine for skilled workers and the priceless timber of Libanus and other luxury goods.

To give the organization of one of the simpler tribes of today, let us consider the Bambara peoples.[10] The Bambara are not primitive

---

[7] *Quadragesimo Anno*, p. 28 (*QA*, 29).

[8] *Ibid.*, p. 27 (*QA*, 29).

[9] Cf. Gen. 4:2, 17, 21, 22.

[10] Cf. Henry, J., *l'Ame d' un peuple africain:* Les Bambara; Monteil, Ch., *Les Bambara de Ségou et du Kaarta, et al.*

but their culture is decidedly of a low order. Their history goes back to the seventeenth century, when they fled from the southern highlands of Upper Gambia, to escape their enemies, and settled among a tribe to the east of that territory, in the French Sudan. They remained in the Sudan ever since that time, and as the peoples they settled with had adopted the religion of Islam, the Bambara, too, adopted this religion. The Bambara are pre-eminently agriculturists. Both the men and women work in the fields, but so far as the division of labor is concerned, the women do the lion's share of the work. They are not slaves, however. They enjoy full liberty, and divide the hard work among themselves in such manner that each has her free week to go to the market, and there speak to her neighbors in the public places and where she will. In addition to the work in the fields, the men cut the necessary wood for household purposes, and they do the sewing. During the dry season they pass their hours sewing, plaiting rushes, straw, or millet stalks, and weaving. Their output is small, however, and fishing, works of art such as the forging of jewelry, wood carving, pottery, tooled leather have all been left to the non-Bambara peoples near whom they live. Some of the men belong to hunting associations and occasionally hunt the hyena and other animals. Although the men cut the wood, the women have the hard work of carrying it. To the women also falls the lot of cookery, cotton spinning, beer making, the pounding of sorghum and millet, and the care of the poultry yard. Despite her life of hard work, the Bambara woman "keeps her hut and her interior court clean, and if she has only a rag to give her children, at least she washes them, and anoints them with oil and butter, so that the Sudan cabins are not filthy as are the Algerian Arab huts."[11]

At various times within the history of man, slave systems have regulated labor. Such was true in the time of King Hammurabi, and in the economy of Ancient Egypt, Greece, and Rome.

One of the best known of the later organizations of economic life is the manorial system of feudal times, which took the place of the later Roman system. Within the Roman Empire of later days all persons had been equal before the law, the only distinction being temporary tenure of office; ownership of the land was absolute, freely passed by inheritance; the arts and literature flourished. This relatively high material development was ended by the rude nomadic tribes who overran the plains of Gaul, Spain, Italy, and the rest, coming from the countries now known as Germany, Scandinavia, and Russia. Keeping

---

[11] Henry, *op. cit.*, p. 9.

their hold by military rule, the feudal system arose, and under it the former absolute ownership of land was destroyed. Land was then held by the king, who ceded it to the various lords to be used in return for a promise to provide men in case of war. Highly developed agriculture, based on a militaristic social system was the characteristic of these times. It was during these times that woman lost her rights of person and property except insofar as she was protected by the Church.

Another well-known system of the Western world is the guild system of the towns, which developed side by side with later feudalism. The craft guilds, private associations of small craftsmen; and the merchant guilds or organizations of merchants, had a self-protective element somewhat similar to modern trade-unions, insofar as they protected themselves against the dominion of the kings and nobles. But they were an occupational organization of a kind which has not been duplicated in history. The craft guilds in particular aimed at preserving and fostering the best workmanship, and honesty in the material, character, and time of the work; they tried to secure, too, the religious and physical wellbeing of the workers and their families. In addition, therefore, to securing fair wages, and helping unemployment, they also guaranteed good work in return, and they saw that the wages were well spent. Even though the journeymen had their separate organizations, their rights and those of the apprentices were definitely watched and safeguarded. The abuses that crept in and helped ultimately to bring about the downfall of these guilds does not detract from the utility of their ideals for a well-ordered economic organization based upon the natural dignity of man and work.

Space does not permit the outlining of other economic systems which have existed within historical times. The organization of economic life as it exists today in the Western world is, of course, the capitalistic order. Modern capitalism is characterized by an extreme division of labor in large-scale industry, and by the predominant importance of capital rather than labor; it is based upon a recognition of man's right to own private property, and upon free competition. We shall now examine modern capitalism in some detail.

Economic Organization Under Capitalism

There are four factors in production: Land, labor, capital, and organization.

Land. Land gives support for men and buildings, it provides extension by which men and goods can move from place to place; it gives the geographical aid of rivers, mountains, seas, and plains, and of

THE DIVISION OF LABOR IN THE UNITED STATES (IN 1930)[12]

Occupational Distribution of the Population of the United States in 1930

Occupation	Males	Females	Total	Per Cent All Workers
Agriculture	9,562,059	909,939	10,471,998	21.4
Forestry and fishing	250,140	329	250,469	0.5
Extraction of minerals	983,564	759	984,323	2.0
Manufacturing and mechanical industries	12,224,345	1,886,307	14,110,652	28.9
Transport and communication	3,561,943	281,204	3,843,147	7.9
Trade	5,118,787	962,680	6,081,467	12.5
Public service (not elsewhere classified)	838,622	17,583	856,205	1.8
Professional service	1,727,650	1,526,234	3,253,884	6.7
Domestic and personal service	1,772,200	3,180,251	4,952,451	10.1
Clerical occupations	2,038,494	1,986,830	4,025,324	8.2
Total: all occupations	38,077,804	10,752,116	48,829,920	100.0

electrical forces and explosive power of gases; and it supplies all vegetable, animal, and mineral matters of use in economic life.

Capital. Capital is a fund of wealth — goods made in the past and stored up to aid production in the future. Capital goods are the produced means of production. The resources of nature, intrinsically more important than any other factor in production, are often only utilizable after man has fashioned them or changed them, or transported them from where they are procured in abundance to where they are very scarce. In modern times, with the extreme division of labor, capital goods are needed more than ever before. Originally, of course, capital goods came from the land, but being themselves transformed into tools or machinery, they help to transform other products of the land and are useful in this indirect productive capacity, rather than for direct enjoyment or consumption. There is, for example, the need of an ax, a saw, various types of machinery, varnishes, and many other things to transform the growing tree into a desk; and trucks and trains and storage places are usually needed to get the desk to the final buyer.

Labor. To use the capital goods and to change the raw materials from the land into valuable economic goods, labor is also an essential factor in production. There is no question that the work of man is a necessity of production and is of extreme importance. Whether men

---

[12] *Statistical Abstract of the United States*, 1937, p. 55. Total population of the United States: Males, 62,137,080; Females, 60,637,966; Total: 122,775,046. The percentage of gainfully employed was, therefore, 49.5 per cent. (See *Statistical Abstract*, 1937, p. 10.)

enter into economic activity for the primary purpose of acquiring by
their labor the wherewithal to satisfy their wants; whether it is because of interest in the work for its own sake, because of love of the
distinction, power, or position which may come with the work; or
because of a desire to help their fellow men by their aptitudes and
gifts, labor is the work of a dignified living being, and essentially of
more importance than any other factor. As a result of the extreme
division of labor, the tendency of modern times has been to treat men
as mechanical factors rather than as dignified human beings playing an
important and very necessary role in economic life. Workers are termed
"labor" or "hands," impersonal expressions which sometimes lead to a
lack of human consideration for the laborer himself.

Domination of Capital. Under modern capitalism capital predomi-
nates, and production is undertaken not so much for the use value of
goods, for the mutual well-being of employer and employed, and for
the social character of economic activity, as for the exchange value of
products and the profits to be gained. Large-scale industry has forced
the workers into closely packed urban communities where, despite their
theoretical individual freedom, they are completely dependent on an
uncertain money income to obtain their daily bread. Since faulty organization of banking and industry together with other factors lead to
periodic depressions, this dependence of the worker on the wage system
has disastrous consequences to both his material and his moral well-
being. Modern industry has, indeed, so organized the large-scale production and distribution of products that even the consumer is in some
measure dominated by the corporation directors, who make final decisions as to the type of good to be produced and the price at which
goods must be sold. The unplanned market mechanism of twentieth-
century capitalism has led to great extreme of poverty and riches, and
to an increasing insecurity in the tenure of material goods. With widespread unemployment, poverty, and graft, it is very questionable
whether we are more advanced in non-material ways than under some
of the economic organizations of other peoples or of other times.

It seems apt here to quote Pope Pius XI on the exploitation of labor
by the capitalists, despite the mutual need of these two factors.

"Now the natural law, or rather, God's Will manifested by it, demands that right order be observed in the application of natural
resources to human need; and this order consists in everything having
its proper owner. Hence it follows that unless a man apply his labor
to his own property, an alliance must be formed between his toil and
his neighbor's property, for each is helpless without the other. This

was what Leo XIII had in mind when he wrote: 'Capital cannot do without labor, nor labor without capital.' It is therefore entirely false to ascribe the results of their combined efforts to either party alone; and it is flagrantly unjust that either should deny the efficacy of the other and seize all the profits.

"Capital, however, was long able to appropriate to itself excessive advantages; it claimed all the products and profits and left to the laborer the barest minimum necessary to repair his strength and to insure the continuation of his class. For by an inexorable economic law, it was held, all accumulation of riches must fall to the share of the wealthy, while the workingman must remain perpetually in indigence or reduced to the minimum needed for existence. It is true that the actual state of things was not always and everywhere as deplorable as the Liberalistic tenets of the so-called Manchester School might lead us to conclude; but it cannot be denied that a steady drift of economic and social tendencies was in this direction. These false opinions and specious axioms were vehemently attacked, as was to be expected, and by others also than merely those whom such principles deprived of their innate right to better their condition.

"The cause of the harassed workingman was espoused by the intellectuals, as they are called, who set up in opposition to this fictitious law another equally false moral principle: that all products and profits, excepting those required to repair and replace invested capital, belong by every right to the workingman. This error, more subtle than that of the socialists who hold that all means of production should be transferred to the State, or, as they term it, socialized, is for that reason more dangerous and apt to deceive the unwary. It is an alluring poison, consumed with avidity by many not deceived by open socialism."[13]

Of course capital has been used in productive enterprise ever since the time when man first realized the advantage of storing up some of the goods he produced to aid in future production. The profit motive, too, has always been the average man's incentive to put forth his best efforts in work. The special characteristic of capitalism is not, therefore, the existence of capital and the profit motive! Rather it is the fact that money interests and the profit motive have been allowed to dominate the human aspects of industrial enterprise.

Materialistic profit-seeking is the chief end of modern capitalistic organization, and socially irresponsible corporations are a menace to

---

[13] *Quadragesimo Anno*, pp. 18–20 (*QA*, 19–22).

the consumer, the worker, and the general welfare of the people organized into world-states. Workers may be dismissed because the management finds it more profitable to move the plant elsewhere; they are forced to leave their home and neighborhood to seek work in distant places;[14] they become unemployed as soon as younger men can do their task more quickly; or their work may cease because the entrepreneurs have overestimated the needs of the unascertained market for which modern economic enterprise produces. Workers are individual "hands"; they are not considered as persons with human feelings and human needs. Wages tend to be the minimum the workers' bargaining power can secure. The stockholders (the owners of modern business) and the bondholders who make further capital available for industry's needs, are solely concerned with their dividends and their interest payments; the conduct of affairs is left to the directors and to the working of the falsely named natural law of "free competition." The workers frequently work merely for the wage which their labor will produce, and do not take a pride in their work, to insure a maximum output of the best possible quality. The consumer, whose needs are the object of economic pursuit, must usually pay such prices as are the highest that the "market will bear" because, as we said, competitive prices are largely fixed by corporations with semi-monopolistic power. Although nominally free, there is a large element of slavery in our modern economic life.

Organization. We have now discussed land, capital, and labor as three factors of production. A fourth is organization. A man has little chance to have his own one-man business or small partnership in modern times. Occasionally he can do so, either by himself owning the needed capital and land or by borrowing capital privately, or needing little capital because his services predominate in the work he is engaged in. Such are many professional people, dressmakers, small farmers. However, instances of this kind are rare, and a specialized type of labor, distinct from the ordinary worker has therefore come into being: organizers or entrepreneurs, who find the necessary land and capital, raw materials, and men suitable for creating the utilities involved in production. The entrepreneur's share in the fruits of production is called wages of management and profits. In these times of large-scale production, it is rare for the entrepreneur to provide even two factors

---

[14] In such situations as these the practical sociologist could render much service by pointing out the danger to the stability and well-being of the community when ties of family, home, neighborhood, educational and recreational society are so ruthlessly destroyed.

of production, capital as well as management. Business is on too large a scale for one man or a partnership to secure the necessary finances from personal funds and private borrowing. The average earnings of this rapidly dying type of owner-manager are normally lower than the average salary earnings of people performing the same type of work for a large-scale employer.

Entrepreneurs, therefore, usually provide only the organizing ability, and the capital is secured by stock and bond issues. Since relatively few people have the necessary ability to organize large-scale business for others, entrepreneurs who can take charge of the larger modern corporations often have a high scarcity value, and perhaps can legitimately claim large remuneration. Frequently only the broader managerial policies are determined by corporation entrepreneurs, and hired managers are employed for the detailed direction. Hired managers, of course, are really a "labor" factor in production and not the specialized entrepreneurs. Their interests, however, are on the side of the entrepreneurs and capitalists rather than the workers who labor under their direction, and the share of these higher corporation officers as well as of the entrepreneurs, is frequently out of all proportion to the possible value of their services. The abuse of the power of corporation entrepreneurs over large-scale financial resources is one of the evils of the capitalistic system which calls for speedy remedy, as does the excessive proportion of production's product which goes to the capital owner who, generally speaking, is a "silent partner."

Again, we may quote Pope Pius XI on this subject. Pointing out that particularly in our day man's faculties have been so deranged that he is easily led astray by low desires, and is strongly tempted to prefer the goods of earth to those of heaven, he says:

"For the uncertainty of economic conditions and of the whole economic regime demands the keenest and most unceasing straining of energy on the part of those engaged therein; and as a result, some have become so hardened against the stings of conscience as to hold all means good which enable them to increase their profits, and to safeguard against sudden changes of fortune the wealth amassed by unremitting toil. Easy returns, which an open market offers to anyone, lead many to interest themselves in trade and exchange, their one aim being to make clear profits with the least labor. By their unchecked speculation prices are raised and lowered out of mere greed for gain, making void all the most prudent calculations of manufacturers.

"The regulations legally enacted for corporations, with their divided responsibility and limited liability, have given occasion to abominable abuses. The greatly weakened accountability makes little impression, as is evident, upon the conscience. The worst injustices and frauds take place beneath the obscurity of the common name of a corporative firm. Boards of directors proceed in their unconscionable methods even to the violation of their trust in regard to those whose savings they administer. In the last place must be mentioned the unscrupulous but well-calculated speculation of men who, without seeking to answer real needs, appeal to the lowest human passions. These are aroused in order to turn their satisfaction into gain. . . .

"With the leaders of business abandoning the true path, it is not surprising that in every country multitudes of workingmen, too, sank in the same morass: all the more so, because very many employers treated their workmen as mere tools, without any concern for the welfare of their souls, indeed, without the slightest thought of higher interests."[15]

The most striking picture given us by Pope Pius XI is his description of what he styles the "despotic economic domination of our day." He writes:

"In the first place, then, it is patent that in our days not alone is wealth accumulated, but immense power and despotic economic domination is concentrated in the hands of a few, and that those few are frequently not the owners, but only the trustees and directors of invested funds, who administer them at their good pleasure.

"This power becomes particularly irresistible when exercised by those who, because they hold and control money, are able also to govern credit and determine its allotment, for that reason supplying so to speak, the lifeblood to the entire economic body, and grasping, as it were, in their hands the very soul of production, so that no one dare breathe against their will.

"This accumulation of power, the characteristic note of the modern economic order, is a natural result of limitless free competition which permits the survival of those only who are the strongest, which often means those who fight most relentlessly, who pay least heed to the dictates of conscience.

"This concentration of power has led to a threefold struggle for domination. First, there is the struggle for dictatorship in the economic sphere itself; then, the fierce battle to acquire control of the state, so that its resources and authority may be abused in the economic struggles. Finally, the clash between states themselves.

---

[15] *Quadragesimo Anno*, pp. 41–43 (*QA*, 45).

"This latter arises from two causes: because the nations apply their power and political influence, regardless of circumstances, to promote the economic advantages of their citizens; and because, vice versa, economic forces and economic domination are used to decide political controversies between peoples.

"You assuredly know, Venerable Brethren and Beloved Children, and you lament the ultimate consequences of this Individualistic spirit in economic affairs. Free competition is dead; economic dictatorship has taken its place.

"Unbridled ambition for domination has succeeded the desire for gain; the whole economic life has become hard, cruel, and relentless in a ghastly measure. Furthermore, the intermingling and scandalous confusing of the duties and offices of civil authority and of economics have produced crying evils and have gone so far as to degrade the majesty of the state. The state which should be the supreme arbiter, ruling in kingly fashion far above all party contention, intent only upon justice and the common good, has become instead a slave, bound over to the service of human passion and greed. As regards the relations of peoples among themselves, a double stream has issued forth from this one fountainhead: on the one hand, economic nationalism or even economic imperialism; on the other, a not less noxious and detestable internationalism or international imperialism in financial affairs, which holds that where a man's fortune is, there is his country."[16]

Philosophy of Capitalism and Its Results

Modern capitalism is largely the outcome of a philosophy of liberalism which assumes that all men are equal and should be free to attain their economic ends without restraint. If this philosophy were a correct one, if all men were really equal, and if all were equally responsible, there would be little to criticize in an organization by which some provide land and capital, some labor, and others organization. Certainly capitalism has resulted in an enormous extension of want-satisfying goods and services of a material order which we enjoy as a characteristic of our age. Our present Western civilization is more developed materially than any civilization recorded in the history of mankind. Industry is more scientifically organized, and wealth is much more productive. There are many good features about our modern economic life, with its widespread adoption of industrial and scientific inventions, the cheap and speedy means of travel, the provision of many luxuries and comforts which were unobtainable by the

---

[16] *Ibid.*, pp. 32, 33 (*QA,* 34, 35).

average person before this century. All men are theoretically free, and the able and gifted can rise to wealth and power in a manner rarely possible before. Even workers, by their small stockholdings, can share in the ownership of business — although this function is distinct from the labor they provide in the economic organizations; and they have no control, of course, in any of the enterprises in which they have placed their savings. Scientific progress has been greatly promoted by capital accumulations and the profit incentive which the system has provided. Excellent medical attention and free education are furnished for the masses to a degree which history has never before recorded. By means of airplanes and mass-production supplies, we can assist the victims of any big disaster within an incredibly short period of time.

However, as we pointed out when discussing man's human rights, men differ physically, in mental ability, in moral character, in education, opportunity, the amount of wealth they inherit, and in many other ways. They are not all equal in the sense which capitalism assumes. The natural outcome of the philosophy of liberalism has been individualistic lack of social responsibility, and the unbridled competition has led to the concentration of economic wealth and the powerful domination of the wealthy. In the precapitalistic era of the Middle Ages men did not usually forget that they were all members of the same human race; and they regarded their possessions as bringing with them social responsibilities. The maldistribution of wealth, which was not absent in the Middle Ages, was emphasized when capitalism made possible the securing of raw materials from the ends of the earth, and the marketing of products in the far corners of this globe. It was further increased by corporate organization, so that although there is widespread ownership of the capital concerned, its control is in the hands of a few corporation directors and investment bankers. Trade associations and price agreements have led to an amount of price fixing which entirely destroys "free competition" in many industries, and gives the producers concerned semi-monopolistic power. Materialistic individualism left the propertyless unprotected, and led to the monopolistic abuses which are so evident today, including the risks of unemployment and dependency upon relief measures.

The Legitimacy of Interest

Since the whole capitalistic system is dependent upon the payment of interest upon capital, the question of interest on capital and its monetary equivalent is here of great importance, for its legitimacy is sometimes questioned.

Interest must be clearly distinguished from profits. Profits mean the surplus earned by the entrepreneur of a business over and above the expenses of production, including his wages of management and interest on his capital; or the net income received by stockholder or the owners of a private business after all costs, including wages of management and interest, have been taken care of. Competition tends to make profits disappear, and many organizers and business owners do not make any profits at all, although their business is successful to the extent that rent is paid for the use of land, wages for labor and organization, and interest on the capital needed. Often profits are made because of what is called "good will," which means that repeat orders are received with a minimum of selling cost because people like the producer or his products, and come to rely upon the goods sold under his trade-mark, or upon his recommendation. Good will can only be acquired by the undertaking of business risks in the past, or by a long-continued provision of reliable products and services, and the lack of it is one of the barriers which outsiders must overcome in the establishment of a business. The entrepreneur or the stockholders claim profits because they undertake the risk of producing in anticipation of demand. Frequently anticipated profits are nonexistent because of fluctuations in costs, temporary overproduction, or changes in the social habits of the community, or because production is interfered with in some way. Sometimes monopoly profits arise by reason of patent rights, trusts, pools, or other devices which allow the producer the opportunity of so limiting output that the price will never fall to a point where it is only equal to the cost. Here profits and interest are usually out of all proportion to the common good.

Interest is the payment made for the use of wealth, expressed in terms of money which, generally speaking, belongs to someone else. Interest, therefore, is payment for the use of a certain amount of money (or value or credit expressed in terms of money) for a certain length of time. Although wealth or its monetary equivalent is sometimes borrowed for consumptive purposes, most borrowings are for the purchase of needed capital goods or land, or to provide money or credit for wages and other productive needs; and they may be used for speculation.

Capital exists for two reasons. First, because part of the expenses of production are reserved for depreciation and obsolescence, and these replacement funds are available for investment until needed for their original purpose. Second, because laborers as a whole produce more than they receive, that is, there is a surplus productive power, and this surplus is saved. If laborers received all the surplus product in wages, unless they themselves saved up capital, there could be no production under present-day conditions of the division of labor, with its large capital needs. On the other hand, the difficulty at the present time seems to be the fact that too much capital or its monetary equivalent has been saved by the well-to-do, whereas the wages paid to workers are too inadequate to enable the general public to have sufficient purchasing power to absorb surplus production.

In modern times we use the word *interest* for a normal and reasonable payment, and *usury* for what is considered an unduly large exaction for the use of money. The word was used rather indiscriminately in former times, and interest was often forbidden in the past. The Hebrew, for example, was forbidden by the Mosaic Law to charge interest to his poor neighbor: "If thou lend money to any of my people that is poor, that dwelleth with thee: thou shalt not be hard with them as an extortioner, nor oppress them with usuries. If thou take of thy neighbor a garment in pledge; thou shalt give it him again before sunset."[17] Indeed, it was strictly forbidden to charge usury to any fellow Hebrew, although interest might be taken if money were lent to a stranger — presumably on the grounds that the foreigner himself took interest from the Hebrew when he in turn lent the latter money: "Thou shalt not lend to thy brother money to usury, nor corn, nor any other thing: But to the stranger."[18] Again, interest seems to be positively discouraged in the Psalm, wherein is praised "he that hath not put out his money to usury."[19]

Christ said: "If you lend to them of whom you hope to receive, what thanks are to you? For sinners also lend to sinners for to receive as much."[20] Yet in a parable He put these words into the mouth of the nobleman, who reprimanded his servant: "And why then didst thou not give my money into the bank, that at my coming I might have exacted it with usury?"[21] Quite early in the Christian era, interest was frowned on. Perhaps this was due to Christian charity and religious fervor, or to a reaction against the Roman regime under which usurious interest rates were very common, although both Greeks and Romans considered moneylending a detestable profession.[22] Or perhaps it was a

---

[17] Exod. 21:25, 26; cf. also Levit. 25:36, 37.
[18] Deut. 13:19, 20.
[19] Ps. 14:5; cf. also Ezech. 18:8, 13, 17.
[20] Luke 6:34.
[21] Luke 19:23.
[22] Cf. Cicero, *De Officiis*, I, xlii; Plato, *Laws*, v, 742, 743 *et al.*

reversal to the ancient Greek thought of Aristotle,[23] that money should earn no interest because its purpose was to facilitate exchange, and in itself it was sterile. All the early Church fathers; SS. Ambrose, Jerome, Augustine, Basil, Gregory of Nyssa, John Chrysostom, were against lending and borrowing at interest. As early as A.D. 314 and 325, at the Councils of Arles and Nicaea respectively, Christian clerics were strictly forbidden to charge interest, and in A.D. 848 the Synod of Meaux extended the prohibition to lay people.

The scholastics of the twelfth and thirteenth centuries were especially strong in their pronouncements against it; but this prohibition was probably due to the economic conditions of the time, and there is no indication that obstacles were intended to be put in the way of production. Some of them considered the taking of interest as a sin against charity, but not against justice. Actually there was a dearth of money in Europe until the silver mines of America were utilized some centuries later. Although credit instruments were in use, the widespread use of credit is a feature peculiar to our twentieth century. When money was borrowed in the Middle Ages, it was nearly always for consumptive and not for productive use. Money could not then be invested in land, to earn rent, because nearly all the land belonged to the nobles or clerics, or was leased to them by the king, and they either could not or would not sell: but if a man lent animals or the use of his trees or land to another, it was considered right that a portion of the natural increase should belong to him, and this was not prohibited. Similarly, money could not as a rule be invested in industry, for the guilds regulated trade, and allowed no one to operate a trade unless he himself personally conducted it and worked alongside his journeymen and apprentices. Local home trade was small, and foreign trade extremely limited. There was no prohibition against receiving rent for land, and the sharing of a part of the profits made on a business contract of partnership was not interfered with, even if the partner were a "silent" one, because the money was invested at the owner's risk of there being losses and no profits at all.

But ordinarily, apart from partnership contracts, if a man had surplus money or other forms of wealth, he could do with it only one of three things. First, he could spend it for personal use, buy jewelry or other goods for storage against future needs, improve his castle or his lands, or increase his retinue. Secondly, he could use it for charity, for the relief of the poor, or for the construction of roads, bridges, and

---

[23] Cf. Aristotle, *Politics*, I, III.

similar enterprises. The third alternative was to hoard it. The Church's prohibition was, therefore, adequate for the times, for if money were lent it would nearly always be for consumptive and not for productive needs.

It was after the Black Death in England that money rather than land came to be considered as desirable property, giving the owner a non-Christian sense of absolute ownership which was not present at the time when landowners usually realized their duties toward those who lived on their estates. Apart from any moral issue, industrial and commercial conditions changed, and large loans grew to be a necessity in the conduct of affairs, as production became more roundabout and therefore needed more capital goods. A change then came about in the Church legislation, suited to the new circumstances in the economic world.

The most authoritative of the philosophers of the times, St. Thomas Aquinas, made a distinction in his discussion of interest between fungible and nonfungible goods. Fungible goods are goods consumed in the use, such as food. Aquinas considered that money came under this category for he maintained that its use was in its consumption or alienation, so that its use and consumption are inseparable. Since to sell something and also to charge for the use of it would not be just, St. Thomas stated that to get a fee for the use of money lent as well as to get the return of the money would not be a just equivalence in sale and therefore interest was inadmissible. Nonfungible goods are those in which consumption and use can be separated, such as a house or an ornament, and the charging of a fee for the use of these was considered quite in order. In time, therefore, prohibition was replaced by regulation, and only an unjust interest rate was declared usury and forbidden. At first, interest was allowed because of the supposed loss suffered by the owner in foregoing the personal use of his money during the period it is lent to others (*lucrum cessans*), on the ground that profits ceased which might have been made in a business partnership. Or it was permitted because of the risk incurred in entrusting wealth to the borrower (*periculum sortis*); or because of some loss arising from the loan (*damnum emergens*). Authority was given to a prince to exact interest as a result of his legal authority (*titulus legis*); and sometimes people were allowed to state that a loan must be paid back within a few days of borrowing, and if this was not done then a penalty (*poena conventionalis*) was exacted for the *mora* or delay.

At the present day, various reasons are given by the economists to justify the need of interest payments. Interest is primarily justified because it is not now feasible to store up wealth in grain, precious metals, and other past forms of providing for the future. The acquisition of money and liens on others' debts is the modern method of making this provision for the future. Now there is a demand for the loan of money so that capital goods can be bought, and wages can be paid before labor turns goods into finished products. Interest on money is therefore justified for the use which can be made of the land and capital goods which it can buy. Capital goods increase man's production, are needed to produce other goods, reproduce themselves in the product made, increase productivity or the supply of wealth, and therefore merit a division of the increment which comes from production. Yet it must be admitted that if interest is allowed on this ground alone, it would be difficult to justify the taking of interest on an unproductive loan.

The supply of capital goods or their monetary equivalent is limited, so a second argument in favor of interest payment is this scarcity coupled with the above-mentioned need. While man has many motives for saving, such as a desire to provide for contingencies, ambition for success and social esteem, the interest to be earned on the use of capital, he has many reasons also for not saving. Some people do not produce sufficiently to save; others lack imagination about future needs, or have insufficient will power to provide for them; others, seeing the uncertainty of the future would rather have present enjoyment of their wealth, or do not wish to take the risk of investing it. People's willingness to save varies with the general security and continuity of economic life, on the attitude toward heirs, the expectancy of life, and the productivity of capital goods.

Three less important arguments are the following: First, the discount theory, because a loan may be considered as a sale, and to return an equivalent a year hence some extra amount is needed (since future goods are, generally speaking, worth less to the normal consumer than present goods of like kind and quantity). This theory does not take into account, however, the possibility that price levels may decrease and so enhance the purchasing power, that is, the value of money. Second, the abstinence theory, which considers interest as the reward of waiting, and as a necessary inducement to the lender to discount the future and to sacrifice present consumption to his own future enjoyment or that of his heirs. Finally, the risk taken is given as a reason for the "scarcity of capital," and hence for allowing interest, since not only must the earner of interest forego the enjoyment of goods which his capital would buy, but his savings must be invested with outsiders. Since the losses and gains on investments in our modern society are rarely predictable, interest charges on unsecured loans are frequently very high. On the other hand, since, strictly speaking, interest must be distinguished from profits and their "dividends," interest frequently takes the form of fixed rates on loans secured by mortgages and in other ways, and it seems definitely unjust that the interest takers should bear so little risk, whereas the workers, and consumers (through price fluctuations) bear the brunt of the vagaries of modern business.

It may be argued that money is not always invested in productive purposes, but is sometimes lent for consumption goods, or to purchase stocks of goods to store up — not for the utility to be gained by the storing, but to create an artificial scarcity and so add to the price — or for some similar practice. While the latter seems to be an unsocial reason, and therefore utterly immoral, one may nowadays justify interest on loans for consumptive purposes in general because the same money might have been lent for productive purposes, and therefore the lender loses the chance of interest and profits. Interest on consumptive loans is, indeed, generally higher than on loans for productive purposes, because the risk undertaken by the lender is the greater according as the security offered is less than that possible to the average businessman. Yet frequently consumptive loans are secured by excellent collateral and, as we just said, it seems difficult to justify interest rates on secured loans which thereby have all risks eliminated, insofar as it is possible to eliminate risks in this world. At the present day most of the governments of the world regulate interest rates which may be charged, at least on consumptive loans. Legal rates have been established in the different states of the United States, and the creditor is often punishable by fine and imprisonment for charging higher rates, which are then called usury. These usury laws are usually evaded by charging fees of various kinds in connection with consumptive loans. The "loan shark" is one of the parasites of modern economic organization, whose exploitation of the public is in some way diminished by the establishment of Morris Banks, Co-operative Credit Unions to which we shall again refer in Chapter 19, and other institutions to help the small borrower of consumptive and productive capital to procure his needs at a moderate interest rate.

The present-day justification of interest, as received by bond and mortgage holders and similar investors, may chiefly be said to be that of *lucrum cessans*. If they had not invested their capital in this manner they might have bought stocks[24] or otherwise have become partners in a business, so that their present investments are alternative to receiving profits (usually in the form of dividends) and interest is justified because of the profits which they thereby forgo.

It is not always unjust if wages do not share equally with capital on marginal production, because it is sometimes the efficient use of capital goods which makes for business success, rather than labor skill and productivity. Yet it cannot be denied that on account of the stress given at the present time to the legitimacy of interest and profits, an undue importance is attached to capital (or its monetary equivalent) as a factor of production. This ideology accords but little with a true notion of the dignity of man. In view of the evident contrast when we compare the high interest rates and also profits received by most capitalists, with the lack of material well-being of the unemployed and many wage earners, it is obvious that the whole question of profits as well as interest needs careful consideration and some measure of reform.

Toward a Better Organization

Despite the evils of our present system, which must be evident from the brief discussion made above, many of the abuses of nineteenth-century industrial development have already been greatly remedied. The inequality of bargaining power between worker and employer is somewhat mitigated by trade-unionism; and some idea of collective responsibility is evident in State labor laws for the health and safety of workers, in education and medical services, and in social-insurance measures where these exist. Working conditions were also voluntarily improved when industrial managers feared a too extensive criticism of their monopolistic abuses, or when they realized that happier and more healthy workers produced more goods and led to a diminished labor turnover. Profit-sharing schemes and family allowances have likewise helped to advance the economic status of some workers. Consumers' co-operation and other self-help schemes have been highly successful in many districts.

But not even the most ardent admirer of modern capitalism can deny that its present organization needs a measure of reconstruction, so that the product of industry may be more equitably shared. It has been shown that in the prosperous year of 1929, 21 per cent of the

---

[24] English readers are asked to note that the American term *stock* is the equivalent of the English *share*. The word *bond* is the American equivalent of the English *stock* or *debenture*.

families of the United States, that is, about six million families, had an income of less than $1,000 a year; about twelve million families, or more than 42 per cent of the total had incomes of less than $1,500; while nearly 20 million families, or about 71 per cent of total families had incomes of less than $2,500. Only about 2 million families, or 8 per cent of the total had an income of more than $5,000, and only about 600,000 families or 2.3 per cent of the total had incomes of over $10,000. The 0.1 per cent of the families at the top, with incomes over $75,000 received almost as much as the 42 per cent of the families at the bottom of the scale.[25]

Before we consider how a reconstruction of society can be effected without a major revolution, with the inevitable hardship which this would effect upon worker and capitalist alike, it would seem best to examine some of the social aspects of modern industrial organization at greater length. This we shall do in the last section of this book, which deals more specifically with modern problems. A discussion of the Vocational Group organization often called Corporatism, as propounded by Pope Pius XI in *Quadragesimo Anno* is, therefore, relegated to Chapter 20, instead of being developed here.

---

[25] Leven, M., Moulton, H. G., Warburton, C., *America's Capacity to Consume,* pp. 55, 56.

CHAPTER 13

INTERNATIONAL SOCIETY

International Society: A Primary But Not a Natural Group

WE SHOWED in Chapter 9 that the organization of individuals and families in various parts of the world into a defined area with a common government is natural to man. Yet the State is not an isolated unit in the world, and the higher the degree of civilization which the world attains, the less is it all-sufficing. The more complicated human needs become, the more specialized industry, the more highly developed the means of transportation, so much the greater is man's interdependence upon other men, so much the more complicated the relations between State and State or, as it is termed, "international relations." Indeed, it is only as a member of the community of nations that the State can now fulfill its ends.

By international society is meant organized harmonious co-operation among all the nations of the world: an amicable federation of the various nations of the world, each working not only toward its own good but also for the good of all other States or nations. As Pope Benedict XV said: "It is most desirable that all states putting aside all their mutual suspicions, unite to form only one society, or even better, one family both for the defense of their respective liberties and the maintenance of the social order."[1]

Since such a society does not yet exist, and since nations have not as yet shown any inclination to submit wholeheartedly to any central authority, it does not seem that we can call it a "natural society." Nevertheless the usefulness of international society would appear to prove that it is a primary group, for just as the individual cannot exist without the family, and just as the family needs group life and the State for its protection and its fuller development, so States need each other. International society should logically be the natural development of civil society and so it may be considered to be at least remotely a primary group.

The International Union of Social Studies, following the idea of

---

[1] Pope Benedict XV, encyclical *Pacem Dei Munus Pulcherrimum.*

Suarez in his *De Legibus,* is firmly of the opinion that international society is a natural group.[2] Religiously, this may appear to be true, since all men have a common destiny. One form of worship of God can alone be the true society, and did all men belong to the true Church, all would indeed be united in brotherhood and mutual understanding in the Mystical Body of Christ, "which is the Church, in the enjoyment of the common Fatherhood of God." St. Augustine, apostrophizing the Catholic Church wrote as follows: "Thou joinest together, not in society only, but in a sort of brotherhood, citizen with citizen, nation with nation, and the whole race of men, by reminding them of their common parentage."[3] World peace is, indeed, the natural law.

But world peace and harmony does not necessarily imply the essential naturalness of a true international society, although such society would appear to be highly desirable and even necessary for the peace and well-being of all nations. Yet even if organized international society did exist, wars might still occur. So it seems that international society may be said to be remotely a primary society, but not a natural one.

The primary character of a proposed international society may be shown for several reasons other than the teachings of the prophets of old, of Christ, and of His Church, as regards the brotherhood of all men.

1. Man has a social need of mutual helpfulness. From the social and cultural viewpoint, each nation has its quota to contribute to the world. It is precisely national differences — the culture and spirit of each nation rich in its divergence from the culture and spirit of the rest, and the peculiar distinction of its genius — which produces the highly developed civilization of the world as it is today. Each nation has an individual contribution which it can make to the common needs of man. Pasteur, Marconi, Abraham Lincoln, Shakespeare, Newton, Edison, Goethe, Beethoven, Gounod, Murillo — to name at random but a few of the many thousands of the world's great men — belong to their respective countries, it is true, but they are likewise the inheritance of the entire world. Man would be poor indeed if he could not participate in the fruits of the greatness and the culture of other nations, no matter how rich might be his own State in natural resources, gifted citizens, and cultural traditions.

2. Economically, too, the more advanced the civilization of a nation,

---

[2] Cf. *A Code of International Ethics,* p. 14.
[3] Quoted by Pope Leo XIII, encyclical *Immortale Dei.*

the greater is its dependence upon other States. With improved methods of transportation each State is enabled to give of its cultural advantages to others, and to participate in the pre-eminence of other States. The value of international trade and specialization is, indeed, clearly recognized, despite the sometimes almost impassable tariff barriers erected to impede international trade and commerce, as a consequence of excessive nationalism, fear, and governmental greed, or as a result of the avarice of the heads of business who make use of political corruption to achieve their ends. As Pope Pius XI said: "It would be well if the various nations in common counsel and endeavor strove to promote a healthy economic co-operation by prudent pacts and institutions, since in economic matters they are largely dependent one upon the other and need one another's help."[4]

3. This interdependence leads to relations between States, and hence man has a political need of international society. Despite the theories of some that the State has absolute sovereignty and is not subject to the moral law, as is individual man, it must, nevertheless, be apparent to all sound thinkers that since the State is composed of individuals, it is bound by the same moral law as they, and by the same duties of fraternity, charity, and justice.

"The Church teaches (she alone has been given by God the mandate and the right to teach with authority) that not only our acts as individuals but also as groups and nations must conform to the eternal law of God."[5]

"Nature allows man to defend his right by force and by arms: but what nature does not allow is that force be the source of right."[6]

The State exists for the public welfare and the protection of its citizens to provide for the good of all. In its dealings with other States it is clearly bound by its duties to its own citizens and by the rights of other nations. These duties and rights, and the customs and usages which arise from relations with others, lead to international law.

The oneness of the human race is apparent, as also the fact that all men are brethren to some degree at least, and the world is thus intended to be a single brotherhood. But the very fact that men are not cosmopolitan, but live in distinct States, is proof of the necessity for some machinery by which the dealings of State with State in the comity of nations be controlled, that world welfare be not sacrificed to national aims and ambitions. International law provides this con-

---

[4] *Quadragesimo Anno*, p. 29 (*QA*, 30).
[5] Pope Pius XI, encyclical *Ubi Arcana Dei*.
[6] Pope Leo XIII, *Consistorial Allocution*, 1889.

trol, but it is clear that a means of preserving this law, of determining its meaning, and of settling differences is likewise necessary. It is the function of organized international society to fulfill this purpose: "To exercise juridical and moral control over the activities of the States, especially in the matter of nationality."[7]

"The end toward which the State moves demands the organization of an international regime which would guarantee international order and common good."[8]

4. Man has a certain aptitude for international society, and for at least the past several hundred years has shown a certain propensity for it, although this aptitude and propensity for international relations have been less clearly defined than those implied by organized international society. International relations may be said to have existed as far back as the year 1500. Although by that period, the English, French, Spanish, Portuguese, were each unified peoples, through the influence of common customs, language, literature, domination, and the like, yet they, and the various city states such as Florence, Venice, Antwerp, Genoa, were conscious of the necessity of friendly relations with other powers by the use of diplomacy rather than by the craftiness and connivance which they had hitherto employed. It may be noted, too, that when the Holy Roman Empire, abolished in 1648 by the Peace of Westphalia, was divided into the several Kingdoms of the Germanies, international dependency was acknowledged when each was given equality of State and sovereignty, and hence the power to make alliances with other States. From that time forward the nations of the world have time and again shown that amicable international alliances are for the greater good of society than the destruction of war.

So the remotely primary character of international society is clearly portrayed, even though it does not yet exist in any permanent or universal form.

International Society Is Not Cosmopolitanism

It must not be thought, however, that international society should supersede the State. Were this so, then the latter would not be a natural society, despite the clear evidence that God preordained it in the natural law. It is considered neither possible nor desirable to destroy

---

[7] Cf. "Nationality: Its Place in the Law of Nations." Pronouncement of the Catholic Union of International Studies, quoted in *The Month* (London), January, 1932, pp. 59–61; and reprinted in *The Catholic Mind* (New York), February 22 and March 8, 1932, pp. 86–88, 108.

[8] *Month,* p. 61; *Catholic Mind,* March 8, 1932, p. 108.

national or local societies. Civil society has existed from the earliest times, as we have shown, and patriotism, the love of man for the country of his birth, is a highly desirable and admirable trait. It is indeed a duty incumbent on the citizen, as shown in Chapter 9, to be loyal and patriotic to his country and to lend his State sincere co-operation in its work for the common good. Since God ordained civil society, man's natural love for his country should arise from the same source as his love for his family, and for the supernatural society of the Church.

"The national sphere is for man a natural one, which in its complete form, offers him at the same time an extension of the domestic sphere on a spiritual, cultural, ethnical, and territorial basis. It exercises on him an educative and stabilizing influence which is of great value in the development of the individual. The natural rights enjoyed by nationals and national groups are founded on this service rendered to the individual."[9] "The natural law enjoins us to love devotedly and to defend the country in which we had birth, and in which we were brought up, so that every good citizen hesitates not to face death for his native land."[10]

Yet, as we also said in Chapter 9, nationalism, in the modern sense, sometimes called jingoism and chauvinism, is a vice instead of a virtue, because of the hatred and false pride which it engenders in mankind. This it is of which Pope Pius XI speaks:

"Difficult, not to say impossible, is it for peace to endure between States and peoples, if in place of true and genuine love of country, there reigns — or rages — a hard and egotistical nationalism; that is to say, if envy and hatred supplant mutual desire for good; distrust and suspicion replace fraternal confidence; strife and conflict take the place of concord and co-operation; and ambition for primacy and pre-dominance excludes respect and protection of the rights of all, be they even the smallest and weakest."[11]

But international society does not mean cosmopolitanism. The world is too large and its peoples too varied in their cultures for all national societies to be destroyed and reunited in one large cosmopolitan State, such as is envisaged by the Marxian socialists, or even such as Dante hoped for in his *De Monarchia*, with an emperor watching over man's temporal welfare and the Pope ruling their spiritual destinies. Dante

---

[9] "Nationality: Its Place in the Law of Nations," *Month*, January, 1932, p. 59; *Catholic Mind*, February 22, 1932, p. 86.

[10] Pope Leo XIII, *Sapientiae Christianae*, 1890.

[11] Pope Pius XI, encyclical *Pax Christi*, December 24, 1930.

was but expressing the views of his day, when the world was composed, on the one hand of Christians all under the Church of Rome, and on the other, the infidels who were, on the Turkish side, a severe menace to Western civilization. Such a fusing of interests of all the nations of the world is neither conceivable nor advisable. A federation of nations as international society is quite otherwise, although, of course, all Catholics would welcome Dante's idea of the actual acknowledgment of the spiritual supremacy of the Pope over all man. In international society such as we refer to in this chapter, national patriotism is not, of course, excluded, for just as intercourse with those outside the family does not abolish family love among the members of a family, neither does true international amity exclude one's love of one's native land.

Peace and War

Harmonious international society will be ever at peace. Without organized machinery for the preservation of international law, and without true religious harmony, wars will still occur. There have been some who have glorified war, who talk of its "romance," who extol the strength and the bravery, the unselfishness and self-sacrifice which it engenders, bringing to the fore, they say, all the finer and nobler qualities in man. The ruthlessness and the destruction, the untold sufferings and miseries resulting from the World War are sufficient in themselves to refute the argument without further examples or detailed proofs. And when we consider the methods employed toward the end of that war, when we think, moreover, of the present perfection in aircraft and poison gases, and long-range guns, it cannot but be evident that the next large conflict might even mean extermination for the attacked nation before a chance for reprisals would be had. Neither is war a purely local disturbance, as it once was. International trade is now so complicated in its operation that every war must of necessity be world wide in its consequences. Indeed, the causes of the depression of the early 1930's were largely traced as the inevitable aftermath of the war which terminated almost twenty years before, yet still brought misery to mankind. Much of the present European situation is also due to the effects of the last war. It is perhaps wise to remember, too, the weakened constitutions of many citizens of the belligerent countries, particularly of those who were children during that war, who played no active part in it but were seriously affected by the lack of nutrition and the nervous tension of the times.

For self-protection, if for no other loftier motives, it is incumbent

on the nations of the world, therefore, to devise a means whereby
future wars will, if possible, be avoided. Nor would permanent peace
measures insure the saving of life and money in wartime only. To
protect itself from possible encroachment, each nation at the present
time has its standing armies, navies, air fleets, and the rest. Particularly
during the present times of large-scale armament the cost of these
"defense measures" is appalling in its magnitude. Money thus spent
could well be employed by the State for promoting the welfare of its
citizens and would be of immense advantage to them, whereas at
present the money spent is of no tangible benefit to the people from
whom it is raised by taxation, other than the protective worth of the
armaments in the event of war.

The Causes of War. Let us now examine into the causes of war.
They are, of course, many and varied.

1. The mistaken philosophy that the State is an end in itself and
practically free from the moral law; that it can commit acts — for
example, the seizure of the property of other nations, or the ruthless
invasion of another nation's territory — which would be reprehensible
in the individual but which, by reason of the State's supposed sovereignty is entirely permissible to the government of a people. It is
obvious that the rights of no nation may be violated in the name of
sovereignty. Probably the most fundamental cause of war is the rejection of the true norms which should influence conduct and by which
conduct should be judged:

"To repress ambition and covetousness and envy — the chief in-
stigator of war — nothing is more fitting than the Christian virtues
and, in particular, the virtue of justice; for by its exercise, both the law
of nations and the faith of treaties may be maintained inviolate and
the bond of brotherhood continue unbroken, if men are but convinced
that *justice exalteth a nation.*"[12]

2. The pride of nationalism, which makes a nation intolerant of
others, regards them as inferior, and breeds a hatred of other States
and an excessive sensibility to supposed hurt to national honor, which
often leads to war. Such a spirit in one nation leads to the engendering
of like errors in others, and it further conduces to discontent among the
peoples whom that nation may control. Added to this is the cult of
imperialism: that form of nationalism which is ever anxious to acquire
more power, to absorb other nations and to take possession of further
territories for the sake of the ensuing prestige.

---

[12] Pope Leo XIII, encyclical *Praeclara Gratulationis Publicae.*

We may mention under this heading the mistaken attitude of the victors in the settlement of the last war. There is no doubt that aggressors should be punished for their aggression and the needless misery entailed, but the mistakes of the Versailles Treaty are now well known. To take her colonial possessions from Germany, already relatively overpopulated, gave her an immediate economic problem which had sooner or later to be solved. To set up reparations payments, and then to limit foreign-trade possibilities, created no small amount of difficulty. To divide up countries without sufficient regard to racial composition and cultural background, furnished a ready-made source of national frictions.

3. The possession of excessive armaments by all the nations of the world: Each nation has the right and the duty to protect its citizens against unjust aggression from the outside and from internal disorders, and in times of just warfare it may even conscript men for military service. Until a true comity of nations comes into being, armed force may seem to be essential. Nevertheless, international rivalry in this respect has reached unprecedented and unwarranted proportions. Each year expenditure for armaments increases instead of being curtailed. At the present time (early 1939) about $962 millions are spent in the United States each year in place of the prewar figure of $245 millions in 1913; France has doubled her expenditures but is still below Great Britain and Germany. Great Britain has increased from an expenditure of under $400 millions in 1913, to about $900 millions today; and Germany, who spent under $300 millions in 1913 now has an annual expenditure of over $1,500 millions. National pride has been largely responsible for the increase in expenditure noted above; in turn the increase leads the respective nations to fear that one of them may become stronger than the rest, and so still further arming is undertaken. Thus a vicious circle is formed, for which there would appear to be no remedy but universal and mutual consent among the nations for proportionate reduction of arms. The expenditure of public money in this rivalry is appalling: money which, as we have previously stated, could be put to much nobler and more useful ends. Indeed, even before this present period of increased arming Pope Pius XI showed how this wasteful expenditure of national resources is one of the main causes of depressions:

"Since the unbridled race in armaments, which on the one hand is the cause of international rivalry, and on the other is the cause of enormous expenditure taken out of the resources available for the public well-being, is not the least of the reasons for the present crisis,

We cannot refrain from renewing and making Our own the grave warning of Our Predecessor. We deplore the fact that it has not yet been heeded and We exhort you, Venerable Brethren, to employ every means at your disposal, through preaching and through the press to enlighten men's minds and to incline their hearts to the requirements of right reason and even more, of the law of Christ."[13]

4. The materialistic doctrine which has now been rampant in the world for many years, which sets excessive store by worldly gains and riches and leads to the many economic causes of war.

"It is a grave error to believe that true and lasting peace can rule among men and among peoples so long as they turn first and foremost and avidly in search of sensible, material, earthly things. These being limited, can with difficulty satisfy all, even if no one (which is hard to imagine) should wish to take the lion's share. They are necessarily unsatisfying because the greater the number of sharers, the smaller the share of each. Whence they are almost inevitably sources of discord and opposition as they are of greed and envy. The contrary is true of spiritual treasures — truth, goodness, virtue — which the more widely they are shared, the more they abound and give fruit to the advantage of each and all."[14]

5. One of the most important causes of war is economic imperialism and greed, which is an outgrowth of the materialism just referred to, and the desire of a nation to extend its authority over peoples and territory for the resulting economic advantage. This economic struggle offers several reasons for war:

a) The desire for territorial expansion for the sake of the wealth to be acquired thereby, the potential markets to be gained for the conquering nation's excess production, or the outlet for surplus population. The exclusion of immigrants by rich and underpopulated States is, generally speaking, a breach of charity, though not necessarily a breach of justice.

b) The importance to a country of controlling international shipping, railroad and cable facilities, and the like, and the consequent struggle for the possession of means of communication.

c) Financial investment of one country in another, whether the loans be made direct to the government of that country or to manufacturers, transportation companies, public utilities, and the like. This gives the lending nation an excessive interest in the welfare of the other. It like-

---

[13] Pope Pius XI, encyclical *Nova Impendet*, October 2, 1931.
[14] Pope Pius XI, encyclical *Pax Christi*, December 24, 1930.

wise affords the latter an undue incentive to declare war in the hope of the cancellation of its debts in the event of victory.

d) The struggle for the control of raw materials, since the more civilized a nation becomes the more raw materials it finds necessary for its well-being. No nation possesses all the varieties of goods sufficient for its needs,[15] but since the United States, Great Britain, France, and Russia together control a large part of the world's supply of raw materials, this fact gives great dissatisfaction to other highly populated and industrialized nations. Some of these other nations, and particularly Germany, are now seeking for economic autarchy or self-sufficiency, with the consequent lower standard of living and higher prices for the home population, which provides a further source of friction and antagonism.

e) The struggle for markets as an outlet for excess production consequent upon the lack of agreement among nations regarding foreign trade. This leads not only to a desire to possess other territory but to the erection of unreasonable trade and tariff barriers.

f) The excessive trade and tariff barriers, just mentioned, erected by nations to foster their home industries or to establish economic autarchy. Some goods are denied entrance to certain countries, or only a certain quota is allowed if an import license is procured; others are allowed only upon payment of an exorbitant import duty. Such re-

---

[15] Even the United States, with its wide territory and range of climate needs many goods from abroad which she cannot produce or can produce only in quantities insufficient for the needs of the people. The following is but a partial list of these goods:

Article	Chief Country of Supply	Article	Chief Country of Supply
Antimony	China	Nux Vomica	Cochin China
Camphor	Japan	Platinum	Russia
Cobalt	Australia, Canada, Belgian Congo	Potassium	Germany
		Quicksilver	Italy, Spain
Chromium	New California, Rhodesia	Quinine	Java
Coffee	Brazil	Rubber	Borneo, Brazil
Cork	Algiers, Portugal, Spain		Malaya
Graphite	Mexico	Shellac	India
Hemp	Asia	Silk	Japan
Hides	Argentine, Australia, France, Netherlands, Orient	Sodium Nitrate	Chile
		Sugar	Cuba, Hawaii, Philippine Islands, Puerto Rico
Iodine	Chile	Tin	Bolivia, Borneo, Malaya, United Kingdom
Jute	India		
Linseed Oil	Argentine	Tungsten	China
Manganese	Brazil, Russia	Vanadium	Peru
Manila Fiber	Philippine Islands	Wool	Argentine, Australia, Orient
Mica	India		
Nickel	Canada		

strictions prevent or hinder other countries from finding an outlet for goods which, for one reason or another, they may be able to manufacture more cheaply than the opposing nation. Excess in this regard creates much animosity and international hatred and distrust, particularly where these barriers are directed against some nations, but do not include others, or admit the goods of others on more favorable terms, a form of discrimination known as "most-favored-nation" treatment. The United States, with its after-war tariff policy, is responsible for much of the "tariff war" of the times. Reciprocal high tariffs were imposed by most countries against the goods of the countries which first established such restrictions, until the "war" reached absurd proportions, and led to a lowered standard of living (because of increased import costs) and to a reduction of exports (hence unemployment and a still lower living standard). It is noteworthy, however, that the United States set the example for a diminution of these tariffs by the Reciprocal Tariff Act of 1934, which empowered the President to enter into trade agreements with foreign governments to lower existing tariffs by not more than 50 per cent of existing rates in return for equivalent concessions from the foreign powers concerned. As the United States tariffs prior to this time had, in general, been passed by Acts of Congress and not by reciprocal treaty negotiations with foreign countries, this Act is an important step toward organizing international economic trade.

Occasionally import tariffs on certain goods are necessary, because of a need to foster an industry of some kind.[16] The United States seems to have little reason for tariffs of this nature. Yet to give an example of this kind of justification, it is conceivable, for instance, that England may genuinely need to impose import tariffs on certain foodstuffs because she is overindustrialized and highly populated, and her unemployed must either emigrate or they must produce more foodstuffs for themselves.

Where high import tariffs already exist, it may be necessary to make an economic adjustment before they are abrogated. If this is not done, cheaper goods entering the country from abroad may bring unemployment to a large number of people, which may be particularly serious in its effects if the industry concerned is highly localized. In this latter situation almost the whole of the population of certain districts may be thrown out of employment, with no local possibility of reabsorption

---

[16] For further particulars of arguments for and against protective tariffs, see, Ross, E. J., *What is Economics?* or any standard work on economics which discusses the topic of foreign trade.

in other employment for a more or less lengthy period of time. Since a lowering of tariffs in a situation of this nature would mean cheaper goods for the community at large, the people would have eventually a larger income surplus to spend on other goods and thus would create employment in other fields. The temporary disruption, however, ought to be considered by the government, in co-operation with the employers and workers concerned. The tariffs might be withdrawn gradually, so that sufficient time is allowed for readjustment. New industries might be established in the district and financed by government loan or gift. Or the employers or government might pay a dismissal wage to the workers concerned, to aid them in finding other employment. The temporary transition costs of such a procedure would be regained in the eventual re-employment of capital, organization, and labor in occupations in which the United States has a comparative advantage over production abroad, so that there would later be a relatively permanent increase in national productivity, in addition to the cheaper goods procurable from abroad as a result of the tariff reduction.

A Just War?

The question arises as to whether or not there can ever be a just war at the present time. Some theorists falsely assert that wars are inevitable because man "is aggressive by nature," because war benefits industry, or leads to the survival of the fittest, or is necessary as a solution to overpopulation problems. We may answer these arguments by pointing to the fact that aggression does not seem to be an innate trait of human nature;[17] that the ultimate harm to industry on account of war is much greater than any immediate benefits; that it is the old and the weak who will survive rather than the young and the strong who will usually be in the ranks of active combatants; and that there are many solutions to the overpopulation question other than the appeal to arms, such as improved methods of food production, emigration, experimentation with substitute foods and other products, or securing from the people of underpopulated territories a part of their surplus land.

Because of the possibility of war, however, the moralists have set rigid conditions to determine whether or not a war is a just one:

1. There must be a just cause — an actual and morally certain violation of right on the part of another State.

2. All peaceful means to avoid war must have failed or be impossible. "Nowadays, owing to the development of peaceful methods of con-

---

[17] Cf. Chapter 2.

ciliation and arbitration, we possess a very efficacious criterion for establishing the responsibility of the various parties concerned. At least the party which has rejected from the first all arbitral or judicial procedure which could have established clearly the demands of Right, and pretends to settle the conflict by armed force alone, can never consider itself as authorized to declare war."[18]

3. There must be a reasonable hope of success, that the people may not be made to suffer without any prospect of deriving good from it, whether present or future.

4. The evils involved in the war must not be greater than the evils to be averted by it.

5. The sovereign authority must declare the war, and he must have a right intention. However just the cause, the war would be immoral insofar as a nation had subsidiary ideas of unjust aggrandizement or other wrongful benefit to the victor.

6. The methods employed must conform to the moral law. As we read in the *Code of International Ethics:* "Morality will never allow a belligerent to attack non-combatants directly, so that the enemy may be led, under pressure of its terrorized subjects, to give up the struggle sooner (bombing of open towns, poison gas, bacillary infection, torpedoing of liners, etc.). In all these cases the harm inflicted on innocent people is directly sought as a means of bringing about the more rapid surrender of the enemy, and it is never lawful to do evil that good may result, for the end does not justify the means."[19] However, the Code continues: "War has become a national affair, and all citizens in various ways take a very active part in it. It is sometimes very difficult indeed to distinguish between combatants and non-combatants. Is not the enemy therefore justified in taking the line of least resistance and attacking indiscriminately both civil and military elements, in order to dissolve this compact union?

"The argument is not unreasonable, and belligerents have certainly the right to take into account the part played in modern warfare by the civilian population. The latter has ceased to be 'innocent' in the sense of the older moralists. It is now permissible for the just belligerent to attack the enemy in the vital elements of its economic structure: militarized factories, railways, ports, sources of raw materials, etc. He is also allowed, by means of blockade, to exercise a gradual pressure which will end in the surrender of the adversary.

"But the mass murder rendered possible by chemical or bacteriolog-

---

[18] *A Code of International Ethics,* pp. 75, 76.
[19] *Ibid.,* p. 87.

ical war must be judged quite differently. The extermination of entire populations, which are not given any time to show repentance, is obviously a dreadful crime against the laws of humanity."[20]

It may here be mentioned, too, that at the termination of the war the victor may exact just compensation for losses suffered, but he should be moderate in the prosecution of his rights. He may not aim at destroying the opposing nation, and he may take punitive measures to subjugate the enemy only insofar as they are clearly necessary as a precaution against future attack, where, for instance, the enemy clearly shows an attitude of permanent hostility and a resolve to renew attack at a future time.

Until comparatively recent years, the lack of a recognized agency of peace enabled the sovereign authority of the State to decide whether or not its rights had been violated, and whether, in self-defense or in vindication of a grave injury which had been suffered, war might be declared. While the principles underlying the declaration of a just war have in no wise been changed, their application is at present greatly modified, owing to the greater interdependence of States such as we have previously described, and the unprecedented interests now at stake in any war which might be decreed. For example, we stated one of the conditions of a just war to be that the evils involved in it must not be greater than those evils which are sought to be averted. One may well question the probability that the injury to an individual nation for which no other remedy could be found would counterbalance the terrible bloodshed, suffering, and misery of the world cataclysm which would almost inevitably ensue. A nation can no longer lightly plead the failure of all peaceful means to stop aggression, with the establishment of the League of Nations, the World Court, the Hague Court, and other tribunals for the settlement of disputes by the increasingly popular and more civilized means of arbitration. Some Catholics go so far as to assert that there can never be a just war under modern conditions, claiming that the evils involved will always be greater than the possible good to be procured.[21] The International Union of Social Studies, however, upholds the theory that a war of self-defense may still be just, if the requisite conditions be observed, since it is the duty of the State to protect its citizens from unjust aggression.[22] The mem-

---

[20] *Ibid.*, pp. 87, 88.

[21] Cf. The *Pax* movement in Great Britain, an organization not to be confused with Benedictine publications of the same name, or with the *Pax Romana*, international university student movement.

[22] Cf. *A Code of International Ethics*, pp. 26, 69, 70.

bers of the Union also point to the words of St. Thomas Aquinas: "The pardon of injuries one has suffered oneself is an act of perfection if to do so is useful to others; but to tolerate patiently injuries suffered by others is an act of imperfection and even a vice if it is possible to resist the aggressor."[23] And the same International Union points out that a just war may be possible even in "a perfectly organized international society," because "recourse to arms must be considered as the ultimate means left to the international authority or the community of nations to overcome a State which obstinately disregards the law and disturbs international order."[24]

When there is a war between two States, and organized international society does not yet exist, then the other States must choose between remaining neutral or intervening in the war. States may in justice remain neutral, if they are constituted as perpetually neutral States. If they make only occasional agreements of neutrality, then, if justice or charity does not require their going to war, their neutrality may be "armed neutrality," in which event they will be armed to defend their neutrality if any of the belligerent States attempt to injure their neutral rights, or their neutrality may be conditional to the maintenance of certain conditions which it has previously announced. Other States, however, are sometimes bound to enter a war because of the demands of justice or charity. When a State has made a treaty with another to assist the latter against any unjust attack, then that State has a strict obligation to keep the terms of its treaty and to declare war on any aggressor. Charity requires that other nations should go to the aid of one which is unjustly attacked and which is too weak to defend itself, provided their own citizens are not thereby too greatly endangered.

Civil war may sometimes take place when national minorities or colonies secede from a parent State, or rid themselves of a dominant government, and become independent because of a so-called "right of self-determination." Such an occurrence (which is not, of course, technically a matter of international relations) would be justified only on the conditions stated in Chapter 9. Grave injury must have been done by the parent State or dominant government, no other means of redress must be obtainable, the international common good must be adequately safeguarded, and all other conditions of a just war must be observed.

---

[23] St. Thomas Aquinas, *Summa Theologica*, IIa IIae, Q. 188, art. 3, 1.
[24] *A Code of International Ethics*, p. 70.

Peace Measures

Pope Benedict XV in his letter to the belligerent nations on August 1, 1917, clearly sets forth the measures by which lasting peace may be obtained.

"We now wish to make more concrete and practical proposals and to invite the governments of the belligerent peoples to agree to a consideration of the following points, as a basis for a just and durable peace, leaving to them the task of analyzing and completing them.

"First of all, as a fundamental principle, moral right must be substituted for the material force of arms. Out of this shall arise a just agreement for a simultaneous and reciprocal diminution of armaments, according to rules and guarantees to be laid down hereafter, without impairing, however, the force needed for the maintenance of public order within each State. In place of armed force shoud be substituted a Court of Arbitration with its high peacemaking function, subject to regulations to be established and sanctions to be determined against any State which might refuse either to submit its international disputes to arbitration or to accept an arbitral decision."[25]

1. First and foremost, as we see, His Holiness showed that the fundamental basis of lasting peace is the substitution of moral right for the force of arms. Only when all nations realize that the State is as subject to the moral law as the individuals who compose it, and only when they sincerely wish to carry out this law, will the resulting practice of justice and charity lead to a universal and mutual good will and understanding among all the countries of the world.

2. Pope Benedict then proposed a "simultaneous and reciprocal diminution of armaments," according to an agreement to be reached among nations, "without impairing the force needed for the maintenance of public order within each State." Since a world assembly of nations (international society) might conceivably lead to even greater calamities than the individual exclusiveness of former years and to war alliances on a hitherto unprecedented scale, only by almost total and universal disarmament could this danger be averted, coupled with a universal instruction to instill into the minds both of statesmen and of individual citizens the right attitude toward this all-important question of peace and war.

3. Going yet a step further. The Holy Father advised an agreement among nations for the establishment of norms and guarantees of inter-

---

[25] Pope Benedict XV, *Letter to the Belligerent Nations,* August 1, 1917.

national conduct, and of sanctions or penalties for the nonadherence to these regulations. In this way a comprehensive international law would be created, States would be compelled to submit questions in dispute to an International Court of Arbitration and to accept its awards, peaceful arbitration would take the place of warfare, and the predetermined punishment would deter nations from a transgression of the law. Sanctions, of course, sometimes lead to the outbreak of war, because, as the International Union of Social Studies has said: "In order to impose respect for right on one who is about to violate it, force may sometimes be necessary. If war breaks out, it is not the fault of the states which apply sanctions, but rather of the one whose injustice has obliged them to have recourse to it. . . . But there is no danger of sanctions bringing about an armed conflict if they are applied with resolute unanimity. No state will dare to resist the collectivity of nations if the latter is firmly resolved to demand the full respect of the Covenant."[26] If universal agreements are made among nations, that economic or political pressure be brought to bear upon those threatening war, particularly by means of trade embargoes or boycotts, these will probably act as practical deterrents to any nation contemplating the use of warfare for the violation of another's rights or even the vindication of its own.

All three of the Pope's suggestions were followed to some extent for some period of time. At the present day, further measures toward a goal of international peace would seem to be necessary. Some of the more mistaken measures of the Treaty of Versailles must probably be revised, and in particular, international trade barriers set up by tariffs, quotas, prohibited imports, and the like must be mitigated. Mr. Van Zeeland advocated this diminution of tariffs in his *Report on International Economic Reconstruction*,[27] and Pope Pius XI likewise wrote in his Encyclical on Atheistic Communism: "In international trade relations, let all means be sedulously employed for the earliest possible removal of those artificial barriers to economic life which are the effects of distrust and hatred. All must remember that the peoples of the earth form but one family in God."[28]

An attempt to bring international society into being was made by thirteen important states of the world with the foundation of the League of Nations on January 10, 1920, "to promote international

---

[26] *A Code of International Ethics*, p. 118.
[27] See *International Conciliation*, March, 1938 (Carnegie Endowment for International Peace), pp. 83–109.
[28] *Divini Redemptoris*, par. 76.

peace and security," and with the definite viewpoint that "universal peace can be established only if it is based on social justice." The League comprises a permanent secretariat which deals with all routine matters of international importance, prepares reports, and investigates difficulties; an executive council, consisting of representatives of the member states, which meets three times a year, and the World Assembly, which meets for one month in every year, to discuss all major problems. Soon nearly all the states of the world belonged to it, although the United States always remained aloof, fearing an embroilment in European or Asiatic affairs, with less possibility of being truly influential and helpful in matters of international concern.

In 1920 The Permanent Court of International Justice, called the World Court, was established by the League as a separate organization. This World Court practically superseded the Hague Tribunal which had been established in 1899, for the latter, though effective enough in concluding treaties, was restricted in its power of arbitration between States by the almost universal practice whereby these treaties excluded from arbitration all disputes involving "national honor," "national independence," or "vital interests." The World Court has settled various disputes between nations in a satisfactory manner: a dispute between Finland and Sweden, for example, regarding the boundaries of the Alard Islands, was settled as early as 1920; Memel was given to Lithuania as an international port in 1924; wars were avoided between Italy and Greece in 1923, between Bulgaria and Greece in 1925, between Bolivia and Paraguay in 1928, and other valuable work was accomplished. The League, however, has never had the support of the United States, and various nations have abandoned its membership, so that it is now evident that its present usefulness in the settlement of international disputes for the avoidance of war is very slight.

However, through the International Labor Organization (the I.L.O.), another separate organization affiliated with the League, which has branches in all important countries, and which the United States finally joined in 1934, many unsatisfactory social, economic, and industrial world conditions have been very much improved. The I.L.O. agrees upon "conventions" at its different meetings, which set forth certain minimum standards for the treatment of different aspects of the labor problem. States which are members of the I.L.O. (and these now number more than 50, including some states, such as the United States, which are not members of the League itself) are asked to conform to these conventions. Usually many of the members do so, and the result is, of course, a much greater uniformity of economic conditions the world over, and hence less cause of the economic strife because of the "dumping" of cheap products produced under unfavorable labor conditions. The achievements of the I.L.O. as regards working conditions in Turkey, India, China, Japan, Persia, and other countries have been very notable.

Due to lack of support, and possibly also to its ideals of material prosperity for the world rather than peace resulting from the spiritual notions of the "brotherhood of man" in the "fatherhood of God" as taught by St. Paul and the Church, the League of Nations has failed to prove itself the International Society envisaged at its organization. A league of nations is essential it would seem, to world peace, and required by the rational nature of man. It is now the aim of all those who work for world peace to bring into being a league of nations which will truly carry out its purpose of providing the instrument for the maintenance of world harmony.

Various organizations have been formed to study international problems bearing on this important question of peace. Reports are issued, conferences, lectures, and study circles formed. There is the Carnegie Association of International Peace, the Nobel Peace Prize, and the numerous associations of the League of Nations. Catholics, too, are foremost in this program of dissemination of knowledge of the benefits of peace and the means whereby it may be attained. In the United States the Catholic Association for International Peace, which has its headquarters at the offices of the National Catholic Welfare Conference in Washington, publishes many pamphlets and reports of high scholastic value, organizes students into regional associations which regularly hold their regional meetings, and holds an important annual meeting in Washington at Easter time. The ultimate aim of all these Catholic organizations is: *Pax Christi in Regno Christi* — "the Peace of Christ in the Kingdom of Christ." For to the Catholic it is obvious that no organized international society will succeed in its endeavor unless there prevails in the world a true religious harmony, and unless man is indeed united under the Fatherhood of God. As Pope Pius XI has written:

"Another error against which the apostolic word, divinely inspired, wishes to fortify us, is that of supposing that true external peace can reign between men and peoples where there is not internal peace, where, that is to say, the spirit of peace does not possess the intelligence and hearts, or better, the souls of men — the intelligence so as to recognize and respect the claims of justice, the hearts so that charity may be joined to and even prevail over justice. For if peace, according to the prophet, must be the work and fruit of justice (Isa. 22:17), it belongs, as St. Thomas luminously teaches (2a, 2ae q. 29iii ad 3um) and this is true, by the very nature of things, more to charity than to justice."[29]

"Then only will it be possible to unite all in harmonious striving for the common good, when all sections of society have the intimate conviction that they are members of a single family and children of the same Heavenly Father, and further that they are 'one body in Christ and everyone members one of another.' "[30]

"It is the moral law alone which commands us to seek in all our conduct our supreme and final end, and to strive directly in our specific actions for those ends which nature, or rather, the Author of Nature, has established for them, duly subordinating the particular to the general. If this law be faithfully obeyed, the result will be that particular economic aims, whether of society as a body or of individuals, will be intimately linked with the universal teleological order, and as a consequence we shall be led by progressive stages to the final end of all, God Himself, our highest and lasting good."[31]

---

[29] Pope Pius XI, encyclical *Pax Christi*, December 24, 1930.
[30] *Quadragesimo Anno*, p. 44 (*QA*, 46).
[31] *Ibid.*, p. 15 (*QA*, 13).

CHAPTER 14

EDUCATION AND EDUCATIONAL SOCIETY

Educational Society Is a Primary Group But Not a Natural One

EDUCATIONAL society — the organized group which we call the school or the school system — consists of those who are especially trained to perform the important function of education, and pupils who are entrusted to these teachers by their parents or guardians, or who voluntarily place themselves under instruction in later life. Educational society is not a natural society, because man can gain knowledge and skill and become highly educated without receiving any formal scholastic training. Educational society, therefore, is not as important and fundamental to social life as the family, the Church, the State, and private property rights; neither is it needed with such urgency as occupational society and international society. Yet Cooley and others have pointed out the immediate importance of the school group, together with the family and the play group, in the life of the ordinary individual in his early and most formative years, terming all three, "primary, face-to-face groups." Most people spend many hours daily in a school for at least eight to twelve years of their life, and sometimes continue in it until they attain mature years. The 1930 Census of the United States showed that at that time 26,849,639 students between the ages of five and twenty were attending school in this country, with an additional 1,034,782 students of twenty-one years and older. In view of the importance of the school as a factor in the development of the majority of men, particularly in our present age of specialization and city life, it therefore seems true (as we said in Chapter 4) that educational society can be called a primary, though not a natural group.

The Place of Education in the Development of the Individual

We specifically called this chapter *"Education* and Educational Society" because, as we have said, it is not necessary to belong to any formal school group to secure an education.

In our discussion in Chapter 3 about the factors which lead to human conduct, we showed that although the basis of personality is the hereditary constitution plus the soul, nevertheless conduct is largely due to habit and to one's mental state. Our actual character is the result of the fashioning of our inherited predisposition by the twofold aspect of education. Education is not necessarily instruction. On the one hand, there is the education which is imparted by example, by the habits, convictions, attitudes, and the ideals which we imbibe from the conversation and conduct of those around us, and by all the other types of environment, together with the influence of grace. On the other hand, there is the second aspect of education, and the more usual meaning of the term: the formal training given to us. The word *education* is derived from the Latin, *educere,* to bring out — the unfolding or development of all the physical, intellectual, and moral potentialities of man by transmitting to him the knowledge, ideals, and attitudes of the past. As is evident from this definition, education is not only concerned with the fashioning of our character and moral conduct so that we can live harmoniously in society, and with the development of our intellect and will; but it aims also to lead us into the culture of the civilization into which we are born, so that we receive the traditional possessions of our fellow citizens — their human culture — to the end that we can help carry them forward for the oncoming generation to take up. Animals can manage with little or no formal educational training: they do not transmit a cultural heritage from one generation to the next by precept and example. Man differs from the animal, not only in the possession of a mind which can be developed and nourished with truth, a will which can be exercised, virtues to be fostered, and bad dispositions to be changed, but also in the ability to acquire the accumulated knowledge of past generations, handed down to him by example, by artifacts, and by the written and the spoken word. Man, therefore, does not have to "begin at the beginning" with each generation, but can benefit by the achievements of the past.

First and foremost there is a religious inheritance which is passed on to us: the knowledge of God which He Himself has imparted through Revelation, and which can be found in the Bible, the teachings of the Church, and the writings of holy men; the knowledge, also, handed down by Tradition. Then there is the heritage of habits and customs, ways of doing things, and "polite manners." These are not only of scientific value, for greater speed or comfort, but they also help to give life in society a human value. There is, too, all the accumulated scientific inheritance which makes this twentieth century outstanding for its material achievements. Finally, there is our literary and aesthetic inheritance, including our language. As a more or less mechanical tool necessary for the acquirement of culture, we ought perhaps to place language in the first rank, although intrinsically it cannot be ranked with religion and much of the other knowledge which we acquire.

Man Has a Right to an Education

Unlike the animals, the human child is dependent for many years for the satisfaction of his needs. Not only is there a lengthy period of physical maturation, but his (or her) intellectual powers are not usually fully matured until some years after adolescence, and many years of education are needed for the average individual to attain to the plenitude of his intellectual development. Among the natural rights which man holds in common with all other men, as postulated in Chapter 7, are the rights to life, to truth, and to live socially. We shall briefly consider these in order.

First, as a human being, the child not only has a right to grow and develop bodily, into full health and strength; but he (or she) has a right to a technical training and instruction, in science, industry, one of the professions — necessary to enable him to gain a livelihood (a man should also be able to gain a livelihood for a wife and children), and so to live in a sufficiency of comfort as regards material goods. A woman needs a technical training in the household arts, if she is successfully to conduct the affairs of her own home, or to direct servants in the management of her household; and nowadays many women also need a technical training to take their place side by side with men in the occupational group outside the home.

Second, man possesses an intellect so that he may know truth; and a will so that he may make right choices when the intellect proposes truth to him. The child has, therefore, a right to the truth, which includes a right to know God — a right to a religious education which will teach him about God, about his eternal destiny, and about the Church, and give him a motive power for a high ideal of moral living. It should never be forgotten that the final end of each child is to attain everlasting happiness. All education is futile if it does not help the child to a knowledge of this end and the means to acquire it. "What doth it profit a man if he gain the whole world, and suffer the loss of his own soul?"[1] The child also needs a moral training, so that he will learn to recognize the rights of others and his duties in their regard; to face difficulties squarely, to make wise choices of his own free will; and to shun evil, whatever may be the temporal consequences of his good actions.

---

[1] Matt. 16:26.

Third, the child needs specific training and knowledge for normal social intercourse. He requires some form of cultural instruction, to enable him to appreciate the best and most wholesome things of life. He must be trained in the conventions of polite society, for he will not be an influence for good in the world unless he can conduct himself gracefully as well as morally. As Ruskin said: "Education is not teaching people to know what they do not know, but to behave as they do not behave."

The ideal of every child is a complete physical, mental, technical, moral, cultural, and religious education, sufficient for his welfare in this world and in the next. In all probability he will then become a true social being — a benefit to society — and not antisocial and a hindrance or detriment to other men; his gifts and aptitudes will have been given the opportunity to be fully developed; and he will have been given the means to attain his right to a well-ordered social life, and his right to truth, including that most important of all goals: everlasting happiness.

The Duty of Parents to Provide for the Education of Their Children

We said in Chapter 8 that the family is the most important of all social groups primarily because it insured the continuity of the human race, and preserved the important traditions and accumulated culture of the past (including a knowledge of God) by transmitting these to the children by education. We are not concerned in this chapter with the other important end of marriage: the mutual well-being of husband and wife.

So far as education is concerned, the family is the most important educational agency. Marriage is not merely a matter of bringing children into the world, the children need many years of care and education, and the parents are the natural teachers of their young, and hence divinely appointed for this purpose. It is, therefore, the parents' duty to provide their children with fitting instruction and training. In his encyclical on the Christian Education of Youth Pope Pius XI specifically stated that "The obligation of the family to bring up children, includes not only religious and moral education, but physical and civic education as well, principally insofar as it touches upon religion and morality."[2]

The first and most important source of instruction is the home. First, the child comes under the environmental influence of the home for a longer period than that of any other social environmental factor.

---

[2] *Divini Illius Magistri,* p. 47.

Second, modern psychologists insist that the first five years of a child's life are the most important from the educational viewpoint. Even in the first few months, a child can be grounded in selfishness (to expect attention at the slightest whim) or in a reasonable give-and-take attitude which is so necessary for later social relations. The child is naturally selfish, for at first he is conscious only of himself, but he can be trained from the first few days to give in to others, to sleep and to be nursed at certain times, and that crying will not necessarily procure for him what he wants. The child can learn in babyhood to give in to anger fits and "temper tantrums," or to learn that such behavior is undesirable. At this time, too, he can become fearful of or confident in those around him: fear is part of what seems to be an instinct of self-preservation, and the child who is not adequately protected from sudden unpleasant situations which are unfamiliar to him may easily develop into a nervous individual in later life. Deliberately frightening an older child by threats of unpleasant experiences which will occur if he does not perform a certain required behavior, threats about animals, the police, and the like, are frequent causes of later phobias and other mental disorders. It is also in the earliest days of a child's existence that he may be made nervously unstable or mentally lazy (according to temperament) by leaving him in a monotonous environment for too lengthy periods of time.

It is noteworthy that the early training of the child, which is begun almost immediately after birth, as we have seen, comes from those with whom the child is intimately associated and whom he loves. Thus it has a peculiar power — for the sympathy, love, and understanding which characterize the majority of parents are more important than rewards and punishments, and the more impersonal attitude of others outside the family. Furthermore, the family is the most important social unit of the State, because it is within the family that the individual can get the personal regard and attention needed for complete training, as well as a complete development of many of his individual human qualities. Parents owe it to their children to "keep up with the times," so as to understand their changing points of view. They need to acquire the latest scientific knowledge of psychology, so as to know them the better — to be able to deal with the problems of the "gang age" and the adolescent period. They need the necessary knowledge to guide their children's reading and their choice of companions and entertainments; and to know the content and value of the courses offered in the schools, particularly in the United States during the high-school period, for the multiplicity of choice provides many courses that are useless for those with a definite career in view. Particularly where Catholic children are obliged through circumstances to attend a non-Catholic school, parents should be able to judge of the educational philosophy taught there, and to be equipped to counteract its objectionable features; and when the children are more mature, to be able to discuss it with them.[3] Since education in the United States is not a Federal matter, but one of local responsibility, it also seems advisable that Catholic parents should try to serve on school boards, to obtain a more adequate knowledge of the curriculum taught in the schools, and to have some influence in the choice of teachers and subjects to be taught.

Speaking of the necessity of Christian education Pope Pius XI wrote as follows:

"More than ever nowadays an extended and careful vigilance is necessary, inasmuch as the dangers of moral and religious shipwreck are greater for inexperienced youth. Especially is this true of impious and immoral books, often diabolically circulated at low prices; of the cinema, which multiplies every kind of exhibition; and now also of the radio, which facilitates every kind of reading. These most powerful means of publicity, which can be of great utility for instruction and education when directed by sound principles, are only too often used as an incentive to evil passion and greed for gain. . . . How often today must parents and educators bewail the corruption of youth brought about by the modern theater and the vile book!

"Worthy of all praise and encouragement, therefore, are those educational associations which have for their object to point out to parents and educators, by means of suitable books and periodicals, the dangers to morals and religion that are often cunningly disguised in books and theatrical representations. In their spirit of zeal for the souls of the young, they endeavor at the same time to circulate good literature and to promote plays that are really instructive, going so far as to put up at the cost of great sacrifices, theaters and cinemas, in which virtue will have nothing to suffer and much to gain.

"This necessary vigilance does not demand that young people be removed from the society in which they must live and save their souls;

---

[3] Well-educated Catholic chaplains have been appointed to most of the more important non-Catholic universities in the United States, who, in addition to encouraging Catholic students attending these universities in the development of their spiritual life, are also equipped to discuss difficulties with them. Unfortunately, for a variety of reasons a large percentage of Catholics in such institutions do not meet these chaplains, a circumstance which consequently detracts from the seeming effectiveness of the chaplaincy.

but that today more than ever they should be forewarned and fore-armed as Christians against the seductions and the errors of the world, which, as Holy Writ admonishes us, is all 'concupiscence of the flesh, concupiscence of the eyes and pride of life.' Let them be what Tertullian wrote of the first Christians, and what Christians of all times ought to be, 'sharers in the possession of the world, not of its error.' "[4]

Daily intercourse with their children gives thoughtful parents a special insight into the child's character, and hence a knowledge of the special moral and secular education which each child needs, and which others outside the family may only very imperfectly realize. It is, indeed, for this reason that children brought up in institutions lack the advantages of those who enjoy good home life, affection, and care; although, of course, individual children from institutions may become much better citizens than many others who had normal home surroundings. The responsibility of parents in this matter is clearly stated in Canon 1113 of the New Code of Canon Law, as cited by Pope Pius XI in his Encyclical on the Christian Education of Youth: "Parents are under a grave obligation to see to the religious and moral education of their children, as well as to their physical and civic training, as far as they can, and moreover to provide for their temporal well-being."

The obligation of parents to see to the religious instruction of their children, as just cited in the above canon, involves more than the delegation of this duty to the Church or the school. Although the Church is the official society to occupy itself with the worship of God and with moral teaching, the family is, nevertheless, the first religious school to which the child belongs. Religion is a vital process, and unless the parents hand down to the child a deep religious conviction, by their attitude toward religion as well as their positive teaching, later dogmatic instruction from outside will not normally be an adequate substitute for their lack of attention to this duty. The school and the Church may teach the child his spiritual and moral obligations, but if the parents misguide the child, either positively in their teaching or indirectly by bad example, the child will be much more prone to adopt their attitude than to follow the precepts of those outside the home.

The home, therefore, is not only the best school because of the formal training which it can give to the child in his most pliable years, and because it gives the personal attention needed by the individual, but also because it is in the first few years of rapid development that a child almost completely assimilates the habits and attitudes of his environment — the example of parents and other members of the house-

---

[4] *Divini Illius Magistri*, pp. 67, 68.

hold.[5] If the parents and these others are patient, and forbearing with each other, if they are orderly, good mannered, self-restrained, moderate in their tastes, and if they are honest and truthful, kind and charitable, and have a spirit of mutual helpfulness, self-sacrifice, and legitimate pride in the achievements of other members of the family, then it is most probable that the child will also develop these social and moral virtues.

Those parents who do not worship God and who do not act from supernatural motives, do not usually bring their children to a true recognition of their duties to God and their moral duties toward their neighbor. Emotional parents will probably give very poor example to their children in self-restraint and necessary discipline; the children of selfish parents and of parents who are uncharitable in their attitude toward others, envious or jealous, will not usually be social-minded; thriftless parents and those with weak will are not likely to have self-reliant offspring. Particularly important is the fact that good parents who win the love and respect of their children, who do not lead their children to lose confidence in them by bad example or by deceiving them in various ways, will have no difficulty in inculcating a necessary affection for themselves, and respect for their authority. The Commandment: "Honor thy father and thy mother" will then become easy of observance, and by the practice in obedience and respect for authority at home, the children will easily acquire respect for authority elsewhere. In this connection, however, it must be noted that the parents' duty is to mold and fashion the child, to develop his individual character along the lines of his own personality, and not to crush his individuality in an attempt to form him along rigid, preconceived patterns.

For all these reasons, therefore, it will be evident that good parents perform a valuable service to society, for by training their children not only in needed physical, technical, and other secular knowledge, but also in virtues, including their duty toward God and neighbor, and proper respect for authority, they will be training them to be good citizens of the State.

The Church Is Also a Divinely Appointed Educator

Although the parents have immediate duties and rights in the education of their children, all baptized children belong to the Church by virtue of their baptism, and hence there should be a close collaboration

---

[5] It is, of course, necessary that other members of the household, as well as relatives, be of a desirable character and influence.

between Church and parents, particularly in regard to religious education. The Church's rights over the Catholic child, and its duty to supply the religious education which the parents cannot or do not supply, and hence its duty to establish Catholic schools are based on two reasons: First, Christ conferred on the Church authority to teach and govern all the faithful when He gave the divine command: "Going, therefore, teach ye all nations . . . teaching them to observe all things whatsoever I have commanded you."[6] Second, as we have mentioned, the child has a right to a complete education, and this includes a right to an education which not only insures that he is not learning wrong principles and habits, but which provides him with positive moral and religious instructions and environmental influence.

The majority of parents have neither the time, the ability, nor opportunity to give their children a complete education in all branches without the assistance of others. Even moral training in the home may be more or less haphazard and lacking in the results achieved by expert educators. And since few can afford adequate instruction for their children by private tutors in the home, schools are needed to supplement the family in its work of education. The school is valuable, too, in that it helps the child to cope with social life which is less sheltered than his home life. In the school he learns to adjust himself to varying characters, to face difficulties squarely, and to compete with others.

But the Catholic child brought up in non-Catholic environment during his school hours will form non-Catholic friendships and imbibe non-Catholic ideas, and will usually grow up without a true Catholic spirit, and a complete knowledge of his religion and how to live it every moment of his waking hours. The right of the Catholic child to be sent to a Catholic school when one is available should therefore be observed by his parents and by the State. Although the parents' right to educate their child according to their conscience is inviolable, they do not have an absolute and despotic right. They must always subordinate all other types of instruction to the "last end and to natural and divine law," and it is their duty to see that "the education and instruction of the child" is "in accord with the end for which by God's blessing it was begotten."[7] Pope Leo XIII wrote in an encyclical on education: "It is the duty of parents to make every effort to prevent any invasion of their rights in this matter, and to make absolutely sure that the education of their children remains under their own

---

[6] Matt. 28:19, 20.
[7] *Divini Illius Magistri*, p. 47.

control in keeping with Christian duty, and above all to refuse to send them to those schools in which there is danger of imbibing the deadly poison of impiety."[8] If the parents do not observe this duty in regard to the Catholic child, then it is the duty of the Church to take over their work and to see to the religious instruction of youth.

In this connection, it is noteworthy that the Church is wholly opposed to a Catholic child receiving an education in a non-Catholic school, where religion is ignored, or where it is relegated merely to the instruction period set aside for its teaching. In the first type of school, where God and His rights are completely ignored, the attitude of students toward religion must necessarily be antireligious or at best irreligious, hence the education itself is antisocial. In the second type of school, religion is taught as if it were a "subject" which could be delimited from all other subjects, instead of giving the child the realization that religion, regard for God, obeying His commands, striving to do all things perfectly at all times, as the creature's reasonable use of His gifts, is a vital factor in life which should permeate all his studies and activities.

Pope Pius XI has expressed himself very strongly in this regard in the encyclical on the Christian Education of Youth, and it seems well to quote him:

"When literary, social, domestic, and religious education do not go hand in hand, man is unhappy and helpless. From this it follows that the so-called 'neutral' or 'lay' school, from which religion is excluded is contrary to the fundamental principles of education. . . . We renew and confirm the declarations of Pius IX and Leo XIII, as well as the Sacred Canons in which the frequenting of non-Catholic schools, whether neutral or mixed, those, namely, which are open to Catholics and non-Catholics alike, is forbidden for Catholic children, and can be at most tolerated, on the approval of the Ordinary alone, under determined circumstances of place and time, and with special precautions. Neither can Catholics admit that other type of mixed school (least of all the so-called *école unique*, obligatory on all), in which the students are provided with separate religious instruction, but receive other lessons in common with non-Catholic pupils from non-Catholic teachers.

"The mere fact that a school gives some religious instruction (often extremely stinted), does not bring it into accord with the rights of the Church and of the Christian family, or make it a fit place for Catholic students. To be this, it is necessary that all the teaching and the whole

---

[8] Leo XIII, quoted in *Divini Illius Magistri*, p. 47.

of the organization of the school, and its teachers, syllabus, and text-books in every branch, be regulated by the Christian spirit, under the direction and maternal supervision of the Church; so that religion may be in very truth the foundation and crown of the youth's entire training; and this in every grade of the school, not only the elementary, but the intermediate and the higher institutions of learning as well. To use the words of Leo XIII: 'It is necessary not only that religious instruction be given to the young at certain fixed times, but also that every other subject taught be permeated with Christian piety. If this is wanting, if this sacred atmosphere does not pervade and warm the hearts of masters and scholars alike, little good can be expected from any kind of learning, and considerable harm will often be the consequence.'

"And let no one say that in a nation where there are different religious beliefs, it is impossible to provide for public instruction otherwise than by neutral or mixed schools. In such a case it becomes the duty of the State, indeed it is the easier and more reasonable method of procedure, to leave free scope to the initiative of the Church and family, while giving them such assistance as justice demands. That this can be done to the full satisfaction of families, and to the advantage of education and of public peace and tranquillity, is clear from the actual experience of some countries comprising different religious denominations. There the school legislation respects the rights of the family, and Catholics are free to follow their own system of teaching in schools that are entirely Catholic. Nor is distributive justice lost sight of, as is evidenced by the financial aid granted by the State to the several schools demanded by the families.

"In other countries of mixed creeds, things are otherwise, and a heavy burden weighs upon Catholics, who under the guidance of their Bishops and with the indefatigable co-operation of the clergy, secular and regular, support Catholic schools for their children entirely at their own expense; to this they feel obliged in conscience, and with a generosity and constancy worthy of all praise, they are firmly determined to make adequate provision for what they openly profess as their motto: 'Catholic education in Catholic schools for all the Catholic youth.' If such education is not aided from public funds, as distributive justice requires, certainly it may not be opposed by any civil authority ready to recognize the rights of the family, and the irreducible claims of legitimate liberty. Where this fundamental liberty is thwarted or interfered with, Catholics will never feel, whatever may have been the sacrifices already made, that they have done enough, for the support and defense of their schools and for the securing of laws that will do them justice."[9]

Of course, circumstances arise in certain districts which make it impossible for Catholics to provide special Catholic schools for their children, and then the Church must needs make arrangements for these children to be sent to non-Catholic establishments and to receive their religious instruction separately. So far as higher education is concerned, it is frequently necessary for students to attend non-Catholic colleges and universities for instruction in specialized studies impossible adequately to attain under Catholic auspices. As mentioned in a footnote earlier in the chapter, the Church often appoints special chaplains to these places of learning, so that students will have the advantage of prompt and expert guidance according to their needs.

It is noteworthy, too, that the Church is opposed in principle to the coeducation of adolescents, where this can be avoided. This teaching is not in conformity with the ideas of some educationists that children develop more naturally if members of the two sexes are brought up in each other's company and hence are accustomed to normal social life. Yet there is nothing in Pope Pius XI's encyclical which precludes the normal social intercourse between children of opposite sex in the home, and through meeting the companions of their brothers or sisters out of school hours. So far as the school is concerned, Pope Pius has written the following:

"False also and harmful to Christian education is the so-called method of 'coeducation.' This too, by many of its supporters, is founded upon naturalism and the denial of original sin; but by all, upon a deplorable confusion of ideas that mistakes a leveling promiscuity and equality, for the legitimate association of the sexes. The Creator has ordained and disposed perfect union of the sexes only in matrimony, and, with varying degrees of contact, in the family and in society. Besides there is not in nature itself, which fashions the two quite different in organism, in temperament, in abilities, anything to suggest that there can be or ought to be promiscuity, and much less equality, in the training of the two sexes. These in keeping with the wonderful designs of the Creator are destined to complement each other in the family and in society, precisely because of their differences, which therefore ought to be maintained and encouraged during their years of formation, with the necessary distinction and corresponding separation, according to age and circumstances. These principles, with due

---

[9] *Ibid.,* pp. 63–65.

regard to time and place, must in accordance with Christian prudence, be applied to all schools, particularly in the most delicate and decisive period of formation, that namely, of adolescence; and in gymnastic exercises and deportment, special care must be had of Christian modesty in young women and girls, which is so gravely impaired by any kind of exhibition in public."[10]

Obviously, the Church intends that the lay teachers in Catholic schools should themselves be Catholics, and not merely baptized Catholics practising a minimum religion, but Catholics who are conscious of their privilege in helping to mold the minds and wills of their young charges toward the end for which they were created. Unless Catholic teachers, both religious and lay, fully realize their duty, by precept and example, to give religion its full position in every aspect of life, a so-called Catholic education is of little value, and may do positive harm. As said before, religion cannot be compartmentalized but must be the background of all our thoughts and actions.

The Right and Duty of the State to Promote Education But Not to Dominate It

The State exists for the common good of its citizens, and is bound to protect its members and to supply whatever they cannot provide by their own unaided effort. It is, therefore, the duty of the State to foster and aid education in every possible way: first, because the citizen himself needs an education and has a natural right to it; second, because prosperity, security, and economic and cultural advancement all rest on the education which young citizens receive. No State can prosper unless its citizens are law abiding, hard working, frugal, possessing a high degree of mental, technical, cultural, and moral achievement. It is, therefore, the right and duty of the State to insure to every citizen an opportunity to acquire at least a minimum education suited to his position in life, and to set down certain minimum requirements for the school. That citizens be educated is particularly necessary in a democracy. Only persons with trained minds and a wide knowledge can properly deal with any difficulty which may arise, and regard a situation from all possible angles. In a democracy, therefore, where each man has a vote, and women, too, of late years, it is important that all be given an education to enable them to vote intelligently.

It must be noted, however, that the State's duty is merely that of

---

[10] *Ibid.,* p. 59.

supplying the deficiencies which private endeavor does not, or cannot provide. Its rights, therefore, are not absolute, but limited. The rights both of the parents and of the Church must be respected, and the State must in no way dominate education. However poor parents may be, they have a natural right to educate their children, and if they do not wish their children to attend a particular school, they should be allowed the liberty to send them elsewhere. The school is merely an aid to the family, to supplement and not to supersede it, and therefore despite the importance of the school group, teachers possess only so much authority and jurisdiction over their charges as the parents wish to delegate to them. For their own protection, however, the school may bargain with the parents, and impose conditions on which pupils will or will not be accepted. But even where free education is concerned strict attention should be paid to the parents' natural right to demand that the education given their children shall include at least the minimum requirements, and thus provide for training in morals, and instruction in whatever religion they choose to designate. Only where parents are morally or mentally incapable of educating their children, and no other persons provide what is lacking, should the State supply for their incapability by taking complete charge of their nonreligious education. In every case, of course, the rights of the Church must be respected.

The Educational Facilities of the State Should Be Complete

We said that it is the duty of the State to propose the minimum educational facilities available to citizens. These facilities should take care of the "whole man," and not merely provide for the physical, mental, and vocational education necessary to enable every child to take his place as an economicaly independent citizen in later life, with the requisite strength, mentality, and ability to provide for material progress. We might include adequate grade and high schools in this general need.

Education must not be too theoretical and bookish, and entirely divorced from life; on the contrary, it must be "alive" and adequate for all the varied phases of social life, as well as for all cultural needs. Most important, however, education must primarily aim at the development of character. Law and order, habits of thrift and good workmanship, and true "social-mindedness" within the State, all depend on the character of the citizens. A good character is formed only by long-established habits of virtue, based on high principles, noble ideals, and well-trained strength of will. Since religion and education are inseparable, and religion provides the child with a motive power for his good actions, the State should not neglect to provide its citizens with a program of education which includes time for the acquisition for religious knowledge, and it should do nothing to hinder such an education. To become a true citizen and not to fail in his duty to himself, to his fellow men, and to the State, the child needs a training which makes him realize his allegiance to God. Only prolonged education of the best type can endow citizens with such characters, and it is therefore to the advantage of the State, as well as its duty, to see that the educational system of the country gives its citizens a true moral training. In its educational program, however, the State must not supply merely a minimum education for the ordinary citizens. Special schools or other aids must be provided for the handicapped, the defective, and for those adults who have met with accident or who, for any other reason, such as economic and industrial changes, may require a vocational training. For this reason, too, evening and other part-time continuation schools are needed, so that adults may supply for a lack of earlier instruction and training if they so desire it. Within the State there should also be museums and art galleries, to promote the cultural education of the people, and free public libraries should be within easy access of all, for books are an important means of education.

Private initiative usually provides colleges, universities, summer schools, lectures, conferences, study clubs, correspondence courses, and the like. The National Congress of Parents and Teachers, with its thousands of local associations, and the National Council of Parent Education, founded in 1926 have done much to induce co-operation between parents and teachers in their joint work of educating the child.

Every State, of course, should have a good daily press, and suitable inexpensive weekly, monthly, and quarterly publications, and pamphlets which will provide the citizen with good educational material unstained by undesirable features. It seems advisable that most of these facilities should be privately owned, but the State should guard, by legislation, against objectionable periodicals and other literature. The importance of newspapers in the life of the ordinary individual may be judged by the circulation figures for the United States in 1937[11] which included more than 15 million morning newspapers, over 25 million evening newspapers, and nearly 30 million Sunday newspapers: the sale of morning and evening newspapers was even greater in 1931. The influence of these journals is by no means wholly good. At one time the newspapers catered largely to the so-called "educated" classes, but

---

[11] *Directory of Newspapers and Periodicals* (N. W. Ayer & Sons), 1937.

today their largest sales are from the "masses," as must be obvious from the circulation figures above. Despite the veneer of education which is now given to everyone within the modern States, the average newspaper reader of today needs to be amused, and to be aroused emotionally. Hence the newspaper, with an eye to profits, provides these features, and in so doing is itself a large factor in molding the lives of its readers — arousing their interest in the ephemeral things of life and accustoming them to an emotionalism which is by no means wholly rational. Again, most newspapers are controlled by large corporations or wealthy capitalists, and hence they are usually edited with a view to increased circulation for profits rather than for their intrinsic value. Then, too, the true needs of the subscribers, are very frequently neglected in favor of the policy of the advertisers, who bear most of the production expenses of modern newspapers.

Since the radio and the motion-picture theater are also cheap and almost universally used means of recreation and of indirect education, it would seem that their programs, too, need to be watched over by the State, so that they may be agents of good and not of evil.

The Financing of State Educational Facilities

There is an extensive system of free education in the United States, supported in the usual manner by taxation.[12] Libraries, museums, art galleries are financed by local taxation, except such institutions as are under state control or privately endowed. The elementary schools and public high schools also depend for their upkeep on taxes levied in the particular city or district in which they are situated, but these schools invariably receive a state grant also. All the states have state universities, normal schools, and agricultural colleges, to which they allot yearly financial aid, and all the states have legislation regarding educational requirements and the school-leaving age. The Federal Government supports education in a variety of ways — by laws against the transmission of immoral literature and plays through the mails; by publications; and, under the provisions of the Smith-Hughes Vocational Education Act of 1916, by financial aid to those states which help to support high schools giving vocational courses. The youth of the country are now also helped educationally by funds from the National Youth Administration, established in 1935.[13]

---

[12] In 1934, out of a total number of approximately 31,618,000 children between the ages of 5 and 17, 26,434,193 were attending public elementary and secondary schools (*Statistical Abstract of the United States*, p. 104).

[13] See Chapter 22.

It must be noted, however, that if the members of a state provide an adequate system of education of their own initiative, which satisfies the requirements of the state, then the latter should in no wise interfere. It is the state's duty to see that each child within its realms receives a fitting education, and that adults have adequate facilities for educational development, yet only when good private education is not available is it the state's duty to supply deficiencies. Again, although it is important that there should be as many educated citizens as possible within the state, nevertheless only a "minimum" education need be supplied free of charge to all. The proportion of state and municipal revenue allotted to higher education in this country has been severely criticized by many citizens as being an unduly lavish expenditure of public funds for the benefit of the comparatively prosperous few. Instead of widespread provision of public education in the higher branches, the state might best be served if poorer citizens with the requisite mental ability were assisted in prolonging their educational training by state loans and scholarships.

As we shall show in Chapter 21, a large proportion of rural peoples between the ages of 20 and 44 leave the countryside for urban residence and occupations. As Bishop Muench, of Fargo, North Dakota, has truly said: "The farmer educates and cares for his boys and girls and then, before they are twenty-five, he delivers them to the city at no cost of education to the urban population. Dr. O. E. Baker, Chief Statistician of the United States Department of Agriculture, has estimated that in ten years, from 1920–1930, conservatively calculated, $14,000-000,000 worth of care and education have gone from the farm to the cities."[14] These facts would seem to point to the need of city peoples helping to pay for rural education by scholarships, educational taxes, or other methods.

Catholic Education in the United States

As was pointed out earlier in the chapter, while Catholics recognize the work of the public schools in secular education, and contribute to their support by means of tax payments, nevertheless they claim that they are entitled to give their children a Catholic education because of the lack of religious training in the public system.

There is a widespread Catholic educational system in the United States, entirely supported by voluntary contributions. In private institutions, of course, the students pay fees which usually cover the

---

[14] Muench, Most Rev. A. J., D.D., "Agrarianism in the Christian Social Order," *The Catholic Rural Life Bulletin,* Vol. I, No. 1, May 20, 1938, p. 23.

cost of their tuition. The elementary schools, however, are mainly supported by the parishes (although students are usually charged a small fee in part payment of tuition and textbooks) and the teachers work for a minimum salary. In some parishes the school is able to accept children from needy families without payment, but in poorer districts, where there are large numbers who cannot afford the small cost of Catholic schooling, parents are often obliged to send their children to the local public school, to the danger of their religious training. Many citizens are opposed to supporting sectarian education out of public funds. Yet it does not seem unreasonable to expect, where education is paid for out of the taxation, as in the United States, that those Catholic schools which meet the ordinary demands of the country should receive their share of tax payments allotted for educational purposes. Failing this, it seems that taxpayers should be allowed to decide for which class of schools their tax must be allotted and Catholics could designate Catholic schools for this purpose. And if this is not allowed, where health service and standard textbooks are supplied gratis to public-school children out of public funds, it seems that it would not only be just but also to the advantage of the nation, if such service were likewise given to Catholic students. In very few localities are textbooks provided to Catholic schools by the public authorities, and in many places pupils attending Catholic schools receive no public health service of any kind.

Education Among the Primitives

As among more advanced peoples, the child's training among primitives and those of comparatively primitive culture is largely conducted within the family circle. Yet because of the lack of privacy in primitive social life, the family group is usually larger than our own, and often includes the grandparents, if not other relatives — and the social control exercised by the band or tribe (the neighborhood group as it were) is much stronger among simpler peoples than with others.

Although the major part of the child's education consists of the absorption of the activities of the family and other groups by suggestion and imitation, and there is very little corporal or other punishment of children, this unconscious training in play and other spontaneous activities is usually supplemented at an early age by the direct tuition of parents and grandparents. Such training is given with a definite intent to instruct, even though the systematic school is not there. Instead of learning through the school, the child of simpler cultures acquires a more extensive knowledge of the practical arts of

life from the parents or family heads, than do the children of more advanced culture, since many more articles prepared are made by hand.
The father usually teaches the boy the necessary means to procure
sustenance, to fish, to hunt, and the like. The girls are usually taught
by the women what foods to gather, how to prepare them, and how to
perform other necessary duties. Since the primitive child must often
be able to cope with many privations in later life, his physical training is frequently severe. Among the simpler peoples are very commonly found elaborate initiation rites for their adolescents, and nearly
always these are periods of great trial and fortitude. Fasting for long
periods, painful tattooing and other cicatrizations, tooth extraction or
filing, and many other ordeals mark the adolescent's entrance into a
period of more mature years. While most of these practices may at
first glance appear senseless to our civilized understanding, nevertheless
they supply a very severe but effective training in fortitude, self-restraint, the ability to keep tribal secrets, and necessary matrimonial
and hygiene lore.

Respect for the religious and moral codes of the tribe, for tradition,
for the aged, may be inculcated by proverbs and tales, and particularly
by tribal etiquette, by the often severe taboos, and by magic. Fear of
violation of tribal custom, and fear of the power of magic, are powerful means by which primitives educated their children to maintain
their culture intact, and one of the chief reasons for the relative stagnation of culture so often found. The elaborate ceremonialism of the
various tribal rites helps to emphasize and to crystallize their importance in the regard of all. Eventual affiliation with a "man's house" as
in some tribes, or with age grades, as in others, provides the child with
further training for adult life, for these help to emphasize the solidarity
of the social group, the necessity of sharing food and other goods with
the rest, and in this manner social responsibilities are undertaken for
the necessary social welfare of the group. Sometimes the age grades are
of paramount importance in training children of simpler peoples.
Among the relatively advanced Bambara, for example, the children
more or less educate themselves in the different associations in which
the sexes are separated and through which they advance from the age
of three until they reach the age of about fourteen. During the puberty
rites at about the age of thirteen or fourteen, however, the adults
delegate certain older members of the tribe to instruct them in all
useful knowledge. The boys do not learn how to trap, hunt, fish, gather
vegetables, and the like from their father, but from the old man who
has care of them during these adolescent ceremonies. Once emancipated

from the children's organizations, both boys and girls join adult societies which also exert a powerful influence over them.

To give further details of all the manifold variations of primitive
and semi-primitive educational methods is, of course, impossible here,
just as we have omitted in this chapter all references to the many
pedagogical methods of history and the different educational systems
of modern times. It is evident, however, that all peoples recognize the
need of training the young, and we find a more or less complete formal
instruction in all cultures.

CHAPTER 15[1]

RECREATION AND RECREATIONAL SOCIETY

Recreation Necessary for Man

RECREATION is necessary for man, both as an individual and as a member of society. Throughout infancy and early childhood, random actions and play, to a very large extent, develop muscles and lead to co-ordination as well as to an amount of knowledge of self. Later in childhood, gregarious play appears, and slowly develops into team activity. In adolescence and maturity, one finds this latter aspect in the complex co-operation of competitive activities, combined with an individualized seeking after satisfactions that fill special recreational needs.

In the social life of man, that primary and natural institution upon which all social life must rest, the family can carry out its fundamental ends successfully only when there is a certain amount of joy and relaxation, as leaven in the family circle. The rearing and educating of children, the first matter of the marriage contract, can be accomplished only through directing the solitary play of the child in early years, and through guiding the formation of the later play group. Likewise, in that larger social unit, the State, community of interest in recreation is a powerful factor in cementing people together for more serious political purposes. Perhaps the great American game of baseball has accomplished more by way of true assimilation than all of the so-called "Americanization" classes, "first-paper" procedures, and oaths of allegiance. Modern dictators have subordinated recreational groups in order that the State might profit by the social values of such great sport congresses. It was in gatherings sponsored by the Church that some of the finest leisure-time activities, such as folk song and dance, the plain chant and the drama, and the supreme pageantry of the Church services and processions, found their rise and cultivation. Finally, as was mentioned in the discussion of Occupational Society in Chapter 12, recreation is necessary as a companion institution, in that man cannot work always but, because of his nature, must seek relaxation in periods of purposeful leisure, through which not only the body

---

[1] The author of this chapter is 'Sister Anne Burns; O.S.B., M.A., of the College of St. Benedict, Minnesota.

but also the mind recuperates from the labors of the day and, being refreshed, is prepared to take up the burden later.

Because recreation is such a human need, resting as it does upon the universal needs of the individual, man has everywhere formed habits around this demand of nature, and has crystallized his behavior in this respect into certain relatively permanent forms, structures, or relationships. It is possible, therefore, to regard recreation as a social institution. More than this, man seems always to have formed recreational groups, although of course, he can fulfill his need of recreation, to some extent at least, without belonging to any formal society. Recreational society cannot be said to be a natural society, but it may well be termed a primary group — first, because of its universal character, in which respect it exceeds other minor groups; and second, because of its profound influence in the socialization of the individual. One cannot emphasize too strongly the contribution which recreational associations can make to society, by fulfilling fundamental human needs, and by the more effective developing of man through the formation of social traits that are desirable. These ends, however, will be accomplished only if guidance in the building of recreational interests comes from those structures that are the most essential in human society — the family, the Church, and the State.

Principles for Recreational Society

If the modern period is to attempt to build a recreational society that approximates that permanence and harmony which we can see in past periods, the basic social institutions — the family, the Church, and the State — must furnish as a prerequisite an abiding, consistent philosophy of life. Recreation, then, could not be a thing apart, but would grow out of and be in agreement with the reasoned approach to life found in all the manifestations of society. There would be, first, the presentation of a whole view of life by the Church in which leisure is shown to have a part in the permanent principles that have been mentioned repeatedly throughout this book: That to God as Creator is due man's best service of body and mind, or in the words of St. Paul: "Therefore, whether you eat or drink, or whatsoever else you do, do all to the glory of God."[2]

The home — and its instrument, the school — must assist in teaching the foregoing, but it must, furthermore, make its contribution in guiding its members toward a balanced leisure program in which various activities are increased or decreased according to the needs of the

---

[2] 1 Cor. 10:31.

individual personality. A part of this balanced program will be the type of leisure that is not totally self-centered; for besides fulfilling the basic needs of man's nature and aiding in his achieving his ultimate goal, leisure also promotes the natural benevolence of man, long ago understood and spoken of by St. Thomas. The home with its affectionate bonds can best teach that selfish satisfactions alone cannot be the object of leisure. Our social nature urges us to act for others, and in agreement with this natural urge, the divine counsels direct us to do good not only to those we love but also to our neighbors. In the home and school, then, the individual can come to realize that his recreational group must look upon leisure not only as a time in which to live, to enjoy, to fulfill, but a time in which to serve.

Except that the spiritual factor in recreation is neglected, the following is one of the most inclusive statements available and points out, by inference, that recreational society should be built to serve tastes and interests developed in the home. Leisure is "time to live" and includes:

"The fellowship of the one we love
 Fellowship of our children
 The fellowship of our friends
 Work that expresses an inward urge toward some perfection
 The building up of a home in which we can live, in the full sense
 The shaping of comely and satisfying things with our hands
 Play and rhythmic physical activity
 Gardens, sunlight, the open air, and all old simplicities
 Intimacy with the life of woods and fields
 The reading of books, the reaching out for greater understanding
 The solitary inward growth of thought
 The outward expression of thought in conversation, writing, art
 The attempt to understand what will make a better community,
     nation and world
 And the attempt to make them better."[3]

The final principle, that to all men a minimum of leisure opportunities should be made available, is the province of the State. Aristotle considered the problem some centuries ago and, in keeping with his times, looked upon it as a prerogative of the ruling class. In a Christian society, it must be recognized that work and relaxation form a part of every day if an individual is to have that freedom of spirit necessary to imitate Christ. Nicholas Murray Butler states the secular view: "He who does not work, loses one of the greatest of life's enjoyments,

---

[3] Hambidge, G., *Time to Live,* p. 139 (New York: McGraw-Hill Book Co., 1933).

and he who has no adequate leisure and no knowledge of how to use that leisure is deprived of life's greatest satisfaction."[4] Since in this industrial world so very many must accept what work is available, regardless of their interests or innate capabilities, and often regardless of superior educational preparation, it is needful that we recognize in leisure the possibility of fulfilling one's nature. It might be defined as the time in which one may in truth "have life and have it more abundantly." The phrase has been used to mean greater physical comfort, but it is time to recognize that it was first used to signify the vast realms of spiritual growth man possesses. The State's obligation is to promote such a society, politically and economically, as to make possible the freedom of man's spirit. . . . No matter what a man's vocation may be, what his race, his social or financial rating, his ultimate goal is the same. If his work is such as to cramp and constrain his soul, his leisure should most certainly be filled with releasing and guiding forces.

The principles of recreational society, then, are closely bound up with (1) The Church — teaching that leisure-time activities can be in agreement with the Christian end of life; (2) the home — promoting a balanced program in leisure so as to meet individual personality needs; (3) the State — making available some opportunities for recreation to all men through improving political and economic conditions so as to strengthen the Church and home rather than through competing with them for the interest and time of the individual.

Recreation in the Past Was Institutional

Only a slight knowledge of history is necessary to see that, in those civilizations where the leisure of the people was in keeping with their whole view of life, a progressively fine, high type of human culture existed. It is likewise observable that depraved types of recreation are found in civilizations that have begun to disintegrate because of a lack of consistency in the view of social life and a decrease in the effort expended to make the entire pattern of life according to some ideal.

A view dealing with the origins of play that would completely deny recreation's being institutional is that of Rousseau. He would have the child, Emile, cut off entirely from the social heritage. In this way the child would be "natural," not in the traditional sense, but after the manner of an animal whose instincts, urges, or natural desires are untrammeled by civilization's restrictions. Though the error of this view

---

[4] Butler, Nicholas M., "Leisure and Its Use," *Recreation*, August, 1934, p. 220.

has been pointed out repeatedly, one still finds it inherent in many popular articles on play. It would seem that Rousseau's later writings, in which he civilized his ideal child considerably and made him submit to society's demands, have not had as wide circulation in America as the earlier work.

The unilinear evolutionists' theory of play is typical of the general trend of their thought: they regarded primitive man as given to the kind of play that we are accustomed to look upon as proper to the higher animals — play in which the whole body is thrown about in a capricious manner and the instinctive cravings of his nature, hunger, thirst, sex, are satisfied. One finds play groups and play activities common to man at all times and all places. Among the primitives age grades and other organizations are evidences of institutional growths within this field. There is a great deal of individualistic skill-play that prepares for protection against animals; there is rhythmic movement and some formal dance activity, often connected with ceremonials; and there are mimicry, impersonation, and, to a certain extent, drama. Since group participation and the passing on of this behavior from generation to generation is found, further research will probably result in showing that play has a definite part in the institutional life of the primitives, as is the established belief today in regard to the more basic institutions.

Certainly among the peoples of the ancient world, recreation was definitely a part of their institutional life. Sparta and Athens show this fact; each, however, with a different emphasis. Sparta was primarily militaristic, and the recreational life of the people centered around this interest in the State. To us the custom of the men dining, separate from the women and children, is unnatural and strange. It was, however, in keeping with their emphasis upon the military State. After the meal the men conversed about matters of State within their separate groups and even at times found time for some merrymaking and singing of songs.[5] At other times they and the older boys engaged in gymnastic and military exercises as well as in the study of music, which continued to be a recreational occupation even after the time of schooling was over. Hunting was a special favorite because it contributed to the hardening of the body and thus to the service of the State. There were choruses connected with sacrifice in their religious ceremonial. Women and girls took part in this rigorous program so that in their own sphere they might serve this militaristic State.

---

[5] Cf. Blümner, H., *The Home Life of the Ancient Greeks* (trans. by Zimmern, A.), pp. 177–179.

The spirit of Athens, on the other hand, was quite different from that of Sparta, but in its adherence to an institutional pattern in recreation, it was similar. Harmony is the word that typifies the ideal toward which the Athenian strove in all walks of life. Consequently all of his activities fit into a plan in which the "good life" was the desired end. Though the citizens alone entered into this plan fully, the slaves and foreigners residing in Athens could not but be touched by much in the public demonstrations and, therefore, affected by the thought that motivated it. Balance, a complete lack of any excess, characterized the Athenian's participation in games, music, the dance, poetry, throughout the entire range of physical and intellectual development. Evidence of this is seen in the statement that "the Olympic and Nemean Games . . . were primarily religious festivals . . . and sacrifice, prayer, and choral hymn were the background against which they were set."[6] Later this character of balance was lost when physical prowess became professionalized and was exalted over the rest of life's interests. This coincided with the decline of integration in societal life.

Thucydides records The Funeral Speech of Pericles in which the latter points out many of the virtues of his city at its height: ". . . we provide plenty of means for the mind to refresh itself from business. We celebrate games and sacrifices all the year round, and the elegance of our private establishments forms a daily source of pleasure and helps to banish sadness. . . ."[7] These recreations ranged from philosophical discussions and dramatic ceremonials connected with religious rites, to the developing of architecture, sculpture, music, and the dance, and the gymnastic games of girls and boys, as well as adults, such as the throwing of discus and javelin, running, jumping, boxing. Throughout all of this ran the thread of the highest aesthetic and ethical ideals that they cherished. Neither play, recreation, nor leisure was an expeditious thing to be determined by the whim of the moment; rather it was an important part of life that must fill its place in the entire pattern. This view is expressed in one of Aristotle's remarks: "Even if it is impossible that men should be such as Zeuxis painted them, yet it is better that he should paint them so; for the example ought to excel that for which it is an example."[8] The place of music (and the word was used to include dancing and poetry) as an element in religion is the clearest example of how permanently these interests were inter-

---

[6] Dickenson, G. Lowes, *The Greek View of Life*, p. 139.
[7] Thucydides, *Peloponnesian War*, Book II, pp. 38, 39. Trans. by Richard Crawley, p. 122.
[8] Aristotle, *Poetics*, XXV, 1461, 6, 12. Trans. by J. E. C. Welldon.

woven into the very fabric of institutional life. "A change to a new type of music," says Plato, "is something to beware of as a hazard of all our fortunes. For the modes of music are never disturbed without the unsettling of the most fundamental political and social conventions."[9]

At no time was the leisure activity of the people more definitely a growth from their own interests, individual and societal, than during the Middle Ages. Historical research has provided us with accounts rich with evidence of co-operation between the guild, the local government, and the Church in planning, preparing, and staging the mystery plays. In these plays all members of the various guilds, apprentices, journeymen, and master — each according to his ability — had a chance to perform. For months before Easter, for example, during the time of the year when life might have been dreary with Lenten penances and cold spring thaws, the people were busy with the creative experience of forming the scenes of their plays, devising costumes, designing and executing settings, and most of all in speaking their lines. The language of Scripture, with its dignified, simple but sublime style, with its message of religious truths, and with its insight into human actions, raised the minds of performers and audience above the level of petty gossip and gave to their growing languages a rich store of Biblical quotations which still flavor our speech today. Later the chronicle play and the whole medieval theater as a recreational agency grew out of the simple kind of drama that had slowly evolved from the liturgy of the Church. Finally it was strong enough to have its own place in life, apart from the Church; for it spoke a language the people could understand, and portrayed character and life situations in agreement with the people's knowledge and hopes.

Play, Recreation, and Leisure

Today, those individuals who would aid in building a strong recreational society must have not only a basic, valid philosophy of leisure themselves but must also be aware of the prevalent concepts and their connotations, so that further emphasis may be laid where it is needed and existing emphasis lessened at certain points.

Play is, perhaps, the most widely used word to denote that activity of man which is not devoted to duties and needs. Many still think of play in connection with joyful infant and childhood behavior. In the crystallization of ideas that has taken place in recent years within the

---

[9] Plato, *Republic*, IV, 424 c. Vol. I, p. 333. Trans. by Paul Shorey.

recreation field, it has come to have a wider connotation. There seems to be at present a useful distinction between the words play, recreation, and leisure.

Play came to have a physical emphasis because of the general character of the thought in the nineteenth century. There grew out of the increased emphasis on health, two movements — closely allied — which have greatly affected the type of recreational structure in America. The playground movement, together with the movement for formal preparation in physical education, succeeded in convincing us that it is necessary for young people, particularly, to play in the open air in such a fashion as to exercise vigorously the large muscles of the body.

The value of play, since that time, has been recognized not only in its physical aspect but likewise for its contributing to the development of a wholesome and well-balanced personality. The emphasis on health has certainly led to many excellent results, and play has been accepted as an important factor in producing increased physical efficiency in the entire organism — nerves and digestive functions as well as muscles and lungs. No one will quarrel with the truth of this, yet man is not only a physical organism.

Play, then, of a strenuous character, was considered to be the human need, and construction went forward to meet it. A national organization founded in 1906, the Playground Association of America, shows in its name this emphasis, and still more shows it in the early publications.[10] Some playground instructors, physical-education teachers, and even so-called recreation directors are still responsible for indoctrinating this idea to the exclusion of all others. In many community playground and recreation organizations the boy or girl who is uninterested in or incapable of active participation in vigorous physical activity finds fewer facilities and less capable leadership to serve his needs.

About the beginning of the twentieth century another word began to be used which showed a slightly different idea and demanded some change in the structure already erected; this word was *recreation*. There followed an increased amount of less strenuous sports and some use of activities that would once have been called "parlor games" and had been the province only of those who could afford equipment. Billiards, pool, and cards had long been used by the economically favored classes without having any opprobrium attached to them, since these games were played in private homes. Now, however, they proved themselves to be recreational forms adaptable to small spaces in urban

---

[10] For a complete survey of theories on play at this time, see Neumeyer, M. H. and E. S., *Leisure and Recreation*, pp. 133–150.

areas. Public opinion did not permit the expenditure of public moneys for such recreation. This left a gap which was quickly seized upon by commercial agencies. Today, the comparative lack of publicly supported social centers where games may be played is evidence of the fact that the less strenuous activities are not yet widely accepted by formal recreation agencies[11] and are left to be carried on for the most part where supervision of a constructive character is not provided along with the game.

The word *recreation* must be further mentioned in its original meaning, "re-creation." Though this basic connotation is seldom seen in modern usage of the word, it might well be that we would profit were we to see in it the element of rebuilding the personality. In this sense the term would certainly include all others in the field, for, of course, the object of all play is to re-create the whole man after he has been fatigued by too much attention to earning a living.

Leisure activity, however, seems to be even more satisfactory as the broadest term of all those used in regard to activities of people during the time that they are not working for their living. Play and recreation can be included in it. For instance, to some people, sports alone fill their leisure time; for others, dancing is the chief activity; play is the word used for small children's actions. Now, all of these are recreational activities. Could we say that studying astronomy, making charts of the positions of stars, erecting a laboratory for this purpose is play or recreation? Most people would not consider it such. Amateurs who discover new planets and make notable contributions to science are read of daily. Definitely, these amateurs are studying astronomy as a leisure-time activity. Thus the term *leisure* can include such broad fields as athletics, the arts, study, and crafts.

The word *leisure* has a further advantage over the other terms in that it has reference to the Aristotelian concept that the "good life"[12] is promoted by those who do not have to spend all of their time working to support existence. Would not emphasis on this view bring into our society a constructive idea toward more cultural interests, less of the mass seeking "What to do" and "Where to go" and more of the individual seeking for those deep joys possible only in self-initiated activity?

One could, thus, use the terms *play, recreation,* and *leisure* to represent the growth and increasing breadth of the movement concerned with that portion of man's life when he rebuilds his energies for the

---

[11] See however, *Social Work Year Book*, 1937, pp. 87–90.
[12] Aristotle, *The Politics*, Book VIII.

serious part of life. "Play," though often used to designate the free, spontaneous behavior of childhood which has no reward outside itself, is used more commonly to apply to vigorous sports, social or solitary, but especially competitive. "Recreation" would include, of course, the foregoing and would have reference to all those activities of a less strenuous type wherein the emphasis is not so much on expending energy as on relaxing from the fatigue of vigorous work or play. Finally, "leisure" certainly does not exclude anything that is play or recreation, but it has the value of emphasizing the intellectual and the cultural. For any well-balanced program of leisure-time activities, all types would surely have to be included.

Some Theories in Recreation

We have examined the words *play, recreation,* and *leisure* and attempted to ascertain the content of thought for each. If our institutional structure today is to be constructed in keeping with a whole view of life, the terms must be understood. It is often pointed out that the concept, belief, or idea, plus a structure erected in society in order to carry into fact that idea, is one of the chief characteristics of a social institution. It is most essential that we evaluate ideas and theories before they are permitted to form a part of our institutions. Sometimes it is merely the overemphasis of an idea that is objectionable rather than the idea itself. A number of such cases have been mentioned, such as the inadequacy of a philosophy of leisure that excludes the realization of eternal reward or punishment, the attitude of mere practicality in thinking of recreation as a problem without philosophical implications, and the undue emphasis on strenuous play without a corresponding emphasis on the possible value of other forms of leisure-time activities. Other theories that need consideration are: the "surplus-energy" theory, the "recapitulation" theory, the theory of awards, and the theory on the value of team play.

In the writings at the turn of the century there was an emphasis on the physical to the detriment of the spiritual. A number of authors spoke of man's necessity for expending his surplus energy in some form of play. Though of itself the idea is certainly admissible, one can recognize in writings in the field a sort of withheld judgment that we are compelled by nature to find an outlet for and expend a certain energy that is pent up within us. Very much in agreement with this notion is the emphasis of the instinctivists who once held that somehow play was instinctive in character although it might not be a separate instinct of itself. Again, there is an implied thought that man cannot help but correspond with these instincts. It will be noticed that such a teaching is a denial of man's free will and if applied to small children would lead, decidedly, to a *laissez-faire* treatment that would hardly aid the child in attaining a well-balanced maturity.

A further teaching that occurred within the period when the physical was receiving such emphasis is that known as the "recapitulation theory" in which man is thought of as going through in his play from childhood to maturity the evolutionary stages of the race, and this of necessity, without volition on his part, as though from the so-called "inner law of growth." Further, one advocate of this theory, G. Stanley Hall, foresees dire results if this necessity is frustrated. He writes: "Who knows but that our misers are not those children grown up whom fond mothers and fathers forced into giving away their playthings, into the doing of unselfish acts, in acting out a generosity which was neither felt nor understood."[13] According to this theory we should not hinder the child in his play by putting before him any moral concepts, for fear of his being prevented from carrying out the mythical period when men strove against each other in primeval conflict. The recapitulation theory is quite discredited today, but one finds its implications in many writings on play; namely, that children must be free to play as they please. It is the error of Naturalism.

Another theory is expressed in those definitions of play which require that it involve any kind of pleasurable activity undertaken without thought of a reward beyond the joy of the activity itself. Upon the basis of this view, the entire scouting program is sometimes criticized in that there is an elaborate plan of awards. No doubt it would be well to encourage young people, and for that matter all human beings, to follow the correct course of action simply for the joy of doing the right thing. It does seem, however, that a man's nature frequently requires an incentive to urge him to put forth his best efforts. Many adults show this desire for awards in a marked degree, at the bridge table, on the golf links, and in similar pursuits. It is a strange idea to try to take such things away from children, though of course excessive emphasis on the winning of prizes must be avoided, and in the character formation of children it is best that they should strive for a deferred reward.

A widely held theory is that group play produces certain definite results on the personality. Team activity has been sponsored by

---

[13] Hall, G. Stanley, *Aspects of Child Life and Education* (New York: Ginn & Co., 1907), p. 266.

schools, playgrounds, and social centers, as well as churches, because of this alleged value. Courage, co-operation, willing acceptance of leadership, diminishing of selfishness, and the growth of appreciation for laws, government, and a judiciary which hands down decisions in case of disputes have been said to grow from those sports in which a number of individuals play a game according to a set of rules. The United States has been following this idea for a number of years; and yet the frequent disregard of referees' decisions at public and private games, the discourteous treatment of opposing teams by the spectators, and a general disregard of law today do not point to the great success of team sports. It may be that so many other factors enter into the situation that the blame cannot be laid there; nevertheless, those who supervise play will agree that the problem of good sportsmanship is one that must be handled by the recreational director with great attention to the human being in question, his cultural background, and the extent to which his institutional life has assisted him in seeing the shades of justice and injustice. There is no doubt that team sports have the potentiality for the excellencies attributed to them. Still, these values will not be accomplished in the personality of the player except through the supervision of a functionary representing one of the basic institutions — the family, the Church, or the State — which institution interprets the changeless norms of conduct in terms of play.

Types of Recreation

The types of recreation were formerly considered in connection with age levels. This was an evidence of the nineteenth- and early twentieth-century approach where emphasis upon the physical changes that take place from infancy to maturity are used as the basis for all categories. Such an analysis led to the error of cutting a life into segments so that unthoughtful people looked at recreation as changing with each age in some necessary, fundamental way, rather than as a continuing influence of the whole life.

With age periods as a framework, it is possible to do a great deal of philosophizing and theorizing about play, but it is questionable whether any of these characteristic play activities end with the periods concerned. In fact, it would seem that the chief usefulness of such classifications is in the discussion of relative values possible in various types of recreational activity, rather than in the age-level idea. Our treatment will be primarily according to types of leisure-time activities — such types to include manipulation activities, vigorous play, the arts, team activities, hobbies, and finally, intellectual and spiritual projects

— with some small concession to the chronological order in which they appear.

Manipulation activities include the young child's play experience with toys, within the family circle. These assist him in muscle-co-ordination development and in a realization of spatial relationships. Not only the very young child is interested in working on things with his hands. Very much can be accomplished with slightly older children by developing in them an appreciation for color and design by using beads for patternmaking and similar play materials. The Montessori method took hold of this fact and made a valuable contribution that would seem to call for much wider acceptance in practice than has been the case. Too soon does the school system resort to a purely in-tellectualized approach as a means of obtaining knowledge. This results in young people emerging from our schools with no realization of how to fashion things with their hands, for either immediately useful or purely satisfying purposes. The old principle, so Catholic in its spirit, of educating the head, heart, and hand has been abandoned. In the recently emphasized craft program, a reversion to the more traditional combination of education through the head and hand is seen. Par-ticularly to be recommended in this regard is the renewed interest in the rural crafts — spinning, weaving, candlemaking, knitting, the mak-ing of hook rugs, and the arts of keeping bees, a garden, or an orchard. It is a mistake to look upon such activities only as a means of balanc-ing the family budget. Instead, this factor as a by-product may be recognized after giving first place to the creative joy and the construc-tive experience for the personality involved. In this regard the promoter of crafts, whether he be parent, teacher, or leisure-time director, must bear in mind that artistic excellence is not the objective of the activity and that the greatest personality enrichment may take place where the finished object is far from lovely.

Vigorous play and the joy accompanying it is a discovery made by the runabout child of two or three years, the child often belonging to his first extra-family group at this time, by playing with his neighbors. From tumbling, pushing, and pulling in a somewhat unplanned way, he grows into an appreciation for wagons, tricycles, and later bicycles, skates, and other toys. These and similar interests continue to appeal to large numbers of people throughout life, and he who leaves them behind with the things of childhood is depriving himself of a leisure-time activity in which the expending of one's physical powers gives the fullest possible satisfaction as well as an increase in health. Walking across an open space of country with the sun and wind as companions contributes immeasurably to one's freedom of spirit. Swimming, tennis, hunting, skiing, bowling, and boxing serve in various environments those individuals whose need is for a type of recreation in which personal skill and vigor are a requirement.

The arts — poetry, singing, drama, and the dance, sculpture, painting, architecture, and music, with the aid of any instrument, are appreciated by the very young. Early in childhood dramatic, imitative play will occupy the little person for hours at a time. He will hum to himself as he imagines that he is the father or mother of the house. No action, word, or personal peculiarity will be missed by his impersonation. His zest for stories of fairies or "Alice in Wonderland" are a compliment to his imagination that has not yet been dulled by the blunt reality of motion pictures. The rhythm of swinging, marching, and of poetry lines is native to him. Without sacrificing the vigorous activity needed by the child for physical development and health, these interests could be saved for his future needs by stimulating development of them throughout the grade-school period. The adolescent or adult would then not be so poor in interests and so at the mercy of high-pressure commercial agencies that vie with one another for his leisure hours. For some, maturity would bring a flowering of artistic ability, the fruit of early nurturing and faithful care during the years. America might, finally, be proud of her people building a deep and permanent culture of truth, and beauty, and joy.

Organized team activities probably begin in earnest during the period known as the "gang age." For both boys and girls in this period, no form of play contributes so much toward the ability to live happily in society with others, as the team games. Co-operation, sacrifice, leadership, and ability to follow are character traits which are developed if there is guidance either within or outside the team. But unless conscious effort is made to have the team function in such a way as to bring about personality improvement, it may happen that it will teach the child instead, that in children's play, as well as in adult's work, "bosses," "a pull," and "racketeer's methods" will help one win. Where this is prevented, child, adolescent, or adult will find in team games the opportunity to grow in social adjustment through experience with a variety of people and situations.

Clubs are another result of that tendency to associate in interest groups which makes its appearance during the "gang age" and continues in various forms throughout life. In studies of clubs it has been found that the number of children who belong to spontaneous groups (that is, such as are connected with play interests and formed without adult suggestion) increase about the age of nine years and continue until the age of about fourteen with boys and girls. At this time, they tend to join existing organizations. It often happens that a parent, teacher, or play director attempts to break up these natural cohesive groups. He would be more successful if he would guide this tendency along good lines instead of attempting to stop it. No group is too small to start with and small groups are group controlled. They can grow; the members' power to control will grow with them. If a group starts large, 25 or 30, it is leader controlled and probably always will be. This is not a club; it is an organized activity in which there may be some good, but it does not fill the club need. The intimate association of several people because of natural congeniality is a phenomenon much more difficult to guide than the desire to engage in team games. Games in which a few may play without too much expenditure of intellectual concentration or physical vigor makes possible that easy companionship that many seek at times. No high-pressure club program will fill this need; rather it will force the person into seeking his recreation some place where well-meaning persons are not forever attempting to regiment him. So long as the living wage is still a reform to be accomplished and many people are without warm homes to which they can invite their friends, private or public social centers must make available small meeting places where informal, unorganized groups may gather in happy companionship of play or conversation.

Hobbies form another leisure-time interest of universal appeal that likewise arises at an early age. This form of activity is individual rather than expressive of a need of recreation within the framework of society, although, of course, some hobbyists form their special societies, philatelic and the like. Some time between the ages of about seven and twelve, the boy ceases to have his pockets filled with every manner of thing that can be stuffed into them, but tends to collect but one type of article such as a large assortment of coat-lapel pins or of stamps. He may have boxes filled with birds' eggs, or his room with models of airplanes. His interests may change so often and so radically as to alarm his very stable parents. One might hazard the guess that the young child whose hobby remains the same for a long period of time is responding to a parent's wish rather than to his own interests; for normally the same hobby can hardly be maintained by the very young child for more than a week, and one slightly older cannot be expected to reach the adult span of interest. That permanent and consistent application to one hobby may lead to vocational remuneration in some distant future is probably true, but that is not the primary value of hobbies. They provide consuming interest in life, give a sense of power and achievement, make possible self-expression, and carry a compensation which may be denied one in his work activities; they furnish means of relaxation in mental and physical stress, and form an interest for the time of disability and old age. Psychiatrists point out the value of hobbies for the tired businessman whose only interest has been in making money and who now finds this no longer satisfying.[14]

Perhaps the last type of recreation, intellectual and spiritual projects, unfolds fully as an interest only in maturity, though certain elements of the foregoing types lend themselves to developing these higher faculties of man in the child and adolescent. Zest for abstract problems of the mind, of government, of social well-being is a characteristic not acquired without some guidance and considerable personal effort. Yet the world is greatly in need of men and women who will give themselves in their leisure hours to co-operative endeavors in making the world, nation, and community more fit for human living. The fact that legal justice requires such personal dedication to public causes — after obligations have been dispatched — is often disregarded in the allocation of time to recreational groups.

Spiritual pursuits, too, do not receive as much attention as time and means would often permit. Prayer and the things of God are regarded as part of the serious business of life and so they are, when only the minimum of attention is given to them. Some people, however, find that carrying out works enjoined by the commandment of "love thy neighbor" form their most deeply satisfying recreational activity. In childhood, love of those in one's immediate surrounding is evidenced by small services. Later in life, love should embrace a wider group, and so can be shown in volunteer social work, study-club activity, Christian labor leadership, assistance in youth organization work, in the donation of one's self and talents — insofar as one's obligations permit — to "restoring all things in Christ."

This brief treatment of types of recreation has been under the headings of manipulation activities, vigorous play, the arts, team activities — including team games, clubs, and small cohesive groups — hobbies, and finally intellectual and spiritual projects. It points to the range possible for man because of his physical, intellectual, and spiritual nature. Most individuals have special need of certain types at different times in their lives; some are physically handicapped and thus need special guidance; yet at no time should any one type be cultivated to

---

[14] On the value of hobbies to maintain mental balance, cf., Oliver, J. R., *Foursquare*, pp. 177, 178.

the entire exclusion of the others. A balanced leisure-time program is needed to promote the balanced personality.

The various types of recreation occur not only at all age levels but also in various relationships. We will now discuss recreation in its two-fold association, as leading to groups not only of primary importance, but to those of secondary character as well. The play group is of the primary, face-to-face type, and thus in the same category — for this purpose — as the home, church, school, and neighborhood. Recreational organization of a secondary-group type is seen in such agencies as movies, radio programs, mass recreation, and certain kinds of club associations.

Recreation, a Primary Group

In considering recreation as a primary group it is necessary to note first that it is into the home that the individual is born, and in it he learns the first lessons that play can teach. Only after the age of four or five does the play group outside the home begin to function as an influence in the child's life. Through it he is introduced to the art of adjusting to the relationships in a larger society than his immediate family. Many have thought that it would be well if the amount of recreation enjoyed in the home could be increased since intimate relations, there, make possible more permanent learning. To this end a very progressive section on "Home Play and Recreation" is to be found in the survey made of Buffalo. There is recorded the number of home parties and pets, the amount of back-yard play equipment and gardens, and the prevalency of music and games.[15] Too often recreational agencies compete with the home for the interest of children and young people. Yet it is agreed that the home needs strengthening. Rather than asserting that, since the home has failed, someone else must aid the child, would it not be useful for the formal recreation agencies to assist him in developing leisure interests that can be pursued in the home?

When there is a wage sufficient to provide adequate space and some facilities, the mother and father have it within their power to make available in the home, materials and incentives for the family's leisure hours. Since the wholesale mechanization of household duties has taken place, a mother often has leisure which may be dedicated to her home, community, vocational interests, or mere amusement. The father is in a like position with the advent of the shorter working day. The disposition which the father and mother make of their leisure hours will

---

[15] Weir, L. H., *Recreation Survey of Buffalo*, p. 369.

decide how much leisure time their children will spend in the home and in recreational groups approved of by them. Union of affection and mutual interests will make correction of character defects easy. Society will gain thereby. A special effort, however, is needed today if parents are to create that permanent and fully satisfying center of interest that existed formerly by the necessary oneness in play and work. This is the challenge to young parents in our modern world, as was pioneering in the wilderness in former days. It is a battle in which firmly rooted spiritual principles and a functioning intellect are assets rather than physical brawn.

Play is also of the primary-group type in the neighborhood and playground, where its intimacy and consequent power become evident. After the family, no other membership in life gives so definitely the feeling of "belonging" to a group in the closest social co-operation, and for this reason the urban child's play needs particular safeguarding. He is subjected to disorganization on every side in the form of family instability, economic insecurity, overcrowded living quarters, and a highly mobile population. In such a situation his gang is very likely to constitute the only unit to which he may "belong." Parks, where the grass is rigidly guarded by custodians against small boys, or playgrounds remote from the home with what guidance it provides, rather augment than aid the difficulty. Efforts to make possible wholesome play under such conditions are seen in the increased number of small play spots within approximately each city block, and the organization of boys' clubs in underprivileged areas. Such agencies will do a service to society so long as they do not attempt to become an autonomous institution. Recreational society must be a servant of the home. Play supervisors would do well to have as a principle of action: Give the child back to the home. The development of leisure interests in childhood and adolescence that can in the future be centered in the home to a very large degree will form the basis for a rich adult life, both from the individual and societal point of view.

Another situation in which recreation profits by being a primary group is when it is sponsored by the Church. Common recreation can be organized by, and thus used as a bond in, parish life. It is the Church that assists man to have the whole and balanced view of life and this can be made concrete in a parish recreation center. When recreational agencies fail to provide activity in keeping with the correct view of life, the Church has an obligation to teach it in whatever way may be most effective. "Going, therefore, teach ye all nations"[16] con-

---

[16] Matt. 28:19.

tains the charter for the Church's function. If teaching is best achieved through play at any time or place, it is the proper means toward the desired end. With this intention in mind many dioceses and parishes have instituted recreational programs. These have been successful where they were administered by leaders equally capable in making attractive both the means, recreation, and the end, eternal life. The parish priest, already overburdened, cannot be expected to have the time or training for such work. Young clerical assistants and lay leaders must assume the management of this new field. The Catholic Youth Organization in a number of dioceses attempts to furnish leadership and facilities for play. Boy and Girl Scout troops, Columbian Squires, and parish Sodalities are serving similar needs. Study clubs, sewing circles, and mission sections are interest groups for adults. The older adolescent who has left school and often is not yet absorbed in occupational society, has particular recreational needs. To him Recreational Society, functioning through the Church, could make a large contribution if the program covered all the types of recreation and provided an adequate amount of indoor facilities when outdoor recreation did not fill the need or was not possible. The Grail social and religious movement of Holland, Germany, Great Britain, and Australia fully realizes this value of recreation provided under religious auspices. Its plays are designed to train character as well as to provide recreation outlet for its members. Leading characters in these plays, which are always of an intensely religious nature, are five or more in number; minor characters may number for each 100 or even more. In this way more persons can take part in the activities, the timidity of amateurs is overcome, vanity is not fostered, and the effect of better acting and volume of voice upon the audience is most effective.

The school has attempted to meet the challenge of leisure needs by the increased numbers of recreation groups instituted through extracurricular activities. But it is doubtful whether a teacher, tired after a day's work with young people, has the necessary strength, zest, or originality left to run a recreation program that will compete favorably with commercial agencies. Further, from a purely academic view, the teacher is already carrying the burden of passing on a large part of the social heritage to the child, and the community cannot well afford to overburden him (or her) unless it is willing to sacrifice the excellence of the educational system.

Play and recreation, then, tends for the most part to be centered in group activity which may be said to be primary. Individuals having mutual interests will organize themselves for recreational purposes and meet together. The meeting place will be variously — according to age and economic status — a gang hut in a vacant lot, a commercially run pool hall, a transient shelter, a drugstore, a fraternity house, a club, a friend's home. If these natural cohesive groups are to follow such recreational pursuits as contribute to character improvement and societal stability, adequate places for meeting and responsible leadership must be provided. Wherever the facilities sponsored by the family, church, or private organizations do not meet the need completely, a governmental unit must step in to fill the gap. The important factor throughout all this is that the primary character of play and recreation be maintained by building around the small local center. Someone has said that the unit of human relationships is about two hundred people. Therefore, from the human point of view there is actual inefficiency in the highly centralized, expensive recreation headquarters.

Recreation, a Secondary Group

Today, large numbers of people do not come under the socializing influence of the primary recreation groups where spontaneous interest, attention, and often affection, unite the individuals and furnish them with strong, readily accepted social controls. Rather they spend their leisure hours in secondary groups where the contact is not face to face, where there are rarely direct personal relations, and where the motive is often profit rather than the good of the individual. This is but one fact in the depersonalizing process which is going on to such a degree that it has been said that we no longer live in a human fashion.

A darkened motion-picture house is typical of the way in which we are massed together in large numbers where one rarely knows his neighbor, and where one receives the sometimes powerful lessons of dramatic situations among people whom one does not, and probably never will, know. Many groups have interested themselves in the effect of motion pictures on the behavior of children and young people with the result that data is available showing that social attitudes and values are being greatly affected. This influence appears to be not in agreement with Christian morals.[17] Further, it is estimated that the weekly admissions during 1930 were close to 115,000,000 and that with forty cents as the average cost the annual expenditure was $2,392,-000,000.[18] The following official census figures for 1935[19] of places of amusement charging admission or receiving fees for use of recreational

---

[17] Cf. Hornell Hart, "Changing Attitudes and Interests," *Recent Social Trends,* p. 386.
[18] *Ibid.,* p. 951.
[19] *Statistical Abstract of the United States,* 1937, p. 821.

facilities give a clear indication of the importance of commercial amusements in the lives of American citizens, particularly as they exclude all places of amusement "operated by educational institutions, municipalities, or other governmental agencies, or fraternal or religious organizations."

Kind of Business	Number of Establishments	Total Receipts (thousands of dollars)
United States total	37,677	$699,051
Amusement devices	902	4,360
Amusement parks	303	8,982
Bands and orchestras	708	4,611
Baseball and football clubs, sports and athletic fields, and sports promoters	426	25,273
Bathing beaches	328	2,218
Billiard and pool parlors, and bowling alleys	12,412	43,271
Boat and canoe rental service	939	1,479
Circulating libraries (commercial)	932	3,039
Dance halls, studios, and academies	3,872	14,831
Horse- and dog-race tracks	64	32,466
Riding academies	645	2,448
Skating rinks	345	1,396
Swimming pools	698	1,938
Theaters, legitimate stage and opera; and theatrical productions	158	19,630
Theaters, motion pictures (including motion-picture theaters with vaudeville)	12,024	508,196
Other amusements	2,921	24,913

When the two factors — of social values and extent of practice — are combined with the importance placed upon experiences of an emotional character in a child's life, it becomes apparent that noncommercial recreation of a more wholesome character is necessary. The radio, when furnishing programs of questionable value for the masses, likewise takes on the undesirable character of a secondary group in being intangible, uncontrollable, and irresponsible to individual influence. "Fan mail" of popular performers in both the field of motion picture and radio shows the human desire to make more intimate the contacts of leisure hours and the widespread imitation of the stars' way of life.

Many people spend a large portion of their recreation in attending mass sport displays such as prize fights, the baseball games, and the great football spectacles. All of these depersonalized forms of recreation do not serve any socializing purpose. If not overdone they can be a legitimate form of amusement, but they can never contribute to personality growth in the same degree as activities in which the individual is known and evaluated through participation. Neighborly actions are never exchanged between the individual and the performers, and in life's battle neither seeks the other out in order to reach a helping hand. Mass recreation leaves one alone after the show.

In response to this need for intimate association, not furnished so perfectly by home, church, and neighborhood relationships as it was formerly, a person joins one group after another. By becoming a member of some permanent, continuing organization, he feels that, regardless of whether his friends move away to distant communities or not, he has a group to which he may "belong" even though the members thereof change constantly. Data gathered in connection with President Hoover's Research Committee on Social Trends shows this tendency by such correlated data as the tax receipts on club dues of more than $25 annually was $12,521,091 in 1931;[20] Federal tax on 49,329,062 packs of playing cards was paid in 1931;[21] and membership in luncheon clubs is estimated at 500,000.[22] A further reason, perhaps, that has swelled the number of "joiners" is the need today to be articulate on certain social, economic, and political issues, and the futility of an individual's attempting to exert pressure alone. The organization of labor groups is particularly due to this cause. Again, in this case we see the result of the breakdown of the primary occupational group where the employer and employees knew each other and the needs of each. The recreational aspect of all of these agencies is sometimes secondary and yet it plays a large part in some lives.

For the individual, membership in organizations has varying usefulness. It may be that a necessary sociability is promoted in the rural areas by the formation of some interest group such as the study club provides. In the urban area, it is very probable that the saturation point has been reached long ago and many memberships actually decrease the individual's social efficiency. Our recreational society has been particularly liberal in providing group opportunities, but it is necessary that agencies seek also to develop interests fruitful for the individual when he is alone. But where is this solitude to be sought? The home is the social institution in which those creative types of leisure most conducive to the "good life" can best be pursued. If in adult years it is hoped that the individual will find in his home the source of his joy and relaxation, in youth he must establish the taste and habit for some kind of leisure-time activity for which the home

---

[20] *Recent Social Trends*, p. 934.
[21] *Ibid.*, p. 935.
[22] *Ibid.*, p. 936.

can furnish the equipment. The gigantic network of recreational agencies does not, for the most part, make any effort to strengthen the home, or to promote tastes for games or pursuits that will have a carry-over value for the average home of the future.

We should like to regard recreation as an aspect of social life where the community builds to fill its manifest needs, and that this building is of a foundational, permanent type that rests upon each individual, his ideas, and his activity in agreement with his thought. Recreation is, however, most often thought of as belonging to the problems section of sociology and indeed there are many reasons for so regarding it. Certain problems discussed in the following chapters — high social mobility seen in immigration, rural-urban flow of population, and urbanization; the crime rate among young people; and rapid industrialization — have impeded the growth of recreational society. Yet it is a mistake so to identify recreational society with problems as to disregard the necessity for a positive, institutional approach in order to accomplish constructive change.

Perhaps the social problem most closely related with recreation in America today is the creation of a great propertyless class, dependent upon a periodic wage for subsistence, and the resulting leisure habits as described by Stuart Chase in *Men and Machines*. His recognition of the extent to which man has become subject to the machines which were made to serve him is representative of a general awakening. With the advent and prolonged continuation of the depression and recession has come a healthy realization to thoughtful men and women of the nation. Enforced rest found us chained to a state of mind which might be called a "dollars-and-cents compulsion." Many seemed literally unable to enjoy any activity which was not either of the "getting or spending" variety. Even further schooling had no charms if a job were not guaranteed. When one must live on "relief" without the cash to drive the car to some distant dance, to attend a prize fight, movie, or symphony according to one's tastes, one has "nothing to do." The poor were not alone in this sad plight; leisure without money was as much of a mystery to those of the middle and richer classes touched by adverses. These economic reverses have made us realize that all classes had accepted but two pleasures as ends of life, the making of money and the spending of it. As a nation, we are utilitarians in the extreme.

Obviously, since the difficulty is in the mind and heart, it will not be adequate for society simply to provide bigger and better recreation facilities without a constructive approach in the matter of the end of life and proper means as aids to fulfilling that end, such as are discussed as the postulates of sociology in Chapter 7. It is for this reason that we should regard recreation from an institutional rather than from a purely problematic point of view. Recreation will then take its place with the school, in the institutional structure of society, as an instrument for the good of the individual in the hands of the family, Church, and State.

PART THREE

SOCIAL PROBLEMS

CHAPTER 16

WORKING CONDITIONS AND WAGES

The Importance of Working Conditions

WE NOW come to the more practical division of this book. We have tried briefly to describe the place of man in the temporal world, and have discussed the various factors which affect both individual and group life. We have also outlined the major theories about social life, have shown wherein the social theory of the Catholic differs from many of the materialistic theories of the day. We have studied the fundamental societies to which man belongs. It now remains to make a survey of the principal social problems of our times, and to discuss their causes and the various agencies for their relief.

Not only must the average man spend the greater part of his working day in labor for others, but he depends upon the wages he receives for his work to provide for all the material wants of himself and his dependents. This is particularly true at the present time, when the populations of most "civilized" countries are city dwellers, and thus entirely dependent upon a money wage for the means of existence. The worker is therefore vitally concerned with two factors: the physical and social conditions in which he works, and the wages which he is paid and with which he hopes to provide himself and his dependents with sustenance, a physical home, and all their other needs.

I. *Unhygienic and Dangerous Working Conditions.* The conditions under which a man works are of great importance, and should be compatible with human dignity and human needs. It has long been recognized that when workers are engaged in industry, unsanitary conditions, dangerous machinery, unhealthy work, undue speeding up of a worker's output, long working hours, inadequate lighting and ventilation, all serve to make factory conditions inimical to the worker's health, morals, and efficiency. Public opinion and general improvements in standards throughout the world have led to great improvements since the rapid growth of factory organization some hundred and fifty years ago.

Notable improvements have also been made as "voluntary concessions" by employers. Modern employers have realized that increased production may be obtained not only by installing new and more efficient machinery but by studying the worker also. Scientific management is the name given to this study of increased production at decreasing costs, and the same idea, but considering the worker more as a human being, and not as a mere "instrument of production" is taken up under the name of industrial psychology and mental hygiene. It has been discovered in recent years, therefore, that a happy and healthy worker produces more than a discontented and overworked one; that the worker's day is made agreeable to him, if he is given scientific rest pauses, if he is provided with tools and furniture adjusted for his comfort, with rest rooms and playfields, and if he has shorter working hours and higher wages. Hence, what individual employers should accomplish from higher motives, they often carry out for the selfish reasons of increased production and greater profits. These scientific methods have also demonstrated that good working conditions not only promote efficiency in the workers but, by lessening fatigue and harassment, indirectly result in a decrease in industrial accidents.

Factory legislation has, however, been the greatest cause of improved conditions. Current laws provide for the protection of the worker in all that concerns factory conditions of hygiene and danger. Most states require that working premises be sanitary, and the walls whitewashed or painted at specified intervals; that adequate lighting be provided; that all dangerous machinery be carefully protected with guards; that noxious fumes, gases, dust from grinding and polishing metals be removed as far as possible by the provision of flues and other devices; and that adequate and separate toilet facilities be provided for workers of both sexes. Dangerous occupations have special legislation requiring that those working with lead, arsenic, phosphorous, or other dangerous chemicals are provided with washing facilities and a separate room for eating, and usually workers are not allowed to take meals in the workroom. This legislation is usually rigidly enforced by state factory inspectors.

With the increased use of machinery and large-scale production, statistics show yearly a corresponding increase in the number of workers incapacitated either because of accident or because of industrial disease. Because the employer is often indirectly responsible for these contingencies, and because he is better able to bear the cost of the risks undertaken by workers on behalf of industry, workmen's compensation legislation now exists to provide for cases which are not covered by the common law. This legislation for industrial risks is treated in the next chapter. It must be noted, however, that work-men's compensation acts in general have not only protected the worker by making provision for compensation when he is injured, but they have very materially supplemented factory acts for the general amel-ioration of working conditions. Where the employer insures against his liability, insurance companies charge lower premiums to those who safeguard the worker from unnecessary risks, hence the employer, for his own financial benefit, inaugurates safety-first movements, in-structs the worker in the right use of equipment, sees that all ma-chinery is properly guarded, obnoxious fumes and dust eliminated as much as possible, and takes other like precautions.

For the protection of the workers themselves, as well as for the protection of the public, most states have established health laws re-quiring periodic examination of restaurant workers, hairdressers, and others to disclose those having syphilis, tuberculosis, or other con-tagious diseases.

The Women's Bureau of the United States Department of Labor has summarized its standards for employment as follows:

"An adequate wage, based on occupation and not on sex and cover-ing the cost of living of dependents; time for recreation, self-develop-ment, leisure, by a workday of not more than 8 hours, including rest periods; not less than 1½ days off in the week; no night work; no industrial home work.

"A clean, well-aired, well-lighted workroom, with adequate provi-sion against excessive heat and cold; a chair for each woman, built on posture lines and adjusted to both worker and job; elimination of constant standing and constant sitting.

"Guarded machinery and other safety precautions; mechanical de-vices for the lifting of heavy weights and other operations abnormally fatiguing; protection against industrial poisons, dust, and fumes; first-aid equipment; no prohibition of women's employment, except in in-dustries definitely proved by scientific investigation to be more in-jurious to women than to men.

"Adequate and sanitary service facilities as follows: Pure and acces-sible drinking water, with individual cups or sanitary fountains; con-venient washing facilities, with hot and cold water, soap, and indi-vidual towels; standard toilet facilities, in the ratio of 1 installation for every 15 women; cloak rooms; rest rooms; lunch rooms, and the allowance of sufficient time for lunch.

"A personnel department charged with responsibility for the selec-tion, assignment, transfer, or withdrawal of workers and for the establishment of proper working conditions; a woman employment executive and women in supervisory positions in the department employing women; employees to share in the control of the conditions of employment by means of chosen representatives, some of them women; co-operation with Federal and State agencies dealing with labor and employment conditions; the opportunity for women workers to choose the occupations for which they are best adapted as a means of insuring success in their work."[1]

II. *Long Hours of Labor.* It is important that the wage contract should not enforce long hours of labor on the worker. Man should not be a slave, and his intelligence demands that he should have adequate time for rest and recreation. The length of the working day is, too, an important factor in the health and happiness of the worker. A reasonably short working day reduces fatigue, and hence accidents; it improves the worker's health, physique, and morale as a result of a more human existence; it increases interest in the home and family life; gives time for religious duties, for physical development, recreation, mental improvement, and sociability; and it prevents the moral degeneration so often caused by overfatigue. Often a shorter working day leads to increased production and with the constant development of technological unemployment, at least until necessary adjustments are made, shorter working hours would do much to relieve the problem.

Pope Leo XIII laid down rules which cover most of the conditions as regards hours of work for dignified human labor:

"But if the owners of property must be made secure, the workman, too, has property and possessions in which he must be protected; and first of all, there are his spiritual and mental interests. Life on earth, however good and desirable in itself, is not the final purpose for which man is created; it is only the way and the means to that attainment of truth, and that practice of goodness in which the full life of the soul consists. . . .

"If we turn now to things exterior and corporal, the first concern of all is to save the poor workers from the cruelty of grasping speculators, who use human beings as mere instruments for making money. It is neither justice nor humanity so to grind men down with excessive labor as to stupefy their minds and wear out their bodies. Man's powers, like his general nature, are limited, and beyond these limits he cannot go. His strength is developed and increased by use and exercise, but only on condition of due intermission and proper rest.

---

[1] U. S. Dept. of Labor, Women's Bureau, *Fact Finding with the Women's Bureau,* Bulletin No. 84, 1931, p. 10.

Daily labor, therefore, must be so regulated that it may not be protracted during longer hours than strength admits. How many and how long the intervals of rest should be, will depend upon the nature of the work, on circumstances of time and place, and on the health and strength of the workman. Those who labor in mines and quarries, and in work within the bowels of the earth, should have shorter hours in proportion as their labor is more severe and more trying to strength. Finally, work which is suitable for a strong man cannot reasonably be required from a woman or a child. . . . As a general principle, it may be laid down, that a workman ought to have leisure and rest in proportion to the wear and tear on his strength; for the waste of strength must be repaired by the cessation of work.

"In all agreements between masters and workpeople, there is always the condition, expressed or understood, that there be allowed proper rest for soul and body. To agree in any other sense would be against what is right and just; for it can never be right or just to require on the one side, or to promise on the other, the giving up of those duties which a man owes to his God and to himself."[2]

Labor unions and a certain amount of legislation have improved general conditions, but there is still room for further regulation. Further legislation for reduced hours is dangerous, perhaps, as employers may then recuperate possible losses by making greater use of available machinery, but at least greater uniformity of laws seems to be needed. Public employees practically all over the United States have a legal eight-hour day; several of the states limit the hours of labor in mines, smelters, laundries, and other dangerous occupations. Practically all the states have laws limiting the number of hours daily during which a woman may work. About one third of them prohibit nightwork for women; most of the states exclude women from mining and other dangerous occupations, but farm work and domestic services are generally specifically exempt from regulation. Nightwork in particular should be prohibited to prevent physical and moral dangers. While legislation for men has been contested in the United States as an intrusion of their liberty to make a free contract, it has also been contested on the grounds that it is impossible to fix a standard working day which would be reasonable for all trades, and that in some industries, a shorter working day leads to greatly decreased production which the employer cannot afford. Arguments for hours legislation for women are chiefly based on the importance of their health as the possible mothers of future citizens. It is to be noted, however, that

---

[2] *Rerum Novarum*, pp. 22, 23, 24 (*RN*, 32, 33).

greater uniformity in the various state laws would often be desirable, for while labor conditions are more or less adequately covered in some states, they are most inadequately cared for in others.

The Fair Labor Standards Act of 1938 legislates for a maximum 44-hour week for standard pay for the first year of its existence, a 42-hour week the next year, and a 40-hour week thereafter. However, overtime may be required if at least one and a half times the basic wage is paid to the worker, and an employer may require a longer working period without overtime payment in the following three conditions: if an agreement has been made "as a result of collective bargaining by representatives of employees certified as bona fide by the National Labor Relations Board, which provides that no employee shall be employed more than one thousand hours during any period of twenty-six consecutive weeks," or for not longer than two thousand hours during any period of fifty-two consecutive weeks; thirdly, if the overtime is for a "period or periods of not more than fourteen work weeks in the aggregate in any calendar year in an industry found by the Administrator to be of a seasonal nature, and if such employee receives compensation for employment in excess of 12 hours in any workday, or for employment in excess of 56 hours in any work week, as the case may be, at a rate not less than one and one-half times the regular rate at which he is employed." It must be noted, however, that the Fair Labor Standards Act only concerns industries connected with interstate commerce, and it does not apply to any employee employed in a bona fide executive, administrative, professional, or local retailing capacity; or anyone employed as a seaman, or in the fish industry, or in agriculture; or anyone employed as a carrier by air, or in connection with the publication of any weekly or semiweekly newspaper with a circulation of less than three thousand, the major part of which circulation is within the county where printed and published, or by street, suburban, or interurban electric railway or local trolley or motor bus carrier. Anyone engaged in handling, packing, storing, ginning, compressing, pasteurizing, drying, preparing in their raw or natural state, or canning of agricultural or horticultural commodities for market, or in making cheese or butter or other dairy products, is also exempt; so, too, learners, apprentices, and handicapped workers who possess special certificates issued by the Administrator of the Act.

It may be of interest to quote the findings of the Kellogg Company, Michigan, on their introduction of a six-hour day in December, 1930:

"While the chief advantages to the worker, under the six-hour day, are fairly obvious in the actual operation, we have discovered others which were not so obvious to us before we inaugurated this system. An enumeration of these advantages may prove interesting:

"More leisure time for recreation (embracing both rest and play).

"Opportunity to cultivate farms or gardens especially by those living on the outskirts of the city, affording them both wholesome exercise and a supply of fruits and flowers, vegetables and dairy products for their tables.

"Time to pursue educational courses, music, or other cultural studies.

"Increased incentive to prepare for managerial jobs, as the change from three to four shifts makes necessary an additional full staff of managers, foremen, foreladies, etc.

"Less fatigue due to smaller number of hours of work daily, and longer periods of rest between, resulting in a more healthy, ambitious, alert, and aggressive working force.

"Opportunity for mothers who must support children to earn a living and yet have ample time at home to care for their families.

"Less waste time, due to concentration of work in a single period.

"Decreased cost of living, on account of being able to have all meals at home.

"Greater assurance of a steady job due to the fact that the increase in the number of workers employed absorbs more of the city's working people, makes them earners and consumers, and stabilizes the local industrial situation.

"The list of advantages to the company is almost as impressive:

"Increased daily production from the plant as an operating unit, due to increased production at every station or task, slight in itself but considerable in the aggregate.

"Elimination of meal periods, with their waste, and the expense of a large cafeteria.

"Increased return from the capital invested in plant and machinery, owing to the increased rate of plant operation.

"Opportunity for reorganizing the working force to rectify inequalities and fit all 'pegs' in appropriate 'holes.'

"Decreased overhead due to the fact that the factory produces more packages of cereals per dollar of overhead than under the eight-hour shift."[3]

III. *Woman and Child Labor.* Both Pope Leo XIII and Pope Pius XI have expressed themselves on the subject of woman and child

---

[3] *What of the Six-Hour Day?*, Pamphlet issued by the Kellogg Company, Battle Creek, Michigan.

labor. As Pope Leo says: "Women, again, are not suited to certain trades; for a woman is by nature fitted for homework, and it is that which is best adapted at once to preserve her modesty, and promote the good bringing up of children and the wellbeing of the family."[4] And Pope Pius, disapproving of mothers working away from the home sphere, does not regard unfavorably women and children helping to maintain the family, for idleness is good for none, provided the hours of labor are not too long, the work not too excessive or unsuited to them, and provided also that they can stay at home.

"It is right indeed that the rest of the family contribute according to their power toward the common maintenance, as in the rural home or in the families of many artisans and small shopkeepers. But it is wrong to abuse the tender years of children or the weakness of woman. Mothers will above all devote their work to the home and the things connected with it. Intolerable and to be opposed with all our strength, is the abuse whereby mothers of families, because of the insufficiency of the father's salary, are forced to engage in gainful occupations outside the domestic walls to the neglect of their own proper cares and duties, particularly the education of their children."[5]

As regards the employment of women outside the home, United States Census figures show[6] that the number has greatly increased in recent years and the percentage increase is much higher than the growth in population.

Year	Number	Percentage of all women in U. S. over 10 years of age	Percentage of all persons gainfully employed
1880	2,647,000	14.7	15.2
1890	4,005,000	17.4	17.1
1900	5,319,000	18.8	18.3
1910	8,076,000	23.4	21.2
1920	8,550,000	21.1	20.5
1930	10,752,000	22.0	22.0

Married women present the greatest problem, because it is impossible for a mother, occupied all day away from home, to perform her family duties, and to give adequate care and supervision to her children. The result is only too often that a house is used by the entire family merely as a place in which to eat and sleep. Tired from her day's industrial work, it is well-nigh impossible for a woman to pre-

[4] *Rerum Novarum*, p. 24 (*RN*, 33).

[5] *Quadragesimo Anno*, pp. 23, 24 (*QA*, 27).

[6] U. S. Bureau of the Census, Census of Occupations: Abstract Summary, 1932, 35 pp.

pare nourishing meals, to keep the home attractive, and to give due attention to her husband and children. The average time spent in household duties by the married woman staying at home depends on the number of children, but in the United States 50–60 hours weekly seems to be the average.[7] Obviously, if this is so, a married woman who works outside the home cannot possibly give the same attention to the ordinary household tasks, unless she can afford a maid or a number of laborsaving devices. Infant mortality, poor health, broken homes, divorce, juvenile delinquency, are frequent results of a woman occupying an industrial or commercial position. In these days, also, the temptations for a married working woman to practice birth control are very strong.

Most married women who work do so because of the insufficiency of their husband's wages or because for some reason or other the family depends either wholly or in part on their earnings. The necessity would be greatly diminished with the universal establishment of minimum-wage laws. It would be further curtailed if the practice of some states of paying mother's pensions to widows were extended to all the states of the Union. A further development of social insurance would also frequently eliminate the necessity of married women entering industry. Most effective of all would be, of course, a reorganization of industry on a better social plan.

The Women's Bureau of the United States Department of Labor, which grew out of the Woman in Industry Service of the War Labor Administration, has as its function to "formulate standards and policies which shall promote the welfare of wage-earning women, improve their working conditions, increase their efficiency, and advance their opportunities for profitable employment." Its standards for employment were quoted earlier in the chapter.

So far as children are concerned, the number and proportion gainfully employed has considerably decreased since the beginning of the century. The *Statistical Abstract* for 1930 gives the following:

Year	Number of children in the U. S. between 10 and 15 years of age	Number of these gainfully employed	Percentage
1900	9,613,252	1,750,178	18.2
1910	10,828,365	1,990,225	18.4
1920	12,502,582	1,060,858	8.5
1930	14,300,576	667,118	4.7

[7] Cf. M. E. Pidgeon, *Women in the Economic Life of the United States of America,* U. S. Dept. of Labor, 1937, pp. 31, 32.

Legislation for children is justified on account of their need for the State's protection against neglect or exploitation. As Pope Leo says: "In regard to children, great care should be taken not to place them in workshops and factories until their bodies and minds are sufficiently mature. For just as rough weather destroys the buds of spring, so too early an experience of life's hard work blights the young promise of a child's powers, and makes real education impossible."[8]

In the United States most states specify the age limit below which gainful employment of children is prohibited, and restrict the number of hours a day during which children under sixteen may work, prohibit nightwork and the employment of children under eighteen in dangerous occupations, and require children employed to spend a certain number of hours every week in school. The National Child Labor Committee has done much to forward this legislation. Mention must be also made of the United States Children's Bureau, founded in 1912 to investigate and report conditions relating to the welfare of children and child life. It must not be forgotten, however, that state laws such as the above may become a menace to the power and liberty of the family when not in the hands of a wise administration.

The Fair Labor Standards Act of 1938, mentioned previously, prohibits any producer, manufacturer, or dealer from shipping or delivering for shipment in interstate commerce any goods "produced in an establishment situated in the United States in or about which within thirty days prior to the removal of such goods therefrom any oppressive child labor has been employed." The Act does not apply to any child "employed in agriculture while not legally required to attend school, or to any child employed as an actor in motion pictures or theatrical productions." "Oppressive child labor" is defined by the Act as "a condition of employment under which (1) any employee under the age of sixteen years is employed by an employer (other than a parent or a person standing in the place of a parent) . . . in any occupation, or (2) any employee between the ages of sixteen and eighteen years is employed by an employer in any occupation which the Chief of the Children's Bureau in the Department of Labor shall find and by order declare to be particularly hazardous for the employment of children between such ages or detrimental to their health or well-being." Although Southern children are often engaged in agriculture which is probably less harmful to their health than the industrial and commercial occupations which engaged much child labor in the North, the

---

[8] *Rerum Novarum,* p. 24 (*RN,* 33).

1930 Census statistics show[9] that there is a disproportionately large number of child workers in the states of Alabama, Arkansas, Georgia, Mississippi, North Carolina, South Carolina, and Tennessee.

Child labor is due to a variety of causes: the greed of employers, and the industrial system providing for it; the poverty of parents and economic necessity, and sometimes also their selfishness; the dissatisfaction of children with school life and their anxiety to earn a livelihood.

Its evils are a grave danger to the State. Child labor tends to weaken the moral authority of the parents, and thus disrupts the home and leads to juvenile delinquency. It endangers the children's health and mental development, deprives them of the health-giving properties of carefree play, and dulls their intelligence. Indeed, adolescent children in particular are in great need of the care of parents and the home. Immature in their judgment, lacking in self-control, with the nervous system and other bodily functions especially delicate on account of the great and uneven growth, children in the adolescent period are particularly liable to physical and mental harm as a result of the overstrain, fatigue, and generally injurious surroundings attaching to industrial and commercial labor. Child labor also restricts their education, leads them to blind-alley occupations where they have no opportunity of fitting themselves for the better positions obtainable in later life by the more healthy and the better educated. It also detracts from their efficiency and limits their possibility of increased earning capacity. This is particularly true of service occupations — work in stores and theaters, and as messengers where their youthful speed, charm, or beauty is often their chief attraction to employers and those they serve, and they are not getting the value of the more productive work in agriculture or actual industrial occupations.[10] When girls are employed away from the home at too early an age, not only is their health often seriously affected, but either further strain is put upon their health by the necessity of doing household tasks before or after working hours, or they receive no training in caring for a home and often make poor wives and mothers in later life. In sum, the early employment of children often deprives them of the opportunity of becoming valuable citizens of the State.

IV. *Inadequate Wages.* The remuneration which is paid to man for labor as a part of production is wages. Time wages, payments

---

[9] Cf. *Occupational Statistics of the United States — Summary,* U. S. Bureau of the Census, 1932, p. 95.
[10] Cf. Miriam van Waters, *Youth in Conflict,* pp. 116, 117.

made by the hour, day, week, or longer period are now usually made only where the actual production cannot be mathematically computed, as in remunerating a professional worker such as a teacher, and one who renders such personal services as a domestic servant, or where quality is more important than speed, such as certain types of jewelry work. Payment is more frequently made per unit of output, that is, payment by the piece, or by results.

The problem of wages is twofold: First, it is a problem of enabling the worker to earn his daily bread, and since few people are now able directly to supply themselves with their material needs, they must now usually depend for a livelihood in our capitalistic order upon hiring their labor under a wage contract. Second, it is a problem of distribution: the apportionment of the income of a community among the different members and classes.

It certainly seems consonant with human dignity that a reasonable livelihood should be guaranteed to workers as a first charge on industry, and that a fair day's work should at least produce an adequate income for a man and a normal-sized family to live in reasonable comfort. Yet neither must it be forgotten that land, capital, and organization are necessary in production. Unless these factors are attracted to production we should have to go back to direct production, with its consequent losses of specialized productive power. There should, therefore, be a reasonable equivalence between the wages which go to the worker; the price of products to the consumer; and the rent, interest, profits, which go to the landowner, capitalist, and entrepreneur. Neither the consumer nor any one of the factors of production should benefit at the expense of the rest. Wages should be fixed not only with regard to the capacity of the worker, his general welfare and that of his family, including provision for the danger of unemployment, but also with regard to the welfare of the nation as a whole, including the worker, capitalist, landowner, entrepreneur, and the consuming public. Especially should the human needs of the worker be adequately regarded before the material factors in production are considered.

Definition of a Living Wage

The payment of a living wage for a fair day's work seems to be a first charge upon industry. As Pope Leo XIII said: "As a rule, workman and employer should make free agreements, and in particular should freely agree as to wages; nevertheless, there is a dictate of nature more imperious and more ancient than any bargain between man and man, that the remuneration be enough to support the wage earner in reasonable and frugal comfort. If through necessity or fear of a worse evil, the workman accepts harder conditions because an employer will give him no better, he is the victim of force and injustice."[11] And again we read: "The employer must never tax his workpeople beyond their strength, nor employ them in work unsuited to their sex or age. His great and principal obligation is to give to everyone that which is just. Doubtless before we can decide whether wages are adequate many things have to be considered; but the rich man and masters should remember this — that to exercise pressure for the sake of gain, upon the indigent and destitute, and to take one's profit out of the need of another is condemned by all laws, human and divine. To defraud anyone of wages that are his due is a crime which cries to the avenging anger of heaven. 'Behold, the hire of laborers . . . which by fraud has been kept back by you, crieth; and the cry of them hath entered the ears of the Lord of Sabaoth.' Finally, the rich must religiously refrain from cutting down the workman's earnings, either by force, fraud, or usurious dealing; and with the more reason because the poor man is weak and unprotected, and because his slender means should be sacred in proportion to their scantiness."[12]

In view of the general need to labor for one's livelihood, and because of the essential human dignity of the worker, a living wage should therefore be sufficient to obtain a reasonable livelihood in return for a fair day's work: at least to have a minimum of "reasonable and frugal comfort." And since man is a social being and seems intended by nature to marry and found a family, a reasonable living wage may be construed as adequate to provide for a family of normal size in the community which is being considered. This wage should be adequate to provide food in sufficient quantity and quality to maintain the efficiency of the individual members of the family; sufficient clothes to provide warmth and decency; adequate housing to provide a healthful, moral environment; sufficient fuel to supply warmth; sufficient light for reading and other purposes; sufficient funds to provide for a reasonable amount of recreation, a befitting education, social intercourse, medical attention, church membership, and insurance against life's contingencies, such as an old age provided for without dependence on State or charity. A living wage for a woman may be said to be an adequate income for her to maintain herself in reasonable comfort away from home.

---

[11] *Rerum Novarum*, pp. 25, 26 (*RN*, 34).
[12] *Ibid.*, p. 11 (*RN*, 16, 17).

Pope Leo XIII has well expressed the reasons for the payment of a living wage. "A man's labor has two notes or characters, he says. First of all it is *personal;* for the exertion of individual power belongs to the individual who puts it forth, employing this power for that personal profit for which it was given. Secondly, a man's labor is *necessary;* for without the results of labor a man cannot live; and self-conservation is a law of nature, which it is wrong to disobey. Now, if we were to consider labor merely so far as it is *personal,* doubtless it would be within the workman's right to accept any rate of wages whatever; for in the same way as he is free to work or not, so he is free to accept a small remuneration or even none at all. But this is a mere abstract supposition; the labor of the workingman is not only his personal attribute, but it is *necessary;* and this makes all the difference. The preservation of life is the bounden duty of each and all, and to fail therein is a crime. It follows that each one has a right to procure what is required in order to live; and the poor can procure it no other way than by work and wages."[13]

Of course the value of a person's work may be much more than a living wage, for workers differ in physical strength, in character, intelligence, training, education, and skill. Certain occupations are unusually difficult or hazardous; others demand exceptional intelligence and skill, or such qualities of character as dependability, leadership, extreme honesty, or prolonged application; some are costly to learn, or give the worker greater or less social esteem. Again, some types of work provide employment for part of the year only, or are suitable only for younger men, so that the worker runs risks of permanent unemployment at a relatively early age; or they may give little or great opportunity of future promotion. Then, too, the money equivalent of the required living wage for a family varies according to the size of the family, the domestic ability of the housekeeper, and the locality. In this latter connection, the purchasing power of money and the standard of living of the community must be considered. Prices are cheaper in some districts than in others, so that the real value of a low wage in one place may possibly be much higher than the real value of higher nominal wages elsewhere. And again, since our wants are so largely determined by habit, lower purchasing power in a district with less high material standards may give a worker as much or more satisfaction than higher wages in a locality where material goods are valued to an exaggerated and unnecessary extent. Quite generally nowadays women expect a husband's wages to be sufficient

---

[13] *Ibid.,* pp. 24, 25 (*RN,* 34).

to pay for beauty products, laundry work, soap, ready-made clothing, and a variety of prepared, baked and canned goods, which the house-wife herself made in former years.

At the present time, wage payments depend on a variety of factors, rather than on the social and moral aspects of the payment of a living wage. They may, for instance, depend on what the employer finds it necessary to pay because of the scarcity of labor, or the reverse, and on the marginal worth of labor in comparison with other production factors. They may depend on the bargaining power of the workers; on the interrelation of the demand and supply of labor because of the hazards or difficulties involved, the cost of training, the social esteem attaching to the work, the pleasantness or otherwise of the task in-volved, regularity and long continuity of employment, or chances of promotion and the like.

Pope Pius XI did not fail to note the complicated economic con-siderations involved in the payment of wages, just as he did not fail to stress the necessity of industry's organizing itself to take into ac-count these factors, and in particular the social and moral claim of the worker to a living wage. He writes as follows:

"Entirely false is the principle, widely propagated today, that the worth of labor and therefore the equitable return to be made for it, should equal the worth of its net result. Thus the right to the full product of his toil is claimed for the wage earner. How erroneous this is appears from what we have written above concerning capital and labor.

"The obvious truth is that in labor, especially hired labor, as in ownership, there is a social as well as a personal or individual aspect to be considered. For unless human society forms a truly social and organic body; unless labor be protected in the social and juridical order; unless the various forms of human endeavor, dependent one upon the other, are united in mutual harmony and mutual support; unless, above all, brains, capital, and labor combine together for com-mon effort, man's toil cannot produce due fruit. Hence, if the social and individual character of labor be overlooked, it can be neither equi-tably appraised nor properly recompensed according to strict justice.

"From this double aspect growing out of the very notion of human labor, follow important conclusions for the regulation and fixing of wages.

"In the first place, the wage paid to the workingman must be suffi-cient for the support of himself and his family. It is right indeed that the rest of the family contribute according to their power toward the common maintenance, as in the rural home or in the families of many artisans and small shopkeepers. But it is wrong to abuse the tender years of children or the weakness of woman. Mothers will, above all, devote their work to the home and the things connected with it. Intolerable, and to be opposed with all our strength, is the abuse whereby mothers of families, because of the insufficiency of the father's salary, are forced to engage in gainful occupations outside the domestic walls to the neglect of their own proper cares and duties, particularly the education of their children.

"Every effort must therefore be made that fathers of families receive a wage sufficient to meet adequately ordinary domestic needs. If in the present state of society this is not always feasible, social justice demands that reforms be introduced without delay which will guarantee every adult workingman just such a wage. . . .

"The condition of any particular business and of its owner must also come into question in settling the scale of wages; for it is unjust to demand wages so high that an employer cannot pay them without ruin, and without consequent distress among the working people themselves. If the business makes smaller profit on account of bad management, want of enterprise or out-of-date methods, this is not a just reason for reducing the workingmen's wages. If, however, the business does not make enough money to pay the workman a just wage, either because it is overwhelmed with unjust burdens, or because it is compelled to sell its products at an unjustly low price, those who injure it are guilty of grievous wrong; for it is they who deprive the workingmen of the just wage, and force them to accept lower terms.

"Let employers, therefore, and employed join in their plans and efforts to overcome all difficulties and obstacles, and let them be aided in this wholesome endeavor by the wise measures of the public authority. In the last extreme, counsel must be taken whether the business can continue, or whether some other provision should be made for the workers. The guiding spirit in this crucial decision should be one of mutual understanding and Christian harmony between employers and workers.

"The exigencies of the common good finally must be regulated with a view to the economic welfare of the whole people. We have already shown how conducive it is to the common good that the wage earners of all kinds be enabled by economizing that portion of their wages which remains after necessary expenses have been met, to attain to the possession of a certain modest fortune. Another point, however, of no less importance must not be overlooked, in these days especially, namely, that opportunities for work be provided for those who are willing and able to work. This depends in large measure upon the scale of wages, which multiplies opportunities for work as long as it remains within proper limits, and reduces them if allowed to pass these limits. All are aware that a scale of wages too low, no less than a scale excessively high, causes unemployment. Now unemployment, particularly if widespread and of long duration, as we have been forced to experience it during Our Pontificate, is a dreadful scourge; it causes misery and temptation to the laborer, ruins the prosperity of nations, and endangers public order, peace and tranquillity the world over. To lower or raise wages unduly, with a view to private profit, and with no consideration for the common good, is contrary to social justice which demands that by union of effort and good will such a scale of wages be set up, if possible, as to offer to the greatest number opportunities of employment and of securing for themselves suitable means of livelihood.

"A reasonable relationship between different wages here enters into consideration. Intimately connected with this is a reasonable relationship between the prices obtained for the products of the various economic groups, agrarian, industrial, etc. Where this harmonious proportion is kept, man's various economic activities combine and unite into one single organism and become members of a common body, lending each other mutual help and service. For then only will the economic and social organism be soundly established and attain its end, when it secures for all and each those goods which the wealth and resources of nature, technical achievement, and the social organization of economic affairs can give. These goods should be sufficient to supply all needs and an honest livelihood, and to uplift men to that higher level of prosperity and culture which, provided it be used with prudence, is not only no hindrance, but is of singular help to virtue."[14]

Many workers are paid considerably less than a human living wage. Minimum-wage legislation is one of the methods which have been suggested for quickly raising the wage level of such unfortunates. While it is undoubtedly best that people should take care of their own interests by private endeavor, yet when this is not done or when it seems impossible, then the State has a clear duty to intervene. Minimum-wage legislation was first passed in Australia in 1896, and now exists to a greater or less extent in such countries as Great Britain, Canada, France, Switzerland, and several others. In the United States it was introduced into the State of Massachusetts in

---

[14] *Quadragesimo Anno*, pp. 22–25 (*QA*, 25–27).

1914, for the benefit of women workers and minors. Other states
followed this lead, but in 1923 a decision of the Supreme Court rendered them all non-mandatory, that is, employers could not be prose-
cuted if they failed to obey the law. This decision is to be regretted,
for such laws, when needed, are not merely just, but are positively
demanded, since it is the duty of the State to intervene whenever a
class is unjustly or unreasonably treated, particularly when the matter
is as important as the provision of a decent livelihood for a large
proportion of citizens. With one exception all these laws applied to
women and children only, for it was thought that legislation for men
would infringe upon the liberty of both workers and employers, and
would also infringe upon the employer's rights.

Women are more in need of such laws than are men because the
wage rates paid to them are usually less than those paid to male
workers, even where they produce equal output in equal time. Contrary to much popular opinion, the average woman does not work for
"pin money" but because of economic necessity. With rare exceptions
a woman works because she has herself to provide for, or because her
husband does not earn a living wage; frequently she has others depending upon her, and must take care of her own expenses as well.
Lower wages are paid her for a variety of reasons. First because although women are as well equipped as men, mentally and physically,
for certain occupations, physical disabilities and long-established custom limit her to a smaller number of occupations than men; hence
there is more competition among women for existing work. Second,
since many women look forward to matrimony, and to leaving industrial occupation for home life, they sometimes, though by no means
always, take less interest in their work. Third, many single workers,
as well as married ones, have home duties to perform in addition to
their daily industrial work, and this deprives them of leisure for self-
advancement, and makes them less capable of putting forth their best
efforts during working hours. Fourth, women are more protected by
law than men, and the employer must spend more for women employees on such equipment as rest rooms, seating accommodation,
lavatory facilities, and the like. Fifth, and probably the chief reason,
women are still largely outside trade-union organization and hence
have less efficient bargaining powers than the majority of men.

Arguments in favor of minimum-wage laws for women, therefore,
are chiefly based on their needs, not only because their wages are frequently below the necessary minimum, but also because of the importance of their health as the possible mothers of future citizens. It

is also argued in favor of such legislation that it protects the position of those employers who were already willing to pay a higher wage than the average and thus jeopardize their chances of meeting the competitive prices of other employers with lower wage costs. Then, too, the increased purchasing power of the women increases the market for goods and helps to prevent an economic depression.

Against minimum-wage legislation was expressed the fear that the employer would find wage costs too high, and would attempt to eliminate labor in production to a minimum, to prevent a condition of business bankruptcy; that women would be discriminated against when it came to competition between women and male workers for any particular work; that the necessary development of the collective bargaining power of women would be impeded if they did not feel the present economic need of joining or organizing trade-unions; that the minimum wage fixed would tend to become the maximum actually paid to the worker, regardless of possible superior efficiency; and that workers past their prime would soon be displaced, thus benefiting the young at the expense of the middle aged. It is also argued against minimum-wage legislation that it is difficult to decide on a minimum wage that would be just in all parts of the State, since costs of living vary in the different cities and rural districts. It would also be necessary to guard against the fluctuating purchasing power of money by establishing a sliding scale of wages dependent upon established index numbers, or by monetary reforms which will keep stable within the country the spending value of money, or by provision of a board to meet at frequent intervals to review changing wage needs of the workers.

All these arguments against minimum-wage legislation seem generally ineffective. First, it is a comparatively easy matter to fix approximate budgets for the determination of a minimum just wage in the various sections of the country. Second, although the difficulties regarding the present fluctuating purchasing power of money are very real, frequent reviews could be made regarding the adequacy of established wage rates until such time as monetary reforms are satisfactorily accomplished. Third, if a living wage were paid to all workers by legislation, they would more quickly be enabled to learn of the advantages of labor unionism, because they would have the means to combine effectively and demand, where necessary, still higher wages. Fourth, minimum-wage legislation can easily provide for the payment of smaller wages to the aged, the mentally or physically handicapped, and other persons whose output may be less than a reasonable normal production. Fifth, where minimum-wage legislation has been introduced, it has not resulted in the minimum being considered as the maximum, and women have not been discriminated against.[15] Far from such legislation being inopportune, it would seem that laws should be extended to embrace men as well as women, until such time as minimum living wages are available to all, without the pressure of governmental authority. Under the N.R.A. such a situation did actually occur, for codes embodying minimum wages were urged upon industry, and until they were set up the "blanket" code made provisions for a minimum wage to each worker according to the population of the area in which he was employed.

The Fair Labor Standards Act of 1938, passed after a stormy passage, has established the following minimum-wage legislation for all industries connected with interstate commerce, with the exceptions noted earlier in this chapter. For the first year a minimum of 25 cents an hour for a maximum 44-hour week; the second year, the minimum wage must be 30 cents for a maximum 42-hour week; the third year, a minimum payment of 30 cents an hour for a maximum 40-hour week is to be made; within seven years wages must be at least 40 cents an hour for a maximum 40-hour week, or at the rate (not less than 30 cents an hour) prescribed by the Administrator and the applicable Industry Committee which is to be set up "as soon as practicable" "for each industry engaged in commerce or in the production of goods for commerce." Overtime is to be paid at not less than one and a half times the normal rate, with certain exceptions already noted. The Industry Committees referred to above are to include representatives of employers and employees in the respective industries, together with disinterested representatives of the public, and at any time a committee may decide on the minimum wage of up to 40 cents per hour in the industry concerned. To lower existing wages which may be higher than the minimum established by the Act has been declared illegal. The Act has been much criticized, and it is probable that changes will later be made.

Perhaps even better than minimum-wage legislation, however, would be laws in favor of a family allowance system, since such a measure would the better provide for human social needs. Most standard budgets for minimum-wage rates consider a "family" living wage as based on a family of four or five, on the assumption that an average family will not have more than two or three children. Men whose families are

---

[15] Cf. U. S. Dept. of Labor: Women's Bureau, *Women in the Economy of the United States of America,* p. 111.

more than this figure, and of course a large number of such exist, do not get a living wage for their family under existing family wage rates. Yet if any legal minimum were fixed for more than two to three children, the resultant wages would perhaps be higher than industry could bear. On the other hand, if the minimum wage were made to correspond to the groups of larger families, but employers were empowered to pay lower wages to families with fewer children, there would be a great temptation for them only to employ such men and to refuse employment to those with big families, to whom they would be compelled to pay a higher wage. The conclusion consequently arrived at by many is that current wages for men should be sufficient to provide for whatever may be considered a normal-sized family in the country under question, and that "family allowances" should be paid to those with larger families. Such a system existed by private arrangement among certain groups of European employers before the beginning of the present century. The usual plan was the agreement of a group of employers to pay a specified amount into a common fund, either a percentage on total wages paid or an amount based on the total number of their employees. Workers with families larger than the "normal" were then paid supplementary wages out of this common fund in the form of a fixed amount per child over and above the basic sized family. Belgium, France, New South Wales, New Zealand, and certain other countries have made the existence of such funds obligatory. Family-allowance schemes of this or similar nature certainly help to solve the difficulties of an industry which might otherwise be unable to sustain itself, and at the same time provide satisfactorily for the needs of every family, no matter what may be the number of children. Some such plan seems worthy of consideration for adoption in our own country.

Private schemes for raising wages through profit sharing and cooperation are discussed in a separate chapter.

Sweated Labor. We must not close this chapter without making mention of the oft-used term "sweated labor." Sweated labor is an embodiment of all four evils which we have just described. Under this system, the maximum amount of work is extracted from workers for payment which is less than a just minimum wage, and often under conditions of insanitation and discomfort. It is usually simple work, capable of being done by children or by the sick, for example, sewing buttons on cards or on garments, making artificial flowers, putting cords on pencils, stringing beads, shelling nuts. Cigars, cigarettes, and many clothes are made by sweated industry. Most sweated labor is carried on in the workers' homes, or in small tenement factories where the workers are supervised by a contractor, that is, by the person who is the intermediary between the factory and the worker.

An inquiry made some years ago in New York State ascertained[16] that in that state only 4 per cent of homeworkers were dependent on this type of work for their sole support; 83 per cent were working to supplement the family income; and 13 per cent were doing this type of work to secure extra spending money. The workers are so isolated that it is impossible for them to organize to obtain the advantages of collective bargaining. Sweated labor is usually highly seasonal, so that employment in any one trade is irregular, and the worker may, for instance, shell nuts in the summer, put in souvenir-card cords in the autumn, and sew buttons in the spring.

This seasonal work, when found, must usually be performed at high pressure, and together with the inevitable periods of unemployment between finding one occupation and the next, leads to excessively long hours of labor at irregular intervals, malnutrition, and no opportunity for organization which might lead to improvement. The conditions under which the work is done, in poverty-stricken, unhygienic homes, often by those suffering from contagious illnesses or diseases, lead not only to the ill health of the worker, but also endanger the health of those who buy the goods. It is also extremely difficult for police officers to discover whether or not child labor is employed. Sweated labor is essentially parasitic labor, for usually the class of goods produced is of a kind which could not be sold other than at a low price, and the low price charged the consumer is only possible if the work involved in the manufacture is poorly paid. It is, therefore, a duty of the consumer to pay a just price for goods and to refuse to take goods produced by sweated labor. It is, however, only natural that consumers should buy goods as cheaply as they can be procured, hence the elimination of sweated labor should not be left to the uncertain action of the buyer.

In the United States the National Consumers' League, organized in 1899, brought to the attention of the public the conditions under which many goods were made. This League was preceded by small local associations with similar objects, the first of which was founded in New York in 1890. The League works mainly by publicity, agitating better wages, standards of health, and conditions of work, on the principle that consumers are responsible for the industrial conditions

---

[16] Cf. New York State Dept. of Labor, *Some Social and Economic Aspects of Home Work,* Special Bulletin No. 158, Albany, 1929, pp. 1, 2.

affecting the employment of women and minors. It has also adopted a label which employers are allowed to affix on articles where the League certifies: (1) that state factory laws regarding hygiene and other working conditions have been carried out; (2) that all goods have been manufactured on premises approved by the League; (3) that no overtime was permitted; and (4) that no children under sixteen years of age were employed.

CHAPTER 17

WORKERS' RISKS

Introductory

NOT only does human dignity require that a man work under satisfactory conditions for human living, and be paid a living wage, but his wage should include a sufficient provision for the main contingencies in life which would otherwise cause economic stress to the worker and his family. The worker is prone to a variety of risks during his lifetime or in the course of his employment, the chief of which we shall take in turn.

I. *Industrial Accidents: Industrial Diseases.* An industrial accident is a definite injury suffered by the worker as a direct result of his industrial employment. In the process of production there must necessarily be a constant risk of accidents and often (though these are mostly preventable by attention to the health legislation mentioned in the last chapter) an exposure to one or more occupational diseases, such as lead poisoning or skin troubles due to contact with certain acids.

As such accidents and diseases may entail much physical suffering, inconvenience, and financial burdens resulting from loss of wages and cost of medical care, the matter would be serious if the worker had to rely on his private savings to provide for such contingencies, for unless he had sufficient wages to insure against them, and did actually insure himself, he would normally have to depend upon private or public charity funds for the care of himself and his dependents. He has always had the remedy of suing his employer at common law, if he could prove that the injury was due to the employer's negligence, and that he himself had not contributed to it in any way. But there is no common-law legal redress whatsoever if he has contributed to the risk, or if an accident is caused by a fellow worker.

Under workmen's compensation legislation the employer is now made responsible for accidents or diseases contracted by an employee in the course of or as a result of his employment, but definite scales of payments due are laid down which, being for all types of accidents or diseases, are necessarily on a low level. Generally speaking, if a

worker is in any way injured during his employment, and can prove
the employer's negligence, and no subsidiary negligence on his own
part, the compensation given him at common law would be much
greater than that provided under any state compensation act. As above
stated, however, the workmen's compensation act usually provides the
worker with redress where none would be available at common
law.

The first law of this kind was made in Maryland in 1902, but all
the early attempts to make suitable legislation for industrial accidents
or diseases were declared unconstitutional, until the State of New
Jersey worked out a satisfactory compensation law in 1911, making
it optional for employers to accept the new legislation, or to be sued
for damages in the ordinary way under common law. Other states
passed similar legislation, and at the present time only the workers
of the states of Arkansas and Mississippi, and seamen and interstate
railroad workers are not covered by such laws. The chief disadvantage
of the present system is the lack of uniform legislation in the different
states. Very few states make it compulsory for employers to insure
against their liability under a workman's compensation act. Not more
than about twelve states include occupational diseases, and some include only exceptionally hazardous occupations. The majority of
states exclude domestic servants, agricultural workers, casual workers,
and employers who hire but few employees. Some of the states have
a state insurance fund under public administration, some require employers to insure their liability privately; others, again, require the
employer to provide medical attention in addition to monetary compensation. The percentage of weekly wages to be paid in compensation varies from 50 per cent in some states to two thirds under the
more advanced legislation. Time limits for these payments vary from
210 to 1,000 weeks; also the maximum total amounts paid in compensation has an average range of from $3,000 to $5,000. Most states
fix a greater amount of liability for permanent total disablement than
for death, since the former is more expensive for the worker's
family.

Many of the states have rehabilitation bureaus, where a permanently
injured worker is, if possible, given suitable training to enable him to
take up another career. Congress passed a law in 1921, empowering
the Federal Board for Vocational Education to co-operate with states
which may wish it, to finance this rehabilitation of industrial victims:
of this excellent scheme advantage has been taken by most of the
states, and it has proved very effective in its operation. The Social

Security Act of 1935 also made available increased funds for training the incapacitated, providing for annual federal aid to states of a
total value of $1,938,000.

In some states, claims for industrial injuries go through the courts;
in others all claims are dealt with by a commission, a much more
satisfactory procedure since the commission becomes highly specialized
in its work, and can give much more expert and speedy assistance to
the victim, and at reduced cost. The most advanced industrial accident commissions arrange to be informed of every accident which
occurs; they can notify each injured person of his rights under the
law, and invite him to apply to the commission for assistance if he
does not get the attention which is his due. Where this excellent procedure is in operation, difficulties are usually straightened out by
letter, but if necessary a traveling referee journeys to the injured
man's home to take evidence and meet the employer.

Social Insurance. Other risks to which the worker or his family are
subject are nonindustrial accidents, invalidity, ill health, and maternity
expenses; an unprovided old age; the death of the breadwinner leaving unprovided dependents; burial expenses; and unemployment. If
all workers were paid a living wage, to include adequate insurance
premiums to cover these contingencies, and if all workers did then
insure, there would be no problem to discuss. But when sufficiently
stable employment, with wages adequate to meet future necessities,
and both safe and healthy working conditions are not assured to the
worker, social insurance or state subsidy seem the only possible resorts
which will not pauperize him.

Social insurance is a payment exacted by law as compulsory by
the employer, the employee, or both, with or without an additional
state subsidy, which gives the worker a legally enforceable right to a
certain sum of money, or goods and services in kind, as compensation
for loss resulting from certain specified contingencies which lead to
his not being able to earn as much as before, or to having increased
expenditures. This type of insurance has been current in most of the
industrial countries of the world for many years, but has been law
in the United States only since 1935, and only for certain types of
risks.

The Hierarchy of the United States clearly recognized the need for
social-insurance measures, until a living wage is universally paid, in
their Pastoral Letter of 1919:

"Until this level of legal minimum wages is reached the worker
stands in need of the device of insurance. The State should make

comprehensive provision for insurance against illness, invalidity, unemployment, and old age. So far as possible the insurance fund should
be raised by a levy on industry, as is now done in the case of accident
compensation. The industry in which a man is employed should provide him with all that is necessary to meet all the needs of his entire
life. Therefore, any contribution to the insurance fund from the general revenues of the State should be only slight and temporary. For
the same reason no contribution should be exacted from any worker
who is not getting a higher wage than is required to meet the present
needs of himself and family. Those who are below that level can make
such a contribution only at the expense of their present welfare.
Finally, the administration of the insurance laws should be such as
to interfere as little as possible with the individual freedom of the
worker and his family. Any insurance scheme, or any administrative
method, that tends to separate the workers into a distinct and dependent class, that offends against their domestic privacy and independence, or that threatens individual self-reliance and self-respect,
should not be tolerated. The ideal to be kept in mind is a condition
in which all the workers would themselves have the income and the
responsibility of providing for all the needs and contingencies of life,
both present and future. Hence all forms of State insurance should
be regarded as merely a lesser evil, and should be so organized and
administered as to hasten the coming of the normal condition."[1]

With this necessary preliminary we shall now discuss the risks
other than industrial accidents and diseases, as enumerated in the
foregoing.

II. *Nonindustrial Accidents, Invalidity, Ill Health, Maternity.* Ill
health is a contingency to which more people are prone than industrial
injury. The Social Security Board stated in 1937 that: "Actuarial
expenditure shows that among an average million persons there will
occur annually between 800,000 and 900,000 cases of illness. This
might seem to mean nearly one case of illness to each person. Actually,
however, the economic burden will fall more heavily on some, for
although 470,000 among an average million persons will not be sick
during a normal year, 460,000 will be sick once or twice and 70,000
will suffer three or more illnesses. Of those who become ill, about one
fourth will be disabled for periods varying from one week to an entire
year."[2] It has been computed that "the annual expense to people of

---

[1] *Pastoral Letter of the Archbishops and Bishops of the United States,* September,
1919.
[2] Social Security Board, *Social Security in America,* pp. 315, 316.

the United States for medical services, if itemized and totaled, would read about as follows:[3]

150,000 physicians at $3,000 per annum.........................	$ 450,000,000
140,000 private-duty nurses at $1,000 per annum...............	210,000,000
150,000 practical nurses at $1,000 per annum...................	150,000,000
100,000 attendants at $1,000 per annum........................	100,000,000
50,000 dentists at $3,000 per annum...........................	150,000,000
7,000 hospitals with a total of 860,000 beds..................	750,000,000
Druggists for medicines..	700,000,000
25,000 healers, chiropractors, osteopaths, Christian Scientists, etc., at $2,000 per annum...	50,000,000
Grand Total	$2,560,000,000

The illness may mean only a temporary incapacity for work, or it may lead to permanent disability. One must not think of the worker alone; ill health may visit his wife, or his children. The expenses involved in childbirth are heavy, and without proper care at that time, not only may the wife and child suffer, but the husband and the rest of the household may also be greatly discommoded by the temporary or permanent incapacity of the mother to attend to her household duties. In several Catholic parishes in the United States a maternity fund has been established to help defray the expenses of members at childbirth. This idea has been largely promoted by the Central Bureau of the Central Verein, a German Catholic organization with headquarters in St. Louis.

Although free hospitals and clinics, the benefit features of certain trade-unions and fraternal societies, public health education, and the health care of school children, do much toward the cure and prevention of sickness, these agencies nevertheless do not cover the needs of all workers' families where there are sick needing attention. The benefit features of the associations mentioned usually take care only of those skilled workers, tradesmen, and others earning steady wages who wish to avail themselves of their advantages. Hospitals and clinics cannot always cope with the demand; sometimes they are inconveniently situated for the worker or his family; there is, too, the stigma of pauperism attaching to attendance at these places. The need for proper health insurance to whatever extent existing condi-

---

[3] Rankin, W. S., "The Economics of Medical Services," *American Journal of Public Health,* Vol. XIX, No. 4, April, 1929, p. 360. Cf., also, Social Security Board, *Social Security in America,* p. 315, which says: "Annual money loss caused by sickness in families with incomes of less than $2,500 a year in the United States in 1929 was estimated as nearly $2,500,000,000. Of this huge sum about $1,500,000,000 represented the expenses of these families for medical care and about $900,000,000 constituted their loss of wages resulting from sickness."

tions may call for it, is even greater than for insurance against industrial accidents.

The Social Security Act of 1935 authorized the Federal Government to distribute among qualifying states annually, $3,800,000 for maternal and child welfare, $2,850,000 for aid to crippled children, and $1,500,000 for child welfare organization, particularly in rural districts, to be allotted through the Children's Bureau of the Department of Labor; $1,938,000 for vocational rehabilitation, through the Office of Education; $8,000,000 for public health, through the United States Public Health Service; a maximum of $15 a month to the needy blind, not inmates of public institutions, through the Social Security Board.

Of all great industrial nations, however, the United States is the only country that has thus far made no provision for social health insurance of any kind. Certain trade-unions and fraternal associations have benefit features, but these are not even so well developed as in England, where they work alongside a national compulsory insurance system, contributed to by employers and employees, and with a State subsidy. Private group insurance (socialized medicine) has been inaugurated by some of the hospitals, with some measure of success. Many of the employers most advanced in the adoption of modern methods take care of their sick employees, but usually these workers are compelled, as a condition of their employment, to subscribe to a sickness fund, to which the employer contributes a greater or less amount, according as his charitable instincts may dictate. The American Association for Social Security has drafted a model bill for compulsory health insurance, but no single state has as yet adopted an insurance scheme.

It has been thought that just as industrial risks have been greatly reduced by workmen's compensation legislation, so also sickness could be prevented if employers had to contribute to an insurance fund which would safeguard the health of their workers, the premiums graduated according to the methods adopted to protect workers not only against accidents and occupational diseases, but also against all other ill health and sickness. Such a fund, no doubt, would induce the employer to instruct employees in the proper care of health; and education of this nature, begun in the schools, would be continued throughout the worker's industrial career. It would not solve the problem, however, for those who could not come under the scheme.

III. *Old Age.* A cause of much worry to the worker is the question of what is in store for him when he becomes old and unable to earn a living. This menace, indeed, increases yearly, for with the development of modern high-power methods of production, fewer workers are required, and the young and strong are preferred to the middle aged, so that "too old at forty" has become a byword in industry. It is often argued that a man should reserve sufficient earnings to provide for an almost certain risk. Yet, particularly if he has a family, wages are often too low to permit of any systematic laying aside of funds for old age. And if he be given employment under industrial conditions such as are calculated quickly to wear out the worker, he may indeed wonder if it is worth his while to deprive himself for an old age which he may never attain. Nor can savings invested in stocks or placed in banks be regarded as immune from the risks of the financial world. Then, too, children, if there are any, cannot be depended upon for support. Frequently, they do not earn sufficient to maintain themselves and their own families. Furthermore, the presence of old folks may possibly overcrowd the home: and daughters- and sons-in-law are likely to resent the presence of aged dependents.

Annuities and pensions provided under private insurance schemes reach only a small section of workers; the thrifty in receipt of higher salaries than the average. The same is true of voluntary subsidized insurance for old age, such as the original Massachusetts old-age annuity system. Certain employers, such as the Westinghouse Electrical and Manufacturing Co., and the Eastman Kodak Co., may provide pension schemes for old employees, or provide the older members in their employ with light work of a suitable nature. All employers, are not so generously inclined; nor are the trade-unions much in favor of such plans, for a worker who hopes soon to receive a pension from his employer will probably endure abuses which he would not tolerate if there were no fear of losing a monetary reward. Public employees are usually adequately covered by pension schemes which are part of their employment agreement. It remains true, however, that the majority of the aged workers must rely either on outdoor poor relief, or must enter almshouses or private charitable institutions. Institutional care is never ideal and is often more costly than care in the home. Moreover, in many institutions old couples are separated, a procedure which leads to much unnecessary heartache.

It is indeed but just that the State take care of the aged, where no other provision is made for them, since most of them have been worthy citizens of their community and an asset to the State. In many cases, the assurance of a fixed sum when old would encourage thrift. Workers with this to look forward to would strive to save enough money to supplement the old-age pension or insurance payment and thus enable them to stay in the surroundings to which they have been accustomed. Many an aged couple are welcome in their children's homes, provided they are no financial burden. And if the payment of such an income takes the form of a pension out of taxation funds, the expense to the State is no greater than if the old people come under the stigma of the poor law, and are forced to live an unnatural life in altogether unfamiliar surroundings.

America, backward in all matters of social insurance, lagged behind the rest of the world's industrial nations in old-age pensions also. A few of the trade-unions have pension schemes, such as the International Typographical Union which adopted a plan in 1907; there are pensions for public-school teachers, Federal employees, and most employees of local governments. A number of employers, probably more than the average in Europe, provide pensions for those employees who have grown old in their service. But so far as public pensions are concerned, less than half of the states have pension laws, and some of these are inadequate. It may perhaps be well to mention here that America's slow progress in social insurance or pension plans has been attributed to the fear of paternalism involved in such schemes, to the independent character of the American people, and to the higher wages usually paid to the American worker. A few years of industrial depression, however, have proved that the worker in America has as great a need of provision for his risks as has the European, and that the states owe it to their citizens to see that adequate care is taken of all the contingencies to which the average workman is subject.

The American Association for Old Age Security, organized in 1927, has done much to further state legislation for old-age pensions, and is still actively agitating the passing of old-age security laws in states where no provision yet exists for the care of the dependent aged, other than by charitable organizations. With the inclusion of pension provisions in the Federal Social Security Act of 1935, however, there is hope of a great extension of mandatory laws and state pensions.

The Federal Act of 1935 contained two provisions for the aged. First, an annuities system was established, by which equal contributions by employers and employed are to be made to a central Old Age Reserve Account for all workers other than agricultural workers, domestic servants, casual workers, ship crews, government employees, and employees in nonprofit-making institutions. These joint contributions, beginning at 1 per cent of yearly earnings in 1937, will be increased by ½ of 1 per cent every three years, until from 1949 onwards both employer and employee will pay 3 per cent per annum into the fund. Contributions must be paid for every employee, regardless of his total income, but on salaries over $3,000 only the first $3,000 is taxable. Beginning in 1942, an annuity of from $10 to $85 per month will be paid to everyone over the age of sixty-five years who ceases work at that time, regardless of his income or property holdings. The amount paid depends upon the total income and contributions made from the time the system came into effect until he reached the age of sixty-five. It is seen that only certain classes of workers are eligible for this old-age-security help; that the annuities paid are a tax upon worker and employer alone, so that the wealthy do not contribute anything from the general taxation funds of the government; and that for many years, until sufficient reserves are built up, the younger people of the country and their employers, paying current old-age-security taxes, will bear a large part of the expense of the annuities to older people who in the meantime reach the age of sixty-five.

The second part of the Federal Securities Act relating to the aged, made provision for financial assistance to states which have passed or which will pass laws to care for the dependent aged. Federal assistance is limited to half the amount of the pension received by a dependent aged person from the state, and is not to exceed $15 per person per month. State pension schemes, however, must conform to certain requirements to be eligible for this Federal aid, but undoubtedly many of the states will revise their existing laws or inaugurate schemes which will make them eligible for the Federal grant. Several states have, indeed, already done this.

IV. *Death of Breadwinner, Leaving Unprovided Dependents.* Another risk to which a worker's family is liable, is the death of the breadwinner, leaving unprovided dependents. If a man dies without savings, and is not privately insured for a sufficiently large sum to provide for his wife and children over a necessary period of years, distress almost invariably results unless relatives are willing to help or there is some local scheme for widow's pensions. The mother may be able to secure work, but rarely will she receive a salary sufficient to enable her to keep her home together and pay someone to look after the children during working hours. Sometimes this is possible if relatives can take care of the children, or if there is a day nursery in the vicinity. Suitable provisions must by all means be made that mothers may not be obliged, through reasons of poverty only, to hand over their children to institutions or foster homes.

In the United States provisions have been made for mothers' pensions (mothers' aid as it is sometimes more correctly called) in all the states except Alabama, Georgia, and South Carolina. The Social Security Act of 1935 offered grants to dependent children, not exceeding $6 a month for the first child, and $4 for each additional child, to supplement state aid. The first law of this nature to be enacted was in Jackson County, Missouri, in 1911. Mothers' aid laws vary in each state of course: some give mothers sufficient relief to enable them to remain at home and care for the children; others intend that the mother shall work part of the time to supplement the pension allotted to her, and in some states the pensions are entirely inadequate. Some give grants to children up to the age of 14, others to the ages of 15, 16, 17, or even 18 years. In some states the pensions are administered through juvenile courts; in others through the poor-law administration or by means of a special commission.

Since a pension is strictly a reward for service, the term "mothers' aid" is now more frequently used than "mothers' pension." From one aspect alone, however, it is truly a pension, for the mother who brings up her children to be good future citizens, is performing a service for the country which an institution or foster home could but imperfectly supply. As the worth-while functions of a good mother and a good home are generally recognized, no degrading implication should be attached to this type of relief. Needless to say, mothers' aid should be given only to those mothers who are capable of rearing their children as good citizens. Where a woman is deficient as a mother in any respect, it would be better that public money should be spent in bringing up the child in a satisfactory foster home or institution. Yet mothers' aid is but a form of charity, and in nearly all cases could be supplanted by social insurance if the correct machinery for the latter were established.

V. *Burial.* The expenses of burial are also a contingency which the worker must face. This contingency must now be borne by the individual family. Generally speaking this risk could be taken care of more economically by public insurance than by reliance on private insurance companies, as at present, and many a poor family would be saved much unnecessary anxiety over funeral costs.

VI. *Unemployment.* The greatest and most disastrous risk of all those to which the worker is exposed under the present economic system is, perhaps, to be unemployed, that is, to be unable to find work suited to his capacity. The industrial system has resulted in the majority of workers congregating in towns, and not owning even a square inch of land on which to grow some of their own food. They must consequently look to capitalistic employment for a livelihood, and this livelihood may be taken away from them, not for personal causes, but for some of the many other reasons which we shall attempt to outline below.

The effects of unemployment. Unemployment affects not only the individual, but also his family and the nation. It means a stoppage of wage payments, and with lessened income comes a lowered standard of life. If the worker has no financial reserves on which to draw, he either runs into debt, or he and his family are deprived of the essentials of life. In the latter case the lowered vitality or sickness which results will eventually increase the public burden of hospital and medical charges.

The longer the period of unemployment, so much the greater will be the worker's loss of skill and efficiency, due to lack of practice, impaired physical strength, and the physical effects of worry, discouragement, and depression. A man who is out of work for any length of time develops a sense of failure; he becomes listless, loses his self-confidence, initiative, and sense of responsibility, and often degenerates from the ranks of the unemployed to the state of being unemployable.

It is, indeed, a matter for wonder that a much greater percentage of those who lack work, and are without religious convictions, supernatural faith and hope, do not seek distractions in habits of intemperance and vice; that more do not reach such a state of despair and social demoralization as to lose self-restraint and resort to stealing, murder, or suicide; that a greater number do not become bitter and rebellious against law and order, and develop a hatred of the wealthy and the employing classes.

The family, that most important social unit of the nation, is also seriously affected by prolonged lack of work, in that the responsibility of earning a livelihood shifts from the father to others in the family. The wife must often seek employment, with a consequent impairment of home life and parental discipline, and an increase in personal and behavior problems. Children must leave school at an earlier age, or work between school hours, frequently losing thereby, if not health, at least adequate education and industrial training. Family life is often disintegrated, for jarred nerves and continued worry are not conducive to happiness and harmony.

Industry is also affected, for the unemployed consume less than before, and trade and retailers consequently suffer. Moreover decreased consumption means not only financial loss to the latter, but also yet further increases unemployment. And when a man is re-employed after a prolonged period of unemployment he may never again be able to reach his former state of industrial efficiency.

Finally, the whole social life of the nation is concerned: general insecurity among the wage earners leads to lack of well-being, peace, and prosperity in the country. Periods of prolonged unemployment usually witness industrial and political unrest. Expenses of hospitals, poorhouses, prisons, and public relief agencies increase, with resultant increases in taxation, and dissatisfaction among the taxpayers. As Pope Pius XI expressed it: "Unemployment, particularly if widespread, and of long duration, as we have been forced to experience it during Our Pontificate, is a dreadful scourge; it causes misery and temptation to the laborer, ruins the prosperity of nations, and endangers public order, peace, and tranquillity the world over."[4]

The causes of unemployment. The causes of unemployment vary, of course, with each individual. Certain conditions, nevertheless, may be outlined as indicative of some of the major causes of the problem.

Natural causes such as fires, earthquakes, crop failure, floods, and other disasters, provide the least problem, because they are accidental, and do not arise from a defective industrial, educational, or moral system. Relief measures are usually the only remedy for the unemployment which these contingencies occasion, although man's ingenuity can sometimes foresee and prevent them.

Sometimes the causes of unemployment are *personal*, that is, a man may be unemployed on account of lack of education, or because of inadequate preparation for industry, physical or mental disabilities, illness or accidents, or such moral deficiencies as laziness, untruthfulness, or inability to mix well with other workers.

Bad social conditions or systems are frequently the cause of unemployment. Chief among the causes of this maladjustment may be cited the lack of a spirit of brotherhood and co-operation in the world; the nonadherence of the majority of men to principles of justice and charity; the tendency to greed; the bad distribution of wealth. On the one hand, we have large accumulations of wealth in the possession of the few, who do not buy more goods because either they do not need more, or they do not wish for more; on the other side, the poverty of the masses, who have many needs meriting fulfillment, but no money to provide for them. The low wages paid to so many, contrasted with the high profits and interest which often go to the employer and the capitalistic class are chiefly responsible for this unequal division of wealth. Yet here we may note the sound remarks

---

[4] *Quadragesimo Anno,* p. 25 (*QA, 27*).

of Pope Pius XI, quoted in the preceding chapter: "Opportunities for work (should) be provided for those who are willing and able to work. This depends in large measure upon the scale of wages, which multiplies opportunities for work as long as it remains within proper limits, and reduces them if allowed to pass these limits. All are aware that a scale of wages too low, no less than a scale excessively high, causes unemployment. . . . To lower or raise wages unduly, with a view to private profit, and with no consideration for the common good, is contrary to social justice which demands that by union of effort and good will such a scale of wages be set up, if possible, as to offer to the greatest number opportunities of employment and of securing for themselves suitable means of livelihood."[5]

A man only obtains work insofar as it is necessary to provide for some need: paid work leads to effective demands from the workers. The demand for work is, therefore, of necessity curtailed when the possibility of reasonable purchasing is absent from the great bulk of the world's population — the working classes. And since it is by past or present labor alone that a man can procure the wherewithal to spend, unemployment, as we said before, decreases yet further the demand for the product of labor, and hence unemployment must continuously grow apace.

It may be said, too, that the diminishing population which results from the more widespread practice of birth control at the present day, means a diminution in the consumption of economic goods. This constant decrease in the number of consumers may lead to a very serious unemployment situation as the years continue. Indeed, we are already suffering from the effects of the decreased child population, which is wholly a consumptive one for some twelve to eighteen years.

Defective public education also leads to unemployment, as we explained under personal causes; so does a social system which permits of sweated labor, woman and child labor, poor wages, and unhygienic conditions in the factory and the home, bad housing conditions, improper family life, divorce, and broken homes, which lead to personal inefficiency.

The immobility of labor is another cause of unemployment. Work may be available in one part of the country, and workers may be jobless in another. Yet it is not easy for a worker to know of labor conditions in other parts; and knowing of them, it is not always feasible or possible for him to transplant his home to other places.

Again, political changes may influence employment, and particularly

---

[5] *Ibid.*, pp. 24, 25 (*QA, 27*).

corruption in governments, which leads to a lack of confidence and to excessive taxation. Other causes are alterations in the tariff or tax systems; variations in fashion, custom, and demand of the consumer for particular classes of goods; unsettled economic conditions abroad; internal or external changes in currency systems; war; inadequate methods of settling industrial disputes; a government which does not take sufficient interest in the economic welfare of the nation and which does not provide adequate legislation for the social and economic prosperity of the country: the enumeration might continue indefinitely.

Personal and social causes of unemployment would be largely eliminated by a return to Christian ideals and principles, by governments recognizing their social responsibilities, by proper home and school training in early life, improved housing and working conditions, the more widespread introduction of industrial education into the school system, and an increase in vocational guidance.

Industry, however, seems most responsible for the present widespread unemployment evil. The chief forms of *industrial* unemployment are three: seasonal, cyclical, and technological.

Seasonal unemployment: Men in trades or professions depending on the season or on the weather are unemployed for certain periods of the year; for example, those engaged in the building or painting trades, the summer tourist business, in packing and canning fruit or vegetables, the manufacture of wholesale clothing, or the making of novelties and favors used only about Thanksgiving and Christmas.

While changes in fashion are largely unavoidable, they can be mitigated to some degree by educating the public, through advertisements and other mediums, to adopt one particular style as standard. This was, for example, accomplished by the Hickey-Freeman Company, who standardized their Chesterfield coats.

Some seasonable fluctuations are inevitable, as for example, harvesting, fishing, ice making, and building. They can sometimes be ameliorated, however, by dovetailing occupations and diversifying output, and by finding compensating sidelines and markets. The Dennison Manufacturing Company, for example, extended their highly seasonal manufacture of fancy jewelry boxes which were sold only about Christmas time, to the production of boxes of all descriptions and many other types of paper goods. The Beechnut Packing Company formerly packed only bacon, a work with a very limited season: it now produces a variety of products, such as chewing gum, candy, cookies, and tomato juice. Manufacturers of goods which can be sold only at certain seasons of the year can strive to find outlets in countries or districts where the seasons fall at different periods of the year. The seasons at which house cleaning is done differs in different parts of the United States, and a manufacturer of materials used in house cleaning can develop new markets in the different sections. The General Motors Company arranged for interindustry transfer, and operated also the Frigidaire Company, and the National Cash Register Company. Many periods of overtime work, followed by dull seasons, could be avoided by a better planned distribution of work, and a more careful and intelligent control of production; by securing advance orders, or by forecasting and preparing for rush periods by advance production for stock; by giving employees a broader training so that they could easily be transferred from a department with little work to do, to one where more work is available; by simplifying the number of products manufactured, and working only for an established and steady market; by research into further possible uses for a product by stimulating demand in off seasons by way of increased advertising, or by special discounts for purchases made at those times, or by changing the product somewhat, as for example, is done by the RCA Victor Company which sells portable phonographs in the summer months. We have in the Procter and Gamble Company an example of what can be done by careful management. After an experiment of two and a half years in careful budgeting and producing for stock, this well-known soap-manufacturing concern announced a guarantee to its employees of full pay for 48 weeks in every calendar year. Similar plans have been carried out by a number of other employers.

Seasonal fluctuations in an industry are expensive to the employer as well as disastrous socially. During the rush periods the employer needs a larger number of workmen whom he has to train to do the work; he also has to maintain an industrial plant large enough to take care of the largest number of orders which the company carries. During slack times, part of the plant is idle, despite the capital outlay which has been made in machinery and floor space; the workers temporarily discharged also lose skill and are less competent when they return, on account of the personal evils attendant upon unemployment, which we have already described; new workers may have to be trained, if former employees have found work elsewhere. If production is budgeted, less factory space will be required; the permanent labor force will be smaller, but through regular work and earnings will be more efficient than any fluctuating body of workmen could be, and less likely to lend itself to industrial unrest and agitation; finally, labor turnover expenses will be lessened. Additional warehouse space which might be required, would be amply repaid by lessened expenses in other directions, nor is it usually as expensive as factory buildings.

There must be, of course, certain inevitable rush periods in industry: industry caters to demand, and demand is fickle. In certain occupations casual and irregular labor is a necessity, for example, in loading and unloading freight at docks and at railroad stations. These rush periods will result in a labor reserve, which may be further increased by additional workers who wish to enter a trade on account of the high wages offered to attract workers during these rush periods. Yet the unemployment which later ensues could be mitigated in several ways. First, if employers and trade-unions worked together in harmony, the entrance of workers into any particular trade could be regulated to avoid the accumulation of a large labor reserve. Improved methods of engaging labor could also be devised. Dock laborers and other casual workers might be required to register, work to be given only to registered men, and any known surplus to be turned over to other industries, assisted by vocational training and other means. There might be a common labor reserve in each industrial center from which employers might secure workers when needed.

Probably the best method of handling the engagement of labor is by a system of public employment bureaus. Such a system, by registering vacant jobs and finding employees to fill them would greatly facilitate the mobility of labor; much time would be saved both for the employer in finding a suitable applicant, and for the worker in seeking a job. Private bureaus cannot necessarily be as competent as public ones. In the first place, they work for a profit and may be tempted to take advantage of unemployment situations; second, the installation of a nation-wide scheme would probably be too expensive in the initial stages for any private enterpriser to undertake. Ohio set up a public bureau as early as 1890, followed by Montana in 1895, and New York in 1896. A nation-wide system which was established by the Federal Government in 1917, and which proved very effective, was rendered largely inoperative by a curtailment of financial allocation in 1919. The Wagner-Peyser Act of 1933, however, inaugurated again a nation-wide scheme for the conduct of state employment bureaus, connected with the United States Employment Service.

Technological unemployment is that due to the great advances which have been made in technology, that is, in the invention of labor- and timesaving devices, so that one man, with the aid of a machine, can now do the work formerly performed by many workers. Yet it is noteworthy that workers are not always thereby unemployed. Workers are needed to handle the raw materials of which machines are made, to transport and install them and to perform other services in connection with their supply. Subsidiary products are needed to operate them such as oil and coal, engineers and machine men are needed to work them, repairmen must be available to overlook their performance; and the increased production will call for large supplies of cartons or other packing materials, transportation facilities, and many other services. Invention and improvement lead to cheaper production, and generally to cheaper goods and increased demand, so that although workers are displaced at the time the improvements are installed the consumers benefit by the decreased costs and eventually more workers are required. During the period of adjustment, however, the worker is unemployed, and it is small comfort to him to know that the advance in technology which caused his loss of work will eventually benefit mankind and lead to an increased demand for workmen. The improvement in technique may be such that his trade will never again be made use of. Men cannot easily change their occupation, and even if such a change can be effected, it is not always easy to find another job when it is needed, and of a level of skill comparable to the old one. For example, skilled typesetters who were put out of work with the invention of the mechanical transmission of master typesetting had no other skilled trade to which to turn. There is, therefore, a great need of planning in regard to the adoption of new inventions and improved methods. It seems fair that since industry is responsible for the unemployment caused in this manner, and profits by what is the loss of the worker, then it should compensate the worker in some fashion. This can be done either by some form of insurance, or by the payment of a "dismissal wage." The latter term is used to signify a lump sum paid by way of compensation to enable the worker to have sufficient finances to adjust himself to a necessary change. Nor is money the only compensation that can be given to the worker. Where a change of occupation is necessary, there should be educational provision to give vocational training to enable the displaced man to take up a new line of work. In the United States, the National Education Act which is operated through the Federal Board for Vocational Education assists states to give this type of aid.

It is to be noted that at the present time the financial benefit of technological improvements goes largely to the employer and to the stockholders, and only secondarily to the consuming public; while the worker usually benefits only indirectly, as a consumer. A more equitable arrangement would be to hand some of the financial returns directly to the worker, either in the form of increased wages (which would increase his consumption and give more work to others), or by giving him the same pay but lessening his working hours (which would make his life more bearable and at the same time would provide additional need of workers and thus absorb some of the unemployed). The idea of lessening the average working day to spread employment has been advocated by a number of people for many years, and is one of the provisions of the 1938 Wages-Hours Child Labor Bill, which, as remarked in the last chapter, provides ultimately for a maximum 40-hour work week at the basic rate in many trades and occupations. As we said before, however, spreading work in this manner is not necessarily economically sound.

Cyclical unemployment: In a period of prosperity, manufacturers overstock their goods, and eventually they are forced to employ fewer men and to reduce their prices until the surplus is disposed of. To meet the competition, newly manufactured goods must be sold at lower prices also, and wages are reduced to enable a profit to be made. The greatest number of the world's consumers are the workers themselves, and those who receive reduced wages, or who are unemployed, will then purchase less goods. In an endeavor to induce consumers to buy, prices will be lowered still more, until eventually prices become so low that those with ready funds will undertake extensive alterations and repairs to their buildings, have new buildings erected, and buy goods in anticipation of future needs. Others will be forced to undertake repair and building work neglected during the depression years. These activities lead to increased employment and will make prices rise somewhat. The re-employed workers will purchase more goods than when they were unemployed, and others likewise make more purchases, fearing further advances in prices. These additional purchases will lead to higher prices, and more employment, and thus the upward movement of what is known as the "trade cycle" will begin, and a boom period will be once more in the making which, if allowed to continue uncurbed, will be followed later by another depression time.

A solution to the problem of cyclical unemployment might be partially found not only in the increased usefulness of the public employment bureaus just outlined, but in employers themselves laying aside reserves during prosperous times, not only to maintain dividend payments to stockholders, but also to insure wage payments to workers during slack periods. Truly Christian employers of high principle are not wanting, but on the other hand, we are only too familiar with those in whose eyes it is more important that the stocks of their companies should be quoted high on the stock markets of the world, than that their workmen should receive a living wage, or be retained on the pay roll despite temporary slackness of work. The employer recognizes his "moral duty" of keeping dividend payments fairly stable "to prevent stockholders losing by market fluctuations." It is the fashion to do so; he himself has large holdings of stock which he does not wish to depreciate in value; and finally, the good name of the company often depends not so much on the employer's treatment of those who work for him, as on the high quotations which its stocks merit on the stock exchange. The same employer, however, may not recognize his moral duty to maintain steady or increasing wage rates, or to guarantee stability of employment to those whom he employs. To a large extent unemployment is an outgrowth of our industrial system, hence industry must attempt its solution. When an employer engages a laborer to work for him, not only must the wages be adequate, but unless he stipulates that the work is temporary, he should surely give the competent worker a reasonable assurance of a permanent job.

A certain amount of voluntary private insurance schemes have been worked out by different companies, to insure their employees against risk of unemployment. The Dennison Manufacturing Company, the General Electric Company, Procter and Gamble, the S. C. Johnson Company, and a number of others have plans of this nature. Some of them guarantee a minimum amount of employment yearly, with full wages if the work is not provided; others pay insurance benefits for a certain number of weeks to workers who are dismissed for lack of work. Many of the latter type of insurance schemes are on a contributary basis, that is, both employer and employee pay a stipulated amount to a central fund. The Swope Plan of the General Electric Company is one of the best known of these schemes.[6] The plan, which covers death, disability, old age, and unemployment, is as follows: A trust composed of equal representation from employees and the company administers the three branches of the scheme. (*a*) Employer and employee each pays half the premium on a life and disability insurance having a face value of one year's salary — the premium is much lower than the average insurance of this kind because of the large numbers covered in the blanket policy. (*b*) Employer and employee each contribute annually 1 per cent of the employee's annual salary

---

[6] For details of the other private plans, as also the British unemployment provisions see any modern textbook on labor problems, or Chapter XVI of the author's *A Survey of Sociology.*

into a pension fund, from which the employee shall be paid one half of his annual salary yearly upon retiring at the age of 70. (c) Employer and employee each contributes 1 per cent of the employee's salary for unemployment insurance for all who earn $5,000 or less. After the first two weeks of unemployment employees are to receive insurance at the rate of 50 per cent of their weekly salary for not more than 10 weeks in any consecutive 12 months, the maximum weekly payment to be $20. Provision is also made enabling employees of 6 months' standing to draw loans from the fund not exceeding $200 with or without interest charge, as may be determined by a committee. Most of the voluntary schemes were abandoned in 1935 when the Federal Government inaugurated its social insurance measures.

There are various state and federal schemes for providing for cyclical and other types of unemployment, in addition to the public employment bureaus previously discussed.

One is the deferment of construction work and repairs until slack times. In particular, government bodies should defer until slack seasons, or periods of depression, such undertakings as the improvement and construction of roads and public buildings, slum clearance, reforestation, reclamation of desert lands, irrigation schemes and flood controls, the construction of parks and recreation centers. In these times construction materials are usually less expensive, too, than at other periods. Furthermore, work is indirectly provided by these means for many workers in subsidiary industries, and money which would otherwise be "frozen" in the banks thus comes to circulate in the country. It seems particularly the duty of public bodies to supply work of this kind during periods of great economic stress, provided the work be really needed and not a mere waste of public money. The Roosevelt Administration has tried to effect a relief of unemployment in this manner through such organizations as the Public Works Administration, the National Youth Administration and other government boards, which provide Federal funds for employment which would not otherwise be available.

Although many European countries have had government unemployment-insurance schemes in operation for many years, the United States did not attempt any such measures until 1932, when the State of Wisconsin worked out a highly successful plan. In 1935 the Federal Social Security Act was passed. This Social Security Act provided that all employers of eight or more persons pay a tax of 1 per cent of their pay rolls in 1936, 2 per cent in 1937, and 3 per cent thereafter. Workers employed in agriculture, in domestic service, as seamen, and by the government, relatives, or religious, charitable, and educational institutions, are exempt. Since the government wishes to promote state provision for unemployment, the act has made no provision for the Federal distribution of funds. Instead, states are urged to provide for a certain type of unemployment insurance, to be financed by a pay-roll tax equal or greater than the Federal tax. If this is done, they may be credited with 90 per cent of the Federal pay-roll tax for their own scheme. Moreover, the Federal Government will provide funds for the administration of the state unemployment system. Benefits were not to be paid to workers for a period of two years. They vary in amount in the different states from $5 to about $15 weekly.

Congress is authorized to appropriate annual financial subsidies for the management of the program, through the Social Security Board, yet obviously most of the expenses of the scheme come from the direct tax on employers, and there is much discussion as to whether this additional tax will not hamper industry, and eventually lower wages and lead to further economic distress. Whatever the merits or demerits of this particular scheme, however, it seems that until the widespread insecurity of employment is overcome, and until all workers receive a living wage, some form of unemployment insurance is essential to national well-being. Most of the states of the Union have now passed unemployment insurance acts, which provide for a 2.7 per cent pay-roll tax plus a 0.3 per cent Federal tax, a total of 3 per cent, which equals the Federal tax which would be imposed in the absence of a state law.

Two remedies seem to be outstanding as the only solutions to this grave problem. First, a definite plan of organized occupational groups, as outlined in Chapter 20.

It seems essential to industry that employer and employed should provide themselves with the machinery necessary for the mutual discussion of business problems, and that in these discussions the consumer should also have his part. A guarantee of steady work is only possible if industry is stabilized to a much greater extent than it is at present: to effect this it will be necessary for employers and workers to co-operate in their efforts; neither class must be actuated by greed, but rather by an unselfish interest in the welfare of all — consumers as well as producers; more efficient methods of production must be discussed and introduced; and production must be planned so that all preventable unemployment is eliminated. In other words, there must be a reform in the spirit of capitalists, entrepreneurs, workers, and of the present bargain-seeking consumer who rarely takes the trouble to consider the conditions under which his bargain is made possible.

Second, since it is the scope and purpose of government to protect its citizens and to further their well-being, it is the State's duty to see that all its citizens have the opportunity for this well-being, and consequently, employment on such conditions as will give them a livelihood, provided they are willing to work. It should prevent such combinations as would restrict production and trade in order to efface competition or keep up prices; and such monopolies or mergers of enterprises as would force by unjust means the elimination of small businesses: for the almost inevitable results of these monopolies is to lessen employment; it should not only regulate public works, establish employment bureaus, prescribe unemployment insurance, but should also help and advise industry in its task of reorganization for a planned economic order which will be for the greater social good than our present individualistic capitalism. It seems, too, that the government might strive to prevent a further growth of urban communities, to make life in country districts more attractive, and to help to establish subsistence gardens, so that the unemployed can themselves provide a large part of their food requirements, instead of needing money to buy goods at inflated retail prices.

CHAPTER 18

LABOR AND LABOR UNIONS

The Situation of Labor

WORKING conditions at the present time show a vast improvement over those of the past century. Although legislation and efficiency methods of employers are to some degree responsible, the action of the workers themselves was by far the most influential factor in this change. As early as the eighteenth century workers came to realize their need of organization. The dependency of the laborer upon the fruits of his labor is a narrow one. Except in times of great prosperity workers compete with each other for the work which is available, since there is always a "labor reserve" which is unemployed. The work of the laborer is a perishable commodity, each day of unemployment is a day's work lost forever, and means the loss of a day's wages, too. Without work the laborer and his family are often reduced to relying upon charity or philanthropic aid, for wages are not always sufficient to "save against a rainy day," and unemployment insurance, as yet by no means universal, is at best but a poor substitute for the wages given in exchange for honest toil.

Definition, Types, and Aims of Labor Unions

Freedom of contract is but a phrase when one party, lacking all property, depends upon the wage contract for a livelihood for himself and his dependents. Employers, whether owners, or managers who control the capital supplied by stock- and bondholders, have power over three of the four factors of production. With this power of wealth behind them, and with the knowledge of a man's need of work and the competition of their fellow workers, they can drive a bargain with the workman, involving lower wages and less advantageous conditions than seem just, which the worker must accept to avoid the risk of unemployment and its consequences. One remembers, however, that "capital cannot do without labor"; if, therefore, workers band together and demand just terms of employment, the employer must either accept the workers' conditions, or witness the dwindling away of his capital and the failure of his business.

A labor union is an association of workers who band together to maintain or improve their working conditions. Because of the strength given them by association, they are not forced to make an unjust wage contract through fear of competition or through ignorance of actual labor-market conditions. The labor union aims at the improvement of working conditions by protecting wage earners from the employer's monopoly of providing work, and by enforcing reasonable working hours and fair wages by means of collective bargaining. Collective bargaining may be described as bargaining concerning conditions of employment between the employer, or a group of employers, with employees — either collectively or through a delegate.

The term *labor union* is generally applied to two types of union. First, there are unions which may be called "trade-unions" in the strict sense of the word, that is, groups of workers engaged in the same trade or occupation, such as associations of bricklayers, bakers, teachers, or printers. Second, industrial unions, or associations of those engaged in the building industry, the garment-manufacturing industry, the mining industry. Industrial unions admit of members gathered together in one industry and the men engaged in any one factory or workshop all belong to the same association. Yet such unions must contend with the difficulties resulting from members belonging to different classes of society, each class having diverse interests and aims; with the protests of skilled members who resent the equal representation of the unskilled. The bookkeeper's interests, for example, differ very widely from those of the carpenter, the mechanic, the foreman, and the furnace tender.

A third type of union, the company union, will be discussed later, as it is not a labor union in any way comparable to others: it is an association of all the workers engaged in a particular corporation, and its purpose is to provide an organization which will elect representatives to effect all transactions between the workers and the management.

History of the Labor Unions

The history of labor unionism in the United States is too long and complicated to detail here. The starting point was the year 1825, but there were several organizations of labor before that date. Small unions of printers and other craftsmen existed even before 1800; they were local in character, however, and were chiefly formed to provide benefits for the sick — the betterment of working conditions being a secondary consideration. Between the years 1825 and 1837 several trade associations were organized to unite individual trade groups for common action. In 1830, 116 unions had been formed, with a combined membership of 300,000. They were, for the most part, loosely organized, and became associated with various political and utopian schemes which were unsuccessful. The depression in the year 1837 led to their almost entire disappearance. But three years later the union movement was renewed, and small associations once again arose.

About the year 1850 the industrial development of the country led the unions to see the mistakes of the earlier period, to drop political and reform objects, and to attempt to combine into national affiliations. The trade-union movement proper then began.

The period 1866 to 1886 has been called the period of amalgamation. In 1866, various labor organizations of the country united to form the National Labor Union, which by 1868 had attained a membership of 540,000, but as rapidly declined.

The Knights of Labor were formed in 1869 as a secret society, but the secrecy was abandoned in the United States under the direction of Powderly, a Catholic, in 1878. This association aimed at improving working conditions as a whole by co-operation, political action, and education, rather than by strike or boycott. It admitted any person over sixteen who was not a professional gambler, liquor dealer, banker, or lawyer, and by 1886 had a membership of 700,000. Although possessing a highly centralized government, the organization of the Knights of Labor was too comprehensive for continued united policy and sank to its decline after the year 1886. It has an interesting history for Catholics in that it was condemned in Canada by the Archbishop of Quebec, as a secret society, savoring of socialism. Cardinal Gibbons of Baltimore, personally pleaded the cause of the organization in Rome, and as a result of his representations Catholics in the United States were permitted to maintain their membership. An avowed socialist took the place of Powderly in 1894.

The American Federation of Labor (A. F. of L.), is not a centralized national association, but a federation of national and international (Canadian) trade-unions; certain industrial unions are also members. It is based on voluntary co-operation of the individual unions belonging to it. Unions associated with the A. F. of L. manage their own individual policies of management. In 1935 a number of the union delegates at the annual meeting of the A. F. of L. criticized the federation's policy of not furthering the unionization of such mass-production industries as steel, rubber, automobile manufacturing, so that its bargaining strength was declining with the increased mechanization of industry and the decreased employment of skilled craftsmen. A proposed program to enlarge the policy of the A. F. of L. and promote industrial unions in the United States was defeated. In the same year, however, John L. Lewis, president of the United Mine Workers Union and seven other industrial union presidents formed a "Committee for Industrial Organization," the C.I.O., to hasten the unionization of the unskilled and semiskilled workers in mass-production work. In 1936, the A. F. of L. suspended from membership those unions which had joined the C.I.O. while still maintaining membership with the A. F. of L. ranks, and since that time the C.I.O. has become an independent federation of industrial unions.

The Industrial Workers of the World, founded in 1925, also claims to be organized on an industrial-union basis, but actually it seems to be a loosely bound group of any workers who subscribe to its revolutionary and terrorist methods, and who apply for membership.

The membership of these three union Federations is difficult to compute with any exactitude. The A. F. of L. and the C.I.O. are each said to include some four million members, and the I.W.W. claims about 30,000 members. Two important independent labor unions at the present time are the Big Four Brotherhoods of the railroads, and the International Ladies' Garment Workers.

The Wagner National Labor Relations Act of 1935, designed to take the place of the defeated N.R.A. legislation in protecting the rights of organized labor, specifically states in Section 7 that "Employees shall have the right to self-organization, to form, join, or assist labor organizations, to bargain collectively through representatives of their own choosing, and to engage in concerted activities, for the purpose of collective bargaining or other mutual aid or protection." Section 8 of the same act declares that employers must not, among other practices, interfere with, restrain, or coerce employees in the exercise of the rights guaranteed in Section 7; discriminate in regard to the hire of union members, or make terms or conditions of employment to encourage or discourage membership in any national labor organization; refuse to bargain collectively with the representatives of employees. This Act was, of course, a distinct victory for labor. Other sections will be later discussed.

Advantages of the Labor Union

The chief advantages of collective bargaining by means of labor unions are as follows:

1. Workers whose individual bargaining power is inherently weaker than that of the capitalist or those who control capital, are effectively

enabled to meet employers on more equal ground, and are thus protected from unjust treatment.

2. By means of collective bargaining, labor-union members frequently secure bigger wages, shorter hours, and better conditions than non-union workers; hence labor unionism tends to improve the economic conditions of the masses of the people.

3. Members of trade-unions benefit in their dealing with employers, because they are represented in each district by specialized representatives having expert business knowledge and acquaintance with the labor market and employers. A capable labor-union agent can usually obtain a better bargain from the employer for the workers whom he represents than would otherwise be possible. He can meet on equal terms the trained men hired by employers, and not being in any way connected with the companies in which labor-union members are employed, he has no fear of losing his position — frequently a deterring factor in the driving of a just bargain where the individual worker deals directly with the employer.

4. Where labor unionism is strong, the just employer is protected from the competition of those who treat their workers unfairly, since all employers must pay all unionists the same wage. It is to be noted, indeed, that if wages and hours in any industry are unfair to the worker, unless labor unionism or legal measures force competitive employers to improve their standards, the just employer must almost inevitably lower his own standards, or cease doing business.

5. By making conditions of labor approximately the same over a wide area, or over an entire country, labor unions help to stabilize the working population. The worker has no incentive to mobility, for working conditions, hours, and wages will be approximately the same in his present factory as in any other. This serves to decrease "labor turnover," and consequently to decrease the employer's costs of production. It may be noted, too, that standardized trade-union wage rates eliminate the speculative element in wage costs, to the advantage of more stable business conditions.

6. Strong labor unionism eliminates competition among workers as regards wages, so that skill and efficiency are the determining factors in a man's employment.

7. A labor union pledges itself to keep all agreements made with the employer on behalf of its members: thus employers are spared troubles which often arise when agreements have been made by individual workers without the stabilizing influence of a collective pledge.

8. Labor unionism furnishes the machinery through which the em-

ployer and the employee may cultivate friendly relations and obtain a clearer insight into their individual problems.

Disadvantages of Labor Unionism

While the advantages of labor unionism far outweigh the disadvantages, certain unsatisfactory features must be noted:

1. Labor unions have often been the cause of increased hostility between employer and employed, instead of working toward that cooperation necessary for increased production and social harmony.

2. In certain instances labor unionism has led to a labor monopoly equally as obnoxious as any monopoly of capital, and has resulted in unjust and unreasonable demands by workers from employers.

3. There is a tendency for the union to benefit skilled workers rather than the unskilled and poorly paid, although this situation is now at least partially remedied in the United States by the existence of the C.I.O.

4. The interests of the consumer and the general public are often disregarded when the unionists are seeking to enforce their claims.

5. Some labor unions have abused their semi-monopolistic power to restrict workers' output. Others have charged excessive entrance fees; or have limited the number of apprentices received into the union, without just cause, in order to create an artificial shortage of labor in a particular occupation, and so enable members to demand higher wages. Others again, have demanded equal wages for all men in the union, without sufficient attention to individual efficiency and skill. And there have been many disputes among trade-unions themselves as to membership jurisdiction over workers in particular branches of trades and industries.

In general, however, it may be said that labor unions aim at organizing all workers and in no way constitute a labor trust, since they by no means exclude the many for the benefit of the few. The disadvantages just enumerated largely disappear where trade-unionists remember that excesses of all kinds are to be avoided, and that the employer has rights as well as duties, and these rights must be honestly acknowledged and respected.

Labor-Union Methods

To attain their ends, labor unions make use of the following methods:

1. Many of the unions provide educational facilities, so as to give members a knowledge of economic conditions, of how to conduct meetings and the like, so that they can meet employers on more equal

grounds. The American Federation of Labor has regarded education as a powerful medium for permanent and constructive growth of the trade-union movement, to enable workers to cope with the social and economic problems which affect labor. The Workers' Education Bureau founded in 1920, was affiliated with the A. F. of L., in 1931. It aims at extending the educational facilities of workers by the promotion of study clubs, the issuance of pamphlets, representation on school boards, and general agitation for more widespread public educational facilities. Special courses of higher instruction are provided at such labor institutions as the Bryn Mawr, Barnard, and Wisconsin Summer Schools for Working Women; by the Commonwealth College at Mena, Arkansas; the Brookwood Labor College near Katonah, New York, now under the radical auspices of the Workers Party of the U.S.A.; and the Work People's College in Duluth, Minnesota, which is the educational institute of the I.W.W., and is working toward a communist revolution. Labor unions can do much to develop good qualities of citizenship in its members by holding its meetings at a high level of subject matter and discipline and by fostering education, recreational facilities, and like cultural amenities.

2. Many labor unions have assisted in bettering the worker's condition, by acting as mutual insurance associations for their members. Benefit features may include the provision of medical attendance, homes for sick and aged members, and even vacation homes. Labor banks and credit unions are also run by certain labor organizations to provide savings and loan facilities for their members.

"Among the purposes of a society should be an effort to arrange for a continuous supply of work at all times and seasons; and to create a fund from which the members may be helped in their necessities, not only in case of accident, but also in sickness, old age, and misfortune."[1]

3. Labor unions often make use of political action to attain their ends. The formation of a special party was abandoned in the United States in the early stages of labor-union development, but the unions are naturally interested in the passing of legislation of benefit to the worker, and the A. F. of L. claims to have secured the passage of some hundreds of laws, and to have presented many antilabor laws. There are communist agitators in the ranks of both the A. F. of L. and the C.I.O., but the majority of labor leaders are by no means anxious for any revolution in our economic system.

4. By far the most important form of labor-union action is collec-

---

[1] *Rerum Novarum*, p. 33 (*RN*, 43).

tive bargaining. While collective bargaining may be achieved by individual workers direct, by shop committees, works' councils, or by
other methods, the labor-union procedure is usually the best method
of approach. As just explained, the agent of the union has generally
far greater bargaining power than the individual worker or the shop
committee. He is an expert negotiator, and in the enforcement of his
claims on behalf of the workers has no fear of possible persecution or
dismissal if he does not accept the employer's demands.

Peaceful collective bargaining, with resort to arbitration where the
two parties cannot come to terms, is the ideal method of co-operation
between laborer and employer. "In order to supersede undue interference on the part of the State, especially as circumstances, times,
and localities differ so widely, it is advisable that recourse be had to
societies or boards such as we shall mention presently, or to some
other method of safeguarding the interests of wage earners; the State
to be asked for approval and protection."[2] Yet labor unions often find
it necessary to make use of the strike, picketing, and the boycott, to
achieve their ends. Subsidiary methods of union attack are the closed
union, the closed shop, the use of the union label, and the "unfair
list."

A *strike* is a simultaneous and concerted cessation of work by a
group of wage earners, to enforce a demand upon an employer; the
strikers taking measures to retain the positions they have temporarily
vacated. Because of the hardships which workers usually inflict upon
themselves by foregoing the wages they might earn from current
work, strikes are usually undertaken for serious causes, indicative of
particularly bad industrial maladjustments. The usual means resorted
to, to make the strike effective, are picketing and the boycott.

Picketing is a technical term used in two senses. Usually it means
establishing workers' agents near the employers' place of business to
persuade or coerce non-union labor from taking the work vacated by
the strikers. These non-union workers are popularly known as strike-
breakers, blacklegs, or scabs. Picketing is lawful only when reasonable
methods of moral suasion are applied. Trade-unionism is founded on
the principle of voluntary membership, and any compulsion, particularly through physical intimidation and fear, is opposed to this
principle and interferes with the individual's right of liberty of action.
The same term may also be used in connection with the boycott.

A *boycott* is a combination of wage earners to enforce a demand

---

[2] *Ibid.*, p. 26 (*RN*, 34).

upon an employer by withholding or inducing others to withhold business dealing with him. Boycotting is effected by picketing in its second connotation, when workers' agents are established near the employer's place of business with signs so worded as to be calculated to withdraw business from him. A boycott is sometimes a worse weapon than a strike alone, for it means that the employer's business will decline, either because of his being unable to buy raw materials, or its being difficult for him to find a market for his finished products.

In 1937 strikers developed a new technique in the form of the sit-down strike. Here strikers actually occupied the employer's workplace and refused to move until their demands were acceded to. It was maintained by many that the sit-down strike was an illegal invasion of property rights. Strikers maintained, however, that the sit-down technique was merely the expression of their vested interest in the right to a job under acceptable working conditions, and that this more effective weapon was positively called for because their rights were being questioned by the contesting of the Wagner National Labor Relations Act in the Supreme Court. Since the Wagner Act was upheld by the Supreme Court's favorable decision, the sit-down strike has rapidly disappeared.

Not all strikes are unjust. The employer has always the weapon of discharge. Similarly the worker has the right to refuse work, except where such cessation would lead to grave danger to person or property, and even in these latter circumstances, a strike may sometimes be justifiable. It is considered conspiracy at common law to restrain trade unreasonably or to commit a tort against employers or non-unionists, but Section 13 of the Wagner National Labor Relations Act, after enumerating the procedure to be taken to prevent unfair labor practices, specifically states that nothing in the act is to be "construed so as to interfere with or impede or diminish in any way the right to strike." Where peaceful methods of arbitration fail, and the employer insists on unjust demands, a strike is sometimes the only way in which workers can enforce their claims. A just strike would have the following characteristics:

1. It is called on account of a just grievance, with no malicious intent.

2. Peaceful methods of arbitration must have failed, and no other solution be found possible.

3. It must not involve violence or destruction of property.

4. The benefits expected to result from it must exceed the damage done.

5. There must be a reasonable hope of success, or at least of ultimate advantage to the striker.

Sometimes workers use the sympathetic strike as a method of attacking unfair employers. A sympathetic strike takes place where workers refuse to work for their employer, against whom they have no grievance, in support of other workers who are striking. If the original strike is unjust, the sympathetic strike would, of course, be unjust also. If the original strike seemed justified, the circumstances of the case would determine whether or not the sympathetic strike was likewise just. If those who strike in sympathy are doing this to aid strikers in another department of the same employer's business, it would be less difficult to vindicate their position than where loss and hardship is inflicted on an innocent employer in no wise connected with the original offender.

Pope Leo XIII emphasized the duty of the State to seek to eliminate strikes by just legal measures:

"If by a strike or other combination of workmen, there should be imminent danger of disturbance to the public peace . . . there can be no question that, within certain limits, it would be right to call in the help and authority of the law. The limits must be determined by the nature of the occasion which calls for the law's interference — the principle being this, that the law must not undertake more, nor go further, than is required for the remedy of the evil and the removal of the danger."[3]

But lest the reader be led by this statement to believe that the Pope denies the justice of workers' claims in a just strike, we must hasten to add that immediately following the above statement, His Holiness says that "rights must be religiously respected wherever they are found," and that particularly the rights of the "poor and helpless have a claim to special consideration," and "wage earners, who are undoubtedly among the weak and necessitous, should be specially cared for and protected by the commonwealth."

"When workpeople have recourse to a strike, it is frequently because the hours of labor are too long, or the work too hard, or because they consider their wages insufficient. The grave inconvenience of this not uncommon occurrence should be obviated by public remedial measures; for such paralysis of labor not only affects the masters and their workpeople, but is extremely injurious to trade, and to the general interests of the public; moreover, on such occasions, violence and disorder are generally not far off, and thus it frequently happens that

---

[3] *Ibid.*, p. 21 (*RN*, 29).

the public peace is threatened. The laws should be beforehand, and prevent these troubles arising; they should lend their influence and authority to the removal in good time of the causes which lead to conflicts between masters and those whom they employ."[4]

A *boycott* seems to be just only if it has the same characteristics as a just strike. Unless it be in restraint of trade, a simple boycott against the offending employer is usually legal. A secondary boycott, which is against the merchant who buys or sells goods to the unfair employer, must be considered with the same caution as the sympathetic strike.

Other methods employed by labor unions are various.

The *unfair list* is sometimes used by unions to force employers to make just conditions of labor. A list of manufacturers and dealers who are unjust to trade-unionists is published to warn the public against purchasing goods from them. Its justification depends on the individual circumstances of the case.

A more constructive measure is the *union label,* a mark which some trade-unions ask employers of union labor to affix to their products or to display in their place of business. The public is then urged to buy only products bearing this mark. The use of the label is frequently not only effective in inducing manufacturers to employ union men, but assists the consuming public in knowing whether or not goods are manufactured under just labor conditions; and both the workers and the producers of the goods can thus retain the public confidence in the good workmanship as well as in the sound labor policies under which they were produced.

The *closed union,* which is another weapon employed in collective bargaining is a union which may include practically the whole of the workers in a particular trade or industry, but which does not necessarily offer membership to all qualified workers who wish to join. Such unions are undesirable when members, in order to advance their wages beyond what would be a normal competitive rate, limit the number of workers in the industry or trade by unjustifiable restriction of apprenticeship or output, or by excessively high entrance fees. Restriction of output to prevent undue speeding up and to protect the worker's health is lawful; but all restrictions which unduly limit the number of workers in the union, or increase jobs for workers by unfair restrictive measures or by unreasonably narrow demarcation of work which union members might be permitted to perform, interfere with the rights of both artisans and employer, and are unjust. If prices are increased as

---

[4] *Ibid.,* p. 22 (*RN,* 31).

a result of increased costs of production due to such trade-union measures, then the injustice is extended to the consumer as well. Generally speaking the limitation of output is a selfish policy benefiting a few workers at the expense of others. Sometimes it is due to a belief in the "lump of labor" theory by which workers erroneously maintain that the amount of work is fixed, and so a curtailment of immigration, and shorter hours at the same pay are demanded in order to "spread work." Limitation of output, however, usually discredits labor where it is put into practice.

A *closed shop* is a workshop or factory where only members of a trade-union are allowed to work, and where all non-union workers are refused employment. A closed shop is unfair only when it is used in connection with the closed union. In all other cases it is usually of great benefit to the workers. The organization and executive duties of officials are greatly simplified in a company where all men belong to the same union, and work peacefully together. The closed shop enables the union more easily to enforce agreements; it induces workers to join the union, as otherwise they might lack employment; it gives the union greater bargaining strength; and it protects the just employer; and if union labor is not available employers can hire non-union men who can then join the union. The closed shop should suppose, however, honest union methods that take no unfair advantages and show all due consideration for the common good. Where a labor union dictates to the employer, and gives him practically no power of discharging employees, the dangers of the closed shop become manifest. The power of the union may no more be abused than the power of capital.

Fighting Methods of Employers

Employers as well as employees resort to certain means of achieving their ends. Those most frequently tried are the following:

1. *The Lockout.* We have a lockout when an employer refuses to employ anyone who will not work on his conditions, with the idea of compelling all workers to accept his conditions of labor or alternatively to face unemployment. As the strike is often imperative to obtain justice from an employer, so a lockout is sometimes necessary to force employees to come to reasonable terms, and it is just if the workers' demands are unfair and they will not agree to settle differences by peaceful conciliatory methods. A just lockout has the same characteristics as a just strike.

2. *The Injunction.* In America employers have frequently tried to force workers to come to terms by means of the injunction. An injunc-

tion is an order of the court commanding that certain persons refrain from conduct which threatens to injure property, until the final determination of rights in a court. Workers have sometimes been forbidden in this way to mention even the cause of the strike to anyone. A violation of an injunction is considered a contempt of court, and violators are liable to summary jurisdiction. This method of attack was first used in 1888, and while it has been occasionally necessary to prevent injury to property or to preserve *status quo,* it has often amounted to an unwarranted attack on the liberty of the worker. When used to destroy the influence of a just strike, an injunction is an unjust act on the part of the State. Fortunately, however, the powers of the injunction were limited by the Norris-La Guardia Bill of March, 1932, insofar as the Federal courts are concerned, and most of the state courts follow the Federal court procedure.

3. *The "Yellow-Dog" Contract.* Some employers have fought unionization by forcing what was known as a "yellow-dog" contract on their employees; that is, by forcing every worker to sign a contract stating that he would not join a labor union while in that employer's service, and that he would cease membership in any union to which he might then belong. Such a contract is in direct violation of man's natural right to join lawful associations, but, due to his fear of unemployment, the worker often acceded to the employer's demands. Some of the states had declared "yellow-dog" contracts illegal before the Norris-La Guardia Act just mentioned, also outlawed them. This type of contract cannot now be enforced in any Federal court, although some of the state courts will not follow the Federal procedure. The N.R.A., and Section 8 of the Wagner Labor Relations Act of 1935 both specifically made it illegal to interfere with the right of workers to bargain collectively, so "yellow-dog" contracts are now outlawed by the Wagner Act.

4. The *"blacklist"* is another method of attack sometimes used by employers who belong to an employers' association. It is prepared by the association from lists supplied by members, of certain employees who have been on strike, or who have been discharged because of labor-union activities. The workers on this list are then boycotted by the employers of the association, and are thus unable to obtain work. This lends itself to grave abuses, particularly as the list is secret and the case would be difficult to prove. The justification of a blacklist, as that of a union boycott, depends upon the maliciousness or justice shown in each individual case, while the serious consequences of such an act must be carefully weighed.

5. Certain of the larger corporations have made use of a pernicious *spy* system to discover the men who are responsible for urging their fellow employees to join a union. Organization plans can then be frustrated in various ways, and pretexts can be found to dismiss those workers who agitate for unionization. No comment is needed regarding the ethics of such proceedings. Obviously workers who receive pay for spying on their fellows are of low moral order.

6. In some companies, *company unions* have been set up, with works' councils or shop committees composed of equal representation of employers and workers. Workers and employers are free, of course, to establish whatever machinery they please for the right conduct of the work, without connection with any outside agency. If such unions and committees work side by side with a labor union, they are very advantageous in acquainting the management with the workers' needs, in giving workers an insight into the problems of management, in settling internal disputes, and in deciding local matters of policy which need not always be referred to the outside union. Where, however, the company sets up such company unions and their committees in opposition to trade-unionism, they are a serious menace to the worker's freedom to join any lawful association he may please to associate with, and to his chances of obtaining the benefits of collective bargaining by representatives not on his employer's pay roll. The number of company unions was greatly increased during the N.R.A. period, for in order to qualify for a code, employers were obliged to deal collectively with labor. Yet Section 7 (a) of the N.R.A. specifically provided that the employee was to have the right of joining any union he pleased, and he was not to be "required as a condition of employment to join any company union or to refrain from joining, organizing, or assisting a labor organization of his own choosing." Section 8 of the Wagner National Labor Relations Act of 1935 gave the same protection to labor.

As bargaining agencies, company unions and shop committees are inherently weak. Representatives of the workers cannot be as efficient bargainers as the trained negotiators of the employer, since their shop committee work is necessarily a part-time occupation. As previously mentioned, the agent of the labor union is by far the most effective representative of the worker. Shop committees are also inferior to labor unions in that they cannot provide the educational and insurance benefits which are a feature of many of the union organizations; and they are powerless to enforce legislation favorable to labor, as is done by many of the more prominent unions. Neither does the company union help to protect the fair employer from the competition of those who exploit labor.

7. *Company Towns*. Occasionally company towns, that is, small towns, are entirely owned by a corporation which can then threaten with unemployment and eviction from their home all workers who do not conform to rules regarding labor-union membership, as well as regulations concerning enforced purchases at the company's store (frequently at exorbitant prices). These towns are found especially in connection with the lumbering, mining, and like industries.

Conciliation in Industrial Disputes

We stated earlier in the chapter that peaceful bargaining, with resort to arbitration where the two parties cannot come to terms, is the ideal method of settling labor disputes. Best of all would be a voluntary agreement of employers and employees to submit their differences to private boards of arbitration created by themselves, but such a procedure is rare in the United States. Some of the plans actually in existence in the United States have been as follows:

1. *Compulsory arbitration by a state board,* a system inaugurated in New Zealand in 1894, and adopted in modified form by the State of Kansas in 1920. The Kansas law prohibited strikes and lockouts and established machinery for the supervision of hours and wages in certain specified industries, and created a court of Industrial Relations for compulsory settlement of disputes in the industries affected. Meat packers, who came under the regulations, protested an unfavorable decision made against them, and in 1925 the Supreme Court declared that the act was invalid insofar as the regulation of hours in the meat-packing industry is concerned. In other respects, the law is still operative, although the state has actually allowed it to be in abeyance since 1924.

2. *Voluntary arbitration by public boards*. In the United States several states have provided for permanent state boards of conciliation and arbitration and have adequate machinery for arbitration with voluntary acceptance. This is in entire accord with Pope Pius XI's suggestion:

"Let employers, therefore, and employed join in their plans and efforts to overcome all difficulties and obstacles, and let them be aided in this wholesome endeavor by the wise measures of the public authority."[5]

In numerous cases this voluntary method of dealing with disputes

---

[5] *Quadragesimo Anno*, p. 24 (*QA*, 27).

has resulted in satisfactory settlements between the parties. In 1913 Congress created the Department of Labor with a special Division of Conciliation[6] and authorized the Secretary of Labor to act as a mediator or to appoint commissioners of conciliation whenever in his judgment the interests of industrial peace required it. This department has been very successful in the amicable settlement of thousands of disputes by mediatory methods, although its findings cannot be enforced by law. Most states have also added mediation to the duties of the state departments of labor. The N.R.A. established a Labor Mediation Board composed of three labor representatives, three representatives of "big business," and Senator Wagner to represent the government; seventeen regional boards were likewise established. Under the N.R.A. code system special labor boards were set up in several industries. Very soon after the declaration of the unconstitutionality of the N.R.A. in 1935, the Wagner National Labor Relations Act established the National Labor Relations Board, composed of three members to be "appointed by the President, by and with the advice and consent of the Senate." One of the original members of this impartial tribunal was to be appointed for "a term of one year, one for a term of three years, and one for a term of five years." The purpose of the Act was to make the bargaining power of the worker more nearly equal to that of the employer, and to protect the worker from "unfair labor policies." The duty of the Board is to watch over the operation of the Act, and if any unfair labor practices as set forth in the Act are perpetrated, in interstate industries, then it is the duty of the Board to set a time for the compulsory hearing of evidence on both sides. The decision of the Board is likewise binding on employers. The National Railroad Adjustment Board and the National Mediation Board were created by the Railway Labor Disputes Act of 1934 to amend previous machinery set up in 1920 and 1926 for the amicable settlement of railroad disputes.

The labor unions have not always been favorable to government-enforced arbitration, for they fear a biased judgment in favor of the employer and a possible threat to their ability to carry out a seemingly necessary strike. They also fear that the benefits of the government action will deprive them of some of their arguments in drives for new membership, and that the existence of government boards will prevent the private development of machinery for arbitration and conciliation. It is certain, of course, that the government should only step in when

---

[6] For further details of the work of this division see: Rev. H. S. Spalding, S.J., *Social Problems and Agencies,* Part II, Chap. 7.

private initiative cannot or does not provide the necessary organiza-tion for this important problem. Until such time as adequate private facilities are available, however, public conciliation boards seem essen-tial for the prevention of undue friction between employer and em-ployed, and for the prevention of strikes. If employer and employed would collaborate for the common good, providing the necessary ma-chinery for settling the difficulties arising inevitably out of their op-posing interests, very many of our economic difficulties would be im-mediately solved.

Catholics and Labor Unionism

Both Pope Pius XI and Leo XIII are in favor of Catholic organiza-tions for Catholic workers, who will "pay special and principal atten-tion to piety and morality," for "what advantage can it be to a work-man to obtain by means of a society all that he requires, and to endanger his soul for want of spiritual food?"[7]

Pope Pius XI, however, recognizing that such unions are sometimes impossible, tells Catholics that where "there appears no danger for religion"[8] Bishops may permit Catholic workingmen to join neutral associations:

1. Where the law forbids Catholic societies;

2. Where the peculiar economic conditions of the country make them impossible;

3. Where public opinion is against them; and

4. Where the danger of revolution makes it necessary for Catholics to join forces with non-Catholic workmen "to combat the growing ranks of the revolutionaries."[9]

In the United States and in England (with few exceptions, when for example, communism is all-pervading), trade-unions are of such a character that Catholics need have no hesitation in joining them; nor is there any great opportunity in these countries for the growth of ade-quate workingmen's societies among Catholics, as are extant in Hol-land, France, Belgium, Switzerland, Poland, Czechoslovakia, and other continental nations, particularly the International Federation of Christian Trade-Unions, with its headquarters in Holland. It is to be noted, however, that Pope Pius expressly urges the formation of religious associations for workers who belong to these non-Catholic associations:

---

[7] *Rerum Novarum*, p. 32 (*RN*, 42).

[8] *Quadragesimo Anno*, p. 12 (*QA*, 10).

[9] *Ibid.*, p. 12 (*QA*, 10).

"Side by side with these trade unions, there must always be associations which aim at giving their members a thorough religious and moral training, that these in turn may impart to the labor unions to which they belong the upright spirit which should direct their entire conduct."[10] An attempt has been made to carry out the Pope's desires in the United States by the Association of Catholic Trade-Unionists founded in New York in 1937, and now actively organized in New York, Boston, Detroit, Pontiac, and elsewhere. The aim of the "ACTU" is to organize Catholics who belong to bona fide neutral unions, such as the C.I.O., the A. F. of L., and others, in an endeavor: "(1) to bring the Catholic masses into the labor union, as a work of charity; (2) to spread the social teachings of the Church and prove to the worker, by actions, that the Church is his friend; and (3) to make the Catholic membership in the unions an organized force for sound unionism in the Christian spirit."[11] The Association publishes a biweekly paper, *The Labor Leader*.[12]

---

[10] *Ibid.*, p. 12 (*QA*, 10).

[11] Weber, P., "Actu," *The Christian Front*, Vol. III, No. 12, December, 1938, pp. 153, 154, to which the reader is referred for further details.

[12] Published in New York at 226 Lafayette Street.

CHAPTER 19

INDUSTRIAL PARTNERSHIP AND CO-OPERATION

Profit Sharing, Modification of the Wage Contract

THE worker exercises a natural right when he bands with others in associations for legitimate ends; trade-unions are a necessity in our times, and when conducted along the right lines, are heartily endorsed by the Church, as we have shown. Yet it is far from the Popes' wishes, as expressed in their encyclical letters, that trade-unionism should perpetuate a horizontal division of society, a class conflict between rich and poor, between employer and employed. Pope Pius XI's idea for a vertical integration of industrial society, and a more harmonious co-operation of all mankind in striving for material well-being will be discussed in the next chapter. Here it remains for us to describe the means which have already been adopted by certain employers and in certain industries to bring about a modification of the wage contract.

Some statements of Pope Pius XI seem apposite at this time. He states: "Those who hold that the wage-contract is essentially unjust, and that in its place must be introduced the contract of partnership are certainly in error. They do a grave injury to Our Predecessor, whose Encyclical not only admits this contract, but devotes much space to its determination according to the principles of justice.

"In the present state of human society, however, We deem it advisable that the wage-contract should, when possible, be modified by a contract of partnership, as is already being tried in various ways to the no small gain both of the wage earners and of the employers. In this way wage earners are made sharers in some sort in the ownership, or the management, or the profits."[1]

As the Pope mentions, various forms of profit sharing in business have actually existed for a number of years. What is to be desired is an extension of this to all industries where the wage contract exists.

Technically profit sharing, at least in embryo, exists in five distinct forms:

1. *Welfare Work.* Sometimes employers give pensions to those em-

---

[1] *Quadragesimo Anno*, p. 22 (*QA*, 25).

ployees who have served the company for a fixed number of years; or they add to current wages by the provision of insurance against sickness, accident, death, or unemployment, or they offer recreation centers, elaborate rest rooms, holiday homes, and the like. These "welfare" methods of distributing profits among employees savor too greatly of paternalism, and keep the employee attached to the firm for fear of losing some of the benefits for which he has, perhaps, worked many years. On the other hand, this method of distributing surplus profits is better than no profit-sharing scheme at all, and the worker receives worth-while benefits, whereas he might spend any direct cash distributions very unwisely.

2. *Direct Profit Sharing.* Sometimes direct profit sharing takes place. Employers may divide an arbitrary sum out of profits among the workers, either in proportion to their salary, or equally, irrespective of status in the concern; or after deducting a certain amount of profits as wages of management, they may share the balance with employees in certain agreed proportions. In some companies a percentage of profits based either on profits, price, or output is paid to the workers. Some owners pay the same percentage to wages out of profits as is paid to capital; others divide profits so that the total amount paid as a bonus on wages is proportionate to the total dividend payments on capital; others again, after providing for a fixed profit percentage on capital, divide the remaining profits among the workers, or allow the workers to share the balance with shareholders, either equally, or in a certain fixed proportion. Such schemes are unfairly generous to an employee who takes no interest in the company for which he works. On the other hand, if wages have been paid on the piece-rate system, this disadvantage disappears, and the workers may be encouraged to take a real interest in the business, with the hope of greater money returns.

3. *Co-partnership.* A popular form of profit sharing is to pay part or all of the workers' division of the profits in shares of stock in the company; or to enable workers to purchase shares in the company on favorable terms; or to give workers who are also shareholders in the company additional shares as a bonus, or a preferential dividend on the shares held. Workers are thus induced to become co-partners in the business, and where they are allowed to vote, can have a share in its management. This method has sometimes resulted in the workers owning a goodly portion of the company, if not all of it. Despite the advantages of co-partnership, unless the worker can have full control of his investment in the company, and can sell the stock when needed, he is bound too closely to his employer, and his bargaining power and

mobility are lessened. Again, employee ownership of stock may substantially increase the voting power of the management since the employees are unlikely to vote against the policy of those who employ them. From the worker's point of view, it is also more advantageous to receive cash for his share in the profits, for if forced to sell his stock when in need of finances, a bad stock market at that particular time may result in a great dwindling in size of what he had regarded as "savings." Where the company has arranged, however, for loans on stock at low interest rates, or where it will buy stock from those workers who need or prefer the money equivalent, this disadvantage disappears.

4. *Gain Sharing.* From many points of view the type of profit sharing called gain sharing might be preferred. A standard wage is here fixed for a normal output, after which the worker is paid a bonus in proportion to the excess of his individual production over the normal. Various standard schemes of this nature exist — the Taylor, Gantt, Emerson, Bedeaux, and others. The worker receives his share of the gain in ready cash each pay day, so that his mobility is not impaired and he can, by increasing his output, add substantially to his wages. Gain sharing, however, has only indirect reference to profits made by the company: usually the extra amount earned by the worker is not large, and is certainly not in proportion to the extra profits gained by the company for increased output. Then, too, such systems usually lead to undue "speeding up" of work and to inhuman "efficiency" standards.

With all profit-sharing schemes, it has been found best that the percentage of profits to be shared, or other standard of division, should be arranged in advance, to avoid all possible misunderstanding. From the employer's point of view, profit sharing in general has the disadvantage of enabling workers to share in profits, but letting them take no direct part in losses. Large profits enjoyed by shareholders in good years are offset by losses in less prosperous times. Yet the capital owners are the losers if they are to share profits with the workers, but not their losses. Profit sharing has the additional disadvantage of making the worker accustomed to an extra bonus in times of plenty, which is diminished, or which ceases, when profits are reduced; and this reduction in a bonus to which workpeople have been accustomed, may lead to friction between the employer and employee. Similarly, the worker may become discontented with the proportion of profits allotted to him, although a fair allocation and explanation thereof, should obviate this difficulty. Profit-sharing schemes are likewise means of weakening the bargaining power of the employee, and hence of undoing much of the good attained by trade-unionism and collective bargaining. Employees, who have stockholdings in a company which they forfeit if they participate in trade-union activity; and those who hope soon to obtain some benefit under a welfare or profit-sharing scheme, for which they have long worked, are hardly likely to lend their co-operation to collective bargaining which may result in forfeiture of their promised right.

On the other hand, profit sharing has very definite advantages. It enables the worker to participate in some degree in the profits which he helps to make, and if on sufficiently generous lines, leads to a wider distribution of ownership and control of industry. From the employer's viewpoint, most forms of profit sharing lead to an increased output by the worker, not infrequently to increased co-operation among workers and a genuine interest in the progress of the company, and hence to added gains to the capitalist. Unfortunately, with few exceptions, profit-sharing schemes are promoted by employers for their own gain rather than for the benefit of the worker.

It has been suggested that many of the defects of profit sharing would be eliminated if trade-unions were entrusted with the profits allotted to workers, and were permitted to distribute them in some equitable manner. If shares of stock received under co-partnership schemes were held for the workers by the union, and if money received under other schemes were invested by the union in industrial stock, dividends on these stocks could be paid to the workers, and the shares of stock held for them by the union would gradually be increased until eventually the workers, through their trade-union, would control a substantial percentage of industry. In the meantime, the mobility of the individual worker would not be impaired. Yet in a union of any size, and certainly in a federation of unions, the individual worker would have no chance to control union policies. He would merely be forced to rely on a corporationlike union in place of a capitalistic corporation. It would be almost impossible to insure the election not only of the type of union officers who would ably take care of the workers' stock interests in the public meetings of the companies concerned, but also those who would be immune to "graft."

It seems certain, however, that no profit-sharing scheme should be considered until a fair wage is assured to all workers. Profit sharing should be introduced alongside the wage contract, to supplement wages, and in no way to supersede them. Profits fluctuate — sometimes they are large, sometimes small, and again, they sometimes disappear. With their capital holdings as a breakwater against the penury of lean years, entrepreneurs, high-salary corporation officials, and shareholders can usually tide over profitless times, with the hope of recuperating their losses in future periods of prosperity. Of necessity, the worker can do no such thing. For his own maintenance, and for that of his family, he is dependent upon the money received in exchange for his labor. He needs to have a regular fixed income on which he can depend, and profit-sharing schemes are possible from the worker's standpoint, only if they fill this need. A fixed and fair wage must always be presupposed. It is also essential that in such schemes industry must consider fair prices to the consumer, adequate remuneration to other factors of production, and the welfare of the people of a country as a whole.

Co-operation

I. *Producers' Co-operation.* Another way of changing the wage-contract system to some extent is by producers' co-operation. Producers' co-operation is one of the three types of co-operation, and is the term given to undertakings where the workers are at the same time either complete or controlling owners of a productive enterprise. Producers' co-operation is of two kinds. Either it is a voluntary association of industrial workers who seek to eliminate the employer and to provide for themselves capital, labor, and management for their enterprise; or it is a voluntary association of small employers and agriculturists who, by pooling their resources, can buy and sell more advantageously and obtain credit which might otherwise be difficult or impossible for them to command.

1. Co-operation of workers in the division of labor within a social group is universal. It is found among even the most primitive tribes of today, and has been in existence throughout human history. It is fundamental in the economic organization of every society. But workers' co-operation in the technical sense is of a different order and very recent in development.

The real beginnings of productive co-operation may perhaps be said to have arisen directly out of the first profit-sharing schemes, which were introduced by Frenchmen, the Leclaire house-painting establishment in 1833, and the Godin stove works in 1840, since these schemes resulted in ownership of the entire business by the workers. While the complete transfer of a business, as a result of profit sharing, from the employer's to the workers' hands is rare — insofar as it is possible only where the original owners of the business are exceptionally generous — instances of workers owning a substantial proportion of the business are much more frequent.

In general, however, productive co-operation of workers has not arisen from profit-sharing schemes. It is a co-operation between workers who themselves own the business. They usually appoint a committee of management, and for remuneration depend either upon a division of profits, or upon an agreed wage for each worker plus a division of surplus profits. Although one can point to highly successful workers' co-operative ventures, the plan has several important disadvantages which prevent its widespread adoption.

a) Workers cannot normally provide the large outlay of capital necessary in large-scale production; yet this outlay is usually essential for successful competition with capitalistic organizations. Not having the necessary collateral, they are also very often handicapped in the obtaining of credit, which is an indispensable element of modern business. Co-operative banking, however, may effectively solve these credit difficulties.

b) Even if sufficient working capital is obtained, the workers lack sufficient reserves to carry them over periods of depression and members of these associations run the risk of losing their capital during depression times, whereas a similar loss in a normal capitalistic enterprise would be borne by a large number of stockholders.

c) Workers usually dislike taking necessary orders from foremen and others in command, and frequently they are unable to find men in their ranks to fill these offices. Thus they are forced to hire experts to organize, and to buy and market the produce, and the higher wages commanded by these experts and other executives are not seldom the cause of resentment. Jealousies of this kind can lead to failure.

d) In times of prosperity more capital is needed, yet if more workers are taken into partnership, profits have to be divided among a greater number, which may mean very little money for each individual partner if a depression follows. The tendency, therefore, is to hire workmen under ordinary conditions of wage payment during prosperous periods, and under these circumstances, true workers' co-operation in the technical sense is no longer present, and the enterprise becomes a form of capitalistic partnership.

2. Producers' co-operation would appear to be most successful where the association is one of small employers, or cultivators. Here it is the small capitalist who benefits, and any workers employed are hired on the wage system and do not usually participate in the profits. By eliminating the services of the middleman or wholesaler, and by purchasing raw materials collectively in greater quantities than would be possible for an isolated buyer, members of these co-operative or-

ganizations can effect very substantial gains. Similar gains can be made by collectively grading, packing, and marketing the product of their individual toil. Generally speaking, agricultural co-operation differs from productive co-operation, or at least workers' co-operation, in that it is not usually connected with any political doctrine or end. Workers' co-operation, in European countries, has too frequently had a socialistic aim. It must be noted, too, that the agriculturist is not deprived of private ownership of productive goods, in favor of collective ownership by the co-operative, as is common in ordinary productive co-operation. Instead, agricultural co-operation enables the small capitalist to increase his ownership in a way which would not be possible under any other system, and has removed the one-sided advantages of modern capitalism. In most countries where this type of co-operation is to be found (among these, Belgium, Czechoslovakia, Denmark, Ireland, and certain districts in the United States), the system has been the salvation of the small farmer as an economic unit. It originated in the 1860's in Germany, was adopted by Denmark in 1882, and by Belgium and other countries shortly afterwards. Producers' co-operatives in the United States are exempt from Federal income taxes, and many of the states exempt co-operatives from license fees and certain other taxes. The reader is referred to Chapter 21 on Rural Society for further details of this type of co-operative.

II. *Credit (Bankers') Co-operation.* We mentioned the need of credit in connection with producers' co-operation. This need has been in large part supplied by credit co-operation. Credit co-operation is of various kinds, and by no means always connected with producers' co-operatives. In general it may be said to be an association of individuals who have small amounts of capital to save. They pool their savings and thereby accumulate sufficient funds to eliminate the profits of banker or moneylender, by granting either short-term or long-term loans to members at equitable interest rates. Profits are divided among members in proportion to their capital savings; sometimes in proportion to their borrowing. In this way the disabilities of the wage earner and of the smaller co-operative producer are overcome. Where credit banking is made use of by small producers' co-operatives, it frequently makes it possible for them to remain in business, competing with capitalistic business which has readier access to ordinary banking channels.

Credit co-operation has been chiefly developed in Germany, Italy, Belgium, and the United States.

The first known instance of credit banking as such is the *Montes Pietatis* of Italy. The first *Mons Pietatis,* or Bank of Charity, was founded by a Franciscan in Perugia, Italy, in 1462. Money was collected from the rich, and lent to the poor at interest rates only sufficient to defray administration costs. The object of this enterprise was to save the poor from the extortionate usury of the Jews and Lombards. These banks spread rapidly throughout Italy, and one was established in Paris by the year 1593. Later, however, they disappeared.

Credit for the foundation of co-operative banking proper must be given to Germany. The year 1846–47 was a period of famine in that country. To assist the poor at this time, a Mr. Schulze founded a society in his small native town of Delitsch, to give grain free to the poor, and to sell it at half price to the richer members of the community. This venture gave him the idea of founding a self-supporting loan establishment at Eilenburg, to extend credit to wage earners. His scheme was attempted in 1850, and was so successful that there are now many hundreds of Schulze banks all over Germany which provide credit for artisans, shopkeepers, small businessmen, and other middle-class town dwellers. Each Schulze bank is an association of small savers who supply the initial capital and make themselves severally and individually liable for all the debts of the society. On the strength of this capital and members' unlimited liability obligation, the directors of the association, who are skilled bankers and paid for their services, borrow money from ordinary banks and institutions, obtaining lower interest rates for the larger amount borrowed than would be possible if the individual members in need of credit approached these sources for small loans. Only members can borrow from a Schulze bank, and those members who are in need of funds obtain them at a rate high enough to cover the rate paid for the money, plus a margin for administration expenses. Surplus profits are distributed among the members in proportion to their borrowings, which makes the borrowing rates lower than the original fixed interest.

During the same year, 1846–47, Mayor Raiffeisen of Flammersfeld formed a consumers' co-operative association to help the poor of his township to obtain cheaper bread, and in 1849 he founded his first rural credit and loan society in the same town. The Raiffeisen banks have also been highly successful, and have thousands of branches all over Germany. Their object is to receive the small savings of rural peasant proprietors, and to lend them money at low interest cost. No money is lent except to members: these subscribe to the capital of the local Raiffeisen bank, but are often given money grants by the government. Directors of these banks are unpaid, and loans are made for longer periods than in the Schulze urban banks.

The Schulze banks were introduced into Italy by Luzzanti in 1866. Austria had its first co-operative bank in 1885; France and Belgium in 1892, and the movement spread rapidly to other European countries.

In 1901, a Catholic French-Canadian, Alphonse Desjardins, after an extensive study of the Italian and German credit bank, founded the first *Caisse Populaire*, or Co-operative Peoples' Bank, in his native parish at Levis, Quebec. As in Europe, the system spread rapidly throughout Canada.

The first credit bank to be formed in the United States was organized by Desjardins, in 1909, in St. Mary's Catholic parish in Manchester, New Hampshire. It was authorized by a special act of the New Hampshire legislature. The credit of passing the first general "credit-union" law, however, must go to Massachusetts. In 1908, Edward A. Filene, a well-known Boston businessman and philanthropist, and Pierce Jay, Bank Commissioner for Massachusetts, invited Desjardins to draft a credit-union law. This was passed by the Massachusetts legislature the following year. In 1921, Filene established and financed the Credit Union National Extension Bureau, to promote the establishment of credit unions. As a result of this Bureau's efforts, most states now have laws authorizing credit unions. The promotion of credit unions was particularly advocated by the National Catholic Welfare Conference, and in June, 1934, a Federal law established a Federal Credit Union Bureau in the U. S. Farm Credit Administration, to which fifty or more persons may at any time apply for a Federal charter to establish a credit bank. The Credit Union National Association was established in 1934, and in 1935 this Association took over the Credit Union National Extension Bureau, which was then liquidated.

Credit banking does not interfere with ordinary banking business of the community, because surplus funds are nearly always invested in the local banks. Membership is restricted to persons of good character who have a community interest, i.e., who have some pre-existing bond of interest with the credit-union group, for there is usually unlimited liability, so that each member is responsible for any losses through bad debts. One of the fundamental principles of one of the most important types of credit banking (the Raiffeisen system) is a restricted area of operations; and the ideal unit is a local church group, although successful credit unions have also been established among factory and municipal employees, in village communities, and through trade-unions. Loans are restricted to members, and they are usually made only for productive or constructive purposes. Although collateral is required where possible, loans are also made on character and needs. Capital requirements for membership are low, or even nil, and shares (if any) may usually be paid for by installments. Any member, no matter how small his capital investment, may obtain a necessary loan. The bank is owned and managed by its members; the government is democratic, and no member is entitled to more than one vote. Directors give their services without charge. Profits on loans are payable as dividends on all fully paid shares of capital stock, while loans are obtainable at low rates of interest, so that both lender and borrower share in the earnings.

The chief advantages of credit banking are:

a) It enables interest to be earned on small savings, and makes it possible for the lender to put his tiny capital to constructive uses;

b) It enables loans to be secured which might be too small in amount to be handled by the local bank;

c) It enables a person who lacks the financial standing necessary to secure a bank loan, to procure necessary credit;

d) It maintains the independence and self-respect of members, who without credit facilities thus provided might be forced to abandon their business enterprise, or to resort to charity;

e) It prevents a man in need of money from entering into the clutches of a usurious moneylender — often described by the expressive term "loan shark";

f) It enables a person to obtain money for productive purposes, which will earn profits for him in time;

g) It educates members in the right use of credit, for proof must be given of true need before a loan is granted;

h) It helps to promote honesty among members of the bank, because only those who lead an honorable, regular life can borrow money from it.

III. *Consumers' (Distributors') Co-operation.* This type of co-operation differs from the producers' and credit co-operation just outlined in that it affects the consumptive, rather than the productive, side of economic life. It is an association of consumers, who seek to eliminate the middleman and his profits by arranging to supply themselves with goods instead of buying from private retailers.

Whereas the main purpose of the other schemes we have outlined has been to increase the nominal wages of workers and small capitalists, consumers' co-operation aims directly at increasing the real wages of the lower-income groups by increasing the purchasing power of their money. Nearly all successful consumers' co-operatives, however, have developed producers' co-operation to provide themselves with at least part of the goods they would otherwise purchase from middlemen; most successful co-operatives have also developed a banking business to take care of their financial needs. The development of consumers' co-operatives in Great Britain and Sweden, where they have been most successful, is fully outlined in a number of recently published books.

The first successful consumers' co-operative venture was that of the Rochdale Equitable Pioneers' Society founded in 1844 in a small English manufacturing town by twenty-eight indigent workmen. These men each saved a few cents a week for about a year, and with the minute capital thus secured, purchased collective supplies of such stable commodities as flour, butter, and sugar at wholesale prices. Without one penny subsidy, and without expert advice in any form, these poverty-stricken and uneducated workers devised the whole consumers' co-operative scheme which today in England alone comprises a membership of over six and a half millions.

The usual plan of a consumers' co-operative is as follows: There is unrestricted membership with capital shares of about $5, payable at the option of members in installments. Interest is paid on capital shares at market rates, but each member is strictly limited as to shareholding, the maximum allowed being usually around $1,000,[2] because capitalistic control is considered the antithesis of co-operation. The government of the enterprise is strictly democratic, each member having only one vote, regardless of his capital investment, and the management being elective.

Goods are purchased, and sold to members in conveniently located stores at current market prices.[3] Employees who work in the stores are hired under the wage-contract system and are in no way partners in the organization, unless they themselves are consuming members. Since the co-operatives usually employ only labor-union members, they can render very material assistance to the improvement of the workers' position in economic life. All sales are strictly on a cash basis. After deduction for depreciation, reserves, and perhaps an allocation for educational purposes in the field of co-operation, the remaining profits are divided among members, not in proportion to capital holdings, but in proportion to the amount of goods purchased. Computation of

---

[2] In Great Britain, the amount is fixed by the *Industrial and Provident Societies Act* at £ 200 ($1,000).

[3] Actually the philosophy of co-operation is purchasing *for* members rather than merely selling *to* them.

profits is usually made quarterly, and these profit sharings are quarterly payments, entitled "dividends" in England, and "savings returns" or "rebates" in America. Usually these dividends are 10 per cent, sometimes less, the rate being fixed as a result of long custom; any additional surplus is placed on reserve or used for the development of the business.

Generally speaking, the retail co-operative stores form district societies, which make the purchases for them and are themselves small producers,[4] owning bakeries, local farms, and employing tailors, shoe repairers, and the like. Their profits are large because of the large-scale purchasing involved in the joint orders which the various local stores place with the district society. The co-operative organization of Sweden and Great Britain is well known. In Great Britain, the majority of retail stores belong to one of the two great wholesale co-operative societies: the English Co-operative Wholesale Society founded in 1864 or the Scottish Co-operative Wholesale Society founded in 1868. Local retail stores are members of these wholesale establishments in the same way as individual consumers are members of the retail organizations. Each retail society subscribes to a certain amount of capital, is paid the minimum market rate of interest on this investment, and receives but one vote, regardless of the finances involved. Member stores have the privilege of purchasing their supplies through this wholesale organization at customary wholesale prices. They are not, of course, obliged to make use of the purchasing facilities of the Wholesale Society if they find they can buy at a greater advantage elsewhere. Profits achieved through their co-operative efforts are divided among them in accordance with their purchases as in the case of individual members in the retail establishments. Most of the retail stores also do their banking through the banking department of the Wholesale Society, which is quite a financial power in Great Britain, and owns and operates huge factories, warehouses, transportation facilities, vast tracts of agricultural land, tea plantations, and other means of production. No such important organizations exist in the United States, although the co-operative movement is slowly spreading, largely owing to the efforts of the Co-operative League of the United States, founded in 1916, and to the Consumer Distribution Corporation established by Edward A. Filene in 1936.

It has been objected that consumers' co-operation eliminates the

---

[4] Although consumers' co-operatives may be producers as well as retail distributors of goods, producers' co-operation does not take place, since the production is undertaken to gain additional savings for consumers, and employees are hired.

small tradesman, particularly as such co-operatives are usualy exempted from paying state license fees, income taxes, and incorporation dues. This is true to some extent in poorer districts, although even here many of the poor cannot take advantage of co-operation because they rely on their credit at the local stores, and co-operative business is usually done on a strictly cash basis; and some people, of course, prefer private enterprises. In the wealthier districts, privately owned concerns are nearly always preferred. Co-operative stores, since they cater to the poor more than any other class, supply the general demand and also increase their profits by carrying only a limited number of the more popular brands of goods. Monied people usually like a greater choice of goods, and they also like the individual attention which a private storekeeper will give in helping them with their personal preferences and the supply of goods which are out of the ordinary or not in great demand. There may be, too, a high degree of honesty and personal responsibility. In any event, the chain store has, in many cases, already taken the place of the small tradesman.

While consumers' co-operative schemes sometimes fail as a result of lack of cohesion among the members, petty jealousies, scarcity of able businessmen, technicians, and others necessary to enable the enterprise to compete with capitalistic venture, the advantages of such co-operation are many. First, the cost of living for members is reduced, for by this form of co-operation they take advantage of the economics of large-scale buying and eliminate the profits of the middleman. This increases their purchasing power for other things. Second, habits of thrift are promoted, for not only must members pay for their purchases in cash, but they automatically accumulate savings in the form of dividends which, being paid quarterly, are often left in the society to draw interest as capital. Third, not only does it give the workers an incentive to thrift, but it educates them in habits of self-restraint, co-operation with others, charity, initiative, and unselfishness. Fourth, by attending the periodical business meetings, voting for managers and on questions of policy, members become conversant with some of the technique of government and the intricacies of business management and, through the experience thus acquired, become more fitted to take their place as intelligent members of society. Finally, by means of co-operation, large owners of capital are bereft of their powers, while the poorest member of a co-operative store, by the very fact of his membership, becomes an employer of labor and has an active share in the business. The poorer classes are thus put in the way of acquiring capital and property, and the discrepancies between workers and the capitalistic class are therefore to some extent diminished. We might say, indeed, that all these advantages of consumers' co-operation are likewise advantages of co-operation in general.

It is obvious that co-operation differs from a joint-stock company in several very important particulars. The true spirit of co-operation is "each for all, and all for each," every member working for the benefit of all the others, without the individual profit motive looming too large. The capital of corporations, and the number of shares outstanding, are fixed and regulated, but the ownership of the shares may rapidly change hands. In a co-operative enterprise, membership and capital are variable, and the shares are generally nontransferable. While joint-stock companies are a union of individuals whose capital ownership is of most importance, and they themselves of little or no account, in co-operation there is a union of persons, and the individual person is of greatest import, no matter how little money he may own. Yet consumers' co-operation has sometimes become an instrument in the hands of the socialists, instead of being the nonpolitical organization of mutual help which most of the supporters of co-operation would have it.[5] In this case, instead of promoting small property ownership among the members, for the sake of their greater security of existence, the object is to deprive the wealthy of some of the sources of their wealth by the only means allowed them by most of the governments of today. The philosophy of true co-operation, however, seems quite otherwise.

---

[5] Cf. Warbasse's definition of co-operations: Warbasse, *What Is Cooperation?* Foreword; cf. also *ibid.*, p. 23.

CHAPTER 20

REORGANIZATION OF OCCUPATIONAL SOCIETY
PROPOSED ECONOMIC REFORMS

VARIOUS ideas have been propounded to change the capitalistic order. They have in common that they have arisen out of dissatisfaction with existing conditions. This does not mean to say, however, that all are equally satisfactory from a practical viewpoint, or are advisable on social and moral grounds. Certain of these modifications of capitalism have already been put into practice; some still remain in the realm of fancy. At best we can give in this chapter only the briefest particulars of a few of the outstanding proposals which have been made.

I. Collectivism

Collectivism is a general term which may be used to designate the desire to have a collective ownership of wealth, either productive wealth alone, or else both productive and consumptive goods. There is a good collectivism, and a bad. Collectivism is an ideal condition when a group of persons voluntarily agree to pool their possessions in order to bring about a better distribution of material goods within the group and possibly also to give the members in general a greater freedom from the cares which come from property ownership. Collectivism, for the purpose of charity and not of production, existed in the early Christian Church; under another form it exists today among the members of the religious orders; and at various times in the world's history voluntary collective societies have existed, although, apart from the religious orders, they nearly all came to a very speedy end. Collectivism presupposes an ideal man who will wish to share equally with others, forego his own advantages, and show the same concern for the common goods as he would if they belonged personally to himself. Yet man's nature does not change so easily. If he be rapacious, or lazy, in modern capitalistic society, he will never be different under a collectivist system to which he is forced to belong. The brotherhood of man can exist only when motivated by the lofty ideals of religion, and even with these most men need natural incentives, too, as aids in his seeking after a higher life. Apart from a few very idealistic persons, man needs the spur of self-interest in the acquisition of property, prestige, and the like, to make him industrious and efficient for any prolonged period of time.

In addition to this idealistic collectivism, there are two other collectivist systems called, respectively, socialism and communism. The varieties of socialism are so numerous that it is impossible to do more here than give a very brief outline of the best known types and the most important points in the history of the movement.

Generally speaking, all socialists claim that class distinctions and the great discrepancies between the rich and the poor, the capitalist-employer and the penurious wage earner, are the sole causes of evil in the world today. These discrepancies, they maintain, will be done away with by the compulsory collective ownership of at least some of the means of production, distribution, and exchange. The more idealistic of them think that hatred, envy, bitterness, selfishness, greed, the spirit of commercialism, will forthwith be abolished. Man will belong to a universal brotherhood; he will love activity for its own sake, not for the acquisition of wealth as he does so often today. They claim that the present unnecessary duplication of work, wasteful competition, unscrupulous exploitation and overproduction, will be eliminated. Under a socialistic era industry will be more scientifically organized, they say, and production will be more carefully estimated to avoid unnecessary expenditure of energy and wealth. The result will be an entirely reformed world, universal contentment, greater leisure for the masses, and a larger total of wealth than at present to be divided among all.

No one would wish to quarrel with the socialists in their desire to make production for use rather than for profit, to bring about a better distribution of the world's wealth, and a more equal opportunity for all. Certainly no Catholic would contradict official Catholic social teaching, which has ever been against the exaggerated individualism of Liberalism and Protestantism, and has always urged man to use his property as a sacred trust, and to do all possible to bring about a modicum of material well-being for all. The danger of socialism lies in its philosophy; and in certain socialistic systems the means, too, are contrary to the norms of morality and reason.

However mild a particular form of socialism may be, it is dangerous because of its crass materialism. Here, Pope Pius XI shows the difference between Catholic social teaching and that of the socialists: "For according to Christian doctrine man, endowed with a social nature, is placed here on earth in order that, spending his life in society, and under an authority ordained by God, he may cultivate and evolve to the full all his faculties to the praise and glory of his Creator, and that by fulfilling faithfully the functions of his trade or other calling, he may attain both temporal and eternal happiness. Socialism, on the contrary, entirely ignorant of and unconcerned about this sublime end both of individuals and of society, affirms that human society was instituted merely for the sake of material well-being."[1] Another danger of socialism is its general teaching that society makes man, instead of the true contrary that man makes society. Finally, it denies man's right to at least some, and sometimes all, forms of private property in productive goods. Once a system based on this false philosophy is allowed, there is always the danger that it may be extended, and eventually more violent measures may be taken to usurp all property rights. Those types of socialism which advocate greater State control would also be extending governmental bureaucracy, which might be stultifying to continued material progress and which might eventually lead to the abolition of individual freedom and private initiative and enterprise.

Communism is a more extended and more radical form of socialism. It differs from socialism in that it aims specifically at a classless society where no incomes are derived from the possession of instruments of production, and where material well-being is to be secured by community control over both production goods and goods that are used in consumption. If peaceful means are insufficient, force and violence are to be used. Whereas the socialists wish the world's wealth to be divided among people according to their services, communists want the division to be made according to their needs.

1. *Utopian Socialism.* Leaving aside the various utopian schemes of the ancient civilizations, the "utopian" socialism of the early Christians and of religious orders of today, and the various schemes in literature, such as those of St. Thomas More, Campanella, and others, already mentioned in Chapter 6, the term *utopian socialism* is usually given to various theories which flourished at the beginning of the nineteenth century. This "utopian socialism" was the precursor of the "scientific socialism" of our day; in philosophy it was built upon the growing materialism of liberalism, while at the same time it wished to counteract some of the worst evils which had been the practical outcome of that very philosophy. Original leaders in this movement were Saint-Simon (1760–1825) and Charles Fourier (1772–1837) in France, and Robert Owen (1771–1858) in England and Scotland. In general they may be said to have held that the evils of

---

[1] *Quadragesimo Anno*, p. 37 (*QA*, 39).

the day were due not to any inherent evil in man (as some philosophers believed) but to a misguided capitalistic system. By popular education and by the example of economists, philosophers, and other scholars, they hoped that man would eventually arrive at a voluntary reformation of the property system. In particular they wished to reform the system of inheritance, to replace the antagonism between capital and labor by brotherly affection, and thus to establish a world Utopia.

The theories of all three leaders were dangerous. Saint-Simon and his followers (who originally included Comte, who was Saint-Simon's secretary for several years) made of their doctrines a kind of religious cult. They strove to prove that their theories, if carried into practice, would result in a universal social organization to which all religious societies, including especially the Jewish, had supposedly been leading. The government would be controlled by industrial leaders and by scientists, to take the place of what was termed the waning authority of the Catholic Church.

Fourier, believing that man's present instincts are revelations of the Divine Will, wished all men to have the opportunity to gratify them. To achieve this end, he planned the co-operative organization of labor into phalanxes of from 400 to 2,000 people, these to be subdivided into smaller groups of seven to nine people each, all of whom were to live in great communal barracks on some 5,000 acres of land. The Brook Farm Phalanx, founded in West Roxbury, Massachusetts, in 1841, in imitation of this plan, was supported by such famous people as Horace Greeley, James Russell Lowell, Nathaniel Hawthorne, Ralph Waldo Emerson, and Charles A. Dana.

Robert Owen was more practical than the Frenchmen. A professed atheist, his idea was that men should form co-operative groups, in which their characters were to be trained without religious aids, and where service to others rather than the profit motive was to prevail. The productive capacity of men in these colonies was to be increased by careful organization, so that eventually, by a universal communism based on mutual-benefit co-operatives there would be an abundance of goods for all. Owen was a forerunner of the modern environmental determinist schools. Coming to America, he put his theories into practice and established a co-operative colony at New Harmony, Indiana, in 1924, but it was unsuccessful and lasted only two years. Similar colonies founded on his teachings were equally short-lived. His personal influence, however, was very great. The "Rochdale Pioneers" conceived their idea from his co-operative organization of workers at the mills of which he was manager in New Lanark, Scotland, from 1800 onwards, so that he is called the "father of co-operation." In addition, his zealous work for factory legislation to reform working conditions, gained him the title "father of factory legislation."

2. Louis Blanc (1813–1882) represents a transition stage between the earlier utopian idealists who wished to spread their doctrine by mere teaching and example, and the more radical doctrines of Marx, Proudhon, and those who followed. Blanc's adherents were primarily students and economists who occupied themselves with economic theorizing, agitating for the "right to work" and proposing that the people, aided by the State, ought to take over all the banks, insurance companies, and large capitalistic concerns, the power of the State thus bringing about the compulsory co-operative organization of occupational society.

3. Syndicalism took its rise in France as a result of the teachings of Proudhon (1809–1865), later continued by Georges Sorel (1847–1922), Pelloutier (1867–1901), and others. The word is taken from the French *syndicat,* meaning a trade-union. Proudhon taught that economic life is all important, that property is theft, and that the class system should be abolished. Originally an anarchist, he abandoned this extreme viewpoint in 1852, and favored rule by leaders chosen by the masses.

The aim of the syndicalists is to form a society controlled by workers organized in trade-unions. First they hoped to organize non-political industrial unions, and then by means of strikes and sabotage, first to improve immediate conditions, and secondly to prepare for a general strike. The word *sabotage* comes from the French *sabot* or wooden shoe: "put a shoe in the machine," or, to give the American equivalent: "throw a monkey wrench into the works." Sabotage is any means employed to injure the employers' property — the wrecking of machinery, incendiarism, and other acts of violence. In this way the syndicalists hope to intimidate employers and to give workers growing confidence, so that when a general strike is declared all the industries of a country can be taken over by self-governing groups of workers, and henceforth the workers in each trade or industry would own all the means of production in that industry. The various unions would then be federated into a syndicalist government. It needs no comment to explain how illegitimate and unethical is the whole syndicalist plan. On account of its anarchistic notions very few trade-unions are syndicalist, and few workers have followed the idea. In the United States, however, the I.W.W. is a syndicalist organization, but its membership is very limited.

4. Most important of all socialists from the point of view of influence is Karl Marx (1818–1883), a German Jewish journalist who was expelled from his country in 1845, and went first to Paris, where he came under the influence of Proudhon, and who finally settled down in London in 1849. In collaboration with his disciple, Friedrich Engels (1820–1895), he issued the *Communist Manifesto* in the year 1848, and established what is known as the School of Historic Materialism.

The real beginning of socialist organization of note occurred in 1864, when Marx formed the International Workingmen's Association, generally called the First International, whose members included Russian anarchists and radicals of all kinds, including some of the very mild type of British trade-union radicals. It ceased to exist in 1876. In 1867 appeared the first volume of *Das Kapital*, "the bible of socialism," to be followed by a second volume edited by Engels in 1885 (two years after Marx died), and a third, compiled by Engels from Marx's notes in 1895. Although many socialists no longer hold Marx's extreme doctrines, nevertheless *Das Kapital* has had an enormous influence on the history of socialism.

Marx's main doctrine is twofold. First, the theory of surplus value, which he borrowed from the Labor Theory of Value held by the liberal economists of the time. By this he meant that since the value of goods supposedly depended upon the amount of labor expended upon them, and since the worker's wages were less than the value for which the goods were sold, there was a surplus value which was taken by the capitalists as profits which really belonged to the worker. The worker was therefore considered as being exploited, and Marx's cry was: exploit the exploiter — take away from the capitalist his ill-gotten gains. It may be said here that the labor theory of value has been proved to be incorrect, and to attempt to put it into practice would not be practicable. First of all, since men differ in strength, education, ideals, character, and dexterity, each item would have to be calculated entirely on an individual basis. Sometimes the least labor is expended on the most valuable good. Sometimes labor is misdirected, and the amount of work put by a clumsy worker into a spoiled article, might be much greater than a piece of exquisite workmanship performed by a skilled and speedy worker. Sometimes it is scarcity of workers in one type of needed labor rather than skill which counts in labor costs. Again, capital equipment such as tools and machines, and the labor of organization, must be included, and yet it would be difficult to apportion the exact amount of this indirect use of labor to be allocated to any one piece of finished work, although, of course, modern cost systems do try to effect this accuracy as regards "overhead" expenses.

The second main tenet of Marx was his materialistic conception of history, for which his main source was the philosophy of Hegel. He postulated for this theory that history follows a certain dialectical process, that is, that history came about because of the workings of certain natural laws of change to which man is inevitably subject, because he is, in Marx's view, a wholly material being. Out of a continuous dynamic flux, he thought, various types of economic society arose: first primitive communism; then slavery, serfdom, the wage system of capitalism; and finally there would be communism. For Marx, each of these societies prior to communism represented a "thesis" which was only partially good, and so an "antithesis" would arise, caused by a class environment and a struggle between groups of men organized in various classes. In the course of time a new society would come into being, a "synthesis." Out of each synthesis, which formed a new thesis, yet another class antithesis would evolve until, after a final revolution, communism, the classless economic millenium, would be reached. And since the State is considered by Marx merely as an instrument to enforce the ideas, domination, and status of the ruling class, when complete communism is attained, in the final stage of the Marxian dialectic, then the State would no longer exist, for there would be no ruling class and no need of domination. Finally, when all class societies throughout the world are abolished, Marx expected that all national sovereignties would be abolished, too, so that there would come into existence a peaceful international world union of people bound together by economic life.

In these ideas, of course, Marx completely ignores the psychology of human character. He thought that the present antithesis was between bourgeois capitalists, both large and small, and the propertyless workers — the proletariat (from *proles* — a child), a word which he coined to be descriptive of the masses, whose chief use under capitalism is supposed by the socialists to be the bearing of children as future workers. This class struggle for a livelihood was considered by Marx to be the sole end of human society; so that for him economic life determined all other social life, even the societies of religion and the family.[2] For this reason Marxism is often called economic determinism.

---

[2] Morgan's theory of the evolution of marriage is widely used by followers of Marx, as is also, strange as this may seem, St. Thomas More's *Utopia*.

There is, of course, some truth in the influence of economic life upon human thought and institutions, as we showed in Chapter 3, but such a theory of complete economic determinism postulates that only matter exists, and that man does not differ from the brute creation. It denies that man is composed not only of matter (his animal being) but also of a spiritual soul whose life is immortal and so transcends our present earthly existence. In denying all dualism it therefore denies all the tenets of the Christian and Jewish religions, and it abjures spiritual values of any kind. This is a universal error of socialism.

The followers of Marx have ceaselessly striven to force the acceptance of their doctrine by political means, so as to be able to carry into legal effect the ending words of the *Communist Manifesto:* "expropriate the expropriators." They have also striven, indirectly at least, to abolish religion, which Marx considered as the "opium of the people" and the most important single institution which upholds capitalism and keeps the people contented with an inferior position. Its development into Bolshevism we shall consider later.

5. Quite other than Syndicalism is the diluted radicalism of *State Socialism.* State socialism took its rise in Germany in the teachings of Karl Rodbertus (1805–1875) and Ferdinand Lassalle (1825–1864), and was somewhat a reaction against the impractical side of Marxism which at that time was high-sounding verbiage but had little by way of program to offer its adherents. Lassalle is particularly famous for his theory of the Iron Law of Wages. It was his idea that it is inevitable that wages should always stay at a subsistence level. If wages increase, he said, owing to a lack of supply of laborers in any industry, workers will have larger families and also more labor would be attracted to that particular industry, which would bring about an oversupply of labor to the industry and a consequent diminution of wages again. On the other hand, if wages fall below the subsistence level many workers are incapacitated due to insufficient nourishment, and the death rate rises; workers will also tend to go into other types of occupation or other industries, and so labor will automatically become scarce and wages will be increased once more. This "law" has of course, long since been disproved, although it has had a great influence on certain socialists even to this day.

State socialism in its original plan, aimed merely at an increased amount of State legislation and regulation of industry, and the establishment of workmen's producers' co-operative groups, which were to be subsidized by the State, so that gradually, by their competition, the downfall of capitalism would be achieved.

6. *Fabian Socialism.* The Fabian Society was established in England by a group of middle-class students and professors in 1883, headed by Professor Thomas Davidson. It included such well-known people as Sidney and Beatrice Webb, Phillip Snowdon, George Bernard Shaw, Annie Besant, Graham Wallas, G. D. H. Cole, and J. Ramsay Mac-Donald (who headed the British Labor Party which was in power in Great Britain from 1924 to 1925, and from 1929 to 1931). They believed that the development from capitalism to socialism could not be brought about by any sudden revolution such as Marx predicted, but only by the peaceful and gradual means of ethical reform through education and propaganda. (They took their name from that of the Roman general Fabius Cunctator, the delayer, who defended Rome from Hannibal by "delay.") They also rejected Marx's economic doctrines, particularly his idea of the theory of surplus value, since they adhered to the teachings of John Stuart Mill, and of Jevons and other "orthodox economists" of the marginal utility theory of value. In the gradual transformation of economic society, the Fabians were in favor of State control of certain public utilities, and a redistribution of incomes through progressive taxation and heavy inheritance duties, and especially taxation on land. The group went into politics and the Fabian Society was broken up in 1917 when some of the members objected to this practice. G. D. H. Cole and others joined the Guild Socialist movement at this time.

7. *Guild Socialism,* a movement begun in England by the publication of Arthur J. Penty's *The Restoration of the Guild System,* in 1906. As the name of his book implies, Penty's idea was to restore the medieval guilds by the creation of national guilds to control large-scale industry. Guild Socialism was finally organized in 1915, when G. D. H. Cole seceded from Fabian Socialism in favor of Guild Socialism, joined by such other intellectuals as S. G. Hobson, R. H. Tawney, Bertrand Russell, and Maurice Reckitt. Although highly critical of the bureaucracy of State control, the Guild Socialists provide for a democratic State and look to a certain amount of State ownership of education, roads, canals, bridges, social service, and similar national but non-economic activities. The building trades of Great Britain adopted this form of Socialism after the war, with the foundation of the National Building Trades Guild. The lengthy industrial depression in that country, however, greatly mitigated the influence which it might have wielded. In the U. S. A., the Plumb Plan was a similar scheme. It was planned directly for the railroads, though it was intended to extend to other industries. The government was to be the owner, but the em-

ployees were to manage and operate the railroads, receiving wages and then dividing surplus profits with the government. The interests of the public were to be represented by a minority share in the management.

8. *The Single-Tax System* of socialism has been discussed in Chapter 10 on Property.

9. *Bolshevism*. In 1891 a Second International was formed of two different parties — Marxists, who wanted workers to undertake direct political action to socialize all the means of production as rapidly as possible; and "Revisionists" or German Marxists, led by Edouard Bernstein (1850–1932) who did not wish to participate directly in any political movement but wanted to help a gradual transition by such active means as press propaganda, education, and the like. The Second International had a number of meetings before the Russian Revolution. Then in 1917, the Russian revolution was effected, Bolshevism was established there, and a final split between the Marxist adherents then occurred. In 1918 a republic was set up with the avowed purpose of bringing about the transition stage between capitalism and communism. The Bolshevists considered that in this transition stage planned mechanism and government coercion is needed to overcome the inevitable friction until classless society is finally established. A Third International was formed in March, 1919, when thirty-two foreign delegates from twelve different countries met in Moscow. This Congress established the Communist International or *Comintern* and adopted the policy of the Communist Manifesto, asserting the need for the dictatorship of the masses.

The communists tried to abolish private productive property under every form, to forbid private industry, to abolish the use of money, and to have everything owned in common among the people. The State owned every form of industrial enterprise and became the sole distributor of products. Wages were the same for all workers, whatever their functions and ability. Payment for labor was made by labor tickets, giving the owner right to exchange these at government stores for goods involving the same number of hours of labor.

This very extreme program was a complete failure, and was abandoned in 1921, when the N.E.P., or New Economic Policy was established. Money was used once more. The wage system, with extra payments for merit, was introduced, and bank deposits were allowed, so that in many ways business was once more run on capitalistic lines. In 1928, to bring about better material conditions and greater economic success, economic life was carefully planned under what is known as the Gosplan or the first of the five-year economic plans. This included a special farm program, to bring about large-scale mechanization of small peasant farms, to urbanize rural districts as much as possible, and to abolish the middle-class farmer. State planning on a large scale still continues, and it must be said that special provision has been made for improved health and sanitation. Technical and scientific progress has been considered of highest importance, and education for the workers is very considerably improved.

The U.S.S.R., which is now composed of seven federated republics, is ruled by the All-Union Congress, to which the people elect their representatives. Although less than one quarter of the large population is urban, industrial workers have a much larger political representation than the rural people. The clergy, middlemen, private traders, all who are not considered as doing socially useful work, have no vote at all. Yet not even the workers have control over economic and industrial resources. The Bolshevik (majority) party maintains complete power by the use of force and an extensive spy system: a position which is rendered easier to maintain because for generations before the present regime the people were habituated to autocratic government rule.

In their desire to destroy all precommunist institutions which might oppose the absolutist claim of the present State, the ruling party has attempted to dominate education, religion, and family life. It is true that many more Russians now have an opportunity of receiving an education than under the former regime, but the school has been made atheistic, and atheistic youth societies have been established with the avowed purpose of breaking the power of the supposed "opium of the people." Although private religious worship is to some extent allowed, no religion is to be taught publicly, and no one under eighteen years of age can be instructed in religion at all. The State claims prior rights over the parents in the upbringing of children. Lifelong marriage is not insisted upon. Consent between husband and wife is sufficient grounds for divorce, although husbands are obliged to make provision for the children and their mother before the final decree is granted. However, registered marriage gives no legal privileges to the children, and illegitimacy is not distinguished from "legitimate" birth; incest is not punished as in any way harmful to society.

Summing up, we may say that Bolshevist communism is completely nondemocratic. Bolshevists in power do not consider that the State exists because of the need of individuals and families for organized mutual development and protection. They regard themselves not as representatives of the people, but rather as holding a necessary weapon of State dictatorship to bring about the practical application of their ideas. Families and individuals are said to exist solely for the good of the State, so long as the State is needed to bring about full international communism. A totalitarian State exists, therefore, in the fullest meaning of the word. The State is considered all-important and all-powerful, and dominates over the individual for the supposed good of society. Instead of being a person, the individual is considered merely as a puppet with no needs other than the material, and no aim or hope in life beyond the grave.

II. Fascism

Although Fascism aims at opposing communism, and at upholding the capitalistic position of the bourgeois middle class, it is very similar to communism in that its main purpose is a wider distribution of property by means of a totalitarian State organization.

1. First and most famous of the Fascist regimes is, of course, that of the Mussolini dictatorship in Italy. Aware of the need for better distribution of property, Mussolini's aim was to rebuild capitalism, not by State ownership, as in communism, but by State intervention and State control. As in communism, it is assumed that the welfare of the State as a whole is prior to the needs of individuals: the State is considered an end in itself, instead of as a necessary means whereby families and individuals may attain their full development in orderly society. In Fascism, therefore, all classes and all economic interests are subordinated to the public authority of the State for the greater well-being of the people as a whole.

The word *Fascism* comes from the Italian *fascio,* a bunch or bundle, signifying the close association of the Fascist group, knit together by the common tenets of the movement. Two years after the rise of Fascism as a patriotic and antisocialist campaign, Mussolini marched on Rome in 1922, abolished all conflicting parties, and established the one-party Fascist regime to insure the material well-being of the people and the unification of State aims. All married men over 18 have a vote; all single men over 21 have also a vote, provided they are civil servants, ministers of religion, pay taxes, or own some property in State bonds. The choice, however, is between personalities proposed for office, and not between parties.

Instead of aiming at communist-class predominance, Fascism works for the glorification of the State by class collaboration. The Fascist hope is that by stressing the unification of the nation, and by a national movement for economic development and State glory, the pre-eminence of the Italy of the past will be re-established. In Fascist Italy, therefore, political, social, and intellectual freedom is abolished in the interests of the economic and political freedom of the State. Education is considered as primarily a matter of State and not of parental control. Religion is tolerated, but is somewhat though not wholly subordinated to State interests. Naturally, production is counted as a matter of national concern, and a public service which, although left in private hands, must be submitted to strict regulation and control by the strong central government. Capital levies are made for the unemployed. Higher wages are decreed to increase purchasing power, not for the more widespread acquisition of property. All the major branches of economic life are divided into twenty-two corporations, composed of equal representatives of workers and employers, plus technical experts and representatives of the Fascist party. Workers and employers are both given a status by their permanent place within a trade or profession. Although individual enterprise is allowed within this corporate organization, and limited profits are assured, the corporations are not autonomous as were the medieval guilds, which were subject to a minimum of "State" supervision.[3] Instead, they are the instruments through which the Fascist government carries out the regulation of production for the political power and prosperity of the Italian people. Strikes and lockouts are forbidden and disagreements must be settled by private arbitration and by State labor courts. Mussolini is the president of each of the corporations, so that although he delegates his power to a vice-president, by means of the corporations he can intervene in any department of economic life. In fact, Article VI of the Fascist Charter of Labor specifically declares that the corporations are organs of the State. Strictly speaking, therefore, private enterprise in Italy is abolished, and the corporations are identical with the State.

2. Of the other Fascist nations, Germany is probably of most importance. German Fascism, launched in 1922, seemed temporarily to have failed when the leaders, Adolph Hitler and General von Ludendorf, were punished after the Beer Hall Putsch of 1923. By 1932, however, the party had a voting strength of nearly fourteen millions. In January, 1933, Hitler became Chancellor, and at the elections of March the same year, his party had an absolute majority, and he was given dictatorial powers for four years. As the vote in Germany is at present the same as in Italy, there is a one-party rule, and the choice is between personalities alone. There is little likelihood that either Mus-

---

[3] The Italian corporate State is also to be clearly distinguished from the organization of autonomous corporations or vocational groups proposed by Catholic sociologists and to some extent carried out in practice in Portugal.

solini or Hitler will lose their office. Austria was incorporated into the German State in 1938.

German Fascism is best known as Nazism, a word derived from the term *National Sozialistische Deutsche Arbeiter Partei* (National German Socialist Workers' Party). It has nothing in common with socialism, if by socialism is meant the abolition of capitalism, since it was founded to protect capitalism against socialism and communism. Nazism has, however, gone much farther than Italy in the development of a complete dictatorial regime. To weld the people together for the greater success of his program, Hitler has stressed neither the communist one-class ideal, nor the Italian political unity, but rather the racial unity of the German peoples. A form of race worship has been inaugurated, based entirely on false biological notions of the Nordic race and its supposed supremacy, and on false ideas of German "race purity." Among the "Twenty-Five Points" issued by Hitler in May, 1926, we read: "Only he who belongs to the nation can be a citizen. Only those who are of German blood can form part of the nation, whatever be their religion. No Jew can therefore be part of the nation. . . . Only citizens will have the right to participate in the government and the legislation of the state."

Religion ranks as a secondary matter, to be permitted only as the State does not consider it to be detrimental to the good of the nation. The State completely dominates the life of the people. Education is entirely a State matter for the development of good Nazi leaders (and Nazi followers). Since woman's best service to the State is considered to be that of providing a home, and raising future citizens, the freedom of women has been greatly curtailed. Productive labor is expected from all, for as the tenth point of Hitler's Twenty-Five Points clearly states: "Manual or intellectual work is the first duty of every citizen. The activity of the individual must not harm the interests of the collectivity, but must be developed in the whole for the profits of all." Although the government has the power to create cartels in any industry, no corporate State has yet been established. However, certain of the larger trusts were to some extent nationalized, and there is a strong bureaucratic control. Labor unions were changed by law into the Labor Front, and Nazis are placed in all positions of authority. Nazi cells have been formed in each factory, as the instrument of party policy within their own field — the cells being grouped into larger territorial units, all under the authority of the Nazi Minister of Labor.

So far as land is concerned, some control over its inheritance has been made, but the land of peasant proprietors is protected from the usual legal measures of creditors, and there is a tendency to create a permanent peasant class on the land.

There is no need to dwell on the completely authoritarian aspect of the Nazi regime as above outlined, and of the similarities between the philosophy of Fascism (in Italy and elsewhere) and communism. The ends of communism and Fascism are entirely opposite of course. The one wishes to abolish the aristocracy and the bourgeois class in favor of the workers, for a material millenium. The other wishes to uphold a modified capitalism, and the bourgeois class, against communism, for material well-being based upon a political or racial idealism. But both Fascism and communism are antipersonalist, consider the State of paramount importance,[4] and work for the good of the collectivity of the State rather than for the well-being of the individual as well as the group. Both are maintained by an authoritarian government which controls every department of the private life of the citizens. In both, one party reigns supreme, and within the party the will of one man is paramount.

More hopeful for the preservation of man's liberty and of his natural rights to private property ownership at the same time corrective of the abuses of modern capitalism, are several other schemes.

III. Co-operation

Of all non-totalitarian schemes, by far the most widespread in its practical application is "co-operation," which we have already somewhat fully described in Chapter 19. Briefly we may state here that co-operation in its technical sense means a voluntary association of people for the attainment in common of some business purpose of production or distribution, with socialization of profit and mutual service as the motive of the enterprise. It is claimed that co-operation enables the worker to obtain more goods and services than would be possible under the normal organization of a capitalistic regime; and that it also enables the small producer to compete favorably with mammoth capitalistic enterprise. It works no sudden revolution; it does not abolish capitalism, but it changes our economic order, extends property ownership among the masses, and above all, it substitutes for the profit motive of the capitalist, an ideal of mutual help within the group. The modification of the capitalist system which is inevitably brought about at least to some extent by co-operation, has advanced in some countries more than in others. Some people see in its progress a more extended

---

[4] This is true of present-day communism, although, as earlier explained, the communist ideal is the eventual abolition of the State.

capitalism in the more widespread ownership of productive goods. Others believe that eventually, realizing the advantages of co-operation by actual association, co-operators will spontaneously decide to try a federated collectivism.[5] At the present time, however, co-operation merely tries to make groups of neighbors as self-sufficient as possible, and co-operative societies are merely organizations of neighbors who aim at doing as much as possible for themselves locally.[6]

IV. Distributism

Still in the realm of theory is the proposal of the Distributists. Distributism had its rise with the publication in 1912 of Hilaire Belloc's *Servile State*. Belloc was of the opinion, not only that free competition leads to the monopolistic abuses of small groups of business and financial magnates and to the extension of a propertyless proletariat, but that the system is so unstable that the worker is a slave to the possible work provided by the so-called "risk takers," and that his very means of livelihood can be affected by the selfishness and greed of manipulators or speculators on the financial and produce markets. Only property owners are really free in our capitalistic era, wrote Belloc, since all others must be slaves to the wage system. Social insurance and employers' liability laws are merely evidence, he thought, that we are rapidly developing a servile state of socialistic collectivism. As the only possible alternative to this latter system, he proposed a policy of social and economic reform called Distributism. Belloc's ideas found many followers even prior to the 1914–18 war, including Cecil Chesterton, who founded *The New Witness* in support of the program, a publication which went out of existence soon after its founder's death. In 1925 G. K. Chesterton came forward as a proponent of the theory, with the publication of *G. K.'s Weekly* (now called *The Weekly Review*) and the organization of the Distributist League. The chief organ of Distributism in the United States is *Free America*.

The Distributists wish each family and each nation to become as self-sufficient as possible. Because they consider the downfall of capitalistic industrialism to be imminent, they urge as many as possible to settle on the land. They do not wish to abolish cities, nor do the majority wish to do away with all large-scale production, but they look for an extension of small factories to be either partially owned by employees, or organized as producers' co-operatives. This change is to

---

[5] Cf. Laidler, H. W., *Consumers' Cooperation*, p. 8: "The cooperative movement helps to lay the foundation for a future cooperative commonwealth."
[6] Cf. Warbasse, *What Is Cooperation?*. p. 106.

be rendered possible by taxing the large corporations, who will then be obliged to go out of business or else to charge more for their products (and in this way lose one of the important advantages of large-scale production). A much greater percentage of the population is to work on small plots of land purchased with the savings which the payment of a living wage to present workers would enable them to lay aside, and assisted by co-operative marketing and banking schemes. In the rural areas, the small peasant proprietor and the yeoman farmer would take the place of large-scale farming and inadequately farmed estates. Wherever possible, small family stores and workshops are to provide for local needs, the local market being the medium of exchange for the farmers' surplus produce and the work of the craftsmen and purveyors of other needed articles. Industries which cannot be "distributed" in this manner, such as State services, mining, railroads, shipping, the manufacture of chemicals and armaments are to be nationalized, to avoid the evils of private trusts. Thus property ownership would be spread over a large number of families; population would be better distributed over the countryside instead of being highly concentrated in cities; consumption would be for the most part near the place of production; power would be decentralized, and much of the present economic and human waste brought about by mass production would be avoided.

Although it would seem that in a Distributive State we should have to forego some of the present luxuries of our present urban civilization, Distributists claim that we shall only avoid the definite evils of our modern system. They point to the gains to be attained by a more stable natural civilization, with the personal liberty and initiative of the individual restored by the better distribution of property, the practical recognition of the family as the fundamental social unit, and the average worker and his family no longer dependent on the provision of work by large semi-monopolistic corporations, and by profit-seeking and amoral capitalists.

Some of the more extreme Distributists have already set up certain land-colonization schemes. The practical difficulties in the way are, however, almost insurmountable. Workers have become accustomed to commercialized city life, and it would take many years for most such colonists to be acclimatized to the slower tempo of the country. Successful farming requires an accumulation of knowledge which cannot be acquired in a short period; and the arduous duties of the farmer would be distasteful to most people not brought up from childhood to consider long hours of toil as part of the normal round of life. It seems to be a distinct loss to mankind, too, if large numbers are to forego the use of many of our mechanical inventions of the day; and if chemists and engineers progress rapidly in "dirtless farming," where chemical preparations take the place of soil, one wonders if the Distributists would have us forego the benefits of their researches also. Yet the Distributist State might well be established in the future if the right kind of long-distance planning, educational as well as economic, is attempted on a sufficiently large scale. In particular, a following of the Distributist ideals may well help to maintain the rural character of many of the western, southern, and middle-western states in the United States, and so prevent a too rapid increase in urban populations.

V. Corporatism

Another scheme for the reorganization of economic life, and one of most interest to Catholic students because it is the official program of Pope Pius XI, is what has been called Corporatism or the Corporate Order, to which we have already referred in Chapter 7. Aware that economic life lost its organic form when the guild organization of the Middle Ages disappeared in 1884, Catholic sociologists under the leadership of Cardinal Mermillod in the Union de Fribourg, stressed that the grouping of men according to their community of natural interests and social functions would be far better for the economic well-being of the people than the existing capitalism.[7] Léon Harmel, in his "Christian Corporation" at Val des Bois had already established a vertical organization as the nucleus of a more ambitious scheme. Bishop von Ketteler, Vogelsang, Hitze, the Solidarists, had all stressed the need of such a plan. In 1922, the Christian Trade Union International included a corporative organization of industry in its official program, anxious that associations of employers in each branch of production should unite with labor-union members as equals in a corporation, to regulate all undertakings, both internal and with others.[8] This idea of

---

[7] Cf. Declaration of the *Union de Fribourg*, 1884.

[8] It is noteworthy that quite apart from Catholic endeavors, the Whitley Council scheme of Great Britain was inaugurated in 1917 to form shop committees in various industries, with equal representation of employers and workers, linking these up by district industrial councils, and a national Joint Industrial Council. The main object of these councils, however, was the fostering of better relations between employers and workers, and although they represent a notable progress in industrial organization, and some ninety industries have such councils, they have confined themselves largely to the settlement of industrial disputes and the collection of statistics. The corporations legally established in Italy in 1927, and finally put into effect in 1934 are organs of the State (Fascist Charter of Labor, article 6) and not a true corporate order.

the corporate organization of society was finally elaborated by Pope Pius XI in May, 1931, in his encyclical letter *Quadragesimo Anno.*

In the *Quadragesimo Anno,* the Pope hopes that workers and employers organized voluntarily into trade-unions and into employers' associations, according to their trade or profession, will form vocational groups for each trade or profession, to bind the two interests together vertically. In this manner existing classes in society would be united by function, not merely to settle disputes which arise between them, but for the orderly conduct of their mutual interests. In contradistinction to the usual class feeling which exists when trade-unions and employers' associations meet under capitalist organization, human society would then be built upon vocational associations as were the guilds of the Middle Ages, instead of on hostile classes. Such vocational groups would not suppress initiative and would not destroy private enterprises which work for legitimate commercial profit. It would have nothing to do with the ownership of property and business enterprise and would not even require profit sharing, although the Pope praised the latter system in the *Quadragesimo Anno,* too.

As the members of the Catholic *Semaines Sociales* explained at the end of their Annual Meeting in 1935 at Angers: "In production and trade the Vocational Group would regulate economic life and would adapt products and services, in quantity as well as quality, to the needs of consumers. It would arrange for markets and for the rational distribution of goods. It would establish peace, based on justice, between the various interests engaged in industry and would regulate competition. For the class struggle it would substitute professional organization, which would give due representation, with effective guarantees, to the various interests. Ultimately there would be regulation of the relations between industries, the aim being the proper co-ordination of all branches of activity in the economic life of the nation."[9] The same pronouncement of the *Semaines Sociales* asserts that the reason for Vocational Groups is to take care of the common good, and it is very insistent that the Vocational Groups envisaged are autonomous bodies, and not a political system, to be identified with the State, as are the Italian "Corporations." The State will give a charter to the Vocational Group, but it does this not as creating the authority of the Vocational Group, but as acting in the office of a judge to determine the boundaries of jurisdictions and naming a special authority competent to settle such questions reasonably. The State recognizes the

---

[9] *The Catholic Social Yearbook,* "The Guild Social Order" (Oxford, 1936), pp. 52, 53.

authority of the Vocational Group and confers upon it the necessary legal powers without either absorbing it or supplanting it. The Vocational Group relieves the State which, when there is no intermediary between itself and private industry, has to meddle with functions not properly belonging to the political authority. The Vocational Group, like all other groups intermediary between the State and the individual, is subordinate to the State, which uses its authority to control or affirm the authority of the Vocational Groups as occasion requires."[10]

Pope Pius XI emphasized in his encyclical that the State is to use its power to supplement the activities of individuals and social groups, and not to supersede them. There is no question, therefore, of a totalitarian State. He showed clearly, however, that for the orderly conduct of social life, and the well-being of society, the State should carry out its function of "directing, watching, stimulating, restraining, as circumstances suggest and necessity demands."[11] This function of the State has been amplified by the Catholic International Union for Social Studies, of Malines, as follows: "The State, while in principle leaving to individuals the ownership and management of enterprises, lawfully interferes either to protect these enterprises against foreign competition (by custom duties of a compensatory but not prohibitive kind), or to help it to enter foreign markets (through consular services and commercial agents). It belongs to the State to give a general direction to the national economy, and for that purpose to set up a national economic council representative of the corporative organization, which will enable the public authorities to keep in close touch with qualified and competent representatives of every branch of production. Special reasons may urge the State to take over the entire management as a State monopoly, of certain industrial, commercial, or agricultural undertakings. But in general it should avoid absorbing the country's economic life in this way. If the nature of a service requires that the undertaking shall not be wholly in private hands, the State should endeavor, preferably to conducting it as a State concern, to retain a partial interest through some form of leasing out or granting concessions. In such cases private initiative may take a suitable share with the public authority, and under its supervision, in the management of services or undertakings of public interest such, for instance, as railways. . . . In any case, the central authority should not act as though it were itself alone the State, for the State is the organized nation with

---

[10] *Ibid.*, pp. 53, 54.
[11] *Quadragesimo Anno*, p. 27 (*QA*, 28).

all the living forces that compose it. A co-ordination of all these forces
is particularly necessary in great undertakings of public importance
which tend to develop the national resources, such as the control of
rivers, canals, harbours, oil-wells, mines, and forests."[12] The same
source, showing that "The different States are mutually dependent in
the economic order," says that they "should pool their experience and
efforts by means of suitable institutions, in order to bring about, along
with occupational and inter-occupational organization, international
economic co-ordination."[13]

How such a corporate order should be worked out within existing
political systems, is left by the theorists for the individual countries
to decide. On account of the present power of the monopolists, an
authoritarian government would seem to be almost essential to in-
augurate such a plan. Instead of waiting for a spontaneous growth from
within, Belgium shaped a semi-corporative state from above;[14] Austria
did the same in the days before it was taken over by the German
Nazis; so too did Dr. Salazar in Portugal, for he inaugurated the system
there in 1935, and still guides it with a firm hand, though he cannot be
strictly called a dictator.[15] In Portugal, whose corporative organization
most closely resembles the Pope's ideas, the corporate regime may
rather be said to be authoritarian, though not completely totalitarian.
In the hands of profit-seeking and amoral (if not immoral) politicians,
however, such an authoritarian State might well end in disaster. The
Corporative Order outlined by Pope Pius XI is primarily of economic
concern. Its connection with politics is only, as it were, incidental,
necessitated by the fact that economic life can function only within
a well-ordered civic association. Whether it can grow within a demo-
cratically organized nation, or whether an authoritarian (but not
totalitarian) government is needed, is a matter for individual peoples
to work out. Yet the intelligent and careful choice of political leaders
is a task which most voters have yet to learn. Undoubtedly a planned
economy is essential to a system which retains an urban economy and
the benefits of the division of labor by large-scale production. Undoubtedly, too, man will enjoy more liberty if his economic life is
privately organized and maintained. If a government can induce the
citizens of a State to organize themselves into autonomous groups, with

---

[12] *A Code of Social Principles* (Oxford: Catholic Social Guild, 1937), p. 62.
[13] *Ibid.*, p. 63.
[14] Cf. Roger, C., *Economic Control — The Experiment of Belgium.*
[15] Cf. Derrick, M., *The Portugal of Salazar;* also "On the Corporative Society,"
Central-Blatt and Social Justice, October, 1938, pp. 193, 194.

the machinery for ample intergroup relationships, such as advocated by the Pope, then its work of directing and advising these groups for the benefit of the nation will never unduly interfere with man's liberty of decision and action, yet will eliminate the disastrous consequences of *laissez faire*.

VI. The N.R.A.

The N.R.A. bore some resemblances to the corporate organization above outlined. Among the provisions of the National Industrial Recovery Act of June, 1933, Title I urged all trades, industries, or subdivisions of trades or industries to draw up voluntary codes of fair competition. The trade or industrial associations or groups drawing up these codes were to be truly representative of their class, and were to plan in the best interests of all — employers, workers, and consumers. The codes were not to promote monopolies, neither were they to eliminate and oppress small enterprises. They were to set up reasonable standards for hours, wages, and conditions of employment, with due regard to retail prices. Hours of labor were to be less than were the average working hours at the time of passing the Act, with the idea of giving employment to as many jobless as was practicable. Standard minimum-wage payments set up by the various codes were to be sufficient to provide the worker with a "living wage." Even a minority in any trade, industry, or subdivision, who might have contested the setting up of a code, was to be held by its provisions once the President was satisfied that the particular code in question was just and equitable. Violation of any duly approved code was to be punishable by law.

If a trade or industry, or subdivision of a trade or industry did not draw up its own code voluntarily, then after due notice and a public hearing, the President had power under this Act to impose a code on that trade, industry, or subdivision. Violations of an involuntary code of this nature were also to be punishable by law.

To assist in the operation of the Act special advisory boards were set up by the President, one each for employers, workers, and consumers. A Labor Mediation Board was likewise appointed to act as arbitrator in the event of disputes between employers and labor, with subsidiary local committees working under this national board in various parts of the country.

The Act did not cover professional people, executives, domestic servants, agricultural workers, and engineers. It must be mentioned, too, that codes drawn up under this Act, whether voluntary or involuntary, were to take effect for two years only, so that mistakes discovered in them could be rectified.

The main difficulties about the successful working of the N.R.A. were five. First, the area of the United States is so vast, and conditions vary so greatly in different parts of the country, that it was difficult to set up codes which would be equitable under all conditions. Second, the ramifications of modern industry and trade and the overlapping of many tasks, sometimes made it very difficult to decide upon the jurisdiction of certain of the codes. Third, since the codes involved price fixing, in the last analysis it was the employers who alone could furnish the necessary cost accounts, and their figures were frequently to their own profit advantage; an increase in monopolistic tendencies was also seen in the restriction of output. Four, a great deal of bureaucracy was entailed in the examination of the hundreds of codes which were established, and in their supervision, particularly as many employers who subscribed to the code evaded their restrictions whenever possible. Finally, there was no provision made for the necessary co-operation between all industries and trades. Yet an interrelation among all the widespread ramifications of economic life is essential, if no one industry is to profit at the expense of a disruption in the plans of the rest.

Within too short a period for the N.R.A. to prove its worth, its legality was contested in the courts, and the Supreme Court declared it unconstitutional in 1935.

Space does not here permit the detailing of further reconstruction plans such as that of Townsend, who thought that the economic ills of the country could be solved by the giving of an old-age pension of $200 a month to all who reached the age of sixty; the Douglas Credit Scheme, whose fiat money plan was attempted in Alberta, and various other monetary plans.[16]

It is evident that a reform of our economic institutions is a radical need; but it is equally evident that man needs a change of heart before any economic reform can be socially effective. Until selfishness, profit seeking, and greed in economic life and in politics give place to a greater degree of brotherly love, with international and interracial understanding, the problems which confront us today will be changed with a changed economic system, but they will not be eradicated. Corporatism seems the most hopeful of all current schemes — it does not do violence to the present monopolistic trends, yet it promotes man's economic well-being in a natural and practical fashion, preserves his

---

[16] See the author's *What Is Economics?*, Chap. XIV, or similar economics books for a brief discussion of some of these schemes.

liberty, and makes of economic life a living, vital organism, whereby families, living within the State, maintain a dignified material existence in true happiness and harmony. There is, too, much to be said in favor of the Co-operative and the Distributive schemes. In any event, to evaluate any of the above proposals for economic reform, a deep knowledge of both practical and theoretical economics is essential, which this book could not pretend to furnish.

CHAPTER 21

RURAL PROBLEMS

Importance of Rural Society

THE reader may have observed that in discussing occupational society, rather undue emphasis was laid upon the industrial section of this large and important social group, and only passing reference was made to agricultural society, despite the fact that of the 48,829,940 persons reported as gainfully employed in the 1930 census, 10,722,467 or 21.9 per cent were engaged in agriculture, forestry, or fishing. The reason for this seeming omission was twofold: first, many of the problems of industrial life similarly affect rural occupations, so that specific mention of the agricultural situation was not called for; second, rural society is of its nature so entirely different from the industrial, that it provides problems which of necessity must be considered apart from other aspects of occupational society.

Of all occupational groups it may be said that the agricultural group is of most fundamental importance. Modern industry might be termed unnecessary, insofar as we could exist without the automobile, the radio, the electric light, hot and cold water, factory-made furniture, chinaware, and the rest. We should, however, fare extremely badly without the produce of the land — without the wheat, vegetables, meat, dairy produce, cotton, wool, hides — and all the other products with which the agricultural worker provides us.

"Nature owes to man a storehouse that shall never fail, the daily supply of his daily wants. And this he finds only in the inexhaustible fertility of the earth."[1]

Setting forth the economic evils of excessive capitalism, Pope Pius XI wrote: "It is true that even today these economic conditions do not everywhere exist exclusively, for there is another economic system which still embraces a very large and influential group of men. There are, for instance, the agricultural classes, who form the larger part of the human family and who find in their occupation the means of obtaining honestly and justly what is needful for their maintenance."[2]

---

[1] *Rerum Novarum*, p. 4 (*RN*, 6).
[2] *Quadragesimo Anno*, p. 32 (*QA*, 33).

Of all occupational groups, the agricultural is the most natural, for its unit is the family, and its life the least artificial. Yet continuing the quotation just given, Pope Pius stated with truth: "This system, too, has its difficulties and problems."[3]

A study of rural life is therefore of importance. First, agriculture provides man with basic sustenance. Second, insofar as modern large-scale industrial methods and excessive capitalization have invaded the field, there are definite economic problems which must be considered. Third, since it is chiefly an industry where small units prevail, where men obtain, in the words of the above quotation, "honestly and justly what is needful for their maintenance," it is useful to consider it as a potential-idea society, to devise means for its extension, and to seek to eliminate its "difficulties and problems."

Rural society, however, is not important for these three reasons alone. In another sense, it is of even wider significance. Statistics of births and deaths show that city dwellers will soon have a declining population, and will not even maintain themselves at a stationary level. It is the rural population which makes up for the deficiencies.

On the average, rural families are much larger than in the city,[4] and are frequently superior to the town bred in strength and vitality, and often in mentality as well. The reason for the frequent superiority must be at once clear. In the country, children generally lead wholesome, healthy lives away from the artificiality of modern town existence. They have good food to eat, pure, fresh air to breathe, the fields to play in, nature to observe, and a sufficiency of simple tasks about the farm to give them the training which work alone can supply. These, then, are the children who form the wellspring of the nation, and prevent the depopulation of our cities. That their physique, mentality, and morals be of high type is, therefore, of the utmost importance.

The Advantages of Rural Life

Man was not intended by nature to inhabit tenements in slums, or

---

[3] *Ibid.*, p. 32 (*QA,* 33).

[4] Cf. Age Distribution Statistics, 1930. (See *Statistical Abstract of the United States,* 1937, p. 19):

Class	Under 5 years	5 to 9 years	10 to 14 years	15 to 19 years	20 to 44 years
Urban Population					
Total Urban......	5,626,360	6,211,141	5,949,693	6,015,411	29,071,885
Per Cent of Total	8.2	9.0	8.6	8.7	42.2
Rural Population					
Total Rural......	5,818,030	6,396,468	6,055,184	5,536,703	17,951,362
Per Cent of Total	10.8	11.9	11.3	10.3	33.4

even to live in hotels and apartment houses. Nor is it natural for a man to work in a factory or a skyscraper office all day long, away from his wife and children, so that he sometimes sees the latter awake only at week ends: one or one and a half days out of the seven. As we said above, of all the groups which come within the category of occupational society, the agricultural group is the most natural, for in rural life the economic and the social form one harmonious whole.

On the farm the family is more truly the unit of society as God seems to have intended it to be: a harmonious co-operation or partnership between parents and children, who derive their sustenance from the soil in the surroundings of nature, and not in the artificial atmosphere of the office, factory, and workshops. In particular, where a man has his own small holding of land, he works near his home, with his wife doing the homework within call, and his children around to perform the odd jobs, or "chores," in the American idiom. The children thus prepare for their lifework under wholesome conditions by their parents' side — the boys early learning the intricacies of their manly tasks, and the girls their womanly occupations. Husband and wife become true helpmates to each other, and their common interests about the farm keep them from the disharmonies of married life which seem to arise more frequently in the city, if we are to judge by comparative divorce statistics, which show that in 1930 only 0.9 per cent of rural peoples, male and female, were divorced, whereas in the city 1.3 per cent of the total male population, and 1.6 per cent of the total female population were divorced.[5]

In the country, too, man is better able to cope with the unemployment crises which periodically arise in occupational society, for at least he can usually grow enough foodstuffs to keep himself from starvation or reliance on charity funds. This gives the children a greater security in life — a true need for happiness and sane mental development.

Rural Needs

Despite the fundamental advantages of rural living, there is a steady influx of population from the country to the cities. This decrease in rural population will be amply evident from the following two tables, from which it will be seen that whereas in 1880, 71.4 per cent of the total population was rural, in 1930, only 43.8 of the total population lived in rural areas, and it was estimated that in 1935 the percentage had declined to 43.1.[6]

---

[5] *Statistical Abstract of the United States,* 1937, p. 47.
[6] *Ibid.,* p. 574.

DISTRIBUTION OF RURAL-URBAN POPULATION[7]

Year	Urban Population	Rural Population	Total Population
1880	14,358,167	35,797,616	50,155,783
1890	22,298,359	40,649,355	62,947,714
1900	30,380,433	45,614,142	75,994,575
1910	42,166,120	49,806,146	91,972,266
1920	54,304,703	51,406,017	105,710,620
1930	68,954,823	53,820,223	122,775,046
1935	72,320,000	54,832,000	127,152,000

One must, of course, in part account for the influx by the need of the city for increased workers, by the frequent absence of congenial work for all in the country, sometimes the absence of any type of work, due to the increased mechanization of the farm, and, though probably in rarer cases, by the growing cult of materialism and the glamour which urban life so often presents to the young. There are, nevertheless, many disadvantages to living in the country: disadvantages which, on account of the rural society in the world, need the very serious study and attention of each and every nation.

ESTIMATED MOVEMENT TO AND FROM FARMS OF THE
UNITED STATES, 1920–1934[8]

Year	To Cities from Farms	To Farms from Cities	Net Movement Farm to Cities	Net Movement Cities to Farm
1920	896,000	560,000	336,000	
1921	1,323,000	759,000	564,000	
1922	2,252,000	1,115,000	1,137,000	
1923	2,162,000	1,355,000	807,000	
1924	2,068,000	1,581,000	487,000	
1925	2,038,000	1,336,000	702,000	
1926	2,334,000	1,427,000	907,000	
1927	2,162,000	1,705,000	457,000	
1928	2,120,000	1,698,000	422,000	
1929	2,081,000	1,604,000	477,000	
1930	1,723,000	1,740,000		17,000
1931	1,469,000	1,683,000		214,000
1932	1,011,000	1,544,000		533,000
1933	1,178,000	951,000	227,000	
1934	994,000	783,000	211,000	

These needs are emphasized by the *Commission on Country Life,* which was appointed by President Theodore Roosevelt in 1908, and

---

[7] *Report on Population 1930 Census,* U. S. Dept. of Commerce, Bureau of Census, Vol. 1, p. 8.

[8] *The Agricultural Situation* (Washington, D. C.: May, 1935), p. 4. Births and deaths not taken into account.

which presented its report to the United States Congress on July 21, 1910. Although written so many years ago, one may say without exaggeration that this report is one of the most constructive attempts at understanding rural problems and needs, and is still as up to date and complete as if it had only lately been prepared. The Roosevelt report has undoubtedly resulted in improvements, but it still calls for earnest study and for a true practical appreciation of the recommendations it has to offer. The keynote to rural needs is to be found in the following excerpt:

"We must picture to ourselves a new rural social structure, developed from the strong resident forces of the open country; and then we must set at work all the agencies which will tend to bring this about. The entire people need to be aroused to this avenue of usefulness. Most of the new leaders must be farmers who can find not only a satisfying business career on the farm, but who will throw themselves into the service of upbuilding the community. A new race of teachers is also to appear in the country. A new rural clergy is to be trained. These leaders will see the great underlying problem of country life, and together they will work, each in his own field, for the one goal of a new and permanent rural civilization. Upon the development of this distinctively rural civilization rests ultimately our ability, by methods of farming requiring the highest intelligence, to continue to feed and clothe the hungry nations; to supply the city and metropolis with fresh blood, clean bodies, and clear brains that can endure the strain of modern urban life; and to preserve a race of men in the open country that, in the future as in the past, will be the stay and the strength of the nation in time of war, and its guiding and controlling spirit in time of peace.

"It is to be hoped that many young men and women, fresh from our schools and institutions of learning, and quick with ambition and trained intelligence, will feel a new and strong call to service."[9]

We shall now proceed to examine rural needs in greater detail.

1. *Economic Needs.* First of all, we must state that the rural population is as mixed in the occupational group as any city population. Statistics show[10] that of the 53,820,223 rural peoples in 1930, only 30,445,350 or 56.6 per cent actually lived on farms. In 1935 the estimated inhabitants of farms was 31,800,907, or 58 per cent of the total rural population. To these figures, however, must be added "farm laborers and their families who, while not living on farms, lived outside

---

[9] *Report of the Roosevelt Commission on Country Life,* 1910.
[10] *Statistical Abstract of the United States,* 1937, p. 574.

the limits of any incorporated place."[11] The number of farms declined from 6,448,343 in 1920, to 6,288,648 in 1938, but increased to 6,812,350 in 1935.[12] These farms include those rented as well as owned, commercialized farms, worked for the profit of the owner or stockholders; family farms (the ideal rural unit); and poverty-stricken farms which do not even yield a subsistence. The percentage of tenant farmers in 1920 was 38.1 in 1928, and had increased to 42.4 in 1930, and decreased to 42.1 per cent in 1935.[13] The percentage of land acreage operated by tenants shows a still greater increase: from 27.7 per cent in 1920 to 31.1 per cent in 1930 and 31.9 per cent in 1935.[14] If, however, we compare the number of private rural families owning their own dwellings, as compared with the number renting them, it is seen that rural peoples are much better off in this respect than is the urban population. Of the 29,904,663 families of the United States in 1930 (excluding all institutions and hotels), 7,432,554 or only 42.8 per cent of the total 17,372,524 urban families owned their own dwelling houses, whereas 6,569,520 or 52.4 per cent of the total 12,532,139 rural family houses, were owned by the families who lived in them.[15]

We shall here confine ourselves chiefly to the owner-farmer or renter of the family farm, for this is the ideal farm unit which all interested in rural life are very anxious to extend. At present, the position of this type of farmer, as of the subsistence farmer, is a poor one. Agriculture is "industry's poor relation," and prices are so low that the farmer can make little or no profit on his goods. This situation seems to be due to three main causes:

First, taxation on farm land has increased so much and so speedily within recent years, that not seldom most of the profits must go to pay taxes. This increase in taxation has been brought about by the rapid building of expensive roads suitable for automobile traffic, with heavy state assessments on adjacent farms. Then, too, rural districts often have been forced to share with city taxpayers in the costly public buildings and other civic improvements erected during the course of this century, with their necessary officials, employees, and cost of upkeep. Not only has this general property tax been a severe drain on the farmer's resources, but existing tariffs have likewise increased his burdens, while operating directly for the benefit of urban industry. The United States

[11] *Ibid.*, p. 574. Note, however, that the 1930 and 1935 statistics include all persons actually living on a farm, without regard to occupation.
[12] *Ibid.*, p. 574.
[13] *Ibid.*, p. 588.
[14] *Ibid.*, p. 588.
[15] *Ibid.*, p. 574.

tariff usually increases the cost to the farmer of the manufactured goods which he has to buy, and the consequent retaliatory import tariffs of other countries increase his sales costs abroad.

Second, the small-scale farmer, at least, sells his produce to the wholesale merchants, who in turn sells it to other wholesalers, or to the retailer or consumer direct, at greatly increased prices. This development of the urban middleman and his organizations has so regulated prices that the profits have been diverted from the small-scale producing farmer to the distributing middleman, and the farmer has been reduced almost to destitution.

Third, the renter or owner of the small farm is at once capitalist, manager, buyer, salesman, and worker. Not only does he require money to carry on his undertakings, but he needs organizing ability, expert knowledge of markets and of buying and selling, practical manual training for farm work, and the scientific knowledge of agriculture which is necessary if he is not only to cope with the vagaries of nature, but also to compete with others in these days of specialization. Obviously only a trained man of unusual ability can deal single-handed with all these multiple problems. Obviously, too, such versatility is rare, more especially when we come to consider that the youth or girl with best brains in the farming family is more likely to migrate to the town, where the professions and large-scale industry offer larger scope for social, cultural, and financial advancement. Farmers generally buy as they think best, frequently at a disadvantage; they often borrow capital from ordinary commercial banks and other loan sources which charge them the same or a higher rate of interest than they obtain from the city financial merchants, and industrialists, despite the fact that the risk to the lender is as a rule considerably smaller. Because of money scarcity they cannot provide themselves with up-to-date and scientific farming methods and appliances which are daily being elaborated in the agricultural colleges, and for this reason and general methods of marketing, they receive smaller returns from their land than might otherwise be possible. They are forced, unless co-operatively organized, to entrust the marketing of their produce to the middlemen or dealers above referred to, who are experts in the speculative field, manipulate the markets to give themselves the highest income yield, ignore the justice which is due both to the seller and to the consumer, and consequently bring periodic economic disaster upon the world.

In Europe, the dependency of the farmer upon the agricultural dealer is not so great, for he usually lives near a small township, where he can dispose of most of his produce on market days, direct to the consumer, or to the middleman who supplies local needs and has no such large interests at stake as the dealer connected with the great grain and other markets of the world — nor the temptations to greater profits. As a disunited unit in the industrial world, however, the farmer needs close co-operation with his fellow farmers if he is to eliminate the present cutthroat competition and the ascendancy of the middleman, and to reap the advantages of large-scale buying and selling. Yet his notorious individualism and even stubbornness — due, no doubt, to his isolation from continued social contact which characterizes the town — makes any universally adequate organization seem but a vague hope.

For all the economic evils just enumerated, however, co-operation and education provide a remedy. (We omit the possibility of large-scale organization on capitalistic lines because although such organization, to a certain degree at least, is a necessity for industry, it seems both undesirable and inappropriate for the majority of agricultural pursuits.)[16] The American farmer might, with greater advantage, learn much from the co-operative organization of agriculture to be found in Denmark and in Belgium and, in a lesser way, in Nova Scotia — which we shall later describe. Adequate finance is one of the primary needs of agriculture. This the farmer might obtain through a parish or other local credit bank described in the last chapter. He might purchase his machinery, seed, and other supplies at much lower cost through a consumers' co-operative society, also detailed in the last chapter. Finally, he might make use of producers' co-operation, and ally himself with his farming neighbors for the installation of co-operative dairies, grain elevators, tobacco and cotton warehouses, and the like. For co-operative marketing he might make use of such organizations as the California Fruit Growers' Exchange, and the advice available from the American Farm Bureau Federations, the Grange, the Farmers' Educational and Co-operative Union of America, and similar undertakings.

To provide the intellect necessary for the sadly needed organization of agriculture on a scientific basis, of which mention was made above, born leaders from rural society must be provided with sufficient attraction to keep them from the city and, by similar inducements, must be led from city business and industrial life to the farm. Particularly is it necessary to make some occupational provision for the unmarried countrywoman who may dislike housework, and under present conditions be thus almost driven to the town. A variety of forces are needed

---

[16] To protect the family farm, the State of Kansas has prohibited the formation of "corporation farms."

to achieve these ends. First, the social life of the country must be made more attractive, as we shall presently explain. Second, agriculture must be so organized that leadership will be adequately remunerated, with the resultant mitigation of the present financial ascendancy of the city. Third, special technical instruction must be provided in the rural schools, and education in the agricultural colleges must be maintained at a high practical level. Extension lectures should also be available to keep the adult farmer in touch with technical progress in agriculture. The colleges must not have as their primary object the training of persons with academic minds for teaching, journalism, or laboratory work — though all three classes are useful. Rather they must aim at the preparation of men and women who will esteem the practical side of rural life, who will be fired with zeal to become leaders, and will uplift and maintain agricultural society at a high level of efficiency and attainment. Fourth, farmers should supply their own subsistence needs, for excessive dependence on cash crops has led to times of starvation in some rural communities where one-crop farming prevails.[17] Fifth, small rural industries might be established to keep those not interested in agriculture on the soil. This would have the double benefit, first, of decentralizing industry, so that industrial workers would be enabled to enjoy the benefits of the country, and their children, growing up in rural surroundings, might become attached to the soil and make it their lifework (the hope of the Distributists) ; second, of creating a new vitality in rural life, with a more varied and less narrow individuality of outlook. Such village industries are to be found in France, Belgium, Germany, and several other European countries.

One of the main difficulties of the farmer is the unusually long period for which he needs his "short-term funds" and his difficulties in meeting interest charges on loans for longer periods. Manufacturers and merchants can usually anticipate a quick turnover on their investments in circulating capital, raw materials, and consumers' goods. Farmers, being dependent for their annual income upon the vagaries of nature as well as of man, need special consideration for the renewal of loans which cannot be paid when they are due. The Federal Government has been largely responsible for the establishment of suitable institutions to take care of these special needs.

In 1916 the Federal Farm Loan Act was passed to make provision for the farmers' long-term credit. Twelve Federal Land Banks were established by this Act, under the direct control of a Farm Loan

---

[17] Cf. Rawe, Rev. J. C., S.J., "Homesteading Solves the Problem of Farm Decline," *America,* Dec. 3, 1938, pp. 201, 202.

Board. These banks do not lend money direct to the farmer (with certain exceptions since 1933), but farmers who wish to borrow up to 50 per cent of the value of their land, or 20 per cent of the insured permanent value of improvement on the land, must form a Farm Loan Association of ten or more members. This Association may then borrow for each member from $100 to $50,000 on the security of a first mortgage on the property, for such specific purposes as the purchase or improvement of farm land, or farm buildings and equipment needs, fertilizers, and the like. The Bank lends such money to the Association on the joint credit of all the members, and the individual farmer who receives the credit gives his note to the Association, secured by the mortgage; this note the Association then hands over to the lending bank. The vast increase in applications for loans during the early 1930 depression years necessitated a reorganization, which included the amalgamation of the various individual Associations formed. At the end of 1937, 828 joint offices had been established, involving 3,064 Associations.[18] The present improved economic position of the farmer is evidenced by the fact that whereas in 1934, 402,829 applications had been made to the Federal Land Banks for loans of a total of $730,367,-000 which were granted; in 1935, 162,968 applications were received by the banks, in 1936, 84,030, and in 1937 the total loans applied for were only 60,836, the total volume being $63,092,000. At the end of 1937, the 12 banks had 635,776 loans outstanding for $2,035,307,000.[19]

Banks, known as Intermediate Farm Banks, created by the Agricultural Credits Act of 1923, provide the farmer with short-term credit on his produce or stock. These banks are also twelve in number, one in each of the twelve farm loan districts, and were likewise placed under the Federal Farm Loan Board. Interest at but 2 per cent per annum is charged on short-time debentures, issued at 1½ per cent. The total volume of debentures issued during 1937 amounted to $354,-775,000, and the amount outstanding at December 31 that year was $174,050,000.[20]

The Federal Farm Mortgage Corporation, established in 1934, took over the 200 million dollar fund allotted under the provisions of an Emergency Farm Mortgage Act of 1933, amended by the Farm Credit Act of 1937, and is responsible for the operation of the two types of

---

[18] *The Fifth Annual Report of the Farm Credit Administration,* 1937, U. S. Government Printing Office, 1938, p. 4.

[19] *Ibid.,* p. 5.

[20] *Ibid.,* p. 8.

land banks we have just discussed. The Farm Credit Administration, founded in 1933 supervises the two banks dealt with by this Corporation, and the act which brought it into being provided for two additional groups of institutions: Production Credit Associations, to supervise the short-term credit needs of the farmer, and Banks for Co-operatives, to take over all loans to co-operatives, formerly made by the Federal Land Banks or the Intermediate Credit Banks. There were 550 Production Credit Associations in operation at the end of 1937, which had made 245,799 loans during the year, in the amount of $286,578,000.[21] Farmers' co-operatives borrowed $87,584,000 from the Central Bank for Co-operatives in 1937.[22]

The Federal Farm Credit Administration also administers the Federal Credit Union Act of 1934. This Act created a Credit Union Section within the Farm Credit Administration to charter, regulate, and examine credit unions. On September, 1930, there were 2,356 credit unions, with a total enrollment of 422,826, and of these 1,995 were Federal organizations.[23]

So far as production is concerned, an Agricultural Marketing Act of June 15, 1929, was passed, to curb speculation and inefficient and wasteful methods of distribution of farm products. A Federal Board was created (composed of eight members, each representing one or more major agricultural products), especially designed to promote the co-operative marketing of agricultural goods by assisting in the creation of stabilizing corporations and clearinghouse associations, and by providing a revolving fund of five hundred millions of dollars, appropriated from Congress, to be used as loans to approved co-operative societies. The Federal Farm Board was responsible for dealing in wheat futures and buying up wheat to the subsequent loss to taxpayers, and greatly reduced prices to the farmer.

Other schemes to help solve the farmers' production difficulties were proposed by the Agricultural Adjustment Act of 1933, one of the N.R.A. sequence of Acts which were declared unconstitutional in 1936. The AAA provided for voluntarily curtailed production of cotton, wheat, corn, hogs, rice, tobacco, and milk, to be compensated for by the proceeds of processing taxes, which met with much opposition from manufacturers and meat packers. At the present time, crop control is reserved to the local state governments, but the Soil Conservation Act of 1936 provides Federal appropriations.

---

[21] *Ibid.*, pp. 9, 10.
[22] *Ibid.*, p. 11.
[23] *Ibid.*, pp. 105, 106.

Still other governmental economic aid has been given to the farmer by the Subsistence Homestead Agency, succeeded by the Resettlement Administration which was established as a separate corporation in 1935, but placed under the direction of the Department of Agriculture in 1937. The main work of the Administration is threefold: first, to help families to become self-supporting on the land; second, to establish some specially organized communities in rural and suburban areas; third, to administer the Bankhead-Jones Farm Tenant Act, and make loans to farm tenants, farm laborers, share croppers, and others for necessary repairs and improvements to their property.

The farmers themselves have provided a number of organizations for their own economic improvement, which have usually included also wider social programs. Of these mention may here be made of the following:

First, the Patrons of Husbandry, or the Grange, as this institution is generally called. The Grange has had great influence in all four fields of politics, economic life, education, and the promotion of social intercourse. Both men and women, and children over fourteen years of age, may become members. Founded in 1867 by Oliver Hudson Kelly, it was primarily intended to give the farmers a larger control over legislative affairs and thus to break the powerful capitalistic monopolies, especially the railroads, which the Grangers believed were discriminating unfairly against the smaller farmer. By 1875 the Grange had one million members, and in the early days it wielded such great political influence that many states were, in fact, dominated by it. After 1875 it declined somewhat in power and prestige, but at the present time it still has about 600,000 members. The Grange has been largely responsible for the great extension of the United States Department of Agriculture; for the establishment of the free rural postal delivery service, the parcel-post service, and the postal savings bank; and for the passing of pure-food laws, and also tax reforms in several states. The Grange has also promoted better agricultural methods, co-operative manufacturing, warehousing and shipping companies, mutual fire-insurance concerns, and similar enterprises. From the educational standpoint it has always aimed at self-education of the farmer, which it has promoted by the educational program which has been a feature of all the weekly or biweekly meetings which are held; indirectly it has also helped to develop many of the agricultural colleges. At all the meetings of the Grange social intercourse has had, of course, adequate recognition. Many of the local organizations have debating societies, a club theater, a library, and other activities.

Another institution which has had a great influence is the American Farm Bureau Federation, a federation of State farm bureaus, whose first organization began in Broome County, New York, in 1911. In 1914 the Smith-Lever Agricultural Extension Act inaugurated county agents, to assist farmers, and it is these agents which made the bureaus of nation-wide importance. The County Bureau is composed of a county farm agent and a membership of progressive farmers in the district, the latter paying membership dues. The first state federation of these farm bureaus was formed in Missouri in 1915. This amalgamation scheme was soon imitated by other states, and in 1919 the national American Farm Bureau Federation was inaugurated, to extend co-operative marketing and reduce production costs, and to protect the rights and needs of the farmer. These farm bureaus have done much useful work. They have encouraged farming interests and a higher rural standard of living and education, particularly by practical demonstration. They are also largely responsible for the passing of the Capper-Volstead Act of 1922, which exempted agricultural co-operative societies from most of the restrictions placed on foreign and interstate commerce, and for the Agricultural Credits Act of 1923 and the consequent establishment of the Intermediate Farm Banks.

We might here mention, too, the Farmers' Educational and Co-operative Union of America, founded in Texas in 1902, and now comprising some 300,000 members, organized in state unions, and federated into the national group. Formerly its membership was much larger. Although predominantly founded to help cotton interests in the South, this organization has aided farms both in production and in marketing, and was quite influential in the establishment of the Federal Farm Loan System and for the Intermediate Farm Credit Banks already discussed.

2. *Educational Needs.* No society can attain a high level of proficiency and social worth without adequate provision for the pursuit of culture. Almost inevitably the country school is at a disadvantage in comparison with the city institution. The paucity of pupils leads to one teacher having to instruct children at varying stages of proficiency, perhaps even the entire school; because of the same lack of students, school-board authorities rarely pay a salary which is of sufficient inducement to the best brains of the profession to devote themselves to rural needs; finally, the narrow localization is not conducive to the mental competition generally to be found among students in the city school, and which is usually a prerequisite for the training of an alert mind. Moreover, standardized educational methods usually leave no

room in the curriculum for the special subjects which are of interest, and which are indeed needed in the rural community. Subjects which are of use to the town-bred student may be utterly valueless for one living in the country. If the country school is adequately to fulfill its purpose of training the child for adult life, then teachers must be specially prepared to fill the need; they must be adequately remunerated, and must, moreover, realize their high calling and take up their work of teaching the rural child as a true life vocation. So far as Catholic rural teaching is concerned, as Father Schmiedeler points out,[24] only too frequently the Sisters of teaching communities have had urban ideals inculcated in their preparatory training and so they are not sufficiently interested in their rural work. In addition to the above scholastic facilities, adequate provision is also needed for the transportation of children to and from their homes to the district school, which calls for the provision of good roads, and probably a local bus service.

Rural education must have as its aim the development of a satisfactory rural community. With this object in view, it must provide rural children with an education which will prepare them for rural life, not only by giving them adequate vocational training, but also by making them appreciate the country so that they will wish to remain there and will not have their imagination fired with the so-called advantages of city life. Indeed the chief need of rural society seems to be the overcoming of the mental domination of the city. If only country folk can be brought to realize the dignity of their profession, its worth and need, then rural civilization will come into its own, and the children of the countryside who take up their abode in the cities will bring with them a better civilization. Both physically and from the social and cultural viewpoint, they can bring new life and vigor to the nation, a rejuvenation which seems a vital need.

Rural education has been promoted especially by the Smith-Hughes Vocational Education Act of 1917, which authorized annual financial appropriations from Federal funds to those states which established vocational agricultural instruction for trades and teacher training, as a part of their permanent public educational program. In 1936 vocational education was further developed by the George-Dean Vocation Act, providing for an annual subsidy of 12 millions, beginning from July, 1937, to be allotted to the states for rural vocational needs, provided the states themselves provide an additional 50 per cent of the allotment yearly until 1942, with a 10 per cent increase in the allot-

---

[24] Cf. Schmiedeler, Rev. E., *A Better Rural Life*, p. 28.

ment yearly thereafter until 1946, from which time onward states receiving the Federal grant must match it by a 100-per-cent expenditure. In addition to these financial aids, the Bureau of Home Economics and Extension Division of the U. S. Department of Agriculture sends practical demonstrators into rural areas for the instruction of farmers and their wives. There are over 500 extension agents employed by the Department of Agriculture to give instruction in home management, dietetics, child care, credit facilities and other rural home problems. The work of these agents is supplemented by voluntary workers. These extension lectures and home demonstrations are especially needed to develop adult vocational proficiency, including domestic economy for the women; and to give the rural inhabitant a fuller mental life, with an intellectual provision sufficient to retain the alert-minded on the farm and not to make them anxious for the cultural amenities of the city. The Farmers' Institute established in 1862 should be mentioned here as of special importance in the development of rural educational extension work. It has special sections for men, women, and children. The states have aided the organization with financial appropriations, and the Federal Government has helped by the provision of expert lecturers and the promotion of agricultural colleges. The American Country Life Association, with its annual conference, and the Catholic Rural Life Bureau of Washington, have, too, done much to further rural thought and education, as have the juvenile 4-H clubs.

The Department of Agriculture has also been very active in the provision of free literature of technical interest to the farmer, a service which may be said to be more extensive than in any other country.

In this latter connection it must be said that the farmer and his family have a particular need of adequate provision of libraries. Books are a necessity for the agricultural advancement of rural peoples, as well as for the recreation of those who value the entertainment a book may provide. Sometimes there are local libraries initiated by a storekeeper, the church, or a public-spirited citizen. Many of the states operate free public libraries for the whole state, not the usual local community, and have a system whereby a citizen may borrow books by mail upon payment of the postage charges; or they provide an extension service in the smaller country towns, where boxes of books are sent at regular intervals for the use of citizens in a district. On the whole, however, library facilities for the countryman are very poor. The Roosevelt Commission previously referred to pointed out the valuable service which the library can perform by stimulating and directing reading habits and by co-ordinating village social life through the

provision of reading rooms, study clubs, and traveling libraries. As the
Commission puts it: "This may mean that the library will need itself
to be redirected, so that it will become an active rather than a passive
agency; it must be much more than a collection of books."[25] Not only
does each country district need a library, but no rural community can
be considered satisfactory without a village hall, with a meeting room
and stage equipment. The ideal social center is probably that attached
to a church.

It seems in place to mention in this section the International Institute of Agriculture, a project originated by David Lubin, a California
merchant, and financed by 74 nations of the world. Originally 40
nations agreed by treaty in 1905 to establish an international bureau
for collaboration and co-operation in technical matters pertaining to
agriculture, and the Institute came into being in 1908 with headquarters in Rome. Two monthly reviews and two yearbooks of statistics
are published, in addition to the expert statistical and information
service which it renders, and the very complete library it maintains
for the use of the general public.

3. *Domestic Needs.* The domestic disadvantages of rural life are
many. Not only is it necessary to work for the cultural advantage of
the male worker, if rural life is to come into its own as a respected and
honorable profession, but the farmers' wife must also share in an improved standard of living, and in a fuller existence. Only too often at
the present time the lot of the woman on the farm is one continuous
and monotonous round of domestic toil. As the Roosevelt Commission
clearly showed: "Her life is more monotonous and more isolated, no
matter what the wealth or the poverty of the family may be."

This situation, then, must be improved. First of all, farming needs
to be better planned, so that the hours of toil may be lessened and the
farmer himself may have greater leisure to devote to social intercourse
with his wife. Then, if he be a hired laborer, his wages should be increased to a standard which will enable him to provide his wife with a
modest amount of present-day domestic conveniences. We cannot do
better than once again to quote the Roosevelt Commission.

"The relief to farm women must come through a general elevation of
country living. The women must have more helps. In particular these
methods may be mentioned: development of a co-operative spirit in
the home; simplification of the diet in many cases; the building of
convenient and sanitary houses; providing running water in the house,

---

[25] *Report of the Roosevelt Commission on Country Life,* 1910.

and also more mechanical helps; good and convenient gardens; a less exclusive ideal of money getting on the part of the farmer; providing better means of communication, as telephones, roads, and reading circles; and developing women's organizations. These and other agencies should relieve the woman of many of her manual burdens, on the one hand, and interest her in outside activities, on the other. The farm woman should have sufficient free time and strength so that she may serve the community by participating in its vital affairs."[26]

The overcrowding in the small rural cottages is sometimes appalling, and apart from the purer air and more abundant food of the countryside, conditions among the poor in many of the villages might be considered almost as bad as in the city slums.

We might consider under this heading also the greater need of health facilities for rural communities. In general there seems to be a great need of instruction in the schools in the simple laws of sanitation and hygiene. This would educate the public in the bad consequences of the lack of proper sanitary conveniences to insure adequate sewage disposal and an unpolluted water supply. It would also impress upon the people the necessity for as strict a quarantine of contagious diseases in the country, as in the towns where the possibility of evasion of health laws is but slight. Similarly the people would come to realize the importance of calling in medical assistance in times of sickness — for particularly among children, the death rate in the country, and the frequency of sickness, is very much greater than might be supposed. Rural society needs an extension of the system of district nursing, it needs the establishment of a rural hospital, dental clinics, and other medical facilities within comparatively easy reach of all communities. There is a need of an organized health service for country school children in every state. Until such time as the country child receives the same health care as the town dweller, country life for the child, no matter how ideal the conditions otherwise, will be inadequate and a severe indictment of the state which allows such conditions to exist.

4. *Social Needs.* While, as we said, family social life of the country is generally superior to that of the town, nevertheless social intercourse with others is not only a necessary form of recreation and a protection against stagnation, but it is likewise essential for the development of community spirit with which is bound up the solidarity and the welfare of a community, and ultimately of the nation.

The isolation of country life is now largely overcome by many of

---

[26] *Ibid.*

our modern inventions. The increased use of the telephone and the newspaper has done much to achieve this end. Then, too, the progress of the radio has been an immense boon to the rural household from the recreational and even from the educational standpoint. The wider use of automobiles, the provision of better roads and more extended bus services, have also opened a wider field to the farming community from the social viewpoint.

There is, of course, a wide divergence of village social facilities. Some communities are exceptionally well equipped; in others, recreational provision is very limited.

For American youth the organization of most far-reaching national importance has been the 4-H clubs, established by the United States Department of Agriculture, and now numbering more than one million members. The avowed purpose of these clubs is to develop the "head, the hand, the health, and the heart," and to foster a spirit of co-operation, leadership, group responsibility, and loyalty. The clubs are supported by Federal funds and are conducted by the agricultural extension departments of the various state universities, with the aid of volunteer leaders. In order to establish a club there must be five members between the ages of 10 and 20, and an adult club leader. Besides the more purely recreational side of the club activities, boy members of each club are instructed in various rural arts, and girls learn dressmaking, cooking, and other useful accomplishments, so that from the standpoint of vocational training alone, they are extremely valuable. There is ample opportunity for Church leadership in these 4-H clubs, if seminaries and colleges will train their students for the work.

The Farmers' Institute and the Grange, earlier described, have also done much to promote friendly intercourse between the rural population.

5. *Religious Needs.* Rural peoples are also frequently placed at a disadvantage from the spiritual point of view. Ministers or priests are too often town bred, or have acquired urban sympathies, so that they do not enter sufficiently into the lives of their people. Frequently there is no church at all, or the church is at too great a distance for regular attendance. For Catholics, the absence of a Catholic school, and frequently even a priest to give their children religious instruction, is of very grave consequences. Many a Catholic country family has moved to the town on account of the lack of spiritual facilities in their former community. Again we cannot do better than to quote the Roosevelt Commission's Report on the great value of the church as a social agency, and the need of a specially trained rural priesthood, working

not only to lift the people to a higher spiritual plane, but to raise them economically and socially as well.

"It is especially important that the country church recognize that it has a social responsibility to the entire community as well as a religious responsibility to its own group of peoples. . . .

"Any consideration of the problem of rural life that leaves out of account the function and the possibilities of the church and of related institutions, would be grossly inadequate. This is not only because in the last analysis the country-life problem is a moral problem, or that in the best development of the individual the great motives and results are religious and spiritual, but because from the pure sociological point of view the church is fundamentally a necessary institution in country life. In a peculiar way the church is intimately related to the agricultural industry. The work and the life of the farm are closely bound together, and the institutions of the country react on that life and on one another more intimately than they do in the city. This gives the rural church a position of peculiar difficulty and one of unequaled opportunity. The time has arrived when the church must take larger leadership, both as an institution and through its pastors, in the social reorganization of rural life. . . .

"The country church doubtless faces special difficulties. As a rule it is a small field. The country people are conservative. Ordinarily the financial support is inadequate. Often there are too many churches in a given community. Sectarian ideas divide unduly and unfortunately. While there are many rural churches that are effective agents in the social evolution of their communities, it is true that as a whole the country church needs new direction and to assume new responsibilities. Few of the churches in the open country are provided with resident pastors. . . . The social activity of the real country church is likely to be limited to the short informal meetings before and after services and to suppers that are held for the purpose of raising funds. . . . The range of social influence is therefore generally restricted and there is likely to be no sense of social responsibility for the entire community. . . . The rural church must be more completely than now a social center. This means not so much a place for holding social gatherings, although this is legitimate and desirable, but a place whence constantly emanates influences that go to build up the moral and spiritual tone of the whole community. The country church of the future is to be held responsible for the great ideals of community life as well as of personal character. . . . The country pastor must be a community leader. He must know the rural problems. He must have sympathy with rural ideas and aspirations. He must love the country. He must know rural life, the difficulties that the farmer has to face in his business, some of the great scientific revelations made in behalf of agriculture, the great industrial forces at work for the making or the unmaking of the farmer, the fundamental social problems of the life of the open country.

"Consequently, the rural pastor must have special training for his work. Ministerial colleges and theological seminaries should unite with agricultural colleges in this preparation of the country clergyman. There should be better financial support for the clergyman; in many country districts it is pitiably small. There is little incentive for a man to stay in a country parish, and yet this residence is just what must come about. Perhaps it will require an appeal to the heroic young man, but we must have more men going into the country pastorates not as a means of getting a foothold but as a permanent work. The clergyman has an excellent chance for leadership in the country. In some sections he is still the dominating personality. But everywhere he may become one of the great community leaders. He is the key to the country church problem."[27]

In the Catholic sphere, much has already been done for the rural Catholic. The Catholic Rural Life Bureau, a part of the National Catholic Welfare Conference,[28] has given excellent service, not only in the spiritual and moral field, but also in extending educational facilities for the Catholic rural dweller, in educating the parent in problems of the rural child, in extending the co-operative movement, the establishment of recreational clubs, better health facilities, better conveniences in the rural home, and many other activities. The National Catholic Rural Life Conference, founded in 1923, has also been instrumental in awakening the interest of Catholics in rural activities and rural needs. This it does by means of an annual conference held in different parts of the country, in cities where strong rural interests prevail in the district, and by the publication of a magazine. For some years the Director of the Catholic Rural Life Bureau was *ex officio* Executive Secretary of the Conference, but since 1936 the Executive Secretary has been Reverend James A. Byrnes of St. Paul, who now devotes his whole time to the undertakings of the Conference. The original publication of the Conference was a monthly entitled *St. Isidore's Plow*, which later became the *Catholic Rural Life*, but was suspended in 1930. Later a small quarterly called *Landward* was issued,

---

[27] *Ibid.*

[28] See Chapter 28 for a description of the activities of the N.C.W.C.

but since Father Byrnes's active reorganization of the work of the Conference within the past two years, the quarterly has been enlarged and revised as the *Catholic Rural Life Bulletin*,[29] and promises to be an important vehicle of Catholic thought and action in the rural sphere. A committee was formed by the Conference in 1937 to prepare a statement on the Catholic attitude toward rural life.[30] This statement should do much to clarify Catholic thought on the subject, and to make the Catholic viewpoint more widespread in the country.

For several years now, religious vacation schools have been held in various parts of the country where no parochial school was established. Popularized by the Rural Life Bureau of the N.C.W.C., and by the Catholic Rural Life Conference, the work of these schools has been largely taken over by the Confraternity of Christian Doctrine since 1936. The object of such schools is to provide intensive religious training for the child during a few weeks in each summer. The school is held in the local parish hall, or village school, or even in the church or in the open air. It is conducted by a priest, with the assistance of teaching Sisters and students from seminaries and colleges. Where these centers have not been possible, by reason of the scarcity of Catholics in a neighborhood, religious correspondence courses have been inaugurated. These latter have also been useful in giving the child a year-round religious education even where the vacation school is a regular feature. Lessons and questions based on them are regularly sent to parents, who instruct their children in the truths propounded, so that the child learns its religious knowledge from those best fitted by nature to instruct them. Answers written by the children are then forwarded to a central office to be corrected by a priest or by Sisters, though sometimes the local pastor undertakes this work. The Missionary Catechists of Huntington, Indiana, and several other religious communities have also promoted lay instruction in rural districts. In some rural towns year-round catechism schools have been established, where three or four Sisters teach religion all day long to groups of children of all ages who are excused from their public school for a short period on several days of the week. In place of formal religious instruction, high-school students are often taught sociology in these schools, as they are, too, in many Catholic high schools.

The Catholic resettlement plan of Granger, Iowa, under the direction of Monsignor Ligutti, and the work of the Reverend George Nell, at

---

[29] The first number of the *Catholic Rural Life Bulletin* was issued on May 20, 1938.
[30] Published under the title, *Manifesto on Rural Life* (Milwaukee: Bruce Publishing Co., 1939).

Effingham, Illinois, are outstanding Catholic achievements in the United States.

One ought perhaps to mention, too, the work which can be done by communities of priests or religious who settle in backward rural districts, gather around them a Catholic village, with the monastery or convent as its center, and set the standard in technical achievement, culture, and high spiritual ideals. Such work has already been accomplished by communities of Benedictines, Franciscans, and others, but an increase in their number could not but be of benefit to whatever countryside is fortunate enough to have them settle there. The importance of this work is: First, to create and foster a Catholic rural culture; second, since the Catholics of the United States are predominantly to be found in urban communities, to insure that the influx of Catholics from the country to the town comprises those strong in religious ideals, and already well grounded in their religious beliefs.

Three Rural Organizations Abroad

It seems advisable to outline here the agricultural system of Denmark and Belgium, as well as the local Catholic co-operatives of Nova Scotia, for the extension of their practices would be beneficial in almost any country of the world. A similar achievement has been made in the Irish Free State, which has been practically transformed within recent years from a country of landlords and tenants to one of peasant proprietors. The work of Monsignor Ligutti at Granger, Iowa, and the co-operatives established by Reverend Duren at Westphalia, Iowa, Reverend Schnellenberger at Celestine, Indiana, and Reverend Aloisius Fischer, O.S.B., at St. Anthony, Indiana, and others, though small in scope, are definitely worthy of study and imitation.

Denmark

The famous agricultural system of Denmark began only in 1875, when the government passed a law for the creation of State-aided credit banks to assist the worker to acquire small holdings of land. Today the country is composed almost entirely of small landholders, who are at the same time capitalists, middlemen, and workers. At first the large estate owners seriously opposed the movement, by making the holdings of land so small that the owners were compelled to accept part-time work on these large estates to eke out their livelihood. Despite their powerful influence and opposition, however, an Act of Parliament in 1899 voted an appropriation of two million kroner as a revolving credit for farmers, and similar acts in later years increased the fund, the money being used to acquire land to allot to small home-steaders, and to lend them up to 90 per cent of the value of needed improvements. In 1919 the movement was still further promoted by an act permitting landowners — whose estates had been granted to their ancestors on the condition that they were handed down in their entirety to posterity, and never sold — to sell part or the whole of their estates in return for a 10-per-cent levy of land, and an additional levy of 10 per cent on the capital value of the whole property. The land and money thus obtained has been used for establishing workers on small holdings. The workers do not actually own the property, but they obtain all the benefits of ownership by the payment of a 4½ per cent tax annually to the government on the assessed value of the land exclusive of improvements. It is noteworthy, however, that there is a higher tax on intensively cultivated land than on larger estates of extensive cultivation.

Danish farmers are not successful merely because they can acquire the benefits of ownership cheaply. The well-known co-operative system, although begun only in 1881, with the establishment of a co-operative dairy, now extends to co-operative marketing, buying, and banking. There is an abundant provision both for short- and for long-term loans, and through credit societies, which are government assisted, as mentioned above, small holders of land have been enabled to enlarge and improve their holdings and their stock, and to modernize their buildings. As a result of widespread education in co-operative principles, the co-operative buying and marketing establishments have been so well conducted that the farmer, though by no means wealthy, obtains an ample return for his labor.

Not only has the land-tenure system, and the co-operative organization, helped the Danish farmer, however, but the Danish educational system is probably the most extensive and the best planned in the entire world. It aims deliberately at a peasant culture, and is designed to give the child the best possible preparation for agricultural life, and to keep the adult well informed in his profession. Both the government and the farming associations give grants to many agricultural colleges, where the fees are extremely moderate and students can attend intensive technical courses in the winter months when they are not needed on the farm. Model farms are attached to these schools. The boys take a five months' course in the practical phases of farming in which they are most interested. The course for girls is only of three months' duration, and is intended to give them a thorough knowledge of all phases of domestic farm education. Extensive lectures and less comprehensive courses make ample provision for the poorer farmer who cannot afford the more extended program.

Belgium

Of greater interest from the social viewpoint, as well as of particular concern for Catholics, is the development of agricultural co-operation in Belgium.[31] In this country, the majority of farmers are Catholics. Their farms are small, and are worked by the farmer and his family, with the occasional assistance of hired labor. These small peasant farmers were in desperate plight at the end of last century — the soil was poor, their costs were high, their methods very antiquated, and they were vainly attempting to compete with the cheaper produce of more recently developed and more fertile land in the United States, Canada, and elsewhere. Not only was the whole community in dire economic distress, but the young people were deserting their native villages for the work to be had in the rapidly developing industrial centers. A few local co-operatives were formed from 1870 onward, without much success. The salvation of all rural Belgium was to come from a co-operative formed as a result of the zeal, foresight, and organizational ability of a poor parish priest.

The Abbé Mellaerts (1845–1925) saw the needs of his parishioners of Goor and tried to persuade them to follow the co-operative methods of Denmark, and of the farmers in the German Rhineland. After much difficulty he finally prevailed upon members of the local St. Vincent de Paul Society in 1887 to establish a co-operative for the purchase of animal feed, fertilizer, machinery, and farm implements. Two years later, he recounted the story of his parishioners' material improvement at one of the famous Belgian social congresses at Malines. Two laymen, one a professor at the University of Louvain, the other the head of a flourishing Louvain bank, were fired with enthusiasm at this possibility of economic and social salvation for the Belgian farmers, and together with the Abbé Mellaerts, they founded the *Belgische Boerenbond* (League of Belgian Peasant Farmers) in 1890. Today, despite financial reverses within the past eight years, the *Boerenbond* is probably the largest and most influential co-operative in the world.

---

[31] For further details the reader is referred to articles by the present author in *The Catholic World*, November, 1935; *The New Review* (Calcutta), April, 1938; *The Catholic Rural Life Bulletin*, August, 1938. The author has completed a book on the subject, which is to be published by the Bruce Publishing Company (Milwaukee) later in 1939.

Approximately two thirds of the 312,000 exploiters of commercial farm holdings[32] in Belgium, belong to farm co-operatives, and of these three fifths (about 120,000 farmers) are members of the *Boerenbond,* a predominantly Flemish organization; another one sixth belong to the *Alliance Agricole Belge,* the Walloon counterpart of the *Boerenbond,* to which the latter has given both impetus and direction; and most of the rest are in some degree under Catholic auspices.

Belgian farmers today produce from 75 to 85 per cent of the total agricultural needs of the dense population, although, of course, this statement must not be misconstrued: Belgium produces less than she needs in some lines of agriculture, but her exports of such other branches as horticultural produce, dairy produce, meat, cattle, horses, are very considerable. The *International Yearbook of Agricultural Statistics* shows that the yield per acre in Belgium compares very favorably with yields in other countries; the milk yield per cow is exceeded only in Holland and in Denmark; and only in Great Britain, Holland, and the Irish Free State is the average egg yield higher than in Belgium. The percentage of land owned directly by cultivators has increased from 27.9 per cent in 1895 to 40.94 per cent in 1930, leaving only 59.06 per cent rented in 1930, as compared with 72.1 per cent rented in 1895.[33] This great change from widespread and almost hopeless depression to a notable relative prosperity, and a high state of scientific efficiency, seems to be almost wholly due to co-operative enterprise, although a certain amount of governmental aid must also be taken into account.

Through the *Boerenbond* the farmer can fill all his farm needs, including the purchase or hire of machinery at advantageous prices. He can send his produce to be graded at local centers, and can have it sold for him in all the important centers of Europe. Technical experts visit him to give advice. Insurance sections take care of his insurance needs. Credit banks enable him to borrow money at the lowest cost and to undertake small savings. (The first credit bank in Belgium was established in 1892 and now it controls over two thirds of the country's 1500 or more local banks.) A consumers' co-operative provides for cheaper household supplies. Economists and technical experts watch the position of Belgian agriculture at home and in the world markets, and protect the farmers' political interests in the legislative assemblies of the State. Since grain production was seen to be un-

---

[32] Cf. Henry, A., *La Rentabilité de l'Agriculture,* Comité Central Industrial de Belgique, Brussels, 1936, p. 39.

[33] Cf. *Annuaire Statistique de Belgique, 1899–1900,* pp. 276, 277; *Ibid.,* 1936, p. 163.

profitable, the *Boerenbond* persuaded its members to specialize in egg
production, in the raising of horses, in the extension of fruit orchards,
and particularly in horticultural produce — a type of farming particularly suited to the small acreage of the average Belgian farm. The
promotion of hothouse growing of cherries, grapes, and peaches, and
the production of early crops of good quality cauliflower, asparagus,
witloof, and early potatoes is also attributable to the *Boerenbond* — a
development which has had a remarkable success when one considers
the poor quality of the soil and the very unfavorable climate of the
country. Weekly and monthly publications supply *Boerenbond* members with technical knowledge, and keep them up to date in general
matters as well as in *Boerenbond* concerns. Schools have been established, and the children of members encouraged to look upon a farming
career as a true vocation. Lectures, films, picnics, dances, organized
games, hiking parties, and pilgrimages provide the members, their
wives and families, with appropriate diversions. Monthly sermons and
periodical retreats and pilgrimages supply the spiritual needs of the
members.

As must be evident, the *Boerenbond* aims at the spiritual, intellectual, economic, and social development of the members; in other
words, its specific purpose is the development of the whole man.
Nothing, of course, could be more completely in line with Catholic
teaching, and nowhere in the world has Catholic thought so important
a place in the rural development of a country.

Nova Scotia

The Catholic co-operatives of Nova Scotia are perhaps of greater
interest to readers in the New World, although much smaller in scope
and less involved in detail.[34] Largely through the work of the Reverend J. J. Tompkins, the lobster fishermen began to take an interest
in co-operation in 1923. Father Tompkins was later helped by the
adult-education extension work of the Reverend M. M. Coady and the
Reverend A. B. MacDonald and others of St. Francis Xavier University of Antigonish, and within recent years a new economic system
has been established not only among the fisherfolk, but in farming
communities and coal-mining areas of the Province.

Today, the fishermen own their own lobster canneries and fish-
processing plants, market their fish direct in Boston and elsewhere,

---

[34] For further details see: Fowler, Bertram B., *The Lord Helps Those* (New York:
Vanguard Press, 1938); also Fowler, B. B., "The Lord Helps Those," *Survey Graphic*,
June, 1938, pp. 340–343.

have their own consumers' co-operative stores, their own credit unions, and, above all, they insure a permanent economic improvement by continuing their studies in the evenings, and by establishing high schools for the better education of their children. The miners have established co-operative housing plans and co-operative credit. They are developing subsistence farming, to cut their costs of living and to provide for depressions in the coal industry. They, too, continue their education so as to learn of other outlets for their products and their skill, as well as to experience the enjoyment which comes from cultural pursuits. The farmers have their own credit, purchasing, and marketing co-operatives, and have learned to improve the quality of their poultry and stock. In 1923 the fishermen were entirely dependent upon middlemen, illiteracy was prevalent, and their economic condition was poor in the extreme. Even as late as 1930, the whole of eastern Nova Scotia was in economic penury. Today, practical sociologists and social workers journey from far and wide to study the methods by which the people of the district were brought to relative economic security and to hope for an improved future. Protestants work side by side with Catholics in the newly established co-operatives, education has progressed to an almost unbelievable extent, and peace, contentment, and security are the social effects of this new economic planning.

Conclusion

"There is the immense army of hired rural laborers, whose condition is depressed to the extreme, and who have no hope of ever obtaining a share in the land. These, unless efficacious remedies be applied, will remain perpetually sunk in the proletariat condition."[35]

"The law, therefore, should favor ownership, and its policy should be to induce as many people as possible to become owners.

"Many excellent results will follow from this: and first of all, property will certainly become more equitably divided. . . . Another consequence will be the great abundance of the fruits of the earth. . . . And a third advantage would arise from this; men would cling to the country in which they were born; for no one would exchange his country for a foreign land if his own afforded him the means of living a tolerable and happy life."[36]

These words of the Popes are indeed true. We need the extension of property owners, and the small rural landholders, whom all interested in rural life hope to see increased in number, must be made happy,

---

[35] *Quadragesimo Anno*, p. 21 (*QA*, 24).
[36] *Rerum Novarum*, pp. 26, 27 (*RN*, 35).

contented, and efficient, if they are to remain on the soil and not eventually turn to city life, or be reduced to penury by the competition of large-scale farming. It behooves all Catholics, therefore, to think most seriously of the advantages of country life, and to make provision for a strong *Catholic* rural population, which will uplift the country communities to a higher level, and will supply the city with stanch Catholics, well versed in their religious and social duties, and strong in health and educational accomplishments. This Catholics can do by means of a greater consciousness of responsibilities; by specially trained priests; by an extension of the Catholic land associations; by an increase in monastic farming communities; and, it might be suggested, by an extension of the work of the Catholic Rural Life Bureau or of the National Catholic Rural Life Conference along the lines of the successful, practical form of Catholic Action exemplified in the Belgian *Boerenbond* and the co-operatives of Nova Scotia.

We may conclude with the apt opening lines of Goldsmith's *Deserted Village:*

> "Ill fares the land, to hast'ning ills a prey,
> Where wealth accumulates and men decay;
> Princes and lords may flourish, or may fade,
> A breath can make them, as a breath has made:
> But a bold peasantry, their country's pride,
> When once destroy'd can never be supplied."

CHAPTER 22

POVERTY, DEPENDENCY, AND RELIEF

Definitions

THIS chapter deals with the general problem of poverty and dependency, and its solution. As Pope Leo XIII pointed out in his encyclical forty years ago, "the enormous fortunes of individuals and the poverty of the masses" is one of the primary problems of the social and economic world. And "all agree, and there can be no question whatever, that some remedy must be found, and quickly found, for the misery and wretchedness which press so heavily at this moment on the large majority of the very poor."[1]

While conditions may be slightly better than in Pope Leo's days, it is certain that the "poverty of the masses" is a crying evil of our times, and that remedies for the "misery and wretchedness" have still to be "quickly found."

The study of poverty has a twofold aspect: the collective poverty of a large group of poor people, the causes and remedies of which are largely social; and the poverty of the individual person, which is an individual problem needing individual care.

To define our terms before continuing the discussion:

Poverty means the deprivation of something necessary for subsistence and physical efficiency. It is a vague and relative term, for some people consider themselves poor if they are unable to afford an automobile, or the education of a son or daughter at an expensive private school; others, and with more cause, regard themselves as poor because they cannot buy the clothes necessary for their station in life, or because they can afford little amusement or diversion, and cannot take a yearly vacation; others, again, are poor because they lack the resources to provide themselves with sufficient food, clothing, or shelter to maintain full bodily vigor.

Destitution, on the other hand, is a positive term. It means the entire deprivation of the means of subsistence. A person without the means to purchase food, or clothing, or shelter, may be termed desti-

---

[1] *Rerum Novarum,* p. 2 (*RN*, 2).

tute, and since man has a right to life, it is the duty of society to take care of him.

A *pauper* is one who, being poor and destitute, seeks public aid, that is, aid from the state or local civic community. The word *pauper*, however, is now little used, and the much kinder name of *dependent* is usually given to all who are unable to provide themselves with the necessities of life and who seek assistance of others. The word *dependent*, therefore, is not used in this chapter in the sense of one dependent upon another, such as a child on its parents, but in the more specific connotation of one who receives private and even public charity assistance from others than the immediate family.

It must be remembered, of course, that a very large number of the poor are neither paupers nor dependents. They manage to subsist without outside relief, frequently to the detriment of their physical well-being.

The Causes of Poverty

It is a sad blot on our civilization that there are still so many people in the world who have to subsist without what may be termed even the necessities of life, while others have much more than enough for their needs, or are even fabulously wealthy. The causes of poverty, however, are so many that a discussion of them is almost impossible. In turn, poverty is itself a leading source of economic and social problems. It is impossible to ascribe poverty to one main cause alone, as did Malthus, who attributed it to the pressure of population upon food supply; or Henry George, who blamed the private ownership of land; or Karl Marx, who complained of the unjust appropriation of the fruits of labor by capitalistic production. To obtain an idea of the many reasons for individual poverty, we shall group some of the more important causes under two main heads:

1. *Objective Causes.* By far the most important causes of poverty are objective, and not the fault of the individual poor person. All the causes of unemployment — natural, social, and industrial — enumerated in Chapter 17, are also sources of poverty, for irregular, insufficient, and poorly paid employment is perhaps the greatest cause of the evil.

All the other risks to which the worker is subject, unprovided old age, death or disability of the chief wage earner, unprovided widowhood, orphanhood, and the like, also frequently result in poverty.

Environment, too, comes in for its share of responsibility, for very often poverty is the outcome of insufficient natural resources, bad surroundings, poor housing, and undesirable associates.

Poverty is likewise sometimes due to ineffective education and legislation, or to an inadequate or nonconstructive punitive system. A philosophy of education which does not recognize clear norms of morality, of charity and justice toward one's dependents, one's employers or one's employees, and toward one's associates, is bound to lead to character defects which may result in individual poverty. Finally, even philanthropy, if it be unwise or indiscriminate, may perpetuate or increase the condition which it seeks to relieve.

The extensive poverty in the world would be largely eliminated by the universal payment of a living wage, and until that time by the provision of social insurance against all risks to which the worker is exposed; by the improvement of working conditions; by the extension of vocational training to every citizen; by the amelioration of inadequate housing; by the provision of adequate hospital, medical, and health facilities for all; and by a return to a true Christian family life with more competent moral training at home and in the schools (although adequate home training is practically impossible in slum districts in our cities). It would also be greatly mitigated if as many urban workers as possible had subsistence gardens around or near their homes, where they could grow their own foodstuffs and save much of the money now expended on prepared or partially prepared foods. In other words, a reorganization of our industrial and social system is needed if widespread poverty is to be abolished.

2. Subjective Causes. The causes of individual poverty may proceed from any of the above conditions, but the situation of each individual may be aggravated, and sometimes caused by, individual circumstances and inequalities. Character defects and moral handicaps rank high among personal causes of poverty. Idleness and laziness at school or in later life, extravagance, waste, shiftlessness, a roving disposition, poor judgment, an ignorance of domestic economy, are frequent causes of individual poverty. Many a steady working laborer has been reduced to poverty by the vanity, incompetency, or laziness of his wife, where a more capable partner would have been able to make both ends meet. Many a man has been thrown out of employment, has had only irregular work, or has been forced to accept inferior positions, because he could not "get on" with his fellow workers, or was lazy, careless, and inefficient.

Bad habits, such as intemperance, immorality, dishonesty, betting, gambling, and vice of every kind almost invariably lead the comfortably well off to poverty, and the poor to pauperism. Indeed, the effects of overindulgence in alcoholic drink are a very important cause of pauperism.

Discord in family life also frequently results in poverty: children who are neglected or brutally treated by their parents or relatives, or who grow up in an atmosphere of disharmony, are rarely fitted in later life to compete with those who have enjoyed the discipline and affection of a normal home.

Again, physical or mental handicaps may bring about individual poverty — for they hinder the child and adolescent from taking full advantage of educational training when at school; they render the handicapped worker unable to compete with wage earners who are mentally and physically normal.; and they add an extra burden of medical and hospital expenses to the weekly budget.

The Effects of Poverty

At the risk of repeating what has been expressed earlier in this book, we shall say that while the moral effects of poverty are not always detrimental, nevertheless poverty almost invariably undermines physical and mental ability. Bad housing conditions, overcrowded rooms, lack of air and imperfect sanitation, worry and malnutrition, all lead to ill health. And the moral effects of poverty are sometimes so grave as to result in a lack of self-assurance and initiative — so necessary to make a way in life — discouragement, depression, and even habits of vice and crime.

The Church teaches that poverty is not so great an evil as many suppose, that it often produces greater attachment to God's Will than does affluency, and in His wise dispensation of Providence God seems to permit poverty to some for the enhancement of their spiritual life. A large proportion of canonized saints have been very poor in this world's wealth,[2] and although there have been holy men in all stations of life, wealth brings with it many temptations and the means of satisfying evil desires. "It is easier for a camel to pass through the eye of a needle, than for a rich man to enter into the Kingdom of Heaven,"[3] said Christ. Yet the history of the charitable activities of the Church is sufficient proof that the Church is actively interested in alleviating the condition of the really poor. It is the Church's teaching that the

---

[2] It must be noted, however, that the poverty of the saints was not, as a rule, the sordid poverty which must be endured by so many of the poor today in the unnatural and humanly undignified life of city slums.

[3] Matt. 19:24.

rich are but stewards of the possessions which God had entrusted them; they must make right use of their property, and see that at least some of the surplus over and above that necessary to maintain themselves and their families according to their station in life, accrues in some way to the benefit of the less fortunate; and all men must strive for the betterment of society.

Yet poverty can never be entirely eliminated. It will always exist, since there will always be inequalities among mankind, and man will always be prone to character defects, and the victim of unforeseen circumstances. "For the poor you have always with you,"[4] said Christ. It is society's duty to see that all citizens possess at least a minimum of material goods necessary for well-being, for apart from the universal law of charity, no State can prosper if it has any large numbers of unprovided poor in its midst. The modern method of helping the individual poor person is by social case work, which we shall next describe.

Social Case Work

The practical application of the principles of sociology and psychology in the relief of the poor and in provision for the sick, the handicapped, the defective, and the delinquent, is called social work, or social service. It is being increasingly recognized that the poor are not always helped in the most effective manner by the giving of private alms, and many private and public charity organizations have adopted what is known as scientific case work.

Modern social case work comprises much more than a mere dispensation of alms or provision for immediate needs; while relieving needs, the social worker tries to prevent them by removing the causes from which they arise, so that they will not recur in the future. As stated, poverty is due to a variety of causes, and each "case" must be treated in accordance with the poor person's need. It is not always necessary to give money; sometimes the help needed may be sympathy and patience in changing a character; on the other hand, it may be a complete change of environment, an expensive operation, the finding of employment which the case worker must try to effect, or even, as a last resort, the breakup of a home.

Social case work consists first in the discovery of persons in need of help; nor is it always advisable to wait until the poor themselves apply for help, for then they may have already reached a state of

---

[4] Matt. 26:11; John 12:8; Mark 14:7.

destitution too advanced for constructive assistance, and so become a costly burden to the community. The second step consists in interviewing the person needing help, to determine the causes of his poverty. If necessary, his family and other individuals and groups must be interviewed, so that all possible information is secured.

Third, the case must be diagnosed, taking into consideration not only that need which is most visible, but also all the multiple contributing factors, so that a complete understanding of all needs is arrived at. Last, comes the treatment of the needs as a unit, using the individual's own resources where possible, and also all available community resources which may be necessary. During this process, temporary relief of chronic poverty is, of course, often necessary.

Outdoor and Indoor Relief

Poverty may be relieved in two ways, technically known as outdoor and indoor relief. Outdoor relief means the care of the sick and the poor in their own homes, or in foster homes. Indoor relief is the care of the sick and needy in institutions. There are, of course, various advantages and disadvantages in each method. As a general rule it may be said that, wherever feasible, outdoor relief is preferable to indoor: the home is not broken up, and the needs of the family can be more carefully ascertained and provided for; it is also generally considered that this form of relief can be administered more economically. On the other hand, outdoor relief has certain disadvantages. It is easier to obtain, and has few of the unpleasantnesses attendant upon the entering of an institution, hence the number of applicants is increased. It likewise tends to discourage thrift and to retard progress toward payment by employers of a living wage — workers know that if they become indigent they can obtain relief, and employers are aware that if their workers lack some of the necessities of life, in all probability they will apply to local charitable associations for assistance. Much more extensive administration work is also required for scientific outdoor relief, and discrimination between deserving and undeserving cases is often practically impossible. Yet the merits and demerits of outdoor and indoor relief must be judged in each individual case. If all the poor and dependents were forced to enter institutions, in depression periods there would not be enough room for them all. And the people themselves would become demoralized and "institutionalized"; they would be made unfit for ordinary life; and domestic society would be completely broken up.

Institutions versus Colonies

A modern type of institution is the colony or cottage system. Instead of living in an ordinary institution, where everyone must follow a routine life, and where individuality and initiative of every kind is avoided for the sake of discipline and good order, inmates live in groups of thirty or less, each group in an individual house. Each house is in charge of a matron or house warden, who supervises the whole establishment. The group lives near enough for centralized management, but the life they lead is as near a normal family life as possible. Every member is encouraged to take a personal interest in his or her particular cottage, and at the same time individuality is allowed full play. A spirit of loyalty to the group is fostered, as also mutual kindness and self-helpfulness. Necessary work in the cottage is usually performed by the members, according to their individual capacities. Some do housework, others gardening; others, again, work in the colony workshops, so that they learn skilled trades. Not only does the cottage plan make the life of an inmate much more happy and normal, but it can also be made to reduce the cost of upkeep, when each member becomes practically self-supporting. In addition, whereas institutions often render their inmates unfit to take their place once more in normal surroundings, the cottage system accustoms them to the give and take of close association in family life.

Although modern in its present widespread application and more scientific technique, the cottage system originated in France and Belgium in the Middle Ages, and was not connected with the poor. The most famous colony was at Gheel, 26 miles east of Antwerp. In this village was the shrine of St. Dympna, an Irish girl martyr who became known for the cures effected through her intercession. Defectives came from all parts to visit the shrine, the villagers grew accustomed to their presence, and gradually an increasing number of defectives were left in the charge of foster families, with the hope of their subsequent cure. Thus the villagers became skilled in the care of defectives, particularly the mentally deficient, and at the present time over three thousand mental deficients are being cared for in Gheel and the surrounding villages. Although the patients are brought up in foster homes, yet the system is more properly a colony or cottage plan, for the entire region is devoted to the work under the direction of a centralized bureau of medical men.

Since the family is a divinely appointed natural society, no institution, however perfect, can ordinarily take its place. When persons have to be taken from their family circle, therefore, for poverty or any other reason, the nearer the substitution approaches family life, the happier and more natural will be their mode of living. Foster homes are usually next best to the family itself, but some cases are better cared for under more constant supervision than is possible in an ordinary home. It should, of course, be borne in mind that not all those who must be placed in institutions are necessarily poor or dependent. The violently insane, some of the worst cases of mental deficiency, seriously delinquent persons, drug or drink addicts, the crippled and defective who need constant medical care, can be more adequately provided for in an ordinary institution. On the other hand, the cottage system has been found most effective for orphans, the aged, and for such cripples, deaf, dumb, or blind, as cannot live at home and are unable to find foster homes, but who are not in need of the special medical care which only an institution could provide. The cottage system is also the most effective way of training many juvenile delinquents and those suffering from the milder forms of mental deficiency or insanity, and it is certainly the kindest way of segregating epileptics. The value of the system has only lately been realized, but an increasing number of institutions are adopting it, and it will probably become much more widespread within the next few years.

The History of Relief

It is beyond the scope of this present book to examine in detail the history of charity in pre-Reformation times.[5] Briefly, however, we may here premise that the Church very adequately performed its function of caring for the poor, both through relief at monasteries and at convent gates, through guilds, and also though the parish priests. In the parishes, there was, during the Middle Ages, a highly developed form of relief, as shown by the following quotation:

"Contrary to the ordinary opinion, the management of the parish was not left to the parish priests, but was in the hands of a deliberative assembly. This elective body taxed the parishioners, supervised the spending of income, and every year gave a balance sheet which in most respects would meet the requirements of a modern business firm. . . .

"We mention the income of the parish because we wish to insist on the fact that the parish, as such, took care of every form of social work, although very frequently its ministrations passed through the guild

---

[5] For a brief history of charity from pre-Christian times to the present, see the *Catholic Encyclopedia*, "Charity and Charities," Vol. III, pp. 593–604.

members. Thus in England there were two great systems of social activities, those of the monasteries and those of the parishes."[6]

When the Church's activities were necessarily curtailed after the Reformation, the various municipalities were constrained to find some method of dealing with the poor, to supplement the restricted help then given by the Church. Their methods generally took the form of prohibiting begging and creating a system of compulsory taxation to provide a fund to help those in distress. The fact that charity was again financed and organized, even as it had been in the earlier ages, was not in itself bad. Nevertheless the spontaneity of charitable donations which had ever been a feature of the Church's alms was somewhat eliminated. In place of giving alms for the love of one's fellow men, who are likewise God's children, and because Christ Himself had said, "As long as you did it to one of these My least brethren, you did it to Me,"[7] the majority of donors then gave because they were compelled to. Poverty came to be looked upon as a disgrace; and indeed, from the Reformation times right down to the end of the past century, the indigent and unemployed were regarded as lacking in those moral qualities which were accredited to the "respectable poor" who were fortunate enough to be employed.

The beginning of modern scientific methods of relieving the poor by outdoor relief is generally credited to the Hamburg system. Under this system, which was promoted in the city of Hamburg in 1765, the giving of alms to beggars was strictly forbidden, but a central bureau of relief of the poor was established. The city was divided into districts with an overseer over each; an industrial school was provided for the training of the unemployed; the sick were cared for in hospitals; the unemployed were assisted to find work, or, if it was considered that they were not willing to work, they were driven from the town. After having operated for thirteen years the system declined, chiefly because the overseers were too overworked to attend to their duties with efficiency.

The Elberfeld system is usually considered to be the next attempt at modern case work, although the organizations founded by St. Vincent de Paul, and some of the Sodalities of Our Lady, were just as scientific in their dealing with "cases."[8] Nor must we forget the Society

---

[6] Rev. H. S. Spalding, S.J., *Chapters in Social History,* pp. 258, 259.

[7] Matt. 25:40.

[8] See Rev. H. S. Spalding, S.J., *Chapters in Social History* (Heath and Co., 1925); also, Rev. Augustus Drive, S.J., *The Sodality of Our Lady, Historical Sketches* (Kenedy and Sons, 1916).

of St. Vincent de Paul, founded by the 20-year-old Frédéric Ozanam in 1833. And as regards indoor relief, as early as the fourth century St. Basil had housed the sick and dependent in separate buildings and thus obviated many of the conditions to be found even in the modern poorhouse.

The Elberfeld system just mentioned originated in the city of Elberfeld, Germany, in 1852. It was an elaboration of the Hamburg system. The city of Elberfeld was divided into 564 sections, each with a population of about three hundred. An almoner, appointed for a period of three years, was placed over each of these sections, and gave his services free. The position of almoner was considered highly honorable, and was usually the steppingstone to political preference. Almoners, therefore, usually remained in office for a considerable number of years, and through long experience could give expert service. It was the almoner's duty to keep himself informed as to the needs of all those in his area, and the needy applied to him for relief. Great attention was paid to the prevention of poverty and also to rehabilitation. The almoner provided medical help, found employment for the workless, gave advice, and, where needed, furnished material assistance. For every group of fourteen sections a district overseer was appointed, and a central committee of nine had control over all the districts, and also over the prisons and institutions furnishing indoor relief. Almoners met every two weeks to discuss matters of policy, this meeting being followed by a meeting of the central committee. There was, therefore, a high degree of centralization and control. The system was, and still is, very successful, and in modified form has been adopted by many countries and municipalities.

The United States. When, in early colonial days, the need of public help for the poor became apparent, the British workhouse system was adopted. Provision for public relief was hastily made by the purchase and remodeling of farms. In some instances the poor were given into the custody of the lowest bidder. Indoor relief was usually inadequate both as regards housing and food. No provision was made for rehabilitation, and the workhouse became an institution for all classes of needy, without regard to the necessity of separating the young from the old, the aged and the sick from the well, and the innocent from those of evil repute.

In modern times, of course, relief of the poor varies in the different states and municipalities. Generally speaking the public almshouses are reserved for the aged poor and for vagrants. The management of many of these almshouses leaves much to be desired. Social workers continuously urge that to be of use they should be situated on a farm; that a social-service department should be provided for attempted rehabilitation of vagrants and single men who are unemployed; and that superintendents should be properly qualified, and should receive adequate remuneration and recognition for good work rendered, as an incentive to better service.

On the other hand, the organization of private and semiprivate local charities in the United States has been most notable. Case-work methods have been highly developed, and a large proportion of social workers have received training in techniques in one of the several qualified Social Work Schools in the various parts of the country. Their methods of co-ordinating and financing relief will be discussed shortly.

Since the depression, however, private charity and even semipublic city charities, were unable to cope with the enormous amount of relief which was necessary to take care of the unemployed and their families. For this reason the Government stepped in with a series of mammoth projects for providing employment by the construction of public works, through the Works Progress Administration (WPA) which was established in 1935, after the liquidation of the Civil Works Administration (CWA) in 1934, and the Federal Emergency Relief Administration (FERA) in 1935. Adults incapable of heavy work have been provided with clerical jobs in connection with the construction activities, or have been financed in the carrying out of approved projects in various professional and research lines. Young people were assisted by the National Youth Administration (NYA) established as part of the Works Progress Administration in June, 1935, and by the Civilian Conservation Corps (CCC) which was created in 1933. The purpose of the NYA is to finance suitable clerical and other occupations, to help young people of both sexes, between the ages of sixteen and twenty-five, to pay for a high-school, college, or even postgraduate course, and thus increase their ability for future employment, and prevent their being added to the ranks of the unemployed at the present time. The CCC is designed to provide temporary work under healthful conditions for young men between the ages of sixteen and twenty-five who do not wish to complete their education, or who do not find the NYA payments sufficient to enable them to do so.

Public versus Private Charity

The merits and demerits of public and private charity is a matter of some controversy. Public or State charity is the provision of charity by local State or municipal authorities. Private charity is the giving of alms and social service either directly by the alms-giver or through private organizations not connected with the State. It is the duty of the State to care for the indigent, and some people are of the opinion that the service it can render is much greater than is possible by private endeavor, by reason of the greater amount of funds which it can command, and the possibilities of eliminating duplication and waste through its centralized and co-ordinated organization. Most people, however, agree that despite duplication of effort, skilled service is to be found much more frequently in private charity agencies. Private charity is also more personal: it is less subject to political corruption and the "red tape" of public institutions and less pauperizing in its effects, since it is more hidden from the public. Moreover, the motive of almsgiving should be the religious motive of love of one's neighbor for God's sake, in fulfillment of our Lord's command to love our neighbor as ourselves, with the hope of no reward other than the eternal: "Come ye blessed of My Father, possess you the kingdom prepared for you from the foundation of the world. . . . As long as you did it to one of these My least brethren, you did it to Me."[9] Charity, therefore, should be dis-pensed with humility and secrecy; with justice, mercy, and discretion; with cheerfulness and generosity. The State should not interfere where private charity is sufficient. But when the State is obliged to intervene, everyone is bound to contribute his fair share of the public burden for charity relief, and a man should not refuse to provide his share on the plea that he has given private alms.

The justification of private Catholic social agencies hinges upon the important supremacy of eternal values over the material, and the neces-sity for a Catholic receiving relief to be aided in a supernatural ap-proach to his problem, to have adequate opportunity to practise his religion and learn its truths. In most areas, but not in all, it is possible for parents and guardians to specify the denomination of the institu-tion to which children in their charge are to be sent. In general, Cath-olic agencies look for a much greater degree of active support and intelligent understanding than they receive from the majority of the Catholic laity.

Co-ordination of Private Charities

1. *Organization.* The need of private charities to co-operate with each other in the formulation of programs and the delimitation of

---

[9] Matt. 25:34, 40.

work, is provided for in most cities by local Councils or Federations of Social Agencies. Through these Councils social workers in the district meet regularly to exchange views and to prevent overlapping of existing or projected social undertakings. The result is usually a much greater unification and co-ordination of charitable assistance in the locality.

In the handling of specific cases, the work of the Councils of Social Agencies has been rendered more efficient and complete by the installation of a Social Service Exchange (sometimes called a Central Index, or a Confidential Exchange). As the Rev. H. S. Spalding points out,[10] duplication of work was rare when Frédéric Ozanam and M. Bailly drew up the rules for the Society of St. Vincent de Paul, because their charity was limited to a city where all social activities came under the administration and supervision of the Church. With so many agencies for public and private relief, it is now almost impossible for local social workers to detect fraud or to prevent duplication of investigation, without some sort of central organization. Where several agencies have been concerned with the same person or family, co-ordination is also an effective means for the determination of the correct diagnosis and the proper remedy. The first Social Service Exchange organized for the purpose of co-ordination was established in Boston in 1876 by the Boston Provident Association, and a similar organization is now to be found in all large cities in the United States, as well as in certain rural and semirural districts. Over 300 Exchanges were active in 1936.[11] The Exchange is valuable not only to those welfare societies giving outdoor relief, but also to hospitals, public health services, children's agencies, and many other social organizations. Its aim is to enlist the co-operation of all the public and private agencies in the district, and it functions as follows:

If any agency gives assistance to its applicant, or investigates a "case," it records at the Exchange the name and address of the person investigated or helped, to indicate that it has information to supply, upon application, to other members of the Exchange. Records are open only to authorized representatives of Exchange members, so as to protect the poor from the curiosity of those not immediately concerned with giving them relief. If a new case comes to the notice of an agency, its first step is to inquire at the Exchange if it is known to other organizations. Then, if a record of the person or family is found,

---

[10] Rev. H. S. Spalding, S.J., *Social Problems and Agencies*, p. 143. The organization of the Society of St. Vincent de Paul will be outlined in Chapter 28.

[11] Cf. *Social Work Year Book*, 1937, p. 481.

the inquirer communicates with the agencies noted, obtains all available information from these sources, and thus obviates duplication of investigation. Through the Exchange, an agency can also sometimes collaborate with other organizations in rendering assistance to the needy. This union of forces leads to greater service efficiency and prevents duplication of assistance.

2. *Finances.* It would seem advisable that not only should the administration of private charities be unified and co-ordinated, but that there should also be federated finance. As we have already pointed out, one of the advantages of public over private charity is the larger amount of funds at the disposal of public authorities. Group financing of private charities seems to be an effective manner of providing funds.

The first recorded federated financing took place in Liverpool, England, in 1873. Certain philanthropists induced a group of agencies to make a joint appeal for funds, so that they could make their charitable contributions to one central office and save themselves the inconvenience of solicitation from a number of social organizations. There are now in Great Britain various associations of charitable agencies which make a joint appeal and divide the proceeds in quotas previously agreed upon; but community, rather than group financing, that is, common appeal by all the charitable associations in a district, is essentially American. The history of federated finance, in the United States, dates back to the Charity Organization Society, which began in the United States in 1875, and which followed the Liverpool idea. Incidentally, it may be mentioned that this organization is also credited with the development of case-work methods, although as far back as thirty years before its formation, the Society of St. Vincent de Paul had introduced these methods into the country. In 1887, social agencies in the city of Denver, Colorado, formed a federation to solicit funds, but this association likewise maintained a joint bureau for the dispensation of relief. In 1910 the Federation of Social Agencies of Elmira, New York, was established, but it was only a partial federation, since all local social agencies did not participate.

The increased number of Councils of Social Agencies in the various cities finally led the way to Community Chests, which is the name given to the central money-raising organization for financing all the social work in a community. By 1917, fourteen cities had partial federations for joint financing. Then the urgent necessities of the local charities to maintain subscriptions in 1917–18, despite the appeal of war needs, led to the establishment of War Chests. These War Chests, by the increase in total subscriptions over previous efforts, demon-

strated the value of co-operation in finance, and the first Community
Chest proper was started in Cleveland in 1919 as a direct outgrowth
of the Cleveland War Chest. Many other cities then followed suit, and
by 1929 there were 330 Community Chests in the United States and
Canada. Most of these Community Chests belong to the Association
of Community Chests and Councils, founded in 1918 "to assist in the
improvement of joint finance and joint planning of social work through
committee activities, research, correspondence, field visits, local studies
of chests and councils, conferences, direction of financial campaigns,
and publications." Since 1925 the Association has also assumed responsibility of the work formerly done by the American Association of
Social Service Exchanges, organized in 1920.

A Community Chest proper presupposes the co-operation of all social
agencies in the district. The participating agencies usually appoint
representatives to the Board, which also includes prominent bankers,
businessmen, and others, who serve as representatives of the local contributors. Prior to the yearly campaign each participating agency is
required to prepare a budget for the coming year. This involves planning ahead not only for current expenses but also for necessary exten-
sions; it generally involves also the adoption of uniform accounting
systems. Next come extensive preparations for the systematic solicitation of donations from all citizens, use being made of up-to-date publicity methods to insure as large a contribution as possible. The Chest
then makes a joint appeal for funds during a fixed period of one or
two weeks. The goal aimed at is the amount of the combined budget
demands, and an intensive drive is made to reach, or even exceed, this
figure. Proceeds are divided among the participants in the agreed
amounts, and usually contributors to the Chest are promised immunity
from further solicitation by agencies within the federation during the
ensuing year.

Charitable contributors benefit from this system of co-ordinated
charity finance in several ways. A well-organized Community Chest
guarantees the efficiency of the social agencies represented. The public
is educated as to the local needs of the poor and the best way of making provision for them; and since all citizens are urged and persuaded
to contribute according to their ability, the charitable do not then
have to bear an unfair burden of local charity programs. A community
spirit is engendered and fostered, and personal prejudices tend to disappear. Furthermore, the participating social agencies have each a well-
defined field of operation; improved standards of operation and finance
are encouraged; a steady income is insured, and thus freedom from the

worry involved in promiscuous giving; and the greater publicity and driving power afforded by the Chest invariably results in larger financial returns.

It must be noted, however, that there is the danger of autocratic control of charities by the Community Chest administration, and a sacrifice of the interests of the minor members of the administration to those of the strong and powerful. If, however, care is taken at the outset to insure that the Chest officials will respect the policies of each of the participating agencies, this danger will disappear. It has also been objected that by contributing to a central agency, the individual donors lose interest in the particular activities of the individual charities. This difficulty can be obviated by attention to the publication of news regarding the special achievements of each of the charities concerned. In many localities Catholic organizations have belonged to the Chest, and have found membership to be of decided advantage to themselves. They have learned improved methods through exchange of ideas; they have learned to understand the problems and ideals of other denominations; they have secured financial stability; and they have brought their interest before the non-Catholic public, and succeeded in diminishing prejudice. In some cities, however, it has been decided that since Community Chests are essentially local in character, and since many Catholic charities are necessarily diocesan in their scope, it is more advantageous for Catholics to organize and subscribe to their own diocesan funds. In certain cities also, Catholics have been of the opinion that membership in the Chest would lead to friction, and not to a better understanding between themselves and other secular or denominational organizations; that they would be discriminated against in the allotment of funds; and that their principles would not always be respected. Evidence seems to indicate, however, that the advantages of the Chest organization of charity usually outweigh the disadvantages in districts with a fair representation of donors and participants on the local Chest Board. In most of the large cities, Catholic charities co-operate with the local councils of social agencies.

Classification of the Needy and Their Relief

We said previously that one of the causes of poverty is unwise and indiscriminate philanthropy. Although the best manner of relieving poverty must vary with each individual case and, indeed, the keynote of modern charity administration is differentiation in treatment, we can make certain general statements as to the means which are probably the best for helping the chief classes of dependents.

1. *The Aged.* We have previously discussed old-age pensions in the chapter on Workers' Risks. Undoubtedly the best method of dealing with the aged poor is to allow them to remain in their own homes or in the homes of their children, or, this failing, to place them in suitably selected foster homes. Some old people, however, need special nursing attention and medical care, which may be unobtainable in the home. Often, too, suitable foster families are not available. Where the aged are placed in institutions, humanity requires that husbands and wives should be allowed to live together and to retain at least a few of their household possessions, and that relatives and friends should be permitted to visit them as frequently as possible. Institutions for the aged poor may be classed as two: almshouses or poorhouses for those with no financial resources, and private institutions where the inmates of their friends make small periodical payments, or provide a lump sum of money at the outset. The Little Sisters of the Poor are the best-known Catholic order of religious noted for the care of the aged poor; they do not seek remuneration for their services, and the attention their clients receive is, of course, vastly superior to that available in public poorhouses.

2. *The Feeble-Minded, Insane, Epileptic, Drug Addicts, Permanently Ill, or Crippled.* The best treatment for the poor thus afflicted will be fully outlined in the following chapters. The best institutional care for such classes can be provided in residential institutions or mental hospitals on the cottage plan, where each should get proper care and attention suited to his particular case. As mentioned in the next chapter, special schools should be provided for mentally deficient children, so that later in life it may be possible for them to become in some measure self-supporting.

3. *The Deaf, Blind, and Dumb.* Treatment for these, too, will be fully detailed in the next chapter. When there is no danger of "spoiling" at home, and when special schools are available in the neighborhood, it is naturally best that young people afflicted in this manner should lead a life as nearly normal as possible. At times, however, it may be advisable that young deficients should be placed in institutions, where vocational training and other help can be adequately provided. When older, these deficients should, where possible, remain at home or be placed with foster families.

4. *The Poor Who Are Temporarily Sick, or Unable to Provide for the Prevention of Sickness.* Public or private hospitals offering services free or at a low cost, dispensaries, clinics, and visiting nurses are a necessity: the moral and mental status of a nation depends largely

upon the physical well-being of its people. It is therefore the duty of the State to supply the deficiencies in its public health measures and to lay especial stress on good sanitation, health laws, and public health education, indispensable necessities for every nation. Health insurance as outlined in the chapter on Workers' Risks is likewise highly advisable. Since sickly children seldom grow up to be strong and robust, it is particularly to the advantage of the State to provide special health facilities for them.

The laws vary in each state of the union, but most states or municipal authorities make provisions for the health inspection of every child of school age and for treatment of deficiencies. It is to be noted, however, that where such provision is made under the direction of school boards, children in parochial schools are sometimes deprived of this service. For several years in St. Louis, Missouri, Catholics themselves bore the entire financial burden of an elaborate health service for Catholic school children; in some cities the municipal authorities provide parochial-school children with the services of physicians or nurses or both, particularly where the health services are given by the public health department instead of by the school-board authorities. Free meals are also provided to school children in many districts, either out of the public funds or from private charities. Such measures, however, can readily be carried to excess.

The White House Conference on Dependent Children resulted in the establishment of the Federal Children's Bureau in 1912 which, as an outcome of its investigations, has provided valuable data on all phases of child care. A second Conference held in 1919 led to the passing of the Sheppard-Towner Act for the promotion of the welfare and hygiene of maternity and infancy, which became a law on November 23, 1921. This act was repealed in 1929, but it resulted in an expansion of birth and death registration areas, in the establishment of state child-hygiene bureaus, the provision of permanent health consultation centers, and a great increase in appropriations of public money for health care of children and mothers. The act operated through the Children's Bureau, and during its lifetime the bureau administered an annual appropriation from the Federal budget of $1,240,000 for distribution among the states which co-operated with its program. The principle to be remembered here is that the State or municipality should not assume duties which can be taken care of by parents or private groups, but should merely supply deficiencies. Similarly, the Federal Government should not be allowed to assume the tasks that belong to the sovereign states. That tendency has been toward a wrong conception of these relations in the United States, though whether or not Federal or state grants are actually needed at the present time, to supply public health needs, is a matter for debate.

As mentioned in Chapter 17, the Social Security Act of 1935 authorized the Federal Government to distribute among qualifying states annually, $3,800,000 for maternal and child welfare, $2,850,000 for aid to crippled children, and $1,500,000 for child-welfare organization, particularly in rural districts, to be allotted through the Children's Bureau of the Department of Labor; $1,938,000 for vocational rehabilitation, through the Office of Education; $8,000,000 for public health, through the United States Public Health Service; and a maximum of $15 a month to the needy blind not inmates of public institutions, through the Social Security Board. Thus it may be said that the Sheppard-Towner Act has been re-established, though in different form. By the end of 1936 all the states of the Union had submitted programs which qualified them to receive the Federal grants.

The dependent ill are sometimes also assisted by visiting housekeepers provided by certain public and private charitable administrations. Certain religious Orders, such as the Little Sisters of the Poor also visit the sick in their own homes, nurse them, look after the domestic duties, and generally perform the duty of a mother to the children during the illness of the parents.

It seems appropriate to say a few words here about hospital social service. Until comparatively recent years hospitals were mainly concerned with their specialized medical work, and did not realize how social-service technique could come to their assistance. An almoner was first appointed in an English hospital in 1895. In the United States, paid social workers were introduced into outpatient departments and were gradually extended to hospital wards some ten years later.

Many hospitals now have a special social-service department whose work is usually as follows:

a) It obtains reports of the home conditions of the patient, so that doctors can be aware of any contributory causes of the malady, and so that dependents needing financial support may be put in touch with relief agencies. This latter often materially helps the patient on his way to recovery, by relieving him of worry as to the welfare of his family. The inquiry into family history is of the utmost value in diagnosing and prescribing for mental disabilities.

b) The second most important work of the social-service department is to follow up the patient after he has left the hospital. Doctors may prescribe certain medicines or surgical appliances for which patients are unable to pay. The social-service department would discover this lack of monetary resources and would see that means were obtained to follow out the doctor's orders. Often, too, patients either do not know how to carry out the doctor's orders, or do not fully understand them; again, they receive advice from the visitor sent them from the social-service department.

c) Sometimes home or work conditions need to be improved if the patient is to recover completely, and here too the social worker can do invaluable work in explaining the case to relatives or employers, or in seeing that the correct agencies are informed, who can then be responsible for seeing that the improvements are made.

d) Again, hospitals cannot usually keep convalescent cases, and it is often the duty of the social-service department to see that a patient receives proper care during the period of convalescence and that finances are obtained for a change of air or residence in a convalescent home, where this is needed.

e) Where mental deficients, epileptics, or other defectives are placed in foster homes, the social-service department of the hospital or medical institution to which they have been attached usually sends a regular visitor to visit the patient and be sure that everything is progressing satisfactorily.

As the foregoing merely suggests some of the most important branches of the work carried on by hospital social service, the reader is referred to other sources for more detailed information.[12]

5. *Families in Need Because of Unemployment, Sickness, or Poor Wages of the Breadwinner.* While the payment of a living wage, and at least until then a reasonable establishment of social insurance, such as circumstances may call for, should largely prevent this type of poverty, nevertheless there should be adequate private and public charity provision for the relief of poor families in their own homes, in accordance with the best modern methods of scientific case work.

6. *The Poor Who Are Forced to Live in Inadequate Dwellings.* Undoubtedly, poverty leads many to live under housing conditions which are unfit for human habitation, and which lead to much ill health, as well as to undesirable social attitudes. This important need is discussed in Chapter 25.

7. *Unmarried Mothers and Children Born Out of Wedlock.* During

---

[12] See *The Social Work Year Book*, 1929, pp. 202–205; Also: Warner, Queen, and Harper, *American Charities and Social Work*, Chapter XXII and Bibliography, p. 588. For England, the best reference is: *The Hospital Almoner*, Published by a Committee of the Hospital Almoners' Association, 1932 (2/–).

confinement, unmarried mothers should, where necessary, be able to obtain free medical care, and this is available in all modern communities. It was formerly the general practice, however, to separate the unmarried mother from her child soon after the baby was born, and to place her offspring in an institution or foster home. It is now recognized that where the mother is physically and mentally fit, it is best not only for the child, but also for herself, that she should be kept near her baby as long as possible. Where feasible, a case worker meets the mother as soon as she comes to the notice of a social agency, and tries to discover her plans. All means are taken to persuade her to nurse the child herself, since it is realized that this awakens mother love and is of high value in the moral rehabilitation of the parent. Special hostels are available in many large cities where, if relatives are not willing to receive them, mother and child can be kept together at least for a few months. Later the mother is encouraged to work for the child, the latter being placed in a foster home or institution near by, and the mother given every facility to visit it and concern herself with its progress. Where adoption is considered the better course, it is essential for a Catholic mother to realize that she surrenders her right to control the child's religious faith, and to see that the adopter is a Catholic and in every way capable of the task undertaken. All Catholic adoption agencies take care of these important features of adoption.

8. *Widows with Young Children, Wives Deserted by Their Husbands, Wives with Sick Husbands, Mothers Who Need to Work to Maintain Themselves and Their Families.* Normally this type of contingency should be covered by social insurance, but where this is not the case mothers' pensions, such as outlined in Chapter 16, are highly necessary, so that the home may be kept intact and the children remain under the mother's care. Often a mother prefers to work, rather than receive the help of charity. On the other hand, it sometimes happens that a husband's earnings, charity help, mothers' pensions, or insurance payments are not sufficient to enable the mother to remain at home without supplementing the family budget by her earnings. Where a mother has to work to maintain her family, and where the children are not of school age, day nurseries are a necessity.

The first day nursery or *crèche* was established in Paris in 1844. Madame de Pastoret, a charitable Catholic lady, was one day attracted by a child's cries, and upon investigation found a baby with a broken arm, locked in a room of a tenement house. She at once established a day nursery to take care of the children of working mothers, and the success of this charitable work immediately proved that it filled a long-needed want. Later it was taken over by the Sisters of Charity of St. Vincent de Paul, and by 1853 there were fourteen day nurseries in Paris alone, caring for more than 600 children. The first permanent day nursery in the United States was founded in Troy, New York, in 1858, and at least one is now to be found in every important city in the United States and Europe. Many American cities have associations of day nurseries, to promote co-ordination of efforts, and as early as 1898 the National Federation of Day Nurseries, Inc., was founded in New York to unite day nurseries in a common body and to assist them to develop the best possible standards and methods, and to work with a common aim.

In the morning, mothers bring their children under school age to the nursery before going to work. In some instances, the nursery sends a conveyance to call for the children before the mother leaves her home. The earlier nurseries merely cared for the physical needs of the children, and were simply places where they were safeguarded and fed during working hours. They have now, however, taken on the character of nursery schools, where attention is paid to the moral and personal habits of the child through supervised play and recreation, and simple schooling along kindergarten lines. Particular attention is given to the child's health: special food is furnished when necessary, and medical supervision is provided for the correction of physical defects and diseases, and the performing of requisite dental work, operations, and the like. Although by no means universal, parent education is also an important part of the work of many day nurseries, the mothers being helped in their dealings with childhood's behavior and health problems. In some day nurseries a mothers' club is formed which provides needed recreation for the parent, and also an opportunity to talk over the many problems which may arise. Catholic day nurseries can often do good work by searching out Catholic families neglectful of their religious duties, and bringing them back to a recognition of their spiritual needs.

Day nurseries should not, however, take the place of home life for the child, where the mother is not obliged to work, or is in no way incapable of caring for her children during the daytime. They should be regarded as a temporary shelter only, and everything possible should be done to enable the mother to remain at home to care for her little ones. This help to the mother may take the form of procuring work for the husband, or of securing expert medical aid or necessary industrial rehabilitation to enable an incapacitated husband to resume his duties as breadwinner; it may mean urging forward compensation claims, or rights to a pension, the education of the mother in her duties toward her children, or an adjustment in domestic or industrial life. And where circumstances render it necessary that day nurseries look after the children, they often prevent them from being sent to institutions or foster homes, and insure that they receive a good start in life from the viewpoint not only of physical health, but of sound training in physical and moral habits. From the foregoing enumerated services which the day nurseries render society, it is clearly evident that their role is an important and necessary one.

9. *Dependent and Neglected Children.* In 1933 there were 242,929 dependent children in institutions and foster homes. Of these, 140,352 were in institutions; 31,538 were in "free" foster homes; 66,350 were "boarded out," and 4,689 were working for their board in foster homes.[13] At the White House Conference on Child Health and Protection held in Washington in 1930, President Hoover proposed the following Children's Charter as an ideal to be aimed at in child care and protection:

a) For every child spiritual and moral training to help him stand firm under the pressure of life.

b) For every child understanding and the guarding of his personality as his most precious right.

c) For every child a home and that love and security which a home provides; and for that child who must receive foster care, the nearest substitute for his own home.

d) For every child full preparation for his birth, his mother receiving prenatal, natal, and postnatal care.

e) For every child health protection from birth through adolescence including: periodical health examinations and, where needed, care of specialists and hospital treatment: regular dental examinations and care of teeth; protection and preventive measures against communicable diseases; the insuring of pure food, pure milk, and pure water.

f) For every child from birth through adolescence, promotion of health, including health instruction and a health program, wholesome physical and mental recreation, with teachers and leaders adequately trained.

g) For every child a dwelling place, safe, sanitary, and wholesome, with reasonable provisions for privacy free from conditions which tend to thwart his development; and a home environment harmonious and enriching.

---

[13] Cf. *Statistical Abstract of the United States,* 1937, p. 78.

h) For every child a school which is safe from hazards, sanitary, properly equipped, lighted, and ventilated. For younger children, nursery schools and kindergartens to supplement home care.

i) For every child a community which recognizes and plans for his needs, protects him against physical dangers, moral hazards and disease; provides him with safe and wholesome places for play and recreation, and makes provision for his cultural and social needs.

j) For every child an education which, through the discovery and development of his individual abilities, prepares him for life, and through training and vocational guidance prepares him for a living which will yield him the maximum of satisfaction.

k) For every child, such teaching and training as will prepare him for successful parenthood, homemaking, and the rights of citizenship; and, for parents, supplementary training to fit them to deal wisely with the problems of parenthood.

l) For every child, education for safety and protection against accidents to which modern conditions subject him — those to which he is directly exposed and those which, through loss or maiming of his parents, affect him indirectly.

m) For every child who is blind, deaf, crippled, or otherwise physically handicapped, and for the child who is mentally handicapped, such measures as will early discover and diagnose his handicap, provide care and treatment, and so train him that he may become an asset to society rather than a liability. Expenses of these services should be borne publicly where they cannot be privately met.

n) For every child who is in conflict with society the right to be dealt with intelligently as society's charge, the court, and the institution, when needed, shaped to return him whenever possible to the normal stream of life.

o) For every child the right to grow up in a family with an adequate standard of living and with the security of a stable income as the surest safeguard against social handicaps.

p) For every child protection against labor that stunts growth, either physical or mental, that limits education, that deprives children of the right of comradeship, of play, and of joy.

q) For every rural child, as satisfactory schooling and health services as for the city child, and an extension to rural families of social, recreational, and cultural facilities.

r) To supplement the home and the school in the training of youth, and to return to them those interests of which modern life tends to cheat children, every stimulation and encouragement should be given to the extension and development of the voluntary youth organizations.

s) To make everywhere available these minimum protections of the health and welfare of children, there should be a district, county, or community organization for health, education, and welfare, with full-time officials, co-ordinating with a state-wide program which will be responsive to a nation-wide service of general information, statistics, and scientific research.

Were this charter to be carried out to the full, all children would grow up with their rightful heritage of moral and physical well-being. We cannot in the present book discuss all childhood's needs, and all provision for their fulfillment. Certainly no child should be deprived of home care unless its parents are morally and physically unfit to look after it. Even then, good social work requires that an investigation be made to discover the possibility of relatives coming to the rescue, or of an adjustment of family life under the supervision of a case worker, or the maintenance of the children in the home if one of them is old enough to take over domestic duties, possibly under the supervision of a visiting housekeeper. Where, however, it is necessary for a child to receive foster care, then, as pointed out in the third clause of the Children's Charter, he has a right to "the nearest substitution for his own home." This, of course, means placement in a foster home wherever possible, or alternatively, his care in institutions run on the cottage plan.

When placing in a foster home is the method resorted to, the child-placing agencies must, in all cases, of course, ascertain that the foster father and foster mother are people of good character, able to offer the child a real home and good training, under at least a minimum of desirable economic conditions. Some foster families offer their services free, with or without the promise of later adoption; others are paid by the social-service agency, or expect the child to render some previously arranged definite services in return for the home offered. In any event, the agency sends a visitor to the foster home at regular intervals, to assure that both the family and the child are happily adjusted and that everything is satisfactorily progressing for the child's welfare. Needless to say, it is essential that a Catholic child be boarded out in a Catholic family, and failing this it is much better for it to be placed in a Catholic institution, where it will not be deprived of the benefits of its religion. In all cases the child's relatives and friends should be encouraged to write and visit him, in order that previously existing natural ties will not be broken, and the child, when returned to normal society, will not be utterly friendless.

The Social Security Act of 1935 has made available Federal funds to supplement state programs for the aid of dependent children under sixteen years of age, whose parents are dead, incapacitated, or have abandoned them. The maximum Federal grant to supplement those of the states is $6 a month for the first child in a family, and $4 for each additional child.

10. *The Poor Who Need Some Provision for Social Life, for Recreation, for Cultural Development, and for Certain Types of Education.* Despite the cheapness of commercialized recreation, many of the poor are so poverty stricken that they cannot afford to avail themselves of it. However, as was pointed out in a previous chapter, commercialized recreation is not very desirable. Parks and open-air playgrounds should be a feature of every community, other than the smallest. But outdoor amusement is not always feasible, particularly in the winter and during inclement weather, hence there are needs for other social facilities. These needs may be satisfied by local clubs, such as are attached to many of the churches — clubs for mothers, children, boys and girls, and workingmen. They may also be filled by social settlements or, as they are sometimes called, community houses, neighborhood clubs, or community centers.

A social settlement is a group of people who have enjoyed cultural and social advantages; who settle in a poor neighborhood for the purpose of obtaining personal knowledge of the residents and their problems; who share with them the advantages which they have had; who attempt to break down class barriers and provide needed help; and who receive in return an enlarged vision of social life, a development of personality, and the friendship which their poorer neighbors have to offer. As settlement workers aver, their work is not merely service, it is an exchange of mutual help.

The settlement house originated with the Reverend Samuel Barnett, a clergyman of the Church of England, who was appointed vicar of a poor London parish in Whitechapel in 1872. Lecturing on the needs of his parishioners to the undergraduates at Oxford University, the Reverend Barnett interested a young student, Arnold Toynbee (1852–1883), who spent his summer vacation of 1875 and all his university vacations thereafter, living the life of a workingman in Barnett's parish. After his graduation in 1873, Toynbee devoted the greater part of his time in lecturing to workingmen and otherwise showing his practical interest in the poor. He married in 1879, and his poor health necessitated his living abroad for a considerable portion of the year, but when he died (at the age of 31), his zeal and the activities of the

Reverend Barnett led to the idea of creating settlement houses of university men in all large cities. A fund was raised in Toynbee's memory, and the first social settlement was founded by Canon Barnett in Whitechapel, in 1884, under the name of Toynbee Hall. At the present time there are numerous settlement houses all over England, both denominational and nonsectarian.

Americans interested in the poor soon recognized the great possibilities of Barnett's work. In 1886, Stanton Coit, an American student doing graduate work in England, lived in Toynbee Hall. In 1887, together with Charles B. Spahr, he established the first American settlement on the lower east side of New York, early known as the Neighborhood Guild, and later as the University Settlement. In 1888, Miss Jane Addams likewise visited Toynbee Hall, and in 1889, in conjunction with Miss Ellen Gates Starr (afterwards a convert to Catholicism), founded the famous Hull House on Halstead Street, Chicago. Other settlements in America quickly followed. In 1929 there were 160 members of the National Federation of Settlements, Inc., the latter having been founded in New York, in 1911, to provide for co-operation of effort and standards among these community centers.

The personnel of a settlement house is usually made up of voluntary resident and nonresident workers, who devote part or all of their time to the work: but there are generally one or more trained social workers who are paid to devote their full time to directing the settlement activities. These activities are many, since the aim of the settlement is to discover and to fill all the needs of the community in which they are placed. Probably their most important function is club work — the provision of a home, as it were, where the people of the neighborhood can congregate for a few hours to forget their troubles, or to discuss them with understanding social workers who endeavor to find suitable remedies. There are usually separate clubs for boys, girls, mothers, and workingmen; dramatic groups, athletic associations, and summer camps. Depending upon local demands and local needs, there are besides, study circles and various classes for instruction in cultural subjects: music, sewing, cooking, carpentry, and the like.

Usually the settlement house provides a day nursery, and often a cafeteria where cheap meals can be obtained, and also bathing and washing facilities if the housing conditions of the neighborhood are deficient in these respects. Frequently, too, the settlement workers put those of their neighbors who are in distress in touch with social agencies giving financial relief, and help them to make the best use of community charitable resources. In America, settlement houses have done invaluable work, both in helping the foreign born to adjust themselves to American conditions and ways of living, and also in stimulating them to preserve the best in the culture brought with them from their native lands; their folklore and dances, their language, and their distinctive occupational pursuits. In a word, the settlement house gives its neighbors a richer and more interesting existence, with good, wholesome recreational, cultural, and instructional facilities; it supplies gaps in local organizations; it is often the means of inducing local authorities to remedy deficiencies of various kinds; and it helps its neighbors also to learn community resources and to make full use of them.

There has been some controversy as to whether or not settlement houses should be denominational in character. Although most settlement houses profess to be sympathetic toward the religions of the people in their neighborhood, yet they usually wish to ignore sectarianism; and there have been, indeed, many complaints of alleged proselytizing, of the fostering of religious indifference or hypocrisy, and of the hiring out of the settlement rooms to distinctly antireligious or at least anti-Catholic gatherings and entertainments. In Catholic and Jewish neighborhoods at least, settlement workers cannot ignore religion, for it is a fundamental part of the lives of the people, who cannot be truly understood, nor truly assisted in their needs, unless the definite precepts and tradition of their religious faith form an intrinsic part of all their activities. Although settlement workers usually deplore the foundation of denominational houses, nevertheless, Catholic settlements are essential if the religious faith of the Catholic poor is not to be weakened or undermined. There are settlement-house workers who sincerely strive to help the religious needs of the community, and who give all possible help to the local ministers. In general it may be said, however, that where parish clubs and activities are not sufficient to meet the people's needs, Catholics should themselves establish settlement houses, or they should found joint settlements with other parishes, not too far away from the neighbors to be served. And if the Catholic community cannot establish a settlement house of its own, or should not do so because of a previously existing nonsectarian settlement which amply furnishes all material assistance needed, then the clergy of the parish or their competent representatives should cooperate with the established settlement, thus preventing any spiritual abuses of the nature just described.

CHAPTER 23

THE TREATMENT OF DEFECTIVES

The Needs of Defectives

BECAUSE of hereditary defects, or environmental causes (including illnesses and contagious diseases) there will always be found some people
who are physically or mentally handicapped, and thus prevented,
through no fault of their own, from taking their normal place in this
world as independent social beings. It is, of course, the duty of the
families of those with defects to try to fit them to become as normal
as possible, by special hospital treatment, care, and education, and, if
necessary, by providing them with vocational guidance and training
which will enable them to be as economically independent as possible
in adult life and as happy as they can be despite their handicaps. The
formulation of a constructive program for defectives is, therefore, a
positive necessity. Particularly is this needed where their families cannot help them, either through lack of interest or, as is frequent,
through lack of facilities, and above all on account of poverty. When
this is so, it is the duty of the State to provide all necessary aid for
their welfare, if private agencies do not themselves supply the deficiencies of the family.

In this chapter we shall give a brief outline of some of the problems
connected with those who are blind, deaf, dumb, crippled, mentally
deficient, or insane.

The Blind

The official census of 1930 reported a total of only 69,593 blind persons in the United States.[1] This figure is recognized as being incorrect.
The *White House Conference Preliminary Committee Report* gave an
estimate of 60,000 children alone, who are either blind or with but partial vision,[2] and the *Social Work Year Book* for 1937 is of the opinion
that there are about 100,000 blind persons in the United States at the
present time.[3] Blindness, is, therefore, a serious problem as regards

---

[1] *Statistical Abstract of the United States,* 1937, p. 79.
[2] *White House Conference Preliminary Committee Report,* p. 447.
[3] *Social Work Year Book,* 1937, p. 40.

number, as well as an important social and economic question which has not yet been adequately solved.

The causes of blindness are varied. Some blindness is congenital, as a result of heredity or a prenatal environmental condition, such as venereal disease of the mother. Consanguineous marriages may, of course, result in blindness if there is a hereditary defect in the family. The fact that less than one tenth of the blind are under 20 years of age, and over three fifths are sixty years or over would seem to point to environmental causes, but, of course, it must not be forgotten that inherited blindness need not appear at birth, but may be a progressive defect, for example, nearsightedness. At least 80 per cent of blindness is, however, said to result from environmental causes, such as lack of attention to the eyes at birth, injuries, accidents, venereal conditions, inflammation following measles or other diseases, or degenerative changes due to old age.

The two chief problems of the blind are the necessity of training in order to live socially, and the difficulty of earning a livelihood. Eyesight is essential for most occupations, so that the blind are always limited in choice, and the most appropriate positions are usually overcrowded, and consequently the wages paid in them are very low. Even when blind persons are suitably trained and adept at a particular type of work, it is often difficult to place them because they are usually slower and more inaccurate than those who can see. Then, too, there is always a prejudice against employing the handicapped, and insurance companies often refuse to insure employers against work risks when handicapped persons are employed.

Although under the Christian era there were special hospices provided for the blind as far back as the fourth century, systematic training began only in 1784, when Haüy founded an institution for the training and care of the blind in Paris. A similar school was opened in England in 1791, and other European countries quickly followed suit. The first American institution was founded in 1832. After many attempts to devise a suitable alphabet for the blind, or to adapt the ordinary sight alphabet by line methods, there are now two special alphabets in almost universal use: the Braille method, devised in 1829 by Louis Braille, a blind pupil of Haüy's school, and the New York point system invented in 1868 by Mr. William B. Wait, an American blind teacher. Both methods have led to the translation of many books, and there are now special libraries for the use of the blind. The American Printing House for the Blind was established in 1879 and is given a Federal appropriation. The American Foundation for the Blind produces special phonograph records for blind use, also with the aid of a Federal appropriation. The latter organization sponsors research work to discover approved appliances to help the blind, and conducts an information bureau and other services. Other aid is given to the blind by the American Association of Workers for the Blind and by the American Association of Instructors for the Blind. With the aid of the books, phonographs, and special oral instruction, blind persons have been graduated from college in the same average length of time as for the ordinary student who is not handicapped.

It is now generally recognized that the blind need special training and care at the beginning of their scholastic career, which can be secured only in schools set apart for that purpose. This training should begin with kindergarten work, for best results are obtained from those who have had their senses of touch and sound developed in their early years. Such scientific training cannot be provided at home, and although day schools for the blind benefit many (and there are still too few available) it is often best that patients should not be left with their own families.[4] Early training may be neglected at home, or they may be pampered and otherwise spoiled for fighting their own way in the world in later years. Yet institutional life is almost equally detrimental for later life in the world, for there is the danger of "institutionalization," so that the problem needs to be individually settled in every case. The training of "seeing-eye" guide dogs has been a real boon to many an independent blind person. The Germans began training dogs as guides in 1916; a Mrs. Harrison Eustis adopted the same method in Switzerland soon afterwards; and in 1928 Mr. Morris Frank, a blind man from Tennessee went to Switzerland to be trained with a dog, and then established "The Seeing Eye" center in Morristown, New Jersey, with Mrs. Eustis' help. In training the blind, particular attention is now paid to physical education, and instruction in music and in industrial or commercial arts, such as massage, typewriting, sewing, basketmaking, weaving, and metalwork. Many blind persons have made excellent success in industry, commerce, or one of the professions, such as law, although, as we have said above, they are particularly handicapped in obtaining employment, and generally need the help of an institution to find them work. On account of their peculiar difficulties in the occupational group, many states provide a pension for

---

[4] Statistics for 1932 report 47 state schools for the blind, with 4,510 students; 95 public day schools with 5,308 students; and 11 private schools with 1,020 students (*Statistical Abstract of the United States,* 1937, p. 121).

the blind at an early age. The Social Security Act of 1935 provided for a maximum Federal grant of $15 a month to the needy blind, not inmates of public institutions, in those states with state pension programs which needed supplementary finances.

Modern care of the blind does not end with the provision of libraries, special schools and training, and early pensions. Since most blind persons do not become blind until a relatively advanced age, preventive work is more important than alleviation of the condition. The National Committee for the Prevention of Blindness, organized in 1915, is concerned solely with the investigation of the causes of blindness or impaired vision, to advocate measures for their elimination, and to extend preventive work. The increase of skilled medical attention for all children of school age, and the free testing of eyesight and provision of glasses, with "sightsaving classes" — special schoolrooms and apparatus for those with seriously impaired vision — greatly help to diminish preventable blindness, even when the impaired sight is a hereditary defect. Appropriate factory laws have greatly diminished eyestrain also, and the number of accidents at work. Babies' sore eyes due to gonorrheal infection (*opthalmia neonatorum*) has been practically eliminated in almost every country by laws making it compulsory to drop a weak (1 per cent) solution of nitrate of silver into every infant's eyes at birth.

For the Catholic blind, Catholic literature is provided in the United States through the Xavier Free Publication Society for the Blind, in New York City. There is great need, however, for the extension of these services, for translations of suitable books, for the establishment of more Catholic schools and societies for the blind to provide the necessary Catholic environmental influence, and also for a greater number of Catholics to take a friendly interest in blind persons living in their neighborhoods. Many Catholic college students are doing admirable voluntary work, translating books into Braille.

The Deaf and Deaf-Mutes

It has been estimated that there are at least 90,000 deaf persons in the United States, and about ten million persons who are "hard of hearing";[5] the 1930 census reported 57,193 deaf-mutes in the country.[6] Although deafness is a severe handicap in life, it does not provide so great a problem as blindness, and can be overcome.

There are various causes for deafness, principally meningitis, brain

---

[5] Cf. *Social Work Year Book*, 1937, pp. 119, 120.
[6] *Statistical Abstract of the United States*, 1937, p. 79.

fever, primary ear disease, and various contagious or infectious diseases, such as measles and diphtheria. Deaf-mutism and otosclerosis (which develops in later life) may be due to heredity. Heredity, however, is responsible for only a small percentage of deafness, because, as mentioned in Chapter 2, there are many types of deafness and as the defect is a recessive characteristic, it does not become dominant unless two people who marry have the same inheritable defect, as is likely to take place in consanguineous marriages. As with blindness, increased facilities for the medical inspection of children is greatly diminishing deafness caused by lack of expert care or other environmental factors, particularly when the deafness is due to primary ear disease.

A Catholic priest in Paris, the Abbé Charles Michel de l'Epée, invented sign language and founded the first school for the deaf in Paris about 1760. Braidwood in Edinburgh, and Heinicke in Dresden, adapted articulate speech, taught lip reading, and founded schools about the time of the Abbé de l'Epée's death in 1789. In 1815 an American, Thomas Hopkins Gallaudet was sent to Europe to study methods of teaching the deaf, by a private fund originating in Hartford, Connecticut. Gallaudet wished to observe the methods of teaching lip reading in Scotland, but Braidwood refused to divulge his system: a refusal which seriously retarded the instruction of the deaf in the United States. Gallaudet then went to the Paris school, at that time under the charge of the Abbé Sicard, where he was given every assistance. Sicard gave him his best pupil, Laurent Clerc, to help establish schools for the deaf in the United States. The first school was founded in Hartford in 1817, and several others were soon established in various states. In 1864 Gallaudet's son, Dr. Edward M. Gallaudet, founded a college for the deaf, under the title of the National Deaf-Mute College. In 1894 the name was changed to Gallaudet College and the college provides courses leading to the degrees of B.A. and B.S., as well as special training for teachers of the deaf.

The deaf who are taught lip reading or a combination of lip reading and sign language, together with physical training, can usually take their place in the world and suffer little from their handicap. Special schools, however, are needed to give them this necessary help, particularly as the deaf are often physically subnormal (and should not, therefore, be educated with the blind).[7] Usually special instruction is provided in those arts and industries where deafness is least a handicap.

---

[7] Statistics for 1932 show 57 state schools for the deaf and hard of hearing, with 12,408 students; 116 public day schools with 4,434 students; 27 private schools with 2,482 students (*Statistical Abstract of the United States,* 1937, p. 121).

Most of the deaf become self-supporting; the majority find work in manufacturing and mechanical occupations, but some also succeed in the professions. In certain tasks, where concentration is particularly valuable and where hearing is not required for the receiving of frequent instructions, a deaf person is more efficient than one who has the distractions which come from hearing.

The deaf and dumb are, of course, in a much more serious position, but it has been discovered in modern times that mutism is frequently due merely to lack of adequate training. If the deafness occurred in childhood and there was no special training, the deaf person is necessarily mute, for we learn to speak largely through hearing others.

The national organization for social work among the deaf is the American Federation of Organizations for the Hard of Hearing, founded in 1919, as an extension of an earlier society. Vocational rehabilitation for those who become deaf or hard of hearing in later life is provided by many of the states, aided by Federal funds through the Vocational Education Act of 1921, the George-Ellzey Act of 1934, and the Social Security Act of 1935.

It is interesting to note that the telephone was invented by Dr. Alexander Graham Bell in his efforts to discover a device which would enable the deaf to hear. With the 25,000 franc Volta prize awarded him by the French government, Dr. Bell established in Washington the "Volta Bureau for the Increase and Diffusion of Knowledge Relating to the Deaf."

There are several Catholic schools for the deaf and dumb in the United States, the first being founded by the Sisters of St. Joseph in St. Louis, Missouri, in 1838. There is also the Catholic association of the Knights de l'Epée, which has branches in most large cities. In addition to providing special chaplains for work among the deaf, this association maintains a fund for the education of the deaf and for the relief of the deaf poor and widows and orphans of deceased members. Unable to hear oral instruction, and often forced to attend special schools under non-Catholic auspices, the deaf are in great need of Catholic missionary work. Certain churches, however, are now installing in some of their pews apparatus for the hard of hearing, so that sermons and other instructions can be heard, but better provision for the Catholic deaf is an urgent need.

The Crippled and Permanently Bedridden

The *White House Conference Preliminary Committee Report* estimated the number of crippled children in the United States as between 289,000 and 365,000,[8] but the Social Security Act of 1935 gave the number of crippled in the country as approximately one for every 100 population, or a total of about 1,250,000.

The causes of crippling are many, and range from hereditary defects, to deformities due to tuberculosis, rickets, paralysis, arthritis, prenatal injury, birth accidents, and accidents after birth. Happily the number of children who are crippled as a result of malnutrition and other effects of poverty is now greatly diminished due to the more widespread medical and material assistance offered to mothers and prospective mothers. Yet much still remains to be done.

The treatment of cripples is, of course, provided mainly through hospitals. Yet more than medical treatment is needed to make a patient happy and financially independent in adult life. Adults who become crippled, are often capable of receiving vocational training so that they can return to the occupational group, though not necessarily in the trade or profession they formerly pursued. This rehabilitation work receives state aid in the majority of states; help is needed, too, to assist the crippled person to overcome the difficulty of adjustment.

Handicapped children can sometimes be completely cured, if their treatment and special dietary needs are attended to in time. The Social Security Act authorized the Children's Bureau of the Department of Labor to allocate $2,850,000 yearly for aid to crippled children in states with appropriate state programs. The Shriners maintain a chain of hospitals with a large number of beds for crippled children; crippled children are also aided by many of the Rotary Clubs, Junior Leagues, and local clubs belonging to the National Federation of Women's Clubs and the National Congress of Parents and Teachers. In 1921 the International Society for Crippled Children was founded to act as an information bureau and clearinghouse for organizations interested in crippled children. This Society publishes the magazine *The Crippled Child*, bimonthly. Handicapped children not only require medical treatment and correct diet, but they also need an education compatible with their state of health, particularly to help them adjust themselves to their inability to take part in the normal activities of the able-bodied; they must often be helped to become accustomed to whatever orthopedic appliances they may have to wear; and they need an industrial training to fit them to earn a livelihood. Sometimes visiting teachers are sufficient for their needs, or day schools, possibly with the provision of transportation and suitable desks and other equipment; but sometimes it is best for the physical well-being of a child to

---

[8] *White House Conference Preliminary Committee Report,* p. 453.

become a resident in a special institution, despite the danger of the "institutionalizing" effect.

Catholic cripples are better provided for than other Catholic defectives. There are numerous Catholic hospitals and institutions in the United States to take care of them. Yet Catholics can assist cripples not only by seeing that every Catholic patient in a non-Catholic institution has adequate provision for the practice of his religion, but by visiting those afflicted and helping to make their lives a little brighter, and by providing them with suitable employment whenever possible. To be able to assist in the cost of his own support has brought joy and a new interest in life to many a cripple. Then, too, some cripples would be just as well cared for in a foster home as in an institution, and Catholic families who would volunteer such assistance would assuredly be performing an act of mercy.

Treatment somewhat similar to that outlined above is needed for those who are permanently sick and disabled, though not necessarily crippled.

Mental Deficients

Mental deficients are those who have never been of average intelligence. Their bodies may have normal growth, but their brains are either underdeveloped from birth, or development ceases at a very early age. The most recent classification of mental deficients, now in general use, is that adopted by the American Association on Mental Deficiency in May, 1934, and used by the United States Bureau of the Census since 1935.[9] Mental deficients are classed into three main types:[10]

1. "An 'idiot' is a mentally defective person usually having a mental age of less than three years or, if a child, an intelligence quotient of less than 20." In other words idiots are unable to preserve themselves from ordinary physical dangers.

2. "An 'imbecile' has a mental age of 3 to 7 years inclusive, or an intelligence quotient from 20–49." Imbeciles are therefore never able to manage their own affairs.

3. "A 'moron' has a mental age of 8 years or upwards, or, if a child, an intelligence quotient between 50 and 69." Morons do not exceed the mentality of a child of 12 years.

---

[9] In England mental deficients are called feeble-minded, and are generally classified as of low or high grade.

[10] Definitions taken from *Mental Defectives and Epileptics in Institutions, 1936*, U. S. Dept. of Commerce, Bureau of the Census, 1938, p. 14.

It is noteworthy that moral defectives are frequently but not necessarily mental deficients, and a distinction should be made between the two.

Since there is no sharp dividing line between the normal person and the high-grade moron, it is difficult to estimate the number of mental deficients in the United States. Statistics show the following numbers in hospitals and institutions for mental defectives and epileptics at the end of 1936, but the Census authorities urge that: "It should be clearly recognized, however, that statistics relating to patients in institutions for mental defectives and epileptics do not furnish even an approximate measure of their total number, either in the country as a whole or in the various States. The institutions established for the care of mental defectives and epileptics contain only a small part of the total number of such persons. Many are inmates of prisons and reformatories;[11] others are in almshouses; and some are confined in hospitals for the insane. The vast majority of them, however, are not confined in institutions but live at large in the community."[12] It is also noteworthy that certain hospitals did not make a return.[13]

MENTAL DEFECTIVES AND EPILEPTICS IN THE U. S.[14]

Institutions	Totals		In Institutions		On Parole or Otherwise Absent	
	Mental Deficients	Epileptics	Mental Deficients	Epileptics	Mental Deficients	Epileptics
State	89,473	18,254	76,550	16,421	12,923	1,833
City	622	1	622	1	....	....
Private	3,733	595	3,605	592	128	3
Totals	93,828	18,850	80,777	17,014	13,051	1,836

Private estimates state that the number of mentally deficient and insane persons together probably exceeds one in every 250 of the population, with about one moron to every 500 of the population, and about one idiot and imbecile to every 2,000 of the population.[15]

---

[11] Readers are asked to note that while "many are inmates of prisons and reformatories," nevertheless this is not true of the majority of mental deficients and epileptics, as the next sentence in the above quotation makes quite clear: "The vast majority ... live at large in the community."

[12] Mental Defectives and Epileptics in Institutions, 1936, U. S. Dept. of Commerce, 1938, p. 4.

[13] Ibid., p. 5.

[14] Ibid., p. 4.

[15] Cf. Dr. Charles Bernstein, The Social Care of the Mentally Deficient, p. 5; Cf. also Stanley P. Davies, Social Control of the Mentally Deficient, p. 56; G. B. Mangold, Social Pathology, pp. 369, 370.

As mental deficiency is a legal concept rather than an accurate biological term, it is difficult to classify border-line cases. It is recognized that some mentalities are of slow growth, and for a child to be "retarded" or "dull" does not necessarily mean that he is of low mentality. Lack of interest or attention is often misinterpreted by teachers as lack of memory or understanding. While the majority of dull children do not grow up more brilliant than their early promise, yet such well-known personages as Newton, Darwin, Sheridan, and Wellington, were very poor scholars in their youth. Catholics will be particularly interested in the story of the late Reverend Dr. Shields, formerly head of the Education Department of the Catholic University of America, whose extraordinary intelligence was discovered only by accident, after he had long been thought of by his family as an imbecile.[16]

Generally speaking, mental deficiency is now determined more or less scientifically by the giving of mental tests to school children, to discover their Intelligence Quotient.[17] These tests are the most accurate method yet devised to discover the mentality of a person, and should lead to the detection of a greater number of mental defectives. Nevertheless, they are by no means wholly accurate, for no standardized results can be obtained in tests which have some bearing at least on the subjective reactions of the person tested. Since the exact nature of the intelligence is not known, to attempt to measure it in terms of performance in tests devised for the purpose can never be wholly accurate. Moreover, the tests are given through the medium of language — a culture trait which some children will not have attained to the degree reached by others, though they will not necessarily be less intelligent than those others. For example, the child of mentally deficient or entirely illiterate parents will not have had the environmental opportunities of those who enjoyed normal social surroundings in early years, with proper attention paid to their mental needs. It is very difficult to distinguish native ability from acquired skill due to past experience and habits. Again, the one tested may be of a nervous disposition, or may not react normally on the day the test is given: the will and the emotions both affect the intelligence, and under greatly changed environmental conditions it is very possible for a person's intelligence to differ from a previous state. And the individual tester

---

[16] Cf. Shields, Rev. T., *The Making and Unmaking of a Dullard.*

[17] The Intelligence Quotient is commonly known as the "I.Q." and this is found for children as follows: $\dfrac{\text{Mental Age}}{\text{Chronological age up to 14}} \times 100.$

himself may differ from other testers by his manner of giving the test; or some details of his findings may be different from the conclusions which would have been reached by another.

As for the cause of mental deficiency, while inheritance of a defective physical brain or glandular deficiency undoubtedly plays an important part in mental deficiency, there are many other causes also. Before birth there may be such environmental causes as undernourishment due to malnutrition or mental worry of the mother; maternal poisoning due to alcohol, lead, drugs used in contraceptives, and by disease such as nephritis and syphillis; X-ray treatment of the mother's pelvic organs; inadequate thyroid secretion in the mother, which may lead to cretinism, as discussed in Chapter 2; exhaustion of the mother's powers of reproduction; prenatal injuries such as trauma due to prolonged labor at child birth and the use of instruments. Mental deficiency may also be due to such postnatal environmental causes as accidents, malnutrition, infections which may attack the central nervous system, as a result of such diseases as encephalitis, poliomyelitis; convulsions, postnatal syphillitic infections, and even measles.

Mental deficients need protection from harmful influences all their life, for they rarely attain the measure of prudence necessary to take care of their own affairs. Where patients can be adequately cared for at home, special schools are often provided for them by local education authorities, so that their potentialities can be discovered and developed to the fullest possible extent. Sometimes foster homes are found for them. More often, mental deficients are placed in colonies or in institutions, where they are happy among those in the same situation as themselves, are adequately trained to procure a livelihood, and are protected from meeting persons of the opposite sex (often depraved persons who take advantage of their slow comprehension) and possibly contracting unhappy marriages, or immoral associations. Since mental deficients are more dependent upon the acquisition of life patterns by the formation of habit than are the more intelligent, it is obvious that they need careful education. If given an education in some suitable employment, such as agricultural work for boys, and domestic service for girls, and if trained in good habits, high-grade morons are capable of earning their own living, and of leading useful lives in the world, with a minimum of supervision.[18] A certain amount of supervision is, however, necessary, for they never attain normal prudence and social

---

[18] Statistics for 1932 show 80 state institutions for the mentally deficient with 12,171 students; 483 public day schools with 75,099 students; and 50 private schools with 1,615 students (*Statistical Abstract of the United States,* 1937, p. 121).

stability. The Gheel colony system in Belgium has already been described. In the United States a colony established for mentally deficient girls by Dr. Charles Bernstein at Rome, New York State, is the best known. The members work in the city as domestic servants, or in a factory, in charge of a matron, and they live in small houses, carefully supervised, until such time as they have acquired sufficiently stable habits to enable them to be paroled. The cost of maintaining girls and women in such a colony is considerably less than institution costs.[19] From the Catholic point of view, the education of mental deficients involves the problem of adequate religious instruction and training in morality, and maintaining moral integrity despite the attempts to exploit them which are often made by moral perverts of normal mental ability.

The Insane

In its legal connotation the word *insanity* means a condition which renders a person incapable of managing his own affairs. Medically the term is used to describe the condition of those who are not born mentally defective, but whose mind becomes deranged later in life. Yet, of course, it must be noted that insanity does not always have a mental basis, since many persons who are cured after an attack of insanity are as intelligent as before. At the end of 1936, census figures show the following statistics for the insane in hospitals or on parole:

NUMBER OF INSANE IN THE UNITED STATES IN 1936[20]

	Total	In Hospital	On Parole or Otherwise Absent
State Hospitals (including 2 Federal Hospitals)	411,432	364,403	47,029
Veterans' Administration Hospitals.	23,983	21,960	1,333
County and City Hospitals[21]	38,103	34,743	3,360
Private Hospitals[21]	11,624	11,025	599
Totals	485,242	432,131	52,321

Insanity is a relative term, based on a norm of "average" conduct and intellectual power which is very elusive in definition. The sane are those who are in touch with reality, those who can control their

---

[19] Cf. Charles Bernstein, M.D., "Colony and Parole Care for Dependents and Defectives," *Mental Hygiene*, July, 1923, pp. 449–471.

[20] *Patients in Hospitals for Mental Disease*, 1936, U. S. Dept. of Commerce, Bureau of Census, 1938, p. 2.

[21] Five county and city hospitals and private hospitals failed to report and are not included in the statistics given (*Ibid.*, p. 1).

thoughts and emotions, who are capable of self-management and of adjusting themselves to their environment, reacting reasonably to situations in the manner which the situation calls for. Insanity may be temporary, of short or of long duration, and it may be permanent. There are various types of insanity, and many persons living a "normal" life may have certain symptoms of insanity which may or may not develop into serious deviations from the normal so that they are a problem to society. It has been estimated that only about 30 per cent of insanity is due to an organic disorder, that is, to brain destruction, injury to the nervous tissue, glandular deficiencies or malfunctioning, an infection which has attacked the nervous system, and similar organic injuries. By no means are these disorders always due to inheritance. By far the greater percentage of insanity is functional in nature, and is not due to any damage or deficit in the nervous system, bur rather to faulty mental and emotional habits which lead to mental difficulties.

The various types of insanity may be roughly classified as follows:

1. *The Psychoneuroses and Neuroses,* which are a mild form of mental disease: nervous disorders, usually caused by fears, anxieties, and obsessions. Sometimes general fatigue or an emotional shock develops into a psychoneurosis as a result of faulty mental habits. This type of mental disorder includes:

a) Neurasthenia — in its mild state this is evidenced by constant fatigue, inability to sleep, lack of concentration, and the like; in its more dangerous form, the neurasthenic complains of suffering from bodily ailments for which no physical cause can be found. Neurasthenia is usually accompanied by digestive disturbances.

b) Hysteria, a morbid state of emotional instability produced by psychological induction and often leading to temporary paralytic conditions, digestive disorders, and the like. Other hysterical conditions are aphasia, or the temporary inability to speak, due to loss of memory and the meaning of words; auditory aphasia, or forgetting the meaning of words heard, or even temporary loss of hearing; visual aphasia, or the temporary inability to see correctly; and agraphia, or the temporary inability to write. It has been said that about 10 per cent of the breakdowns among combatants during the war was due to hysteria.

c) Hypochondria, or the continued "enjoyment" of ill health and imaginary complaints.

d) Psychasthenia, or abnormal fear of high places, dirt, fire, closed-in places, sin (resulting in religious scruples), and the like.

e) Obsessions of various kinds in their milder forms, which obtrude themselves constantly on the patient's consciousness.

2. *The Psychoses,* which are grave mental disorders, and include a wide variety of types, of which the following are some of the most important (no attempt is here given to enumerate them all):

a) Traumatic psychoses, which results from brain injury due to accident and includes delirium and various types of mental enfeeblement.

b) Senile psychoses: various types of mental disintegration probably due to old age, including simple deterioration and forgetfulness, delirium, senile dementia (agitation or melancholia, accompanying general deterioration), paranoia (delusions of grandeur, persecution, and hallucination), and other types.

c) Manic-depressive psychoses, which include such types of marked emotional disturbance as great excitement; excessive despondency; the "circular type" of excitement followed immediately by a depression stage, or vice versa; the catatonic type, or alternate stages of excitement and of negative stupor accompanied by inhibited muscular movements.

d) Dementia praecox (*dementia* means absence of mind) — the premature dementia of the young, which includes paranoia, the catatonic type, the hebephrenic type, or emotional dilapidation, resulting in a "silly" confusion, depression, delusions, and the like.

e) Paresis or general paralysis, beginning with a slight mental disorder and leading to complete dementia and general paralysis.

f) Involutional melancholia, or grave morbid depression, usually resulting in stupor.

g) Toxic conditions with or without psychosis, resulting from alcoholism, drug addiction, or other toxic poisons.

h) Psychoses accompanied by other physical diseases, such as a tumor, cerebral arteriosclerosis, infectious diseases such as influenza, diseases of the ductless glands.

i) Epilepsy with or without psychosis.

As must be evident from the above classification, insanity may be due to a variety of causes. Sometimes it is inherited, that is, one may be born with a predisposition to become insane at about a certain age. In many cases the exciting cause of insanity is a shock or violent emotion, but in these cases of functional disorder there are always other predisposing causes, such as a period of prolonged emotional disturbance or worry, which preceded the final cause of the breakdown, or a lack of training in will power and adjustment to difficulties. Sometimes insanity is caused by a direct injury, or it may be caused by an injury or illness in other parts of the body, such as defective glands, arteriosclerosis, or by an infection such as influenza. It may be caused by worry or excessive fatigue due to overwork; it may be due to venereal diseases, or excessive indulgence in drugs or alcohol. Even those who fear an inherited tendency toward insanity have the future largely in their own hands. Often, though of course not always, a healthy life, freedom from excesses, training in will power, care to suppress any tendency toward hysteria, and above all a sane outlook on the inevitable contrarieties of life, will prevent insanity from making headway.

At one time insanity was considered by some as a curse from God. In reality it is a disease to which all may be more or less liable, and one for which there is often a remedy, if the disease is functional, provided the patient is put under skilled observation at an early stage. Most mental hospitals now receive voluntary patients, for effective treatment can usually be procured only in the hospital itself, and not when the patient lives at home. Indeed, it is often home environment, plus faulty early training, which is the occasion of the malady, and the sooner a patient is removed from that environment, the greater are his chances to have the disease arrested and cured.

Of recent years very rapid strides have been made in the treatment of insanity. It is not so very long ago that the insane were treated in an extremely inhuman fashion. So far as the United States is concerned, the Society of Friends was the first to care for the insane in separate hospital wards, for they established such wards in 1752. Dorothea Dix (1802–1887) was responsible for the establishment of the first state hospital for the insane, at Williamsburg, Virginia, in 1868; but Clifford W. Beers (b. 1876) through his book: *A Mind that Found Itself* (1908) and the resulting mental-hygiene movement has done more than anyone else to change the attitude toward the insane, to improve the methods of treatment, as well as to prevent the condition becoming serious in many thousands of cases, by the improved scientific recognition and treatment of symptoms in their early stages. Trained psychiatrists now inquire into the patient's history, and strive to probe into the exact causes of the mental disorder. Once the cause is discovered it is often only a question of time and careful treatment to effect a cure. It is a true sign of progress that the stigma which once attached to insanity is gradually disappearing; and the time seems to be approaching when a doctor will be as loathe to pronounce a person with a functional disorder as incurably insane, as he is now reluctant to state that any other illness baffles him. Another advance in the treatment of the insane is the practice of some institutions of placing chronic but harmless patients under the "cottage system," where suitable work is provided for them to support themselves, so that they may be happy, and at the same time are not a burden on the community. Since the depression, however, grants to hospitals and other organizations for the treatment of the insane have been somewhat curtailed, so that the rapid progress of the earlier part of the century has not been continued in many districts.

Mental Hygiene. More important than all attempts to cure insanity is, however, the means taken to prevent it. It is especially this work which is the finest achievement of Clifford Beers and the National Committee for Mental Hygiene which was established in 1909, as a result of Beers' book. Beers, a Yale graduate, became a manic-depressive insane person at an early age, and spent three years in mental hospitals in Connecticut. The treatment accorded to him was so unscientific and lacking in understanding of his needs that he has devoted the remainder of his life working for a greater understanding and better treatment of the insane, as well as for the prevention of disorders. The work of the National Committee has been greatly extended since the interest taken in it by the Commonwealth Fund in 1931, and in 1928 the mental-hygiene movement was further extended by the establishment of the American Foundation for Mental Hygiene to raise an endowment for this purpose.

The aim of mental hygiene is, of course, the prevention of mental disorders, and a recognition of early symptoms so that their development can be checked. Just as it is impossible for physical hygiene to eliminate all types of illnesses, or even all cases of preventable types, so mental hygiene will never succeed in preventing all people from becoming insane. Nevertheless, the early training of a child to meet people and social situations with correct reactions, is bound to help him to become a well-balanced individual — one who is not unduly egocentric, who can successfully combat excessive fears, daydreaming, and emotional reactions, who can adjust satisfactorily to the inevitable unpleasant situations which will arrive, and who can keep his emotions in control and maintain his poise even under exceptional provocation. On account of the varying situations of life in society, the frailties of human nature, and the delicate adjustment of the nervous system, some persons will always fail in meeting situations in the manner called for, and character difficulties may result, symptomatic of a lack of true mental health.

The first psychiatric clinic in this country was established in Chicago in 1874. At the present time such clinics, particularly those which deal with "difficult" children and juvenile delinquents, perform a very worth-while work in attempting to help persons in their adjustments to life and society. As the soul of the human being is such an all-pervading part of him, Catholics will always prefer the assistance of Catholic specialists when advice of this nature becomes necessary. Actually, the correct attitudes which are influenced by the sacraments and grace, and instilled by Catholic teaching and the help provided in the confessional, give the earnest Catholic who tries to follow these teachings and inspirations the best possible assistance in the avoidance of incorrect attitudes which may lead to a mental breakdown.

Psychoanalysis. Other methods of dealing with functional insanity are those of the psychoanalysts, whose aim is to eliminate undesirable conduct due to mental disturbances, and to improve the mental condition of mankind.

Psychoanalysis, properly so called, was initiated by Sigmund Freud (b. 1856), an Austrian Jew, and a pupil of the well-known French doctor, Charcot, who treated mental cases by hypnosis. Freud's chief idea[22] is that abnormal conduct is largely due to sexual repression, and to predetermined hereditary complexes, which leave us without psychic freedom. He believes that the mind is composed of two parts. First, an unconscious, passionate, and immoral Id, which is the supposed source of our psychic energy, and which is presumed to be in constant warfare because it is composed of two factions, the instinct toward death and destruction, and the Eros impulse or yearning toward life. Second, the Ego, which includes our will, and is the medium through which the Id can reach the external world. Freud thinks that not only is there a warfare within the Id, but there is also a constant warfare between the Ego and the Id, for the Ego checks the Id, and the Id is pleasure-loving, pain hating, instinctive, and unmoral. Above both the Ego and the Id, is the Super-ego, which is almost synonymous with conscience, but includes also remorse and feelings of guilt. The Super-ego is the chief force which socializes the individual, and is the seat of the ideals taught by the family and society. Not everyone has a Super-ego, for criminals are said to be without it.

Freud is of the opinion that the primitive instincts of man are fundamentally sexual, and that it is sex which is at the base of all our urges. He thinks that we are heterosexual when we are born, but selfish and only interested in ourselves and in our "erotogenic zones." We sup-

---

[22] Cf. Freud, S., *The Interpretation of Dreams* (1901), *Psychopathology of Everyday Life* (1901); *The History of the Psychoanalytic Movement* (1917); *The Ego and the Id* (1922).

posedly develop from narcissistic self-interest, into homosexualism, and only later into heterosexualism. This so-called development into heterosexual life is said to come about by boys becoming increasingly, though unconsciously, infatuated with their mothers, and girls transferring their affection to their fathers, and having unconscious incestuous feelings toward them. Freud believes that the stories of Electra and Oedipus are symbolic of the early history of mankind, and are re-enacted, in part at least, by all of us. Electra incited her brother to kill his mother, for she hated her: Freud considers that all girls hate their mothers in early life. Oedipus killed his father and married his mother by mistake and was filled with remorse. Freud considers that we carry similar conflicts in our unconscious self, and that the Electra complex and the Oedipus complex are at the basis of all social life (including religion) and all morality. However, Freud thinks that our supposed youthful preoccupations with sex, and the later homosexualism are frustrated when we are very young by our parents and teachers whom he considers to be the origin of our consciences and the Super-ego. Later, the wishes or desires of the Id are relegated to the background, because we have transferred our affection to people other than the parent of the opposite sex, because of lack of interest due to preoccupation with other pursuits, or the passage of time, or because we forced ourselves to forget them, or were forced by our parents and the Super-ego which they engendered. They therefore become embedded in the unconscious Id, and after a period of adolescent autoeroticism we become heterosexual again. But in sleep our Ego is dull, the unconscious self (the Id) is released, and our suppressed desires become translated into the images about which we dream. According to Freud, therefore, everything we dream about is a male or female sex symbol. We may dream of dancing, ships, shoes, knives, keys, wardrobes, landscapes, but they will always reveal our interest in sex. Not only dreams, but slips of the tongue, temporary forgetting of names or situations, losing articles, and many other signs are supposed indications of this preoccupation within our unconscious self.

If there is a harmonious balance between the Super-ego and the Id, and the external reality which is maintained by the Ego, then, Freud says, we are mental normally. If the Id has been greatly repressed, or if, for one reason or another, our psychic life is unbalanced, then we develop one or other of the forms of insanity. Freud thinks, however, that if we can be brought to analyze our past experiences, we shall discover sooner or later an incident whose conscious or unconscious repression was sufficiently important to cause this lack of balance, and we can then adjust our attitude in a fashion which will help us back to mental normalcy.

Freud did not teach that all sex repression is physically bad, and that we must give full rein to our passions, as the popular idea of Freudianism holds. He did, however, stress the influences of sex in our lives to an unwarranted extent, and postulated a universal early homosexual desire in mankind, and in these hypotheses he is unscientifically incorrect. Homosexualism is not a universal tendency, and sex is by no means the preponderant human drive. His method, however, has had definite value in that it has aroused research and study in the causes of mental disease, and he has shown us that the experiences of childhood are responsible for many conduct difficulties in later life. It is possible, too, that one may attribute to Freud the more reasonable modern attitude toward sex of those who have not become too naturalistic in outlook and exaggeratedly sex-conscious. It is, of course, true, that sex is at the basis of certain human conduct. The present-day exaggerated naturalistic attitude toward sex in the motion-picture theater and in literature, and elsewhere, sometimes gives mental and moral shocks to the child which may greatly influence his conduct and character; again, a person may steal to buy clothes to attract the opposite sex for later sex satisfaction, and sex enters into conduct in other ways. But pride and fear are much more important conduct drives than sex. Neither are all repressions bad and productive of "complexes." Rather, repressions are valuable for the development of human character, and it is only forced repressions which may sometimes have a deleterious mental effect.

Alfred Adler (b. 1870), an early disciple of Freud, founded a new school of "Individual Psychology" in 1912. His theories are contained in his books: *The Neurotic Constitution* (1917), *A Study of Organ-Inferiority in its Physical Compensations* (1917), *Individual Psychology* (1924), *Understanding Human Nature* (1927), *Problem of Neurosis* (1930). He does not deny the importance of sex in conduct, but correctly denies that it is a fundamental cause of human behavior. His idea of the basic urge in human nature is not sex, but pride of life. There is a continual conflict within us, he thinks, because on the one side there is the will to achieve or the will to power, of our egocentric nature, and on the other side, there is our inability to succeed, because of inherited inferior organs. To satisfy our frustrated Ego, Adler is of the opinion that we attempt to "compensate" for it. In making this adjustment, we may succeed instead of failing, and a weak organ may in this way become stronger than a healthier one. Demosthenes stuttered, yet later became one of the world's greatest orators; Beethoven was deaf, Mozart had an imperfectly developed ear, yet both became famous musicians. Such are examples which he cites of satisfactory compensation. If we do not overcome our supposed feeling of inferiority in a satisfactory manner, if our egocentric nature cannot express its ego in some fashion, then Adler thinks that a neurosis will develop. We may desire to run away from the situations which we encounter, and escape in phantasies which are imaginary gratifications of our Ego, or we may pretend to be superior and develop paranoia or similar mental disturbances. Dreams, however, Adler thinks to be related to the future, rather than Freud's notion that they are connected with the past as fulfillments of former desires.

There is, of course, much truth also in Adler's theory. He shows the great part that fear plays in childhood, and the influence of our ego and pride. However, he fails to consider the motives of human conduct and frailties, other than pride and fear, and therefore provides a very incomplete explanation of human activities.

Charles Gustave Jung (b. 1875 in Zurich) is another member of the psychoanalytical school, and author of *Collected Papers on Analytical Psychology* (1920), *The Psychology of the Unconscious* (1921), *Psychological Types* (1923), *Contributions to Analytical Psychology* (1928), and other books.

He regarded Freud as one-sided, rejected the notion of sex as the basis of human conduct, and considered searching for a hypothetical childhood difficulty, to the neglect of matters of immediate importance, to be extremely harmful to the mental patient. His main interest was the actual exciting cause of mental disease, rather than predisposing causes, and he considers that the unconscious attitude of a person toward his present problems does not reveal old sex wishes, but the reason for the current difficulty. It is this which he considers it to be the task of the psychoanalyst to ascertain. His idea of the libido is energy or vital force, not sex. For him, the father and mother in the Electra and Oedipus myths are merely mythical presentations of our attempt to free ourselves of our desires for the unattainable, in order to become independent. There are two main types of individuals, he thinks (the "Psychological Types") : extroverts (dominated by feeling, and turned outward in social attitude) and introverts (dominated by thought, inclined to daydream, and turned inward in social attitude). He also provided for a middle type: the "ambivert." His idea of character types has had a wide adoption in psychological literature. So far as insanity is concerned, Jung considers that if we cannot free ourselves of our frustrated desires, a neurosis may develop, and according as we are one or the other type, so we shall regress into different childish adjustments.

Undoubtedly the method of all the psychoanalysts has been productive of good results, in dealing with certain types of mental derangements, although the underlying hypothesis of all three is one-sided and not in any way scientifically proved. Yet to ask patients to analyze themselves, and to delve into past experiences as well as present attitudes, is one that takes a long period of time, and which can, therefore, be afforded only by the well-to-do; moreover, only intellectual peoples are able to discuss their past and present experiences of a psychical nature, for the majority of the uneducated think only in terms of the concrete. The inference of the work of the psychoanalysts is that the more intelligent a person is, and the better he can grasp situations and can adjust to them so much the better will his conduct be. While there is, of course, a correlation between ignorance and conduct, the behavior of intellectuals is very frequently quite other than reflection would lead them to pursue or what intelligence would suggest to them. Psychoanalysis has many achievements to its credit, but it is by no means the solution to the cure of the mentally crippled, or to the prevention of mental ills.

Epileptics

Epilepsy is a serious disease which has long been known to mankind (Hippocrates described it in the fifth century B.C.), but little exact knowledge is even now available. It is a nervous disorder, which may result in a momentary loss of consciousness, or in severe convulsive fits. It is a group of diseases rather than one type, for some forms of epilepsy are accompanied by a psychosis, and some are not; in some people the cause may be definitely traced to local disease of the brain, illness such as meningitis, or a head injury with fracture pressing on the brain, and in others there is no apparent exciting or predisposing cause. The number of epileptics in United States hospitals was quoted in the section on mental deficiency. As there mentioned, the statistics are not accurate, and the actual extent of epilepsy in the United States is not known. Epilepsy nearly always occurs before the patient is twenty years of age, and if it is not cured it often results in a mental defect connected with the nervous system, and sometimes in moral disintegration. In any event, epileptics are subject to more or less frequent recurring attacks of convulsions, automatism or other symptoms, although during the intervening period many of them are often completely normal. Because of these attacks, epileptics are handicapped both socially and economically. With the exception of the worst mental and moral cases epileptics are best cared for under the colony system, when adequate attention cannot be given to them at home. In this way they can lead as nearly a normal life as possible, they can become self-supporting, and the segregation will obviate the danger of marriage. As about 50 per cent of the cases of epilepsy seem to be due to inheritance, probably as a recessive characteristic, epileptics should never marry.

Drug Addicts and Alcoholic Degenerates

Too great and prolonged indulgence in drugs or alcoholic liquors invariably results in physical and mental deterioration, and mental derangement with or without a psychosis develops. Patients then need long care and supervision if they are to recover. Best care can only be given in an institution, where addicts should be separated into mental, immoral, and criminal classes, and treatment given accordingly. Often a period of scientific treatment will effect a cure, and patients can return to their former position in the world. They need careful supervision and aftercare, however, for most addicts are weak willed, and there is always the danger of their succumbing to temptations to return to their former habits. The practice of the tenets of religion is one of the most effective measures to insure against recurrence of the habit.

The United States suffers from a veritable "drug peril." The per-capita consumption of narcotic drugs in the United States is about 36 grains a year, and is higher than in India, the chief producing country, where the per-capita consumption is less than 27 grains a year. Annual per-capita consumption in France is only about 4 grains; in England, about 3 grains; and other European countries seem to take less. Accurate statistics are, however, unavailable, particularly as a cheap domestic source of a narcotic has now been discovered in the marijuana weed. This plant is grown in many parts of the United States and its use is not available in statistical form. The saddest feature of the drug traffic is that boys and girls of school age at times become a prey to the habit. Having once taken the drug, a person almost invariably wants more, and without extremely strong will power he is apt to become a "dope fiend" within a comparatively short time. Once a drug has obtained a hold over a person, he loses all ambition because he wishes to maintain the drugged state with its lack of conflicts, his will is weakened, his mind quickly becomes impaired, and generally he soon finds it impossible to keep in employment. To obtain money to procure supplies, he will often resort to desperate measures, and begin a criminal career. It is said that close to one quarter of the total prisoners in the United States are drug addicts. It must not be forgotten, however, that while morphine was only discovered about one hundred years ago, cocaine about fifty years ago, and heroin (the most dangerous) in 1898, opium has been in use for several thousand years, and is an extremely valuable drug for medicinal purposes. There is nothing morally wrong with the alleviation of pain by lawful means. God seems to have provided drugs for this purpose and their use is sanctioned by Scripture, where it is said that the "physician shall cure and shall allay their pains."[23]

The effects of drunkenness are not quite so virulent as drug addiction. In any case, liquor is cheaper to obtain than drugs, so that the social effects are possibly less harmful. As drunkenness is, however, more widespread than drug taking, its social effects are in some way much greater, and much poverty and family distress are often directly attributable to habitual drunkenness. Although "prohibition" was certainly not a satisfactory solution to the problem, drunkenness is an evil which merits the serious attention of social reformers and practical sociologists, as an adequate remedy for it has not yet been found.

---

[23] Ecclus. 38:7.

CHAPTER 24

EUGENICS AND POPULATION PROBLEMS

Eugenics

THE theory of eugenics has a direct bearing on the problem of defectives. Eugenists are of the opinion that for too long a period man has been more preoccupied with breeding good strains of plants and animals than he is in perfecting the physical quality of the children born to him. Somewhat ignoring such questions as personal and sex attraction, they advocate selective breeding among those whom doctors pronounce to be the best fitted physically for the task of bearing offspring. Their hope is to raise a nation of "supermen," who are such by heredity. With this end in view, they advocate also: (1) the practice of euthanasia, or painlessly putting to death of the old, the crippled, the deformed, and all who are a "burden" on society; (2) the checking of the propagation of the "unfit" — paupers, and defectives, such as the blind, the dumb, the deaf, cripples, epileptics, mental deficients, criminals, and even juvenile delinquents, and all whom they consider likely to produce offspring which would be of poor stock and detrimental to the fitness of the human race; (3) the limitation of offspring by artificial birth control, so that parents may have more time and money to devote to their children than would be possible with a larger family, thus giving the children a better chance in life.

Eugenics is no new idea. The word itself comes from the Greek, meaning "well born." The Spartans practised it many centuries before Christ; later Plato advocated it, and many theorists have touched upon it since. The idea is modern only in that Sir Francis Galton (1822–1911) and his followers gave it popular vogue. In 1883 Galton initiated what is now an ever-growing interest in the cult of the body, as representing the whole man, instead of taking into account also man's mind and soul. Although there is very much truth in eugenism, nevertheless in its modern exaggerated form it has become a doctrine of materialism carried to the extreme, and one which it is the duty of all right-thinking persons to oppose as strongly as possible.

Euthenics is the study of how to improve, not the heredity, but the environment of man, so that environment of all types: geographic, biologic, economic, social, and cultural, will be such as will foster the fullest possible development of man's desirable inherited predispositions. If spiritual and not material motives are the aim of euthenics it is, of course, a program which is highly desirable and fully in consonance with human intelligence and dignity.

We just said that there is much truth in eugenism, despite its shortcomings. Indeed, in its highest sense, eugenism is an idea with which the Catholic Church is wholly in sympathy. The Church in no way condemns any proposal of eugenism which subordinates temporal to spiritual welfare. Far from being an evil, measures seeking the improvement of the human race by lawful means are highly praiseworthy. None are more interested than is the Church in the welfare of the human race. That every person be "well born" with the best endowments of body, soul, and temporal goods, is the Church's most sincere wish. She forbids the intermarriage of close relatives, and consanguineous marriages are certainly often productive of defective offspring because of similar defective genes in both mates. Young people are taught to consider the welfare of their future offspring before they enter into the sacred state of matrimony, and the Church will ever warn them that love should be ruled by reason.[1]

The Church, therefore, is not averse to "selective breeding," when the selection of partners is a prudent one on the part of the partners themselves; nor does it advise a marriage in any way dangerous to possible offspring. But, as we have often stated, man's eternal salvation is far more important than his temporal welfare: the Church is

---

[1] Cf. *Casti Connubii*, p. 15. Giving the Church's views on this matter, Pope Pius XI says:

"To the proximate preparation of a good married life belongs very specially the care in choosing a partner; on that depends a great deal whether the forthcoming marriage will be happy or not, since one may be to the other either a great help in leading a Christian life, or a great danger and hindrance. And so that they may not deplore for the rest of their lives the sorrows arising from an indiscreet marriage, those about to enter into wedlock should carefully deliberate in choosing the person with whom henceforward they must live continually: they should, in so deliberating, keep before their minds the thought first of God and of the true religion of Christ, then of themselves, of their partner, of the children to come, as also of human and civil society, for which wedlock is a fountain head. Let them diligently pray for divine help, so that they may make their choice in accordance with Christian prudence, not indeed led by the blind and unrestrained impulse of lust, nor by any desire of riches or other base influence, but by a true and noble love and by a sincere affection for the future partner; and then let them strive in their married life for those ends for which the state was constituted by God. Lastly, let them not omit to ask the prudent advice of their parents with regard to the partner, and let them regard this advice in no light manner, in order that by their mature knowledge and experience of human affairs they may guard against a disastrous choice."

the guardian of faith and morals, and it cannot sanction enforced selective breeding, for this would encroach on man's personal liberty; nor can it sanction any acts against the natural or positive divine laws, merely for the sake of man's temporal happiness; nor again can it sanction practices which infringe on the exercise of man's natural rights, unless the common good is apparent with the utmost certainty.

Euthanasia

Turning now to the program of the Eugenists, let us first consider euthanasia. Eugenists advocate euthanasia, the chloroforming or otherwise disposing of the old, those in pain, and all infants who are born crippled or deformed. They justify their idea by asserting that it is an act of charity to put out of their misery those who are in pain or without a chance of ever enjoying life. For adults, however, they make the modification that one must first obtain the consent of the person whose life it is proposed to end.

Undoubtedly, it often seems that those in misery might best be relieved in this manner, yet to do so would be to infringe on man's right to live and his duty to maintain his life until God chooses to take it from him. First of all, no man has full dominion over his own life, hence he cannot consent to its elimination under a legalized form, for since we have no right over our own life, there is no right which can be transferred to others. Indeed, although we are not bound to take extraordinary care of our life, we are obliged to take reasonable means to preserve it, and we are prohibited from taking it. Second, the State's right over the lives of its citizens is strictly limited. The authority of the State is based upon the necessity of order, and the need of supporting the law of God for the preservation of order: "For he is God's minister: an avenger to execute wrath upon him that doth evil."[2] Only in the punishment of crime can the State lawfully take away the life of a citizen.[3] Third, the problem of pain is involved.[4] Without the Christian solution that God permits it in expiation of our own sins or the sins of others, this question would be insoluble. As it is, how can we criticize what God allows? The particular pain suffered may be of inestimable value, and to deprive a person of it may result in irretrievable loss to himself or another. God's ways are not our ways. He has permitted pain, and the suffering of Christ has given

---

[2] Rom. 13:4.

[3] Cf. Chapter 26 on capital punishment.

[4] Cf. D'Arcy, M., S.J., *Pain and the Providence of God* (Milwaukee: The Bruce Publishing Co., 1935).

us an example of how pain should be borne and made meritorious. Of course, we ought to make use of our intelligence to seek methods of alleviating pain, but to eliminate it by methods which are contrary to natural law cannot be lawful. Fourth, if euthanasia were allowed, and sufferers could be legally eliminated in this way, there would probably be a laxity in searching for causes and remedies of deficiencies and degeneration. Fifth, if sanctioned by law, euthanasia might lead to many an abuse. Consent to submitting to it might be forged or obtained by force, and many murders might be committed in the name of kindness to the afflicted. Sixth, a defective and handicapped child may grow up to give glory to God or to perform a great service to humanity. Caesar was an epileptic, Milton was blind, Beethoven was deaf, and Byron was lame. To permit the disposal of infants would lead to grave abuse of the "unwanted child."

Sterilization

Another tenet of the eugenists is compulsory sterilization. The term *sterilization* means the performance of an operation on the sexual organs, so that the person operated on will be rendered sterile, that is, incapable of procreation. Sterilization in no way diminishes sexual instincts and desires. In the male, the necessary operation, called vasectomy, is very slight, and merely involves the cutting of two small tubes. For the woman, a major operation, called salpingectomy, is needed, for the Fallopian tubes must be cut and cauterized. Over half of the states in the United States, and a number of other countries, already have laws which permit the legal sterilization of persons under certain conditions, some even allowing compulsory sterilization. It is often said that sterilization has a beneficial influence on the health of those who have it done, particularly on the male, though this is by no means certain.

The Eugenists advocate the compulsory sterilization of all those with a disease or defect which is capable of transmission by heredity, such as the blind, deaf-mutes, and those with other inherited physical deformities, and particularly the mentally deficient, the insane, and the epileptic. Some Eugenists also advocate the sterilization of moral defectives, criminals, and juvenile delinquents, and particularly girls guilty of sexual immorality, and go so far as to wish to sterilize the poor who apply for financial relief and have large families. They claim that all these types tend to have children who will perpetuate their condition and be either a menace or a burden to society. By sterilizing these persons Eugenists hope that the "unfit" and "undesirable" will be eliminated, so that a physically and mentally superior population will eventually result.

There are three aspects to this question: the medical, the social, and the moral.

Medically, the theory rests upon our knowledge of the inheritability of these defects, about which much yet remains to be learned. As we noted when discussing their causes in the last chapter, very many blind, deaf, crippled, mentally deficient, insane, and epileptic persons are defective because of prenatal or postnatal environmental causes, or because of glandular disturbances in the mother or the child, which could be cured. The increase in insanity, for example, is much more certainly due, not so much to inheritance as to the modern rush of city life, modern economic insecurity, faulty education and habits. Furthermore, the increase of such cases on hospital records (to which the Eugenists point) is due to the realization today that mental illness may possibly be cured if properly treated. Actually, a weakened nervous system may be inherited, and a predisposition toward insanity, but not insanity itself. The exciting cause of insanity in any person may not be present for the children of that person, even though they inherited a predisposition for the development of the malady. Sometimes one identical twin may become insane, and not the other. Often it is by no means easy to differentiate persons with nontransmissible though undesirable characteristics, from those with an inherited deficiency. It is true that certain classes of physical defects are obviously inherited, and it is likewise true that a large proportion of the children of the insane, epileptics, and mental deficients seem to inherit the defect, or the predisposition to it. Scientifically, where inheritance is clearly the cause of the deficiency, sterilization will indeed eliminate the inheritance of the defective strain. Yet all biologists are agreed that too little is known about heredity to prophesy a definite inheritance as regards any individual characteristic. We are not yet sure that inherited defects may not be gradually eliminated from a family stock by correct training and care. Small mutations are constantly occurring, which may have a marked effect on an inheritable characteristic. The defect may, for some reason or other, die out, and the carriers of recessive characteristics may themselves be normal or even superior persons. Environment and food may change the development of a potentiality. Again, a defect may seemingly be inherited, because one of the parents has a similar characteristic, whereas actually the child may have the same defect merely by chance, as a result of an environmental factor.

Eugenists who advocate the sterilization of the "unfit" are usually of the opinion that mental deficients in particular will invariably have mentally deficient children, and that they tend to be very prolific. These opinions are inaccurate. Not all deficients are defective by inheritance in which case their children will probably be born of normal mentality. Children are often thought to have inherited mental deficiency, whereas in reality their deficiency may be caused by untoward environment and neglect. If the mother or both parents are mentally deficient, even though the child does not inherit the defect, home life can hardly give him the mental alertness found in children of normal parentage, and a mentally deficient mother may entirely neglect her child's welfare. Heredity undoubtedly plays an important part in mental deficiency, but in many cases it provides only a tendency, which can be eradicated with correct training and care. Where one parent only is affected, or the defect is inheritable only from one of two defective parents (on account of the environmental cause of the deficiency of the one) then there are chances that the children may receive the characteristics of the normal parent. As an inherited defect, too, it is not a unit character but is most probably due to a combination of a large number of genes;[5] also it is a recessive and not dominant, and may remain hidden in the germ plasm without ever becoming phenotypic. It has, indeed, been computed that if there is now one mental deficient to every one thousand population, it would take sixty-eight generations, or two to three thousand years, to reduce the proportion to one in ten thousand, if only actual mental deficients are sterilized.[6] Always there will be the possibility of defective genes arising for one cause or another in individuals who were previously normal, and many persons would have been sterilized whose possible offspring might in no way have been defective. It is interesting to note that of 312 children of mentally deficient mothers in the well-known Rome State School and Colony, New York, Dr. Bernstein, the founder and superintendent reports as follows: "Ten per cent were adjudged to be defective (though not definitely of low grade). . . . Sixty per cent appeared to be normal children and thirty per cent were on the borderline. The progress of these children has been checked at regular periods, and the great majority are developing normally. They are average students at school and measure up in every way to other normal chil-

---

[5] Cf. Popenoe, P., "Heredity and Mental Deficiency," *Mental Hygiene,* 1931, pp. 570–575.

[6] Cf. Fisher, R. A., "Elimination of Mental Defects," *The Journal of Heredity,* 1927, pp. 529, 531, quoted by H. S. Jennings, *The Biological Basis of Human Nature,* pp. 241, 242.

dren.''[7] As regards prolificacy, although it is true that some mental deficients do marry and raise large families, often of inferior type, nevertheless many deficients are not capable of reproduction, some die in their youth, and they often do not marry, particularly if they are of the lower grades of mental attainment.[8] Indeed, the majority of low-grade deficients are necessarily kept in institutions, and then sterilization is entirely unnecessary, for segregation of the sexes is an easy matter.

As for the inheritance of moral defects. So far as pauperism is concerned, it is true that this condition is often due to character defect, such as lack of judgment, laziness, or incompetence. Yet we have shown the very many other possible causes of individual poverty in Chapter 22. The condition of most poor persons is much more probably due to lack of healthy surroundings and nourishing food, and to the daily worry and deprivations of decent human living conditions, whose devitalizing influence may well affect the character of those who were originally normal. Robert Burns, Giotto, Faraday, Abraham Lincoln, and many others came from poor families, and were neither dull nor moral perverts on account of it! The inheritability of crime has long been definitely disproved. Character traits are not inherited as such, although predispositions to certain character types may have an inherited basis. We have already shown that environment is of much greater importance in character formation than is heredity. The children of criminals, drug addicts, inebriates, or moral degenerates are frequently entirely normal. Sexual perverts, if sterilized, may be a greater menace to society than not. The sterilization of persons with undesirable character traits would be a cruel punishment, unjustified by the natural law, and for which there is no scientific foundation. It must also be noted that the Report of the Departmental Committee of Sterilization in Great Britain, published in 1934, as also the Report of the Committee of the American Neurological Association, published in 1936, are both opposed to eugenical sterilization upon scientific grounds.

Actually, some of the current ideas about the inheritance of mental deficiency and certain moral characteristics are due to certain studies which have been made, such as *The Kallikak Family* (1912) and *Feeblemindedness, Its Causes and Consequences* (1914), by H. H. Goddard; *The Hill Folk,* by Davenport and Danielson (1912); and *The Jukes,* by Arthur H. Estabrook (1915). For example, in his book

---

[7] Cf. Charles Bernstein, M.D., *Problems in Mental Deficiency,* Pamphlet No. 2, p. 22.
[8] Cf. *Ibid.,* Tabulations, pp. 26–29.

on *Feeblemindedness* Goddard gave a table (p. 555) which shows that feeble-mindedness is a perfect example of a simple Mendelian recessive character. Yet his conclusions are based merely on superficial personal examinations of children said to be feeble-minded, no use being made of objective data. So far as the Kallikak family is concerned, a Martin Kallikak married a supposedly mentally deficient barmaid while he was a soldier in the civil war. As a result of this union there were numerous descendants, of whom 480 have been traced, and only 46 of these were found by Goddard to be normal, while the rest were mentally deficient, moral perverts, alcoholics, criminals, and the like. Later, Kallikak married a woman of good family, and of the 496 known descendants there were no mental deficients, no immoral women or illegitimate children, and only three men who were somewhat degenerate. Yet Goddard discovered that all the daughters of the first marriage were defective, whereas mental deficiency seems to be a recessive trait, so that the defect should not have been manifested in any of them. Further, the unscientific character of any conclusions to be drawn from this study about the inheritability of mental deficiency and moral worthlessness lies in the fact that the progeny of the first union were not only branded with the stigma of illegitimacy, but they had not the social and economic advantages of the descendants of the later marriage, so that it is impossible to decide whether heredity or environment is more surely the cause of the divergence of family type. Moreover, the reputation of those who are dead rests on secondary evidence which, of its nature, is not scientifically accurate, and may be almost wholly unreliable.

The study of the Jukes, compared with the achievements of the Edwards family, is similarly of little worth in a consideration of the inheritability of characteristics. Juke, who was born in 1720, is known to have left some 1,200 descendants, many of whom were thieves, murderers, professional paupers, and the like. Jonathan Edwards, born 1703, is famous as a President of Princeton University. By the year 1900 his descendants numbered such socially useful persons as senators, judges, college presidents and professors, clergymen, lawyers, and the like. Yet as for the inheritability of moral qualities, it has been discovered that an ancestor of the original Edwards was an Elizabeth Tuthill who was anything but a desirable character, and in the account of the successful descendants, no mention is made of those who did not succeed or who had less desirable positions or characters.

Socially, it is argued in favor of the sterilization of mental deficients in particular, that there are many "high-grade morons" who would be

capable of living a normal life in the world and of maintaining themselves, if there were no danger of their marrying and propagating their
kind: hence, these defectives, if sterilized, would cease to be a burden
on the public in an institution, and could take their place in the world,
and even marry, without danger of any defective offspring who might
in their turn become a burden on the State. Hence it is claimed that
sterilization has an economic argument in its favor, as well as being
of eugenical benefit. Yet many "high-grade" morons in institutions are
self-supporting, and those under parole are wholly so. Society can
make use of many persons who are not "normal" physically or mentally. Sometimes the highly gifted are badly integrated emotionally,
insane, drug addicts, addicted to alcoholism, but the world benefits by
their brilliant contributions to culture. A defect may be compensated
for by good characteristics of other kinds; many defective persons,
even the mentally deficient or insane, have had civic careers of high
usefulness, although, of course, such persons while holding office, have,
sometimes, been responsible for undesirable events. Again, mental deficients of the ordinary kind are often very happy and efficient at
certain simple, if monotonous tasks. The world is certainly not losing
if these people reproduce their like; indeed, with the growth of mechanized industry, they may be more suited to many economic tasks,
than the more mentally gifted, who are irked by the routine of mechanized tasks.[9] While no sane person would deny that good physical
inheritance is desirable, nevertheless, the eugenic program stresses the
necessity for the production of a good physical type, and neglects to
note that it is far more important for society that people be of moral
worth. Character traits, not being inherited, religious and educational
programs and other means of moral training are intrinsically and socially of greater importance than breeding people of good physique.

It must also be noted that legal sterilization carries with it three
real dangers to society. First, mental deficients with sexual tendencies
will be a great menace to society, even though the danger of procreation be eliminated: extramarital relations will probably be increased,
and there will be an increased danger of infectious "social diseases."
Those suffering from these tendencies should certainly not be at large
in the community. Second, the world may be deprived of many useful
citizens, even if sterilization were only applied to those known to have
an inherited defect, or to be carriers of such a defect. Third, the
sterilization of certain persons might be carried out for emotional

---

[9] Cf. Haldane, J. B. S., *Heredity and Politics* (New York: W. W. Norton & Co.,
1938), pp. 108, 109.

reasons: people might offer to be sterilized for a material benefit of some kind; political or other enemies might be declared as defective in order to punish them by sterilization. The distinction between the normal and abnormal is so unscientifically subjective, and so much a matter of opinion or current ideology that the determination as to who should be sterilized is one which cannot be accurately determined. Even though the determiners endeavored to be scientifically accurate in designating only those of known inherited defects, errors would be made. There is also the danger of sterilization entering into the political sphere, as already stated, and if a demagogue were in power in any country, political opponents might be sterilized, or it might even be decided that those who profess a religious belief are inferior intellectually, and merit sterilization.

Apart from the above medical and social considerations, the practice of sterilization is to be condemned because it is entirely opposed to the natural law. One cannot deprive a person of his right to marry and live a normal family life with wife and children, for a mere probability of harm to a future generation. The State has no complete domination over man, and cannot deprive him of a natural function of the body for any economic or other benefit to others. Only as a possible punishment for a crime is mutilation by the State justified, and then only in proportion to the crime, if administered justly and with full consideration of all the objectives of punishment to which we shall refer in Chapter 26. Moreover, a man cannot voluntarily deprive himself of any part of his body, unless such sacrifice is imperative for his physical good. The Church forbids the marriage of the insane, for marriage is a contract, and the insane are incapable of making a contract. The Church also forbids the marriage of close relatives, which has the effect of preventing inherited recessive characteristics within a family from almost certainly becoming expressed openly, due to reduplication of the defective characteristic. Then, too, she strongly advises abstention from marriage for those with what is considered an inheritable disease or defect, although she does not forbid such a marriage. Man's liberty of action must not be impaired by bodily mutilation. The State may, indeed, take reasonable and lawful measures to prevent a possible degeneration of the race, but in so doing it cannot justly deprive a man of a function given him by God. The right of man to seek his happiness in marriage is a fundamental right, and the interest of the public demands that as many as possible should marry, since man is free to make use of this right, or to forego it, as he pleases, provided prudence is observed.

The only possible solution to the real problem provided by defectives is to search for the large number of those who are still unrecognized by medical authorities, and to provide correct medical care, training, and supervision, before such attention is too late. Certain deficients such as the seriously insane, some of the epileptics, and low-grade mental defectives might well be placed in colonies or institutions, and segregated from the opposite sex, so as to eliminate all possibility of marriage and perpetuation of their stock, without sterilization. In the same manner, society could be protected from those who persistently commit sexual offenses. Only in this way, and by sane counsel, can those with almost certain heritable defects be lawfully restrained from exercising their natural right to marry.

Pope Pius XI has written about sterilization as follows: "That pernicious practice must be condemned which closely touches upon the natural right of man to enter matrimony but affects also in a real way the welfare of the offspring. For there are some oversolicitous for the cause of eugenics, who not only give salutary counsel for more certainly procuring the strength and health of the future child — which, indeed, is not contrary to right reason — but put eugenics before aims of a higher order, and by public authority wish to prevent from marrying all those whom, even though naturally fit for marriage, they consider, according to the norms and conjectures of their investigations, would, through hereditary transmission, bring forth defective offspring. And more, they wish to legislate to deprive these of that natural faculty by medical action despite their unwillingness; and this they do not propose as an infliction of grave punishment under the authority of the State for a crime committed, nor to prevent future crimes by guilty persons, but against right and good they wish the civil authority to arrogate to itself a power over a faculty which it never had and can never legitimately possess.

"Those who act in this way are at fault in losing sight of the fact that the family is more sacred than the State and that men are begotten not for the earth and for time, but for heaven and eternity. Although often these individuals are to be dissuaded from entering into matrimony, certainly it is wrong to brand men with the stigma of crime because they contract marriage, on the ground that, despite the fact that they are in every respect capable of matrimony, they will give birth only to defective children, even though they use all care and diligence.

"Public magistrates have no direct power over the bodies of their subjects; therefore, where no crime has taken place and there is no cause present for grave punishment, they can never directly harm, or tamper with the integrity of the body, either for the reasons of eugenics or for any other reason. St. Thomas teaches this when, inquiring whether human judges for the sake of preventing future evils can inflict punishment, he admits that the power indeed exists as regards certain other forms of evil, but justly and properly denies it as regards the maiming of the body. 'No one who is guiltless may be punished by a human tribunal either by flogging to death, or mutilation, or by beating.'

"Furthermore, Christian doctrine establishes, and the light of reason makes it most clear, that private individuals have no other power over the members of their bodies than that which pertains to their natural ends; and they are not free to destroy or mutilate their members, or in any other way render themselves unfit for their natural functions, except when no other provision can be made for the good of the whole body."[10]

Birth Control

The most widespread of the eugenist tenets is the right of married people to restrict their offspring by artificial means, to a number which will permit the best possible care, education, and training, according to their state in life. Three reasons are usually given in justification of this doctrine of controlled births by artificial birth prevention:

1. *Economic Reasons.* It is stated that if people who cannot afford children forego having them, then no children will be brought into the world who cannot be given adequate training and care; those children who are born will then be wanted, and the care given them will insure that they will grow up strong, healthy, and happy. These economic reasons really had their rise in the writings of Thomas Robert Malthus (1766–1834) which we outlined in Chapter 6. Malthus' idea was that food supplies tend to increase only arithmetically, while population increases geometrically, unless there be such preventive checks to population increase as famine, disease, epidemics, and urban congestion. To avoid such disasters he advocated later marriages and marital restraint, and not the artificial controls which are now advocated under the name of "Neo-Malthusianism."

Yet so far as these economic arguments are concerned, it is noteworthy that conditions in the world at large are quite otherwise than those which Malthus envisaged: the population of the world is rapidly becoming stationary, instead of increasing, and if the present decline

---

[10] *Casti Connubii,* pp. 95, 96.

in births in many countries continues in the same proportion the world will have a decreased population to cope with.

Economically, too, a large population does not necessarily mean an unfavorable situation, for if men are more productive because of the development of their skill, or improved methods of work and the use of machines, a large population may lead to more income per head, instead of less. With a decreased population, less competition may well make progress much slower than the present time. A decreased population will lead to the need of fewer houses, and also less production, at least of the basic products of relatively inelastic individual demand (even if we keep on the same economic level and do not decline), hence demand will decrease for these basic products, including agricultural goods such as milk and flour, and the capital invested in agriculture and in the industries concerned will expect to get the same return as formerly. The present investments of capital in the then large amount of unneeded fixed capital goods will make fixed charges disproportionate to production and prices of goods will be increased; as the supply of capital will be greater than the demand, interest rates for new investments will be decreased; fewer people will, of course, be engaged in industry and trade; and the decreased demand for houses, and eventually for factories will bring about further unemployment in the building trades and all the heavy industries.

It may be said that if the economic savings resulting from machine-made goods are divided among a smaller population, it may well be that all will have a greater income than before to spend on a wider range of luxury goods, and that employment and capital in these newer industries will be benefited. Yet a decrease in births at the present time means a decrease in women of marriageable age in the future, and so even if the birth rate does not decline yet further, there will be a marked decrease in total births in the following generation. Internal markets, therefore, will be continuously reduced, and with the lessened international trade which seems likely to continue, there will be no expanding foreign markets to buy the surplus products, and unemployment and other economic disturbances will be the inevitable result. Moreover, with each new generation smaller than the last, and with the increased expectancy of life of people at the present time, the number of older people compared with young will be disproportionately greater with each generation. Added to the numbers of those normally considered old, will be those whom the mechanization of industry yearly causes to be retired from lucrative employment at a much earlier age than in former times. Unless their income has been sufficient to provide for such contingencies as old age and unemployment, these persons will be a charge on the younger members of the family, or upon the tax resources of the State. Each succeeding generation, therefore, will be obliged to shoulder an added burden of taxation and expense for the upkeep of the older generation. Temporarily, individual families which restrict their offspring may be better off from the economic viewpoint than their more prolific neighbors, but eventually the economic effects of restricted families will be disastrous.

2. *Physiological Reasons.* Another justification cited for the practice of birth control is that the wife's health is often seriously endangered by the sufferings and cares entailed by frequent childbirths, and a large family. Yet for the average woman the wear and tear is not in the childbearing, but in the child rearing, especially if a family attempts to "live up to the Joneses." Indeed, the health of the mother is usually actively promoted by conception, for in pregnancy a woman attains her complete physiological consummation, and the absorption of certain substances in sexual union have beneficial effects on her metabolism. A woman happily married and leading a normal married life is usually improved in health and general psychical welfare, for her whole system naturally and favorably reacts to marriage and conception, and often the mothers of large families live to a happy old age. As to frequent births, nature's spacing is generally about two years if a mother nurses her own child, for conception during the nursing period is the exception rather than the rule. It is, of course, well known that for the child itself numerous advantages are the result of natural nutrition. There is also another side to the picture: first, birth-control devices are not absolutely infallible, and children may still come from an irregular union where birth control is practised; second, the use of contraceptives may result in positive physical injury to the woman, and it often leads to permanent sterility, so that when children are wanted they are not obtained.

Yet it is true that some women are physically worn out by frequent childbearing, and Pope Pius XI has shown that he is fully aware of the dangers which sometimes threaten a mother's life: "As regards the evil use of matrimony, to pass over the arguments that are shameful, not infrequently others that are false and exaggerated are put forward. Holy Mother Church very well understands and clearly appreciates all that is said regarding the health of the mother and the danger to her life. And who would not grieve to think of these things? Who is not filled with the greatest admiration when he sees a mother risking her life with heroic fortitude, that she may preserve the life of the offspring which she has conceived? God alone, all bountiful and all merciful as He is, can reward her for the fulfillment of the office allotted to her by nature, and will assuredly repay her in a measure full to overflowing."[11]

3. *Social Reasons.* The third reason given in favor of birth prevention is the greater advantage which a smaller family usually possesses over a larger one in economic and social life. Eugenists claim that much of the poverty of the world is due to large families and many children to feed, clothe, and educate. Yet it is precisely those with larger incomes who usually have smaller families than others, although the reasons for this may be in no way connected with birth control, and if it were, the temptation to limit offspring may be very great because the middle class have to meet standards of education, clothing, and other expenditures, which poorer people are not "obliged" to incur by social convention. It is common knowledge, too, that those who practise this evil do not think so much of the welfare of the race, and of their offspring, as of their own personal comfort and convenience. Eugenists are aware of the dangers of a declining birth rate. Their aim is to improve the race and to keep the birth rate stationary. But how insure that those who are considered best able to bear children will have the requisite number of offspring to maintain the race at the present level? Because some people do not marry, die young, or are sterile, an average of 3.3 children per married couple seems to be necessary to insure that a nation's population will be maintained at a stationary level. Yet too many families have no children or none at all, or a maximum of one or two, and not since 1860 has the birth rate attained this 3.3 average, as the following statistics will show:

SIZE OF AVERAGE FAMILY IN THE UNITED STATES[12]

Year	No. of Persons Per Family
1860	5.3
1870	5.1
1880	5.0
1890	4.93
1900	4.69
1910	4.54
1920	4.34
1930	4.10

[11] *Casti Connubii,* p. 92.

[12] *Fifteenth Census of the U. S. Population,* Vol. VI, U. S. Dept. of Commerce, Bureau of the Census, 1933, p. 10. The term *family* includes husband, wife, children, and other relatives, visitors, and servants in the household at the time the census was taken. The actual population increase in the United States during these years is due, of course, to immigration and the increased expectancy of life at the present time.

Nor are the economic or social disadvantages of a large family greater than the moral benefits which accrue to parents and children in a good-sized family. In this daily life of such a household all the members learn to subordinate their wishes to those of others, they learn the virtues of unselfishness, devotion to others, self-reliance, self-control, in the very best and most natural of schools. There is less divorce among those with large families than among couples with few or no children as we shall show in the next chapter. And we might note that Washington was the first child of a family of six; Thomas Jefferson was the third child of a family of ten; Jefferson Davis was the tenth child of ten; Washington Irving the eleventh child of eleven; General Pershing the first of eleven; Nelson, the sixth child of eleven; Napoleon the fourth of ten; Sir Joshua Reynolds the seventh of eleven; Kant the fourth of nine; William Morris the third of nine; Carlyle the first of nine; Scott the fourth of twelve; Tennyson the fourth of twelve; Coleridge the tenth of ten; Beethoven the second of twelve; St. Francis de Sales the first of thirteen; St. Ignatius the thirteenth of thirteen; and St. Catherine of Siena, one of the greatest women of history, the twenty-fifth child of a family of twenty-five.

It must be pointed out, indeed, that an extension of knowledge of birth-control measures seems invariably to lead to an extension of immorality — certainly such practices destroy self-control and foster self-indulgence. That some feel justified in resorting to birth-control measures for economic reasons is, of course, true, but the remedy lies, not in the extension of knowledge of these measures, but in an improvement of the condition which makes them seem advisable.

The Natural Law. Thus far we have only given natural reasons why birth prevention is to be abhorred. There is, however, a more weighty reason to be found in the natural law. As we said at the beginning of Chapter 8, the sexual desire was implanted in man to give him an incentive for sexual intercourse, in order to insure the propagation of the race, just as we are given a hunger appetite to insure eating for bodily strength. Now, it is clearly contrary to reason to use an object for any other than its natural end. Birth-control measures make sexual pleasure, instead of the procreation of children, the basic purpose of the marriage act. They defeat the end of marriage, and degrade it to the level of an animal instinct. As we said earlier in the chapter, however, the Church does not teach that parents should bear children without thought of their welfare. She has ever advocated marital chastity, and has taught that self-discipline and self-denial form the basis of all happy unions, and that love should be ruled by reason. Marriage is a serious responsibility, and as far as possible human prudence should control the bringing of children into the world. Therefore, while birth-prevention measures can never be undertaken without sin, there is no sin, it is rather a virtue, that husband and wife should mutually agree to refrain for a time from the legitimate pleasure which is theirs by lawful marriage. When, therefore, for any reasons whatsoever, a couple find it advisable not to have children for a time, the only possible birth control that is allowed by the law of nature is the exercise of self-restraint. This is true birth control: the birth control which is thus described in popular language is birth prevention and the mere exercise of lust.[13]

EXCESS OF BIRTHS OVER DEATHS[14]

Year	Excess of Births Over Deaths	Rate Per Thousand of Population Births	Deaths
1920	672,742	23.7	13.1
1921	888,750	24.2	11.7
1922	836,366	22.3	11.8
1923	800,409	22.2	12.3
1924	923,620	22.4	11.7
1925	848,362	21.5	11.8
1926	762,557	20.7	12.2
1927	961,031	20.6	11.4
1928	871,162	19.8	12.0
1929	800,163	18.9	11.9
1930	882,591	18.9	11.3
1931	811,355	18.0	11.1
1932	780,773	17.4	10.9
1933	739,126	16.5	10.7
1934	770,733	17.1	11.0
1935	762,353	16.9	10.9

Current Population Problems

Although some countries are overpopulated today, the problem of most nations is not the fear of Malthus, that famine and other checks must needs limit a population rapidly outgrowing its food supplies, but rather that the diminishing birth rates will soon increase an

---

[13] With certain reservations involving the primary end of marriage, it is, of course, permissible to make use of the so-called "safe period": to practise abstinence during those days of the month when conception is more certain. This does not involve the use of contraceptives, with their risk to physical and mental health; sex love finds its natural expression; and continence is practised. For further details the reader is referred to such books as H. Sutherland, *The Laws of Life;* Coucke & Walsh, *The Sterile Period in Family Life* (New York: Jos. Wagner); L. J. Latz, *The Rhythm* (Chicago: Latz Foundation).

[14] *Statistical Abstract of the United States,* 1937, p. 85.

economic problem such as we discussed under the topic of birth control. The size of the average family in the United States has very steadily declined for the past seventy years, as the statistics already quoted have shown. The decline in the rate of population growth is also evidenced by census statistics, which demonstrate the decrease in the birth rate, and the increase in longevity. Unless the present restrictions on immigration are modified, it would seem that within another generation deaths will balance births.

PERCENTAGE OF POPULATION SIXTY-FIVE YEARS
OF AGE AND OVER[15]

1880	1890	1900	1910	1920	1930
2.3	3.8	4.1	4.2	4.7	5.4

The birth-rate decline of recent years is due to a variety of factors: First of all, there is the question of artificial limitation of families by birth control. Although birth control in one form or another has been known for a very long period of time,[16] nevertheless it seems true that its practice is more widespread today than in times past, and certainly more widespread than in the immediate past. A number of reasons seem to be responsible for this increase in immorality. Most important of all reasons is the decline in religious principles and hence in supernatural motives for self-control. Another reason is the higher standard of living of today, the rise in living costs, and the growth of individualistic selfishness, which makes it seem economically advantageous to have small families, or none at all, so as to avoid the added burden of expenses due to bearing and raising children. The present judgment of worth by success also leads many to ambition, success for themselves and their children, and to gain this end through family limitation. Again, the restriction of child labor, coupled with the tendency to live in cities, means that children are an expense until a relatively late age, and are usually unable to help the family's economic situation by working around the home, or to add to the family finances by outside employment. Restricted city housing accommodation may also be a consideration in the limitation of offspring, on account of the expense of room rent, or the impossibility of finding adequately large houses or apartments where landlords will consent to the presence of children. Still another factor may be the present lack of effective

---

[15] *Fifteenth Census of the U. S. Population:* Vol. II, U. S. Dept. of Commerce, U. S. Bureau of the Census, 1933, p. 566.
[16] Cf. Gen. 38:8–10.

restrictions against sending birth-control literature through the mails, despite the Federal Postal Law of 1873. Local authorities now allow birth-control appliances to be sold in stores, articles to be published in magazines, and centers to be established where information is obtainable. Besides, a number of medical schools now instruct student doctors in birth-control practices. The feminist movement of this century has led women to seek financial independence, with consequently greater numbers of them working outside the home. Some women desire to maintain this independence after married life, and restrict their family in order to be able to do so. Again, some married women must work because their husbands cannot or do not earn a living wage, and restrict the number of their children so as to be free to continue in their employment. Mrs. Barbara Wootton's severe indictment of our modern economic system seems amply justified. She says with truth: "The decline in reproduction rates of industrial peoples tells its tale; for it is difficult to believe that a pattern of life is satisfying — more satisfying than any imaginable alternative — when those who adopt it are everywhere found, sooner or later, unable or unwilling to reproduce their numbers. Whether the explanation of declining fertility is itself physiological or psychological, it is sufficient criticism on any civilization that it should spell extinction for those who live under it. There must be something — and something pretty fundamental — wrong, if our ways of living are such as to inhibit our normal animal function of reproduction; and there must be something equally wrong, if our judgment of the world that we have experienced is so adverse that we are reluctant to beget children into it."[17]

It must not be thought, however, that birth control is wholly responsible for the declining birth rate. The rate in Ireland is equally on a decline, and yet birth-control practices seem to be practically unknown there. Autopsies show that the female organism is producing the same number of ova as before, but there may be a fundamental biological process by which when the activity of the protoplasm reaches a level of reproduction, it may decline. Women are probably less fertile than they were formerly, on account of the increased strain under which they live, particularly in our cities. Certainly the dimensions of their pelvis is reduced in size, and of recent years there is a marked deterioration in the female organism. Then Doubleday's law may be operating: that the birth rate tends to fall under conditions of ease and to increase under harsher circumstances. The better living

---

[17] Barbara Wootton, *Lament for Economics* (Farrar & Rinehart, 1938), pp. 205, 206.

conditions of today may bring about this effect. Rising standards in living and in education, and the greater emancipation of women, have also led to marriages being postponed to a later date than formerly, and since women are more fecund in the earlier years, later marriages not only lead to proportionately fewer children, but even to fewer children than the number which might be deducted because of the portion of the mature period which was passed in celibacy. Abortions, of course, also decrease births, and the number of these is said to be great, although they certainly cannot be accurately computed. Abortion is murder, and can never be tolerated.[18] A number of natural evils also attend the practice of abortion: the danger of infection is very great, and sometimes the woman is permanently disabled or rendered sterile; moreover, her nervous system receives a shock which may render her emotionally unstable and lead to mental disorders.

As must be evident to the reader of this chapter, the whole question of population presents problems of biology, psychology, economics, and sociology which merit much deeper study than could be given here.

---

[18] Cf. Gen. 4:10; Exod. 23:7; Matt. 19:18.

CHAPTER 25

PROBLEMS OF FAMILY LIFE

Materialism, the Root of Family Problems

IN RECENT years there have been drastic moral, economic, and social changes in family life. Domestic society lacks its former unity and affectionate cohesion. There are fewer children, and often none at all, to cement the parents' love and provide a bond to preserve family unity despite the misunderstandings that inevitably occur. By many, divorce is considered the natural remedy for what might be only passing conjugal misunderstandings. Economic and social changes have inevitably led to a disruption of harmony and co-operation. Indeed, it seems mainly the philosophy of *laissez faire* and of materialism which has led to the current situation. In our present economy of production for exchange rather than use, and under our present standards of material well-being the gaining of money is considered more important than decent human living.

The seriousness of the situation is evident when it is realized that if the family, the most important social unit of society, lacks harmonious integration, individuals will grow up without discipline and without respect for authority and will inevitably act as a disintegrating force within the State, so that the State will also come to lack necessary order and social union. The essence of happy and orderly home life is harmony.

Economic Changes in Family Life

Just prior to what is called the industrial revolution, with the advent of the modern capitalistic regime, the economic order was known as the domestic system. The majority of people were not herded together in cities, as now, but lived by the cultivation of the soil. Even those who were engaged in industry carried on their occupation in or about the home. Thus, all day long, the family was united; parents and children worked and played together. Although there were many defects in the system, nevertheless the economic and social interests of all the members of the family were identical. Mutual helpfulness, co-operation, and trust were the results.

With the growth of the capitalistic organization of economic life, there came a change from family production to production in workshops and factories. The result was the congregation of families in towns, to be nearer the father's business. Not only did this lead to overcrowded housing conditions and unnatural family life, but it broke up the interdependence and unity of the family circle. The average father, at the present time, must needs spend the greater part of the day working outside the home, in order to gain a livelihood. When he returns after his day's work, he is too tired to take full advantage of the enjoyment he might derive from the society of his family. The wife, also, frequently seeks remunerative employment outside the home, and so leaves the children for long periods to their own devices. Married women sometimes work because home life is irksome to them, but usually because under our present economic system the husband does not earn a living wage. In earlier times the wife could supplement her husband's earnings by growing garden produce, and by making the family's clothing, soap, canned provisions, and many other household supplies. Today, most of the household needs are purchased in their finished state, because housing accommodation is often too limited to permit of such activities, and also because mass production enables them to be purchased cheaply, and extensive advertising successfully induces the housewife not to make homemade supplies. Mechanized appliances in the home in conjunction with the smaller sized houses of today, also give women more free time, which they sometimes choose to spend in remunerative work outside, or in outside amusements and recreation. For some women, the interests apart from the home give them a greater ability to create an interesting home environment. Often, however, their homemaking capacity is impaired by the lesser attachment of many modern women to the affairs of their family circle. The laborsaving devices of today also give the children fewer tasks to perform to aid their parents, so that the spirit of cooperation fostered by such duties is not developed. And again, under modern capitalism girls who formerly would have stayed at home to learn houshould management can find remunerative employment at office work and other occupations, and so grow somewhat apart from the family circle and its training as future homemakers.

Indeed, one of the anomalies of our present system is that mothers and children often work outside the home, to earn money with which to purchase ready prepared goods, whereas if they stayed at home, raised vegetables in a garden, canned their own food, made many of the goods now bought in stores, the necessary savings would be effected, and they would be enabled to remain in the natural environment of the home instead of the artificial atmosphere of the factory and workshop. Economic ideology and economic conditions are largely responsible for the fact that family life is much less stable than in former years.

The Effects of City Life

We have already stated that where men work in cities, away from the family circle, the unity of the family is affected. City life, however, has other evil effects. To the moral and physical influence of overcrowded housing conditions we shall refer separately. Moreover, it must be noted that city life is unnatural to man, who develops best in spacious surroundings and fresh air. Recreation is essential for man's well-being, and in city slums, and even in the apartment houses of the well-to-do, facilities for healthful recreation are limited, if not wholly absent. Members of the family, therefore, must spend their leisure hours largely outside the home. For the satisfaction of their recreational needs they are, indeed, for the most part at the mercy of commercial undertakings. Not only do morals suffer as a consequence of this, but the interdependence of the various members of the family, already affected by the changed economic system, decreases still more.

The provision of commercialized recreation outside of the home and the lack of normal family life have also led to a great restlessness among the population. People crave for ever-increasing pleasure and enjoyment, and the mother and other members of the family become increasingly less attached to the home. Obviously, in these circumstances there is less adequate home training of children and less unity within the family circle.

City life has also led to social competition, with the result that a person's worth is more often judged by the wealth he possesses or appears to possess, than by his moral qualities. Thrift and frugality have become almost forgotten virtues in many city homes, and thus the family becomes less and less united, and dissensions and disputes are more frequent.

Lack of Adequate Preparation for Married Life

Economic life, at present spent mostly outside the family circle, in factory, workshop, office, or store, has had an extremely harmful effect on the preparation of children by parents for marriage and bringing up children. Away at school or at work for the greater part of the day, during the years when this training would be more naturally obtained, modern boys and girls do not learn the requisites of homemaking. The family certainly has more chances of success if the man can turn his hand to household matters when occasion demands, but this training is essential for a woman, on whom homemaking more naturally devolves. An adequate knowledge of how to run a house and care for husband and children is not easily learned, and requires more time than is normally possible under present-day conditions. In some aspects, housekeeping today requires much more training than in previous years, for in place of the more or less trustworthy local dealers, the modern woman must choose her supplies from among an almost bewildering number of labeled brands, and must usually purchase them in stores run by managers hired by corporations who do not always pay attention to her needs as formerly.

Again, although every mother should, of course, have some time for recreation, nevertheless, where she is occupied around the home for the greater part of the day, she provides a family bond, and earns an appreciation from her husband and offspring, which normally does not lead to a disrupted home. It is to be noted, however, that even where a girl does not go out to earn her livelihood before marriage, but stays at home, the cramped living quarters of most city dwellings, the labor-saving devices, and other amenities of modern life obviate any thorough training in domestic duties. This means the probable elimination of the spirit of co-operation which such duties foster. It means, too, that women have more leisure time at their disposal which, to be pleasantly employed must, under normal city conditions, be spent outside the home, thus destroying one other bond of family union.

Nor is our present school system wholly without blame. Although we cannot but welcome the extension of education, nevertheless, the family bond was much more stable and enduring when the child was at home during a great part of the day. His presence at home from his earliest years also insured an early training in domestic needs. A remedy, of course, lies in the school giving more attention to studies which engender homemaking qualities, both moral and manual.

Changed Religious Ideals

Side by side with economic and social transformations within the family, have grown up spiritual change. Many parents no longer possess the spirit of filial piety toward God which once was usual. This loss of religious spirit has resulted in a lack of true understanding of the holiness of family life, and of the moral duties and obligations of parents and teachers.

Family life entails many sacrifices, and with the waning of religious ideals has come a decline in the spirit of self-forgetfulness which is necessary on the part of all members of a family for the maintenance of family unity and love. The decadence in religious ideals has, therefore, loosened family bonds to the detriment of domestic society. The increase of selfishness, the decline in filial respect, the diminution of parental sense of responsibility toward their children as charges for which they are responsible to God, have all led to a lack of reverence toward the sacredness of family life. Where parents do not control their emotions and their moods, there can be no adequate harmony in the home. Children who are not brought up in a spirit of reverence toward their parents, are not inclined to obey authority in other quarters, be it that of the State or of a minor social group. Children and parents who do not exercise a sense of social responsibility and co-operation within the home circle, cannot be expected to be good and useful members of society, reverencing and recognizing the social rights of others, and fulfilling their social obligations.

Imprudent Choice of Marriage

In a passage in the *Casti Connubii* encyclical, already quoted in the earlier chapter on the Family, Pope Pius XI clearly showed the necessity of prudence and foresight before marriage. We should not like to go back to the times when parents chose husbands for their daughters, and wives for their sons, without consulting their children (a practice still to be found in many countries), yet it is surprising to note that these "arranged marriages" seem to have been proportionately more successful than many present-day marriages undertaken by children without parental consent. It would seem that more prudence and foresight in the choice of a mate might avert many possibly unsuccessful marriages.

Smaller Families Have Also Caused Domestic Disunion

The decline in the number of children in the modern family is, of course, due to a variety of causes. Cramped living quarters are an inducement to limit the size of the family; working wives and also the selfish and pleasure-seeking often do not have children. Then again, the rush of modern-day life and later marriages are responsible for fewer births. Children cement parental love, and oftentimes preserve unity in a family when the parents disagree. Divorces are not so lightly undertaken if there are children to be thought of. They are much more likely to occur if there is only one child to arrange for, or none at all.

The following table shows the truth of these remarks (Official statistics later than 1932 are not available).

NUMBER OF CHILDREN IN FAMILIES TO WHICH DIVORCES WERE GRANTED[1]

	1932	1931	Per Cent 1932	1931
No children	88,449	103,882	55.4	57.0
One child	34,598	38,608	21.7	21.2
Two children...................	15,831	18,079	9.9	9.9
Three children...................	6,113	7,185	3.8	3.9
Four children...................	2,521	3,147	1.6	1.7
Five children...................	1,058	1,249	0.7	0.7
Six children	498	595	0.3	0.3
Seven children..................	234	275	0.1	0.2
Eight children..................	96	103	0.1	0.1
Nine or more children...........	66	78		
No report as to children.........	10,246	9,002	6.4	4.9
Totals	159,710	182,203	100.0	100.0

Lax Divorce Laws and Marriage Legislation

Unhappy marriages are much more frequent when the legal ceremony is easily arranged, without the safeguards afforded by the publication of bans and by the requirement of parental consent for those under age, and a certain minimum time of residence in the district. Lax marriage legislation is the outcome of the exaggerated individualistic liberalism of modern times, from which spring most of our present economic and social problems. The good and the rights of the many, of society, are submerged in this individualism, and "living one's own life" is the logical consequence, with the supposed right to choose, reject, and interpret the laws of Church and State according to individual desire. Such legislation leads to hasty unions, with consequent incentive to lack of prudence. Similarly, husband and wife will be tempted to give reign to their emotions and to seek divorce on very slight pretexts when divorce is easily obtained. If it is difficult to secure divorce, there is much more likelihood that quarrels and dissensions will be forgiven when time has softened the misunderstanding.

Most larger communities in the United States now have what are known as Courts of Domestic Relations, of which the first was founded in Buffalo, New York, in 1910. Usually these special courts deal with all cases involving domestic quarrels and dissensions, nonsupport of wife and family, and bastardy. There is usually a social-service de-

[1] Cf. *Marriage and Divorce,* Eleventh Annual Report, 1932. U. S. Dept. of Commerce, 1934, p. 6.

partment attached to these courts, whose members examine each case which comes before it for divorce or separation, and endeavor to show the husband and wife where compromise is possible. The department's efforts often result in private reconciliations without any ensuing court trial.

Since the welfare of the State depends upon the integrity of family life, it is to its own interests to protect the sanctity of marriage and not to foster a low regard for marriage nor make divorce easy to obtain. And since the protection of families and individuals within them is the *raison d'être* of the State's existence, as we have so often said, the State should do all it can toward eliminating conditions which weaken the family, and toward building up favorable conditions for healthy family life. Of course, this does not mean that the State should interfere in family life in an unnecessary manner, but merely that it should carry out its duties of protection and development where this aid is needed and positively required.

Housing and Its Effects on Family Life

It seems in place to digress somewhat at this moment to discuss the important modern problem of housing conditions at the present time. It is easy to realize that four walls and physical environment do not make the "home" and that luxurious surroundings are not essential or even desirable for a family's welfare and happiness; too often these things impart a hotel atmosphere, and the home spirit is lacking. The word *home* describes something difficult to define but the meaning of which all understand; it should never be a place in which merely to eat and rest, but rather the inner sanctuary of the family, the abode where all members of the family delight to be, where they can meet in privacy, enjoy one another's company, and develop a normal family social group which is the most intimate and most important of all social groups in the world. It should be the most comfortable and satisfying abode for the parents and adult members, and the happiest of all places for children. If the home is a failure, the family is disorganized; and if the families of the State are not united in peace, harmony, and contentment, the State will never prosper. Although we ought not overestimate the importance of environment, nevertheless social and psychological environmental influence is very closely bound up with one's physical surroundings. Joy, domestic contentment, industrial efficiency, high standards of morality, good health, all depend in large measure upon favorable housing conditions; that is, upon the provision for each family of a modestly comfortable and comely home.

Minimum housing requirements. The ideal to be aimed at in housing is that every family should live in clean and decent surroundings, with accommodations providing at least the essentials for health, family life, and the preservation of morality. Every family should have a house which furnishes protection against the elements of nature, with a kitchen and separate sleeping accommodation for the sexes. There should be windows in every room, so that there is enough light and air; and no families should be obliged to sleep in cellars or dark rooms without windows. Water should be obtainable within the house, and in tenement buildings it should be in an easily accessible and public place if each family is not provided with its own supply, which is, of course, desirable. Every family should have its own bathroom and toilet, and, preferably, its own garden also. To insure good air and recreational facilities for children and adolescents, open spaces and, if possible, supervised recreation grounds, should be easily accessible.

Actual conditions. There still exist in all civilized countries thousands of poor families who live under entirely inadequate housing conditions. Often they inhabit tenements where, perhaps, each room is made to house an entire family and serve the triple function of kitchen, parlor, and bedroom for all; where there are filthy yards, halls, stairways, and public toilets; and where the water supply is a long way from each "home." Sometimes rooms which house families have no windows; other rooms look out on narrow sunless courts; frequently public authorities add injustice to the lot of these slum dwellers by bad provision of street lighting and cleaning; odors arise from all sides; there is often excessive noise in the streets and in neighboring rooms; and since the rooms themselves are poorly ventilated, overcrowded, and dirty, the air in them is vitiated and the surroundings drab and cheerless. The serious overcrowding makes it impossible to provide for the proper separation of the sexes, to keep the home clean, or to have any privacy in those times when a short period of solitude would prevent the incessant close association of others getting on one's nerves. Land overcrowding results not only in lack of air, but also in inadequate parks or open-air playgrounds, so that the street is the only alternative to the probable unhealthy and uncongenial atmosphere of the home. Sometimes single-family houses in the country may have conditions as bad as those we have just described, with serious overcrowding of rooms, insufficient protection against the elements, the extremes of heat and cold, impure water supply, and inadequate drainage and sanitation. In the country, however, the spirit of a person is not so stultified as in the city, with the lack of nature's beauty, fresh air, and other advantages of country life.

The grave social results of bad housing. Because of such conditions as we have described, few precautions can be taken against contagion, and the very atmosphere makes for a poor physical condition, so that it is small wonder that disease of all descriptions is rife in slum areas, and ill health is the rule rather than the exception. The worker in poor health, without the relaxation from his labor which would be provided by a peaceful home, and unable to get refreshing sleep, becomes inefficient at his work, and thus costs the country money not only in reduced economic output, but also in poor relief. It is little wonder, too, that many adults turn to drink, gambling, and narcotics as a temporary distraction from their surroundings; that parents, with jarred nerves, treat their children cruelly, or resort to divorce or separation; that since those of the opposite sex must sleep in the same room, immorality is frequent; that children, with no joyful home to attract them, with the street as their playground and bad companions as their playmates, often grow up undisciplined, become rebellious against law and order and those better off than they, too often develop habits of delinquency, crime, and immorality. Indeed, the cost to the State for the upkeep of hospitals, prisons, reformatories, and the relief of the poor, in consequence of bad housing, is appalling.

The causes of overcrowding. Again, it would seem that our modern capitalistic ideology and economic organization are responsible for the evils we have noted. The introduction of the factory system was one of the earliest causes of bad housing conditions, leading as it did to a desire for accommodation near the place of work, and hence to a scarcity of building space. The poorer workers seeking to live near their place of employment in order to save time and traveling expenses as well, could afford only a minimum of rent in return for a roof over their heads. The desire for accommodation in these factory areas, and for many years the great influx of immigrants to the poorer quarters of large cities, led to competition for room space and hence to greatly increased rents. These high rents charged to workers resulted not only in what is known as land overcrowding, but also in room overcrowding, families even being obliged to share one room with a lodger to help them pay the rent. Workers tolerated these conditions either because they were ignorant that better conditions might be found elsewhere, or because they were unwilling to move to the suburbs and thus cut themselves off from the friendliness of neighbors and the brightness and distractions provided by the crowded city streets; sometimes they were unable to pay the cost of removal or the daily traveling expenses entailed by residence in another district of the town.

The greed of landlords is another frequent cause of bad housing conditions. The provision of housing has nearly always been left to private enterprise, and the landlords who built for profit were anxious to make as much money as they could. They therefore charged the highest possible rents, and usually gave in return a minimum of improvements and repairs. In the rural districts, where only low rents were obtainable because of the poor wages paid to the farm laborers, landlords did as little repair work as they could in order to get what they considered a fitting return on their capital.

The payment of a living wage and better housing legislation would largely eradicate these two causes of the housing evil. If our economic system were different from the present one, if all workers received a living wage, they could pay the higher rents necessary for better accommodation, and could also afford to take advantage of the new cheaper traveling accommodation to the suburbs of all our large towns.

The absence of improved housing legislation, which is indeed, a third cause of bad housing, is chiefly due to the indifference of the voting public. Citizens should see to it that town planning and zoning are undertaken by all cities, so that overcrowding will not take place in the future. This will be possible if, together with these zoning plans, they likewise insist on legislation to make landlords conform to city development plans, setting forth minimum requirements for all new buildings, and specifying improvements which must be made in existing slum areas. Citizens should see that competent and reliable building inspectors are appointed, and they should foster co-operative building-and-loan societies which enable workers to buy their own homes.

While the foregoing causes are the main reasons for bad housing, the tenants themselves are sometimes responsible for the conditions. The way to overcome their deficiencies is principally by suitable education of children in the schools, through some educational work which can be done through parish societies, settlement houses, or other agencies. Particularly a girl needs to realize that since the home is the woman's workshop, and she spends more time in it each day than the rest of the family, it is to her own advantage to keep it clean, healthy, beautiful, and comfortable. She needs also to realize that it is not only to her advantage to do this, but also her duty, for she is the central pivot of the family, and only if there is a bright and cheerful house for her children and husband to come to, will her family be united, satisfied, and safe from the dangers of recreation sought outside the home. Courses in homemaking are sometimes provided for girls in the school. All students need to be taught that in the home the tenant has actual duties and responsibilities, not only toward himself and his family, but also toward his neighbor and his landlord. Yet it may well be better if, apart from a general philosophy of homemaking and social responsibility to family, landlord, and all other persons with whom one has dealings, the school devoted itself mainly to the task of imparting the more theoretical knowledge to which it confined itself in former times. The adult education of girls and mothers might well be much more successful from the practical viewpoint, than the expenditure of money on younger people to obtain skills in the schools. The mothers might be taught how, in turn, to teach their children the skills of homemaking, and in this way the home itself would be strengthened, and desirable results obtained.

Landlords whose tenants are to blame for much of the dirty and unsightly conditions of slumland, might perhaps find it to their advantage to employ intelligent women rent collectors. These could be specially trained not only to instruct the tenant in homemaking, but also to observe any necessary repairs which the landlord himself should make. With the help of Ruskin, this idea was first carried into effect in England in 1865, by Miss Octavia Hill, and her well-known organization still continues the work. In the United States, the Better Housing League aims at educating tenants and the public in better housing conditions. Visiting housekeepers in poorer districts can perform a similar service, but they do not collect rents.

Another remedy of the housing question lies in the provision of cheap residential clubs for poorly paid unmarried men and women, where they can live in congenial surroundings at a minimum of cost.

Finally, where overcrowding in an area is beyond improvement, city authorities may find it necessary to formulate a settlement plan, and help families from slum areas to settle in the suburbs or in rural districts elsewhere.

The Federal Government has done much to improve housing conditions in the United States within recent years.[2] The Home Loan Bank Act of 1932, the Home Owners Loan Act of 1933, and the Federal Housing Act of 1934 have all helped home owners to get loans on their property, or to maintain existing mortgages on which they were tem-

---

[2] Cf. *Fourth Annual Report of the Federal Housing Administration,* Year ending Dec. 31, 1937. U. S. Govt. Printing Office, Washington, D. C., 1938.

porarily unable to meet the charges. Loans were also encouraged by
Federal aid for the construction of new buildings, and the newly
established Division of Subsistence Homesteads which was made part
of the United States Department of the Interior under the NRA legislation in 1933, has done much to alleviate economic distress among
certain groups, by assisting them to establish themselves on
the land.

The important United States Housing Act of 1937 amended in 1938,
was passed to assist those localities who wish to do so to eliminate
unsafe and insanitary housing conditions, to abolish their slums, and
to provide "decent, safe, and sanitary dwellings for families of low
income." It is administered by the United States Housing Authority,
and it is hoped that the Act will stimulate business activity, and
eliminate unemployment, too. All Federal housing projects, funds,
property, and employees of the Federal Emergency Administration of
Public Works has been transferred to the new United States Housing
Authority, which is empowered to make capital grants for the construction of low-rent-housing and for slum-clearance projects.

Need for a Re-establishment of Higher Family Ideals

It will be evident from the foregoing discussion of some of the
causes for present-day decadence in family life, that a re-establishment
of higher ideals regarding the family is essential to the true progress
of society, as is also an improvement in the economic condition of the
poor. We might summarize by saying that the first requisite for reform is the restoration of religious ideals and a true comprehension
of the dignity of successful married life and of parenthood, as discussed
at the end of Chapter 8. When this dignity is realized once more,
preparation for marriage will become more adequate, there will be
greater prudence in selecting a partner, divorce will not be considerd
as an honorable way out of a domestic difficulty, parents and children
will come to regard the home as a home in the true sense of the word,
and will be less inclined to seek friendship and amusement elsewhere.
To attain all this the sure remedy would be a restoration of religious
principles. Such a remedy would not only affect man's aspirations and
his outlook, but his family life would be improved in other ways. If
high ideals of justice and of the human worth of the individual could
also be inculcated into citizens, we might then see the general payment
of a living wage, sufficient to maintain a wife and children in the home;
housing conditions would be improved; and more material incentives
could be provided within the home to attract the members to it.

Divorce

Since the greatest evidence of family disintegration is the increasing number of divorces of the present day, we shall devote the rest of the chapter to a consideration of this subject. The percentage of divorces in the United States is so very much higher than in any other country in the world that it is proving a severe menace to family life here, and of necessity must soon affect the welfare of the entire nation.[3]

The increase in divorce will be evident from the following tables. Unfortunately official statistics later than 1932 are not available for the exact ratio of divorces to marriages, as the Department of Commerce ceased to issue them, for reasons of economy, after the year 1934. A private endeavor was made to bring these statistics up to date for the years 1933, 1934, and 1935,[4] but as all the states were not included these findings are of value only in indicating trends generally.

Year	No. of Divorces Per 1000 of Total Population[5]	No. of Divorces Per 100 Marriages Performed[6]
1890	0.53	5.9
1895	0.58	6.5
1900	0.73	7.9
1905	0.82	8.2
1910	0.90	8.8
1915	1.05	10.4
1920	1.60	13.4
1925	1.53	14.8
1930	1.56	17.0
1931	1.48	17.3
1932	1.28	16.3

---

[3] Comparative divorce rates have been computed by Strachey, R., "Current Social Statistics: Marriage and Divorce," *The Political Quarterly,* Vol. VIII, Jan.–Mar., 1937, pp. 93, 94. Giving "the latest figures available" he quotes the following number of divorces per 100 families in each country:

United States	16.3	Finland	4.9
Austria	14.4	Jugoslavia	4.7
Japan	10.1	Norway	4.4
Latvia	9.5	Belgium	4.0
Switzerland	9.4	Australia	3.9
Denmark	8.6	Czechoslovakia	3.9
Germany	8.3	Portugal	1.8
New Zealand	7.5	Scotland	1.5
France	6.6	Canada	1.4
South Africa	6.4	England and Wales	1.3
Netherlands	5.2		

[4] S. A. Stouffer and Lyle M. Spencer, "Marriage and Divorce in Recent Years," *Annals of the American Academy of Political and Social Science,* November, 1936, pp. 56–69, quoted in the *Statistical Abstract of the United States,* 1937, p. 93.

[5] *Marriage and Divorce,* Eleventh Annual Report, 1932. U. S. Dept. of Commerce, 1934.

[6] *Ibid.,* p. 1.

COMPARATIVE MARRIAGE AND DIVORCE STATISTICS[7]

	1930	1931	1932
Population, estimate of July 1..............	123,191,000	124,070,000	124,822,000
Marriages	1,126,856	1,060,194	981,903
No. per thousand of population...........	9.15	8.55	7.87
No. per thousand of population 15 years old and over.................	12.95	12.10	11.13
Divorces			
No. per thousand of population...........	191,591	183,664	160,338
No. per 100 marriages...................	17.00	1.73	16.3

CAUSES FOR DIVORCES GRANTED IN 1932[8]

Divorce Granted to Husband	Per Cent of Total Causes	Divorce Granted to Wife	Per Cent of Total Causes
Desertion	42.6	Cruelty	45.6
Cruelty	36.3	Desertion	22.8
Adultery	9.8	Adultery	6.2
Drunkenness	0.3	Failure to Provide.........	5.7
Combination of above causes	4.1	Drunkenness	1.8
All other causes...........	6.9	Combination of above causes	9.5
		All other causes...........	8.4
Total	100.0	Total	100.0

Marriage is not a private contract to be left to the consent and good pleasure of both parties, and to be dissolved for any reason whatsoever. It is a social obligation freely undertaken by two persons because of the need implanted in man for married life and for domestic unity and love. Just as it is plain that the family can only best develop when it is monogamous so it must be evident that where divorce can be obtained on the slightest pretext, the whole family suffers. We showed in Chapter 8 that for natural reasons alone it may be proved that the family was originally intended to be monogamous, and that wherever polygamy is permitted it is never the best for society as a whole. Divorce is thus against the natural law of monogamy. Strict monogamy no longer exists in a comunity where frequent divorce occurs, and the present permission given by civil authority for divorce

---

[7] Estimates for 1933–1935 give marriage and divorce statistics as follows (cf. *Statistical Abstract of the United States*, 1937, p. 93):

Year	No. of Marriages	No. of Divorces Per 100 Marriages
1933	1,098,000	15.0
1934	1,302,000	15.7
1935	1,327,000	16.4

[8] *Marriage and Divorce*, Eleventh Annual Report, 1932. U. S. Dept. of Commerce, 1934, p. 6. It is, of course, to be noted that the "causes" for divorce are often agreed upon by the parties concerned, as convenient reasons to give the courts.

is, therefore, contrary to man's natural welfare. Divorce is, indeed, one of society's greatest evils. The children in a divorced family suffer most, for they are deprived of the loving care and help of a normal family life. The training of both the father and the mother ordinarily are needed for the complete development of a child: the mother's influence is, perhaps, strongest in the earlier years of childhood, and the father's during the adolescent period, but the influence of both parents, with their differing outlooks and temperaments, is, as we said, needed for full development. Moreover, there is greater security and peace in marriage if neither party has to fear that one will be unfaithful and leave him unsupported in old age. The child, too, grows best in an atmosphere of tranquillity and stability, so that he can have loving confidence in the support of his parents, and has no uncertainty about the interest of his parents in his welfare or is not torn with doubt as to the respective merits of either. Many children of divorced parents fail to receive the training necessary for useful social and economic life. Others, unable to respect their parents, develop a disrespect for all law. Only too often the cause of juvenile delinquency, crime, and poverty, may be traced to the lack of a normal home life in early years. Frequently, too, the child's mental health is seriously impaired, for not only is there the serious adjustment to be made after the divorce has taken place, but one must take into account the "scenes" which preceded it, the insecurity, suspicion, and hostility which the parents most probably displayed before the child on many occasions before separation was agreed upon. Some people consider that divorce is better for the child's mental health than the scenes which may occur between those temperamentally unsuited to each other, who remain in wedlock. It is very true that parents should not permit themselves seriously to lose control of their emotions before their children. Yet one must further take into consideration the effects of the public scandal of divorce, no less than the attitude and the gossip of neighbors and relatives, which cannot escape the child's notice, and may intensify his feelings of inferiority and insecurity. Pope Pius XI clearly shows the natural reasons why divorce is to be avoided:

"To revert again to the expressions of Our Predecessor, it is hardly necessary to point out what an amount of good is involved in the absolute indissolubility of wedlock and what a train of evil follows upon divorce. Whenever the marriage bond remains intact, then we find marriages contracted with a sense of safety and security, while, when separations are considered and the dangers of divorce are present, the marriage contract itself becomes insecure, or at least gives ground for anxieties and surprises. On the one hand we see a wonderful strengthening of good will and co-operation in the daily life of husband and wife, while, on the other, both of these are miserably weakened by the presence of a facility for divorce. Here we have at a very opportune moment a source of help by which both parties are enabled to preserve their purity and loyalty; there we find harmful inducements to unfaithfulness. On this side we find the birth of children and their tuition and upbringing effectively promoted, many avenues of discord closed among families and relations, and the beginnings of rivalry and jealousy easily suppressed; on that, very great obstacles to the birth of children and their education, and many occasions of quarrels, and seeds of jealousy are sown everywhere. Finally, but especially, the dignity and position of women in civil and domestic society is reinstated by the former; while by the latter it is shamefully lowered and the danger is incurred 'of their being considered outcasts, slaves of the lust of men.'

"To conclude with the very important words of Leo XIII, since the destruction of family life 'and the loss of national wealth is brought about more by the corruption of morals than by anything else, it is easily seen that divorce, which is born of the perverted morals of a people, and leads, as experiment shows, to vicious habits in public and private life, is particularly opposed to the well-being of the family and of the State. The serious nature of these evils will be the more clearly recognized, when we remember that, once divorce has been allowed, there will be no sufficient means of keeping it in check within any definite bounds. Great is the force of example, greater still that of lust; and with such incitements it cannot but happen that divorce and its consequent setting loose of the passions should spread daily and attack the souls of many like a contagious disease or a river bursting its banks and flooding the land.'

"Thus, as we read in the same letter, 'unless things change, the human family and the State have every reason to fear lest they should suffer absolute ruin.' All this was written fifty years ago, yet it is confirmed by the daily increasing corruption of morals and the unheard-of-degradation of the family in those lands where communism reigns unchecked."[9]

There are also positive divine reasons why divorce must not be allowed. The Church does not sanction divorce, as we detailed in Chapter 8, first, because it is against the clear teaching of Christ, and second for the subsidiary reasons to be found in the very nature of marriage,

---

[9] *Casti connubii*, pp. 105, 106.

which we have just given. It is claimed that her attitude inflicts severe hardship on those who wish to break the marriage bonds. It is true that some innocent people suffer when they obey the Church's law. It may seem unjust that a marriage contract cannot be dissolved, if afterwards the parties find their characters unsuited for the life partnership. The injustice may seem the greater when one of the partners meets someone better suited to his tastes, but cannot marry because of the existence of the first partner. Yet in all these cases it must be remembered that the exceptions do not prove that the doctrine is based on a weak foundation. Church laws are made either because of a fundamental natural law, or for the sake of good accruing to the majority (where, of course, the good is in harmony with the natural law). The Church cannot, for the sake of benefit to a few, change a precept which is grounded in the natural law, in the welfare of society, and on the solemn words of Christ Himself.

Though it does not sanction their remarriage until the death of one of the partners, to prevent a worse evil the Church allows married people to live separately from each other in the following cases:

1. Where one of the parties commits adultery.

2. Where one of the parties is in danger of body or of soul.

Yet the Church urges partners to bear with each other's defects, and advises separation only when further forbearance is impossible. Separation — not divorce — is also allowed when, by mutual consent (the children having been duly provided for) one of the parties, with dispensation of the Holy See, enters religious life or receives Sacred Orders.

In no instance will the Church annul a validly contracted Christian marriage. It does, however, declare certain marriage ceremonies null and void in the following two categories:

1. When a purely natural marriage was previously performed between non-Christians, but later one of the parties becomes a Christian and the other party raises serious objections to his embracing the new faith. This is called the Pauline privilege, and is based on the Scriptural reference: "If any brother hath a wife that believeth not, and she consent to dwell with him, let him not put her away. And if any woman hath a husband that believeth not, and he consent to dwell with her, let her not put away her husband. Otherwise your children should be unclean but now they are holy. But if the unbeliever depart, let him depart. For a brother or sister is not under servitude in such cases. But God hath called us in peace."[10]

---

[10] 1 Cor. 7:12–15.

2. When the marriage contract which took place was really null and void, and no real contract, either through error or lack of free consent, or through physical or moral or legal (i.e., Church laws) incapacity for marriage. "The annulling impediments to marriage are: Insufficient age, impotence, existing marriage bond, disparity of worship, Sacred Orders, solemn religious profession, abduction, crime (a technical term that includes adultery with a promise to marry or civil marriage, adultery and murder of consort, murder of consort alone), consanguinity, affinity, public propriety, spiritual relationship, legal adoption if civilly it voids marriage."[11]

---

[11] Davis, Rev. H. D., S.J., *Moral and Pastoral Theology* (New York: Sheed & Ward, 1938), Vol. IV, p. 104, to which author we refer for the exact meaning of the terms used.

CHAPTER 26

CRIME AND DELINQUENCY

Definitions and Importance of the Subject Matter

THE subject matter of this chapter is a brief survey of the fields of criminology and penology. Criminology is a scientific inquiry into the factors which determine crime and delinquency. Penology is a scientific study of the treatment of criminals and delinquents. Both these sciences are important branches of sociology, and the problems concerned can be discussed only very inadequately in one chapter.

Basically, the problem is one of sin. When there is disharmony between man's conduct and the right moral order, the result is called by the moralists "sin." Sin is defined as any thought, word, act, or omission contrary to the divine law. A habit of committing certain types of evil actions is called vice — which is the opposite of virtue, or the habit of performing a certain kind of good action.

If, instead of remaining merely an individual problem, the disharmony of sin and vice affects fellow beings, an exterior social problem results, and it is a question of crime or delinquency. A delinquent act is a willful violation of the laws of the State by act or by omission. As we said in the chapter on the State, the State exists to promote the welfare of the people living within its territory, and to protect them under the divine law. To promote law and harmony, the government of the State must promulgate all necessary laws, and it is the duty of citizens to obey them. Sometimes, for the preservation of order, and in carrying out its duties of promoting the common good and protecting its citizens, the State makes laws of a lesser kind. Laws that are purely penal are not binding in conscience, except insofar as one should always obey legitimate authority in all that is not sin, but the penalty when inflicted must be accepted. Occasionally, a State may make a law which is beyond its function and which enjoins sin, instead of promoting law and harmony under the divine law; in such an event, of course, the citizen must disobey the human law, in order not to break the divine law, of which human law is but a part.

Human law is divisible into two chief kinds: the *lex gentium* or the *law of nations,* and the *municipal law;* in the wide sense of the term, *municipal law* can be subdivided into constitutional law, statute law (written law), and common law (unwritten law). Commercial law is in large part derived from the common law, both the unwritten law of municipalities and the unwritten law of nations. Both statute law and common law may be further classified as to kind: civil or criminal. It is with this latter type of law that we are here concerned, the breaking of which comes under the jurisdiction of the criminal or the civil courts. Another type of municipal court is called a Court of Equity. The Court of Equity originated at the end of the fifteenth century, when Henry VII ruled that if the common-law courts did not provide a just remedy to an injured person, then that person could apply directly for relief to the King's chancellor, who, by proposing a remedy to fit the nature of the wrong, would see that justice (equity) was accomplished.

Delinquency may also be divided as to offenses against person, against morals, against religion, against government, against property, against public peace and order, against the health of citizens, and against such resources of society as communal property, animals, and above all, children.

Serious delinquency, such as burglary, robbery, homicide, brutal assault, treason, and arson is known as a felony. Crimes which are lesser violations of the law are called misdemeanors. The dividing line between felonies and misdemeanors varies in different countries, and in different states of the United States. Sometimes, presumably in an effort to eliminate the particular type of delinquency concerned, crimes which are comparatively insignificant in themselves are called felonies, such for example, as the strict laws in certain states against selling lottery tickets; or the prohibition laws of 1913–1933 period against the sale of intoxicating liquors.

The seriousness of crime cannot be measured by the number of persons who are arraigned in the courts, or by the number of persons in prisons or reformatories, for many delinquents pay fines, or are "on probation," or they are paroled, or discharged for technical legal matters. Then, too, many delinquents and criminals have never been discovered or apprehended. The most serious aspects of crime are, of course, that it usually involves sin against God. From the human viewpoint the main problem is the social maladjustments and problems which result. But there is also an economic side whose magnitude cannot be accurately determined, but which certainly amounts in the United States to an annual loss or expenditure of some billions of dollars.[1] Such expenses include the cost of maintaining the court system, a police force, prisons, and reformatories; they also include losses by theft, and by wanton destruction from incendiarism and other vandal acts; and they include the tremendous cost of insurance, the provision of safes, burglar alarms, armored cars, and all the other protective devices of which there is an increased need in our "civilized" era.

Factors Leading to Crime, and Remedies Proposed

The reader will remember from the discussions in the first part of this book, that there is certainly no unit cause of conduct. Man acts in a certain way for a variety of different reasons. While it is evident that heredity is not responsible for crime, nevertheless, as it was pointed out, not only is everyone born with certain predispositions to evil by reason of original sin, but some are born with physical defects, a weakened nervous system, or glandular disturbances which may handicap the will in making right choices.

Conduct, as we said, is the outcome of our mental attitudes and ideals, and the habits we have built upon them. These, in turn, are influenced by emotional disturbances, instincts, the nervous system, our state of health, and particularly by our environment.

Most delinquent acts are due to a defective moral or mental attitude, resulting from lack of true notions of rights and duties toward God, toward one's neighbor, and toward oneself, and to a neglect of training in habits of virtue and self-restraint. A delinquent act may have been performed on the spur of the moment, or may be an isolated crime committed for one reason or another; or it may be but one of a long series of acts committed by one to whom such conduct has become habitual; it may, of course, be committed by one mentally deficient or insane, who was not responsible for the act, but who needs medical or institutional treatment and care.

It is true that every mentally normal person is endowed with free will, and with sufficient grace to overcome defects in his education and external training. Nevertheless man is an imitative animal and, as we showed in Chapters 3 and 4, his environment and training in early youth cannot but play an important part in the molding of his character. He is not rigidly determined by environment and heredity, but he is much affected by them. This fact the Church is ever emphasizing in her insistence that everyone must avoid "the occasion of sin" insofar

---

[1] Cf. National Commission on Law Enforcement: *Report on the Cost of Crime,* No. XII, Washington, D.C., 1931. Especially pp. 438–443.

as this is possible, and in her constant teaching of the important value of a good Christian home and parents.

The chief factors which lead to delinquent conduct and the remedies which may be proposed to eliminate these occasions may be listed as follows:

1. Defective religious and moral education. This could be eliminated by a more widespread teaching of the principles of religion and of sound ethics, by precept and example. Religious influence has been greatly weakened in our materialistic era, with consequences which even those who only see in religion a means of "social control" do not fail to recognize. Knowledge of right and wrong, and training in right conduct, are primarily acquired in the home, with the subsidiary assistance of the school. These institutions, then, are principally responsible for the inculcation of wrong attitudes and ideals, and for the establishment of mental conflicts. If the home life of a child is defective, or if the educational system neglects its duty to promote religious and moral education, the child runs a serious risk of becoming a delinquent.

2. Defective home life. Neglect in the home proceeds from a variety of sources. Some parents are shiftless, ignorant, lacking in self-restraint, selfish, emotional, immoral, or delinquent, and for these reasons neglect to train their children in habits of virtue, giving them instead the disadvantages of bad example and bad environment. Quarrels and conflicts between the parents are bound to affect the growing minds of the children and to lead to imitative conduct. Death or desertion of the father, nonrealization of maternal duties, or dire economic need, often lead a mother to work away from home, leaving her children to their own devices during working hours. Many mothers, too, spend too many hours in social activities, shopping and the like, which had better been given to attention to the children's needs. The Gluecks said of Boston that: "More than nine-tenths of juvenile delinquents came from broken or poorly supervised homes."[2] Divorce is a very potent occasion of crime, for a broken home often leads to the children being deprived of adequate home life and attention, to lack of family discipline, or to disrespect of parental authority.

It must be noted, too, that many parents are themselves the victims of false philosophies and a lack of Christian principles. Led astray by the modern "naturalistic" ideas, to which Rousseau gave impetus, and which the Freudians have fully exploited, many mothers fail to give

---

[2] Glueck, S. and E. T., *One Thousand Juvenile Delinquents* (Harvard University Press, 1934), p. 82.

their children a correct training in modesty and truth. Unless juvenile delinquents are led to reform their way of living, they continue their unsocial conduct in later years.

A large number of juvenile delinquents come from homes where the parents are foreign born, and there is also a disproportionate number of Negro delinquents. Speaking of 1930 conditions in Boston, the Gluecks said: "There is a considerable incidence of foreign born parentage among our juvenile delinquents, only one-fifth of the fathers having been born in America."[3] The question of immigration is discussed in the next chapter. The demoralizing effect of the conflict which frequently arises between the customs of parents from the Old World, and the customs the children learn from their playmates in the New, constitutes a problem which is commonly recognized but difficult to deal with. Frequently, too, immigrant families have been forced to live in unfavorable surroundings, which is an added factor against which the children must struggle, yet is a situation which very frequently is beyond the parent's control. It is this latter factor which is the greatest cause of Negro delinquency. Many Negroes, too, became city dwellers within recent years, and the transition from rural life in the South to the industrial conditions of the North creates almost as many adjustment needs as the immigrants' difficulties in settling in a different cultural environment from the one to which they had been accustomed.

3. Another important factor in crime is poverty, which frequently brings with it lifelong economic handicaps, overcrowded housing conditions, a lack of recreational facilities, and possibly unwholesome psychological conditions.

A very large number of delinquents come from poor families, but it must not be thought for this reason that the poor are more criminal as a class than those better off. As a matter of fact, the percentage is not much more than the general percentage of poor people in relation to the rich. Delinquents come from all classes of society, and a rich delinquent is often shielded or not discovered. Since the majority of citizens are poor, and considering the terrible handicaps of poverty, and the greater temptations to which the poor are subjected, it is surprising that the percentage of poor delinquents is not much higher than it is.

A lack of vocational training contributes to crime in some instances. A man without a trade is usually forced to adopt some occupation which will give him less than a living wage. Nowadays, with the very

---

[3] *Ibid.*, p. 80.

visible discrepancies between the rich and the poor, with parked cars so frequently left unattended, with the increasing display of cheap articles produced under our methods of large-scale production, and with the lack of personal supervision in mass-production businesses, and taking into consideration present-day materialism and the over-valuation of wealth, the temptations to steal, embezzle, and commit frauds are often very great.

Bad housing conditions and uncongenial home life not infrequently result in children having the street as their playground, with almost invariable association with bad companions, and possibly an ultimate criminal career. It is well known that at times local street gangs are schools of crime. Even some modern so-called model housing estates lack opportunities for healthy recreation and amusement. Yet facilities for wholesome games and recreation are of extreme importance for young and old.

Most of these factors could be eliminated to a large degree by better planned economic organization and by an increased realization by the community of its duties toward society. Both rich and poor must mutually recognize their duties and their rights. There is a need of more scientific relief of unemployment and poverty, of better education to provide vocational training, and training in economic household management, of improved community recreational facilities, of the elimination of slums, and of legislation, when needed, to provide minimum wages, family allowances, and allowances to dependent mothers and children. Since most of the circumstances we have enumerated lead to crime at an early age, the handling of juvenile delinquents is a very important factor, which has only been adequately realized in late years. Juvenile delinquency, indeed, forms a separate and important problem in the solution of adult crime, and it will be separately treated at the end of the chapter.

4. Much crime is suggested by newspaper reports, motion pictures, books, and plays. In themselves, of course, news, literature, and the theater are by no means harmful! Rather, in addition to its recreational value, the Aristotelian idea of the uses of the drama seem very true. By presenting certain immoral types of conduct, followed by retribution or a correct moral issue, the playgoer cannot only rid himself of bad emotions in this vicarious manner, but he experiences some good emotions to take away with him.[4] The same might be said of literature. Yet many of our modern books, magazines, and plays are so

---

[4] Cf. Aristotle, *Poetics*, vi, 2; also Butcher, S. H., *Aristotle's Theory of Poetry and Fine Art* (London: Macmillan Co., 1927), pp. 245, 246.

immoral that they cannot but be harmful to all except those who have willed in most strong fashion always to maintain an ideal of virtue. It is for this reason that various Catholic organizations publish lists of acceptable motion pictures and plays, and the Cardinal Hayes Literature Committee writes a quarterly report.

Gambling, alcoholism, drug addiction, also lead to crime by weakening the morale and conscience and inciting to anger, lust, and thieving to obtain money to continue the vice; also by loss of self-respect and efficiency and hence decreased earning power, and sometimes eventually to vagrancy and total economic dependency.

Most of these circumstances, too, can be largely eliminated by improved community organization and social laws; by the provision of wholesome noncommercial recreational facilities; by stricter supervision and more scientific treatment of drink and drug addicts; and by a sane censorship of the screen and of the press. In this latter connection it may be said that one has the right to one's opinions, but not necessarily the right to publish them. The press and the movies must have liberty but not license. In the publication of opinions is involved: first others, that is, society, and it may not be injured; second, the moral law, and this may not be violated.

5. The moral attitude of a community toward crime, the integrity or corruption of local police institutions, and just or lax court procedure, naturally influence the prevalency of crime. The police system of certain districts can be criticized because the force is unskilled or of poor quality intelligence. Discipline standards may be low, and appointments made by political influence rather than on merit. Sometimes the police of rural districts in particular are so poorly paid, or so dependent upon fees and fines that they are greatly tempted to accept graft, and sometimes do so; and city police are also sometimes remiss in this respect. In some places the police force is insufficient in numbers for the community's needs, or the right type of equipment is lacking. Again, judicial institutions are not always free from the taint of bribery and corruption; delinquents sometimes are dismissed on technical grounds, even though they are proved guilty. The unconvicted are allowed their liberty on bail, if their financial resources are sufficient, or if they can persuade the court authorities to accept an often financially incompetent bondsman, so that only the unconvicted poor must go to jail to await trial. Often, an accused prisoner must wait many months in jail before the trial and, of course, he may be innocent. On the other hand many actual criminals try to prolong the period before the trial is held with the hope of finding a way to avoid

punishment. Judges have only short terms in office because of their political positions, and the ineffectiveness of much of our penal action is due to a demagogic judiciary seeking popularity by its leniency. Lawyers are allowed to make emotional appeals to a jury which is often incompetent to sift evidence and testimony, which latter is, in any event, frequently falsified opinion rather than statements of actual fact.

6. Physical and mental disabilities are sometimes factors in crime. All scientists are now of the opinion that crime itself is not inherited, although one may inherit predispositions to criminal acts. The National Commission on Law Observance and Enforcement gives the following conclusions in its report: "Two general conclusions stand out from the consideration of the literature on mental factors in crime. First, it has not been determined to what extent either defective intelligence or any other mental abnormality is present in the criminal population. Secondly, even where defective intelligence and mental abnormalities are present in criminals a necessary and inevitable causal relationship has not been demonstrated."[5]

Epileptics and the insane are often subject to criminal tendencies on account of their mental and emotional instability. Encephalitis leaves lesions in the nervous system which may result in behavior disorders. A defective gland may make fear or anger more or less paralyze the workings of the brain, and the unfortunate possessor may thus have greater temptations than many other people. It must be said, however, that the exercise of will power which is largely a matter of correct environment and training, could usually overcome these defects. The same might be said of those who indulge their sexual instincts in an illegitimate manner, possibly because of an overdevelopment of this physical characteristic: a man in such circumstances may steal to procure money to go out with women; or a woman may steal to buy clothes to attract men. In none of these cases, however, is the physical condition directly responsible for the delinquency. Again, physical or mental defectives are often neglected, discriminated against, and sometimes develop an antisocial character and a distorted view on life. This attitude can, of course, be eliminated by more scientific education in early youth.

7. Although as explained in the chapter on environment, geographical factors are not a major cause of delinquent conduct, climate does influence the conduct of certain persons. Humidity, intense heat, elec-

---

[5] National Commission on Law Observance and Enforcement, *Report on the Causes of Crime* (Wickersham Report), Vol. I, pp. 60, 61.

trical conditions in the air, may lead to nervousness and irritability, and hence sometimes to crimes of violence.

Catholic Criminals

It seems advisable here to say a word about the number of Catholic delinquents arraigned before the courts, or forming part of prison and reformatory population. It is generally held that Catholics as a class are more delinquent than members of other denominations. Actual statistics are hard to find, but one Catholic investigator has tabulated the percentage of Catholic prisoners in forty-five unselected prisons.[6] These prisons represented every section of all states of the Union with the exception of the eleven states of Alabama, Delaware, Georgia, Kentucky, Maine, Montana, Nevada, North Dakota, Rhode Island, South Dakota, and Virginia, and included prisons in the most densely populated states which in many cases have a greater percentage of Catholic population than the others. As the investigator pointed out, the states not included would probably lower the percentage of Catholic prisoners, since most of them have a comparatively small Catholic population. The results show that "the percentage of Catholic prisoners in the forty-five prisons tabulated was 26.76 per cent or a little more than one-fourth of the total population of these prisons . . . a figure which even in its most damaging construction is far removed indeed from confirming the assertion sometimes made that 'Catholics fill our prisons.' "[7]

The percentage, nevertheless, is disproportionate. Another Catholic statistician, giving 1932 statistics for an unnamed Western state showed[8] that Catholic delinquents in the state present about 30 per cent of total delinquents, whereas according to the statistics in the *Catholic Directory*, Catholics only formed 12 per cent of the inhabitants of the state. He shows, however, that the *Catholic Directory* statistics are most probably in error, pointing out obvious errors in the 1932 edition, where Catholic births for the state are given as 30.2 per cent of the population, while only 13.6 per cent of recorded marriages were Catholic.

Actually, of course, even a lapsed Catholic will generally acknowledge his former religious affiliation, whereas those of other denominations will not usually go to the trouble of giving their former religious

---

[6] Cf. Kalmer, Leo, O.F.M., and Weir, E., O.F.M., *Crime and Religion* (Chicago: Franciscan Herald Press, 1936).

[7] *Ibid.*, p. 72.

[8] Kenny, T. F., "Catholic Criminals," *The Commonweal*, April 3, 1936, pp. 624–626.

belief when once they have abandoned it. The early training of a Catholic usually leads even the worst to have the intention of coming back to the fold on his deathbed. While this fact will increase Catholic statistics, the fact remains that the number of Catholic delinquents needs serious consideration on our part. Whether the number is due to the fact that so many recent immigrant and thus "underprivileged" groups are Catholic in religion, whether it is because the greater number of Catholics are city dwellers, and there is such a small proportion of rural Catholics, or whether there is something in the moral training of Catholics which is defective is not at present decided.

The Punishment of Crime

As already stated, to insure good order and the carrying out of the natural law, the government of the State has the power and the duty to make just laws. If it is necessary for the State to enact laws, to carry out the end of its existence, it is the duty of citizens to obey the laws, and the complementary duty of the State to see that the laws are executed.

Punishment is based on the rational nature of man. There can be no just punishment if there is no freedom of will. There is no sin if the intention to commit sin is lacking, although of course we may have committed the offense through habit, and the habit, unless established in our earliest youth through lack of care or training by our elders, was at one time begun by a deliberate action. If we were not rational beings, and could not therefore know the difference between good and evil, we would not be responsible for our choices, and punishment would then be unjust. God sustains us by His creative and sustaining power. We rebel against Him when we violate the moral order, and since God cannot surrender His sovereignty, He must act against rebellion by punishment. He who sinned of his own will, is punished against his will, and thus equilibrium is restored. In the spiritual order, repentance may take the place of punishment, and the merits of others may be applied to our souls. The State takes the place of God in maintaining order upon the earth, and if its laws are just, it has direct authority to punish acts which are injurious to society. Yet only insofar as a delinquent act is an offense against society has civil punishment any justification for its existence; and at the base of all punishment is retribution.

Delinquent conduct, according to Catholic teaching, should be punished with four objectives in view. First, punishment should be *retributive,* as we have just explained. The first aim of society must be to restore order and to prevent hurt to society. Expiation, however, should not be excessive, nor necessarily in proportion to the crime.

Second, punishment should have a *deterring* effect. Punishment should be as unpleasant as is compatible with justice and the other objectives of punishment, so that the offender himself will refrain from committing the same crime a second time; and society will be protected because others also, knowing the punishment applicable to crime, will be deterred from committing it.

Third, punishment should be such that by it a barrier will be erected to *prevent* others from committing crime.

Fourth, although the State's first duty to society is the common good, secondarily it must work for the good of the individual as a member of society. After retributive justice has been effected, there-fore, and the deterring and prevention side of punishment has had its part, the State should seek to *reform* the offender. Punishment is in vain, so far as the delinquent is concerned, if it does not teach him to make better future choices, if it does not make him desire and like to be good. When once a man comes before the court, the problem should cease to be the general one of the elimination of crime, and becomes the particular problem not only how to punish him in a fitting manner but also how to prevent that individual offender from repeating the same offense. Punishment should certainly be strong enough to pre-vent others from wishing to commit a similar crime, and to insure that the prisoner realizes the gravity of his offense; but sometimes reforma-tion is effected more readily without imprisonment, or by a more lenient sentence. When punishment is too severe, feelings of revenge may be engendered, and the delinquent may become permanently antisocial. "Socialized courts," where the individual offender is treated as a social unit presenting a problem which should be solved for the benefit of the community and of the individual himself, are still only in the developmental stage. They will render good service, if they bear in mind the true ends of punishment, and if they are not sentimental in their outlook, but realize the responsibility of the normal man in relation to his conduct. The aim in reform should generally be toward the strengthening of desirable subjective and environmental conditions, the supply of such factors where they are lacking, and the elimination of undesirable conditions wherever possible, or at least a mitigation or substitution of some kind.

We may mention here the controversy as to the legitimacy of capital punishment. Of course, God is the author of life and death, and the State can administer the most severe of all punishments, that of depriving a man of his life, only when the offense is very grave, when the offender's guilt is clearly established, and when it is necessary for the public good (e.g., to deter others from committing a similar heinous crime). The State is not bound to give punishment adequate to meet a crime of magnitude, hence it is never bound to administer capital punishment, however depraved the criminal may be. Again, it must be remembered that there may always be extenuating circumstances which lead a man to perform a certain type of crime, and these a governing authority should always try to take into account as much as possible. As to whether capital punishment satisfactorily deters others from crime, and whether or not other methods of punishment would be more effective is still a debatable question. In many cases it seems more humane than prolonged punishment of other types. And many a man will settle his affairs of conscience with his Maker if death is certain, instead of an event which will happen at an indefinite future time. Those who are opposed to capital punishment must admit, however, that in certain circumstances the State's right to administer retributive justice for the protection of society clearly justifies the taking of a criminal's life.

Changing Attitudes Toward Crime

1. *Retribution.* Under the early Talic law, retribution or vengeance was the dominant idea when dealing with criminals: the miscreant was meted out the same treatment as he had given to others, in accordance with the well-known non-Christian maxim: an eye for an eye and a tooth for a tooth.

2. *Repression.* In the later Middle Ages there was an increasing tendency to regard repression as the best way to punish crime: would-be criminals being deterred by fear of the consequences if they were discovered. This was a time when judges were allowed to pass arbitrary sentences of the most severe kind, and when severe punishments were often imposed for comparatively slight offenses. Horrible tortures were inflicted on suspected criminals; summary punishment was meted out at the whipping post, the pillory, or by means of the ducking stool; ordeals, capital punishment, banishment, and penal transportation were common. Third-degree methods of the present day are reminiscent of this period.

3. *The Classical Theory of Penology.* Neither retribution nor repressive measures were successful in dealing with crime. An Italian Catholic, the Marquis of Beccaria (1735–1794), appalled by the system of repression and arbitrary punishment, which had increased in severity

after the Middle Ages, was the first effectively to challenge its wisdom. Thoroughly imbued with the ideas of liberty of Rousseau, Montesquieu, and Voltaire, he thought that the so-called contract was necessary to make social life a possibility, and taught that the individual criminal tries to destroy the social contract when his ideas of personal freedom tend to overstep its bounds; the delinquent must, therefore, he said, be judged by his act and punished accordingly. He believed in the criminal's individual responsibility for his act, and he wished especially to attack the evils of arbitrary punishment. Returning to the old idea of retribution, he published a book called *Crimes and Punishment* in 1764, in which he argued that punishment should fit the crime, and not be disproportionate to the gravity of the offense: that a fixed and speedy sentence following upon a delinquent act would have a greater deterring effect than severity, and would be more in accordance with justice. To insure that an exact punishment would be meted out, he taught that there should be no uncertainty in the punishment: it should be definitely fixed by statute, and it should be promptly executed by the judge. The judge's business would be merely to execute the law, not to interpret it.

4. *The Neoclassical Theory of Penology.* When it was seen during the French revolution that it was impossible to enumerate all types of crime and to settle upon fixed penalties for them, a new school of penology arose. This school followed Beccaria's main line of teaching but demonstrated that the nature and mental condition of the accused should be taken into some account when dealing with a delinquent. They admitted the advisability of a fixed punishment, but asked that individuals should be exempted therefrom if freedom of will was absent, as in the case of the insane; and reduced, if freedom of will was partially absent, as when a child committed an offense, or an adult did so when drunk, or as a result of seemingly justifiable anger.

Our modern classification of crime as felonies and misdemeanors and many of our punishments such as fixed fines for certain offenses, date from the teachings of the classical and neoclassical theorists. Its teachings are clearly evident, too, in the Baumes Law of New York which, passed in 1926, allowed judges no alternative but to impose lifelong imprisonment on an offender indicted of the fourth felony, thus removing all judicial discretion in the treatment of such offenders. The number of offenses was changed from four to six in 1930.

Undoubtedly there is much in the theory of the neoclassical school to commend it to the reader. It recognizes the average man's responsibility for his conduct, it allows of mitigating circumstances, and it prevents bribery and corruption of judges. On the other hand, a high type of judicial authority can often effect the ends of punishment more readily by having some liberty in setting the individual delinquent's punishment.

5. *Prison Reforms*. Conditions brought about by the extremes of *laissez-faire* individualism did not improve the conditions of prisons, which remained as bad as during the time when the repression of crime was at its height. Humanitarian movements, however, did much to attempt a reform. An Englishman, John Howard (1726–1790), spent the years from 1773 to his death visiting prisons and advocating more humane treatment of prisoners. His work was followed by many others including Elizabeth Gurney Fry (1780–1845) who began her agitation for the better treatment of women prisoners in 1810.

In the United States, William Penn (1644–1718) influenced the formation of the Philadelphia Society for Relieving Distressed Prisoners in 1776. This society adopted the idea that the object of the punishment of crime should, above all, be reformation of the prisoner — not retribution or repression. It decided that reformation would be more speedily accomplished by putting prisoners in solitary confinement, so that they could meditate on their misdemeanors and come to salutary conclusions. In the years 1790–91 the Society transformed a jail to deal with the worst offenders in Philadelphia in this manner, although the less serious offenders were allowed to work together in silence.

Other prisons adopted a modified form of the Pennsylvania scheme, the most famous of which was at Auburn, New York, a new prison erected in 1816. It was realized that the complete isolation of prisoners was a kind of refined cruelty and had serious mental and physical effects. The new Auburn system kept prisoners in solitary confinement at night, in inside cells of a very unsanitary type, but during the day prisoners were allowed to work together, though they were obliged to keep perpetual silence.

Catholics will be interested to note that as early as the year 1703, Pope Clement XI erected a model prison, St. Michael's with individual cells, for the reform of male prisoners, who worked in common during the day, but were isolated at night. Pope Clement XII built a similar prison for women in 1735.

A much more progressive step toward the practical reformation of prisoners was the inauguration of the "Crofton Irish system" with the foundation of the Elmira State Reformatory for youthful offenders in 1876. This system had already been satisfactorily established in a

British penal colony in Australia for a number of years, but had been introduced into Ireland by a Sir Robert Crofton and became known by his name. The main idea of the system is that prisoners should be reformed and made fit to return to society through scientific individual treatment, education, work, and religious instruction. It embodied the merit or progressive-stage system of rewarding good conduct, a final period of comparative freedom during the last stage of imprisonment, and conditional release of prisoners on parole, which will be discussed later in the chapter. Later developments of the line of thought engendered by this system have led to other improvements, such as the indeterminate sentence, some of which will also be later described.

6. *The Positive or Italian School of Penology.* In addition to the classical and the neoclassical schools of penology, a third and most influential system of thought is that founded by Lombroso (1836–1909) with the publication of *The Criminal in Relation to Anthropology, Jurisprudence, and Psychiatry,* in 1876. As the name of the system implies, the positive school denies human responsibility for its acts, it makes a man a mechanism, entirely dependent upon heredity and its development in the environment in which he lives. The theories of even the neoclassical school may seem inhuman to the student who realizes the many complex motives which lead to conduct, and the unequal opportunities of men. But insofar as the classical and the neoclassical schools do not basically deny man's freedom of will, they are infinitely to be preferred to the mechanistic theories of the Positivists, which make man merely an evolved atom, which are based on theories which are biologically unsound, and which are against the teachings of the modern physical anthropologists as well as the findings of correct philosophy. Lombroso maintained that a criminal has no control over his actions because he is influenced both externally and physically. His chief theory, based upon an examination of Italian soldiers, was that criminals inherit a predisposition to crime to such an extent that they belong to a criminal class, which may be distinguished by certain marked physical characteristics such as heavy jaw, receding forehead, and large ears. He classified delinquents as born criminals, insane criminals, epileptoids, criminals from passion, and the occasional criminal or criminaloid. Lombroso agreed that the parents might not be criminals, but propounded that crime not due to immediate heredity would be attributable to atavism, that is, a renewed manifestation of heredity after it had remained dormant for one or more generations. He modified his views somewhat in later years, but his theories have led to a vast amount of sentimentality in

dealing with criminals. With this line of thought punishment would not seem to be applicable, but Lombroso admitted punishment as necessary for the protection of society, and allowable as self-protection in the same manner as precautions against forest fires and floods are desirable. Instead of wanting punishment to fit the crime, however, as do the classical theorists, he wished punishment to fit the criminal. The main constructive part of his teachings is that he pointed to the necessity of modifying conditions which tended to develop criminal conduct.

Ferri (1856–1929), one of Lombroso's chief disciples, denied free will and believed in hereditary causation of crime, but he added physical and social factors. In his well-known books *The Homicide* and *Criminal Sociology,* both published in 1884, he showed that he was particularly in favor of environmental programs to help to abolish crime. With this end in view he advocated better housing, better lighted streets, and an increase in the number of savings banks. Among his unscientific demands for the elimination of crime was his desire to see birth-control propaganda more widespread, and the advocation of other eugenical measures.

Garofalo (b. 1852), the third founder of the positive school, thought that the criminal was not a free moral agent, but a product of his time, and should therefore be treated with understanding. He denied conclusive evidence of a criminal type, but thought that some men were born with an inborn tendency to perform criminal acts. His justification for punishment was in fact that the criminal could be punished by being expelled from the group by imprisonment, just as one can expel a club member who refuses to conform to the customs of a club.

Lombroso's theory has been definitely disproved by an English physician, Charles Goring (1870–1919), who made a painstaking biometric analysis of three thousand unselected British convicts and came to the conclusion that there is no "criminal type." Moreover, Goring continued his measurements on university students, and found many highly moral students with the exact physical characteristics which Lombroso had attributed to criminals alone.[9] All scientists are now of the opinion that crime cannot be inherited, as we have before explained, although certain predispositions may have hereditary basis.

With the Positivist school one can, strangely enough, class the followers of Behaviorism, for although the Behaviorists correctly deny any important hereditary basis of conduct, they do not give sufficient attention to heredity as a cause of conduct, unduly stress the me-

---

[9] Cf. Goring, C., *The English Convict* (1913).

chanical influence of environment upon man, and deny human responsibility, the soul, and grace.

7. *The Prevention of Crime.* Following the work of the later prison reformers, that reform rather than retribution or repression should be the aim of individual punishment, the fourth phase in the attitude toward delinquency was that prevention is better than cure, and that society owed it to itself not merely to punish and reform the criminal, but to prevent crime, for the more complete protection of citizens.

How to prevent the large incidence of delinquency is one of the greater problems which social workers are trying to solve. We have already enumerated the major methods which are or ought to be applied, when we discussed the chief factors which enter into delinquent conduct. It is certain that many crimes would not occur if transgressions were almost certain to be followed by immediate arrest and speedy and just prosecution. It is certain, too, that many delinquents would not be confirmed in their wrongdoing if prisoners were always separated according to age and sex; if first offenders were never placed with habitual criminals; if minor offenders did not associate in prison with greater criminals; and if the unconvicted were never placed with the convicted. Community planning is also badly needed, and in many districts changes need to be made in the educational system, in housing, recreation provisions, and the like.

Present-Day Methods of Dealing with Criminals

There are three kinds of penal institutions in the United States for older offenders. Those awaiting trial go to the county jail, as the local prison is called. Here women are separated from men, but the unconvicted and the convicted are not as a rule separated, and first offenders and the unconvicted come into contact with those suffering from contagious diseases, drug addicts, sex perverts, the sick aged, and with habitual or incorrigible criminals. Upon conviction, those sentenced to small periods of imprisonment, up to nine months or so, usually remain in the county jail or local workhouse, whereas others either pass to a state penitentiary, or, if they have broken a Federal law (a law binding on all citizens of the United States), they go to a Federal establishment. Many of our prisons today are too large and overcrowded, and the building of a number of smaller ones would seem advisable.

The best modern penal methods aim at reforming the delinquent, not merely hardening him; in building up his morale, instead of breaking it down, and in teaching him to help himself. In the more advanced districts, the social history of each accused person is examined, and an endeavor is made to discover the factors which entered into his supposed delinquency, so that proper remedies may be applied. Often physical, psychiatric, and psychological examinations are given before trial to determine physical and other causes. In this way physically or mentally undesirable persons, and the worst types of criminals, can be separated from prisoners of other categories and can be given special treatment. In Massachusetts the Briggs Law was passed in 1921 requiring a psychiatric examination for every individual brought up for capital offense, or at any time after the first occasion. Psychiatry has not yet reached a scientific stage, however, and on account of differing opinions of the board of psychiatrists, their number is strictly limited. When these social, medical, and mental examinations take place, it should not be forgotten that trial should follow arrest as quickly as possible, and that it is a precept of law that everyone is innocent until he is proved to be guilty.

Some delinquents escape with mere fine. Fines have the advantage of costing the State nothing and being, instead, a source of revenue. They can be adjusted to the offense, and are a punishment in that they affect one of the chief modern interests of man — his monetary accumulation. They are, however, unduly hard upon the poor, as they are fixed in relation to the offense and do not take sufficiently into account the ability to pay.

Probation. Other delinquents are not fined or imprisoned, but are punished by being placed on probation. Probation is a modern and distinctly American method of dealing with prisoners. Its origin is accredited to the Boston cobbler, John Augustus, who in 1849 asked in court that a young man charged with drunkenness be committed to his supervision, and he pledged his responsibility for him. The judge consented, and there and then probation began, for John Augustus, encouraged by his first success, continued his function as self-appointed probation officer for many years thereafter. Later, in 1878, a similar instance occurred when Rev. Fr. Cook, a Catholic priest of the same city, appealed to a judge to give an offender another chance, promising to take the delinquent under his supervision. Again the plan proved successful. That year the first probation law was passed, a Massachusetts law which required Boston to appoint a probation officer.

At present the Federal Government and all the states save one include probation in their system of handling juvenile offenders, and as a method of dealing with certain types of adult prisoners. The method of granting and directing probation varies in the different states.

An offender on probation is allowed to remain free, but is under the supervision of a court official called a probation officer. In some large cities the St. Vincent de Paul Society or other Catholic organization provides Catholic probation officers. In others the state or local authorities place Catholic probationers under Catholic officers. The officers, of course, should be specially trained and paid by local authorities or by the State. Unfortunately, their appointment is sometimes prompted by political considerations.

The probationer has to report to his officer at regular intervals, and he is usually restricted in his associations, recreation, and presence on the streets at night. If he fails to carry out the probation regulations, he is taken before the court again, and usually committed. Success in probation work depends to a very large extent upon the type and training of probation officers. The probation officer's duty is to help the offender to reform, by taking a friendly interest in him, finding him work where necessary, and looking after his material and mental welfare to the best of his ability.

In many cases probation has been a very effective institution according to extenuating circumstances in connection with the crime and the personal character of the offender. Probation prevents the stigma of a former prisoner attaching to the offender, and so it avoids the danger of his being unable to obtain work on that account. It does not break up the offender's family, or cause suffering to innocent members because of the withdrawal of the wage earner. It keeps the delinquent out of touch with prison inmates who may be more criminal than himself. That it is also cheaper than sending him to prison would be a greater consideration, if all probation were successful. Many students of crime have pointed to a great amount of recidivism among probationers and former probationers. It is not, of course, advisable to apply probation to every delinquent. Generally careful examination is given to the offender's social history and to the probable results of the probationary sentence before he is given a chance to reform in this manner. Although it is intended mainly for first offenders and minor misdemeanants, the disposition of some offenders is such that even with their first "caught" offense it may be too lenient a measure. And again probation officers nearly always have too many cases to take care of to make it possible for them to carry out the ideal of careful individual treatment.

Prison Conditions

If a prisoner is convicted, and is not placed on probation or dismissed with a fine, then he goes to prison to serve his term of conviction. In 1935, 65,723 persons were sent to State and Federal prisons, and the total population in these prisons was 138,316.[10] In all prisons attention is usually given to the physical training of prisoners so that they are put into good physical condition; to their education, because illiteracy is a big handicap in the modern world, and the majority of prisoners have had a minimum of education; to their industrial training, so that they can earn an honest livelihood when freed; and to their moral and religious instruction. Volunteer instructors and visitors are welcomed, and there are also paid teachers and chaplains attached to the majority of prisons. The educational facilities of some prisons is very wide, so that the inmates can learn a variety of subjects if they choose. Sometimes they are permitted to take correspondence courses. The idea is not only to equip them better for later life in the world, but also to keep their mind on wholesome thoughts and thus avoid the temptation to brood, or to concoct plots of escape or further crimes. Some prisons provide well-chosen lecture programs and musical recitals; Sing Sing equips its cells with radios. The building up of character and morale in prisons depends largely upon the type of prison warder, and upon the guards who watch over them for discipline and take note of any signs of insurrection.

Prison Labor

Unconvicted prisoners cannot be compelled to work, but those convicted are usually given some form of work which will keep them occupied during the greater part of the day.[11] Under an ideal prison system each man would be trained in work which would fit him to take his place in the outside world when he is released. The question then arises as to what should be done with the product of prison labor. Obviously the needs of the prison should be provided for, but if a man is a skilled craftsman, and his work is not suitable for use in the prison itself, it could often be profitably sold to outside agencies. Yet prison labor is of its nature cheaper than outside labor, and if prison work is put on the market at cheaper rates, it provides serious competition with goods manufactured under normal conditions. On the other hand, there should be no reason why prison authorities cannot make the fullest possible remunerative use of their prisoners, compatible with the welfare of the prisoners themselves.

The employment of prison labor varies considerably in the different

---

[10] *Statistical Abstract of the United States,* 1937, p. 74.

[11] For fairly recent details of prison labor, see *Handbook of Labor Statistics,* 1936 ed., pp. 697–706.

states. Some states forbid the products of such labor to be sold on the market; others permit it. In some states only "state use" is allowed for the product of prison labor, that is, prisoners are only engaged in the construction and repair of public works such as public buildings, roads, parks, and bridges, and reforestation projects, and the manufacture of articles whose use or sale is restricted to state institutions. Sometimes this latter type of work leads to giving men work which is not of use to them in later life, such as knitting and the type of garmentmaking which is usually pursued by women workers; this kind of employment is repugnant to men skilled in other trades, and does not help them to keep in physical form for later re-employment. In other states, there is the "public account" system, and the prisons conduct factories and sell their products on the market. The Hawes-Cooper Bill of 1930 was passed to prevent interstate shipment of prison goods, after 1934, and has prevented the lucrative use of prison labor to a very large extent. In a few states the "contract" system applies, or the "piece-price" system. In the contract system a contractor engages for the labor of convicts by the day or hour, and then tries to get as much labor as possible from them. Under the piece-price system the contractor supplies the prison with raw materials, and then buys back the finished product at a given price per piece, and here, too, the tendency is to exploit prisoners. Both these systems, as also the chain-gang system sometimes employed in state-use public works, have now practically disappeared.

An ideal to be aimed at in regard to prison labor is that the work of the prisoners would enable the prison to become self-supporting; that prisoners would have an incentive to work by payments of a small amount of wages which they are allowed to spend as they please; that a certain portion of their earnings would be sent to dependents or, if the prisoner has no dependents, then to accumulate against release from prison. If prison-earned wages can be sent to dependents, then these need not become a charge on public charities. Yet there is a danger in such systems of the means overshadowing the end of prison labor. Idleness is certainly to be avoided, and work is salutary for any man. Yet as we stated before, it is the duty of prison authorities to do all possible to help a prisoner to reform. Work is a means toward this end: but excessive labor, or labor unsuited to the individual, imposed in order to make the prison "pay," is much more harmful than a system whereby the prisoner's work would be a scientific assistance toward building his character and helping him to reform, even though entirely unproductive financially.

Prison Camps

Prison camps and farms do much to build up the health and morale of delinquents. They originated as a result of overcrowding in prisons and the necessity of finding additional accommodation. In these camps offenders live in huts and work on the construction of new roads, the reclamation of land, or afforestation. This system costs the community much less than the expensive upkeep of prisons and the best type of camps are much more helpful than ordinary prison conditions for building up morale and physical strength. A similar plan is that of the farms which are sometimes attached to prisons, where prisoners live in houses after the cottage or colony plan detailed in Chapter 22.

Woman Prisoners

Women prisoners are often cared for in prison colonies. Women prisoners in the United States were not housed in a separate institution under women officers until 1873, after Rhoda Coffin, a Quaker, had induced the governor of Indiana to sanction a special prison for them in 1869. The second women's prison in the United States was established in 1877 in Massachusetts. Today imprisonment for women has been practically abolished in some districts, and particularly when they come under the Federal administration. They are cared for instead, on the cottage colony system, and the results of this system, by which they learn to take care of a home, and make home life more attractive, have been particularly encouraging.

Release from Prison

In most states, a prisoner can gain a certain number of months less imprisonment each year by good conduct, and thus earn unconditional release before his full sentence has been served. This is in accordance with the Elmira plan already mentioned.

Some prisoners are pardoned from the punishment originally allotted to them. This possibility allows political favor and graft to enter into the prison administration; it also makes it possible for a judge to feel that he can unjustly favor the emotional judgment of people about a prisoner during the trial period, and then later undo the wrong done to some extent by obtaining a pardon for the accused. Pardons, of course, are necessary if an error in justice occurred.

Parole

Parole, like probation, is a feature of modern penology, and is chiefly associated with the indeterminate sentence. The first law in the United States which sanctioned the indeterminate sentence was passed in the State of New York in 1889. Under this sentence a minimum and a maximum period of imprisonment is usually imposed. After the expiration of the minimum term, the prison administrative board or the court judge, has the option of releasing the prisoner on parole at any time up to the fixed maximum term of imprisonment. Thus a man with a sentence of two years minimum and ten years maximum may be released on parole at any time from the second to the tenth year. Laws sanctioning parole are now on the statute books of all states except three: Florida, Mississippi, and Virginia.

Parole is not pardon. A prisoner on parole is subjected to the same supervision as a person on probation, and he receives the same assistance. Usually work is found for him before he is released, his home and workplace are visited regularly, and he is obliged to report to a parole officer at fixed intervals. If he does not behave properly, the parole may be withdrawn at any time before the maximum sentence has expired, and he is returned to prison to serve his full term of imprisonment.

To earn parole, a prisoner must show a sincere reformation. This is generally measured by the merit or progressive-stage system, which allows a prisoner to obtain certain privileges, or to lose privileges, depending on his behavior. This system is particularly successful in helping the reformation process and in making the prisoner self-reliant. The higher the grade he attains, the greater the measure of liberty he is allowed, and in many states the final stage before parole is a stay on the prison farm, where prisoners wear civilian clothes and have very few restrictions.

The parole system is stated to have been instrumental in effecting true reformations, for prisoners can thereby be kept in custody for a sufficient length of time to make scientific treatment of individual needs both possible and of value. It has various disadvantages however: the system permits of possible bribing of guards or others to report good behavior and to recommend parole; it also sometimes permits of friends of the prisoner offering fictitious positions to secure his release; and occasionally an employer will make use of his knowledge of the parolee's prison record to exploit him unjustly. The general advantages of the system however, in effecting reform, seem to outweigh the disadvantages.

Recidivism

Habitual criminals or recidivists are a special problem. They may appear incorrigible, and society needs greater protection from them than from the occasional offender. Some states, such as Michigan and New York, deal with recidivism by enforcing imprisonment for life after a certain number of felonies have been committed. Where the felonies have been singly of relative unimportance, this punishment would seem to be excessive, particularly as the judge has no power to mitigate the sentence. But repeated serious violations of the law may in certain cases involve either a contempt for it, or a neglect or reformation after repeated opportunities, or both; and the menace to society by injury to its law or to its members may be such as to justify the permanent removal of the menace. Such laws have, then, a great deterrent value.

Juvenile Delinquency

As most criminals begin their delinquent career before reaching maturity, if the reformation of young criminals can be successfully accomplished, and if the young can be shielded from the temptations of criminal acts, a great number of potential crimes will be obviated.

A real attempt is now being made to improve the social conditions which make for juvenile delinquency, and to take a social interest in each delinquent child so as to help him to adjust his conduct to norms of right action. One of the aims of the Children's Charter, proposed at the White House Conference on Child Health and Protection, held in Washington in 1930, was the following: "For every child who is in conflict with society the right to be dealt with intelligently as society's charge, not society's outcast; with the home, the school, the church, the court, and the institution, when needed, shaped to return him, whenever possible to the normal stream of life."

The occasion of delinquency is often inadequate training and defective home life, over which the child himself has no control. Parents, therefore, are more frequently to blame for a child's delinquency than is the child himself; and much delinquency must also be charged to communities which allow defective housing systems to exist, inadequate recreational facilities, and educational systems which omit religious and moral training and inculcate false naturalistic and materialistic philosophies into young people soon to be parents themselves. There is, too, our defective economic system. Our present organization of occupational society often necessitates mothers working to help the home financially; the payment of poor wages and the necessity of a family living near the place of employment frequently lead to uncongenial and poverty-stricken surroundings. These and other factors which enter into crime causation have already been enumerated at the beginning of this chapter. A greater interest in the child at school, the establishment of clubs, recreation centers, child-guidance clinics, have proved successful in avoiding many a serious conduct disorder. An analysis of all the cases of delinquency in 1930 brought before eighty-eight juvenile courts in the boys' cases, and eighty juvenile courts in the girls' cases, showed the following results:

Reasons for the Delinquency[12]	Boys' Cases Total Per Cent	Girls' Cases Total Per Cent
Total	100	100
Automobile stealing	6	less than 1
Burglary or unlawful entry........................	11	less than 1
Holdup	1	less than 1
Other stealing	26	12
Truancy	8	13
Running away.......................................	5	15
Ungovernable	6	25
Sex offense	2	21
Injury to person....................................	2	2
Act of carelessness or mischief....................	27	8
Traffic violation	3	1
Use, possession, or sale of liquor or drugs..........	1	1
Other reasons......................................	3	1

	Delinquency Cases					
	Totals		Boys		Girls	
Color and Nativity of Child[13]	Number	Per Cent Distribution	Number	Per Cent Distribution	Number	Per Cent Distribution
Total cases	53,757	...	45,374	...	8,383	...
Color reported..	53,750	100	45,367	100	8,383	100
White	43,898	82	37,361	82	6,537	78
Native	38,786	72	32,671	72	6,115	73
Foreign born..	919	2	765	2	154	2
Nativity not reported	4,192	8	3,925	9	268	3
Colored	9,852	18	8,006	18	1,846	22
Color not reported	7	...	7	...	......	...
Total cases[14] ...	36,766	100	30,853	100	5,913	100
Native parentage	19,395	53	15,698	51	3,697	63
Foreign or mixed parentage	17,371	47	15,155	49	2,216	37

It will be seen from the above tables that stealing and acts of carelessness are the chief reasons for the boys' arraignments; and that sex

[12] *Juvenile Court Statistics 1930,* Bulletin No. 212 (Washington: Children's Bureau Publications, 1932), p. 14.
[13] *Ibid.,* p. 7.
[14] *Ibid.,* p. 7.

offenses and incorrigibility (chiefly connected with sex, as a general rule) are the major causes of girls' offenses.

So far as Negro children are concerned, some interpretative remarks in the next chapter will point to mitigating circumstances. Neither must one neglect to take into account that there is a smaller age group of whites than of Negroes, in the lower ages, because of restricted families among white people in recent years, a fact which is not so noticeable among the colored, although it must be said that the Negro child mortality rate is higher.

On account of the lessened immigration around 1930, the few delinquents of foreign birth would be expected. It is noteworthy, however, that of the native-born group, about half the boys and nearly two thirds of the girls were of foreign parentage.

When a child has actually committed a delinquency, it is best to deal with him, when possible, with speed and understanding. England was the first country to recognize the advisability of summary dealing with juvenile delinquents, and the Juvenile Offenders Act of 1847, amended by the Summary Jurisdiction Act of 1879 (still in force) gave judges power to give summary trial to all juvenile delinquents other than those accused of homicide. Similar laws were also passed in other countries, and judges sometimes tried children's cases separately from the ordinary court sessions. However, as a result of some agitation on the part of the Catholic Visitation and Aid Society, the Women's Clubs of Chicago, and the Chicago Bar Association, a bill was successfully presented before the Illinois Legislature, for the establishment of the Chicago Juvenile Court in 1899. This special children's courthouse and its program for the systematic treatment of all neglected, dependent, and delinquent children revolutionized the care of the child delinquent. Although the well-known Chancery Courts in England, founded in 1705, had exercised the parental authority of the State when the parents of a child were dead, absent, or neglectful, the Chicago court was the first to take systematic care of delinquents also, and to provide specially trained workers to study childhood's needs. Holland followed Chicago's lead in 1901, and England in 1905. The juvenile-court system is, at least in the statute books, more highly developed in the United States than elsewhere, and today only the two states of Maine and Wyoming have not legally established special courts for juvenile delinquents. Generally speaking, however, these courts are only to be found in the larger cities.

Although most people agree that it would be a better practice to treat of dependency and relief cases elsewhere, the juvenile court usually has several departments, these dealing with (1) the placing out of delinquents, orphans, and neglected children in foster homes and institutions; (2) the supervision of pensions to mothers of dependent children (see Chapter 18); (3) the supervision of families which look after foster children, or where children have been neglected but are not yet taken from the parents; (4) the investigation, trial, and supervision of children charged with delinquency, and placed on probation, in foster homes or institutions, or on parole.

Under the term *juvenile* are usually included children up to the age of sixteen or eighteen. Delinquents older than juveniles, but under twenty-one years are often treated more leniently than adults, however, and special attention is usually paid to them as "young persons."

Juveniles who come to the attention of the court are allowed to stay at home, if this is feasible, until they are brought to the court for examination and trial. If it is impossible to keep them at home, they are often placed in the bad atmosphere of the county jails, although in many cities they are placed in special juvenile detention homes, and some cities place delinquents in foster homes where these are available. In Boston, delinquents are always placed in foster homes, and it is hoped that in this way they will not come in contact with the contaminating influence of other delinquents, as so often happens in institutions. As soon as possible after notification of an offense, juvenile-court officials study the case from the point of view of social history; they also give psychiatric, psychological, and physical examinations where these are necessary. If the child is physically or mentally defective, steps are taken to remedy these defects. If possible, an attempt is made to adjust the child to normal behavior by placing him on probation or in a foster home. Probation is, of course, to be preferred, as in this way the child continues a normal home life, and also does not become a charge on the community. Special probation officers make it their duty to be a real friend of the child, to visit him regularly, and to do everything possible to help him, whether he be on probation with his own family, or in a foster home.

"Young persons" who need institutional supervision are generally sent to special reformatories, which are usually based on the Elmira plan in the United States. Many of the institutions for juveniles are on the "cottage-system" plan, which most readers will agree to be better for the young than the larger institution. Great care is always made in institutions not only to train the delinquent's character, but to teach him a trade which will enable him to earn a decent livelihood in later years.

So far as Catholics are concerned, in many cities they have founded special institutional homes where boys or girls who come from reformatories and similar places of detention may live happily under supervision until they get a chance to adjust themselves once more. There are also a number of special Catholic reformatories and detention homes where the court sends Catholic delinquents who come under the heading of "juveniles" and "young persons," and where everything possible is done to induce them to wish to live up to the principles of the Church. Nor must one forget the work done by the St. Vincent de Paul Society, the Knights of Columbus, the Catholic Women's League, and similar Catholic societies, who detail certain members to take an interest in the aftercare of Catholic offenders of all ages. Many Catholics belong to "Big Brother" and "Big Sister" organizations — the former founded in New York in 1904, and the latter organized by Mrs. Vanderbilt in 1908. These organizations send representatives to be present at all juvenile-court hearings, to protect the interests of the young accused. They take a very special interest in their young charges and generally do all that a real elder brother or sister would do for an erring younger member of their family.

CHAPTER 27

IMMIGRATION AND RACE PROBLEMS

Brief History of Immigration

No OTHER country in the world is composed of people of so many different nationalities and races as the United States. We all know that the Indians are the native Americans, but from the advent of Columbus in 1492, right down to the present day, people of all races and nationalities have been continually arriving. First came the English, Scottish, Irish, Dutch, Spanish, and French; Negroes were brought in as slaves, though some members of this race entered as freemen (a fact which is sometimes forgotten). At the time of the establishment of the Republic, however, 3,172,444 persons, 80.7 per cent of the population, were white and of these 82 per cent were English and Welsh. The period from 1789 until 1870 is known as the period of "old immigration," during which time nearly 10,500,000 immigrants entered the country, the majority of them coming from the north and west of Europe: Great Britain, Ireland, Germany, the Netherlands, and Scandinavia. In 1850 the census returns showed that of the 50,155,783 total population, 6,679,943 or 13.3 per cent were foreign born. Then began what is called the "new immigration," when large numbers of immigrants from southern and central Europe: Russia, Poland, Italy, Hungary, Bohemia, Serbia, and other countries entered the United States. At the census taking of 1890, nearly 21 million people or 32.8 per cent of the total population were foreign born, but of these nearly 70 per cent were British, Irish, and Germans. Between 1900 and 1910 alone, almost 9 million immigrants came to the United States, and although this was the highest figure for any decade, there were over 4 million immigrants in the 1921–30 period. The report of the Commissioner of Immigration shows that the total number of immigrants between the years 1820 and 1930 was 37,762,012. Of these, 32,276,346 came from Europe; 4,241,429 from Canada and South America; 903,-195 from Asia; and 341,042 from other countries.

The 1930 census shows that 34,703,183 inhabitants or about 32 per cent of the total population at the time, were white people of foreign parentage. Over 21 million of these were born in the United States, but

IMMIGRATION INTO THE UNITED STATES[1]

Year	Number of Immigrants
1821–1830	143,439
1831–1840	599,125
1841–1850	1,713,251
1851–1860	2,511,060
1861–1870	2,377,279
1871–1880	2,812,191
1881–1890	5,246,613
1891–1900	3,687,564
1901–1910	8,795,386
1911–1920	5,735,811
1921–1930	4,107,209
1931–1936	256,538

13,366,407 were foreign born, although the 1930 Report of the Commissioner of Naturalization stated that 58.5 per cent of the latter category were already naturalized, and an additional 9.3 per cent had taken out "first papers." Few foreigners have come into the country since this time, and many more have become citizens, doubtless induced to do so by reduced naturalization fees and the restriction of old-age pension and many relief monies to citizens only. Besides these white people of foreign parentage, there were living in the United States in 1930, according to the census report, nearly 12 million Negroes, about 139,000 Japanese, and 75,000 Chinese as well as several thousand other colored peoples.

POPULATION OF THE UNITED STATES[2]

	1930	1920
White	108,864,207	94,120,374
Negro	11,891,143	10,463,131
Other	2,019,696	1,126,115
Total	122,775,046	105,710,620

The total number of foreign-born peoples, both white and colored, in the United States in 1930 was 14,202,149, or about 12 per cent of the total population, and of these 864,865 or 6.6 per cent were unable to speak English. Since 1930 no foreigners have been admitted as aliens who were likely to become public charges, and as a result the number of immigrants has dropped considerably; from 241,700 in 1930, to 97,139 in 1931, 35,576 in 1932, 23,008 in 1933, 29,470 in 1934, 34,956

[1] *Statistical Abstract of the United States,* 1937, p. 95.
[2] *Ibid.,* p. 11.

in 1935, and 36,329 in 1936. Not only is the present immigration negligible compared with that of former times, but the number of departing foreigners exceeds the arrivals. Many of these departing aliens are deported, but the majority have left voluntarily, for a variety of reasons, chiefly because of the lack of unskilled work here, since foreigners do not qualify for many of the relief projects; because their savings will be able to keep them for a longer period in their own country, or because of unemployment insurance available abroad.

EXCESS OF ADMISSIONS OVER DEPARTURES OF ALIENS[3]

Period Ended June 30 —	Immigrant Over Emigrant	Total (including non-immigrants and non-emigrants)
1930	191,039	173,789
1931	35,257	— 10,237
1932	— 67,719	— 112,786
1933	— 57,013	— 93,074
1934	— 10,301	— 13,268
1935	— 3,878	— 9,329
1936	512	— 2,385

The Causes of Immigration

Immigrants came to the United States for many reasons. Some had been banished from their country for political, religious, or other reasons, and took up their social life again in the New World. Others came voluntarily because of differences at home regarding politics or religion, or because they were malcontents, or had a roving disposition and a spirit of adventure, or most frequently, for economic reasons — because their country did not offer them a livelihood (as when the Irish came in large numbers after the famine of 1845), or because they thought there were greater opportunities for self-advancement in the United States.

Immigration Restrictions

At first the country welcomed everyone who wished to come, but the number of immigrants of all types, races, and characters increased so rapidly that since the year 1882 several laws have been passed to prevent certain types of immigrants from entering the country. Chinese came to the country in large numbers from the time of the California gold rush which began in 1849, and because of the disproportionately large number, Chinese Exclusion Acts were passed in 1882, 1884, and

---

[3] *Ibid.*, p. 95. Excess of departures is indicated by a minus sign.

1888 which prohibited the immigration of Chinese laborers and imposed other restrictions. In 1885 a law was passed forbidding the immigration of "contract labor," foreigners who had bound themselves by a labor contract before entering the country. This was designed to prevent the competition of cheap foreign labor, for the ignorant were very often exploited by Americans, and signed contracts for wages in the belief that the purchasing power of money here was higher than it actually was.

In 1888 a law was passed to provide for the deportation of aliens who were illegally in the United States. In 1891 admission to the United States was denied to polygamists and all suffering from contagious diseases, and this law was extended in 1903 and 1917. In 1917 a head tax of $8 was imposed on each immigrant entering the country, or reentering it after an absence; and a law was passed that no alien who could not read or write English or some other language should be allowed to enter. In 1921 the number of people of any nationality who could be admitted as immigrants each year was restricted to 3 per cent of the number of that nationality which was recorded in the census of 1890. In 1924 a Japanese Exclusion Act was passed, similar to the earlier laws excluding the Chinese. In the same year the 3 per cent "quota" was reduced to 2 per cent, and immigration was forbidden to all aliens who are ineligible to citizenship. This law applied to all countries except those of North and South America. It was very far reaching in its effects. First, only "free white persons" and persons of African nationality and descent are eligible to become naturalized citizens, and so all Asiatics were *ipso facto* completely excluded. Secondly, the "quota" entirely excludes immigration from certain southeastern countries, and discriminates to some extent against the Latin races, the Slavs, and the Irish, because the greater proportion of peoples in the United States in 1890 were of British and German extraction. The law was, indeed, specifically designed to favor "Nordic" immigration, an attitude resulting from the false doctrines of Lothrop Stoddard, Madison Grant, and others, to which we referred in Chapter 5. Indeed, 42.75 per cent of the total number permitted to enter the country in any one year are allowed to come from Great Britain and Northern Ireland, 16.08 per cent from Germany, and 11.61 per cent from Ireland; 82.7 per cent of the total is allocated to the countries of "old immigration" and only 15.8 per cent of the total yearly immigration may come from countries in southeastern Europe.

Further restriction makes it necessary for every immigrant to present a health certificate and a certificate of good character, to be able to read and write and, finally, to be in possession of a definite amount of money upon arrival which, as we mentioned before, has considerably checked the number of immigrants coming here.

Despite the quota law certain non-quota immigrants are admitted as immigrants, such as the wives and unmarried children under eighteen years of age of citizens of the United States, certain professional persons, and students for the period of their studies.

Immigration Problems

Since the number of Negroes in the United States is so great, and since the majority of them have been here for generations, we shall discuss separately the problems they face and the difficulties involved in the adjustment of race relations, and shall confine our attention for the moment to the immigrant. The problem of Oriental immigration is omitted, because the relative number of Orientals in the country is small, and also because they are largely confined to the Pacific Coast.

Although immigration is now practically at a standstill, it will nevertheless be useful to discuss the difficulties which arise from the influx of foreigners to the country, because the immigration laws will probably be relaxed again in the future, and also because many of those who came within recent years are still a social problem. It must not be forgotten, however, that many of our best known public men have been immigrants, for example: Mary Antin, Russian author and lecturer; Charles Proteus Steinmetz, from Germany, famous electrical engineer; Michael Pupin, from Hungary, noted professor of physics and mathematics at Columbia University; Joseph Pulitzer, from Hungary, philanthropist and patron of letters; Jacob Riis, from Denmark, who worked so successfully in connection with slum clearance in New York; John Muir, from Scotland, naturalist and explorer, particularly in Yosemite; Andrew Carnegie, from Scotland, criticized indeed for his manner of making a fortune from the steel industry, but whose later philanthropies toward the cause of peace, and the establishment of numerous libraries have been of great worth not only to the United States but to the world at large. It must be noted, too, that many immigrants have been professional people and highly skilled craftsmen, and far from creating a problem, they have been of the highest worth to the citizens of the country. Even the poorer and less endowed classes have been of high value to the development of the United States, for they have supplied the demand for labor and have done necessary work which many native-born Americans did not wish to perform.

As might be expected, many social, economic, and political problems have resulted from the continued influx into the country of large numbers of peoples of different culture backgrounds.

The first difficulty with the entry of immigrants into the United States is the fact that many have been without resources and have spoken little or no English. Although most of them came from rural districts, or were small-town artisans, upon arrival they have usually settled in the poorer quarters of large cities, and because most of them were unskilled in industrial occupations, they have welcomed any occupation they could find, and have taken up the most menial and underpaid occupations. Ignorant of the language and the law, people of their own race have frequently exploited them under the guise of friendship, finding them miserably paid employment and exacting fees out of proportion to the services they rendered. Contract labor was forbidden by the law of 1885, but the exploitation by labor agents of immigrant laborers, especially the Italians, has been an open scandal. Eventually many immigrants took advantage of better conditions in places other than that of their first settlement, moved to other districts, and found employment for which they were more suited by training and ability. However, sweated labor, woman and child labor, an increase in slum population, juvenile delinquency, disunion in family life, and destitution, have been the inevitable results of the immigrant's need of earning a livelihood immediately upon arrival. Their poverty and need of relief has often been a drain on a particular community.

One of the worst consequences of the exploitation of immigrants was a practical debauching of a democracy's most essential safeguard, the right of suffrage. Especially in the larger cities, immigrants were quickly helped by politicians or their henchmen through the process of naturalization and given the right to vote. Though coming from a country which had problems in no way similar to the economic and social problems of the United States, and though ignorant of the language through which they might have informed themselves, they were taken to the polls to vote on momentous, often civically vital, affairs. Very frequently, in their ignorance of reading and writing, they had to be "aided" in the marking of their ballot. This was almost inevitably cast for the candidate this assistant favored, and the candidate was often an unworthy one. Sometimes this "foreign" vote was large enough to sway municipal or state elections, and generally it led to the formation of "national" groups, seeking national privileges without consideration of the good of the country as a whole.

The assimilation of immigrants into the life and customs of the country presented a problem of a different type. If the people of a country are to form a unified social group within the State, they must be at least somewhat homogeneous in habits and outlook. Yet while many immigrants have been of an educated class, have spoken the English language, and have been able to adapt themselves readily to American ways, very many others have been illiterate, or have come from countries whose language, laws, customs, and ideals may be equally as satisfactory as the American, and yet differ widely from them. As we said, immigrants usually settled in the larger cities, and as they were generally joined by their relatives and friends they have formed colonies where those of the same nationality live in close association, speak their own language, eat their national foods, and follow their own social customs. Their conservatism and clannishness has been a great obstacle to their absorption and Americanization. Orientals provide the worst problem, for their notions of God, of marriage, the home, and the State are all different from our own concepts; they lose the restraints of the sanctions of their own country, and they frequently fail to understand and to conform to ours. The problem is one which is not easy of solution. On the one hand, it is desirable that immigrants should adopt our culture patterns so that a closer understanding will be reached, and the nation will be one in mind and spirit. On the other hand, when immigrants lived together in these national groups, they were provided with the companionship of those they understood, and the transition from their own way of living to the American mode of life was much less painful. Moreover, it seems very advisable that immigrants should be encouraged to preserve the best in the culture which they have brought with them from their native lands: their folklore and dances, their language, and their distinctive occupational pursuits, for it is precisely the mixture of peoples in the country which makes the rich and varied culture of the United States.

A third problem of immigration is a domestic one. The children of immigrants attend American schools and thus come into contact with American ideals and customs much more quickly than do their parents. Naturally wishing to conform to the school and play groups to which they belong, they frequently come into conflict with their social life at home, and even lose respect for their parents because of their differing social habits. Moreover, they speak English as well as any child of American parents, and often fail to learn the language used by the older members of their family. Often, therefore, they grow up undisciplined outside school hours. Disrespect for their parents leads to disrespect for the law, so that the children of immigrants very frequently become delinquent in this manner. Then, too, the quota immigration laws have led to much domestic distress because of the separation of families. Relatives of immigrants already here have been unable to come because they do not conform to quota laws, or could not furnish the necessary certificates of health and literacy. Other members of immigrant families have been deported on arrival, and even if a deportation is for a purely technical reason, perhaps due to the fault of American officials in other countries, a deportee is never allowed to enter the country again. Such family separations lead to bigamy, desertion, and cases of nonsupport of families left in our midst. Until the current restrictive ruling forbidding the entry of immigrants without sufficient means to insure their not becoming a public charge, a much greater proportion of male immigrants came to this country than females. The lack of stable family life which necessarily resulted, created certain social problems, but the situation is already much improved because about 60 per cent of the immigrants since 1930 have been the wives and female relatives of male immigrants who have already been here some time and are in a position to support them. The stabilizing influence of the homes thus set up will eliminate much of the restlessness of the young male immigrant.

Provision for Immigrant Needs

Immigrants are particularly in need of friendship on their arrival in the country — the friendship of people who will find them a suitable dwelling place and occupation, who will teach them, help them to understand American culture patterns, and find them friends among their own national groups.

The Immigrant Publication Society, founded in 1914, collects and distributes practical information, and has greatly helped immigrants through such books as the *Guide to the United States for the Immigrant* and *Makers of America*. Settlement houses, the Knights of Columbus, the Kolping houses, the Y.M.C.A., and the Y.W.C.A., the foreign literature sections of many of our public libraries, and the special classes for foreigners in citizenship and in the history of the United States, have also given them invaluable aid. Since the great decrease in immigration of the poorer and uneducated classes since 1930, the need of classes in citizenship has much declined. Evening classes are still available in most of the larger cities, but there seems to be a need of afternoon classes in English, citizenship, and national affairs, for women who are free from their domestic duties only at that period of the day. Catholics are well provided for by the N.C.W.C. Bureau of Immigration. This bureau establishes working contacts with responsible Catholic welfare societies in many countries abroad, is notified of the date of arrival of Catholic immigrants, and aids them from the time they begin their journey until they are happily settled over here. All immigrants are free to call upon this bureau for information or help in connection with deportation troubles, re-entry into the country after a vacation abroad, or any other matters in connection with their life in the United States.

Because Catholic immigrants who sometimes settle in non-Catholic or anti-Catholic environments, are ignorant of the whereabouts of the local church, cannot understand the language, and are sometimes given the impression that to be a good citizen they must abandon their religion, special interest should be taken in them by American Catholics. Although there is very little need of such help at the present time, on account of the restrictions, yet when immigrants do come to a parish, Catholics should do all that is possible to help them. A few Catholics in each parish should make it their special duty to help all immigrants on their arrival in the district, to give them advice, introduce them to the parish priest, acquaint them with the hours of church services, find them suitable Catholic friends, and show them that it is not necessary to abandon their religion in order to be American citizens — rather, that their religion will help them to become good citizens, and that many of the best Americans are at the same time zealous Catholics.

Naturalization Requirements

Provided his immigration papers are in order, every immigrant may remain in the country as long as he wishes, whether or not he attains citizenship by naturalization. He is given the protection afforded to citizens, and must, of course, pay his share of the taxation of the country. In order to vote, however, and obtain the privileges of a citizen of the United States (ability to apply for certain types of work, certain scholarships, state pensions, and the like), he must renounce his allegiance to his own country and become a naturalized citizen of the United States. Any time after arrival he may go before a court and take out his "first papers," provided he is at least 18 years of age, pays a fee of $5, and promises to renounce his allegiance to any other government. After he has been here five years, but not less than two years after taking out "first papers," the immigrant may again go before the court and ask to be declared an American citizen. His request must be accompanied by a fee of $10 and an affidavit given by two citizens who certify that he is 21 years of age, or over, and they have known him to be a resident of the state where the application is made for one year or more, and that he has been a resident of the United States for at least five years. He must also pass a short test in American history and citizenship. Ninety days after this request has been filed, the immigrant may again appear before the court and receive his naturalization papers, making him an American citizen. Foreign-born children automatically become citizens upon the naturalization of their father, and any child who is born in the United States, even though his father be an unnaturalized foreigner, is considered an American citizen by birth.

Some foreigners do not become citizens because of the expense entailed with the process: the loss of time and earnings for himself and his sponsors during the several court visits that are required, and traveling expenses which may be quite considerable in some of the rural districts of the country. To induce a greater number of unnaturalized aliens to become citizens, in 1934 the naturalization fees were reduced from much higher amounts than the figures given above.

The Situation of the Negro

At the present time there are more than twelve million Negroes in the United States: a number which cannot be ignored when one realizes that this Negro population comprises 10 per cent of the total. There are towns and cities where Negroes are comparatively rare. In some states of the South, he almost equals the white inhabitants;[4] in the North, he forms one tenth or one eighth of the population of such cities as Detroit, Chicago, St. Louis, and Washington. Despite his color, the Negro is an American citizen, as truly American as any white man, and often more American, for he at least has been in the country for several generations, whereas many a white man has not yet mastered the intricacies of the English tongue. Moreover, recognition should certainly be given to the Negro's influence on American prosperity. In days gone by one must consider the fishers, the rum trade, and the slave trade of New England, the tobacco and corn work along the Southern Atlantic States, and the sugar and cotton work in the South (the antebellum sources of wealth). In later times the Negro's labor in both South and North, especially during the late World War,

---

[4] The largest percentage of Negro population is found in Mississippi (50.2); South Carolina (45.6); Georgia (36.8); Louisiana (36.9); Alabama (35.7); North Carolina (29.0); Florida (29.4). Cf. *Fifteenth Census of the United States:* Population, Vol. IV, pp. 41–45.

has also been a signal contribution to the country's wealth — and a reason also for the great migration of the Negro to the North. Yet whereas the white man, as a foreigner, or with merely his "first papers" is treated as an equal by the American-born white, the Negro, however educated, is more often than not treated with unfavorable discrimination. Details of this situation, an examination of the reasons for it, and a discussion of the principles involved, is our consideration in the remainder of this chapter.

History of the Negro in America

Though Negroes are not indigenous to American soil, it may be said that, next to the aboriginal Indians, they probably form the oldest social body in the United States, since some writers authoritatively assert that they came from Africa to America long before the voyage of Columbus' ship in 1492.[5] Their advent as slaves may be traced to the year 1495, when the slave traffic first began with the exportation of Negro slaves from Africa to Europe by Prince Henry of Portugal. This profitable venture was imitated by Spain. With the discovery of the West Indies, the climate being found too hot for the exploitation of the islands by Europeans, the Spanish court allowed a large number of Negroes to be transported to the newly discovered lands as early as 1511. England soon followed suit, and eventually the English slave trade assumed such proportions that in 1672 the Royal African Company of England sold two thousand slaves to Jamaica alone. As regards America, Negroes came in 1526 with the Spanish expedition of Vasquez de Ayllon, which settled near the site of Jamestown (established in 1607). Twenty slaves were brought to Jamestown itself by the Dutch in 1620. In 1671, numbers of slaves were brought from Barbados to South Carolina, to cultivate such crops as sugar, tobacco, rice, indigo, and cotton — work for which they were more fitted than the white man. The biggest impetus to slave importation took place, however, after Eli Whitney had invented his machine in 1793, which permitted the spinning of American short-fibered cotton. Cultivation of cotton then began on an enormous scale, and with it the demand for slaves.[6]

Nominally abolished in 1808, the slave trade continued until the end of the Civil War, when it was entirely done away with as a legal insti-

---

[5] Cf. *The Negro Year Book,* 1931–32 edition, p. 305; also Professor Leo Weiner (Harvard), *Africa and the Discovery of America.*

[6] In 1790 there was a total of 575,181 Negroes in the United States, of whom 59,557 were free; in 1860, the total was 4,441,830, of whom 448,070 were free (cf. *The Negro Year Book,* 1937–38, p. 244).

tution by the Thirteenth Amendment to the Constitution in 1865. Then followed what is known as the period of reconstruction. Before 1865, even those Negroes who were free were not allowed to vote, but in 1868 the North sponsored the passing of the Fourteenth Amendment, giving Negroes all the rights and privileges of citizens; and in 1870 the Fifteenth Amendment forbade any state to deny a citizen the right to vote on account of "race, color, or previous condition of servitude." Quite naturally some of the newly emancipated slaves abused their power, while others were exploited by the white carpetbaggers sent down from the North.

Although the Federal Government intended to insure by the Fifteenth Amendment that Negroes should not be denied full franchise rights, nevertheless, this Amendment left many loopholes by which the South could restrict voting privileges, which it did, despite the fact that it was precisely the Southern Negro who needed the protection which could be afforded by his adequate representation in Government. From 1875 onwards the Southern states began a system of legal evasion of the Fifteenth Amendment, and enacted laws which, without going entirely against the letter of the American Constitution, imposed suffrage restrictions on Negroes, yet in no way eliminated the electoral privileges of the whites. The Southern states contended that though they could not deny a Negro the right to vote because of his color, they could deny all citizens the right if they failed to fulfill certain legal enactments which they inserted in their state constitutions, such as: the requirement that all voters should own a certain amount of property; have paid a poll tax; be able to read and write; or be capable of understanding and interpreting any section of the constitution of the state. Such provisions effectively denied voting privileges to the majority of Negroes, who had been unable to adjust themselves to conditions of freedom, and were mostly poor, vagrant, and often uneducated. These laws, however, also excluded many of the poor white population, against whom no discrimination was intended. In 1898 Louisiana was the first state to devise what is known as a "Grandfather Clause." Thereafter, Southern states began to insert into their constitutions enactments which would, during a certain period, enable persons disqualified by suffrage legislation to be placed upon the roll of voters if they or their ancestors had voted in the state before 1867.[7]

---

[7] Louisiana, 1898. Art. 197, sec. v: "No male person who was on January 1, 1867, or at any date prior thereto, entitled to vote under the Constitution or statute of any state of the United States wherein he has resided, and no son or grandson of any such person not less than twenty-one years of age at the adoption of this con-

Most white people could qualify under this provision, whereas Negroes who could not qualify under other clauses were still effectively excluded because citizenship rights had not been given to them until the year 1868. While "grandfather clauses" are now mostly inoperative, except in Virginia, Alabama, and Texas, in the South, as we have already mentioned, the voting privilege is still indirectly denied to many Negroes. The individual's capacity to vote may be determined by the general governmental body insofar as age, educational, and other reasonable requirements are concerned, and a man may forfeit his right to vote by crimes against society; but the vote should not be denied solely because of unreasonable or unjust racial discriminations.

The reason why the majority of Negroes were unable to measure up to the standards of property and literacy is not hard to find. The slaves came to America with their own primitive culture, and did not, of course, possess the specialized education of the European meaning of the term. Here they were forced to work hard, sometimes under the most cruel taskmasters. This increased their docility, but in no wise made them industrious. The work they were given to do was mostly of the unskilled kind; they could possess nothing of their own and as the masters were supposed to provide them with everything, they were not required to use foresight in providing for emergencies and old age. Their ignorance was not enlightened by education, for beginning with 1740 the various states had passed laws forbidding the instruction of slaves, and imposing penalties on those who taught them.

Nor were their morals safeguarded in any way: "American slavery placed few restraints upon the Negro's sex life, and failed to offer any efficacious substitute for the taboos and interdicts of the African Village."[8] Under slavery the masters often failed to respect or give protection to the virtue of their female dependents. Marriage ties were lightly regarded, and frequently slaves were sold without regard to the ensuing separation of husband, wife, or children. Quite often, too, the marriage contract was considered unnecessary and the marriage ceremony entirely omitted. In fact the morals of the Negroes were deliberately broken down for breeding purposes, since the more prolific the slaves, the wealthier became the owner. Negro women also were wholly at the whim of white masters and overseers, and the failure of these latter to guard the virtue of their female dependents is amply

---

stitution . . . shall be denied the right to register and vote in this state by reason of his failure to possess the educational or property qualifications presented by this constitution. . . ."

[8] Rev. Francis J. Gilligan, *The Morality of the Color Line*, p. 10.

evidenced by the large percentage of American Negroes who are known to be partly white — a percentage which could not be accounted for wholly by voluntary miscegenation.

There were, of course, Negroes of high moral standing, who had come in touch with missionaries, who had been taught surreptitiously by Christian masters, and who had natural gifts and abilities which they had fostered.[9] Others also, and particularly mulattoes, were often employed in the master's house and had observed their ways and imitated them. Often, too, since the whites were responsible for the mixed race, many of the masters saw to it that mulattoes received an education. At the time of the emancipation, however, the great body of the Negroes, especially in the South, were uneducated and indolent. And although some had received an industrial training, the majority had performed only the most unskilled tasks and were utterly incapable of earning a livelihood.

With the disfranchisement of the Negro by the various voting laws, there was naturally much bitterness on the part both of the slave and of the owner. The majority of the former masters disliked the practical equality with which the Negroes were vested by the amendments to the Constitution. The Negroes, on the other hand, resented the vote discrimination and the way they were treated by the white race. And, of course, as previously mentioned, some Negroes inevitably abused their newly gained freedom and incurred the condemnation of the whites. But the worst effect of the emancipation was economic. Deprived of the protection and guidance of their masters, and generally discriminated against in favor of recent immigrants, many Negroes became entirely destitute. Poverty has a cumulative effect. Within a few months the economic status of the ex-slaves was appalling. The situation was intensified by the strong resentment which the Southern whites showed toward Negroes. When mastery was destroyed, the slaves were ostensibly made equal. The poorer white people in the South, who were always hostile to the colored, now felt the competition of the freedman. Personal work became a necessity for many of the former slave owners, to whom the ownership of Negroes had represented wealth. The sudden and violent methods of the politicians of the reconstruction period not only caused dismay but increased the resentment. Peonage and exploitation in the South, and prejudice and opposition in the North, excluded the Negro from business oppor-

---

[9] Among the Catholic slaves there were by no means a few who were distinguished by holiness of life, e.g., Pierre Toussaint in New York, and others noted in Maryland mission records.

tunities everywhere, led to discriminative wages, and to social segregation.

For many years the so-called Negro problem was principally of Southern concern. But gradually the Southern Negroes migrated. In 1910 there were over a million Negroes in the Northern states. Then came the World War with its shortage of labor, and the ensuing demand for Negroes in the industries of the North. Their migration was hastened by crop failures, and more than a half a million moved North between the years 1910 to 1920, and an equal number in the five years following. This large influx of labor, mostly into a few such cities as St. Louis, Chicago, and Detroit, led to a severe housing problem, and intensified the Negro question in the North.

A Comparison Between Negroes and Whites

The notion is rife among many members of the white race that the whites are superior to the colored, intellectually, morally, and manually, and that Negroes and whites in the United States can never live together in amity. Let us examine the facts.

The reader is asked to refer to the middle section of Chapter 5, which deals with Racial Origins and Modern Race Theories. It will be remembered that we showed that there was no scientific evidence whatsoever to prove that one race is by nature superior to any other. History and anthropometry both reveal the constant intermixture which occurred in no small measure between whites and the Negroes within the brief history of the United States. The fact that there is definitely no "pure" race in the world today, is, in itself, a witness to the inaccuracy of the theories of racial superiority. Africa is the second largest continent in the world, and has a greater number of diverse peoples, with their differing cultures, than has Europe. Of the Negroes in the United States today, we have no scientific record of those who are "pure blacks" or descended from mixed racial stock; those who are Negroes, or merely Negroid. Census statistics up to the year 1920 reported on the Negro population under the divisions "black" and "mulatto," the term *mulatto* being used as descriptive of those who had some proportion of white blood.[10] In 1920, of a total of 10,463,131 Negroes, 8,802,577 or 84.1 per cent were classified as "black" and only 1,660,554 or 15.0 per cent as "mulatto." These figures were, however,

---

[10] The general meaning of the word *mulatto* is a person who is descended from one parent who is "pure" white, and one parent "pure" black; *quadroon* is the term given to a child of a mulatto who marries a white; the word *octoroon* describes the offspring of a quadroon and a white; *mustifee* is the name given to the child of an octoroon and a white person.

most arbitrarily determined, as the Bureau of Census itself noted.[11] And since the 1920 census takers reported a smaller percentage of mulattoes than in 1910, it was realized that the classification had little value, and so the distinction was discontinued. Actually the number of Negroes of pure stock in the United States is very limited, and certainly far less than the percentage of 84.1 which was recorded in the 1920 census. Herskovits, an authority in the anthropological field, after studying the genealogies of Negroes at Howard University and in Harlem, gave statistics[12] which lead to the conclusion that this sample testing of race mixture shows: "the astonishing information that instead of 80 or 85 per cent of the American Negroes being wholly African in descent, only a little over 20 per cent are unmixed, while almost 80 per cent show mixture with white or American Indian or with both stocks."[13]

In Chapter 5 we also took up the general question of racial achievement. Here we shall compare the achievement of the American Negro and the American white, as the popular opinion on the subject is nearly always, and quite unscientifically, in favor of the whites.

To consider first the question of Negro intelligence. Performance in intelligence tests is one of the criterions by which a judgment is made that Negroes are of inferior intelligence to the whites. Yet the findings do not appear to present a true picture of the situation. First of all, length of stay in city environment makes for ease or difficulty in passing such intelligence tests, since the manner in which they are given, and the words and concepts involved, are designed for those accustomed to city life. As a group the Negro population of the United

NEGRO POPULATION AND PERCENTAGE LIVING IN URBAN
OR RURAL COMMUNITIES[14]

Year	Total Number	Percentage of Total U.S. Population	Percentage Rural (towns of 2,500 inhabitants and less)	Percentage Urban
1890	7,488,676	11.9	80.2	19.8
1900	8,833,994	11.6	77.3	22.7
1910	9,827,763	10.7	72.6	27.4
1920	10,463,131	9.9	66.0	34.0
1930	11,891,143	9.7	56.3	43.7

[11] *United States Census*, Vol. II, p. 16.
[12] Melville J. Herskovits, *The American Negro: A Study in Racial Crossing* (New York: Knopf & Co., 1928), p. 10.
[13] *Ibid.*, p. 9, cf., also *ibid.*, pp. 11–13.
[14] *Fifteenth Census of the United States:* Population, Vol. II, p. 34; also *The Negro Year Book*, 1937–38, p. 256.

PERCENTAGE DISTRIBUTION OF GAINFULLY EMPLOYED NEGROES
10 YEARS OF AGE AND OVER, 1890–1930[15]

Occupation Groups	1890	1900	1910	1920	1930
Agriculture and allied occupations.............	56.6	53.9	49.0	45.1	36.7
Mining	0.6	0.9	1.4	1.5	1.4
Manufacturing and mechanical industries........	5.6	5.7	14.0	18.4	18.6
Trade and transportation.....................	4.4	4.9	8.3	9.4	10.6
Clerical service	0.3	0.3	0.4	0.8	0.7
Domestic and personal service.................	31.2	32.8	24.9	22.1	28.6
Public service not elsewhere classified...........	0.2	0.3	0.5	1.0	0.9
Professional service...........................	1.1	1.2	1.5	1.7	2.5
Total per cent...............................	100.0	100.0	100.0	100.0	100.0

States has been largely rural for several generations, but has moved into the cities in great numbers during and after the War. This change from rural districts and agricultural employments to the city and industrial life is amply evidenced by census figures for the past forty years.

Another consideration in appraising the performance in these intelligence tests is the widespread racial prejudice and the fear many Negroes experience in their contact with white officials, so that a "rapport" is not established between the subject of the test and the one who gives it, the latter almost invariably being a white person. Then, too, on account of this prejudice, it is by no means certain that the tests are given to Negroes in the same manner as to whites, or that they are evaluated in as favorable a manner.

Again, a greater percentage of Negro children than white children have had the poor cultural surroundings attendant upon poverty and the lack of educated parents. Even intelligent children can be dulled by the drab surroundings of poverty, by the disease which often comes from malnutrition and inadequate medical care, by despair for their future progress, and by the absence of intellectual stimulus provided by parents with education and leisure and the means to provide cultural objects of various kinds. If grandparents or parents are illiterate, almost inevitably there is an absence of alertness in the home training of the child, which may color his whole mental outlook and his achievement in later life. The poor economic situation of Negroes, often due to discrimination in obtaining employment, in the wages paid to workers, and in opportunities for training, is well known. In addition to this, many Negroes have failed to procure an adequate education for, as we shall later discuss, the education available to Negro children

[15] *Ibid.*, Population, Vol. IV, p. 24; also *Negro Year Book,* 1937–38, p. 260.

in the Southern states is often inferior to that received by whites. The performance on the tests given to Negroes would be comparable to the results on the same tests given to white children, only if both had similar opportunities and environment.

Some people have cited in favor of the theory that Negroes are less intelligent, the fact that nearly all the members of the race who have been successful are of mixed white and Negro stock, and not of "pure Negro parentage." This situation is probably due to the greater opportunities which were given to the lighter colored Negroes in slave days, and have continuously been given to them since that time. Light-complexioned Negroes can often receive an education, or take a position of a type which may be denied to those of more obviously Negroid type.

Yet by no means all Negroes fail to achieve average results in the intelligence tests, or fail in the practical business of life. Far from considering the Negro as unintelligent, whites should marvel at the enormous progress which has been made by American Negroes since their emancipation in 1863. In all history, there is no such record of swift, silent, peaceful, almost unobserved progress as the Negro has made in America in the past seventy years, with the migration of more than 2,000,000 Negroes to the North during and immediately after the World War — despite his handicaps socially, in economic life, in education, and every other way.

Culturally, Negroes have always had a passion for education, sought in a pathetic heroism in slave days, and even now despite the restrictions and humiliations to which they are subjected. Each year thousands of Negroes receive college or university degrees, many of these obtained from state or private institutions in the North, and on the same academic conditions as the white students, though frequently under great financial and other sacrifices. In the South they have their own universities, colleges, and schools, including such notable institutions as Howard, Fisk, Atlanta, Hampton, and Tuskegee. In literature, music, and the other arts, Negroes are extraordinarily well represented. They are regular contributors to all the better American periodicals, and their volumes of poetry, fiction, and essays, stand well among American literary works. William Stanley Braithwaite is an arbiter of American poetry, and Paul Laurence Dunbar, James Welldon Johnson, Countee Cullen, Langston Hughes, Claude McKay, all Negroes, are ranked high among the poets. Tanner the painter, and Meta Warwick Fuller, the sculptor, are fully recognized by connoisseurs of art. Booker T. Washington's *Up from Slavery*, *The Souls of Black Folk* by

W. E. B. DuBois, James Weldon Johnson's *Autobiography of an Ex-Colored-Man*, are American classics, as distinguished for their technique as they are for their notable expositions of American life. Stephen Perry and Paul Robeson, the actors; George Carver, an agricultural chemist of high distinction; Thomas W. Turner, also an agricultural chemist with an international reputation; Alain Locke, Harvard graduate and Rhodes scholar; Charles S. Johnson and Robert R. Moton, writers and social reformers — all are men of whom America may well be proud. The number of Negro inventors and those who have attained degrees and special honors is also impressive.[16] Foreign Negroes of distinction include such persons as Alexandre Dumas and Alexander Pushkin, whose literary ability at all events will not be questioned, and the notable composer, Samuel Coleridge Taylor.

Despite the severe economic and social discrimination to which he has been subjected, the Negro's economic progress has also been impressive. As far back as the year 1900, Booker T. Washington organized the National Negro Business League to encourage the Negro to enter business fields. The Negro now owns many business enterprises, banks and insurance companies, and in many towns and cities has organized his own Chamber of Commerce.[17] The Negro has also formed such associations as the National Medical Association, the National Bar Association, the National Association of Teachers in Colored Schools, the National Press Association, and the National Association of Negro Musicians. There are also two influential societies for the promotion of Negro welfare: the National Association for the Advancement of Colored People which has been particularly active in the defense of Negro rights, and the National Urban League which has rendered signal service in the solution of problems of recreation, employment, and housing.

It is sometimes specifically stated that the Negro in industry is relatively less efficient than the white worker. *Quod gratis asseritur, gratis negatur.* So far as actual statistics are concerned, the United States Bureau of Labor Statistics reports that in 1920 the Chicago Commission on Race Relations interviewed 93 employers of Negro labor, of whom 71 "considered the Negro as efficient as white workers, and 22 reported the Negro as less efficient; the first group, however, included nearly all the large employers of Negroes."[18] Three other and more

---

[16] Cf. *The Negro Year Book,* 1937–38, pp. 1–14.

[17] *Ibid.,* pp. 90–95.

[18] *Handbook of Labor Statistics,* 1936, "The Negro in Industry," U. S. Bureau of Labor Statistics Bulletin No. 616, p. 576.

recent inquiries, discussed by the United States Bureau of Labor Statistics show equally favorable returns:

EFFICIENCY AND REGULARITY OF NEGROES AS COMPARED TO WHITE WORKERS, ACCORDING TO OPINIONS OF EMPLOYERS[19]

Efficiency and Regularity	Detroit Bureau of Government Research Survey		Pennsylvania Department of Public Welfare Survey		J. Tinsley Willis Survey	
	No. of Firms Reporting	Number Employed	No. of Firms Reporting	Number Employed	No. of Firms Reporting	Number Employed
Degree of Efficiency						
More efficient ...	11	5,102	14	1,780	1	1,200
Same efficiency..	68	12,631	32	6,400	3	13,677
Less efficient	24	2,729	10	1,120	0	......
Not reported....	17	1,109	..	.....	3	454
Total	120	21,571	56	9,300	7	15,331
Degree of Regularity						
More regular ...	7	199	3	431	0	......
Same regularity .	68	8,864	28	6,321	5	12,754
Less regular[20] ...	33	11,587	25	2,548	1	2,177
Not reported....	12	921	..	.....	1	400
Total	120	21,571	56	9,300	7	15,331

Again, the Negro has frequently earned higher premiums under the Bedeaux system than white employees — the premium being payable strictly on excess of fixed output.[21]

Then there is the question of morals to be considered. A greater number of Negroes, both adults and juveniles, come into conflict with the law, if one takes the percentage of total population into consideration. That this fact is due to a greater inherited criminal propensity is, of course, not true. The reasons are probably social. Undoubtedly racial discrimination has led to a greater number of indictments of Negroes and to a more severe attitude being taken toward their offenses, and also, unfortunately, conviction on not too substantial evidence.[22] It is notorious that judges are frequently more severe with the Negro than with the white offender, so deeply rooted is the idea

---

[19] *Ibid.*, p. 577.

[20] "Recent migration was felt to be responsible for the high rate of irregularity. Labor turnover, for Negro employees was thought to be generally less than that for white employees." *Ibid.*, p. 577.

[21] Cf. *Ibid.*, pp. 577, 578.

[22] Cf. *Negro Year Book*, 1937–38, pp. 147, 148.

that the Negro is a "born criminal." Racial prejudice of the police, perhaps unwittingly, also seems to enter into the situation on occasions, for statistics show that a very high proportion of Negro arrests are dismissed through lack of substantial evidence. Again, racial discrimination has undoubtedly not only kept the Negro in the low-income group, but has confined him in overcrowded districts with all the added temptations of poverty and the disabilities of living in an overcrowded neighborhood. More Negroes than whites are arrested in poolrooms and other places of bad repute simply because the Negro often has no other place to go for relaxation. A great proportion of Negro mental deficients are not cared for by institutions as are most of the whites, and hence there is a greater possibility of their becoming delinquent. The continuing effect of the poverty, discrimination, racial despair, and environmental influence of slave days still has its influence, as we said, upon the grandchildren or the great grandchildren. Added to this, the influence of the migration of large numbers during and after the War, from the Southern rural districts to the large industrial areas, must be considered. Whereas 6,903,658 Negroes (13.4 per cent of the total rural population) lived in rural districts in 1920, only 6,697,230 (12.4 per cent of the total rural population) lived there in 1930, while Negro town dwellers increased from 3,559,473 to 5,193,913 in the same period.[23] Undoubtedly this change has created adjustment difficulties which would account for a greater amount of delinquency and crime.

Illegitimacy rates among Negroes are also much higher than for white people. For example, the number of illegitimate births per 1,000 total births in 1933 was 20.9 for whites, and 156.0 for Negroes. These higher rates may probably be accounted for in large measure by the earlier age at which Negro girls usually begin work, the low wages paid to them, and the percentage who take up city employment with all its temptations for the underpaid and lonely country girl or woman.

Negro children also show a greater tendency toward delinquency if the number of those arraigned in the courts is taken as a criterion, as shown by statistics in the last chapter. Yet, as we said, one must not neglect to note that there is a smaller proportion of white children than of Negroes according to relative population, because of restricted families among white people in recent years, a fact which is not so noticeable among the colored,[24] although it must be said that the

---

[23] *Statistical Abstract of the United States,* 1937, p. 19.
[24] *Ibid.,* p. 50.

child mortality rate is higher with the latter. Also, Negro delinquency in general is more striking for its frequency than its gravity. And a prominent feature of the graver Negro crimes is that they are usually committed on impulse, and rarely from conspiracy or plotting. The general opinion of Catholic priests who have ministered to Negro parishes, or in neighborhoods of large Negro population, seems, indeed, to be very favorable toward the morality of the Negro when properly trained in true ideals of conduct. This opinion is borne out by the study made in New York of delinquent and neglected Negro children brought before the New York Children's Court: "On the basis of population the proportion of juvenile delinquents among Negroes is considerably greater than among the whites, but whereas the most common charge against the white boys is stealing, that against Negro boys is disorderly conduct; the offense second in importance among Negro boys is desertion of home, whereas among white boys who are brought to the Children's Court it is burglary."[25] It may well be less difficult to eradicate a large percentage of Negro crime — when some of the gross injustices to the race are eliminated — than to reform the average white criminal.

It would seem that because white people have such limited opportunities of knowing Negroes adequately, and are usually restricted to such sources of information as biased newspapers or casual acquaintance with Negro employees, they need to be on their guard against forming a stereotype of the Negro, and of grouping all Negroes under this fantastic picture. In their 12,000,000 or more, there are as many grades or castes as there are among whites, with the highly cultured and the uneducated, the refined and the crude, the deeply religious and the careless, the well-to-do and the impoverished.

Negroes and Human Rights

All men, whatever their color, are sprung from the same stock — the stock of Adam, and all mankind is essentially the same, as we showed in Chapter 5. All men, not those of one color only, were redeemed by Christ and were created for a like destiny in heaven. Hence in their human nature and their eternal destiny, the primitive and the civilized, the white and the colored, are all equal. And however inferior a man may appear to be in relation to other men, he has certain natural rights which are the same as, and as sacred as, those of his seeming

---

[25] *A Study of Delinquent and Neglected Negro Children,* Joint Committee on Negro Child Study in New York City, 1927, p. 6.

"superiors."[26] The Negro, even as the white, has, therefore, a right to life, to liberty, to truth, to live socially under duly appointed authority, to property, and to justice. His right to all these goods is seriously impaired when he is not allowed to earn a decent livelihood, or must accept unjust conditions; when he is deprived of an adequate opportunity to avail himself of public education; when his health and recreation needs are not provided for in the same manner as for whites; when legal justice is denied him; when he is deprived of full rights of citizenship in proportion to his natural rights and the sacrifices he has to make. If the members of one race deny to another justice and its complementary duty of charity, there is a serious moral wrong, for, as Pope Leo warned: "No man may outrage with impunity that human dignity which God Himself treats with reverence, nor stand in the way of that higher life which is the preparation for the eternal life of heaven."[27] Instead, as Pope Pius XI wrote: "It is the work of Catholic Action to unite Catholics of every social class . . . in thought and action."[28]

Negro Problems

The Negro himself rightfully claims that *he* is no problem, and he resents being considered and called one. As he says, he is simply a human being and an American citizen, with his natural and civil rights; and all that he demands is that these rights be respected. There is no problem in this. For him, therefore, the problem is a white problem — for the white man to overcome his assumed sense of superiority, a traditional antipathy and a cultivated prejudice, and, with this rational readjustment of himself, to grant the Negro his rights. But though the Negro may not be the cause, he is the occasion of the Negro problem, or the interracial problem, as it might better be called. We shall now discuss some of the principal problems which Americans must face by reason of 10 per cent of the population belonging to the Negro group.

1. *Miscegenation.* Miscegenation, the mixture of races, is one of the major problems resulting from the presence of a colored race in the United States. Biologically there is nothing proved against interracial marriage: from the biological standpoint, indeed, a mixture of races is often beneficial, although, as we said in Chapter 5, it may result in

---

[26] Cf. Chapter 7, on man's rights and duties according to the postulates of Christian sociologists.

[27] *Rerum Novarum*, p. 23 (*RN*, 32).

[28] Pope Pius XI, "Letter to Cardinal Bertram," *Catholic Mind*, p. 82.

physical disharmonies. From the social viewpoint, however, miscegenation is not at present to be desired, either by the Negro or the white man. The present attitude toward the Negro often make relations difficult between the respective relatives of such a marriage. Loss of social prestige not infrequently makes the white party regret the step he took in marrying the other. Children born to the union, if of different colors, may feel the difference in race acutely, and live in disunity and strife. Or the children, as sometimes happens, take sides against the white parent, if they see the colored parent is discriminated against. Misunderstandings between husband and wife may give rise to a long-forgotten former race aversion. Only too often, aversion, hatred, and despair are the custom of such marriages. Therefore, while the Church does not forbid interracial marriages, since to do so would be a sin against justice and charity, yet such marriages add grave dangers to the normal risks of wedded unity. Parents of white children of marriageable age are consequently justified if they refrain from inviting the colored of the opposite sex to their houses or social gatherings. To do so is possibly to foster a union which will normally lead to much unhappiness, and it is a parent's duty to shield his offspring from pitfalls of this kind.

The racial prejudice which causes the peculiar problem of miscegenation is not, of course, an innate trait in mankind. Prejudices, of their nature, can only be acquired. In France this antipathy is practically nonexistent, and the colored people from the French dependencies can be seen mixing on equal terms with the Frenchmen. Children do not experience it, and many a white child brought up with a black nursemaid retains his affection for her long after childhood days are past. The "color line" as practised at the present time is almost ridiculous in its anomalies. White people have Negro nurses, cooks, maids, domestics of all kinds, but will give no recognition to a Negro of their own social or cultural status. This prejudice may have arisen originally because the whites, conscious that they have done the Negro a wrong in slavery days, feel a moral guilt and rationalize this by developing a feeling of repugnance. When adults adopt an attitude of antagonism and aversion to the colored, children inevitably acquire the same bad habits, and so the lack of justice and charity toward the Negro becomes a fixed traditional convention.

The question of Negro segregation in public places does not as frequently arise in the North. In the South, however, existing conditions are different. Because of deep-seated prejudices, the larger proportion of Negro population, and the possibility of miscegenation with its unhappy social consequences, the current opinion among the white population of the South is that the maintenance of separation is advisable for the continuance of peace and well-being, although it sanctions and perpetuates racial antagonism, the arrogance of the white man, and the resentment of the Negro, while its restrictions are accepted practically by the Negroes in order not to lose even those benefits that they can gain under the segregated system. Separation of social groups *merely as separation* does not in theory mean discrimination. In theory, groups can be separated and yet receive equal rights as citizens. Indeed, if justice is not to be violated, in any scheme of separation all citizens must be affected equally, nor should the restrictions be to the detriment of one particular group alone. Separation on the ground *of race alone,* however, owing to its inherently unreal basis, is bound to work out to the detriment of particular groups, especially when it is pursued as a policy for large numbers of people over a long period of time and extended to an almost infinite variety of situations. Apart from the injustice of the situation, the white people do themselves an injury when they crowd large numbers of fellow citizens, merely because of their different color, into undesirable districts, pay them inadequate wages, and deny them normal social life. Such segregation not only leads to a group within the State, with poor health and education and low consuming power, but it breeds discontent. Under this system, too, the better educated of both races are denied the opportunity of mutual understanding and of helpful co-operation.

Even though quite a large amount of miscegenation takes place at present, a "brown America" is certainly not so imminent as some alarmists try to prove, for miscegenation is not ever likely to be on a larger scale than now, and Negroes of mixed race tend to become whiter in color. Contrary to the popular belief, indeed, it is now confidently held by many that where the colored party is an octoroon, the offspring (sometimes called "mustifees") will definitely "pass the line" and will actually belong to the white race.[29] Others still question whether sufficient experimental evidence exists to warrant an assertion that the "passing over" will be inevitable. But the former hold that it has now been definitely shown that white characteristics, and not the black are dominant; that "mustifees" really belong to the white race, and that their offspring again, and all future generations, will inevitably be white if no new mixture of Negro blood is brought into the family.

---

[29] Johnson, C., "Crossing the Color Line," *Outlook and Independence,* August 26, 1931, p. 526. Cf., also Embree, Edwin R., *Brown America,* p. 46.

2. Discrimination in Education and Educational Opportunity. In 1860, of the 247,149 free colored persons over 20 years of age, the United States census report shows that 62.9 were literate. The slaves, by law, were deprived of an education. In 1861, the first day school among the freedmen was opened, and various others were established in 1862. The big impetus to Negro schooling at the time was, however, given by the Freedmen's Bureau, created in 1865 with the education of freedmen as one of its main objects. During the five years of its existence the number of Negro students in school increased from 90,778 to 149,581.[30] In 1870, 2,789,689 Negroes, or 81.4 per cent of the total Negro population, could not read or write. By 1931–32, the average daily attendance of Negro students in public elementary and secondary schools was 1,802,928.[31] The 1930 census showed that only 1,513,892 or 16.3 per cent of the present Negro population were illiterate. Great as is this progress, it compares very unfavorably with the general percentage of all illiterates in the country in 1930, including the foreign born, for this general figure was but 4.3 per cent, so that Negroes as a group are definitely less educated than other groups.[32] Public-school education in the North makes little difference, if any, between the white and the colored. In the South, however, conditions are quite otherwise. Many Negro children live too far away from a school to get an education. Negroes are entirely excluded from many of the public schools, and where separate schools are provided out of public funds, there is a great disparity between expenditure on the white children and on those of Negro blood, and an adequate training for higher educational pursuits is very often completely lacking. The salaries paid to Negro teachers are usually wholly inadequate, and the buildings and equipment very poor. In addition, the Negro school year is usually over a month shorter than the school term for the white children, because the children's services are needed on the farm, due to family poverty. Fifty per cent of the Negro schools in six Southern states have school years of less than 150 days. An extreme example of disparity in expenditure for the education of white and colored children was quoted by Charles S. Johnson in 1930: At that time, in the states of South Carolina and Mississippi, Negroes, who make up about 50 per cent of the population, were allotted only slightly above 10.5 per cent of the total public expenditure on education.[33] It would certainly seem that

---

[30] Cf. *The Negro Year Book*, 1937–38, p. 161.
[31] *Ibid.*, p. 167.
[32] Cf. *Statistical Abstract of the United States*, 1937, p. 41.
[33] Charles S. Johnson, *The Negro in American Civilization*, p. 262.

since the Negro and the white man bear equal tax burdens, justice requires that they have equal educational advantages. Since it is to the advantage of a State to have educated citizens, the lack of equal educational facilities for all citizens is to the detriment of the well-being of America as a whole. Of course some Negroes come from highly cultured home surroundings, and have the advantages of an adequate private education. The disparity in expenditure on the public education of the poorer Negro has been so flagrant as to make a strong appeal to private philanthropies. To a very limited extent this public deficiency has been made up from private funds, such as the Julius Rosenwald fund. But the discrimination is there, and on the whole the Negroes are the losers. And it is hardly to be expected that the Negro will equal the white man in attainments, if handicaps of this nature are continuously imposed on him.

In the North, all state universities and colleges are open to the Negro, and most of the distinguished private institutions, such as Yale, Harvard, Cornell, Bryn Mawr, the University of Chicago — to name a few. The great majority of Catholic institutions, however, were closed to Negroes, until about 1935. Since that time, the Catholic University in Washington has opened its doors to colored students, also, and gradually a number of other colleges and high schools are doing likewise. But although the situation is being rapidly remedied, in many localities Catholic Negroes are still forced to attend non-Catholic schools, and the subsequent defection from the Church by reason of this is inevitable.

3. *Discrimination in Public Places.* Discrimination in theaters, restaurants, hotels, street cars, railroads, and even churches, takes place in certain districts. Such discrimination is sadly lacking in Christian charity, and often involves injustice as well. Probably the worst offense in this regard is the "Jim Crow" car of the Southern railroads. The occupants pay the same as white people, but are given inferior accommodation. The railroad company, in other words, profits by the local prejudice. This segregation is a particular hardship to many Negroes traveling at night, who, although willing to pay for Pullman accommodation, which is one of the amenities of modern travel, are prevented from availing themselves of this privilege. The railroad is the loser on these occasions, it is true, but its action involves unnecessary hardship for our colored population.

4. *Economic Discrimination.* It may be well here to quote Leo XIII on the subject of the right of a worker to earn his livelihood: "Without the results of labor a man cannot live; and self-conservation

is a law of nature, which it is wrong to disobey. . . . The labor of the workingman is not only his personal attribute, but it is *necessary;* and this makes all the difference. The preservation of life is the bounden duty of each and all, and to fail therein is a crime. It follows that each one has a right to procure what is required in order to live; and the poor can procure it in no other way than by work and wages."[34]

The Negro is discriminated against in the matter of work in several ways, all of which are serious. Some employers refuse to give them work at all; others employ them only for work of an inferior nature. Others again pay them a lower rate of wages than is given to white men for similar services. The refusal of labor unions to allow Negroes to become members also prevents employment in some occupations. As Pope Leo pointed out in the foregoing quotation, the poor can live only if they obtain work, and the variety of types of human intelligence and gifts would point to the justice of allowing the Negro to secure the work for which he is by nature and training best adapted.

Various reasons are given by employers for discrimination against the Negro. In the first place, they assert that the white man is a superior worker. This is a question which we discussed earlier. Statistics of the attitude of employers of Negro labor, as well as the results of actual performance, as shown by weekly payments on the Bedeaux plan, show that if each Negro be judged on his individual merits, many can and do prove equal to such a test. A second reason alleged for discrimination against Negro workers is that the white men will not work with the colored. This is often true. Yet no man may deprive a fellow being of his right to earn a livelihood. Third, many employers will not hire Negroes because of the refusal of specific labor unions to allow Negro workers to become members. Strong resolutions have been passed by national labor conventions against the exclusion of Negroes from local unions, but little practical effect has been given them. The Negro should continue his efforts to be admitted into existing unions, but this failing, he should himself organize unions for his own protection, and to help himself attain equal opportunity with the white man. Lastly, some workers fear that if the Negro be given employment as an equal, the wage standard will be lowered, and with it their existing standard of living. This argument is fallacious, because the non-union Negro laborer is encouraged to work for a lower wage, and this "cut-rate" competition tends to lower the wage of the white laborer. The remedy for these conditions is, of course, for both em-

---

[34] *Rerum Novarum*, p. 25 (*RN*, 34).

ployer and worker to realize that there should be no wage discrimination in regard to Negro labor.

5. *Discrimination in Housing.* Everywhere in the United States, Negroes are restricted in their choice of residence. Many districts are entirely barred to Negroes, either by segregation laws, or, more generally, by a universal opposition of white occupants to Negro neighbors — partly because of racial antipathy, and partly because of fear of property depreciation. The housing that is available for Negroes is mostly dilapidated and grossly overcrowded. A district becomes a "colored section" either when the houses are in such disrepair that the white families have begun to move to other parts of the city, or when a proprietor with an eye to the profits has sold his property to Negroes at a price higher than the market. When Negroes move into a district, race prejudice, and sometimes the overcrowded conditions which Negroes are forced into because of high rents and lack of accommodation, usually leads neighboring white families to migrate to another locality, and Negroes take their place. The fear of depreciation in value of property if rented to a Negro is based on past facts. Yet these facts have very logical explanations. Where houses made available to Negroes are in a state of dilapidation, they are often difficult to put or keep in repair; and the lack of housing accommodation for the race makes for rapid congestion which necessarily increases the normal rate of dilapidation. The same is true of houses which may reach Negro hands in good condition: serious lack of housing makes for rapid overcrowding of most available residences. Apart from the great need of houses for the Negro worker, however, it is obvious that the restriction in their choice of residence implies hardship to many of the professional and other classes, who naturally may desire the same social environment as middle-class white people. It is a problem which needs serious study.

6. *Discrimination on Recreation and Health Facilities.* Even in the North, most clubs, golf courses, tennis courts, and so forth, are barred to Negroes, even many of those which are publicly owned. This, too, may become a serious detriment when it excludes necessary recreational facilities. A child without adequate provision for recreation cannot become fully developed, and play in the streets frequently leads to an early initiation into crime. Similarly, the adult may be led into crime through lack of recreational opportunity.

Johnson states[35] that he made specific inquiries in 75 cities of largest

---

[35] Charles S. Johnson, *The Negro in American Civilization*, p. 21.

Negro problem as regards facilities for recreation for Negroes. Returns were received from 32, and Johnson says: "Summarizing these returns briefly, it appears that in both the North and in the South one important condition of free participation in play facilities is separation; that where public support is not sufficient for an adequate dual system, the Negro facilities suffer; and that in 28 of the cities there are means for accommodation of not more than 8 per cent of the Negro children. . . . A feature which should be noted is the consistent opposition to Negroes in swimming pools and on golf courses."[36]

Several large cities, such as Cincinnati, Cleveland, Detroit, and New York, have taken definite steps to solve the recreation problem for the Negro, and the Playground and Recreation Association of America has a special bureau of colored work, and is doing much to promote facilities. Interracial committees have also helped to develop facilities in various towns as, for example, the one in Orlando, Florida, "which stimulated the city to provide a playground, club house, and bathing beach for Negroes."[37]

As for Negro health, the Bureau of Census reported in December, 1936, that out of 100,000 Negro male babies born alive, 91,268, as compared with 93,768 white male babies, will complete the first year of life; 82,903 Negro males and 88,621 white males will reach the age of 21; and 14,419 Negro males and 29,471 white males will reach the age of 75. Infant mortality is therefore greater among Negroes than among whites, and the life expectancy of Negroes is considerably less than for whites.[38] These discrepancies cannot, of course, be laid entirely to the economic and social condition of the Negroes; and yet their poor economic position, overcrowded conditions, and the like, undoubtedly have an influence on Negro health and mortality. Undoubtedly, too, the Negro is not so well cared for as the white in regard to hospital and similar facilities. In 1926 a study of the Negro hospital situation disclosed that in hospitals for white persons there was one hospital bed for each 139 white members of the population, compared with only one hospital bed for each 1,941 Negroes in hospitals for Negroes. The effect of this situation is not so bad in the North, where Negroes are admitted to many public hospitals in certain districts, but in the South Negroes are frequently denied admission to any hospital other than those specially designated for them.[39]

---

[36] *Ibid.*, p. 320.

[37] Quoted in the *Negro Year Book*, 1937–38, pp. 286, 287.

[38] *Statistical Abstract of the United States*, p. 82.

[39] Cf. W. D. Weatherford and C. S. Johnson, *Race Relations* (Boston: D. C. Heath, 1934), pp. 50, 51.

Catholics and the Negro

For Catholics, the problems of the Negro in America are perhaps the most tragic. Very many of the early Negroes in the United States in the sixteenth and seventeenth centuries were Catholics, under the tutelage of the Spaniards and the French. Very many, if not the majority of Negroes in the eighteenth century were Catholic also: although in the English colonies, they had been brought from the West Indies. In the year 1860 there are said to have been 250,000 Catholic Negroes in America, mostly in the states of Louisiana and Maryland. Today, at most only 270,000 of the total twelve millions in the United States are reckoned as Catholics. The numbers cannot be accurately given, for the Catholic statistics are notoriously defective, since many Catholic Negroes attending churches are not tabulated, and many, by reason of the widespread miscegenation are not recognizable as Negroes. The reason for this small number of Catholic Negroes compared with the millions of Negroes belonging to other denominations seems to lie first in the very sparse number of priests devoted to Negro missions, although this number is being increased yearly, and second, to the apathy of white Catholics, and their easy accommodation to the prejudice aroused and fostered by greed and ignorance and a blind conformity to convention. The prejudice toward the Negro shown by northern Catholics is more difficult to understand, on historical grounds, than that of the Southerners, when one considers that few were ever slave owners, and that non-Catholics have given more liberty to their colored missionary endeavors and to educational institutions for Negroes. We have already mentioned the leakage due to the discrimination shown to Negroes in Catholic schools, a situation which is but gradually improving.

What might be the remedy? First, on the material side, a better understanding of the Negro: a realization that he is no being of lower status and inevitable criminal tendencies, but an American citizen, honorable in every way. Second, the manifestation of an ordinary Christian attitude. A recognition on the part of Catholics that the

---

NOTE BY GENERAL EDITOR: In regard to Catholic hospitals in the United States, an official investigation into the number of Catholic hospitals accepting Negro patients was made by the Catholic Hospital Association, in its annual questionnaire sent out in 1936. About six hundred hospitals, representing 85 per cent of the entire number answered the question concerning acceptance of Negro patients. Of these hospitals 74 per cent declared definitely that Negro patients are accepted by them.

Further details regarding these statistics can be obtained from the Headquarters of the Catholic Hospital Association, located at St. Louis University Medical School, St. Louis, Mo., where the documents are filed.

Negro is their equal in the spiritual sphere; he possesses an immortal soul, was redeemed by Christ, and is a child of the same heavenly Father, bound for the same destiny as the white man. These are elementary truths of the Catholic faith. The Negro is the white man's neighbor, to be "loved as himself," and much practical zeal is necessary for the adequate support of his Catholic missions, charities, periodicals, and other works.

As a practical recognition of these truths many efforts are being made by various Catholic organizations and institutions. The community of the Sisters of the Blessed Sacrament was founded to work for Negroes and Indians, and began its labors as early as 1894. There are three religious communities of colored women: the Oblate Sisters of Providence (founded in 1829), the Sisters of the Holy Family, of New Orleans (1842), and the Handmaids of the Most Pure Heart of Mary (1920). There is a fraternal organization entitled the "Knights of St. Peter Claver," with its Ladies' Auxiliary, as also the Federated Colored Catholics whose official organ was *The Chronicle,* a publication later taken over by the Catholic Interracial Council and developed into the monthly *Interracial Review.* As was formulated at the sixth annual meeting of the Federation in 1930: "The Federation's prime objective is to unite all colored Catholic parishes and already existing colored Catholic societies for the purpose of national Catholic Action in all its phases." The Catholic Interracial Council just mentioned was organized in 1934 by Reverend John LaFarge, S.J., and a number of white and colored laymen. This newly organized interracial movement has led to some effective social developments. The Council itself maintains an active speakers' bureau whose members have addressed numerous Catholic colleges and societies, while it has called into being a number of Catholic intercollegiate Interracial Conferences.

The Industrial Conferences under the auspices of the N.C.W.C. have always supported the Negro cause. Resolutions regarding interracial justice have been passed by the Catholic Student Mission Crusade, the National Catholic Alumni Federation, and at conventions of the Students' Sodality of Our Lady. Catholic priests, too, have formed their own Clergy Committee for Negro Welfare. Scholarships for suitable Negro candidates have been offered by some of the Catholic colleges; and the Catholic press has recently displayed an increasing interest in Negro news and Negro needs.

CHAPTER 28

CATHOLIC ACTION

Definition of Catholic Action

As SOCIAL beings, needing the help of others because none of us is self-sufficient, a reciprocity is required of us, and we have an obligation to further the progress of society so far as we are able. Our previous study has shown us that most of the world's evils are due to a lack of attention to social rights and duties and the dictates of the moral law, and it is evident to all right thinkers that no progress is possible without consideration to God, and therefore to religion. For the Catholic, the best way to fill his duty to society is by spreading the Kingdom of God to bring all men to a knowledge of God and to His service. This is the specific purpose of Catholic Action. Within the past decade, Pope Pius XI has continuously stressed the important part which must be borne by the laity — the vast majority of Catholics — in the work of extending Christ's Kingdom upon earth. Atheistic communism is being spread by carefully organized plan; Catholicism is largely judged by the words and deeds of the laity who are those with whom non-Catholics most frequently come in contact; priests and religious cannot reach into all the spheres where an apostolate is actively required and the active work of the laity is urgently needed. For all these reasons Pope Pius has realized that the laity must be urged to undertake an active apostolate, and for the effective carrying out of such an end, organized and concerted effort is required. Catholic Action has therefore been constituted as the official organization of the Catholic laity in the apostolate of the hierarchy: the organized participation of the laity in the work of the Church, under the guidance of the bishops and priests. Priests and religious have their own work within the Church, by which they assist the hierarchy, and so they cannot form a part of Catholic Action — though Catholic Action units may be established as auxiliaries to their undertakings.

Fundamental to Catholic Action, therefore, is the organization of Catholic laity into societies approved by the hierarchy for special ends, and maintained under the authority and direction of the hierarchy. Frequently, the immediate direction of a Catholic Action unit is a suitable member of the laity, but unless he works with the direct authority and approbation of his Bishop, the organization, however laudable, is not a part of Catholic Action. It is to be noted, moreover, that organized Catholic groups whose main purpose is social, cultural, economic, or political, are not part of Catholic Action, for the main purpose of a Catholic activity approved as Catholic Action by the bishop must be, of its nature, mainly spiritual and supernatural in character.

The Work of Catholic Action

As Pope Pius XI has repeatedly affirmed, the first end of Catholic Action is the "pursuit of personal Christian perfection."[1] "Its first consideration should be to make good Christians,"[2] he says. Since our most important duty to society is that of good example (we showed in Chapter 3 the great importance of social environment in the molding of character and the influencing of attitudes and ideals) we must first make use of all the means given by God for our personal perfection in virtue. This important fact, Pope Pius has continuously expressed in official pronouncements and in semi-private letters to particular members of the hierarchy, and to special organizations. He pointed out to the Bishops of the Argentine Republic: "The axiom *nemo dat quod non habet* (one cannot give what one does not oneself possess) precludes from the work of the apostolate all who lack a formation in Christian virtue, without which Catholic Action will not only prove fruitless but lifeless."[3] The liturgy, therefore, has a fundamental role in Catholic Action, since active participation in the corporate services of the Church, and particularly the Mass (including the frequent reception of the sacraments) is the chief source of spiritual formation and sanctification for the Christian. Good schools, and the education which can be supplied to the laity by zealous priests, are, too, essential in this preparatory work of Catholic Action. This basic work of Catholic Action needs the auxiliary helps provided by membership in sodalities, and affiliation to one of the great Orders of the Church, such as the Oblates of St. Benedict, or the Tertiaries of the Carmelite, Franciscan, Dominican, or other orders — of which the

---

[1] Pope Pius XI, Letter to Cardinal Bertram of Breslau, quoted in the *Catholic Mind*, March 8, 1929, p. 82. (Permission to quote granted by the Press Department of the National Catholic Welfare Conference.)

[2] Pope Pius XI, Letter to a Catholic Society in Belgium, quoted in the *Catholic Mind*, January 22, 1930, p. 38.

[3] Pope Pius XI, Letter Addressed to the Bishops of the Argentine, 1931, quoted in *Central-Blatt and Social Justice*, December, 1937, p. 267.

Franciscan Tertiaries are, perhaps, the most active in formation for external works. However, it is especially participation in the liturgy of the Church which will give Catholics not only their own personal formation to sanctity, but a true realization of the social bonds which exist between mankind, bonds with which the Church, through Christ, helps to bind its members closer to God. True realization of the meaning of the liturgy, and of the Church as the Mystical Body of Christ, will always lead to a correct social attitude on the part of the participants, to a love for all men (of all races, creeds, and social conditions), and to a desire to spend oneself in external activity of some kind, for the good of others. Again, to quote the late Holy Father: "Truly, whoever loves God cannot fail to want others to do as much, and whoever loves his neighbor cannot fail to work for his eternal salvation. Such is the foundation of the Apostolate, which is nothing other than the practice of Christian charity, and this binds all men. Apart from the motive of charity, the apostolate is binding upon us as a thankoffering for graces received. Moreover, when we enable others to share these spiritual gifts we fulfill the wishes of the Most Sacred Heart of Jesus, whose one wish is to be known. 'Ignem veni mittere in terram, et quid volo nisi ut accendatur?' (I have come to spread fire upon the earth, and what more do I wish than that it be kindled?)"[4]

So concurrently with the essential work of personal sanctification, Catholic Action supposes an active apostolate. "The Christian once trained, must spend outside of himself the life that he has received. He ought to carry everywhere this treasure of Christianity, and make it live in every field of life, in the family, and in public life, not excluding politics. For what We wish is that Christ rule on earth as He rules in heaven and that His Kingdom over the world become effective."[5] As the Scriptures put it: "And this commandment we have from God, that he who loveth God, love also his brother."[6] And again: "He that hath the substance of this world, and shall see his brother in need, and shall shut up his bowels from him: how doth the charity of God abide in him?"[7] We must "do the truth in charity."[8] "Faith without works is dead."[9]

Catholic Action, then, "consists of a true *apostolate* in which Cath-

[4] *Ibid.*, p. 267.
[5] Pope Pius XI, Letter to a Catholic Society in Belgium, quoted in the *Catholic Mind*, January 22, 1930, p. 38.
[6] 1 John 4:21.
[7] 1 John 3:17.
[8] Ephes. 4:15.
[9] James 2:20.

olics of every social class participate, coming thus to be united in thought and action around those centers of sound doctrine and multiple social activity."[10] It involves, first of all, the discovery of our vocation in life (the priesthood, religious life, marriage, or the single life in the world),[11] the development of our gifts, the doing of all our actions as perfectly as possible. It involves prayer for others. It involves not only active work in the development of our gifts, but an acquisition of knowledge necessary for conversation with others, and for participation in the complex social and political affairs of the day. As Pope Pius XI has said: "To give this social activity a greater efficacy, it is necessary to promote a wider study of social problems in the light of the doctrine of the Church and under the aegis of her constituted authority. If the manner of acting of some Catholics in the social-economic field has left much to be desired, this has often come about because they have not known and pondered sufficiently the teachings of the Sovereign Pontiffs on these questions. Therefore, it is of the utmost importance to foster in all classes of society an intensive program of social education, adapted to the varying degrees of intellectual culture. It is necessary with all care and diligence to procure the widest possible diffusion of the teachings of the Church, even among the working classes.[12] The minds of men must be illuminated with the sure light of Catholic teaching, and their wills must be drawn to follow and apply it as the norm of right living in the conscientious fulfillment of their manifold social duties. Thus they will oppose that incoherence and discontinuity in Christian life which We have many times lamented. For there are some who, while exteriorly faithful to the practice of their religion, yet in the field of labor and industry, in

---

[10] Pope Pius XI, Letter to Cardinal Bertram of Breslau, quoted in the *Catholic Mind,* March 8, 1929, p. 82.

[11] Cf. For example, Rev. D'Arcy, M. C., *Christian Morals* (London: Longmans, Green, 1937), p. 35; also Goodier, Archbishop, S.J., *Introduction to Ascetical and Mystical Theology* (New York: Benziger Bros., 1938), p. 105 *et seq.* The Dutch movement for girls and women, called *The Grail,* now active in Holland, Great Britain, Germany, Australia, and elsewhere is an especially well-planned Catholic Action organization working toward this end. Members pray daily to know their vocation; they take especial pains to discover and develop their gifts, so that they may the more effectively make themselves useful for God's work as mothers of families or for whatever other vocation in life seems to be theirs. The Belgian *Jociste* movement (Young Christian Workers) and its allied groups for students, agricultural workers, and others, also has somewhat similar aims, and has an extensive membership in Belgium, France, Great Britain, Canada, and other countries.

[12] The reference here may be taken largely to mean the European worker who has a less extensive general education than the majority of workers in the United States many of whom are high-school graduates.

the professions, trade, and business, permit a deplorable cleavage in their conscience, and live a life too little in conformity with the clear principles of justice and Christian charity. Such lives are a scandal to the weak, and to the malicious a pretext to discredit the Church."[13]

In this same Encyclical Pope Pius stresses the power of the press in spreading a knowledge of Catholic doctrine. "In this renewal the Catholic Press can play a prominent part. Its foremost duty is to foster in various attractive ways an ever better understanding of social doctrine."[14]

Pope Pius has also pointed out the special need of Catholic Action work among the workers who, on account of economic and social difficulties and their lack of understanding of principles, have often thought to better their condition by the spread of communism. He has therefore urged parish priests, "while providing of course for the normal needs of the Faithful," to "dedicate the better part of their endeavors and their zeal to winning back the laboring masses to Christ and to His Church."[15] In the *Quadragesimo Anno* the Holy Father showed that: "In order to bring back to Christ these whole classes of men who have denied Him, we must gather and train from among their very ranks auxiliary soldiers of the Church, men who know their mentality and their aspirations, and who with kindly fraternal charity will be able to win their hearts."[16] He showed, too, how "Undoubtedly the first and immediate apostles of the workingmen must themselves be workingmen, while the apostles of the industrial and commercial world should themselves be employers and merchants."[17] This thought he has re-iterated in his encyclical on *Atheistic Communism:* "Here We should like to address a particularly affectionate word to Our Catholic workingmen, young and old. They have been given, perhaps as a reward for their often heroic fidelity in these trying days, a noble and an arduous mission. Under the guidance of their Bishops and priests, they are to bring back to the Church and to God those immense multitudes of their brother-workmen who, because they were not understood or treated with the respect to which they were entitled, in bitterness have strayed far from God. Let Catholic workingmen show these their wandering brethren by word and example that the Church is a tender Mother to all those who labor and suffer, and that she has never failed,

---

[13] Pope Pius XI, encyclical *Divini Redemptoris,* par. 55.
[14] *Ibid.,* par. 56.
[15] *Ibid.,* par. 62.
[16] Pope Pius XI, *Quadragesimo Anno,* p. 46 (*QA,* 48).
[17] *Ibid.,* p. 46 (*QA,* 48).

and never will fail, in her sacred maternal duty of protecting her children. If this mission, which must be fulfilled in mines, in factories, in shops, wherever they may be laboring, should at times require great sacrifices, Our workmen will remember that the world has given them an example not only of toil but of self-immolation."[18]

In addition to all these phases of Catholic Action, it involves, too, a participation in one or other of the existing Catholic Action organizations. These are, of course, many.

First and foremost, in the United States, comes the work of the National Catholic Welfare Conference, established first as the National Catholic War Council during the Great War. The chief work of this Conference is to act as the central organization of Catholic Action in the United States — to unite Catholic lay organizations throughout the country. It comprises the following departments: First, an Executive Department, which publishes the monthly journal *Catholic Action;* and conducts a Bureau of Immigration, to assist immigrants; a Bureau of Historical Records concerning Catholics during the War; a Bureau of Publications; a Bureau of Publicity and Information; a Youth Bureau; and various other works. Second, there is a very important Press Department, whose news service provides the majority of Catholic papers in this country with reliable news from home and abroad. Third, the Social Action Department, to whose work we referred in Chapter 7. This Department is responsible for the publication of a number of important pamphlets, and out of it three auxiliary independent committees have developed: the Catholic Conference on Industrial Problems, the Catholic Association for International Peace, and the Catholic Rural Life Bureau. Fourth, the Lay Organizations Department, including the National Council of Catholic Men, and the National Council of Catholic Women, with their many local branches throughout the country. The Men's Council has been responsible for the development of the radio program, the *Catholic Hour.* Fifth, the Education Department including a Teachers' Employment Bureau. Sixth, the National Catholic School of Social Service for the Training of Catholic social workers.

Not all lay organizations are, however, linked up with this National Catholic Welfare Conference. Most Catholic Action units are parochial, but others are wider in scope. Of these, perhaps most stress should be given to the Society of St. Vincent de Paul, which has been in existence for over one hundred years. The Society of St. Vincent de Paul is a lay organization of Catholic men, founded in 1833 by Frederic Ozanam

---

[18] Pope Pius XI, encyclical *Divini Redemptoris,* par. 70.

and a small group of fellow students at the University of Paris, under the inspiration and direction of M. Bailly, the editor of the *Tribune Catholique*. Its beginnings were very unpretentious, and Ozanam himself had, at first, no notion of founding a society, still less one which would find its place in practically every Catholic parish the world over, with thousands of members paying hundreds of thousands of visits yearly to the poor. The object of this small band of charitable youths was the sanctification of its members by mutual encouragement in a Christian life, and the visitation of the poor in their own homes. The guiding spirit of these visits was to be sympathy and service, that is, the moral and spiritual improvement of the families visited, and the employment of every effort to remove or alleviate their physical needs. The idea spread rapidly throughout France. In 1836 a branch was even established in Rome; in 1844 the society was organized in England, and in 1845 in St. Louis, Missouri.

In organization, the Society of St. Vincent de Paul very closely resembles the Elberfeld system which followed it, as mentioned in Chapter 22, with the exception that its funds for charitable distribution are obtained from the private donation of members and of the parish, instead of from compulsory public contributions. It is based on the organization of the Church: the parish is the unit, but no Conference (as each parish branch is called) is organized without the direct approval and co-operation of the pastor. A characteristic of the Society is, indeed, complete submission to, and respect for, ecclesiastical authority. Members of the Conference meet weekly, recite the prescribed prayers, report on the charitable undertakings of the past week, carefully consider the needs and circumstances of applicants for aid, and decide upon the coming week's program. In localities where three or more Conferences exist, Particular Councils are formed, membership being made up of Presidents of the Conferences represented, and such additional persons as may be necessary.

The work which is too extensive or unsuitable for the parish Conferences is put in the hands of the Particular Councils. These are entrusted with such work as the establishment of institutions and necessary central charitable bureaus; the extension of the Society in parishes where no Conferences exist; the provision of paid and trained workers to advise and direct the usual volunteer members, and the distribution of mutual financial assistance, so that the wealthier Conferences may help the Society in those parishes where the funds are insufficient to care for those in need.

Where there is more than one Particular Council in a diocese, a

Diocesan Central Council is formed, and the various Particular Councils in ecclesiastical provinces unite in forming Metropolitan Central Councils. These Central Councils are merely administrative and supervisory in character. They, in turn, are under the jurisdiction of the Superior Council for each country, which is likewise solely administrative in its function. The Superior Council is the connecting link between the National Councils and the Council General in Paris.

The work of the St. Vincent de Paul Society is Catholic Action in its highest sense. It embodies harmonious co-operation with the Church for the personal holiness of the members themselves, for the extension of Christ's kingdom among others, and for the scientific performance of the corporal works of mercy. It would be impossible to enumerate all the Society's activities, but among them we may cite: (1) spiritual training of youth and young men; (2) visiting and relieving the poor in their own homes; (3) advising the poor and needy, and finding employment for the workless; (4) visiting the inmates of public institutions, prisons, hospitals, almshouses, and the like; (5) placing children in foster homes; (6) maintenance of orphanages, day nurseries, convalescent homes, summer camps, clubs for boys, schools for the juvenile delinquent, residences for homeless boys, and chaplains for public institutions; (7) aid to discharged prisoners and juvenile delinquents; (8) care of distressed travelers and immigrants; (9) circulation of good literature.

To a great extent the Society of St. Vincent de Paul supplements the work of the parishes in needed interparochial services. Many of the larger enterprises, however, are provided by religious communities who undertake charitable works as they appear to be necessary or in accordance with the traditions of their congregation, often with little regard for overlapping of service provided by similar communities in the same district. A central diocesan charity organization seems, therefore, to be almost essential, if duplication of effort and needless expense is to be avoided. A highly efficient plan which seems to be worthy of imitation elsewhere, was inaugurated in the Diocese of Fargo, North Dakota, which has a predominantly rural population, in 1936.[19] This plan links up specific parish social service with a central office which is in the hands of a capable and trained director. Other dioceses also have these diocesan charity organizers. In particular, the annual meetings of the National Conference of Catholic Charities, organized in 1910, provide an important clearinghouse for exchange of views be-

---

[19] Cf. Ryan, Very Rev. V. J., "The Fargo Plan," *Catholic Rural Life Objectives*, 1937, p. 133.

tween the foremost Catholic social workers of the country and the superiors of all the important Catholic institutions. Since 1930 there has been a special division of the conference reserved to religious orders engaged in social activities other than teaching. The monthly *Catholic Charities Review* is the official organ of the Conference.[20] By the publication of surveys, study outlines, and other valuable aids, the Department of Social Action of the National Catholic Welfare Conference also assists the national outlook of Catholic charities in the United States.

The Knights of Columbus, the largest society of Catholic men in the United States, established in 1882 mainly as a fraternal organization, devote a portion of their activities to charitable works. They performed great service during the World War, and after 1918 entered actively into work for boys, providing clubs, Boy Scout troops, summer camps, playgrounds, aid to the delinquent, and finally establishing a junior order, called the Columbian Squires, for boys 14 to 18 years. The Ladies of Charity, founded by St. Vincent de Paul himself in 1643, are foremost in charitable endeavors and volunteer work; as also are such other organizations as the Legion of Mary, founded in Ireland in 1920 and now world wide in its work; the Catholic Women's League, the Christ-Child Society, and many similar groups.

The Catholic Central Verein of America, founded in 1858 to coordinate existing German Catholic societies is now an official organ of Catholic Action. The work of this bureau consists in the monthly publication of the *Central-Blatt and Social Justice;* the maintenance of a unique and excellent library and information service on social and economic matters, and on questions of more particular interest to German communities in America; the support of a settlement house; the distribution of Catholic literature; the issuance of pamphlets on social problems, and other activities almost too numerous to note.

The Catholic Youth Organization of Chicago, New York, Milwaukee, and other cities and dioceses are also Catholic Action groups, founded especially for the Christian orientation of youth.

Catholic Action Is Not Political

Before concluding the chapter we must say a few words on the nonpolitical character of Catholic Action, for since the controversy between the Pope and the Italian Government in 1931, many people

---

[20] Cf. O'Grady, Very Rev. John, *An Introduction to Social Work,* Chapter XV for further information regarding diocesan and national organization of charities in the United States.

have misunderstood this question. Catholic Action is in no way a move on the part of the Church to attain political influence. Pope Pius indeed said that "The Christian . . . ought to carry everywhere this treasure of Christianity, and make it live in every field of life . . . not excluding politics"[21] but he meant no more than that a man imbued with Christian principles could not but be a good citizen, worthy of exercising civic office within the State. This His Holiness made quite clear in other pronouncements on the subject. "In view of the public good, which is principally moral and religious, Catholic Action will not exclude the participation of its adherents in public life in all its phases. On the contrary, it will render them better fitted for public office by a serious preparation for holiness of life and the fulfilment of their Christian duties. Catholic Action, indeed, was born for the purpose of giving to the State its most honest and able officials."[22]

Since Catholic Action aims at making men holy, how could their personal holiness be entirely divorced from their life in the State? Yet the same Pope makes the following most solemn statement: "We have repeatedly and solemnly affirmed and protested that Catholic Action, both from its very nature and essence (the participation and collaboration of the laity with the Apostolic hierarchy) and by Our precise and categorical directions and dispositions, is outside and above every political party."[23]

Conclusion

As we said in the first chapter, sociology in itself is in no way connected with ameliorative programs, but is merely concerned with the examination of human society, its customs, institutions, and their development. Nevertheless, applied sociology most certainly has its place, and Catholics who take part in Catholic Action will the better be able to carry out applied sociology in practice.

---

[21] Pope Pius XI, Letter to a Catholic Society in Belgium, quoted in the *Catholic Mind,* January 22, 1930, p. 38.

[22] Pope Pius XI, Letter to Cardinal Bertram of Breslau, quoted in the *Catholic Mind,* March 8, 1929, p. 82.

[23] Pope Pius XI, encyclical "On Catholic Action," quoted in the *Catholic Mind,* July 22, 1931.

APPENDIX

BIBLIOGRAPHIES AND QUESTIONS

NOTE: The Bibliographies which follow are intended merely to provide some indication as to references for further study of each particular subject. A general library of sociology books in the Catholic college would include as a minimum the books starred. Catholic books which should be considered as essential are designated by two asterisks; non-Catholic by one. It must be noted, however, that Catholic books starred in any one chapter are not necessarily the best references for the subject matter of the chapter; *neither is it to be considered that non-Catholic books which may be starred are scientifically accurate in all particulars, or unobjectionable from the Catholic viewpoint.*

In addition to the books indicated by asterisks in the various chapters, the following general references and periodicals would be advisable:

**Dictionnaire de Sociologie: Familiale, Politique, Economique, Spirituelle,* Générale, Rev. G. Jacquemet, ed. (Paris: Librairie Letouzey et Ané).

Encyclopaedia of the Social Sciences (New York: Macmillan Co., 1934–35).

**Sixteen Encyclicals of His Holiness Pope Pius XI 1926–1937* (Washington, D. C.: The National Catholic Welfare Conference, 1312 Massachusetts Avenue, N.W.).

Social Work Year Book, biannual, 1929, 1931, 1933, 1935, 1937, 1939 (New York: Russell Sage Foundation).

Statistical Abstract of the United States, annual (Washington, D. C.: U. S. Department of Commerce).

At least three or four of the better known non-Catholic texts on sociology, such as:

Bogardus, E. S., *Sociology* (New York: Macmillan Co., 1934).

Davis, J., and Barnes, H. E., *Introduction to Sociology* (Boston: Heath & Co., 1931).

Dawson, C. A., and Gettys, W. E., *Introduction to Sociology* (New York: Ronald Press, 1935).

Groves, E. R., *An Introduction to Sociology,* rev. ed. (New York: Longmans, Green, 1932).

McIver, R. W., *Community* (New York: Macmillan Co., 1927).

Park, R. E., and Burgess, E. W., *Introduction to the Science of Sociology* (Chicago: University of Chicago Press, 1921).

Ross, E. A., *Principles of Sociology,* rev. ed. (New York: Appleton-Century Co., 1930).

Sumner, W. G., Keller, A. G., and Davie, M. R., *The Science of Society,* 4 vols. (New Haven: Yale U. Press, 1927).

Sutherland, R. L., and Woodward, J. L., *Introductory Sociology* (Philadelphia: Lippincott & Co., 1937).

Wallis, W. D., *An Introduction to Sociology* (New York: Crofts & Co., 1927).

The author's high-school text, *Rudiments of Sociology* (Milwaukee: Bruce Publishing Co., 1934) will furnish pictorial illustrations for many of the topics discussed.

PERIODICALS

GENERAL

American Journal of Sociology, bimonthly (Chicago: University of Chicago Press).

American Sociological Review, bimonthly, official journal of the American Sociological Society (Pittsburgh: University of Pittsburgh).

Annals of the Academy of Political and Social Science, bimonthly (Philadelphia, Pa.).

Character and Personality, quarterly (Durham, N. Car.: Duke University Press).

International Labor Review, monthly.

Journal of Juvenile Research, quarterly (Claremont, Calif.: California Institute of Juvenile Research).

Mental Hygiene, quarterly (New York: National Committee for Mental Hygiene).

Midmonthly Survey, monthly (New York: Survey Associates, Inc., 112 E. 19 Street).

Rural Sociology, quarterly (Baton Rouge, La.: Louisiana State U. Press).

Social Forces, quarterly (Baltimore, Md.: Williams and Wilkins Co.).

Sociology and Social Research, bimonthly (Los Angeles: U. of Southern California).

Survey Graphic, monthly (New York: Survey Associates, Inc., 112 E. 19 Street).

The Family, 10 issues yearly (New York: Family Welfare Association, 130 East 22 Street).

The Monthly Labor Review, monthly (Washington, D. C.: U. S. Bureau of Labor Statistics).

CATHOLIC

America, weekly (New York: 53 Park Place).

Catholic Action, monthly (Washington, D. C.: National Catholic Welfare Conference, 1312 Massachusetts Avenue, N. W.).

Catholic Charities Review, ten issues yearly (Washington, D. C.: The Catholic University of America).

Catholic Educational Review, ten issues yearly (Washington, D. C.: The Catholic University of America).

Catholic Family Monthly, monthly (Huntington, Ind.: Our Sunday Visitor Press).

Catholic Rural Life Bulletin, quarterly (St. Paul, Minn.: National Catholic Rural Life Conference, 240 Summit Avenue).

Catholic Worker, monthly (New York: 115 Mott Street).

Central-Blatt and Social Justice, monthly (St. Louis, Mo.: 3835 Westminster Place).

Christian Democrat, monthly (Oxford, England: Catholic Social Guild).[1]
Christian Front, monthly (Villanova, Pa.).
Commonweal, weekly (New York: 386 Fourth Avenue).
Interracial Review, monthly (New York: 20 Vesey Street).
Labor Leader, biweekly (New York: 226 Lafayette Street).
National Conference of Catholic Charities, Annual Reports of Proceedings (Washington, D. C.: Catholic University of America).
Primitive Man, quarterly (Washington, D. C.: American Catholic Anthropological Society, Catholic University of America).
Review of Politics, quarterly (Notre Dame, Ind.: University of Notre Dame).
The Wanderer (St. Paul: 128 E. 10 Street).
Other periodicals such as the *Catholic World, The Sign, Blackfriars* (Oxford, England), *The Month* (London, England), have frequent articles of interest to the sociologist.

CHAPTER 1

SOCIETY AND THE SOCIAL SCIENCES

RECOMMENDED READINGS

Beard, C. A., *A Charter for the Social Sciences in the Schools* (New York: Charles Scribner's Sons, 1932).
——— *The Nature of the Social Sciences* (New York: Charles Scribner's Sons, 1934).
——— *The Open Door at Home,* Chaps. 1 and 7 (New York: Macmillan Co., 1935).
*Bernard, L. L., *The Fields and Methods of Sociology* (New York: Farrar & Rinehart, 1934).
*Borsodi, R., *Prosperity and Security* (New York: Harper & Bros., 1938), pp. 224–228.
**Cahill, Rev. E., S.J., *The Framework of a Christian State* (Dublin: M. H. Gill & Son, 1932).
Encyclopaedia of Social Sciences, Introduction, Vol. I.
**International Union of Social Studies, *A Code of Social Principles,* rev. ed. (Oxford: Catholic Social Guild, 1937).
Lundberg, G. A., Bain, R., and Anderson, N., *Trends in American Sociology* (New York: Harper & Bros., 1929).
**Muntsch, Rev. A. J., S.J., and Spalding, Rev. H. S., S.J., *Introductory Sociology* (New York: Heath & Co., 1928).
**Murray, Rev. R. W., C.S.C., *Introductory Sociology,* Chaps. 1, 2 (New York: Crofts & Co., 1935).

---

[1] The subscription price of the *Christian Democrat* is 2/6 (two shillings and sixpence) yearly. Readers are, however, strongly urged to become members of the Catholic Social Guild. For the small annual subscription of 5/- (five shillings) members receive the *Christian Democrat* monthly, the *Yearbook* of the Catholic Social Guild, which is always a substantial publication of considerable worth to the Catholic student of social affairs; also all publications of the Catholic Social Guild which are sixpence or less in price for period of subscription. The address is: The Catholic Social Guild, Oxford, England.

Odum, H. H., and Jocher, K. C., *Introduction to Social Research* (New York: Henry Holt & Co., 1929).

Park, R. E., and Burgess, E. W., *Introduction to the Science of Sociology* (Chicago: University of Chicago Press, 1921).

Report of the Commission on the Social Studies, Conclusions and Recommendations (New York: Charles Scribner's Sons, 1934).

Shenton, H. N., *The Practical Application of Sociology* (New York: Columbia U. Press).

QUESTIONS

1. Show that man is social by nature.
2. Give a definition of a society. What are its common elements?
3. What is the difference between society in general, and "a society"?
4. Explain the fact that animals are not sociable although they may be gregarious.
5. Give a definition of sociology. Compare this with others given in some of the current standard textbooks. Do you agree with the definition given in this present book, or do you prefer some other definition? Discuss. (NOTE: It would be useful to refer to this question again at the end of the course.)
6. Discuss the two methods of attaining a knowledge of the truth.
7. What are the main branches of pure sociology? Applied sociology?
8. What are the main sources of sociological data (*a*) where induction is used; (*b*) where deductive methods are also employed?
9. What is a social science, and how does it differ from other sciences?
10. Give a brief definition of the major social sciences, and show their relation to sociology.

CHAPTER 2

BIOLOGICAL INHERITANCE

RECOMMENDED READINGS

*Bruno, F. J., *The Theory of Social Work* (Boston: Heath & Co., 1936).

*Encyclopaedia of the Social Sciences, article on Heredity.

Harris, J. A., ed., *The Measurement of Man* (Minneapolis: University of Minnesota Press, 1930).

Jennings, H. S., *Prometheus* (New York: Dutton & Co., 1925).

—————— *The Biological Basis of Human Nature* (New York: Norton & Co., 1930).

*Klineberg, O., *Race Differences* (New York: Harper & Bros., 1935).

*Schwesinger, G. C., *Heredity and Environment* (New York: Macmillan Co., 1933).

Shull, A. G., *Heredity* (New York: Macmillan Co., 1926).

Stockard, C. R., *The Physical Basis of Personality* (New York: Norton & Co., 1931).

Sutherland, H., *Laws of Life* (New York: Sheed & Ward, 1936).

Thompson, W. R., *Science and Common Sense* (New York: Longmans, Green, 1937).

Willemse, W. A., *Constitutional Types in Delinquency* (New York: Harcourt, Brace, 1932).

QUESTIONS

1. Why is a knowledge of biology essential for an understanding of man's conduct in society?
2. What is heredity, and what does it include?
3. Who was Mendel, and what are his "laws"?
4. What is the importance of a knowledge of "recessive" inheritance in connection with the inheritance of defects?
5. Discuss Mendel's idea of the inheritance of unit characters in the light of later research.
6. What are the major defects about which we have some positive knowledge regarding inheritance? Why is it impossible to predict the inheritance of an unborn child even in the light of this knowledge?
7. What are the main characteristics of man? What is meant by the statement that man is "dual by nature"?
8. What is meant by the statement that at birth man's mind is a *tabula rasa?* To what do we owe our ideas?
9. If it is correctly stated that environment is more important than heredity, why is it essential to consider heredity at all?
10. What are the ductless glands? Enumerate the most important of these glands and state how they may influence conduct.
11. Why would it be incorrect to attribute the abnormal conduct of a person with a hyperactive thyroid or adrenal gland, wholly to the physical defect?
12. Would it be scientific to attribute to heredity every case of a defective ductless gland? Discuss.
13. What is Kretschmer's theory of the influence of body build upon character? Can you justify this theory scientifically?
14. What is the main theory of McDougall as regards the inheritance of human characteristics? What is the major criticism of his theories?
15. What are W. I. Thomas' "Four Wishes"? In how far may they be said to be incomplete or inaccurate in a consideration of the cause of human conduct?
16. From your study of this chapter why would you consider it necessary to make a study of the characteristics of man and of human conduct in order to arrive at a correct appraisal of the theories of many of the sociologists?
17. Discuss the statement: "The 'nature versus nurture' controversy is still a matter of scientific debate."

CHAPTER 3

CHARACTER, PERSONALITY, AND ENVIRONMENT

RECOMMENDED READINGS

**Allers, R., *The Psychology of Character* (New York: Sheed & Ward, 1930).

Allport, F. H., *Social Psychology* (Boston: Houghton Mifflin, 1924).

Aveling, F., *Personality and Will* (New York: Appleton-Century Co., 1931).

Barrett, Rev. J. F., *Elements of Psychology* (Milwaukee: Bruce Publishing Co., 1930).

*Boas, F., ed., *General Anthropology* (Boston: Heath & Co., 1938).

*——— *The Mind of Primitive Man*, rev. ed. (New York: Macmillan Co., 1938).

**Brennan, Rev. R. E., O.P., *General Psychology* (New York: Macmillan Co., 1937)

Fearon, A. D., *The Two Sciences of Psychology* (New York: Prentice-Hall, 1937).

Gruender, Rev. H., S.J., *Problems of Psychology* (Milwaukee: Bruce Publishing Co., 1937).

Harris, J. A., ed., *The Measurement of Man* (Minneapolis: University of Minnesota Press, 1930).

Hull, Rev. E. R., S.J., *The Formation of Character* (St. Louis: Herder Book Co., 1929).

Huntington, E., *Civilization and Climate* (New Haven: Yale University Press, 1924).

——— *The Character of Races* (New York: C. Scribner's Sons, 1925).

Le Piere, R. T., *Collective Behavior* (New York: McGraw-Hill Book Co., 1938).

Lindworsky, Rev. J., S.J., *The Training of the Will* (Milwaukee: Bruce Publishing Co., 1938).

Moore, Rev. T. V., *Dynamic Psychology* (Philadelphia: J. B. Lippincott Co., 1924).

Phillips, Rev. R., O.P., *Modern Thomistic Philosophy*, 2 vols. (London: Burns, Oates & Washbourne, 1934).

*Schwesinger, G. C., *Heredity and Environment* (New York: Macmillan Co., 1933).

*Thomas, F., *The Environmental Basis of Society* (New York: Appleton-Century Co., 1925).

Wolfe, Rev. J. M., *Human Conduct and Character* (New York: Benziger Bros., 1930).

QUESTIONS

1. What is the difference between character and personality? (See Allers, R., *The Psychology of Character*.)
2. What is the basic error in Behaviorism, and why is this error of such importance?
3. What are the elements which make conduct? Where does the function of the soul enter in?
4. Which is most important in the formation of attitudes and ideals: heredity or environment? What is the part played by grace?
5. What are the main types of environment which affect the individual? Write a few lines about each.
6. Why is it correct to say that not all the characteristics of a newborn child are due to heredity?

7. What is the importance of physical environment — what does such environment include?

8. If economic environment is correctly stated to be of great importance in the development of a person, what is the error of the majority of sociologists who call attention to this fact?

9. Name some of the most important writers who stressed the influence of geography in human conduct.

10. What are the main ideas of modern geographical determinists? Wherein may they be said to be in error?

11. Of what value is Father Frenay's study of Suicide? (Cf. Frenay, Rev. A. D., O.P., *The Suicide Problem in the United States,* Washington, D. C.: The Catholic University of America, 1928.)

12. What is meant by psycho-social environment? Why would you consider it more important in the causation of conduct than other types of environment? Why is it not all important?

13. Which sociologists wrote about the "consciousness of kind," the "we feeling," and "syngenism"? What did they mean by these terms?

14. What is the exaggeration in the theories of Durkheim and Le Bon about the influence of the crowd?

15. Give a report on one of the following: Durkheim, E., *Elementary Forms of Religious Life,* 1920; Gumplowicz, L., *Outlines of Sociology;* La Piere, R. T., *Collective Behavior,* 1938; Le Bon, G., *The Crowd,* 1925; McDougall, W., *The Group Mind,* 1920; Martin, W., *The Behavior of Crowds,* 1920.

16. After a study of this chapter and considering differing hereditary characteristics and the different workings of grace what would you consider to be ideal environment for the upbringing of a child? Would this necessarily be of a so-called high material standard? Why?

CHAPTER 4

MAN AND CULTURE

RECOMMENDED READINGS

Benedict, R., *Patterns of Culture* (Boston: Houghton Mifflin, 1934).

Boas, F., *Anthropology and Modern Life* (New York: Norton Co., 1932).

*———— *The Mind of Primitive Man,* rev. ed. (New York: Macmillan Co., 1938).

Chapin, F. S., *Cultural Change* (New York: Appleton-Century Co., 1928).

Childe, V. G., *Man Makes Himself* (New York: Ryerson Press, 1936).

Driberg, J. H., *At Home with the Savage* (New York: Morrow, 1932).

Encyclopaedia of Social Sciences, articles on Culture, Culture Area.

Goldenweiser, A., *An Introduction to Primitive Culture* (New York: Crofts & Co., 1937).

———— *Early Civilization* (New York: A. A. Knopf, 1922).

Leyburn, J., *Frontier Folkways* (New Haven: Yale University Press, 1935).

Linton, R., *The Study of Man* (New York: Appleton-Century Co., 1936).

Lowie, R. H., *Are We Civilized?* (New York: Harcourt, Brace & Co., 1929).

—— *Culture and Ethnology* (New York: P. Smith, 1929).

—— *An Introduction to Cultural Anthropology* (New York: Farrar & Rinehart, 1934).

*—— *Primitive Society* (New York: Boni & Liveright, 1920).

Murdock, G. P., *Our Primitive Contemporaries* (New York: Macmillan Co., 1934).

*Ogburn, W. F., *Social Change* (New York: Viking Press, 1922).

Ross, E. A., *Social Control* (New York: Macmillan Co., 1904).

Ross, E. J., *Social Origins* (New York: Sheed & Ward, 1936).

—— "Do Primitives Fill a Gap in History?" *Central-Blatt and Social Justice*, Vol. XXXI, No. 10, January, 1939, pp. 301–304; No. 11, February, 1939, pp. 339–342.

Sapir, E., *Time Perspective in Aboriginal America* (Canada: Geological Survey, Memoir No. 90, 1916).

*Sumner, W. G., *Folkways* (New York: Ginn & Co., 1906).

Thomas, W. I., *Primitive Behavior* (New York: McGraw-Hill Co., 1937).

Tozzer, A. M., *Social Origins and Social Continuities* (New York: Macmillan Co., 1925).

Wallis, W. D., "Social Anthropology," in Schmidt, E. P., *Man and Society* (New York: Prentice-Hall, 1937).

*Wissler, C., *The American Indian*, rev. ed. (New York: Oxford University Press, 1922).

—— *An Introduction to Social Anthropology* (New York: Henry Holt & Co., 1929).

QUESTIONS

1. What is meant by the word *culture* as used by the sociologist?
2. If culture differs in all social groups, explain why it is incorrect to say that all culture traits are but relevant, and that no norms exist by which they may be judged?
3. Why is high material culture not necessarily the best for the development of mankind? Would you therefore wish to abolish the amenities of Western civilization? Discuss.
4. What is meant by a culture trait?
5. What is a folkway? Distinguish between folkways and mores.
6. Discuss the following terms giving examples of each: natural society; perfect society; primary society.
7. Wherein does the Catholic viewpoint differ from that of most non-Catholics in a consideration of the basic nature of certain societies?
8. What is meant by the terms, culture complex and culture area?
9. Discuss the probable culture of Adam and Eve.

10. How did culture develop or evolve? What proofs, if any, have we of such development?
11. Distinguish between the idea of cultural development as expressed in this book, and that elaborated by the unilineal evolutionists.
12. What is meant by the terms *parallelism, convergence, diffusion,* and *acculturation* when applied to cultural development? Give examples.
13. Discuss the possible effect of culture borrowing upon a natural institution.
14. Explain the meaning of the terms: culture threshold; culture horizon; syncretism; social control.
15. Distinguish between the social and the cultural.
16. Discuss the notion of many of the cultural sociologists that the influence of culture is entirely mechanical. How would such an idea agree or conflict with the Catholic philosophy of man and the teachings of Christianity? Does this differ from Bagehot's idea of the "cake of custom"?
17. What is meant by a culture lag? Is a culture lag necessarily harmful? Give examples.
18. What is meant by the term *age area?*
19. What is the *Kulturkreistheorie?* What are the major criticisms of this theory?

CHAPTER 5

THE ORIGIN OF MAN

RECOMMENDED READINGS

**Allen, V. T., *This Earth of Ours* (Milwaukee: Bruce Publishing Co., 1939).

*Boas, F., ed., *General Anthropology* (Boston: Heath & Co., 1938).

Boyle, M. E., *In Search of Our Ancestors* (Boston: Little, Browne & Co., 1928).

Burkitt, M. C., *The Old Stone Age* (New York: Macmillan Co., 1933).

Caiger, S. L., *Bible and Spade* (Oxford: Oxford University Press, 1936).

Carr-Saunders, A. M., *The Population Problem* (Oxford: Oxford University Press, 1922).

**Cooper, Rev. J. M., "The Scientific Evidence Bearing upon Human Evolution," *Primitive Man,* Vol. VIII, Nos. 1 and 2, Jan.–Apr., 1935.

**Dawson, C. H., *The Age of the Gods* (New York: Sheed & Ward, 1933).

Dumas, G., *Nouveau Traité de Psychologie,* Vol. I, Chap. 1, Perrier, R., "La Place de l'Homme dans la Série Animale," pp. 1–54; Chap. 2, Rivet, P., "Les Données de l'Anthropologie," pp. 55–101 (Paris: Félix Alcan, 1930).

Eyre, E., ed., *see* Schmidt, Rev. W.

*Garth, T. R., *Race Psychology* (New York: McGraw-Hill Book Co., 1931).

**Haas, Rev. F. J., *Man and Society* (New York: Appleton-Century Co., 1930).

Hankins, F. H., *The Racial Basis of Civilization* (New York: Knopf & Co., 1931).

*Hertz, F., *Race and Civilization* (New York: Macmillan Co., 1928).

Hooton, E. A., *Up from the Ape* (New York: Macmillan Co., 1931).

Hrdlicka, A., *The Skeletal Remains of Early Man* (Washington, D. C.: Smithsonian Institute, 1930).

Johnson, Rev. H. J. T., *Anthropology and the Fall* (New York: Benziger Bros., 1926).

*Klineberg, O., *Race Differences* (New York: Harper & Bros., 1935).

Kroeber, A. L., *Anthropology* (New York: Harcourt, Brace & Co., 1923; 1933 Supplement).

*Lowie, R. H., *A History of Ethnological Theory* (New York: Farrar & Rinehart, 1937).

MacCurdy, G. G., *Early Man* (Philadelphia: Lippincott Co., 1937).

———— *Human Origins* (New York: Appleton-Century Co., 1924).

**Messenger, Rev. E. C., S.J., *Evolution and Theology* (New York: Macmillan Co., 1932).

**Murray, Rev. R. W., C.S.C., *Introductory Sociology*, Chaps. 13–15 (New York: Crofts & Co., 1935).

*Osborn, H. F., *Men of the Old Stone Age*, 3rd ed. (New York: C. Scribner's Sons, 1924).

Radin, P., *Primitive Man as a Philosopher* (New York: Appleton-Century, 1927).

Schmidt, Rev. W., S.V.D., "Primitive Man," in Eyre, E., ed., *European Civilization*, Vol. I (Oxford: Oxford University Press, 1934).

Trever, A. A., *History of Civilization* (New York: Harcourt, Brace & Co., 1936).

*Wallis, W. D., *An Introduction to Anthropology* (New York: Harper & Bros., 1927).

QUESTIONS

1. What evidence do we possess regarding prehistoric times: (*a*) as to plants and animals; (*b*) as to man as a physical being; (*c*) as to man's culture?
2. What do we know of the times prior to evidence of man's habitation on the earth? Give a chart to show the names assigned to the various eras, and the plants and animals which are attributed to them.
3. Give a chart to show the various culture "stages" which are evidenced by prehistoric findings.
4. Why is it unscientific to attribute any definite date to these stages, and to think that we may have discovered the whole of the culture of these times?
5. What evidence do we have of prehistoric man in Java? Why is it incorrect to say that the remains found there are "missing links"?
6. Outline briefly the prehistoric findings near Peking.
7. What remains were found (*a*) at Piltdown; (*b*) at Heidelberg; (*c*) at Rhodesia?
8. Why is it incorrect to describe the people of the Neanderthal race as "missing links"?
9. Who were the Cro-Magnon peoples?
10. Distinguish between the Old and the New Stone Ages.

11. What do we know of the early Neolithic period and of the late Neolithic period?
12. What is a race? Why is it impossible to make more than very general classifications of race?
13. What is the evidence for the "oneness of the human race"?
14. Cite some of the theories as to the origin of the different races.
15. What seems to be the most scientific theory as to the origin of races?
16. What arguments would you bring to support a refutation of the theory of Nordic superiority?
17. Why is it incorrect to say that until comparatively recent times, Christians thought that the world was created only 4,004 years before Christ?
18. What is the evidence which may be brought in support of a theory of evolution?
19. Why is it incorrect to hold that there is conclusive evidence of evolution?
20. If a Catholic considers that the evidence in support of evolution outweighs the evidence against it, how would he justify his position with regard to the Church's teaching that God created all things, man included?
21. Show how the story of the Creation as given in Genesis does not necessarily run counter to the theory of evolution.

CHAPTER 6

BRIEF HISTORY OF SOCIAL THOUGHT

RECOMMENDED READINGS

Barnes, H. E., "Sociology Before Comte," *American Journal of Sociology*, Vol. XXIII, September, 1917.
———— and Becker, H., *Social Thought from Lore to Science* (Boston: Heath & Co., 1938).
*Bernard, L. L., *The Fields and Methods of Sociology* (New York: Farrar & Rinehart, 1934).
Bogardus, E. A., *A History of Social Thought* (Los Angeles: University of Southern California Press, 1928).
———— *Contemporary Sociology* (Los Angeles: University of Southern California Press, 1937).
Bréhier, E., *Histoire de la Philosophie*, Vol. II, Parts I and II (Paris: Librairie Félix Alcan, 1930, 1932).
*Davis, J., *Contemporary Social Movements* (New York: Appleton-Century Co., 1930).
**Delos, Rev. J. T., O.P., *et al.*, *Comment Juger la Sociologie Contemporaine* (Marseille: Editions Publiroc).
Dunning, W. A., *Political Theories from Luther to Montesquieu* (New York: Macmillan Co., 1905).
———— *Political Theories from Rousseau to Spencer* (New York: Macmillan Co., 1920).

Ellwood, C. A., *Methods in Sociology* (Durham, N. Car.: Duke University Press, 1933).

Hertzler, J. O., *The Social Thought of the Ancient Civilizations* (New York: McGraw-Hill Book Co., 1936).

———— *The History of Utopian Thought* (New York: Macmillan Co., 1923).

Höffding, H., *A History of Modern Philosophy*, Vols. I and II (London: Macmillan Co., 1900).

*House, F. N., *The Development of Sociology* (New York: McGraw-Hill Book Co., 1936).

Husslein, Rev. J., S.J., *The Bible and Labor* (New York: Macmillan Co., 1924).

Ideal Commonwealths (New York: The Colonial Press, 1901).

**Jarrett, Rev. B., O.P., *Social Theories of the Middle Ages* (Boston: Little, Brown & Co., 1926).

*Lichtenberger, J. P., *Development of Social Theory* (New York: Appleton-Century Co., 1923).

Panunzio, C., *A Student's Dictionary of Sociological Terms* (Berkeley: University of California Press, 1937).

Park, R. E., and Burgess, E. W., *Introduction to the Science of Sociology* (Chicago: University of Chicago Press, 1921).

Parsons, T., *The Structure of Social Action* (New York: McGraw-Hill Book Co., 1937).

Phelps, H. A., *Principles and Laws of Sociology*.

*Rice, S. A., ed., *Methods in Social Science* (Chicago: University of Chicago Press, 1931).

Seth, J., *English Philosophers and Schools of Philosophy* (New York: E. P. Dutton; London: J. M. Dent, 1912).

*Sorokin, P., *Contemporary Sociological Theories* (New York: Harper & Bros., 1928).

Spencer, H., *The Study of Sociology* (New York: D. Appleton-Century Co., 1896).

*Tawney, R. H., *Religion and the Rise of Capitalism* (London: John Murray, 1929). *Now obtainable in the Penquin Series, price 6d.*

QUESTIONS

1. Distinguish between social thought and sociology (see Chap. 1 for a wider use of the word *sociology*).
2. Make a report on some of the social teachings of (*a*) Plato, (*b*) Aristotle.
3. Make a report on the social teachings of the major Jewish prophets. Wherein did the social teachings of Jesus Christ differ from those of the prophets?
4. Make a report on the *City of God* of St. Augustine. Look at some of the criticisms of this work made by Pareto in *The Mind and Society* and discuss these.
5. Make a report of the major social teachings of St. Thomas Aquinas.
6. Outline one of the major Utopian theories.
7. What was Machiavelli's main doctrine? Wherein did it err? What was its influence? (Cf. Macaulay's essay on Machiavelli.)

8. What was the influence of the "Protestant revolt" on social thought?
9. Who were the social-contract theorists, and what was their basic idea? Why are sociologists interested in their notions, as well as political economists?
10. Who was Montesquieu and what was his influence?
11. Give the theory for which Thomas Malthus is most famous.
12. Write an essay on either (a) Comte and his influence, or (b) Herbert Spencer and his influence.
13. Write brief notes on Lilienfeld, Schaeffle, and Spengler.
14. What is meant by sympodial development? Write a brief note on the sociologist who used this term.
15. Make a brief report on Gumplowicz and Ratzenhofer.
16. Read and give a critical appreciation of Veblen's *Theory of the Leisure Class.*
17. Who was Le Play, and what was his major doctrine?
18. Evaluate the influence of W. I. Thomas on certain trends of sociological thought.
19. For what sociological theories are the following most noted: the "Chicago school"; C. H. Cooley; the "cultural sociologists"; F. Giddings; R. M. McIver; V. Pareto; Edward Alsworth Ross; Albion Small; Sorokin.

CHAPTER 7

BRIEF HISTORY OF SOCIAL THEORY: THE CATHOLIC POSITION

RECOMMENDED READINGS

*Beard, C. A., *The Open Door at Home,* Chaps. 1 and 7 (New York: Macmillan Co., 1935).

**Brauer, T., *The Catholic Social Movement in Germany,* pamphlet (Oxford: Catholic Social Guild, 1932).

**Cahill, Rev. E., S.J., *The Framework of a Christian State* (Dublin: Gill & Son, 1932).

Chesterton, G. K., *What's Wrong With the World?* (New York: Dodd, Mead & Co., 1910).

**Crawford, V. M., *Catholic Social Doctrine 1891–1931,* pamphlet (Oxford: Catholic Social Guild, 1933; out of print).

D'Arcy, Rev. M. C., S.J., *Christian Morals* (New York: Longmans, Green, 1937).

Déploige, Rev. S., *The Conflict between Ethics and Sociology* (St. Louis: B. Herder Book Co., 1938).

Furfey, Rev. P. H., *Fire on the Earth* (New York: Macmillan Co., 1936).

** ———— *Three Theories of Society* (New York: Macmillan Co., 1937).

Glenn, Rev. P. J., *Sociology* (St. Louis: B. Herder Book Co., 1935).

**Haas, Rev. F. J., *Man and Society* (New York: Appleton-Century Co., 1930).

**International Union of Social Studies, *A Code of Social Principles,* rev.

ed., pamphlet (Oxford: Catholic Social Guild, 1937).

Leclercq, Rev. J., *Leçons de Droit Natural: I: Le Fondement du Droit et de la Société*, 2nd ed. (Louvain: Société d'Etudes Morales, Sociales et Juridiques, 1934).

**McEntee, G. P., *The Social Catholic Movement in Great Britain* (New York: Macmillan Co., 1927).

Metlake, G. (Rev. J. J. Laux), *Christian Social Reform* (Philadelphia: Dolphin Press, 1912).

Michel, Rev. V., O.S.B., *Human Rights*, pamphlet (Collegeville, Minn.: St. John's University).

————— *Social Concepts and Problems*, pamphlet (Collegeville, Minn.: St. John's University).

————— *St. Thomas Today*, pamphlet (Collegeville, Minn.: St. John's University, 1936).

————— *The Social Question*, Series of nine pamphlets (Collegeville, Minn.: St. John's University, 1936).

**Moon, P., *The Labor Problem and the Catholic Social Movement in France* (New York: Macmillan Co., 1931).

Mounier, E., *A Personalist Manifesto* (New York: Longmans, Green, 1938).

O'Kane, Rev. T. J., *A Catholic Catechism of Social Questions*, pamphlet (Oxford: Catholic Social Guild, 1936).

O'Hea, Rev. L., "The Christian Trade Union International," *The Christian Democrat*, October, 1938, pp. 152–155.

**Parkinson, Rev. H., *A Primer of Social Science*, 6th ed., rev. (Oxford: Catholic Social Guild, 1936).

Ring, M. I., *Villeneuve-Bargemont* (Milwaukee: Bruce Publishing Co., 1935).

Ross, E. J., *A Survey of Sociology* (Milwaukee: Bruce Publishing Co., 1932).

————— "Ladies of the Grail," *The Christian Front*, February, 1937.

————— "Successful Youth," *The Commonweal*, November 6, 1936.

Ross, Rev. J. E., *Ethics*, rev. ed. (New York: Devin-Adair, 1938).

Somerville, H., *Studies in the Catholic Social Movement* (London: Burns, Oates & Washbourne, 1933).

Watt, Rev. L., S.J., *Capitalism and Morality* (London: Cassell & Co., 1929).

————— *Catholic Social Principles* (New York: Benziger Bros., 1930).

QUESTIONS

1. Write an essay on Frederic Ozanam and the social influence of the Society of St. Vincent de Paul.
2. Write brief notes on the major German Catholic social thinkers of last century.
3. What is the major social teaching of the late Reverend Henry Pesch, S.J.?
4. Write brief notes on the major French Catholic social thinkers of last century and this.
5. What was the Union de Fribourg?

6. What were the immediate antecedents of the publication of the *Rerum Novarum* encyclical?
7. Discuss the theory of Personalism.
8. What is the work of the Catholic Social Guild in England? In what respects do you think such work is being carried on with equal, greater, or less success in the United States?
9. Write an essay on the social teachings of Msgr. John A. Ryan.
10. Read the late Dom Virgil Michel's *A Christian Social Reconstruction,* and such articles as contained in *Orate Fratres,* Vol. XIII, No. 3, January 22, 1939; Ward, Rev. L. R., C.S.C., and Hynes, E., "Virgil Michel," *Commonweal,* Vol. XXIX, No. 9, December 23, 1938, pp. 237, 238, and evaluate his social teachings.
11. Discuss the position of those who maintain that sociology is exclusively an inductive science and evaluate the place of deductive work in this field.
12. What is a postulate? Discuss whether or not postulates are necessary as a correct basis of sociology.
13. Discuss the validity of the postulates given in the text. Are any superfluous? Ought others to be included?
14. What is the moral law? Why is it essential to note such law when considering man's social life?
15. What are the major rights of man?
16. What are man's major social duties?
17. Write an essay on St. Paul's doctrine of the Mystical Body of Christ and show wherein this doctrine affects the thought of the Catholic sociologist.

CHAPTER 8

MARRIAGE AND THE FAMILY

RECOMMENDED READINGS

**Haas, Rev. F. J., *Man and Society* (New York: Appleton-Century Co., 1930).
**International Union of Social Studies, *A Code of Social Principles,* rev. ed., pamphlet (Oxford: Catholic Social Guild, 1937).
**Joyce, Rev. G. H., *Christian Marriage,* rev. ed. (New York: Sheed & Ward, 1938).
Leclercq, Rev. J., *Leçons de Droit Naturel: III: La Famille* (Louvain: Société d'Etudes Morales, Sociales et Juridiques, 1933).
*Lowie, R. H., *Primitive Society* (New York: Boni and Liveright, 1920).
**Lynch, Rev. A., O.P., *This is Christian Marriage* (Union City, N. J.: The Sign Press, 1933).
**Pope Leo XIII, encyclical, *Arcanum Diviniae Sapientiae,* 1880.
**Pope Pius XI, encyclical, *Casti Connubii,* 1930.
***Primitive Man,* Vol. III, Nos. 3, 4, July–October, 1930 (Washington, D. C.: Catholic Anthropological Conference).
Ross, E. J., *Social Origins* (New York: Sheed & Ward, 1936).

**Schmiedeler, Rev. E., O.S.B., *Readings in the Family* (New York: Appleton-Century Co., 1931).

*Westermarck, E. A., *A Short History of Marriage* (New York: Macmillan Co., 1926).

Wissler, C., *An Introduction to Social Anthropology* (New York: Henry Holt & Co., 1929).

Zimmerman, C. C., and Frampton, M. E., *Family and Society* (New York: D. Van Nostrand Co. Inc., 1935).

Questions

1. Distinguish between the terms marriage and the family.
2. What is the importance of (*a*) marriage and (*b*) the family as social institutions?
3. Upon what basis is the assertion made that the family is a natural institution?
4. What are the two principal forms of marriage?
5. What is meant by the terms *exogamy* and *endogamy?*
6. What is the difference between the terms *clan* and *gens?* What is a sib? What are age grades?
7. What is the "romantic fallacy" as regards marriage?
8. What is a matriarchal family? Distinguish between matriarchy and matrilineal family organization.
9. What is the avunculate?
10. What is the levirate; the couvade?
11. Discuss the theories of the origin of the family.
12. Give a brief refutation of the theory of the unilinear evolutionists.
13. Discuss the Christian ideal of marriage and the family.
14. Why is the family the most important social unit?
15. Discuss the Catholic doctrine of virginity and chastity.

Chapter 9

THE STATE

Recommended Readings

*Boas, F., ed., *General Anthropology* (Boston: Heath & Co., 1938).

**Cahill, Rev. E., S.J., *The Framework of a Christian State* (Dublin: M. H. Gill and Son, 1932).

**International Union of Social Studies, *A Code of Social Principles,* rev. ed., pamphlet (Oxford: Catholic Social Guild, 1937).

**Haas, Rev. F. J., *Man and Society* (New York: Appleton-Century Co., 1930).

**Husslein, Rev. J., S.J., *The Christian Social Manifesto* (Milwaukee: Bruce Publishing Co., 1931).

Leclercq, Rev. J., *Leçons de Droit Naturel: II: l'Etat ou la Politique,* 2nd ed. (Louvain: Société d'Etudes Morales, Sociales et Juridiques, 1934).

**Pope Leo XIII, encyclical, *Immortale Dei,* 1885: encyclical *Sapientiae Christianae,* 1890; encyclical, *Rerum Novarum,* 1891.
**Pope Pius XI, encyclical, *Quadragesimo Anno,* 1931.
Ross, E. J., *Social Origins* (New York: Sheed & Ward, 1936).
**Ryan, Rev. J., and Millar, Rev. F. X., S.J., *The State and the Church* (New York: Macmillan Co., 1922).
Somerville, H., *A Course of Social Study, First Year,* pamphlet (Toronto, Can.: Canadian Extension Office, 67 Bond Street, 1936).
Watt, Rev. L., S.J., *The State,* pamphlet (Oxford: Catholic Social Guild, 1938).

QUESTIONS

1. What is the distinction between the words *State* and *government; State* and *nation?*
2. Why is the State to be considered as a natural society?
3. Distinguish between true and false nationalism.
4. What are the major forms of State organization?
5. Discuss the authority of the government of a State from the viewpoint of the natural law.
6. What should be the relations between State and Church?
7. What are the chief functions of the State?
8. What are the chief duties of the State in the light of the State's functions?
9. What are the rights of the State?
10. Discuss the duty of the citizen toward the State as regards tax payments. (Cf. *A Code of Social Principles;* Ryan and Millar, *The State and the Church.*)
11. What are the chief duties of citizens?
12. Has an educated Catholic any special duties to perform as regards the State?
13. Discuss the citizen's right to a vote.
14. What are the arguments for and against votes for women?
15. How did states arise?
16. What is Hegel's main idea as to the State, and what is his influence at the present time?
17. Can it be said that there is a State among the primitives? Discuss.

CHAPTER 10

RELIGIOUS SOCIETY

RECOMMENDED READINGS

*Boas, F., ed., *General Anthropology* (Boston: Heath & Co., 1938).
Boullaye, Rev. P., de la, *l'Étude Comparée des Réligions* (Paris: Beauchesne, 1922).
Briault, Rev. M., *Polytheism and Fetishism* (St. Louis: B. Herder Book Co., 1921).
Burtt, P. A., *Types of Religious Philosophy* (New York: Harper and Bros., 1939).

Encyclopaedia of the Social Sciences, article on Culture.

Johnson, Rev. H. J. T., *Anthropology and the Fall* (New York: Benziger Bros., 1923).

Karrer, O., *The Religions of Mankind* (New York: Sheed & Ward, 1936).

**Le Roy, Rt. Rev. A., *The Religion of the Primitives* (New York: Macmillan Co., 1922).

*Lowie, R. H., *Primitive Religion* (New York: Boni & Liveright, 1924).

**Messenger, Rev. E. C., S.J., *Evolution and Theology* (New York: Macmillan Co., 1932).

———— *Studies in Comparative Religion,* Vol. I (London: Catholic Truth Society, 1934).

**Muntsch, Rev. A. J., S.J., *Cultural Anthropology* (Milwaukee: Bruce Publishing Co., 1934).

**Primitive Man,* Vol. II, Nos. 3, 4, July, October, 1929 (Washington, D. C.: Catholic Anthropological Conference).

**Schmidt, Rev. W., S.V.D., *The Origin and Growth of Religion* (New York: Dial Press, 1931).

———— "Primitive Man," in Eyre, E., ed., *European Civilization* (Oxford: Oxford University Press, 1934).

Questions

1. Distinguish between religion and religious society.
2. Upon what facts does the Catholic base his belief that the Church is a supernatural and primary society?
3. What characterizes the religion of the primitives?
4. Why is it impossible that religion could have arisen from atheism?
5. Have primitives any notion of morality? Discuss.
6. Discuss the validity of Frazer's idea of the origin of religion from magic.
7. What is fetishism? Discuss the theory of Comte and others as to the origin of religion from fetishism.
8. Distinguish between animism and animatism.
9. What was Spencer's Ghost Theory? Discuss.
10. What is totemism? Who are the chief exponents of the totemistic origin of religion? Discuss their theories.
11. Is it possible to formulate with any certainty a theory of the origin of the different forms of religious belief at the present time?
12. Does a study of anthropology refute or uphold the theory of the "evolutionary" theories derived from anthropological data? Discuss.

Chapter 11

PROPERTY

Recommended Readings

**Haas, Rev. F. J., *Man and Society* (New York: Appleton-Century Co., 1930).

**Husslein, Rev. J., S.J., *The Christian Social Manifesto* (Milwaukee: Bruce Publishing Co., rev. ed., 1939).

**International Union of Social Studies, *A Code of Social Principles,* rev. ed., pamphlet (Oxford: Catholic Social Guild, 1937).

*Lowie, R. H., *Primitive Society* (New York: Boni & Liveright, 1920).

**Michel, Rev. V., O.S.B., *Christian Social Reconstruction* (Milwaukee: Bruce Publishing Co., 1938).

O'Kane, Rev. T. J., *A Catholic Catechism of Social Questions,* pamphlet (Oxford: Catholic Social Guild, 1936).

**Pope Leo XIII, encyclical, *Rerum Novarum,* 1891.

**Pope Pius XI, encyclical, *Quadragesimo Anno,* 1931.

Ross, E. J., *Social Origins* (New York: Sheed & Ward, 1936).

Ryan, Rev. J. A., *The Christian Doctrine of Property,* pamphlet (Washington, D. C.: National Catholic Welfare Conference).

** ———— *Distributive Justice* (New York: Macmillan Co., 1919).

Sommerville, H., *A Course of Social Study,* pamphlet (Toronto, Ont.: The Catholic Register, 67 Bond Street).

Watt, Rev. L., S.J., *Capitalism and Morality* (London: Cassell & Co., 1929).

QUESTIONS

1. Give a definition of property.
2. Distinguish between consumptive and productive property.
3. Write an essay on property ownership among the primitives.
4. Prove that private property ownership is a natural right.
5. Discuss the important point that the right to own private property is a limited right only.
6. How does the Christian conception of property ownership differ from (*a*) the legal system of today; (*b*) socialism and communism?
7. Give a brief outline of the single tax system of socialism, showing (*a*) the element of truth in its teachings; (*b*) wherein the fundamental error lies; (*c*) the practical impossibility of carrying out its plan.

CHAPTER 12

OCCUPATIONAL SOCIETY

RECOMMENDED READINGS

Allen, A. A., *The Lords of Creation* (New York: Harper & Bros., 1935).

Belliot, Rev. A., O.F.M., *Manuel de Sociologie Catholique,* 2nd ed. (Paris: Lethielleux, 1927).

Benvenisti, J. L., *The Iniquitous Contract* (London: Burns, Oates & Washbourne, 1937).

Berle, A. A., and Means, G. C., *The Modern Corporation and Private Property* (New York: Macmillan Co., 1933).

*Boas, F., ed., *General Anthropology* (Boston: Heath & Co., 1938).

Borne, E., and Henry, F., *A Philosophy of Work* (New York: Sheed & Ward, 1938).

*Borsodi, B., *Prosperity and Security* (New York: Harper & Bros., 1938).

Briefs, G., *The Proletariat* (New York: McGraw-Hill Book Co., 1937).

Burns, A. R., *The Decline of Competition* (New York: McGraw-Hill Book Co., 1936).

**Cave, R., and Coulson, H. H., *Source Book for Medieval Economic History* (Milwaukee: Bruce Publishing Co., 1936).

Fallon, Rev. V., S.J., McNalty, Rev. J. L., and Goss, B. C., *Principles of Social Economy* (New York: Benziger Bros., 1933).

**Fanfani, A., *Catholicism, Protestantism and Capitalism* (New York: Sheed & Ward, 1935).

**Husslein, Rev. J., S.J., *The Christian Social Manifesto* (Milwaukee: Bruce Publishing Co., rev. ed., 1939).

**International Union of Social Studies, *A Code of Social Principles*, rev. ed. (Oxford: Catholic Social Guild, 1937).

Johnson, E. A. J., *Some Origins of the Modern Economic World* (New York: Macmillan Co., 1936).

Josephson, M., *Robber Barons* (New York: Harcourt, Brace, 1934).

**McGowan, R. A., *Toward Social Justice*, pamphlet (Washington, D. C.: National Catholic Welfare Conference, 1933).

**Michel, Rev. V., O.S.B., *Christian Social Reconstruction* (Milwaukee: Bruce Publishing Co., 1938).

—— *The Social Question*, Series of nine pamphlets (Collegeville, Minn.: St. John's University, 1936).

**Nell-Breuning, Rev. O. von, S.J., *Reorganization of Social Economy* (Milwaukee: Bruce Publishing Co., 1936).

**O'Brien, G., *An Essay on Mediaeval Economic Teaching* (New York: Longmans, Green, 1920).

**Parkinson, Rev. H., *A Primer of Social Science*, 6th ed., rev. (Oxford: Catholic Social Guild, 1936).

**Pope Leo XIII, encyclical, *Rerum Novarum*, 1891.

**Pope Pius XI, encyclical, *Caritate Christi Compulsi*, 1932; *Divini Redemptoris*, 1937; *Quadragesimo Anno*, 1931.

Robbins, H., *The Sun of Justice* (London: Health Cranton, Ltd., 1938).

**Ross, E. J., *What is Economics?* (Milwaukee: Bruce Publishing Co., 1939).

**Ryan, Rev. J. A., *Distributive Justice*, rev. ed. (New York: Macmillan Co., 1927).

***The Guild Social Order* (Oxford: Catholic Social Guild, 1936).

Watt, Rev. L., S.J., *Capitalism and Morality* (London: Cassel & Co., 1929).

—— *The Ethics of Interest*, pamphlet (Oxford: Catholic Social Guild, 1926).

—— *The Future of Capitalism*, pamphlet (Oxford: Catholic Social Guild, 1931).

—— *Pope Pius XI and Social Reconstruction*, pamphlet (Oxford: Catholic Social Guild, 1936).

QUESTIONS

1. What is the Catholic idea of work?
2. Why is the division of labor a sign of intelligence in man?
3. If occupational organization has existed from earliest times and if it is necessary for more orderly and scientific production for human needs, discuss its place (*a*) as a primary organization and (*b*) as a natural social organization.
4. Give brief particulars of two economic organizations of the past.
5. What are the essential features of modern capitalism?
6. Discuss the history of the Church's attitude on the taking of interest on loans.
7. How would you explain the Church's present-day attitude which, in general, upholds the theory that a stockholder is justified in taking his dividends, and that a bondholder or a depositor in a bank or building society is justified in taking interest?

CHAPTER 13

INTERNATIONAL SOCIETY

RECOMMENDED READINGS

***Arbitration and the World Court; Agriculture and International Life; International Ethics; Causes of War; Europe and the United States; The Ethics of War; National Attitudes in Children; Tariffs and World Peace; International Economic Life; The Church and Peace Efforts; Peace Education in Catholic Schools*, pamphlets (Washington, D. C.: Catholic Association for International Peace).

*Beard, C. A., *The Open Door at Home* (New York: Macmillan Co., 1935).

Brown, Rev. S., S.J., *International Relations from a Catholic Standpoint* (Dublin: M. H. Gill & Son, 1932).

**Cahill, Rev. E., S.J., *The Framework of a Christian State* (Dublin: M. H. Gill & Son, 1932).

Ellsworth, P. J., *International Economics* (New York: Macmillan Co., 1938).

**Eppstein, J., *The Catholic Tradition of the Law of Nations* (Washington, D. C.: The Catholic Association for International Peace, 1935).

———— *A Catholic Looks at the League*, pamphlet (Oxford: Catholic Social Guild, 1937).

***Foundations of International Order*, pamphlet (Oxford: Catholic Social Guild, 1938).

Gigon, H., *Ethics of Peace and War* (London: Burns, Oates & Washbourne, 1935).

**Haas, Rev. F. J., *Man and Society* (New York: Appleton-Century Co., 1930).

Hayes, C. J. H., *Essays on Nationalism* (New York: Macmillan Co., 1926).

———— *The Historical Evaluation of Modern Nationalism* (New York: Richard R. Smith, 1931).

*Hewett, N., *Toward Better Things* (London: Longmans, Green, 1936).

**International Union of Social Studies, *A Code of International Ethics* (Oxford: Catholic Social Guild, 1937).

Keating, Rev. J., S.J., *Catholics and the Problems of Peace,* pamphlet (Oxford: Catholic Social Guild, 1920).

Pax Pamphlets: Gill, E., *And Who Wants Peace?;* Berdyaev, N., *War and the Christian Conscience;* Sturzo, Rev. L., *Morality and Politics;* Attwater, D., *Bombs, Babies, and Beatitudes;* Watkin, E. I., *The Crime of Conscription;* Vann, Rev. G., O.P., *Commonsense Christianity and War.*

**Pope Pius XI, encyclical, *Nova Impendet,* 1931; *Caritate Christi Compulsi,* 1932.

Robbins, L. C., *Economic Planning and International Order* (London: Macmillan Co., 1937).

**Ross, E. J., *What is Economics?* (Milwaukee: Bruce Publishing Co., 1939).

The Pope's Peace Note, text and comments; Replies to the Pope's Appeal; Free Seas in Peace and War; The Law of Nations: What it is; National Tribunals and International Law; The Restoration of the Law of Nations, pamphlets (Oxford: Catholic Social Guild).

QUESTIONS

1. Discuss the importance of International Society and give your opinion as to whether it is, or is not (*a*) a primary; (*b*) a natural group.
2. Distinguish between the organization of international society as urged by Catholic sociologists, and cosmopolitanism, such as envisaged by communism.
3. Discuss the advantages of international society as opposed to present-day exaggerated nationalism.
4. Outline the main causes of war.
5. Discuss the connection of economics with international friction.
6. Why is it inadvisable from the sociological as well as from the economic viewpoint, to urge high protective tariffs?
7. Can there ever be a just war? Discuss this question in the light of the arguments set forth (*a*) in *A Code of International Ethics;* (*b*) by the members of the *Pax* peace movement in Great Britain as expounded in their various pamphlets.
8. Can civil war ever be just?
9. What are the major peace measures which have been undertaken in recent years?
10. Give a short critique of the League of Nations.
11. Write an essay on the important work of the International Labor Organization in Geneva.
12. Evaluate the importance of student membership in the associations promoted by the Carnegie Association of International Peace and by the Catholic Association for International Peace.
13. Why was it necessary in this chapter to make more use of the deductive than of the inductive method? How would you expect a sociologist

who believed exclusively in the inductive method to criticize this chapter, and how would you answer his charges?

CHAPTER 14

EDUCATION AND EDUCATIONAL SOCIETY

RECOMMENDED READINGS

Bourne, Cardinal, *Education: A Novel Solution,* pamphlet (London: Catholic Truth Society).

**Burns, Rev. J. A., C.S.C., and Kohlbrenner, B. J., *History of Catholic Education in the United States* (New York: Benziger Bros., 1937).

Butler, N. M., *The Meaning of Education* (New York: Macmillan Co., 1898).

Catholic Educational Review, ten issues yearly (Washington, D. C.: The Catholic University of America).

Catholic Encyclopaedia, article on Education.

*Davie, M. R., *Problems of City Life* (New York: John Wiley & Sons, 1932).

Finney, R. L., *The American Public School* (New York: Macmillan Co., 1921).

Fitzpatrick, E. A., *I Believe in Education* (New York: Sheed & Ward, 1938).

Handbook of American Indians, Bulletin No. 30, articles by Mason, O. T., Education; Mooney, J., Child Life; Stevenson, M. C., and Matthews, W., Ethics; Swanton J. R., Puberty Customs.

**Hovre, Rev. F. de, *Philosophy and Education* (New York: Benziger Bros., 1931).

**———— *Catholicism in Education* (New York: Benziger Bros., 1934).

Hutchins, R. M., *Higher Learning in America* (New Haven: Yale University Press, 1936).

**Kane, Rev. W., S.J., *An Essay Toward a History of Education* (Chicago: Loyola University Press, 1935).

**McGucken, Rev. W. J., S.J., *The Catholic Way in Education* (Milwaukee: Bruce Publishing Co., 1934).

Miller, N., *The Child in Primitive Society* (New York: Brentanos, 1928).

**Newman, Cardinal J. H., *The Idea of a University* (New York: Longmans, Green & Co., 1912).

O'Kane, Rev. T. J., *A Catholic Catechism of Social Questions* (Oxford: Catholic Social Guild, 1936).

**Pope Pius XI, encyclical, *Divini Illius Magistri.*

QUESTIONS

1. What is meant by educational society? Why is it considered a primary group, but not a natural one?
2. Under what two aspects may education be considered?

3. Why has man a right to an education?
4. What is the duty of parents as regards education?
5. Why is the family the most important of all educative means?
6. What is the duty of the Church regarding education?
7. What part must the State play in the education of the child? What is the delimitation of its rights and duties in this regard, in view of the rights and duties of State and Church?
8. How is education financed?
9. Give an outline of the Catholic educational system of the United States.
10. Give a brief history of Catholic education in the United States.
11. Wherein does Catholic educational philosophy differ from that of those who do not believe in man's possession of a soul and in his eternal destiny?

CHAPTER 15

RECREATION AND RECREATIONAL SOCIETY

RECOMMENDED READINGS

Addams, J., *The Spirit of Youth and the City Streets* (New York: Macmillan Co., 1909).

Adler, H., & Others, *The Incidence of Delinquency in Berkeley, 1928–1932* (Berkeley, Calif.: University of California Press, 1934).

Bowers, E., *Recreation for Girls and Women* (New York: National Recreation Association).

Burns, C. D., *Leisure in the Modern World* (New York: Appleton-Century Co.).

*Carpenter, N., *The Sociology of City Life* (New York: Longmans, Green & Co., 1932).

Elsom, J. C., and Trilling, B., *Social Games and Group Dances* (Philadelphia: J. B. Lippincott Co., 1927).

*Forman, Henry J., *Our Movie Made Children* (New York: Macmillan Co., 1933).

Furfey, Rev. P. H., *The Parish and Play* (Philadelphia: The Dolphin Press, 1928).

Gardner, E., *Development of a Leisure Time Program in Small Cities and Towns,* pamphlet (Washington, D. C.: United States Department of Labor, Children's Bureau, 1933).

—————— *Handbook for Recreation Leaders,* pamphlet (Washington, D. C.: United States Department of Labor, Children's Bureau, 1936).

*Glueck, S., and E. T., *Preventing Crime* (New York: McGraw-Hill Book Co., 1936).

Gulick, L. H., *A Philosophy of Play* (New York: Scribner's Sons, 1920).

Hambidge, G., *Time to Live* (New York: McGraw-Hill Book Co., 1933).

Hartsough, M., and G. C., *The Relation Between Housing and Delin-*

quency (Washington, D. C.: Housing Division, Federal Emergency Administration of Public Works, 1936).

Lee, J. E., *Play in Education* (New York: Macmillan Co., 1915).

Leisure Hours of 5,000 People (New York: National Recreation Association, 1932).

Lies, E. T., *The New Leisure Challenges the Schools* (New York: National Recreation Association, 1933).

*Mitchell, E. D., and Mason, B. S., *The Theory of Play* (New York: A. S. Barnes Co., 1934).

Nash, J. B., *The Organization and Administration of Playgrounds and Recreation* (New York: A. S. Barnes Co., 1927).

Neumeyer, E. S., and M. H., *Leisure and Recreation* (New York: A. S. Barnes Co., 1936).

Rainwater, C., *The Play Movement in the United States* (Chicago: University of Chicago Press, 1922).

Rural and Small Community Recreation (New York: National Recreation Association).

Sheffield, A. D., *Training for Group Experience,* A Syllabus from a Laboratory Course for Group Leaders Given at Columbia University, 1927 (New York: The Inquiry, 129 E. 52nd St., 1929).

*Steiner, J. F., "Americans at Play" in *Recent Social Trends Monograph* (New York: McGraw-Hill Book Co., 1933).

*Williamson, M., *The Social Worker in Group Work* (New York: Harper & Bros., 1929).

PERIODICALS

Leisure, 683 Atlantic Avenue, Boston, Mass.: $1 per year.

Play in Institutions Bulletin Service, National Recreation Association, 315 Fourth Avenue, New York City: $1 per year.

Recreation, National Recreation Association, 315 Fourth Avenue, New York City: $2 per year.

Recreations Bulletin Service, National Recreation Association, 315 Fourth Avenue, New York City: $2.50 per year.

Rural Recreation Service Bulletin, National Recreation Association, 315 Fourth Avenue, New York City: $1.50 per year.

QUESTIONS

1. Explain the extent to which recreation is institutional, and compare its nature with that of other social institutions.
2. What are the duties of the Church, the family, and the State in regard to the recreational group?
3. Show that recreation in the past was a part of the institutional life of the people.
4. Evaluate recreation as viewed by the Athenian.
5. What effect do you think the recreational life of the people in the Middle Ages would have upon the other social institutions?
6. Trace the change of emphasis in the recreation movement through the use of the words play, recreation, and leisure, and show the values emphasized in each of these words.

7. Why is it important to know the emphasis in certain theories of recreation?
8. Evaluate types of recreation according as they serve age and personality needs.
9. What specific contributions can the home, the neighborhood, the Church, and school make to recreation as a primary group?
10. Evaluate recreation as a secondary group.
11. Justify the treatment of recreation from an institutional point of view.

CHAPTER 16

WORKING CONDITIONS AND WAGES

RECOMMENDED READINGS

*Bruno, F. J., *The Theory of Social Work* (Boston: Heath & Co., 1936).
*Commons, J. R., and Andrews, J. B., *Principles of Labor Legislation* (New York: Harper & Bros., 1936).
**Cronin, Rev. J. F., *Economics and Society*, 3rd rev. ed. (Baltimore: Seminary Bookstore, 1938).
*Daugherty, C. R., *Labor Problems in American Industry*, rev. ed. (Boston: Houghton Mifflin, 1938).
Douglas, P. H., *Wages and the Family* (Chicago: University of Chicago Press, 1935).
*Elliott, M. A., and Merrill, F. E., *Social Disorganization* (New York: Harper & Bros., 1934).
Fallon, Rev. F., S.J., McNalty, Rev. J. L., and Goss, B. C., *Principles of Social Economy* (New York: Benziger Bros., 1933).
*Gillin, J. L., *Social Pathology* (New York: Appleton-Century Co., 1933).
Gray, A., *Family Endowment* (London: Ernest Benn, 1927).
**Haas, Rev. F. J., *Man and Society* (New York: Appleton-Century Co., 1930).
Handbook of Labor Statistics, 1936 (Washington, D. C.: United States Department of Labor, Bureau of Labor Statistics).
**Husslein, Rev. J., S.J., *The Christian Social Manifesto* (Milwaukee: Bruce Publishing Co., 1931).
**International Union of Social Studies, *A Code of Social Principles*, rev. ed., pamphlet (Oxford: Catholic Social Guild, 1937).
Kyrk, H., *Economic Problems of the Family* (New York: Harper & Bros., 1933).
Mangold, G. B., *Social Pathology* (New York: Macmillan Co., 1932).
McGowan, Rev. R., *Women and Industry*, pamphlet (Washington, D. C.: National Catholic Welfare Conference, 1926).
**Michel, Rev. V., O.S.B., *Christian Social Reconstruction* (Milwaukee: Bruce Publishing Co., 1937).
**O'Grady, Rev. J., *An Introduction to Social Work* (New York: Appleton-Century Co., 1928).

Pidgeon, M. E., *Women in the Economy of the United States,* pamphlet (Washington, D. C.: United States Department of Labor, Women's Bureau, 1937).

**Pope Leo XIII, encyclical, *Rerum Novarum,* 1891.

**Pope Pius XI, encyclical, *Quadragesimo Anno,* 1931.

Rathbone, E. F., *The Disinherited Family* (London: Allen & Unwin, 1927).

**Ryan, Rev. J. A., *A Living Wage,* rev. ed. (New York: Macmillan Co., 1920).

**Spalding, Rev. H. S., S.J., *Social Problems and Agencies* (New York: Benziger Bros., 1929).

United States Children's Bureau, Bulletin No. 187, Children in Agriculture, 1929; 188, Child Workers on City Streets, 1929; 197, Child Labor — Facts and Figures, 1930; 227, Children Engaged in Newspaper and Magazine Selling and Delivering, 1935.

United States Department of Labor, *The Commercialization of the Home Through Industrial Home Work,* Bulletin No. 135 (Washington, D. C.: United States Department of Labor, Women's Bureau, 1935).

Vibart, H. H., *Family Allowances in Practice* (London: P. S. King & Sons, 1926).

Viteles, M. S., *Industrial Psychology* (New York: W. W. Norton, 1932).

QUESTIONS

1. Why is the question of adequate working conditions of major importance in a nation?
2. Enumerate the major problems connected with the question of adequate working conditions.
3. Discuss modern methods of eliminating unhygienic and dangerous working conditions.
4. What is the social importance of a reasonably short working day?
5. Outline recent legislation as regards working hours. Are long hours absolutely forbidden?
6. Why is legislation for the protection of working women of importance to a nation?
7. What is the social importance of restricting child labor? What problems are involved in such restriction?
8. Outline recent legislation regarding child labor.
9. What would you consider an adequate definition of a living wage?
10. What is the basis of the Catholic teaching that a man should receive a living wage? How does this theory differ from the theory of the economists?
11. Give a brief history of minimum-wage legislation. What is the present law on the question in the United States?
12. What is meant by the "family-allowance" system? Discuss (*a*) the need, and (*b*) the practicability of such a system in the United States.
13. What is meant by sweated labor? Does sweated labor exist in the United States?

CHAPTER 17

WORKERS' RISKS

RECOMMENDED READINGS

Beveridge, W., *Unemployment, a Problem of Industry,* rev. ed. (New York: Longmans, Green & Co., 1930).

*Bossard, J. H., *Social Change and Social Problems* (New York: Harper & Bros., 1934).

*Bruno, F. J., *The Theory of Social Work* (Boston: Heath & Co., 1936).

Burns, E., *Toward Social Security* (New York: McGraw-Hill Book Co., 1936).

*Commons, J. R., and Andrews, J. B., *Principles of Labor Legislation,* 4th ed. rev. (New York: Harper & Bros., 1936).

*Daugherty, C. R., *Labor Problems in American Industry,* rev. ed. (Boston: Houghton Mifflin Co., 1938).

Douglas, P. H., *Social Security in the United States* (New York: McGraw-Hill Book Co., 1936).

*Elliott, M. A., and Merrill, F. E., *Social Disorganization* (New York: Harper & Bros., 1934).

*Epstein, A., *Insecurity: A Challenge to America* (New York: Random House, 1936).

Falk, I. S., *Security Against Sickness* (New York: Doubleday, Doran & Co., 1936).

Gill, E., *Unemployment* (London: Faber & Faber, 1933).

*Gillin, J. L., *Social Pathology* (New York: Appleton-Century Co., 1933).

*——— *Poverty and Dependency,* rev. ed. (New York: Appleton-Century Co., 1937).

**Haas, Rev. F. J., *Man and Society* (New York: Appleton-Century Co., 1930).

Handbook of Labor Statistics (Washington, D. C.: United States Department of Labor, Bureau of Labor Statistics, 1936).

Mangold, G. B., *Social Pathology* (New York: Macmillan Co., 1932).

Rubinow, I. M., *The Quest for Security* (New York: Henry Holt & Co., 1934).

**Smith, Rev. T. M., S.J., *The Unemployment Problem* (Milwaukee: Bruce Publishing Co., 1932).

Social Security in America (Washington, D. C.: The Social Security Board, 1937).

*Warner, A. G., Queen, S. A., and Harper, E. B., *American Charities and Social Work* (New York: Thomas Y. Crowell, 1930).

QUESTIONS

1. What are the major contingencies in life for which the worker needs provision? Which of these can be somewhat mitigated by foresight and preventive measures; which need financial provision?

2. Since industrial accidents cannot be entirely prevented, on whom should the financial cost of the risk fall? Discuss the employer's liability in this regard.
3. What are the chief kind of health expenses to which the worker and his family may be subject? Discuss how his various risks may be taken care of in the United States. Discuss improvements which may be needed and the possible manner of providing for them.
4. Why is old age a serious risk for the poor?
5. What provisions exist in the United States for the care of the aged?
6. If the aged are taken care of by social insurance will the young have to bear more than their due share of such insurance (*a*) temporarily, (*b*) permanently? Discuss.
7. What provisions exist in the United States for widows and orphans of workers?
8. What is the social importance of unemployment?
9. Outline the major causes of unemployment.
10. What type of unemployment may be said to be due to faulty economic organization? Discuss.
11. What steps have been taken (*a*) by private agencies, (*b*) by the Federal Government to lessen employment due to the following causes: seasonal work; technological improvements; trade depressions?
12. What are the provisions of the Social Security Act of 1935 regarding unemployment? Discuss the terms of these provisions.

CHAPTER 18

LABOR AND LABOR UNIONS

RECOMMENDED READINGS

Brooks, R. R., *When Labor Organizes* (New Haven: Yale University Press, 1937).

Characteristics of Company Unions, 1935 (Washington, D. C.: United States Department of Labor, Bureau of Labor Statistics, Bulletin No. 634, 1937).

**Cronin, Rev. J. F., *Economics and Society*, 3rd rev. ed. (Baltimore: Seminary Bookstore, 1938).

Cummins, E. E., *The Labor Problem in the United States* (New York: D. Van Nostrand Co., 1935).

*Daugherty, C. R., *Labor Problems in American Industry*, rev. ed. (Boston: Houghton Mifflin Co., 1938).

Handbook of Labor Statistics (Washington, D. C.: United States Department of Labor, Bureau of Labor Statistics, 1936).

Handbook of Trade Union Methods, pamphlet (New York: International Ladies' Garment Workers' Unions, 3 W. 16th Street, 1937).

**Husslein, Rev. J., S.J., *The Christian Social Manifesto* (Milwaukee: Bruce Publishing Co., rev. ed., 1939).

**International Union of Social Studies, *A Code of Social Principles*, rev. ed., pamphlet (Oxford: Catholic Social Guild, 1937).

***Labor Leader,* biweekly (New York: 226 Lafayette Street).

Letter from the Sacred Congregation of the Council to the Bishop of Lille on Trade Unions and Employers' Associations (Oxford: Catholic Social Guild, 1929; *Catholic Mind,* January 8, 1930).

**McLean, Rev. D., *The Morality of the Strike* (New York: Kenedy & Sons, 1921).

Patterson, S. H., *Social Aspects of Industry* (New York: McGraw-Hill Book Co., 1934).

**Pope Leo XIII, encyclical, *Rerum Novarum,* 1891.

**Pope Pius XI, encyclical, *Quadragesimo Anno,* 1931.

Shields, B. F., *The Labor Problem* (London: Burns, Oates & Washbourne, 1936).

**Spalding, Rev. H. S., S.J., *Social Problems and Agencies* (New York: Benziger Bros., 1929).

Swanstrom, Rev. E. E., *The Waterfront Labor Problem* (New York: Fordham University Press, 1938).

Walsh, J. R., *C.I.O., Industrial Unionism in Action* (New York: W. W. Norton Co., 1937).

Yoder, D., *Personnel and Labor Relations* (New York: Prentice-Hall, 1938).

QUESTIONS

1. Give a definition of the term *labor union.* What are the two chief kinds of unions?
2. Why do workers need to organize in labor unions under the present economic system? Have the recent Popes spoken adequately of this need, and if so, where?
3. Outline the history of the Knights of Labor; the A. F. of L., the C.I.O., and the I.W.W.
4. What is the legal position of the labor union in the United States today?
5. What are the advantages of labor unions?
6. What are the major criticisms against labor unions?
7. What are the special educational needs of workers for the furtherance of unionism?
8. What are the means taken by labor unions to achieve their ends?
9. Does collective bargaining inevitably involve a strike? Why or why not?
10. Define the terms *strike, picketing, boycott.*
11. When is a strike morally just?
12. Are strikes legal in the United States?
13. What was the argument of "sit-down" strikers regarding the legality of their invasion of the employers' property? Discuss their viewpoint.
14. What is meant by (*a*) a closed union; (*b*) a closed shop? Are these situations just? If so, under what conditions?
15. What is a lockout? Discuss its legality and its justice.
16. What Federal laws have affected the employer's weapon of (*a*) the injunction and (*b*) the "yellow-dog" contract?
17. Give the legal position of the company union.
18. Discuss the use of conciliation in the settlement of industrial disputes.

19. What recent attempt has been made toward organizing Catholic labor unionists, in view of the fact that Catholic labor unions are not feasible in the United States?

CHAPTER 19

INDUSTRIAL PARTNERSHIP AND CO-OPERATION

RECOMMENDED READINGS

Berengren, R. F., *Co-operative Banking: A Credit Union Bank* (Macmillan Co., 1923).

Bowen, E. R., *A Co-operative Economic Democracy,* pamphlet (New York: The Co-operative League).

Carr-Saunders, A. M., Florence, P. S., Peers, R., *Consumers' Co-operation in Great Britain* (New York: Harper & Bros., 1938).

Childs, M. W., *Sweden: The Middle Way* (New Haven: Yale University Press, 1936).

Consumers' Co-operation, monthly (New York: The Co-operative League, 167 W. 12th Street).

*Daniels, J., *Co-operation, an American Way* (New York: Covici-Friede, 1938).

*Daugherty, C. R., *Labor Problems in American Industry,* rev. ed. (Boston: Houghton Mifflin Co., 1938).

*Elliott, S., *The English Co-operatives* (New Haven: Yale University Press, 1937).

*Fowler, B. B., *The Lord Helps Those* (New York: Vanguard Press, 1938).

Handbook of Labor Statistics (Washington, D. C.: United States Department of Labor, Bureau of Labor Statistics, 1936).

Howe, F. C., *Denmark: The Co-operative Way* (New York: Coward-McCann, 1936).

**Husslein, Rev. J., S.J., *The Christian Social Manifesto* (Milwaukee: Bruce Publishing Co., 1932).

Kallen, H. M., *The Decline and Rise of the Consumer* (New York: Appleton-Century Co., 1936).

Laidler, H. W., and Campbell, W. J., *Consumers' Co-operation,* pamphlet (New York: The League for Industrial Democracy, 1937).

Mercer, T. W., *Towards the Co-operative Commonwealth* (Manchester, England: The Co-operative Press, 1937).

**Ryan, Rev. J. A., *Distributive Justice* (New York: Macmillan Co., 1919).

Selekman, B. M., *Sharing Management with Workers* (New York: Russell Sage Foundation, 1924).

**Smith, Rev. T. M., S.J., *The Unemployment Problem* (Milwaukee: Bruce Publishing Co., 1932).

**Spalding, Rev. H. S., *Social Problems and Agencies* (New York: Benziger Bros., 1929).

*Warbasse, J. P., *Co-operative Democracy,* 3rd ed., rev. (New York: Harper & Bros., 1936).

QUESTIONS

1. What is welfare work? (*a*) Is it advisable? (*b*) Does it cover all the workers' needs?
2. What is meant by direct profit sharing?
3. What are the advantages and disadvantages of all profit-sharing schemes? Would their extension solve the "labor problem"?
4. How does co-operation differ from profit-sharing schemes?
5. What are the two forms of producers' co-operation, and why is one of them never likely to be very extensive?
6. Outline one or two major producers' co-operatives in the United States.
7. If producers' co-operatives of the type now growing in the United States ever became very extensive, would our present capitalistic system be much changed, and if so, in what particulars?
8. Is it practicable to urge the extension of producers' co-operation in the United States (*a*) in all branches of industry, commerce, and agriculture; (*b*) in some branches only? Discuss.
9. What is meant by credit co-operation? Give a short history of the movement (*a*) in Europe; (*b*) in the United States.
10. Is credit co-operation in the United States today primarily intended for consumers or for producers?
11. Do you consider the extension of credit co-operation in the United States needed, and would such an extension be feasible? Discuss positive ways by which such an extension might be made (if you consider it feasible).
12. What are the advantages of credit banking?
13. What is meant by consumers' co-operation? Discuss its organization.
14. Give a brief history of consumers' co-operation (*a*) in Europe (*b*) in the United States.
15. Would the extension of consumers' co-operation change the present economic system, and if so, how?
16. What do you consider to be the prospects of a rapid extension of co-operation in the United States?
17. What part do you think Catholics need to play in the extension of such movements?

CHAPTER 20

PROPOSED ECONOMIC REFORMS

RECOMMENDED READINGS

*Borsodi, R., *Prosperity and Security* (New York: Harper & Bros., 1938).
**Cahill, Rev. E., S.J., *The Framework of a Christian State* (Dublin: M. H. Gill & Sons, 1932).
***Catholic Encyclopaedia*, articles on Collectivism, Communism, Socialism, Socialistic Communities.
**Cronin, Rev. J. F., *Economics and Society*, 3rd rev. ed. (Baltimore: Seminary Bookstore, 1938).

*Davis, J., *Contemporary Social Movements* (New York: Appleton-Century Co., 1930).

Dawson, C. H., *Religion and the Modern State* (New York: Sheed & Ward, 1933).

Derreck, M., *The Portugal of Salazar* (London: Sands & Co., 1938).

**Fanfani, A., *Catholicism, Protestantism and Capitalism* (New York: Sheed & Ward, 1935).

Goldwell, F., *Guild Socialism,* pamphlet (Oxford: Catholic Social Guild, 1918).

Gurian, W., *The Rise and Decline of Marxism* (London: Burns, Oates & Washbourne, 1938).

Hoffmann, J. R., *The Will to Freedom* (New York: Sheed & Ward, 1935).

Hollis, C., *Lenin* (Milwaukee: Bruce Publishing Co., 1938).

**Husslein, Rev. J., S.J., *The Christian Social Manifesto* (Milwaukee: Bruce Publishing Co., 1931).

**International Union of Social Studies, *A Code of Social Principles,* rev. ed., pamphlet (Oxford: Catholic Social Guild, 1937).

*Loucks, W. N., and Hoot, J. W., *Comparative Economic Systems* (New York: Harper & Bros., 1938).

*MacKenzie, F., ed., *Planned Society* (New York: Prentice-Hall, 1937).

**Michel, Rev. V., O.S.B., *Christian Social Reconstruction* (Milwaukee: Bruce Publishing Co., 1937).

Political Theories and Forms, pamphlets (Collegeville, Minn.: St. John's University).

**Pope Leo XIII, encyclical, *Graves de Communi,* 1901; *Rerum Novarum,* 1891.

**Pope Pius XI, encyclical, *Quadragesimo Anno,* 1931; *Divini Redemptoris,* 1937.

Prince, J. F. T., *Creative Revolution* (Milwaukee: Bruce Publishing Co., 1937).

Robbins, H., *The Sun of Justice* (London: Heath Cranton, Ltd., 1938).

Robbins, L. C., *Economic Planning and International Order* (London: Macmillan Co., 1937).

Roger, C., *Economic Control of Belgium,* pamphlet (Oxford: Catholic Social Guild, 1935).

Sandée, de la, *Communism and Religion* (New York: Kenedy & Co.. 1938).

Sheed, F., *Communism and Man* (New York: Sheed & Ward, 1938).

Strachey, J., *The Coming Struggle for Power* (New York: Covici-Friede, 1933).

**The Guild Social Order* (Oxford: Catholic Social Guild, 1936).

Watt, Rev. L., *Pope Pius XI and Social Reconstruction,* pamphlet (Oxford: Catholic Social Guild, 1936).

Wootton, B., *Plan or No Plan* (New York: Farrar & Rinehart, 1935).

Van Zeeland, P., "Report on International Economic Reconstruction," reprinted in *International Conciliation,* March, 1938 (New York: Carnegie Endowment for International Peace).

QUESTIONS

1. Distinguish between socialism and communism.
2. Briefly outline the chief theories of the Utopian socialists.
3. Who are the syndicalists?
4. Give Marx's ideas on (*a*) surplus value; (*b*) the materialistic conception of history.
5. What is the distinction between (*a*) State socialism; (*b*) Fabian socialism; (*c*) guild socialism?
6. Give a brief history of Russian communism and state its main tenets.
7. Give a brief history of either Fascism in Italy or nationalistic socialism in Germany.
8. Discuss the main features of the totalitarian State as exemplified in communism and Fascism. Wherein does totalitarianism conflict with the theory of the State outlined in Chapter 9?
9. What is the theory of distributism? Discuss the practical possibilities of distributism in the United States.
10. What is the Corporate State as advocated by Pope Pius XI? What is the essential difference between the corporate order and totalitarianism?
11. Do you consider that corporatism could be organized in the United States without any major upheaval in our political system?
12. Would economic organization in a corporate order change the present economic system, and if so, how?
13. Outline the chief features of the N.R.A. In what important features did it differ from the Corporate Order advocated by most Catholic social theorists?

CHAPTER 21

RURAL PROBLEMS

RECOMMENDED READINGS

Agar, H., *Land of the Free* (Boston: Houghton Mifflin Co., 1935).
**Belloc, H., *The Servile State* (London: T. N. Fonlis, 1912).
*Borsodi, R., *Flight From the City* (New York: Harper & Bros., 1933).
*Brunner, E. de S., and Kolb J. H., *Rural Social Trends* (New York: McGraw-Hill Book Co., 1933).
**Catholic Rural Life Bulletin,* quarterly (St. Paul, Minn.: 240 Summit Avenue).
**Catholic Rural Life Objectives,* Annual Reports, 1935, 1936, 1937 (St. Paul: National Catholic Rural Life Conference, 240 Summit Ave.).
Chambers, M. M., *Our American Youth Problem* (Washington, D. C.: American Council on Education, American Youth Commission, 1937).
Duggan, Rev. R. P., *A Federal Resettlement Project: Granger Homestead* (Washington, D. C.: Catholic University of America).
Farm Credit Administration: Fifth Annual Report, 1937 (Washington, D. C.: U. S. Govt. Printing Office, 1938).

*Fowler, B. B., *The Lord Helps Those* (New York: Vanguard Press, 1938).

Free America, monthly (New York: 112 E. 19 Street).

*Gillette, J. R., *Rural Sociology,* 3rd ed., rev. (New York: Macmillan Co., 1936).

**Haas, Rev. F. J., *Man and Society* (New York: Century Co., 1930).

Hoffer, C., *Introduction to Rural Sociology* (New York: Farrar & Rinehart, 1936).

Holmes, R. H., *Rural Sociology* (New York: McGraw-Hill Book Co., 1932).

Humphreys, H. E., *Liberty and Property* (London: The Distributist League, 1930).

*Kolb, J. H., and Brunner, E. de S., *A Study of Rural Society* (Boston: Houghton Mifflin Co., 1935).

**Manifesto on Rural Life* (Milwaukee: The Bruce Publishing Co., 1939).

**O'Hara, Rt. Rev. E., *The Church and the Country Community* (New York: Macmillan Co., 1927).

Recent Social Trends: Report of the President's Research Committee on Social Trends (New York: McGraw-Hill Book Co., 1933).

Report of the Commission on Country Life, Senate Document No. 705, 60th Congress, 2nd Session, Reprinted in book form (New York: Sturgiss & Walton Co., 1911).

**Ross, E. J., *Belgian Rural Co-operatives* (Milwaukee: Bruce Publishing Co., in preparation).

Rural Sociology, quarterly (Baton Rouge, La.: Louisiana State U. Press).

**Schmiedeler, Rev. E., O.S.B., *A Better Rural Life* (New York: J. F. Wagner Inc., 1938).

Taylor, C. C., *Rural Sociology,* rev. ed. (New York: Harper & Bros., 1933).

The Associated Country Women of the World (Washington, D. C.: U. S. Dept. of State, Government Printing Office).

Ward, F. E., *The Farm Women's Problem* (Washington. D. C.: U. S. Dept. of Agriculture, Extension Circular No. 148).

Yearbook of Agricultural Co-operation, annual (London: Routledge & Sons, Ltd.).

Yearbook of Agriculture, annual (Washington, D. C.: United States Department of Agriculture).

QUESTIONS

1. Why is the welfare of rural peoples of such vital concern to the nation?
2. What are the advantages of rural life from the social viewpoint?
3. What are the chief economic needs of the farmer at the present time? Enumerate the chief measures which are being taken to provide for these needs.
4. Outline the work of the major organizations of national scope which aim at helping the farmer's economic status.

5. Discuss the question of rural education.
6. Why should rural education be considered as a separate problem from urban education? What are the chief needs of rural children?
7. What are the needs of the rural housewife?
8. Why is there a rural recreational problem? What means have been taken to solve it?
9. What are the problems connected with the Church in the country districts?
10. To what type of rural peoples will the *Catholic Rural Life Bulletin* make special appeal? Why is it useful that colleges in urban districts should also read this magazine?
11. Discuss the value of rural religious vacation schools. Read some magazine literature on the subject.
12. Write an essay on the resettlement project at Granger, Iowa.
13. Could the Danish co-operative farming system be extended to the United States? Discuss.
14. What are the main features of Belgian rural co-operation which might be adopted by farmers in the United States?
15. Discuss the Nova Scotia experiment (*a*) from the viewpoint of its educational work; (*b*) as an economic program; (*c*) as a social force.
16. In how far do you think it feasible to emulate these plans in the United States?

Chapter 22

POVERTY, DEPENDENCY, AND RELIEF

Recommended Readings

*Bossard, J. H., *Social Change and Social Problems* (New York: Harper & Bros., 1934).

Breckinridge, S. P., *Public Welfare Administration* (Chicago: University of Chicago Press, 1927).

*Bruno, F. J., *The Theory of Social Work* (Boston: Heath & Co., 1936).

**Catholic Charities Review,* 10 issues yearly (Washington, D. C.: Catholic University of America).

**Catholic Encyclopaedia,* articles on Almsgiving; Charity and Charities; Homes; Hospitals; Monasteries; suppression of; Orphans and Orphanages; Poor, care of by Catholic Church; Poor Law; Poverty; Society of St. Vincent de Paul.

**Cooper, Rev. J. M., *Children's Institutions* (Philadelphia: Dolphin Press, 1931).

*Davie, M. R., *Problems of City Life* (New York: Wiley & Sons, 1932).

*Elliott, M. A., and Merrill, F. E., *Social Disorganization* (New York: Harper & Bros., 1934).

Ford, J., *Slums and Housing* (Cambridge: Harvard University Press, 1936).

—— and Ford, K. M., *The Abolition of Poverty* (New York: Macmillan Co., 1936).

*Gillette, J. M., and Reinhart, J. M., *Current Social Problems,* rev. ed. (New York: American Book Co., 1937).

*Gillin, J. L., *Poverty and Dependency,* rev. ed. (New York: Appleton-Century Co., 1937).

*——— *Social Pathology* (New York: Appleton-Century Co., 1933).

**Haas, Rev. F. J., *Man and Society* (New York: Appleton-Century Co., 1930).

Handbook of Labor Statistics, 1936 (United States Department of Labor, Bureau of Labor Statistics).

*Kelso, R. W., *The Science of Public Welfare* (New York: Henry Holt & Co., 1938).

**Kerby, Rev. W. J., *The Social Mission of Charity* (New York: Macmillan Co., 1924).

Mangold, G. B., *Social Pathology* (New York: Macmillan Co., 1932).

——— *Problems of Child Welfare* (New York: Macmillan Co., 1936).

——— *Organization for Social Welfare* (New York: Macmillan Co., 1934).

May, E. S., *Social Welfare: A Guide for Studying Welfare Facilities of the Local Community,* pamphlet (Washington, D. C.: American Association of University Women, 1938).

**Muntsch, Rev. A. J., S.J., and Spalding, Rev. H. S., S.J., *Introductory Sociology* (Boston: Heath & Co., 1928).

**National Conference of Catholic Charities,* annual proceedings (Washington, D. C.: Catholic University of America).

Norman, M. C., "The Application of Catholic Philosophy to the Practice of Social Work," *Proceedings of the 23rd Annual Meeting of the National Conference of Catholic Charities,* 1937, pp. 59–72.

**O'Grady, Rev. J., *Catholic Charities in the United States* (Washington, D. C.: National Conference of Catholic Charities, 1931).

——— *The Catholic Church and the Destitute* (New York: Macmillan Co., 1929).

**——— *An Introduction to Social Work* (New York: Appleton-Century Co., 1928).

*Phelps, H. A., *Contemporary Social Problems,* rev. ed. (New York: Prentice-Hall, 1938).

Post, L. W., *The Challenge of Housing* (New York: Farrar & Rinehart, 1938).

Pouthier, Rev. E., S.J., "The Philosophy of Catholic Social Case Work," *Proceedings of the 23rd Annual Meeting of the National Conference of Catholic Charities,* 1937, pp. 49–59.

*Proctor, A. W., and Schuck, A. A., *Financing of Social Work* (New York: McGraw-Hill Book Co., 1926).

*Queen, S. A., Bodenhafer, W. B., and Harper, E. B., *Social Organization and Disorganization* (New York: Thomas Y. Crowell Co., 1935).

Schweinitz, K. de, *The Art of Helping People Out of Trouble* (Boston: Houghton Mifflin, 1924).

Social Security in America (Washington, D. C.: Social Security Board, 1937).

*Social Work Year Book, 1929, 1931, 1933, 1935, 1937, 1939 (New York: Russell Sage Foundation).

**Spalding, Rev. H. S., S.J., Social Problems and Agencies (New York: Benziger Bros., 1929).

———— Chapters in Social History (Boston: Heath & Co., 1925).

The Family, 10 issues yearly (New York: Family Welfare Association of America).

United States Children's Bureau, Bulletin Nos. 125, Unemployment and Child Welfare, 1923; 136, Foster Care for Dependent Children, 1929; 142, Causal Factors in Infant Mortality, 1929; 162, Public Aid to Mothers with Dependent Children, 1928; 166, Children of Illegitimate Birth and Measures for their Protection, 1926; 190, Children of Illegitimate Birth Whose Mothers Have Kept Their Custody, 1928; 221, Maternal Deaths, 1933.

*Warner, A. G., Queen, S. A., and Harper, E. B., American Charities and Social Work, 4th ed. (New York: Thomas Y. Crowell, 1930).

*White House Conference on Child Health and Protection, Dependent and Neglected Children (New York: Appleton-Century Co., 1933).

*White House Conference on Child Health and Protection, Organization for the Care of Handicapped Children (New York: Appleton-Century Co., 1932).

QUESTIONS

1. Distinguish between poverty and destitution.
2. Outline some of the major subjective factors which may lead to poverty, and state how they may be avoided.
3. What are the major objective factors which lead to poverty at the present time — which of these, in general, could be avoided by a better social planning, and which can be eliminated only to a small extent? Give reasons for your answer.
4. What are some of the effects of poverty in many persons? Can it be said that poverty is not always detrimental to the poor person? Why?
5. What is social case work?
6. Distinguish between outdoor and indoor relief.
7. What is meant by the cottage or colony system? How does it differ from the usual institution? For what types of needy persons is it most suited?
8. Give a brief history of relief.
9. What was the Elberfeld system of relief?
10. Discuss the pros and cons of private versus public relief.
11. What is the work of a social-service exchange?
12. Give the history and organization of community chests.
13. What is the work of the National Conference of Catholic Charities?
14. What are the chief types of needy people?
15. What are the needs of the dependent sick?
16. Distinguish between socialized medicine and social health insurance.
17. How are needs of dependent sick cared for in the United States?
18. What is the special work of medical social work?
19. Discuss the best method of treating the unmarried mother.
20. Give history of day nursery, and outline chief service it can render.

21. Discuss chief needs of dependent child; how they may be cared for.
22. Why do the poor need provision for recreation?
23. What is the work of the social settlement?

CHAPTER 23

THE TREATMENT OF DEFECTIVES

RECOMMENDED READINGS

Adams, G., *Psychology, Science or Superstition?* (New York: Covici-Friede, 1931).

*Beers, C. W., *A Mind that Found Itself,* rev. ed. (New York: Doubleday, Page & Co., 1923).

**Bernstein, C., *Social Care of the Mentally Deficient,* pamphlet (Washington, D. C.: National Catholic Welfare Conference, 1930).

Best, H., *Blindness and the Blind in the United States* (New York: Macmillan Co., 1934).

*Bruno, L., *The Theory of Social Work* (Boston: Heath & Co., 1926).

*Burt, C., *The Backward Child* (New York: Appleton-Century Co., 1937).

Conklin, E. S., *Principles of Abnormal Psychology* (New York: Henry Holt, 1927).

———— *Principles of Adolescent Psychology* (New York: Henry Holt, 1935).

*Davies, S. P., *Social Control of the Mentally Deficient* (New York: Thomas Y. Crowell Co., 1930).

Deutsch, A., *The Mentally Ill in America* (New York: Doubleday, Doran & Co., 1937).

*Elliott, M. A., and Merrill, F. E., *Social Disorganization* (New York: Harper & Bros., 1934).

*Gillette, J. M., and Reinhardt, J. M., *Current Social Problems,* rev. ed. (New York: American Book Co., 1937).

*Gillin, J. L., *Social Pathology* (New York: Appleton-Century Co., 1933).

Groves, E. R., and Blanchard, P., *Introduction to Mental Hygiene* (New York: Henry Holt & Co., 1930).

**Hauber, Rev. U. A., *Inheritance of Mental Defect,* pamphlet (Washington, D. C.: National Catholic Welfare Conference, 1930).

*Howard, F. E., and Patry, F. L., *Mental Health* (New York: Harper & Bros., 1935).

Jeliffe, S. E., and White, W. A., *Diseases of the Nervous System* (Philadelphia: Lea and Febiger, 1923).

Kreuger, E. T., and Reckless, W. C., *Social Psychology* (New York: Longmans, Green & Co., 1931).

Mangold, G. B., *Social Pathology* (New York: Macmillan Co., 1932).

**McCarthy, Rev. R. C., S.J., *Safeguarding Mental Health* (Milwaukee: Bruce Publishing Co., 1937).

**———— *Training the Adolescent* (Milwaukee: Bruce Publishing Co., 1934).

Mental Hygiene, quarterly (New York: National Committee for Mental Hygiene).

Moore, Rev. T. V., O.S.B., *Dynamic Psychology* (Philadelphia: J. B. Lippincott Co., 1924).

**Muntsch, Rev. A. J., S.J., and Spalding, Rev. H. S., S.J., *Introductory Sociology* (New York: Heath & Co., 1928).

**Murray, Rev R. W., C.S.C., *Introductory Sociology,* Chaps. 11, 12 (New York: Crofts & Co., 1934).

*Oliver, J. R., *Fear* (Macmillan Co., 1927).

*———— *Foursquare* (New York: Macmillan Co., 1929).

Pratt, G. K., *Mental Hygiene Concepts in Social Life; Morale: the Mental Hygiene of Unemployment,* pamphlets (New York: National Committee for Mental Hygiene, 1933.

Shaffer, L. F., *The Psychology of Adjustment* (Boston: Houghton Mifflin Co., 1936).

**Shields, Rev. T. E., *The Making and Unmaking of a Dullard* (Washington, D. C.: Catholic Education Press, 1929).

Social Work Year Book, various articles.

United States Children's Bureau, Bulletin Nos. 143, Child Management, 1928; 202, Are You Training Your Child to be Happy?, 1930; 225, Guiding the Adolescent, 1933.

Wallin, J. E. W., *The Education of Handicapped Children* (Boston: Houghton Mifflin Co., 1924).

*Warner, A. G., Queen, S. A., and Harper, E. B., *American Charities and Social Work,* 4th ed., rev. (New York: Thomas Y. Crowell, 1930).

White House Conference on Child Health and Protection, *Special Education: The Handicapped and the Gifted* (New York: Appleton-Century Co., 1931).

*Woodworth, R. S., *Contemporary Schools of Psychology* (New York: Ronald Press, 1931).

QUESTIONS

1. Why do defectives present a social problem?
2. What are the special needs of the blind, and how are they remedied in the United States at the present time?
3. What is the special problem presented by (*a*) the hard of hearing and (*b*) the deaf and dumb?
4. Give a short history of Catholic work for the deaf in the United States.
5. What provisions are made at the present time for crippled children; for adult cripples?
6. What is the usual classification of mental deficients?
7. Discuss modern methods of ascertaining whether or not a person is mentally deficient.
8. What are the special needs of mental deficients to enable them to live as happily as possible in later life?
9. Distinguish between insanity and mental deficiency.

10. Give a brief classification of the major types of neuroses and psychoses.
11. What is the best method of dealing with the different types of insanity?
12. Discuss the theories of Freud. What is his essential error and wherein is he at least to some extent correct?
13. Outline the main thesis of (*a*) Alfred Adler, and (*b*) C. G. Jung.
14. What would you judge to be the contribution of the psychoanalysts in the treatment of mental disorders?
15. What is the peculiar social problem presented by the epileptic?
16. Discuss the social influence of drug addiction; what measures are being taken to eradicate this evil?
17. What is the social problem presented by drunkenness? Why was not Prohibition an adequate solution?

CHAPTER 24

EUGENICS AND POPULATION PROBLEMS

RECOMMENDED READINGS

*Committee of the American Neurological Association, *Eugenical Sterilization* (New York: Macmillan Co., 1936).
**Cooper, Rev. J. M., *Birth Control* (Washington D. C.: National Catholic Welfare Conference, 1923).
Dublin, L. I., ed., *Population Problems* (Boston: Houghton Mifflin Co., 1926).
Encyclopaedia of Social Sciences, article on Births.
Gucheteneere, R. de, *Judgment on Birth Control* (New York: Sheed & Ward, 1931).
Haldane, J. B. S., *Heredity and Politics* (New York: W. W. Norton Co., 1938).
Hildebrand, D. von, *In Defence of Purity* (New York: Sheed & Ward, 1935).
**Joyce, Rev. G. H., S.J., *Christian Marriage* (New York: Sheed & Ward, 1933).
*Kuczynski, R. R., *The Measurement of Population Growth* (New York: Oxford University Press, 1936).
Landman, J. H., *Human Sterilization* (New York: Macmillan Co., 1932).
*Lorimer, F., and Osborn, F., *Dynamics of Population* (New York: Macmillan Co., 1934).
**Montavon, W. F., *Eugenic Sterilization in the Laws of the United States*, pamphlet (Washington, D. C.: National Catholic Welfare Conference, 1930).
**Moore, E. R., *The Case Against Birth Control* (New York: Appleton-Century Co., 1931).
Morrison, Rev. B., S.J., *Marriage* (Milwaukee: Bruce Publishing Co., 1934).

Myserson, A., and others, *Eugenical Sterilization* (New York: Macmillan Co., 1936).

**Pope Pius XI, encyclical, *Casti Connubii,* 1930.

Popenoe, P., and Johnson, R. H., *Applied Eugenics,* rev. ed. (New York: Macmillan Co., 1933).

Power, E. R., *Population Prospects,* pamphlet (Oxford: Catholic Social Guild, 1938).

Report of the Departmental Committee on Sterilization (London: H. M. Stationery Office, 1934).

**Ryan, Rev. J. A., *Moral Aspects of Sterilization,* pamphlet (Washington, D. C.: National Catholic Welfare Conference, 1930).

Surbled, Rev. G., and Eggemann, Rev. H. J., *Catholic Moral Teaching* (St. Louis: B. Herder Book Co., 1930).

Sutherland, H., *Laws of Life* (New York: Sheed & Ward, 1936).

Wayne, Rev. T. G., *Morals and Marriage* (London: Longmans, Green, 1936).

QUESTIONS

1. What is the meaning of the word *eugenics* and what social problems does it include?
2. In how far may it be said that Catholic social ideals agree with the teachings of the eugenists?
3. What is the social problem presented by euthanasia?
4. What is the philosophical error in the advocation of sterilization of the unfit?
5. Explain why any general sterilization of the unfit would be unsound on medical grounds.
6. What is the fundamental error in advocating sterilization of moral defectives?
7. Upon what social grounds should general sterilization of the unfit be combated?
8. Show how the economic reasons usually cited in favor of birth control are in large measure unsound.
9. What social measures would you propose to remedy those economic arguments in favor of birth control which seem to be correct?
10. What are the physiological and psychological arguments for and against artificial birth control?
11. Discuss the social effects of extensive birth control.
12. Explain the Church's opposition to artificial birth control. What is her attitude toward what may be termed a natural birth control?

CHAPTER 25

PROBLEMS OF FAMILY LIFE

RECOMMENDED READINGS

*Bossard, J. H. S., *Social Change and Social Problems,* rev. ed. (New York: Harper & Bros., 1934).

Colcord, J., *Broken Homes* (New York: Russell Sage Foundation, 1919).

*Elliott, M. A., and Merrill, F. E., *Social Disorganization* (New York: Harper & Bros., 1934).

Gillin, J. L., Dittmer, C. G., and Colbert, R. J., *Social Problems,* rev. ed. (New York: Appleton-Century Co., 1932).

**Haas, Rev. F. J., *Man and Society* (New York: Appleton-Century Co., 1930).

Leclercq, Rev. J., *Leçons de Droit Naturel: III: La Famille* (Louvain: Société d'Etudes, Morales, Sociales et Juridiques, 1933).

Lynch, Rev. A., O.P., *This is Christian Marriage* (Union City, N. J.: The Sign Press, 1933).

Morrison, Rev. B., S.J., *Marriage* (Milwaukee: Bruce Publishing Co., 1934).

*Phelps, H. A., *Contemporary Social Problems* (New York: Prentice-Hall, Inc., 1938).

Pope Pius XI, encyclical, *Casti Connubii,* 1930.

Recent Social Trends: Report of the President's Research Committee on Social Trends (New York: McGraw-Hill Book Co., 1933).

Reuter, E. B., and Runner, J., *The Family* (New York: McGraw-Hill Book Co., 1931).

Sayles, M. B., *Substitute Parents* (New York: The Commonwealth Fund, 1936).

———— *The Problem Child at Home* (New York: The Commonwealth Fund, 1928).

———— *The Problem Child in School* (New York: The Commonwealth Fund, 1926).

**Schmiedeler, Rev. E., O.S.B., *An Introductory Study of the Family* (New York: Appleton-Century Co., 1930).

**———— *Readings on the Family* (New York: Appleton-Century Co., 1931).

———— and McDonough, M. R., *Parent and Child* (New York: Appleton-Century Co., 1934).

The Catholic Family Monthly, monthly (Huntington, Ind.: Our Sunday Visitor Press).

QUESTIONS

1. Show the connection between economic organization and the present problems of family life.
2. Evaluate the difference between family life of a hundred years ago and today.
3. In what way do you think people could be better prepared for marriage and family life than they are today?
4. What have changed religious ideals to do with problems connected with the family?
5. How could the State remedy some of the causes of marital disunion?
6. Discuss the effects of bad housing on family life.
7. What are the main general causes of bad housing conditions?
8. What specific provisions have been made in recent years to eliminate bad housing?

9. Why is divorce a greater problem in the United States than elsewhere? Quote some statistics in support of your answer.
10. Why is divorce a social evil?
11. Discuss the Church's teaching as regards divorce.
12. What is the distinction between divorce and separation?
13. Why does the Church sometimes allow separation, when divorce is impossible?
14. What is the distinction between divorce and annulment?

CHAPTER 26

CRIMINOLOGY AND DELINQUENCY

RECOMMENDED READINGS

Bates, S., *Prisons and Beyond* (New York: Macmillan Co., 1936).

Beard, B. B., *Juvenile Probation* (New York: American Book Co., 1934).

Blumer, H., and Hauser, P. M., *Movies, Delinquency, and Crime* (New York: Macmillan Co., 1925).

*Burt, C., *The Young Delinquent* (New York: Appleton-Century Co., 1925).

Cantor, N., *Crime, Criminals and Criminal Justice* (New York: Henry Holt & Co., 1932).

*Cooley, E. J., *Probation and Delinquency* (New York: Thomas Nelson & Sons, 1927).

*Elliott, M. A., and Merrill, F. E., *Social Disorganization* (New York: Harper & Bros., 1934).

*Encyclopaedia of the Social Sciences, articles on crime; criminology; juvenile delinquency; penal institutions; punishment.

*Ettinger, C. J., *The Problem of Crime* (New York: Farrar & Rinehart, 1934).

**Furfey, Rev. P. H., *The Gang Age* (New York: Macmillan Co., 1926).

Geisert, Rev. H. A., *The Criminal* (St. Louis: B. Herder Book Co., 1930).

*Gillin, J. L., *Criminology and Penology*, rev. ed. (New York: Appleton-Century Co., 1925).

Glueck, S., and Glueck, E. T., *500 Criminal Careers* (New York: Alfred A. Knopf, 1930).

———— *One Thousand Juvenile Delinquents* (Cambridge: Harvard University Press, 1934).

*———— *Preventing Crime* (New York: McGraw-Hill Book Co., 1936).

Hartsough, M., and Casell, G., *The Relation between Housing and Delinquency*, pamphlet (Washington, D. C.: Housing Division, Federal Emergency Administration of Public Works, 1936).

**Kalmer, Rev. L., O.F.M., and Weir, Rev. E., O.F.M., *Crime and Religion* (Chicago: Franciscan Herald Press, 1936).

Lou, H. H., *The Juvenile Court in the United States* (Chapel Hill: University of North Carolina Press, 1927).

———— *Race Mixture: Studies in Intermarriage and Miscegenation* (New York: McGraw-Hill Book Co., 1931).

*Schwesinger, G. C., *Heredity and Environment* (New York: Macmillan Co., 1933).

**Spalding, Rev. H., S.J., *Social Problems and Agencies* (New York: Benziger Bros., 1929).

Thomas, W. I., and Znaniecki, F., *The Polish Peasant in Europe and America* (New York: Alfred A. Knopf, 1927).

Weatherford, W. D., and Johnson, C., *Race Relations* (Boston: Heath & Co., 1934).

Woodson, C. G., *The Mis-Education of the Negro* (Washington, D. C.: The Associated Publishers, 1933).

———— *The Negro in Our History* (Washington, D. C.: The Associated Publishers, 1931).

Woofter, T. J., *Races and Ethnic Groups in American Life* (New York: McGraw-Hill Book Co., 1933).

*Work, M. N., ed., *Negro Year Book 1937–38* (Tuskegee Institute, Ala.: Negro Year Book Publishing Co., 1938).

QUESTIONS

1. Write a brief history of immigration to the United States.
2. Give the main features of the present immigration laws.
3. Enumerate the chief problems which must be solved by citizens of the United States if they receive immigrants into the country.
4. Enumerate the chief problems to be solved by the immigrant and his family at home and abroad.
5. Why is it not always true to say that immigrants will add to the unemployment of United States citizens?
6. What have been the contributions of immigrants to the United States (*a*) since 1930; (*b*) since the beginning of last century?
7. Does your answer to the last question show conclusively how ridiculous is the attitude of those Americans who talk about immigrants, past and present, in derogatory fashion? Explain.
8. If you were asked to attend to the needs of a newly arrived Catholic immigrant and his family, what would be the best method of procedure? What organizations would you advise him to consult?
9. Outline the procedure required of an alien who wishes to become a United States citizen.
10. Why is it essential for a student of American social problems to study the question of immigration despite the present restrictions?
11. Write a brief history of the Negro in the United States.
12. Why may it be said to be unscientific to attribute a higher place to white people than to Negroes in the record of past development of the United States?
13. Why is it un-Christian to have an attitude of superiority and disdain toward Negroes?
14. Is it correct to maintain that the average Negro in the United States is less intelligent than the average white person? Justify your answer.
. Give reasons for the greater percentage of poverty among Negroes than among white persons.

Mangold, G. B., *Social Pathology* (New York: Macmillan Co., 1932).

**Murray, Rev., R. W., C.S.C., and Flynn, F. T., *Social Problems* (New York: F. S. Crofts & Co., 1938).

National Commission on Law Observance and Enforcement, Report Nos. 3, Criminal Statistics; 9, Penal Institutions, Probation and Parole; 10, Crime and the Foreign Born; 11, Lawlessness in Law Enforcement; 12, Cost of Crime; 13, Causes of Crime (2 vols.); 14, Police (Washington, D. C.: Government Printing Office, 1931).

Recent Social Trends, Report of the President's Research Committee on Social Trends (New York: McGraw-Hill Book Co., 1933).

Report of the Select Committee on Capital Punishment (London: H. M. Stationery Office, 1930).

**Spalding, Rev. H. S., S.J., *Social Problems and Agencies* (New York: Benziger Bros., 1929).

*Sullenger, T. E., *Social Determinants in Juvenile Delinquency* (New York: John Wiley & Sons, 1936).

*Sutherland, E. H., *Principles of Criminology* (Philadelphia: J. B. Lippincott Co., 1934).

Thrasher, F. M., *The Gang*, 2nd rev. ed. (Chicago: University of Chicago Press, 1936).

United States Children's Bureau, Bulletin Nos. 142, Juvenile Courts at Work, 1925; 195, Youth and Crime, 1930; 215, Facts About Juvenile Delinquency, 1932; 228, Institutional Treatment of Delinquent Boys, 1933.

*Warner, A. G., Queen, S. A., and Harper, E. B., *American Charities and Social Work* (New York: Thomas Y. Crowell Co., 1930).

*White House Conference on Child Health & Protection, *The Delinquent Child* (New York: Appleton-Century Co., 1932).

Young, P. V., *Social Treatment in Probation and Delinquency* (New York: McGraw-Hill Book Co., 1937).

QUESTIONS

1. What are the different kinds of law?
2. In how far is crime and delinquency (*a*) a moral problem, (*b*) a social problem? Can the two problems be clearly delimited? Discuss.
3. Distinguish between sin, crime, misdemeanor.
4. Discuss the tangible "cost of crime."
5. Why is it correct to say that there is no one cause of any crime?
6. Why is it important to know the major factors which are the occasions of crime?
7. Why is a knowledge of the subject matter of Chapters 2 and 3 a necessary prerequisite for a study of crime causation?
8. What is the inherited basis, if any, of delinquent conduct? Discuss the greater or less inheritance of predisposition to certain types of conduct.
9. What subjective factors other than possibly inherited predispositions toward certain types of conduct might enter into a criminal's acts?
10. Enumerate the chief environmental factors which enter into crime causation.

11. What major social reforms seem needed to eliminate the chief occasions of crime?
12. What is the only basic reason by which society, through the governing body, is justified in punishing the criminal?
13. What are the main objectives of punishment, in addition to its fundamental justification?
14. Give the pros and cons of capital punishment.
15. Outline the major theories in regard to the punishment of criminals.
16. What seems to be the major error in the attitude of those following the "classical" school?
17. What was the theory of Lombroso, and what criticisms can be made thereof?
18. What is the major present-day emphasis on the treatment of criminals in the United States? Is it based on a true or a false philosophy?
19. Give a brief history of probation, and state the major criticisms against it as well as the arguments in its favor. Does a sentence of probation eliminate punishment and/or retribution?
20. What are the arguments for and against prison labor? Discuss the validity of each side and come to a definite conclusion on the subject.
21. Discuss whether or not prison education is an important factor in the reformation of the prisoner.
22. What special treatment is needed in the case of women prisoners with the object of effecting a socially useful reform?
23. Distinguish between parole and probation.
24. What is the indeterminate sentence? What are its drawbacks, and what its advantages in connection with reform?
25. Why is juvenile delinquency of particular concern to the social worker and reformer?

CHAPTER 27

IMMIGRATION AND RACE PROBLEMS

RECOMMENDED READINGS

Abbott, E., *Immigration* (Chicago: Chicago University Press, 1924).

Anderson, E. L., *We Americans* (Cambridge: Harvard University Press, 1937).

Bercovici, K., *Around the World in New York* (New York: Appleton-Century Co., 1924).

Boas, F., *Anthropology and Modern Life*, rev. ed. (New York: W. W. Norton Co., 1932).

*——— *The Mind of Primitive Man*, rev. ed. (New York: Macmillan Co., 1938).

Bok, E., *The Americanization of Edward Bok* (New York: Scribner's Sons, 1924).

*Brown, L. G., *Immigration* (New York: Longmans, Green, 1930).

Carr-Saunders, A. M., *World Population* (Oxford: Oxford University Press, 1936).

*Davie, M. R., *World Immigration* (New York: Macmillan Co., 1936).

Day, C. B., *Negro-White Families in the United States* (Cambridge: Harvard University Press, 1932).

Dubois, W. E. B., *Black Reconstruction* (New York: Harcourt, Brace, 1935).

Eaton, A. H., *Immigrant Gifts to American Life* (New York: Russell Sage Foundation, 1932).

*Elliott, M. A., and Merrill, F. E., *Social Disorganization* (New York: Harper & Bros., 1934).

Embree, E. R., *Brown America* (New York: Viking Press, 1931).

*Encyclopaedia of the Social Sciences, articles on Man, Mental Tests, Race Conflict, Race Mixture.

*Garth, T. R., *Race Psychology* (New York: McGraw-Hill Book Co., 1931).

**Gillard, Rev. J. T., S.S.J., *The Catholic Church and the American Negro* (Baltimore: St. Joseph's Society Press, 1930).

*Gillette, J. M., and Reinhardt, J. M., *Current Social Problems*, rev. ed. (New York: American Book Co., 1937).

**Gilligan, Rev. F. J., *The Morality of the Color Line* (Washington, D. C.: Catholic University of America, 1928).

*Handbook of Labor Statistics, 1936 (United States Department of Labor, Bureau of Labor Statistics).

Herskovits, M. J., *The American Negro* (New York: Alfred A. Knopf, 1928).

**Interracial Review, monthly (New York: 20 Vesey Street).

*Jenks, J. W., and Lauck, W. J., *The Immigration Problem* (New York: Funk & Wagnalls, 1926).

*Johnson, C. S., *The Negro in American Civilization* (New York: H Holt & Co., 1930).

Johnson, J. W., *Along This Way* (New York: Viking Press, 1933).

——— *The Autobiography of an Ex-Colored Man* (New York: A. Knopf, 1928).

Klineberg, O., *Negro Intelligence and Selective Migration* (New York: Columbia University Press, 1935).

*——— *Race Differences* (New York: Harper & Bros., 19).

**LaFarge, Rev. J., S.J., *Interracial Justice* (New York: T Press, 1937).

Lasker, B., *Race Attitudes in Children* (New York: Henr)

Moton, R. R., *What the Negro Thinks* (New York: Dou 1929).

**Murray, Rev. R. W., C.S.C., and Flynn, F. T., *Social York: Crofts & Co., 1938).

Nearing, S., *Black America* (New York: Vanguard

Negro Year Book, see Work, M. N.

Pinsk, J., *Christianity and Race* (New York: Sheed

Ravage, M. E., *An American in the Making* (N Bros., 1917).

Reuter, E. B., *The American Race Problem* (N Crowell, 1927).

16. Discuss the supposed greater delinquency and crime among Negro than among white groups.
17. Make a list of the chief claims that American Negroes are not awarded their just rights (*a*) as human beings; (*b*) as citizens of the United States. State briefly any arguments against these claims and give briefly your conclusions as to the actual justice of the situation.
18. What are the chief problems involved by the presence of Negroes in the United States?
19. Why is it more correct to speak of the interracial problem than of the Negro problem?
20. What are the possible social effects of the discriminations against Negroes in education?
21. Why is it socially and economically unsound to discriminate against Negroes in regard to employment and conditions of work?
22. What have Catholics done to solve the "Negro problem" within recent years? Outline the major work still needed in this connection.

CHAPTER 28

CATHOLIC ACTION

RECOMMENDED READINGS

**Civardi, Rev. L., *A Manual of Catholic Action* (New York: Sheed & Ward, 1936).

**Crofts, A. M., O.P., *Catholic Social Action* (St. Louis: B. Herder Book Co., 1938).

**Cuthbert, Rev., O.S.F.C., *Catholic Ideals in Social Life* (New York: Benziger Bros., 1904).

**Fitzsimons, Rev. J., and McGuire, P., *Restoring All Things: A Guide to Catholic Action* (New York: Sheed & Ward, 1938).

Furfey, Rev. P. H., *Fire on the Earth* (New York: Macmillan Co., 1936).

** ———— *Three Theories of Society* (New York: Macmillan Co., 1938).

Garesché, Rev. E. F., S.J., *Modern Parish Problems* (New York: Jos. F. Wagner, 1928).

Garriguet, Rev. L., *The Gospel and Our Social Problems* (New York: Jos. F. Wagner, 1925).

Harbrecht, Rev. J., *The Lay Apostolate* (New York: Benziger Bros., 1930).

**Kerby, Rev. W. J., *The Social Mission of Charity* (New York: Macmillan Co., 1924).

Lugan, Rev. A., *Social Principles of the Gospel* (New York: Macmillan Co., 1928).

Martin, P. R., *The Gospel in Action* (Milwaukee: Bruce Publishing Co., 1932).

Meyer, Rev. J., O.F.M., *The Social Ideals of St. Francis* (St. Louis: B. Herder Book Co., 1938).

Michel, Rev. V., O.S.B., *The Social Question,* Series of nine pamphlets (Collegeville, Minn.: St. John's University, 1936).

Mounier, E., *A Personalist Manifesto* (New York: Longmans, Green, 1938).

Muntsch, Rev. A. J., S.J., *The Church and Civilization* (Milwaukee: Bruce Publishing Co., 1936).

** —————— and Spalding, H. S., S.J., *Introductory Sociology* (Boston: Heath & Co., 1928).

**Murray, Rev. R. W., C.S.C., and Flynn, F. T., *Social Problems,* Chap. 1 (New York: Crofts & Co., 1938).

**O'Grady, Rev. J., *Catholic Charities in the United States* (Washington, D. C.: National Conference of Catholic Charities, 1931).

** —————— *An Introduction to Social Work* (New York: Appleton-Century Co., 1928).

**Pope Pius XI, encyclical, *Mens Nostra,* 1929, quoted in the *Catholic Mind,* February 8, 1930; "On Catholic Action," 1931, quoted in the *Catholic Mind,* July 22 and August 8, 1931; "Letter to Cardinal Bertram," Archbishop of Breslau, quoted in the *Catholic Mind,* March 8, 1930; Various letters quoted in "Directives for Catholic Action," *Central-Blatt and Social Justice,* December, 1937, pp. 265–268; January, 1938, pp. 305, 306; *Divini Redemptoris,* 1938.

Schumacher, H., *The Social Message of the New Testament* (Milwaukee: Bruce Publishing Co., 1937).

Spalding, Rev. H. S., S.J., *Chapters in Social History* (Boston: Heath & Co., 1925).

Walsh, M. E., *Saints and Social Work* (Silver Spring, Md.: Preservation of the Faith Press, 1937).

Will, Rev. J., S.J., and Hennrich, Rev. K. J., O.M.Cap., *Catholic Action Handbook* (New York: Jos. P. Wagner, 1936).

QUESTIONS

1. Define the term *Catholic Action.*
2. What is the procedure to be undertaken if you would like a society to which you belong to become an official part of "Catholic Action"?
3. Why is it incorrect to say that "anyone who performs a good work or who belongs to a pious society is carrying out Catholic Action"?
4. Why is personal holiness a fundamental requisite for those who wish to take part in Catholic Action?
5. In how far may it be correctly said that an understanding of the liturgy and a participation therein is a powerful aid to Catholic Action?
6. Why is an active apostolate also a prerequisite to Catholic Action, in addition to personal holiness?
7. What part can the press play in Catholic Action? Why is it correct or incorrect to say that the mere publication of a Catholic paper is not Catholic Action even though it may be a highly praiseworthy undertaking?
8. How can the worker take part in Catholic Action among his fellow workers, even non-Catholic? To do this, why must he join a duly

constituted society? If he did not join such a society, why would his work, however far reaching, fail to be a part of Catholic Action as such?

9. What is the organization and work of the National Catholic Welfare Conference?

10. What is the history of the Society of St. Vincent de Paul?

11. How is the Society of St. Vincent de Paul organized?

12. What is the chief work of the Society of St. Vincent de Paul at the present time?

13. Discuss the need of social work in parishes.

14. Give a brief history and description of the Knights of Columbus.

15. Give a brief history and description of the Legion of Mary.

16. Give a brief history and description of (a) the Jociste movement; (b) the Grail youth movement.

17. Why is it incorrect to say that Catholic Action is in any way political? Since this is so, in how far does Catholic Action affect the life of the State?

INDEX

A. F. of L., 378 f., 393; and communism, 382; and education, 382; membership, 379

Abortion, 530; Exodus on, 530; Genesis on, 530; St. Matthew on, 530

Abraham, 91, 222; and polygyny, 163; patriarchal family head, 157

Accidents, industrial, 354 ff.; nonindustrial, 357 ff.

Acculturation, 69

Acheulian culture, 84

Action Populaire, 130 f.

Acts on early socialism, 232

Actu, 393

Adam, 103; and speech, 5; and work, 242

Adam and Eve, 105; and marriage, 153; culture of, 65, 66; origin from, 90

Addams, Jane, 486

Addison's disease, 33

Adler, Alfred, 506 f.

Adolescence, difficulties, 288

Adoption, child, 480

Adrenals, 31, 33

Aesthenic type, 35 f.

Africa and religion, 214

Age, and birth control, 523 f.; and relief, 476; statistics of, 528; *see also*, old age

Age areas, 75 ff.

Age grades, 155; and state, 192

Agricultural Adjustment Act, 442

Agricultural co-operation, 453; Belgium, 455; Denmark, 453 ff.; Nova Scotia, 457 f.

Agricultural Credits Act, 1923, 441, 444

Agricultural Marketing Act, 442

Agricultural Situation of U. S., 435

Agriculture, and Jews, 245; *see also* rural problems, rural needs

Ainu, and levirate, 158; and marriage, 164; and monogamy, 165; and punishment, 200; and religion, 198, 204, 208, 211, 214, 216; and property, 228; and State, 192

Alberta and Douglas credit scheme, 430

Alcohol, effect of, on child, 47; effect of, on health, 48

Alcoholism, 501, 509 ff., 517; and crime, 555; and housing, 539; and sterilization, 519

Algonquin, and religion, 209, 210; and totemism, 212

Alignments, 87

All-Union Congress, 418

Almoner, 409

Almshouses, 469

Alpine peoples, 90

Ambiverts, 507

American Anthropological School, 153

American Anthropologist, 78

American Association for Old Age Security, 361

American Association of Instruction for the Blind, 490

American Association of Workers for the Blind, 490

American Association on Mental Deficiency, 495

American Catholic Anthropological Society, 199

American Country Life Association, 446

American Farm Bureau Administration, *see* Farm Bureau Administration

American Farm Bureau Federation, 439

American Federation of Labor, *see* A. F. of L.

American Federation of Organizations for the Hard of Hearing, 493

American Foundation for the Blind, 489 f.

American Indians, 96; and matriarchy, 157; and religion, 207; inventions, 70

American Journal of Sociology, 120

American Neurological Society, 517

America's Capacity to Consume, 263

Amusement, commercial, 57; *see also* recreation, play

Anarchism, 412 f.

Ancestor worship, *see* ghost worship

Andaman, and monogamy, 165; and property, 223 f., 228; and religion, 198, 209, 210; and State, 191

Andaman Islanders, 4

Andamanese and marriage, 154, 162

Anger and glands, 33

Animal worship and totemism, 215

Animals, and man, 28, 59, 139, 285; gregarious nature, 8; versus man, 43, 44

Animatism, 207 ff.

Animism, 201 f., 207 ff.

Ankermann, 76

Annuaire Statistique de Belgique, 456

Annulment, 547 f.

Anthropogenic society, 121

Anthropology, American Historical School, 77; and religion, 13; and sociology, 12; branches of, 15 f.

Mangold, G. B., *Social Pathology* (New York: Macmillan Co., 1932).

**Murray, Rev., R. W., C.S.C., and Flynn, F. T., *Social Problems* (New York: F. S. Crofts & Co., 1938).

*National Commission on Law Observance and Enforcement, Report Nos. 3, Criminal Statistics; 9, Penal Institutions, Probation and Parole; 10, Crime and the Foreign Born; 11, Lawlessness in Law Enforcement; 12, Cost of Crime; 13, Causes of Crime (2 vols.); 14, Police (Washington, D. C.: Government Printing Office, 1931).

*Recent Social Trends, Report of the President's Research Committee on Social Trends (New York: McGraw-Hill Book Co., 1933).

Report of the Select Committee on Capital Punishment (London: H. M. Stationery Office, 1930).

**Spalding, Rev. H. S., S.J., *Social Problems and Agencies* (New York: Benziger Bros., 1929).

*Sullenger, T. E., *Social Determinants in Juvenile Delinquency* (New York: John Wiley & Sons, 1936).

*Sutherland, E. H., *Principles of Criminology* (Philadelphia: J. B. Lippincott Co., 1934).

Thrasher, F. M., *The Gang*, 2nd rev. ed. (Chicago: University of Chicago Press, 1936).

United States Children's Bureau, Bulletin Nos. 142, Juvenile Courts at Work, 1925; 195, Youth and Crime, 1930; 215, Facts About Juvenile Delinquency, 1932; 228, Institutional Treatment of Delinquent Boys, 1933.

*Warner, A. G., Queen, S. A., and Harper, E. B., *American Charities and Social Work* (New York: Thomas Y. Crowell Co., 1930).

*White House Conference on Child Health & Protection, *The Delinquent Child* (New York: Appleton-Century Co., 1932).

Young, P. V., *Social Treatment in Probation and Delinquency* (New York: McGraw-Hill Book Co., 1937).

QUESTIONS

1. What are the different kinds of law?
2. In how far is crime and delinquency (*a*) a moral problem, (*b*) a social problem? Can the two problems be clearly delimited? Discuss.
3. Distinguish between sin, crime, misdemeanor.
4. Discuss the tangible "cost of crime."
5. Why is it correct to say that there is no one cause of any crime?
6. Why is it important to know the major factors which are the occasions of crime?
7. Why is a knowledge of the subject matter of Chapters 2 and 3 a necessary prerequisite for a study of crime causation?
8. What is the inherited basis, if any, of delinquent conduct? Discuss the greater or less inheritance of predisposition to certain types of conduct.
9. What subjective factors other than possibly inherited predispositions toward certain types of conduct might enter into a criminal's acts?
10. Enumerate the chief environmental factors which enter into crime causation.

11. What major social reforms seem needed to eliminate the chief occasions of crime?
12. What is the only basic reason by which society, through the governing body, is justified in punishing the criminal?
13. What are the main objectives of punishment, in addition to its fundamental justification?
14. Give the pros and cons of capital punishment.
15. Outline the major theories in regard to the punishment of criminals.
16. What seems to be the major error in the attitude of those following the "classical" school?
17. What was the theory of Lombroso, and what criticisms can be made thereof?
18. What is the major present-day emphasis on the treatment of criminals in the United States? Is it based on a true or a false philosophy?
19. Give a brief history of probation, and state the major criticisms against it as well as the arguments in its favor. Does a sentence of probation eliminate punishment and/or retribution?
20. What are the arguments for and against prison labor? Discuss the validity of each side and come to a definite conclusion on the subject.
21. Discuss whether or not prison education is an important factor in the reformation of the prisoner.
22. What special treatment is needed in the case of women prisoners with the object of effecting a socially useful reform?
23. Distinguish between parole and probation.
24. What is the indeterminate sentence? What are its drawbacks, and what its advantages in connection with reform?
25. Why is juvenile delinquency of particular concern to the social worker and reformer?

CHAPTER 27

IMMIGRATION AND RACE PROBLEMS

RECOMMENDED READINGS

Abbott, E., *Immigration* (Chicago: Chicago University Press, 1924).
Anderson, E. L., *We Americans* (Cambridge: Harvard University Press, 1937).
Bercovici, K., *Around the World in New York* (New York: Appleton-Century Co., 1924).
Boas, F., *Anthropology and Modern Life,* rev. ed. (New York: W. W. Norton Co., 1932).
*———— *The Mind of Primitive Man,* rev. ed. (New York: Macmillan Co., 1938).
Bok, E., *The Americanization of Edward Bok* (New York: Scribner's Sons, 1924).
*Brown, L. G., *Immigration* (New York: Longmans, Green, 1930).
Carr-Saunders, A. M., *World Population* (Oxford: Oxford University Press, 1936).

*Davie, M. R., *World Immigration* (New York: Macmillan Co., 1936).

Day, C. B., *Negro-White Families in the United States* (Cambridge: Harvard University Press, 1932).

Dubois, W. E. B., *Black Reconstruction* (New York: Harcourt, Brace, 1935).

Eaton, A. H., *Immigrant Gifts to American Life* (New York: Russell Sage Foundation, 1932).

*Elliott, M. A., and Merrill, F. E., *Social Disorganization* (New York: Harper & Bros., 1934).

Embree, E. R., *Brown America* (New York: Viking Press, 1931).

Encyclopaedia of the Social Sciences, articles on Man, Mental Tests, Race Conflict, Race Mixture.

*Garth, T. R., *Race Psychology* (New York: McGraw-Hill Book Co., 1931).

**Gillard, Rev. J. T., S.S.J., *The Catholic Church and the American Negro* (Baltimore: St. Joseph's Society Press, 1930).

*Gillette, J. M., and Reinhardt, J. M., *Current Social Problems,* rev. ed. (New York: American Book Co., 1937).

**Gilligan, Rev. F. J., *The Morality of the Color Line* (Washington, D. C.: Catholic University of America, 1928).

Handbook of Labor Statistics, 1936 (United States Department of Labor, Bureau of Labor Statistics).

Herskovits, M. J., *The American Negro* (New York: Alfred A. Knopf, 1928).

**Interracial Review,* monthly (New York: 20 Vesey Street).

*Jenks, J. W., and Lauck, W. J., *The Immigration Problem* (New York: Funk & Wagnalls, 1926).

*Johnson, C. S., *The Negro in American Civilization* (New York: Henry Holt & Co., 1930).

Johnson, J. W., *Along This Way* (New York: Viking Press, 1933).

———— *The Autobiography of an Ex-Colored Man* (New York: Alfred A. Knopf, 1928).

Klineberg, O., *Negro Intelligence and Selective Migration* (New York: Columbia University Press, 1935).

*———— *Race Differences* (New York: Harper & Bros., 1935).

**LaFarge, Rev. J., S.J., *Interracial Justice* (New York: The America Press, 1937).

Lasker, B., *Race Attitudes in Children* (New York: Henry Holt, 1929).

Moton, R. R., *What the Negro Thinks* (New York: Doubleday, Doran, 1929).

**Murray, Rev. R. W., C.S.C., and Flynn, F. T., *Social Problems* (New York: Crofts & Co., 1938).

Nearing, S., *Black America* (New York: Vanguard Press, 1929).

Negro Year Book, see Work, M. N.

Pinsk, J., *Christianity and Race* (New York: Sheed & Ward, 1936).

Ravage, M. E., *An American in the Making* (New York: Harper & Bros., 1917).

Reuter, E. B., *The American Race Problem* (New York: Thomas Y. Crowell, 1927).

—— *Race Mixture: Studies in Intermarriage and Miscegenation* (New York: McGraw-Hill Book Co., 1931).

*Schwesinger, G. C., *Heredity and Environment* (New York: Macmillan Co., 1933).

**Spalding, Rev. H., S.J., *Social Problems and Agencies* (New York: Benziger Bros., 1929).

Thomas, W. I., and Znaniecki, F., *The Polish Peasant in Europe and America* (New York: Alfred A. Knopf, 1927).

Weatherford, W. D., and Johnson, C., *Race Relations* (Boston: Heath & Co., 1934).

Woodson, C. G., *The Mis-Education of the Negro* (Washington, D. C.: The Associated Publishers, 1933).

—— *The Negro in Our History* (Washington, D. C.: The Associated Publishers, 1931).

Woofter, T. J., *Races and Ethnic Groups in American Life* (New York: McGraw-Hill Book Co., 1933).

*Work, M. N., ed., *Negro Year Book 1937–38* (Tuskegee Institute, Ala.: Negro Year Book Publishing Co., 1938).

QUESTIONS

1. Write a brief history of immigration to the United States.
2. Give the main features of the present immigration laws.
3. Enumerate the chief problems which must be solved by citizens of the United States if they receive immigrants into the country.
4. Enumerate the chief problems to be solved by the immigrant and his family at home and abroad.
5. Why is it not always true to say that immigrants will add to the unemployment of United States citizens?
6. What have been the contributions of immigrants to the United States (*a*) since 1930; (*b*) since the beginning of last century?
7. Does your answer to the last question show conclusively how ridiculous is the attitude of those Americans who talk about immigrants, past and present, in derogatory fashion? Explain.
8. If you were asked to attend to the needs of a newly arrived Catholic immigrant and his family, what would be the best method of procedure? What organizations would you advise him to consult?
9. Outline the procedure required of an alien who wishes to become a United States citizen.
10. Why is it essential for a student of American social problems to study the question of immigration despite the present restrictions?
11. Write a brief history of the Negro in the United States.
12. Why may it be said to be unscientific to attribute a higher place to white people than to Negroes in the record of past development of the United States?
13. Why is it un-Christian to have an attitude of superiority and disdain toward Negroes?
14. Is it correct to maintain that the average Negro in the United States is less intelligent than the average white person? Justify your answer.
15. Give reasons for the greater percentage of poverty among Negroes than among white persons.

16. Discuss the supposed greater delinquency and crime among Negro than among white groups.
17. Make a list of the chief claims that American Negroes are not awarded their just rights (*a*) as human beings; (*b*) as citizens of the United States. State briefly any arguments against these claims and give briefly your conclusions as to the actual justice of the situation.
18. What are the chief problems involved by the presence of Negroes in the United States?
19. Why is it more correct to speak of the interracial problem than of the Negro problem?
20. What are the possible social effects of the discriminations against Negroes in education?
21. Why is it socially and economically unsound to discriminate against Negroes in regard to employment and conditions of work?
22. What have Catholics done to solve the "Negro problem" within recent years? Outline the major work still needed in this connection.

CHAPTER 28

CATHOLIC ACTION

RECOMMENDED READINGS

**Civardi, Rev. L., *A Manual of Catholic Action* (New York: Sheed & Ward, 1936).

**Crofts, A. M., O.P., *Catholic Social Action* (St. Louis: B. Herder Book Co., 1938).

**Cuthbert, Rev., O.S.F.C., *Catholic Ideals in Social Life* (New York: Benziger Bros., 1904).

**Fitzsimons, Rev. J., and McGuire, P., *Restoring All Things: A Guide to Catholic Action* (New York: Sheed & Ward, 1938).

Furfey, Rev. P. H., *Fire on the Earth* (New York: Macmillan Co., 1936).

** ———— *Three Theories of Society* (New York: Macmillan Co., 1938).

Garesché, Rev. E. F., S.J., *Modern Parish Problems* (New York: Jos. F. Wagner, 1928).

Garriguet, Rev. L., *The Gospel and Our Social Problems* (New York: Jos. F. Wagner, 1925).

Harbrecht, Rev. J., *The Lay Apostolate* (New York: Benziger Bros., 1930).

**Kerby, Rev. W. J., *The Social Mission of Charity* (New York: Macmillan Co., 1924).

Lugan, Rev. A., *Social Principles of the Gospel* (New York: Macmillan Co., 1928).

Martin, P. R., *The Gospel in Action* (Milwaukee: Bruce Publishing Co., 1932).

Meyer, Rev. J., O.F.M., *The Social Ideals of St. Francis* (St. Louis: B. Herder Book Co., 1938).

Michel, Rev. V., O.S.B., *The Social Question,* Series of nine pamphlets (Collegeville, Minn.: St. John's University, 1936).

Mounier, E., *A Personalist Manifesto* (New York: Longmans, Green, 1938).

Muntsch, Rev. A. J., S.J., *The Church and Civilization* (Milwaukee: Bruce Publishing Co., 1936).

**——— and Spalding, H. S., S.J., *Introductory Sociology* (Boston: Heath & Co., 1928).

**Murray, Rev. R. W., C.S.C., and Flynn, F. T., *Social Problems,* Chap. 1 (New York: Crofts & Co., 1938).

**O'Grady, Rev. J., *Catholic Charities in the United States* (Washington, D. C.: National Conference of Catholic Charities, 1931).

**——— *An Introduction to Social Work* (New York: Appleton-Century Co., 1928).

**Pope Pius XI, encyclical, *Mens Nostra,* 1929, quoted in the *Catholic Mind,* February 8, 1930; "On Catholic Action," 1931, quoted in the *Catholic Mind,* July 22 and August 8, 1931; "Letter to Cardinal Bertram," Archbishop of Breslau, quoted in the *Catholic Mind,* March 8, 1930; Various letters quoted in "Directives for Catholic Action," *Central-Blatt and Social Justice,* December, 1937, pp. 265–268; January, 1938, pp. 305, 306; *Divini Redemptoris,* 1938.

Schumacher, H., *The Social Message of the New Testament* (Milwaukee: Bruce Publishing Co., 1937).

Spalding, Rev. H. S., S.J., *Chapters in Social History* (Boston: Heath & Co., 1925).

Walsh, M. E., *Saints and Social Work* (Silver Spring, Md.: Preservation of the Faith Press, 1937).

Will, Rev. J., S.J., and Hennrich, Rev. K. J., O.M.Cap., *Catholic Action Handbook* (New York: Jos. P. Wagner, 1936).

QUESTIONS

1. Define the term *Catholic Action.*
2. What is the procedure to be undertaken if you would like a society to which you belong to become an official part of "Catholic Action"?
3. Why is it incorrect to say that "anyone who performs a good work or who belongs to a pious society is carrying out Catholic Action"?
4. Why is personal holiness a fundamental requisite for those who wish to take part in Catholic Action?
5. In how far may it be correctly said that an understanding of the liturgy and a participation therein is a powerful aid to Catholic Action?
6. Why is an active apostolate also a prerequisite to Catholic Action, in addition to personal holiness?
7. What part can the press play in Catholic Action? Why is it correct or incorrect to say that the mere publication of a Catholic paper is not Catholic Action even though it may be a highly praiseworthy undertaking?
8. How can the worker take part in Catholic Action among his fellow workers, even non-Catholic? To do this, why must he join a duly

constituted society? If he did not join such a society, why would his work, however far reaching, fail to be a part of Catholic Action as such?

9. What is the organization and work of the National Catholic Welfare Conference?
10. What is the history of the Society of St. Vincent de Paul?
11. How is the Society of St. Vincent de Paul organized?
12. What is the chief work of the Society of St. Vincent de Paul at the present time?
13. Discuss the need of social work in parishes.
14. Give a brief history and description of the Knights of Columbus.
15. Give a brief history and description of the Legion of Mary.
16. Give a brief history and description of (*a*) the Jociste movement; (*b*) the Grail youth movement.
17. Why is it incorrect to say that Catholic Action is in any way political? Since this is so, in how far does Catholic Action affect the life of the State?

INDEX